Klaus Storkmann

Homosexuality in the German Armed Forces

De Gruyter Studies in Military History

Edited by
Jörg Echternkamp and Adam Seipp

Advisory Board
Michelle Moyd, Michigan State University
Katrin Paehler, Illinois State University
Sabrina Thomas, Texas Tech University

Volume 6

Klaus Storkmann

Homosexuality in the German Armed Forces

A History of Taboo and Tolerance

Translated from the German Original by Noah Harley

Commissioned by the Bundeswehr Centre of Military History and Social Sciences

DE GRUYTER
OLDENBOURG

Free access to the e-book version of this publication was made possible by the 36 academic libraries and initiatives that supported the open access transformation project in History.

ISBN 978-3-11-107201-2
e-ISBN (PDF) 978-3-11-108269-1
e-ISBN (EPUB) 978-3-11-108307-0
ISSN 2701-5629
DOI https://doi.org/10.1515/9783111082691

Library of Congress Control Number: 2024949446

Bibliographic information published by the Deutsche Nationalbibliothek
The Deutsche Nationalbibliothek lists this publication in the Deutsche Nationalbibliografie; detailed bibliographic data are available on the Internet at http://dnb.dnb.de.

Cover image: © Bundeswehr/Tom Twardy
Copyediting: Ben Dare

www.degruyter.com

Questions about General Product Safety Regulation:
productsafety@degruyterbrill.com

Open-Access-Transformation in History

Open Access for excellent academic publications in the field of history: Thanks to the support of 36 academic libraries and initiatives, 9 frontlist publications from 203 can be published as gold open access, without any costs to the authors.

The following institutions and initiatives have contributed to the funding and thus promote the open access transformation in history and ensure free availability for everyone:

Dachinitiative „Hochschule.digital Niedersachsen" des Landes Niedersachsen
Universitätsbibliothek Bayreuth
Staatsbibliothek zu Berlin – Preußischer Kulturbesitz
Universitätsbibliothek Bern
Universitätsbibliothek Bielefeld
Universitätsbibliothek Bochum
Universitäts- und Landesbibliothek Bonn
Staats- und Universitätsbibliothek Bremen
Universitäts- und Landesbibliothek Darmstadt
Sächsische Landesbibliothek, Staats- und Universitätsbibliothek Dresden (SLUB)
Universitätsbibliothek Duisburg-Essen
Universitäts- und Landesbibliothek Düsseldorf
Albert-Ludwigs-Universität Freiburg - Universitätsbibliothek
Niedersächsische Staats- und Universitätsbibliothek Göttingen
Universitätsbibliothek der FernUniversität in Hagen
Staats- und Universitätsbibliothek Hamburg Carl von Ossietzky
Gottfried Wilhelm Leibniz Bibliothek – Niedersächsische Landesbibliothek, Hannover
Technische Informationsbibliothek (TIB)
Universitätsbibliothek Hildesheim
Universitäts- und Landesbibliothek Tirol, Innsbruck
Universitätsbibliothek Kassel – Landesbibliothek und Murhardsche Bibliothek der Stadt Kassel
Universitäts- und Stadtbibliothek Köln
Zentral- und Hochschulbibliothek Luzern
Universitätsbibliothek Mainz
Bibliothek des Leibniz-Instituts für Europäische Geschichte, Mainz
Universitätsbibliothek Marburg
Universitätsbibliothek der Ludwig-Maximilians-Universität München
Universitäts- und Landesbibliothek Münster
Bibliotheks- und Informationssystem (BIS) der Carl von Ossietzky Universität Oldenburg
Universitätsbibliothek Osnabrück
Universität Potsdam
Universitätsbibliothek Vechta
Universitätsbibliothek der Bauhaus-Universität Weimar
Herzog August Bibliothek Wolfenbüttel
Universitätsbibliothek Wuppertal
Zentralbibliothek Zürich

Foreword

In January 2017, Federal Minister of Defense Dr. Ursula von der Leyen commissioned the Bundeswehr Center of Military History and Social Sciences (Zentrum für Militärgeschichte und Sozialwissenschaften der Bundeswehr, ZMSBw) to write an academic study on the German Armed Forces (Bundeswehr) relationship to homosexuality between 1955 and 2000. After three-and-a-half years, on 17 September 2020, her successor in office Annegret Kramp-Karrenbauer presented the public with the results of the research: "We must not beat about the bush. For decades after its founding in 1955, the Bundeswehr [...] systematically discriminated against homosexual soldiers."

Lieutenant Colonel Dr. Klaus Storkmann has written a pioneering work, one which for the first time considers the relevant legal and regulatory frameworks, illuminates gay service members' day-to-day experiences in the Bundeswehr, and delves into the key topics in political and public debate. In doing so, the author has drawn on extensive written records from the German Federal Archives, numerous rulings at military service and administrative courts, and the testimony of more than sixty contemporary witnesses. Building on this solid foundation, Dr. Storkmann has proceeded to analyze criminal procedures against soldiers' homosexual activity and the Bundeswehr's own internal forms of disciplinary action, the historical status of homosexuality as a security risk, and the professional consequences that discovery of homosexual activity entailed.

Up to the turn of the millennium, homosexuality counted as both grounds for exclusion from a career as an officer or non-commissioned officer – and as a security risk. The author reconstructed a select set of military careers that were impacted by these policies, allowing him to portray the fates of the individual soldiers in detail. The consequences arising out of an otherwise abstract regulatory framework are thus made both palpable and traceable in their effect on the soldiers' professional and private lives.

While presenting the study in September 2020, Minister Kramp-Karrenbauer also laid the groundwork for a law on legal rehabilitation, avowing that "it is not a matter of indifference to us how people were treated at the time." On 25 November 2020, the Federal Cabinet approved the Rehabilitation Act for Homosexual Soldiers Discriminated against in the Bundeswehr and the National People's Army (Nationale Volksarmee, NVA). The Act's inclusion of East German soldiers discriminated against for their sexual orientation can be seen as a further step toward achieving Germany's inner unification.

Lieutenant Colonel Storkmann decided at an early point to go beyond the actual task at hand – considering the Bundeswehr's previous attitude towards homosexuality – and to consider NVA policy as well. In doing so, he adhered to the ZMSBw's methodological tenet of considering both German states and their armed forces in the study of military history after 1945 wherever possible and relevant. *Homosexuality in the German Armed Forces* thus takes its place among a series of composite, often comparative German–German military histories. Dr. Storkmann's historical perspective on previous German armed forces and his lateral view of the armies of other states set the Bundeswehr's practices in a wider context, as do the comparisons he draws with other public service institutions. Sexual minorities' treatment within the armed forces is an illuminating topic for much more than contemporary German history.

Historians' work seldom leads to concrete political decisions, much less new laws. In this case, however, the Federal German Parliament (Bundestag) unanimously adopted the gay and lesbian soldiers' Rehabilitation Act in May 2021. The ZMSBw and the author of the present work can look with pride on what are highly gratifying results for those who experienced discrimination in the past. I would like to thank Lieutenant Colonel Dr. Storkmann for his accomplished research, in addition to the ZMSBw publications department, under the leadership of Dr. Christian Adam, for its dedication and continued professionalism in successfully bringing this English publication into print, and especially to Mr. Noah Harley from the State of New York for his outstanding translation work. I wish this book a wide readership, both throughout the Bundeswehr and among the wider public. May it serve as an impetus for many future studies.

Dr. Sven Lange
Colonel and Commander,
Bundeswehr Center of Military History and Social Sciences in Potsdam

Acknowledgements

When in January 2017 I first accepted the Federal Ministry of Defense's commission to research the history of the Bundeswehr's attitudes and policies towards homosexual soldiers, a colonel and colleague at ZMSBw asked me what qualified me for the job, outside of my own sexual orientation. It was a sharp question, though intended in collegial fashion, and gets at a point that should give us pause for reflection: You do not have to be Roman to write the history of ancient Rome. Still, an interest in antiquity and some knowledge of Latin does not hurt. The same holds true for other topics, those addressed in the present work included.

Empathy and understanding for the topic at hand proved essential in what turned into quite a complicated search for sources and contemporary witnesses. I would like to thank all those who were willing to share highly personal, at times intimate memories and experiences, with me. All of the interviews contributed valuable pieces to the puzzle, so no one will be singled out by name here. Thanks also to those who were not directly affected but shared their observations of how homosexual soldiers were treated – the staff officers, generals, jurists, civil servants and politicians, as well as decision-makers. A complete list of names at this point would go beyond the scope of these acknowledgements, and many expressed a desire not to be mentioned by name.

Beyond the list of interviewees given in the sources section, I would especially like to thank retired State Secretary Peter Wichert, retired Parliamentary State Secretary Brigitte Schulte and retired General Harald Kujat for their willingness to cast light on the decision-making processes as they played out behind closed ministry doors around the turn of the millennium. I would also like to thank retired General Wolfgang Altenburg, whose generous hospitality I still think back to fondly, and with whom I shared a series of illuminating conversations about the Wörner–Kießling affair. My special thanks go to some of the first employees of Military Counterintelligence, whose willingness to talk was of tremendous help in what was probably the most challenging aspect of this research project. Thanks go in particular to retired Colonel Heinz Kluss, who provided a great many helpful insights into MAD's work through numerous conversations, letters and emails starting in 2013. Heinz Kluss unfortunately was not able to witness the publication of this book, as he passed away in January 2019. Retired Surgeon General Dr. Horst Hennig also shared valuable reflections and criticism over a long series of conversations; his perspective as a military physician during the Second World War brought my own research forward. Unfortunately, he did not live to see the publication of this book, either; Horst Hennig passed away in May 2020. Now that the book has been published, I think of both with a great sense of gratitude.

In addition to individual accounts, this study is based on documents from the Federal Archives (BArch) and the Federal Commissioner for the Records of the GDR State Security Service (BStU). I hereby thank all of the employees involved in research at both archives, especially Cynthia Flohr, Christine Reibel, Captain Michael Herden, Master Sergeant Markus Schäfers and Daniel Jost at the Federal Military Archives Department in Freiburg im Breisgau; and Astrid Rose at the BStU in Berlin. Thanks to Dr. Georg Meyer in Freiburg for many entertaining discussions, often accompanied by a good meal and a glass of wine, as well as background information on how the Reichswehr and the Wehrmacht dealt with homosexuality. In Unna I have city archivist Dr. Frank Ahland to thank for sharing sources from the North Rhine-Westphalia State Archives. I am indebted to my colleagues at the ZMSBW's research department for military history after 1945 for a number of insightful and helpful pointers, including to sources beyond the immediate scope of the project: Dr. Jörg Echternkamp, Dr. Dorothee Hochstetter, Dr. Frank Käser, Lieutenant Colonel Dr. Dieter Kollmer, Dr. Bernd Lemke and Dr. Christoph Nübel, as well as those outside my more immediate circle – Lieutenant Colonel Michael Peter, Dr. Thorsten Loch, Dr. Helmut Hammerich, Dr. Heiner Möllers, Dr. Christian Stachelbeck, Navy Captain Dr. Christian Jentzsch and Captain Sebastian Schroeckh. In medical matters, I owe a debt of gratitude to Lt. Col. (MC) Ralf Vollmuth for useful references and background information.

Among others I have Lieutenant Colonel Michael Peter, Michael Lindner, Thomas Odenthal, Vincent Benedikt Seidl and Victor Marnette to thank for casting a critical eye on the manuscript. Government Director Guido Gutzeit and Lieutenant Colonel Wolf Günther Halama at the Center for Leadership Development and Civic Education in Koblenz offered valuable commentary and critique from a legal perspective. I would also like to thank Senior Government Counsellor Hartmut Stiffel in Koblenz for facilitating contact with Michael Lindner in Hamburg as an eyewitness in 2016. Even before the BMVg commissioned this work I had already had an interest in this subject and had begun to assemble sources for a possible future project.

My thanks to Dr. Ursula von der Leyen, Federal Minister of Defense from 2013 to 2019, for her initiative in commissioning the study, as well as to her successor Annegret Kramp-Karrenbauer for resolving to publish the work in a timely manner. My thanks are due as well to State Secretaries Gerd Hoofe, Colonel Dr. Burkhard Köster, Colonel Dr. Sven Lange, Lieutenant Colonel Dr. Rudolf J. Schlaffer and Lieutenant Colonel Dr. Thorsten Loch for their kindly assistance at the ministry in the years leading up to publication.

Such prompt publication of the study would not have been possible without the support of my superiors and colleagues at the ZMSBw, especially for their support, Naval Captain Dr. Jörg Hillmann and Dr. Michael Epkenhans.

My special thanks for facilitating the English translation goes to Colonel Dr. Sven Lange, Colonel Dr. Martin Hofbauer and Dr. Heiko Biehl. Above all I have Professor Dr. Jörg Echternkamp and Dr. Christian Adam to thank for their dedication and continued professionalism in realizing this English translation within a period of just two years, and especially to Mr. Noah Harley from New York State for his outstanding translation work.

In listing all the sources of support, two names are still missing: Dr. Rüdiger Wenzke, the longtime leader of the research department for military history after 1945, and retired Colonel Dr. Winfried Heinemann, the former chief of the research department for GDR military history. It was not just the years they spent accompanying the work, casting both a benevolent and critical eye (Winfried Heinemann was the one who asked the author what qualified him for the research project), it was Rüdiger and Winfried who first opened the doors of academic research to me at the former Military History Research Office (Militärgeschichtliches Forschungsamt, or MGFA) in 2006–2007, and who have remained steadfastly by my side from the very beginning. I have them to thank for much of the academic work I have completed since then. Both have since taken well-deserved retirement; this study is dedicated to them.

Klaus Storkmann

About the Author

Dr. Klaus Storkmann, born 1976, is a lieutenant colonel and leads the subdivision for East German military history within the department for military history after 1945 at the Bundeswehr Center of Military History and Social Sciences in Potsdam. His research focuses on Germany history after 1945 and international relations during the Cold War. Klaus Storkmann is the editor of *Militärgeschichte: Zeitschrift für historische Bildung* (Military history: Journal for historical education).

Select Author Publications

"The long fight for fighting with pride. LGBT Soldiers in the Military History of Australia, Germany, Israel, the Netherlands and the United States," Special issue International *Journal of Military History and Historiography* no. 42 (2022) (edited together with Jacqueline E. Whitt).

"The 'Most Liberal in Nato'? How the (West) German Ministry of Defense Looked to Other Armed Forces' Regulations Concerning Homosexuality (1966 to 1999)." *International Journal of Military History and Historiography* no. 42 (2022): 70–105.

Tabu und Toleranz: Der Umgang der Bundeswehr mit Homosexualität von 1955 bis 2000, Berlin: De Gruyter Oldenbourg, 2021.

"Verbündete auf Distanz: Ostdeutsch-rümanische Militärkontakte vor dem Hintergrund der Politisichen Beziehungen." In *Sozialistische Waffenbrüder? Rumänien und die DDR im Warschauer Pakt*, edited by Jörg Echternkamp, 51–70. Potsdam: Zentrum für Militärgeschichte und Sozialwissenschaften der Bundeswehr, 2020.

"Die DDR als Akteur im 'Globalen Kalten Krieg'? Militärisches Engagement für Afrika und den Nahen Osten und seine Koordinierung mit der sowjetischen Führung." In *Sozialistische Waffenbrüder? Rumänien und die DDR im Warschauer Pakt*, edited by Jörg Echternkamp, 127–48. Potsdam: Zentrum für Militärgeschichte und Sozialwissenschaften der Bundeswehr, 2020.

"Westdeutsche Militärhilfe und Rüstungsexporte in das subsaharische Afrika am Beispiel Kameruns." In *Mission Afrika: Geschichtsschreibung über Grenzen hin weg: Festschrift Für Ulrich van Der Heyden*, edited by Michael Eckardt, 341-351. Stuttgart: Franz Steiner Verlag, 2019.

"Die 'Roten Preußen'? Selbstverständnis und Traditionen der NVA im Spiegel der Traditionsdebatte." *Zeitschrift Für Innere Führung*, no. 2 (2018): 68–73.

"'The powerful China stands firmly on our side'. The strong influence of Maoist ideology on the East German armed forces in the late 1950s." In *World War II and the Development of Warfare in the Twentieth Century*, XLI Congress of the International Commission of Military History in Beijing, China, 2017.

"Operative Personenkontrolle 'Prophet' und IM 'Koran'. Die Überwachung ausländischer Militärs in der NVA durch das MfS." *Gerbergasse 18: Thüringer Vierteljahrshefte Für Zeitgeschichte Und Politik*, no. 1 (2017): 46–41.

Geheime Solidarität: Militärbeziehungen und Militärhilfen der DDR in die "Dritte Welt." Berlin: Christoph Links, 2012.

Die NVA im Traditionsverständnis der Bundeswehr. Bremen: Ed. Temmen, 2007.

Das chinesische Prinzip in der NVA: Vom Umgang der SED mit den Generalen und Offizieren in der frühen NVA. Berlin: Köster, 2001.

Contents

Introduction

"79 centimeters you're gay, 81 centimeters you're a deserter."[1] It is a saying that just about every new recruit, parading in broad formation and lock-step exactly 80 cm behind the soldier in front, would have heard from the drill instructor at some point during initial marching exercises. From a purely statistical perspective there were likely one or two soldiers within that formation who were homosexual; they would have laughed along with the others in order not to attract attention. Gay soldiers were the object of jokes, while the term "gay" served for all kinds of disparaging comments. In 2014 the *Frankfurter Allgemeine Zeitung* (FAZ) looked back on the treatment homosexuals serving in the military could expect from the Bundeswehr and its soldiers in the past: "Deserting fellow soldiers or drawing too near to them – such were deemed the cardinal sins of soldiery. Among recruits, gays occupied a more difficult position than deserters. True, the military police dealt with the latter. Yet at least they were spared the jokes commonly heard among new soldiers."[2]

It did not end with jokes. Soldiers could land other soldiers in jail based on (consensual) homosexual activity. All it took was a report to one's superiors, as occurred on 8 December 1962, a Saturday. As was still common practice in the first decades of the Bundeswehr, Saturday mornings saw soldiers on duty. That afternoon, their shifts now ended, the soldiers celebrated the start of the weekend in the canteen with copious amounts of alcohol. Non-commissioned officer (NCO) K. and Private S. met in the canteen bathroom in a drunken state. The second criminal division at Lüneberg Regional Court summed up the rest with loving attention to detail in its "Determination of crime and guilt":

> In the toilet stall both defendants then engaged in illicit sexual acts. Both had let their pants down. They embraced and grasped hold of each other's genitals [...] ultimately Defendant S. positioned himself behind Defendant K., who was poised bent over with buttocks exposed, and made intercourse-like movements. It could not be determined whether [S.] introduced his member into the anus of K. Nor could other any further particulars of the goings-on be determined.[3]

How did the judges in Lüneberg know what had transpired behind a locked toilet door? The soldiers' comrades had trailed in after the two and peered into the bath-

---

1 Hemicker, "79 Zentimeter sind schwul." The author of this study was still easily able to recall the routine phrase from basic training, as could many of the older soldiers he interviewed.
2 Hemicker, "79 Zentimeter sind schwul."
3 Taken from the court opinion of the 2nd criminal division at Lüneburg Regional Court, 6 June 1963. Cited in Federal Disciplinary Court, 25 August 1964, Az: I WD 69/64.

room stall over the dividing wall. A report to their company chief followed, who in turn alerted the battalion commander. What had been observed in the toilet stall quickly reached division headquarters, at which point the division commander passed the incident over to the state attorney's office. The court sentenced NCO K. to four months prison for full intoxication (conviction under Paragraph 175 did not come under consideration as the accused's state of drunkenness had left him "of unsound mind," in the court's view). The private for his part received a five-month prison term for "illicit sexual acts between men."[4] In appeal proceedings the regional court sentenced the men to a month each in prison, finding that "both defendants met the elements of a crime under §175 (1) of the German Criminal Code by committing illicit sexual acts with each other, whereby each allowed himself to be abused by the other."[5] The decision at the regional court was followed by the Bundeswehr's own disciplinary tribunal; in February 1964 a military service court removed NCO K. from his post and demoted him to the rank of private first class.[6]

On its own, the case points to several key elements for a work of research into the history of homosexual soldiers in the Bundeswehr:

1. The experiential aspect, i.e. individual recollections of how homosexuality and homosexual soldiers were treated among the troops – not just from those who were "directly impacted," but observers as well;
2. The contemporary appraisal of homosexuals' general level of fitness for military service;
3. The matter of homosexual men's conviction under the infamous Paragraph 175 of the German Criminal Code (known formally as §175 StGB), the implications it held for disciplinary law, and how the Bundeswehr punished homosexual acts internally.

The questions raised by the third point set the study within a broader legal and historical context that extends far beyond the narrower subject of sexual minorities' treatment. The reader should keep in mind that both in the past (and today), the armed forces' military tribunals had different legal interests to weigh than the criminal justice system at large. It both was and remains entirely possible, even likely, for an investigation discontinued by the public prosecutor's office still to lead to disciplinary measures in the military. The course of action pursued by the Bunde-

---

4 The original German term "Unzucht" has been translated in what follows as "illicit sexual acts". While a bit wordy, the other option of "fornication" refers specifically to sex outside marriage, while the term "Unzucht" incorporates more than that. – Translator.
5 Federal Disciplinary Court, 25 August 1964, Az: I WD 69/64.
6 Military Service Court C1, Az: C 1 VL 46/63 from 20 February 1964.

swehr's legal staff, military service courts and administrative judges was of course bound by norms of law and justice. Yet those norms were different in the 1960s and 1970s than they are today, in 2022. In 2007 Christian Lutze published a cross-section of the disciplinary and criminal measures used to punish soldiers' sexual activity in the past in the *Neue Zeitschrift für Wehrrecht*.[7]

An early media account of homosexuals in the military appeared in an article "Gays are ousted," published in 1981 in Stern magazine, the "flagship of sexual liberalization",[8] which discussed the case of Michael Lindner.[9] That same year the story of Captain Lindner, who was still serving at the time, also made it into a Rowohlt paperback: *Rosa Winkel, Rosa Listen: Homosexuellen und 'Gesundes Volksempfinden' von Auschwitz bis heute* (Pink triangles, pink lists: homosexuals and "sound public sentiment" from Auschwitz to the present). "For two years," one chapter reads, "Bundeswehr Captain Michael Lindner has been fighting for the same career opportunities as his colleagues. The captain, whose fitness to lead subordinates is denied as it is for all openly homosexual officers [...] will now take early retirement."[10]

The media frenzy surrounding the investigation of General Günter Kießling, who had been denounced as homosexual, turned another early spotlight on how the armed forces treated its gay soldiers; one read about "Soldiers as potential sexual partners," in *Der Spiegel's* phrasing.[11] *Die Zeit*, too, tied its reportage on Kießling in January 1984 to the discrimination experienced by a captain who had since entered early retirement, (critically) posing the question "Homosexuality – A security threat?"[12] Even a cursory look at the contemporary press thus turns up other important questions regarding:

4. The professional repercussions bound up in a soldier being discovered to be homosexual, in this case specifically his fitness for leadership positions;
5. Contemporary assessments of homosexuality as a security risk, and with it the question of how Military Counterintelligence (Militärischer Abschirmdienst, MAD) handled the subject;

---

7 Lutze, "Sexuelle Beziehungen und die Truppe."

8 Schwartz, *Homosexuelle, Seilschaften, Verrat*, 301.

9 Claussen, "Schwule werden abgesägt." Lindner received multiple letters after the article via the editorial staff at *Stern* that were uncomprehending – not of the discrimination he had faced but the circumstances themselves. "A gay captain gets his pension at 37. A 'normie' goes to the grave at 65. It all gives my taxpayer's heart a good chuckle." Signed "Working stiff, also 37." Thanks are due to Michael Lindner for sharing a copy of the letter.

10 Stümke and Finkler, *Rosa Winkel, Rosa Listen*, 377–78.

11 "Soldaten als potentielle Sexualpartner," 22.

12 "Homosexualität – ein Sicherheitsrisiko?"

6. Finally, the point at which the Federal Ministry of Defense (Bundesministerium der Verteidigung, BMVg) altered its stance, and the reasons that proved decisive for this shift.

These six overarching questions can in turn be subsumed under the central research topic at hand, which is to consider for the first time in an academic study how the Bundeswehr and Ministry of Defense dealt with homosexual soldiers in the past. Establishing continuities and discontinuities with earlier configurations of the German military has been a particular interest in the process of the author's research, as is providing a comparative perspective towards the contemporary practices of other nations' armed forces. Past practices in the Bundeswehr are also set within a broader societal frame, a method that proved indispensable in contextualizing the research findings. Everything appears particular and exceptional if one's scope of vision is limited to a single organization. The question of how to approach homosexuality did not fall to the Bundeswehr alone but is one which every society and army has had to contend with, and in many places is still wrestling with. Dealing with this issue was not a problem of the Bundeswehr alone, rather it was a challenge for all armed forces. In comparing the Bundeswehr's approach to earlier German armed forces and those of other countries, it is not the *whether* but the *how* that is of interest.

Brief, introductory historical episodes form the basis of the work. Like any other window that this study opens onto the past, they do not lay claim to be complete but instead serve a need to set the Bundeswehr's historical practices within a broader conceptual and analytical framework. Specific historical vignettes are also introduced at appropriate moments throughout each chapter to complement analysis of the Bundeswehr. These "visual axes" come at particularly telling points, wherever noteworthy continuities could be found. The study concludes by considering the practices of other armed forces in the same era, broadening its scope and, critically, serving to contextualize its findings.

The six elements identified above set the framework for this study. The trajectories they reveal ran highly disparate yet contemporaneous courses that could not be meaningfully depicted in chronological fashion; only a systematic approach to the research could do them justice. Within the study's systematic divisions, changes are worked out roughly over a forty-five-year period between 1955 and 2000, preserving a general chronological perspective.

In opting to work with exemplary cases, it was important that the study not deteriorate into a collection of anecdotes, or the analysis become lost among details. A clear structure and consistent orientation toward the broad issues in this work, as determined by the six overarching areas of inquiry, aimed to guard against this.

1. Sources

At a January 2017 workshop entitled "Sexual identity and orientation in the Bundeswehr," Defense Minister Ursula von der Leyen announced a new research work to reconsider past discrimination against homosexual soldiers. The minister repeatedly underscored the importance of the study in the press, including one August 2017 interview with Munich-based queer magazine Leo:

> Not once has our past handling of the subject been subject to systematic analysis. In preparing for the conference we tried to locate historical examples to present. In the process, we became aware of just how difficult it was to do so. That is why a study that scrutinizes the period between 1955 and 2002 is so important; when somebody was outed, the official cause for discharge was often something totally different. Reasons of health, or something of the sort. This is what makes it so difficult for us to get at the truth by way of the written records.[13]

The vast majority of written sources that proved relevant for this research are housed in the the German Federal Archives (Bundesarchiv, abbreviated hereinafter to BArch), Military Division, in Freiburg im Breisgau. Within the Ministry of Defense it was primarily documents from the Armed Forces Staff (FüS) and the branch staffs of the Army, Air Force and Navy that were pertinent. The author also made use of the archives of the BMVg's personnel directorate (abbreviated as P; formerly the Personnel, Social Services and Central Affairs Directorate, or PSZ), and the Legal Affairs Directorate (abbreviated as R). With few exceptions, data protection regulations alone meant that documents pertaining directly to individuals were not available for research. The same held for documents created in the course of MAD security reviews. Disciplinary measures against a soldier that did not reach the level of proceedings before a military service court or summary dismissals under Section 55 (5) of the Legal Status of Military Personnel Act (Soldatengesetz, SG) were not retained by personnel departments, but entered a soldier's individual file once the matter had been concluded. As a general rule, the end of a soldier's active time in service saw his or her dossier sent to the relevant district recruiting offices, as reservists remained subject to military surveillance.[14] Those files were later transferred to Willich, to the legacy records deposit at the Federal Office of

---

13 Interview with Ursula von der Leyen in multiple outlets of the media group *blu* including *Leo*, August 2017.
14 Information about disciplinary action can in any event only be obtained within the narrow limits set out under Section 9 of the Military Disciplinary Code (Wehrdisziplinarordnung), e.g. by injured parties in order to exercise their rights. Thanks to Governmental Director Guido Gutzeit at the Leadership Development and Civic Education Center for this and other helpful pointers from a legal perspective.

Bundeswehr Personnel Management. The personal dossiers of soldiers from pay grade A15 and up (lieutenant colonel/commander [navy] and higher) were, and still are, made available to the military archives and stored there at the archive's request. Yet even the personnel records that were available for research were not filed under terms like *homosexuality*; looking for incidents related to the topic at hand would have been like searching for the proverbial needle in a haystack. Targeted research based on concrete references provided by contemporary witnesses proved more fruitful, nearly always presaging a "hit."

Court rulings presented another indispensable source. When the author began research in 2017, however, the Federal Archives were still in the initial stages of registering their extensive collection of military service court records, with only a fraction accessible. In light of this gap, which could not be overcome during the course of this research project, the chapter on criminal and disciplinary rulings relied primarily on decisions reached by the military service senates at the Federal Administrative Court (Bundesverwaltungsgericht) and, prior to that, at the Federal Disciplinary Court (Bundesdisziplinarhof). As with nearly every decision handed down at the Supreme Administrative Court, the text of the military service senates' decisions are accessible online for viewing and research at www.wolterskluwer-on-line.de/. Any military service court records that were incorporated into the Federal Archives by 2019 were searched specifically for judgements pertaining to homosexuality, and the findings included in the present work. The author also searched for – and in some cases managed to find – relevant military service court proceedings based on the concrete suggestions and personal files of contemporary eyewitnesses. The legal cases that have been uncovered in the course of research and presented in what follows thus lay no claim to completeness: they do, however, showcase the spectrum of judicial and disciplinary action in effect at the time.

The dearth of personal files meant that "oral histories," or seeking out and speaking with potential eyewitnesses, took on a consequential role. Sources referred to as "ego-documents" in historical scholarship – the personal documents and records kept by such witnesses, as well as any official files related to their person – were also particularly important.

Yet historical witnesses and their individual recollections took on outsized importance for another reason as well, springing from a methodological problem that arose in the course of research. The nature of the written sources that had been preserved – court decisions, disciplinary proceedings, adverse career decisions and the complaints filed against them, and press reports from the era – meant they invariably gave voice to the difficulties homosexual soldiers came up against while in serving. Biographies that did not encounter these difficulties, by contrast, whether due to the tolerance shown by a fellow soldier or commander, or gay soldiers' discretion while in uniform, were obviously never set down on paper in connection with homosexuality. It was precisely the uncomplicated careers that standard sources provided no information on whatsoever, risking a view of the situation as entirely problematic. Presumably this would not have captured the overall image of life in the armed forces at the time but would have resulted in an incomplete, even skewed sketch.

The disciplinary or criminal proceedings that have been archived must therefore be taken for the individual cases they were, albeit cases that allow one to draw inferences about the baseline course of action. Case studies provide characteristic answers to the question of how the armed forces addressed homosexual soldiers in its ranks at a given point in time. Those where soldiers did draw attention (i.e. the intrinsically problematic instances) must be complemented and mirrored by those where a soldier's homosexuality did not lead to problems in service. The challenge lay in uncovering these inconspicuous biographies, with the only path to them being via the people who were there. Aside from written sources, personal interviews thus formed a second key pillar of source work, filling out gaps in the archival material. As the former Defense Minister noted in her 2017 interview, it is "difficult to get at the truth by way of the written records […] which is why we must recruit people to pick up traces along the path to then be able to tell the right stories."[15]

The author interviewed over sixty contemporary witnesses for this study, whether in person, over the phone or in writing. The majority were homosexual soldiers, both former and active, but also included were service members who observed and experienced how their gay comrades were treated. The author also contacted former decision-makers at the armed forces and the Federal Ministry of Defense, among them politicians, government officials, generals and officers. Interviews with previous MAD employees who engaged with homosexuality in an official capacity were particularly valuable, offering insight into the intelligence agency's work on the fraught subject, confirming what few written sources were available and filling out important aspects and details. The author remains indebted to all those he interviewed for the faith they placed in him, for opening themselves up and trusting him with what were in part highly personal and intimate memories. This study would not be possible without them. Historians must take particular care in handling "ego-documents" – all oral and written eyewitness memories underwent critical evaluation as sources, a standard tool in historical scholarship.[16]

---

15 Interview with Ursula von der Leyen in *Leo*, August 2017.
16 Conversation memoranda or notes that interviewees have confirmed can be found in the author's archives, along with any anonymous interviews reproduced here and all relevant data for the person. They are available for viewing to interested parties.

Michael Lindner served as more than an eyewitness, consistently offering invaluable research advice from Hamburg. Captain Lindner first published an account of his time in the Bundeswehr in 1983, one year after departing the service for health reasons.[17] A 1985 essay followed in which Lindner looked beyond his own case to address more general aspects of the issue (or "dilemma," in his words) including "military psychiatry, law and social psychology" – still written of course through the lens of personal experience.[18] Lindner continued to fight for the rights of homosexuals in the armed forces after his own career in the Bundeswehr came to an early end, a struggle which included his own demands for reinstatement and financial compensation. He painstakingly assembled every press account, court decision and document pertaining to his case throughout, giving rise to an extensive collection that Lindner offered to the Bundeswehr Leadership Development and Civic Education Center (Zentrum Innere Führung) in 2016. The Center in turn inquired whether there was interest at the Bundeswehr Center of Military History and Social Sciences (Zentrum für Militärgeschichte und Sozialwissenschaften der Bundeswehr, ZMSBw). The ZMSBw's subsequent acquisition of the collection provided an initial impetus for the present research, even before the BMVg had commissioned the study.

2. The Great Taboo: Contemporary Press and Early Scholarship

"But there wasn't any discrimination in the Bundeswehr – everything went by the book and was vouched for legally, after all." Such was the spontaneous reaction of a staff officer when he first learned about the research topic in January 2017. Holding down the opposite end of the range of opinion are conclusions like the one *Zeit* reached in June 2014: "Since its founding in November 1955 up through the end of the last century, the story of how the Bundeswehr has handled homosexuality has been a dark one."[19]

In January 1984, the newspaper *Nürnberger Nachrichten* placed the Wörner–Kießling affair within the broader context of the armed forces' approach to homosexuality, calling on the Bundeswehr to "finally break down the taboo of homo-

---

17 Lindner, "Nicht mehr mein Weg," 88–102.
18 Lindner, "Homosexuelle in der Institution Bundeswehr."
19 Schadendorf, "Hauptmann Uhlmann ist schwul."

sexuality."[20] Homosexuality has been the great taboo of practically every modern armed force. In the Bundeswehr, the subject was such an anathema that at one point the Army changed its otherwise universal numeration system for battalions, assigning the 17th Mechanized Infantry Brigade stationed in the Hamburg-Lübeck area number 177 instead of 175.[21] Number 175 was too reminiscent of Paragraph 175 of the German Criminal Code, which made homosexual acts between men a criminal offense and – particularly at the table with drinking buddies – ranked as the synonym par excellence for being gay, as in the saying "he's a hundred seventy-five." *Der Spiegel* was already making noises about the irregular numeration in January 1984, noting that when it came to homosexuality, the "Bundeswehr higher-ups got all twisted up in knots even over simple questions."[22] General Günter Kießling's false denouncement as a homosexual and the ensuing media storm first properly turned the armed forces' treatment of gay soldiers into a hot topic: "Soldiers as potential sexual partners," ran the headline in *Der Spiegel*. The article quoted a letter from a gay soldier seeking advice:

> I'm just plain scared, afraid of being found out [...] That's why I hold back, avoid any close contact with the other soldiers, shut down conversation. I'm forced to deny my personality, I always have the image of potential repercussions in front of me [...] There's no more free space for me, I have to keep myself under control 24 hours a day.[23]

In their lead story on the Kießling affair, the editors in Hamburg included a finished, but previously unpublished article from 1982 detailing Captain Michael Lindner's discharge from service:

> The captain had made a decisive mistake. Instead of denying his difference and covering it up in the barracks, the career Bundeswehr officer had admitted his homosexual tendencies, and thus broken a taboo. It was all the same "whether a soldier prefers men, women or animals," one Bundeswehr psychiatrist informed Lindner, all that mattered was that he "kept it to himself." To this day, the school of the nation still operates under this maxim in order to prevent the bothersome phenomenon of homosexuality from ever becoming an issue in the first place.[24]

---

20 Fh., "Das Tabu: Bundeswehr und Homosexualität," cited in Schwartz, *Homosexuelle, Seilschaften, Verrat*, 302–3.
21 The number 176 had already been assigned to the brigade's field replacement battalion. For a history of the battalion, initially deployed in 1959 in Hamburg-Rahlstedt as a field artillery unit and later disbanded in 1993 as a mechanized infantry brigade, see https://pzgrendiv6.de/brigaden/panzergrenadierbrigade-17.html. (Accessed 12 February 2019, German only).
22 "Soldaten als potentielle Sexualpartner," 22.
23 Ibid. quoted at further length in Wickel, "In einer Männergesellschaft nicht hinnehmbar."
24 "Soldaten als potentielle Sexualpartner."

In 2018 the press singled out Captain Lindman as the "first outed gay in the Bundeswehr."[25] He was not. Lindner was, however, the first gay soldier to find attention in the media, though it was not by happenstance but rather active intervention on his own behalf. *Der Spiegel* first reported on Lindner in July 1981; he was at the time a career soldier who had been declared provisionally unfit for service. "Lindner headed a company from 1974 on. The officer first became a case in 1979 when he came out as gay to his superiors. Lindner entrusted those he told with the information because he no longer felt equipped to handle the 'psychological pressure.' In doing so, the captain breached a taboo."[26]

In January 1984 *Stern* magazine also broadened its view of Kießling's case to include the general situation homosexuals found themselves facing in the Bundeswehr, quoting from first-person accounts in a piece entitled, "I put on an act for them." By *Stern's* account it was "common practice" to "immediately remove commanding homosexual officers from their post."[27] Whether that was in fact the case is the subject of this study, and it arrives at a differentiated set of conclusions.

In 1984, the picture of everyday life for gay soldiers painted in the press was riddled with contempt and exclusion. *Quick*, a popular tabloid at the time, ran a multi-page, fully illustrated article about "troops' morale" on the topic. The article quoted a first sergeant as saying "If a guy like that were in my company I'd have a conversation with him to clear things up then send him to the doctor, who would dismiss him from service right away."[28] A lieutenant colonel also spoke up: "We've got no use for homos. Order must prevail. Or maybe you'd like your son to be trained by a homo?"[29]

The first article within the armed forces' internal press to broach the subject of homosexuality appeared in early 1981 bearing an unmistakably negative message. Beneath a conspicuous headline announcing "Current legal cases: A military superior's homosexual tendencies," *Truppenpraxis* magazine reprinted a decision reached at the Federal Administrative Court. "Homosexual tendencies in a military superior," the verdict read, "specifically an officer, preclude his suitability for promotion […] Nothing else applies concerning an officer's fitness for assignment as a superior or further promotion."[30]

---

25 As on the show "Sachsenspiegel," broadcast on MDR-Fernsehen 27 April 2018. Link accessed 4 May 2018.
26 "'Berufliches': Michael Lindner," 176.
27 Krause, "Da spiel' ich denen eine Komödie vor."
28 "Die Moral der Truppe," 20.
29 Ibid., 21.
30 Weidinger, "Homosexuelle Neigungen eines militärischen Vorgesetzten"; discussed in greater detail in chapter 4.

Five years later in 1986 JS Magazin, a publication put out by the Protestant Church's military chaplaincy, broke with convention to publish its own report entitled "Men in the shadows: Gays in the federal government." Written in a matter-of-fact tone, the article gave a concise sketch of the legal and regulatory landscape to shine an empathetic, if cursory, light on the difficulties young gay soldiers encountered in their daily routine. Military leaders with homosexual "tendencies" experienced "additional problems." "In the view of the [defense] ministry," the article continued, "they are fundamentally unfit for the career of an officer or NCO."[31]

In the late 1990s the *Frankfurter Allgemeine Zeitung* (FAZ), *Berliner Zeitung* and *Focus* magazine each published individual portraits of homosexual officers and NCOs who it turned out had been sanctioned by the military. The topic took up less media attention after the military liberalized its stance toward homosexual soldiers in 2000; it was not until 2014, in the wake of reports on the outing of a high-profile soccer player, that media outlets turned again to the present-day circumstances of gay service members, often interspersing reports with historical episodes from the time period established for the present study.

In 2002, the left-wing magazine *Gigi: Zeitschrift für sexuelle Emanzipation* devoted its lead article to the Bundeswehr's newfound liberalism toward sexuality in a piece entitled "A whole man thanks to Scharping," a play on the tagline of a well-known advertisement for dog food that replaced the brand name "Chappi" with that of Defense Minister Rudolf Scharping. The magazine's editors took a long view of the past, beginning in 1961 with the scandal surrounding Parliamentary Commissioner for the Armed Forces Helmuth von Grolman, continuing through the lawsuits filed by a reserve lieutenant from Münster (pointedly described as the "Plein Affair") and the "Wörner–Kießling affair," and concluding with the Bundeswehr's response to HIV and AIDS, denounced in similar terms as the "AIDS affair."[32] (The incident is hardly remembered today, but at the time the media sensation surrounding Parliamentary Commissioner and retired lieutenant general from the Wehrmacht Helmuth von Grolman lasted weeks in 1961: After his homosexual relationship with a seventeen-year-old busboy came out in public,[33] Helmuth von Grolman attempted suicide. He survived. The following day Grolman called for his own dismissal.) *Gigi* repeated the claim that until regulations were changed in

---

31 Wickel, "Männer im Schatten"; see chapter 2 for more detail.
32 Cover title for *Gigi* from March/April 2002: "Ein ganzer Kerl dank Scharping. Sex. Bomb. Sex. Bomb"; in the same issue see also Mildenberger, "Vögeln für Volk und Vaterland".
33 "Die Bekenntnisse des Krull."

2000, homosexuals "were immediately discharged from service in the event their sexual orientation was discovered."[34]

To date the subject has received little to no attention in historical research into the period, with scholarly publications all stemming from the social sciences or sociological writing. One of the first academic papers to consider the professional discrimination homosexuals experienced lamented in 1977 that, as of yet, the military service senates still had not adopted the "liberal turn" taken by the civilian disciplinary senates at the Federal Administrative Court.[35] The article's author, Günther Gollner, took the Bundeswehr to task for continuing "into the present day" to censure "homoerotic activity that would not have constituted a punishable offense even under the earlier version of §175 with the harshest disciplinary measures," and even after consensual homosexual activity between adults had been decriminalized.[36] Removal from service was the standard procedure, Gollner wrote. Four pages down, however, one reads that there had been a "clear decline" in disciplinary rulings on homosexual activity since its decriminalization.[37] The Bundeswehr had also imposed a "hiring and promotion freeze" on homosexuals in leadership positions, "even in instances where homosexual activity could not be proven in the first place."[38] Gollner again: "To avoid misunderstandings – the Bundeswehr should not turn into a 'men's brothel,' of course. Fitness criteria, however, should be both verifiable and concrete."[39]

In 2006, the Working Group for Homosexual Members of the Bundeswehr (Arbeitskreis Homosexueller Angehöriger der Bundeswehr, AHsAB) published a short history of the armed forces' relationship to homosexuality from its founding up through 2005.[40] This was followed in 2007 by an academic piece Karl-Heinz Biesold wrote for the *Zeitschrift für Sexualmedizin, Sexualtherapie und Sexualwissenschaft*. Aside from addressing heterosexual topics related to the armed forces' opening fully to women in 2001, the article was one of the first of its kind to concentrate on the military's approach to homosexuality between 1955 and 2005.[41] Yet with these few exceptions, the same can be said for the present research topic as for research on sexuality and the military in general: "To date there has been astonish-

---

34 Heilmann, "Helm ab zum Sex!"
35 Gollner, "Disziplinarsanktionen gegenüber Homosexuellen im öffentlichen Dienst," 113.
36 Ibid.
37 Ibid., 116.
38 Ibid., 112–13.
39 Ibid., 116.
40 In February 2020 the AHsAB changed its name to QueerBw.
41 Biesold, "Der Umgang mit Sexualität in der Bundeswehr."

ingly little academic research [...] It's a difficult topic that is also subject to certain taboos. People do not venture into it."[42]

Michael Schwartz's work also deserves mention in this context. While his research does not explicitly concern the armed forces or even the Bundeswehr, he covers a good deal of terrain in *Homosexuelle, Seilschaften, Verrat* (Homosexuals, political cliques and betrayal), a study from 2019 that traces the topic's appearance in politics, armies and secret services as a "twentieth century transnational stereotype."[43] Schwartz devotes one chapter to the scandal that enveloped General Günter Kießling in 1983–84 (although his account is based largely on earlier literature and press publications, with the exception of a more recent article by Heiner Möllers).[44] In doing so he looks beyond the affair to consider how the Bundeswehr's attitude toward homosexuals within its ranks was perceived, both at the time and subsequently,[45] and confirms the scandal's enduring effects by documenting the number of reports it received in the press. Those effects continued to make themselves felt in the new millennium, with journalists quickly reaching for the scandal of fifteen years previous to demonstrate just how significantly society had changed since politicians began to openly admit to their own homosexuality, the civil unions law (Lebenspartnerschaftsgesetz) passed and the Bundeswehr fully opened to gays and lesbians in 2000. "Changes in how homosexuality is treated can be made out from the scandals of the past twenty years. In late 1983, General Günter Kießling was fired," wrote the *Tagesspiegel* in June 2001.[46] According to Schwartz's account, by 2001 one no longer had to fear being pilloried in public as mercilessly as General Kießling had been in 1984.[47] He quoted an article from FAZ, which recalled "with stupefaction" that the "witch hunt against General Kießling" lay only fifteen years in the past. "It is precisely because of the speed of the change that a 'contempo-

---

42 Linda von Keyserlingk, an employee at the Military History Museum in Dresden. Cited in Clarke, "Das Militärhistorische Museum Dresden," 34.

43 Schwartz, *Homosexuelle, Seilschaften, Verrat.*

44 See Möllers, "Die Kießling-Affäre." Earlier literature includes Ramge, *Die grossen Polit-Skandale* and Reichard, *Hardthöhe Bonn.*

45 Schwartz quotes historian Katharina Ebner, for example, as saying that the Kießling affair showed that even in 1982, homosexuals were still unwelcome as soldiers in the Bundeswehr. It was "not so much a single person's susceptibility to blackmail and the attendant security risks" that stood behind the scandal "as a general rejection of homosexuality within the Bundeswehr." Ebner, *Religion im Parlament,* cited in Schwartz, *Homosexuelle, Seilschaften, Verrat,* 279–80.

46 Robert von Rimscha writing for the *Tagesspiegel* 22 June 2001, cited in Schwartz, *Homosexuelle, Seilschaften, Verrat,* 324.

47 Schwartz, *Homosexuelle, Seilschaften, Verrat,* 325.

rary history of homosexuality' is so important," it continued.[48] In this respect, the present study hopes to make a contribution to this emerging history.

In 2019 the Kießling affair, "the Bundeswehr's greatest scandal," served as the subject of a monograph from the pen of Heiner Möllers.[49] At the end of that year a far less dramatic but nonetheless "inglorious case study" of the scandal and the fallout for MAD appeared in Hellmut Hammerich's history of the Bundeswehr intelligence agency up to 1990. In his otherwise comprehensive work, Hammerich does not address how the intelligence service dealt with homosexual individuals under its review outside of a single specific instance.[50]

Friederike Brühöfener is responsible for one of the few works that devotes itself explicitly to the legal and professional situation facing gays in the Bundeswehr. It appeared in a 2019 anthology that resulted from a 2015 conference held by the German Studies Association in Washington D.C. Brühöfener focuses on debates in the 1960s and 1970s concerning the 1969 decision to revise §175 and their impact on the armed forces. She also considers the changes made to conscription regulations in 1977 and the possibility, even obligation, that homosexual men have had since to serve in the military. Brühöfener summarized the resulting conflict in the Army's continued refusal at the time to recognize homosexuals as fit for leadership positions with the catchphrase: "Fit to serve, but not fit to command."[51]

Brühöfener had tackled the subject once before in 2015, delving into the sources for an essay entitled the "Discourse about the Moral Conduct of Bundeswehr Soldiers and Officers during the Adenauer Era." She came to the conclusion that West German rearmament had "offered contemporaries an opportunity to stipulate not only acceptable soldierly behavior, but also adequate male behavior in general."[52]

Jens Schadendorf also gave the Bundeswehr careful consideration in "'It's my Bundeswehr too': Queer and an Officer – Dark Tales and Fractious Civilians in

---

48 Allmeier, "Schwul zu sein bedarf es wenig," FAZ 1 August 1998 as cited in Schwartz, *Homosexuelle, Seilschaften, Verrat*, 323.

49 Möllers, *Die Affäre Kießling*. The quote is the book's subtitle.

50 Hammerich, *"Stets am Feind!"* 261–83.

51 Brühöfener, "Contested Masculinities."

52 Brühöfener, "Sex and the Soldier," 523. The article abstract continues: "In the context of heightened concerns about juvenile delinquents (so-called *Halbstarken*), female prostitution, homosexuality, and the distribution of pornographic materials, West German citizens became interested in the social and sexual conduct of Bundeswehr soldiers and officers. Whereas some still considered the military to be a 'school of the nation' and of proper masculinity, others worried about the armed forces as a possible breeding ground for immorality. Partly sharing these concerns, government representatives, members of the Bundestag, church officials, and military commanders sought to guide soldiers' behavior, emphasizing the ideal of the 'complete' (*vollkommene*) Christian male-breadwinner family."

Uniform," a twenty-page chapter from a 2014 book entitled *Der Regenbogen-Faktor* (The rainbow factor).[53] Schadendorf provides a brief overview of the Bundeswehr's first four decades based on interviews with former and active soldiers before pivoting to the changes introduced at the turn of the millennium and the resulting situation for homosexual officers and NCOs. In 2001 Anja Meisner published a concise university seminar paper on homosexuals in the military under the title "Minority in the Armed Forces."[54]

Another early scholarly publication that dealt expressly with homosexuality in the Bundeswehr appeared in 1993. "Homosexuality and Military Service in Germany," written by the former director of the Bundeswehr Institute of Social Sciences (Sozialwissenschaftliches Institut der Bundeswehr, SOWI) Bernhard Fleckenstein, was originally prepared as a lecture in the UK city of Hull. The article only appeared in English despite the fact that an original version in German exists and about which the BMVg received multiple external inquiries.[55]

The author also published a number of articles in the course of his research for *Taboo and Tolerance*, and in November 2017 the work was cited in the *Washington Post* as evidence that the Bundeswehr was giving the subject new consideration.[56] In late August 2019 Bild picked up on the topic in a detailed interview with a private who had been dismissed from the German Navy in 1964 for his homosexual orientation.[57] This book will not go into any further detail at present on the extensive literature addressing the history of homosexuals in Germany before and after 1945, or the past and present situation of homosexual soldiers in other armed forces, although relevant studies will be cited where appropriate.

---

53 Schadendorf, *Der Regenbogen-Faktor: Schwule und Lesben in Wirtschaft und Gesellschaft – Von Außenseitern zu selbstbewussten Leistungsträgern* (The rainbow factor: gays and lesbians in economy and society – from outsiders to self-assured performers). Schadendorf picked up on formulations used by the author of the present work in a 2013 article about the Wörner–Kießling affair and homosexuality written for *Militärgeschichte: Zeitschrift für historische Bildung*, a publication internal to the armed forces. Schadendorf considered the "unequivocal admission of this part of the armed forces' history" an exception in Bundeswehr publications. *Der Regenbogen-Faktor*, 69, in reference to Storkmann, "Ein widerwärtiges Schmierenstück."
54 Meisner, "Minderheiten in den Streitkräften."
55 Fleckenstein, "Homosexuality and Military Service in Germany." For more on Fleckenstein's piece see chapters 1 and 4.
56 Storkmann, "'Don'nt Ask. Don'nt Tell'"; Storkmann, "'79 cm sind schwul'"; Storkmann, "Das große Tabu"; Noack, "As Trump attempts a transgender military ban."
57 Scheck and Utess, "Was wir damals gemacht haben, war kein Verbrechen." The author of the present study conducted an extensive in-person interview with the private, Dierk Koch, in February 2018. Koch also lent the author an unpublished manuscript of his personal memoirs with the working title "Meine Unvergessenen Freunde" (My unforgotten friends) for use in this work.

3. What about Lesbian Soldiers?

When presenting the initial results of his research, the author nearly always encountered one question: "And what about lesbian women?" It is common knowledge that up until the turn of the millennium, women's role in the German armed forces was limited to the medical corps. Historically, this meant that the number of women serving as fixed-term or career soldiers was minuscule in comparison to the total number of people serving in the armed forces. Still, from 1975 on, and in greater numbers after 1989–91, women were able to volunteer for the medical corps and military bands, and there must have been lesbians among them, statistically speaking. With the exception of two cases from 1999 and 2000, the author was unable to locate any documents pertaining to lesbian soldiers within the extensive archival holdings of the BMVg and the armed forces for the established period of research; the same applied for military service court rulings based on sexual activity between female soldiers. It almost seems as though lesbian soldiers entirely failed to surface on the radar of the Ministry of Defense, military leadership and the Bundeswehr judiciary.[58] Nor was any reference found to how inter- or transgender soldiers were treated during the period of investigation. Based on the written sources that were available, the present study had to limit itself to the Bundeswehr's treatment of male homosexuals. The author was and remains aware of this gap. He was able to conduct eyewitness interviews with two women who served in the medical corps during the 1990s.

---

[58] *Magnus*, a magazine dedicated to a gay target audience was still noting in April 1996 that "Lesbians don't so much as enter the minds of superiors." Glade, "In Reih und Glied!" (The BMVg kept a copy of the article for its archives: BArch, BW 2/38355).

Historical Preamble: Homosexuality's Reception in Earlier German Armed Forces

Take your leave, remove yourself, for you do not belong within our ranks!' Yet if he should be caught, gentlemen [...] he must be eliminated.[1]

Despite unfailing stigmatization and the sword of §175 swaying perpetually above their heads, homosexual soldiers were of course active in the Prussian Army. As one "insider" in the late German Empire thought to explain the connection between barracks life and sex drive, "a soldier's sex drive is pressing however; seduction comes easy in a barracks where there are so many young people living together; a man of the people does not think twice about the fact that he's committing an illicit act, the sensation is pleasant – voilà tout."[2]

1. "Sexually Inverted" Soldiers in Prussia and the German Empire

In 1908 the same "insider" posed a question, asking in the parlance of the day whether "homosexuality damages a race's military efficiency?" In his response Karl Franz von Leexow went beyond his initial question to discuss homosexual activity within the Prussian Army and others both past and present. According to Magnus Hirschfeld, one of the fathers of the incipient gay liberation movement of the era, Leexow "had a different name in reality" and came from an "an old noble line of officers." Leexow could be considered a cavalry officer with "all his heart and soul," and a "true authority on the subject."[3] As Leexow writes,

from its highest posts down to its youngest recruits, our army is permeated with homosocial elements. The extraordinary caution with which a sexual invert has to arrange his life naturally makes it a great deal more difficult for the lay person to gain any insight [...] Yet in one infantry regiment I knew of no fewer than seven homosocial officers, in one cavalry regiment of no fewer than three, nor were the numbers much different in other divisions. Thus, I often

---

1 Prussian War Minister General Karl von Einem speaking to the Reichstag on 29 November 1907. See the transcript for the 61st session of the German Reichstag, 29 November 1907.

2 Leexow, *Armee und Homosexualität*, 27.

3 Hirschfeld, *Von einst bis jetzt*, 149.

had the experience that while soldiers may have been well aware, they looked past it with a shrug or a laugh, anxious only to avoid scandal at all costs.[4]

This tacit acceptance toward "sexual inverts," to use Magnus Hirschfeld's phrase, was likely more a case of apathy toward anything that fell outside regulation or criminal law. Yet even the silent indifference unquestionably on display within the Prussian Army had its limits, as Hirschfeld confirmed in quoting from the 1922 memoirs of a detective identified as Major von Tresckow. "July 3 1907. Commanders in the Berlin and Potsdam guard regiments come to me on a near daily basis asking for advice on how they might combat the pederasty that has spread among soldiers in their regiments."[5]

For both Leexow and Hirschfeld, the Eulenburg affair marked a turning point in this fairly common, if unspoken, form of acceptance. A public mud-slinging contest carried out in court starting in 1907 that centered on honor, slander and homosexuality, the affair implicated the "highest circles" of the empire and the Prussian military – people bound by close ties of friendship to the emperor himself. The trial's protagonists were Maximilian Harden, the publisher of the periodical *Zukunft*; the diplomat Philipp zu Eulenburg; and Kuno von Moltke, a high-ranking officer and adjutant to Wilhelm II. In his publication Harden alluded to homosexual relationships among a group in close proximity to the Kaiser, Moltke in particular, decrying it as a "perverted camarilla."[6] In the foreground the scandal revolved around sexuality and the honor of the Prussian military; behind the scenes it was rough-and-tumble political questions that were at stake, namely influence on the Kaiser and the course of German foreign policy.[7] The Prussian War Minister at the time, General Karl von Einem, emerged as advocating a particularly hard line against homosexual officers in the Prussian Army. Speaking before the Reichstag on 29 November 1907, he joined the fray with the words: "I find these people repulsive, I despise them! [...] If a similar man with similar sentiments were in the army,

---

4 Leexow, *Armee und Homosexualität*, 108–9, also cited in Hirschfeld, *Von einst bis jetzt*, 150.

5 At the time, pederasty was a common term for homosexuality among men–between adults that is, rather than being connected with pedophilia, as is common today. The major quoted was Hans von Tresckow (1866–1934), who headed the Blackmail and Homosexuals Department at Berlin Criminal Investigations after 1900. The military rank cited was that of an officer in the reserves. The fact that Hirschfeld introduced the detective with his reserve officer's title shows yet again the superior place automatically reserved for the military, even in civil society. Tresckow's memoirs appeared in print in 1922 under the title *Von Fürsten und anderen Sterblichen: Erinnerungen eines Kriminalkommissars*. See Hirschfeld, *Von einst bis jetzt*, 149.

6 *Perverse Kamarilla* in German. See Tresckow, *Von Fürsten und anderen Sterblichen*, 135.

7 For a detailed account of the scandal see Schwartz, *Homosexuelle, Seilschaften, Verrat*, 16–76; Bösch, *Öffentliche Geheimnisse*, 117–154; Domeier, "Moltke als Schimpfwort!"

I would gladly shout him down: 'Take your leave, remove yourself, for you do not belong within our ranks!' Yet if he should be caught, gentlemen [...] he must be eliminated."[8]

The winds shifted in the Prussian Army following the War Minister's tirade. In his writings on the Eulenburg affair, Hirschfeld spoke of heightened uncertainty among homosexual Prussian officers.

> Following War Minister von Einem's speech calling on homosexual officers to take their leave from the army, some of these gentlemen sought me out to ask whether their own character might not draw notice; there were none among them who had consorted with subordinates, incidentally. They pursued their profession with all their heart and soul, had the prospects of a brilliant career before them and were now facing the fact that if their homosexual disposition were to become public, all that remained was the revolver. "What are we supposed to do if we do take our leave," they said, "a military career is all we've studied for, our families would disown us, mother's pain and father's fury would be boundless" – and a man is supposed to hand himself over to such a fate voluntarily, even willingly?[9]

Hirschfeld had also read in the newspaper that "anxiety was running riot in such circles. But is it any wonder? A deserting officer once wrote to me asking what he was supposed to do now, no way out stood open to him and all because of a drunken act."[10]

When the Kaiser reluctantly appointed Prince Max von Baden Chancellor of the Reich in October 1918, insiders recalled the prince as a homosexual who "had already been put on the relevant 'list' by criminal investigations as a young lieutenant of the guard in Berlin."[11] Upon hearing who the new chancellor would be, General von Einem had responded by saying: "Who could think of Bademax without laughing!"[12]

Other homosexual officers made use of the increasing headwinds during World War I to avoid the hardships and dangers of the front, even submitting letters of resignation with reference to the former War Minister's appeal before the Reichstag and "often withdrawing back home from the line of fire and the military

---

8 Transcript of the 61st Session of the German Reichstag, 29 November 1907.

9 Hirschfeld, "Sexualpsychologie und Volkspsychologie," cited in Leexow, *Armee und Homosexualität*, 106–7.

10 Hirschfeld, cited in Leexow, *Armee und Homosexualität*, 107.

11 Schwartz, *Homosexuelle, Seilschaften, Verrat*, 59, here alluding to Tresckow, *Von Fürsten und anderen Sterblichen*, 240.

12 Schwartz, *Homosexuelle, Seilschaften, Verrat*, 59, here quoting from Machtan, *Prinz Max von Baden*, 387; see also Krause, *Max von Baden*.

bases."[13] At the same time, however, officers were also being tried in military court during the war for crimes connected with homosexuality, and given dishonorable discharge from the army. Hirschfeld cited the case of an "officer with multiple past distinctions" who was brought before a court martial and "sent home in disgrace" all "due to a trifle":

> In the second year of the war a still-youthful squadron leader was taken by surprise on his morning ride in the Argonne when a regimental adjutant galloping alongside gave the lad a kiss. The incident was immediately reported, followed by a mortifying interrogation of the soldier – an earthy farmer who innocently confessed that the kiss had not been the first from his superior.[14]

Hirschfeld went on to report that he had spoken with the mother of the officer at the latter's request, so as to gently explain the reasons for her son's impending return from the war. The mother replied that she would have preferred to receive the news that her son had fallen.[15]

Writing in 1908 with a view to their possible desertion, Leexow advised homosexual soldiers

> it is of course highly unpleasant for a commander and the officer corps alike when an officer incriminates himself under §175. The newspapers will kick up much more dust if the accused commits suicide or goes before court than if he deserts. For this reason, the officer corps likely views the latter option as preferable [...] I would advise any homosexual officer to think through the consequences of desertion carefully at the given moment. I'd warn against suicide; it is preposterous to kill oneself for something that cannot be helped, even if law and society judge it.[16]

The scandal surrounding Austrian colonel Alfred Redl sheds further light on how officers revealed to be homosexual were treated in the past. Redl, former Vice-Chief of the Austrian intelligence service and Chief of sStaff at a Prague corps, was exposed as a Russian agent and took his own life in 1913. As Egon Erwin Kisch reports, Redl's alleged lover was a young lieutenant who received three years in a penitentiary for "illicit sexual acts against nature." Subsequently released when the war began in 1914, he was demoted to NCO and sent to the Russian front, where he drew attention as a "particularly elegant sergeant."[17] Kisch himself could still recall

---

13 Hirschfeld, *Von einst bis jetzt*, 152.
14 Ibid., 152–53.
15 Ibid.
16 Leexow, *Armee und Homosexualität*, 105–6.
17 Schwartz, *Homosexuelle, Seilschaften, Verrat*, 122 and 127 (Kisch).

the "handsome Uhlan."[18] Beauty lies in the eye of the beholder as is well known. These phrases were also likely expressions of a stereotype about good looking, handsome gay men.

Quoting verbatim from a "monthly report" for March 1906, Leexow noted "an effort [was] also underway within military judiciary circles to repeal §175." Military courts would "make do with regulations concerning the abuse of official power" in the "event of homosexual officers' crimes against subordinates," and did not need §175.

> On the contrary, it would be better for officers with homosexual tendencies if the paragraph in question [§175] were repealed. Whereas today a widespread belief exists among homosexuals in the officer class that a certain security presides over their intercourse with soldiers, total exemption from punishment would bring about a shift insofar as they would turn to civilians of similar tendencies so as to avoid coming into conflict with existing paragraphs about the abuse of official power, meaning infractions against undermining discipline would occur to a lesser extent than they have previously.[19]

The effects of criminalizing any and all same-sex activity for soldiers, even if it occurred in civilian garb and without any connection to military service, were the same in 1967 as when Leexow described them in 1907. The civilian criminal code, and consequently military disciplinary law, made all sex between men liable to punishment, so it made little difference to soldiers looking for same-sex activity whether they pursued it in the barracks or not. Sanctions loomed one way or the other. For at least some commanding officers, this made it conceivable to take the next step to sex with subordinates, or even cross the line to abusing soldiers placed in their care. In the event they were hauled up before a judge, conviction was inevitable and dismissal just as likely, a situation which at times lead to crimes of a more serious nature.

For many officers who were dismissed, a new professional start only seemed possible beyond German borders – too great was the force of stigmatization in a country where the army enjoyed high standing and dishonorable discharge was tantamount to expulsion from society. Yet even then, the long arm of the military often reached far beyond national borders:

> A Prussian officer who had been dismissed for homosexuality made his way abroad, as he had not found a single solid offer for a position at home. When he made to enter the civil service of a foreign state whose citizens, incidentally, did not share the same small-minded views of

---

18 Ibid., 122.
19 Leexow, *Armee und Homosexualität*, 108.

sensual love, a German representative felt duty-bound to intervene and cut off the path that was to lead to bourgeois honor for the officer.[20]

In 1958, flight abroad still seemed the only way out for a Bundeswehr staff officer who had been caught having sex with a man one night in a Cologne parking lot. The highly decorated World War veteran succeeded in making a new career abroad, but even at a distance the incident in Cologne caught up with him. Two years after the fact, the Bundeswehr judiciary served the officer, now in the reserve, a written accusation via the consulate of the Federal Republic. Within the small German community of the far-off country where he was living, such an event was fit to leave the reputation of the veteran – and his future – in tatters.[21]

2. The Reichswehr: Fact and Fiction

As throughout the German Empire itself, social disdain paired with a certain ignorance of the subject also existed in the Reichswehr officer corps. More often than not the corps kept its silence as to the apparent preferences of one officer or another. Yet the principle of "see no evil, hear no evil" could only be maintained so long as nothing was in fact seen or heard, or had to be seen or heard. There was no going back once the cloak of silence had been lifted off the open secret. Once the accusation was uttered, the rules of society took hold and what had been tacitly tolerated became a question of honor, and more particularly the honor of an officer. Ignorance turned suddenly into open rejection.

A similar web of gossip spins about Partenau, a gay first lieutenant in the officer corps of a Reichswehr regiment whose name provides the title for Max René Hesse's 1929 novel. As the rumors draw within increasing proximity to the protagonist's own garrison, a major's wife makes little secret of her odium for homosexual officers: "She despised the lieutenant. He paid no serious mind to young women. And she had known why for some time. Her eldest daughter had bitterly announced that such a man should have his head lopped off."[22] Hesse has a young lady issue a similarly stark warning about the homosexual officer to (who she believes to be) an unwitting officer candidate: "Just you take care. There are many such characters in every army [...] Why in the mess hall he even declared that love between men is the

---

20 Ibid., 49.
21 For a detailed account of the Bundeswehr staff officer see the start of chapter 3.
22 Hesse, *Partenau*, 217–18. Thanks to Dr. Georg Meyer (Freiburg im Breisgau) for bringing this Weimar-era novel to the author's attention.

only authentic and real love there is."[23] At another point an older lieutenant speculates as to whether his suspicions about a relationship between Partenau and the cadet hold substance: "Could the impossible really be true?...Such attachment had been a daily sight during his own days in training, but the taste of this cadet! Still, at the end of the day it wasn't happening on his watch."[24] Just a few days later the lieutenant's tolerance is no longer quite as broad-minded as he bluntly warns the cadet about the first lieutenant: "He [Partenau] knows how to disguise everything incomparably well, nor do we ask anything else in the matter. Those upstairs can permit a great deal, but he underestimates us."[25] A short while later he backpedals: "we would never actually lay a finger on him."[26]

The company commander has known his first lieutenant longer – and better – and looks the other way. "I'd also like to let all this dubious *behind that or beneath this* go without further questioning," he warns his wartime comrade as it is already too late, "but you're riding the both of you onto impossible terrain, into the swamp."[27] In the novel's unavoidable conclusion, Hesse's lieutenant lets all pretense drop and summons Partenau and the officer cadet before the assembled circle of regimental officers: "Long-suspected lovers!"[28] With that the curtain of deaf ears and blind eyes is torn down, revealing the scandal with all the ineluctable consequences.

Hesse's novel had a real-world model in Halberstadt's 12th Infantry Regiment. As the story goes, in December 1928 a captain, a company commander in the regiment's third battalion, was first relieved of duty then discharged in January 1929 when a relationship with an officer candidate in his company came out. Until recently, it was unclear whether this came at "his own request" under pressure from above or his fellow officers, or rather by dismissal.[29] The officer's subsequent career spoke against dishonorable discharge and demotion, and more for a gentlemen's agreement: In World War II he was redeployed as a major, eventually rising to the rank of regiment commander and colonel after proving his mettle on the Eastern Front. This earned him a recommendation for the Knight's Cross, although he was reportedly denied the high honor.[30]

---

23 *Partenau*, 189 and 188.
24 Ibid., 206.
25 Ibid., 210.
26 Ibid., 211.
27 Ibid., 239–41.
28 Ibid., 238.
29 Letter from Ret. Lieutenant Wolters to Dr. Georg Meyer in Freiburg on 24 January 1991. The author would like to thank Georg Meyer for the references and sharing the letter.
30 Ibid.

In February 2021 the great-nephew of the Halberstadt captain recognized his great uncle in an advance version of *Taboo and Tolerance* published online, and provided new biographical information based on personnel files provided through the Federal Archives.[31] The files consulted in the Federal Archives at the great-nephew's suggestion offered some clarity on the matter. When the incident was reported in 1928, for example, the homosexual activity in question already lay three and four years in the past. In October 1924 the officer, then first lieutenant and deputy company commander for the 12th Infantry Regiment's mortar company, had asked an enlisted soldier in his unit to "touch him indecently" while under the influence of alcohol. After Private P. had refused these advances, the first lieutenant had tried to "assault" the soldier. In May or June of the following year, the officer had again tried on two separate occasions to touch the soldier "improperly" and pushed him "to do the same with him." In each case the private refused, upon which the lieutenant urged P. "to keep quiet about the incident, as otherwise he would shoot him [the private] and then himself."[32] A number of days later Private P. informed an NCO and relative of his about the incident.

In other words, unlike the account that was initially sketched and later circulated, and deviating significantly from the plot in Hesse's novel, the case did not involve a consensual affair between an officer and a cadet but an attempted assault against a lower-ranking soldier. The incident must be seen in a totally different light, taking its place among many similar instances of assault in the Bundeswehr that this study will consider. The subsequent course of action and eventual outcome also reveal remarkable parallels to the early days of the Bundeswehr, for example in the Halberstadt company's attempts to clear up the embarrassing incident internally and quietly. Ironically enough, it was the first lieutenant himself who as the deputy company commander deposed witnesses in his own case, before then asking them to keep their silence:

> Rumors about Captain M.'s abnormal tendencies had been circulating for months, so NCO D. reported what he had he had heard and been told to [the later] Captain M., who at the time was deputy company commander. In the days that followed the Captain summoned four NCOs including D. to the company reading room and questioned ten company members in their presence toward whom he was reported to have behaved indecently. No one provided incriminating details until P. was questioned, who reported the incidents mentioned above.

---

31 Email from Dr. Andreas Meyer to the author, 4 February 2021.

32 BArch, Pers 6/8771: [Reichswehrministerium, Heeresleitung, Personalabteilung] P2, Betr.: Unwürdigkeitsverfahren gegen Hauptmann M., I.R. 12, undated, 1928. Throughout the report the soldier's rank from 1928 of captain was incorrectly used for the period during which the offenses were committed of 1924 and 1925. Anonymized by the author here and in what follows.

At this point Captain M. ended the hearings without interviewing the remaining (five or so) witnesses. M. then explained to the NCOs that he had in fact made advances on enlisted soldiers, but assured them he had not committed any criminal acts. He intended to do everything in his power to suppress his tendencies and reportedly asked the NCOs to keep quiet about the matter, and respond to the rumors that were circulating. Under heavy psychological pressure from facts which had been proven true and to which he had largely admitted, and out of concern for his position and for his wife and child, Captain M. did not find the resolve to report the matter. A request to be transferred to East Prussia for which he did not give the true cause was denied.[33]

With that, the case came to an initial close; the NCOs (and the enlisted men) kept their silence as requested. In 1927 M. was promoted to captain and chief of the regiment's 12th (machine gun) company, stationed in Magdeburg. In late September 1928 the former NCO D., now a first sergeant, reported the events of 1924–25 to his company commander. The division conducted "unworthiness proceedings" against Captain M. while the senior public prosecutor in Halberstadt opened a simultaneous investigation under §175 of the Imperial Criminal Code, although the latter was suspended in late November 1928. (The older version of §175 only criminalized actual intercourse between men, so the law came nowhere near to applying in the present case of an attempted advance.[34]) Inquiries into possible crimes under §114, §116 (abuse of official power) and §121 (abuse of a subordinate) of the military criminal code were also abandoned. Instead, an internal solution came in the form of an honor council partially made up of battalion, regiment and division commanders, the division's infantry commander and its commanding officer from Group Command 1 in Berlin. The council argued in favor of "immediate" dismissal on grounds of "unworthiness," though a "milder form of elimination [would be] tolerable," and spurned the "dishonorable disposition." (Deviating from the majority vote, the regimental commander further considered "dishonor to be present.")[35] The personnel department also advocated the captain's immediate dismissal in its own statement, reproaching him in particular for trying to win the silence of the officers and enlisted men.

His immoral crime [later emended by hand to read "behavior toward Private P."] has shown him to be unworthy of his position. Making the matter still more serious is his unmanly and dishonorable behavior upon revelation of the incidents from the summer of '25, during which he ["as company commander" was added later] attempted to justify himself before his subor-

---

33 BArch, Pers 6/8771: [Reichswehrministerium, Heeresleitung, Personalabteilung] P2, Betr.: Unwürdigkeitsverfahren gegen Hauptmann M., I.R. 12, undated, 1928.
34 For greater detail on the legal history of §175 see the beginning of chapter 3.
35 BArch, Pers 6/8771: [Reichswehrministerium, Heeresleitung, Personalabteilung] P2, Betr.: Unwürdigkeitsverfahren gegen Hauptmann M., I.R. 12, undated, 1928.

dinates [later crossed out and replaced with "and requested their silence"] [...] Captain M. was ["fully"] aware of his transgressions. He attempted to compensate for these transgressions by especially zealous work, until at last three years later *unavoidable disaster overtook him* [later changed to "his fate caught up with him after all"].[36]

The personnel department cited the officer's military career in World War I as "a mitigating factor," for which he had been decorated with the Iron Cross 1st and 2nd classes and promoted from NCO to lieutenant in 1919 "in recognition of his services." He was further credited with his "frank confession and sympathetic defense," leading the department to propose a more lenient form of dismissal "with the agreement of his fellow service members and superiors." The incidents did mean, however, that the captain's "service qualification" should be "revoked," and that he should be denied "conferral of the uniform," i.e. permission to wear the uniform of a retired officer.[37]

In a document leading up to the decision that ran via official channels through the 4th Division and Group 1 commander up to the chief of Army Command, the personnel department once again emphasized that the "total lack of right moral conception shown in the case of Captain M. has not been remedied. A soldier who errs in such fashion is unworthy of his profession, all the more so when Captain M. should serve as a model as a superior and officer." The captain's attempts to justify himself to subordinates were listed again as aggravating circumstances. "His duty as a leader charged with responsibility and his honor as a man retreated into the background out of weakly concern for his own future. Immediate dismissal would be the requisite expiation."[38] The personnel department would see to his "dispatch" "without uniform" under §26b of the Military Code on 31 March 1929 (§26b governed dismissal for lack of fitness without permission to wear a uniform).[39] As an alternative to active dismissal, it would be left to the captain's discretion whether to apply for his own discharge by year's end 1928, in which case the service would cover his salary through March 1929. The captain chose this latter path; his file

---

36 Ibid., author's emphasis.

37 Ibid.

38 Ibid., "Vorbereitung der Entscheidung," classified a Secret Command Document, notice of receipt from 4th Division on 29 November 1928, Supreme Commander of Group 1 on 3 December 1928 and Army Command on 20 December 1928.

39 An interesting point of constitutional procedure that closely resembled that of the Bundeswehr, playing out even at much higher levels: The captain was to be notified of the decision and his right to appeal to the minister of the Reichswehr within the space of one month. The appeal would then be decided by the Reich president based on a report from the minister. BArch, Pers 6/8771: [Reichswehrministerium, Heeresleitung, Personalabteilung] P2, Betr.: Unwürdigkeitsverfahren gegen Hauptmann M., I.R. 12, undated, 1928.

contains a two-sentence handwritten request for release dated 24 December 1928. On 27 December the regiment sent a telegraph to Berlin: "Agreed upon early release for Captain M. 31.12.28 = Form submission of written consent will come through official channels."[40]

What is not documented, though highly probable given the subsequent course of events, is that the Reichswehr likely offered the captain a way out and a future career as an officer – albeit not in Germany but the German military mission in China. By March 1929, M. had already entered service in Nanjing under the German general advisor to Chiang Kai-shek's National Revolutionary Army. The rapid succession of events leading from the captain's dismissal to his trip by boat to Shanghai and entry into service in March 1929 make a lengthy exchange of letters and formal application process seem unlikely, even impossible in the given timeframe. M. probably boarded the ship to China carrying nothing more than a letter of recommendation from the Reichswehr, able to rest assured that he would be taken in. The case fits in with a recognizable pattern of officers released from the armed forces for homosexual activity who go on to seek a fresh professional start – be it military or civilian – in far-off lands, in many cases even on the other side of the world.

M. returned to Germany in 1938 as the military mission wrapped up its work. (Germany's ally Japan had attacked China in 1937.) In October 1938 he appealed to Wehrmacht High Command for clemency, resulting in recognition of his "character as a major" and permission to wear a uniform.[41] (In the Prussian Army, as in the Reichswehr and the Wehrmacht, this sort of "characterization," or recognition of an officer's rank was standard procedure for conferring the next higher service rank onto a retired officer, albeit without a raise in salary or pension payments. All that was involved was the honor of displaying a higher rank on one's uniform.) The army commander-in-chief did, however, decline to reappoint the officer to active service. A year later in October 1939 Army High Command authorized his assignment as an officer for the duration of the war. By December 1939 M. was a battalion commander, became lieutenant colonel in 1942, and by December of 1942 was made regimental commander and full colonel,[42] though still only temporarily for times of war, not yet for active duty. M.'s division commander had been applying for his active deployment since the late 1930s, with his former superiors

---

40 BArch, Pers 6/8771: Reichswehr Ministry, Navy Intelligence, Long distance input, 27 December 1928.
41 BArch, Pers 6/8771: Order signed in Berchtesgaden 28 October 1938 by Führer and Reich Chancellor Hitler and Army Commander-in-Chief von Brauchitsch.
42 All available in BArch, Pers 6/8771.

in China also calling attention to the matter on multiple occasions, but to no avail – he was not legally called back into active service until 1943. The files also state the reason why – as the personnel department decided more than once, "Chief P 2 *cannot* agree to M.'s transfer from Major on call to active officer; an officer who has repeatedly committed indecent acts against a subordinate is not fit as a commander under conditions of peace."[43] Contrary to what had been reported, the lieutenant colonel did in fact receive the Knight's Cross in 1942.[44]

Things followed a similar course in 1933 when a captain was dismissed as a company chief in Paderborn's 18th Infantry Regiment. Behind hedged talk of "incidents" lay a purported homosexual liaison between the captain and his company's sergeant. The "incidents" did not bring an end to the officer's career, however, but merely put a damper on it. Removed from his position as head of Company 12 in April 1933, the captain was transferred to regimental staff before being appointed to a teaching position that same month at the infantry school in Dresden. By 1942 the officer who had once been removed as commander of a company rose to division commander, reaching the rank of lieutenant general and receiving the Knight's Cross of the Iron Cross.[45]

While novels like Hesse's *Partenau* record how the Reichswehr handled incidents or rumors concerning homosexuality, the story has also come down through archival documents. In 1924 the Army Personnel Office reported seventeen previous cases of "moral misconduct" on the part of officers leading to their dismissal. Fifteen had revolved around the "satisfaction of perverse tendencies" (not explained in greater detail, but clearly classifiable from the context and the harsh censure, as described below), with thirteen committed with or against subordinates. Eight of the cases involved drunkenness.[46] "Drunkenness may exempt one from punishment in court," the office admonished, "[but] in no way lifts the moral responsibility toward one's professional comrades. A man must know himself, and thus the stimulating effects of alcohol on his sex life. Accordingly, in case of uncertainty about his tendencies he has a duty to exercise restraint in his enjoyment of alcohol."

---

43 BArch, Pers 6/8771: P2, 6 November 1940, as well as a preceding note from P2 on request from 83rd Infantry Division on 16 October 1940.
44 BArch, Pers 6/8771: Army Personnel Office, 1st Echelon, Army High Command, 11 May 1942.
45 The author would like to thank Dr. Georg Meyer of Freiburg for this reference as well.
46 BArch, RH 12-1/102: Army Personnel Office to Inspector of Education and Training, 23 December 1924, Secret! For processing only by an officer. The file contains the following quotations. Thanks to Lt. Col. Dr. Christian Stachelbeck of the ZMSBw for sharing archival findings from his study on education in the Reichswehr, and his kind permission to make them available here.

This came followed by a warning about the grave consequences that such "misconduct" held for superiors' authority, and consequently for troop discipline.

> This sort of moral misconduct is always condemnable and disagreeable in and of itself. Yet it is all the more disastrous in a military context for completely undermining discipline like no other action when subordinates are dragged into the affair. It is not simply the soldiers who are directly involved that lose all feelings of respect and subordination toward the accused ranking officer. Anyone else who hears of an officer's moral misconduct – and sooner or later, it always reaches light of day – is forced to reject him as a superior and a comrade.

As this study will show, this assessment from 1924 was nearly identical to those made by Bundeswehr legal staff and military service judges.

The Army Personnel Office offers another example of the fine line separating platonic or comradely affection from homosexual feelings in a series of events from 1926. An officer who had "received especially high marks for bravery and solicitude during the war" had in peacetime "brought himself under suspicion of abnormal tendencies due to his odd behavior when interacting with enlisted men." Specifically, he had caressed them and given them pet names while drunk. He could have remained in the army despite this in the eyes of the personnel manager, but it was no longer possible after he falsely accused other soldiers of "similar misconduct" in his defense.[47] The personnel office gave other examples as to how rumors could arise. An officer who had been involved in a "patriotic youth organization" had subsequently kept up his "free and easy" patterns of interaction with subordinates in the troops. This had led to "ugly rumors about an unnatural tendency" of the officer's, although an investigation had confirmed "their total baselessness."[48]

3. Homosexuality in Wehrmacht, Police and SS: Biographical Examples

Threats of §175 notwithstanding, Harry Pauly (b. 1914) lived out his sexuality in free and unencumbered fashion as a professional actor on the Berlin stage – until, that is, the National Socialists came to power. "It got worse and worse for homosexuals after that. We were really considered the lowest of the low."[49] Pauly was

---

[47] BArch, RH 12-1/102: Army Personnel Office to Inspector of Education and Training, 5 November 1926, Secret Command Document.
[48] BArch, RH 12-1/102: Army Personnel Office to Inspector of Education and Training, 28 August 1925, Secret Command Document.
[49] Eyewitness report of Harry Pauly in Stümke and Finkler, *Rosa Winkel, Rosa Listen*, 313.

drafted into the Wehrmacht in 1939; in 1943 earlier "stories" from Berlin caught up with him when two acquaintances caught in the snares of the Gestapo named names. A military court sentenced Pauly to three years in a penitentiary, which on appeal was reduced to one year and eight months in prison. After his release he was sent to a replacement battalion in Iserlohn, personnel file in tow. "It quickly got around of course that I was a 'warm brother' and had done time for [§] 175."[50] In Iserlohn, and later in France, fellow soldiers would refer to Pauly as the "gay sow," "flushed pig," "gay stallion" or "breech-loader." "It was unbearable," Pauly recalled. "No person alive could have put up with it [...] it made me sick."[51] Pauly deserted, only to be caught. Convicted of desertion, he was sent to serve out his sentence in a penal unit, the Strafbatallion Dirlewanger. Pauly was shot in the stomach during a suicide mission, which he just barely survived in a Wehrmacht hospital in Prague. "All I wanted to do was live, live, live."[52] For Pauly, the end of the war brought true liberation.

May 1945 also meant liberation for Johann-Rudolf Braehler (b. 1914). Called up to serve in a bicycle reconnaissance squadron, in time Braehler became an NCO and was awarded both the Iron Cross 2nd Class and an Assault Badge.

> My advance in the Pan-German Wehrmacht thus seemed assured. There were two other men in the squadron I knew to be homosexual. They knew I was too. It never came to sexual contact though. It was only when two other soldiers came to the squadron in 1942 that I struck up an intimate friendship with them. My trials began [...] I was supposed to be the new squadron sergeant, but things turned out quite a bit different. Suddenly, a rumor surfaced that I spent my time involved in same-sex activity with comrades. My one friend Bruno was so worn down by punishment drills that he confessed to everything. My other friend was apprehended at home and placed under arrest. After that it all went very quickly. They brought Bruno and I under guard to prison in Kassel. Even at this point I still didn't believe they would punish me for a trifle [...] That's why I didn't use my chance to escape when we came under a bomb attack in Hannover during transport to Berlin. We searched out our guards amid all the chaos like blind, faithful sheep and continued on our way.[53]

NCO Braehler was accused of "crimes under §175" and "undermining military morale" and, because his companions were privates, further charged with exploiting his office and "use of force." He was sentenced to two years in the penitentiary; the privates received one year each in prison. Yet Braehler was not sent to penitentiary, instead he was delivered to the Rhede-Brual prison camp in Emsland. "I had

---

50 The term *warme Bruder* is an earlier, generally derogatory term for gay men. – Trans.

51 Stümke and Finkler, *Rosa Winkel, Rosa Listen*, 314.

52 Ibid., 315.

53 Eyewitness report from Johann-Rudolf Braehler in *Rosa Winkel, Rosa Listen*, 316–24, here 318.

lost all sense of naïveté," Braehler recalled, "I no longer deluded myself. The only thing I wanted to do was survive [...] generally speaking the same inhuman terror of the concentration camps reigned at our camp, just without the ovens."[54] While any number of homosexuals were locked up in the camp,

> there was never any homosexual contact [...] we were too worn out and too afraid. My Catholic faith was still deeply rooted in me at the time. I was firmly convinced this was all God's punishment, which had inevitably come down on me because of my serious transgressions. It only became clear many years later just how wrong this attitude was.[55]

In the last weeks of the war the prisoners at Rhede-Brual were enlisted once again as soldiers to join in the final battle. Braehler and a handful of other men quickly deserted, hiding out with the family of a friend in Nordenham until ultimate surrender.[56]

(A necessary postscript: After the war, Braehler failed in his attempt to start a new career at a job center when his conviction under §175 caught up with him yet again. His personnel manager summoned him to make it known that his criminal record had been reviewed in the meantime, and that "the employees at the job center couldn't be expected to work with a homosexual."[57])

One study published in 1991 let eyewitnesses speak for themselves in responding to the question "how did homosexuals feel as soldiers in the Wehrmacht?"[58] As one story goes, in 1936 Air Force Tribunal I in Königsberg sentenced Peter L. to one year and six months in prison for reportedly engaging in same-sex activity around his home in Cologne while serving in the Wehrmacht. Another soldier from Cologne, Werner K., was able to report a "very positive" experience serving as a soldier in the war after his marriage failed. "For me it came as a relief [...] to be in the company of men for once, even if nothing happened." Werner had been aware of the risks and avoided relationships with company members, but had absolutely had "numerous relations in the occupied territories." The study's authors came to the conclusion that "the extreme situation in which every soldier found himself, paired with what was at least the temporary impossibility of living out his sexuality, encouraged same-sex activity. Within a field of latent erotic tension, homosexuals were able to pursue their desires undetected."

---

54 Ibid., 319.
55 Ibid., 321.
56 Ibid., 321–22.
57 Ibid., 323.
58 Ernst and Limpricht, "Der organisierte mann," 65. Also in what follows.

An academic study would not be complete without mentioning that the "Guidelines for handling criminal cases involving illicit sexual acts against nature," issued by Wehrmacht High Command in 1943, prescribed the death penalty "in particularly serious cases."[59] Available research has only documented a limited number of cases of homosexual Wehrmacht soldiers receiving the death penalty, however – and if so it is generally for other charges, usually desertion.[60]

In contrast to Wehrmacht soldiers, homosexual activity, even the tendency itself, *always* stood under the threat of death for the men and police of the SS following a 1941 decree from Hitler, and implementation guidelines the next year from Reichsführer-SS and chief of the German police Heinrich Himmler.[61] Himmler had previously made his position on homosexuality clear in a 1937 speech to SS leaders in Bad Tölz:

> Even today, we still have one case of homosexuality per month in the SS. Throughout the entire SS approximately eight to ten cases will arise annually. I have now decided on the following: These people will be publicly demoted and cast out as a matter of course and handed over to the courts. After serving the penalty determined by the court they will be brought to a concentration camp on my orders then shot while on the run. This will be given on my command to the unit to which the person belonged. In this way I hope to rid the SS down to the last of this sort of person, so as to at least clear a path for what good blood we do have in the Schutzstaffel, as well as the nascent process of restoring the blood that we are pursuing for Germany.[62]

In 1943 the Belgian Eric Vermeer was made to witness what Himmler's words meant for a homosexual SS-man after Vermeer volunteered for the Schutzstaffel

---

59 The directive was issued 19 May 1943 by Field Marshal Wilhelm Keitel, increasing the severity of the current scope of punishment by applying §5a of the Special Wartime Penal Decree (Kriegssonderstrafenverordnung). For more see Lorenz, *Todesurteile und Hinrichtungen wegen homosexueller Handlungen während der NS-Zeit*, 16.

60 Lorenz shows this in detail through the fate of Bernhard Ernst Jung (b. 1919). Jung was drafted into the Wehrmacht in 1939 after multiple arrests by criminal investigations and time spent in prison during his youth. He was arrested for homosexual activity in 1940 while stationed in the occupied Netherlands. He succeeded in fleeing on his way to trial by court martial. His hiding place was later discovered in a Hamburg raid. In February 1941 Jung was sentenced to three years' penitentiary by the court martial of the 110th Infantry Division in Hamburg on two counts of violating §175a. At the same hearing he received a death sentence for desertion. Bernhard Ernst Jung died by guillotine on 6 March 1941. Lorenz, *Todesurteile und Hinrichtungen wegen homosexueller Handlungen während der NS-Zeit*, 17–22.

61 The wording for the decree on "Maintaining the purity of the SS and police," dated 15 November 1941, is available in Lorenz, *Todesurteile und Hinrichtungen*, 14. A facsimile of the implementation guidelines is available in Ernst and Limpricht, "Der organisierte Mann," 63.

62 Himmler, *Geheimreden*, 93–104, here 97–98.

and was assigned to the 6th SS Volunteer Assault Brigade Langemarck.[63] One night while deployed in Ukraine, the men were torn from their sleep by the alarm. Two of their own were then driven before the rows of the assembled brigade.

"These goddam ass-fuckers have sullied German honor," loudspeakers bellow across the courtyard. "They fornicated wrapped up tightly about each other, and now they can go to hell wrapped up tightly about each other!" [...] In a cone of light, six SS go about beating the two men with their rifle butts before the soldiers. Marcel nearly stumbles over the chain, his legs and hands shackled, his face a red pulp by now, the left eye no longer visible. A gunshot strikes him down, and the chain yanks Louis to the ground. Louis takes Marcel's head in his hands and screams. A second shot. Eric Vermeer stands in the first row trying to keep from vomiting, he nearly faints and gives himself away [...] this unit, the one he freely volunteered for, doesn't only kill Jews and Communists, it kills gays as well.

Vermeer was gay.

Eric often hears derogatory comments about "ass-fuckers" and "75ers" [in reference to §175], nobody uses "homosexual" [...] He doesn't visit the military whorehouse along with the others [...] it doesn't go unnoticed. One day an envoy sent by the troops sits down with him. "It's time you went at it with the cook, Maria," the comrade says, handing him a condom [...] Eric doesn't want to chicken out and chases after the cook, a Ukrainian, who flees the soldiers' raucous shouts. Eric lets her go, he's given his performance for now.

Vermeer remained in West Germany after the war, where he "had more to hide than during the war – his homosexuality and his past in the SS."

It was only with a great many blessings in disguise that a gay Berliner drafted into the German police survived the war in occupied France, and that despite being condemned to death.[64] When Hans G. resisted a major's demands to satisfy his sexual desires, the latter reported him for "attempted seduction," if only to protect himself. It was word against word; the officers and Wehrmacht judiciary went with the major's account. The investigation widened to include sexual encounters in Berlin from far back in Hans G.'s past, and the conscripted policeman received three separate death sentences for three previous incidents; as a member of the police, he was subject to Himmler's decree. His father appealed to Himmler for clemency, resulting in the deferral of the son's death sentence and transfer to the Neuengamme concentration camp. He survived both the camp and the war. (Necessary postscript: After the war Hans G. did not risk applying for wartime restitution.

---

63 Wörtz, "Beim Fummeln erwischt." The editors at the *Spiegel* came up with the name Eric Vermeer to protect the identity of the interviewee. The following quotes and information are from there.

64 Eyewitness report from Hans G. in Stümke and Finkler, *Rosa Winkel, Rosa Listen*, 301–6.

"Us gays were still being legally persecuted. There was no way I wanted to go back to prison or a penitentiary."[65])

Like all men convicted under §175 during the National Socialist era, Wehrmacht soldiers who had been convicted of "illicit sexual acts against nature" could not count on mercy even after 8 May 1945. As German Federal Anti-Discrimination Agency chief Christine Lüders writes, "This explains why after the war so many homosexual men who had been freed from the concentration camps found themselves back in prison, where they had to serve out the rest of their terms."[66]

One case involves a man drafted into the Wehrmacht in 1939 at age 30 who was convicted twice under §175 by military courts during the war. In September 1942 the field court martial at Panzer Army High Command III sentenced him to one-year prison and demotion in rank. He served the sentence until it was suspended for the duration of the war in February 1943, but was again convicted by Central Army Court in September 1944 on charges of "attempted aggravated illicit sexual acts between men and illicit sexual acts between men." This time, since he was still on probation, he was given ten years' imprisonment and five months' additional service in a penal unit. The sources show that the man was held at the Dora concentration camp outside Nordhausen until 11 April 1945. In October 1945 the man was apprehended in Unna by the police, who were now under British control, and taken to prison. The British military government ordered him sent to the penitentiary in Werl with nine years and eight months' penitentiary remaining in his prison term. An appeal in February 1946 was denied by the senior public prosecutor in Arnsberg, although his immediate release was ordered later that year in June.[67]

The Unna case was not the exception but the rule; for other Wehrmacht soldiers convicted of homosexuality the end of the war did not mean the end of imprisonment. "You stay here!" liberating U.S. troops told one Luftwaffe soldier detained in Landsberg after inspecting his detention orders. Herrmann R. had to serve out the remaining year of his sentence under new management in the same penitentiary. He was released in 1946.

What had brought Herrmann R. to Landsberg in the first place? After he was called up to the Luftwaffe in 1943, the stage actor was set to work as a personnel

---

65 Ibid., 306.
66 Christine Lüders in her preface to Burgi and Wolff, *Rechtsgutachten zur Frage der Rehabilitierung der nach Paragraph 175 StGB verurteilten homosexuellen Männer*.
67 North Rhine-Westphalia State Archives, Westphalia inventory, Q 926/12138, Werl Penitentiary, Arrest Files for Kurt P., 1945–1946. The file contains the field court martial decision labelled under Pz.A.O.K. 3, St.L. No. 123/42 from 31 August 1942 as well as the decision of Central Army Court, St.L. IX 260/44 from 22 September 1944. The author has Frank Ahland to thank for directing him to the source.

clerk and property administrator at an Air Force staff office in Prague. In the city he gave "free rein" to his "homosexual urges" as he put it. "As will happen, before you know it you're out skating on thin ice."[68] The ice turned out to be extremely thin, and eventually cracked because of a "trifling matter." As a trained actor, R. was sent around for troop support, and after one "colorful evening" involving a great deal of alcohol he had supposedly grabbed the genitals of a Hitler Youth squad leader over the pants.

> To my horror I was immediately arrested and locked up in solitary confinement. When they questioned me I said [...] the whole thing had been foolishness. But it was to no avail. My defender, a crafty court officer [a Wehrmacht jurist] told me that it would help lighten my punishment if I admitted my homosexuality and explained the matter away as a regrettable slip-up. I had no idea about laws at the time, nor did I get that he wanted to take me for a ride [...] The judge sentenced me to three years in the penitentiary for attempted 'illicit sexual acts' and ten years for undermining military morale. The sentence struck me as improbable. Even the two witnesses were startled and apologized to me. It wasn't what they had wanted either.[69]

As became common practice throughout 1944–45, enforcement was "'suspended until the final victory!' [...] Every man was urgently needed, after all." Up until final victory came and the convict entered prison, R. would "prove his worth" on the front in a "penal unit or suicide squad." "I reckoned my greatest chances of survival would be in the camps." At the Wehrmacht prison in Prague, a sergeant helped R. get on a transport to the concentration camp in Dachau instead of a penal battalion. "Czechs out, politicals out, 175ers out," he heard yelled on arrival, at which point a kapo [prisoner functionary, part of the prisoner self-administration in a Nazi camp] bawled back "Gays out, what does 175 mean here?!" With a pink triangle affixed to his striped prison outfit, R's transport continued on to the neighboring camp in Landsberg, an old fortress prison. U.S. troops reached Landsberg on 26 April 1945, and several weeks later a U.S. military commission examined the detention files. "I can still hear the U.S. officer who was questioning me say: 'Homosexual, that's a crime. You stay here!'"[70] Hermann R. was not released until 1946. The British and U.S. officers operated according to the legal practices of their home countries; convicting homosexuals for their sexuality did not strike them as a form of injustice originating in National Socialism, but one that matched their own legal sensibilities.

---

68 Eyewitness report of Herrmann R. in Stümke and Finkler, *Rosa Winkel, Rosa Listen*, 325–30, here 325.
69 Ibid., 325–26.
70 Ibid., 330.

To anticipate one possible question from readers: Within the literature concerning the fate of homosexuals persecuted under National Socialism, the author has yet to come across a single instance of a Wehrmacht soldier who found himself in the Soviet occupation zone in May 1945. This makes it impossible to draw conclusions about how Soviet occupation authorities proceeded. There is one example of a man (not a soldier) previously sent to Sachsenhausen for homosexuality who, like all those freed from the concentration camps, initially received an Opfer des Faschismus (Victim of Fascism) ID card. Yet within a few months his card, and with it his status as victim, was taken away by the new "anti-fascist" authorities in East Berlin after they learned about his internment under §175. As in the Western occupation zones and later in the Federal Republic, gay and lesbian victims of the National Socialist regime were not recognized as victims in the Soviet zone or the later GDR, but remained convicts in the eyes of the law.

I   Unfit to Serve? Evaluating Homosexual Men's Military Fitness

> Consistent homosexuality as manifests in ongoing same-sex relationships represents one form of sexual perversion that on the whole should be classified under psychopathy.[1]

Taken from an internal document prepared by the Office of the Surgeon General of the Bundeswehr in October 1970, the quote's classification of homosexuality as psychopathic, or a psychological illness did not simply reflect the individual views of a staff advisor. Rather, it stood in line with the general regulatory apparatus in effect at the time, appearing in the military's official entrance regulations under ZDv 46/1.[2] And the BMVg or the Bundeswehr were not alone in their position.

1.   Homosexuality as an "Official" Disease

When the World Health Organization (WHO) published the sixth edition of its International Statistical Classification of Diseases and Related Health Problems (ICD-6) in 1948, it designated homosexuality as a psychological illness, specifically a "sexual deviation." As with the subsequent versions ICD-7, ICD-8 and ICD-9, homosexuality was grouped by ICD-6 among "disorders of character, behaviour and intelligence" where it was placed under "pathologic personality." Not until 1992, in the ICD-10, did homosexuality disappear from the list.[3] Since then, homosexuality has not been considered an illness within the international community – since 1992, mind you. It is essential to keep the global framework in mind when casting a narrower and more critical eye toward how the German armed forces related to homosexuality.

---

1 BArch, BM 1/6727: BMVg, InSan I 1, 15 October 1970.

2 ZDv refers to *Zentrale Dienstvorschrift*, or joint service regulations; in what follows the German acronym is used.

3 The ICD-6 dates from 1948, the ICD-7 from 1955, the ICD-8 from 1965, and the ICD-9 from 1975. The ICD-10 was adopted by the WHO in 1990 and used by member states until 1994. Drescher, "Gender Identity Diagnoses," 142. The ICD-10 was new in diagnosing egodystonic sexual orientation as a psychological illness. Egodystonia refers to a condition in which a person does not experience their thoughts, impulses or emotions as being in harmony with their ego, which can lead to panic attacks. In egodystonic sexual orientation doctors recognize the wish to have a different sexual orientation than the one that exists. The direction of the sexual orientation itself is not seen as the disorder. See https://icd.who.int/browse10/2019/en#/F60-F69 under section F66 (accessed 31 March 2021).

A phenomenon's medical perception as an illness raises the question of its treatment. A 1966 conference organized by the BMVg's Office of the Surgeon General, Bundeswehr did just that, addressing a host of medical issues pertaining to homosexuality while also explicitly asking "whether medical treatment of these [types of] soldiers promised results," and "rigorously considering" the chances of success.[4] Surgeon General Dr. Georg Finger had only a handful of "conclusive successes" to report with "treatment" in psychotherapy, and then only in the case of "very mature, i.e. older men" whose fitness for military service no longer came under consideration. The second group with whom Finger reported experiencing "success in treatment" were men who "were not homosexually perverted" but engaged only in occasional same-sex activity. All in all, the surgeon general found the "perversion" to be "practically incurable."[5] Besides prospects for treatment or cure, the symptomology of a condition the medical community firmly believed to be an illness was also logically presented. The government medical director in charge of supervising the medical examination board proceeded with surgical precision, reporting on every deformity in male genitalia conceivable, along with the exact number of incidences found for conscripts born in 1946. In the end, though, it was only to determine that army examiners had not "observed any relationship between sexual perversions and genital deformities," nor did "any appear to exist."[6] The results themselves did not pass muster for the chief medical examiner, so to speak. Instead he informed his colleagues that he would reissue his order to the district draft boards to report any cases that arose so as to gain an "absolutely precise statistical overview."[7]

One former surgeon general of the Bundeswehr recalled his medical course of study in 1958–59 as having "taught us that homosexuals were epidemiological vectors for hepatitis and syphilis, suspected by the police of prostitution and drug trafficking, and thus a part of the criminal world."[8] Ten years later in 1968, a dictionary for psychiatry and adjacent disciplines listed homosexuality as a form of "paraphilia," or sexual desire that strongly deviated from the empirical norm, ranking it as a "perversion" alongside exhibitionism, masochism, necrophilia, nymphomania, sadism and transvestism. Homosexuality generally surfaced in connec-

---

4 BArch, BW 24/3736: Surgeon General Dr. Finger, "Einführende Bemerkungen zu BMVg," InSan: "Beurteilung der Wehrdiensttauglichkeit und Dienstfähigkeit Homosexueller," 1966, here sheet 5.
5 Ibid.
6 BArch, BW 24/3736: "Über die Erkennung von sexuellen Perversionen bei der Musterung." In: BMVg, InSan: "Beurteilung der Wehrdiensttauglichkeit und Dienstfähigkeit Homosexueller," 1966, sheets 35–40, here sheet 38.
7 Ibid., 39–40.
8 Letter from Ret. Surgeon General Dr. Horst Hennig (Cologne) to the author, 17 July 2017.

tion with neuroses, the dictionary stated, and "many homosexuals are neurotic in one form or another [...] which may be explained in one part by the position they (especially men) hold in society."[9] By 1969 the extensive *Brockhaus Encyclopedia* no longer defined homosexuality as an illness but a "common form of deviation from the sexual norm," with four percent of men and one percent of women inclined toward members of the same sex.

The 1970 paper cited at the outset of this chapter also considered the rate at which homosexuality was "diagnosed" during medical entrance exams and in military service. "Clinically speaking," approximately one in a thousand conscripts (or 0.1 percent) born in the years 1946 and 1947 and conscripted in 1965 and 1966, respectively, were determined to be "consistently homosexual" – half during their medical exams and the other half while in service.[10]

The medical service's baseline assumption of two to four percent of the general population being homosexual seemed low to one division doctor, who estimated that the figure "probably lay closer to ten percent than four percent."[11] It likely was not the number of homosexuals that had risen after the criminal code was revised in 1969 "but the number of those openly admitting their homosexuality." Since then, society's view had continued to grow more liberal. "Today [1970] 60% of youth are tolerant of homosexuals, 20% are indifferent and 20% intolerant. Latent homosexuals are the least tolerant."[12]

The conference organized by the BMVg's Office of the Surgeon General in 1966 had also grappled with the fact that the number of young men who had, by whatever means, been identified as homosexual during their medical exams was noticeably lower than the percentage assumed for the general population. The Bundeswehr doctors saw the reason as lying in examinees' either keeping silent about their tendencies or concealing them; in the language of 1966, they were all "plainly of the view that the homosexual's timidity and fear of punishment cause him to stay silent about his illness during examination."[13] Homosexual soldiers led a "double life."[14]

---

9 Haring and Leickert, *Wörterbuch der Psychiatrie*, 284–85, 405, 445, quote on 285.
10 BArch, BM 1/6727: BMVg, InSan I 1, 15 October 1970.
11 BArch, BW 24/7180: Division physician for the 6th Mechanized Infantry Division to the BMVg, 2 April 1970.
12 Ibid.
13 BArch, BW 24/3736: "Über die Erkennung von sexuellen Perversionen bei der Musterung." In: BMVg, InSan: "Beurteilung der Wehrdiensttauglichkeit und Dienstfähigkeit Homosexueller," 1966, sheets 35–40, here sheet 36.
14 Ibid., sheets 56–63, here 59.

At the height of the Wörner–Kießling affair in mid-January 1984, Bundestag deputy Joschka Fischer (Green Party) asked BMVg Parliamentary State Secretary Peter Kurt Würzbach whether he was "aware of homosexual soldiers or ranking officers in the Bundeswehr and if yes, how many." Würzbach replied that while "such soldiers" existed, "we do not keep lists. They are not registered. They are not reviewed. I cannot give you a number."[15] Nor did Würzbach take the bait when another member of Fischer's party followed up to ask if the secretary could "deny or confirm" the number that "German news magazine" *Der Spiegel* had given of 50,000 homosexual soldiers. Würzbach could not confirm the number, nor was he even prepared "to use the number for orientation's sake; it would be speculative."[16]

2. Fitness for Service

Historically, compulsory service meant the military held practically universal biographical importance for men, at the very least on account of the medical examinations that even those who balked at the military and opted for civil service instead had to undergo. The same applied for young men who were not called up for reasons of health or other causes that are fully relevant to the subject at hand.

> There were many paths leading around "service." If someone wanted to take one he would try – with varying degrees of success – to downgrade his state of health for the medical exam, taking medication to raise his blood pressure the day before or hoping to be spared military service by blatantly feigning homosexual tendencies because he had heard gays were not drafted.[17]

Whether or not someone who professed to be gay would in fact be "kept away from the troops" as hoped for was a matter of some debate among those advising men in search of a way out of military service. "'They also get drafted, and then usually stick to their own kind in the troops.' Hearsay, bathroom gossip, words of wisdom."[18] As early as 1964, BMVg jurists were stressing that under no conditions did "the mere profession" of homosexuality suffice to avoid being drafted.[19] §175

---

15 German Bundestag, 10th legislative period, 47th Session, 19 January 1984, typed transcript, 3375.

16 Ibid., 3377.

17 Kulke, "Lieber homosexuell als zur Bundeswehr."

18 Ibid.

19 BArch, BW 1/73389: BMVg, VR III, 3 January 1964. The files from the administration and legal affairs department were introduced under the heading "Homophilic Conscripts."

was still in effect at the time, making all forms of sexual activity between men criminal. This in turn made it easier for medical examination boards to identify possible homosexuals among conscripts, all of whom were required to provide information about any previous convictions and pending investigations or criminal proceedings. §12 (5) of the Military Service Act deferred a man's military service if he had "committed a crime or act of moral misconduct."

a.) Error Code 12 VI: Permanently Unfit to Serve

"Homosexuality is a serious problem in any army, which is why the Bundeswehr refrains from drafting young men with such tendencies," Defense Minister Gerhard Schröder (CDU) explained in 1967.[20] Under previous regulations like the 1965 version of ZDv 46/1, "consistent homosexuality" qualified for "Error Code 12 VI" or "permanently unfit to serve,"[21] where "sexual perversion" and "asociality" are listed under "severe psychopathy" alongside alcoholism, severe neuroses, psychoses and "medium to high levels of mental deficiency."[22] It was here that homosexuality fell. Men turned away on such grounds were not drafted for military service and were no longer subject to monitoring under the National Military Service Act. The regulations also called for soldiers subsequently identified as homosexual while in active service to be deemed "permanently unfit" and dismissed.[23]

The entrance regulations under ZDv 46/1 reveal greater differentiation among levels of fitness during the 1970s, with same-sex orientation – going under the term "homophilia" – assessed at Grade IV, or "provisionally unfit for service." What had applied generally as Grade VI (permanently unfit to serve) in the 1965 version now held true only for "sexual perversions."[24] Nothing changed in practice for young men with a "consistent" same-sex orientation; whether "provisionally" or "permanently," they were considered unfit. Men who only reported occasional sex with other men, on the other hand, were now assessed at Grade III by medical examiners, or "fit for assignment with restriction."[25] Presumably the unspoken concern

---

20 Biesold, "Der Umgang mit Sexualität in der Bundeswehr (1955–2005)," 3; found in Botsch, *Soldatsein*, 135.

21 BArch, BW 1/73389: BMVg, InSan I 5, 4 September 1970.

22 BArch, BM 1/6727: BMVg, InSan I 1, 9 October 1970.

23 BArch, BW 1/73389: BMVg, InSan I 5, 4 September 1970.

24 ZDv 46/1, Guidelines for the medical examination of conscripts at muster and upon entering service, accepting and hiring voluntary applicants and dismissing soldiers, here as an excerpt in BArch, BW 24/5553.

25 Ibid.

voiced itself here that all too many conscripts might evade military duty by referencing occasional or one-time sex with other men.

In the opinion of one Bundeswehr psychiatrist of the era, Dr. Rudolph Brickenstein, "occasional same-sex satisfaction of one's libido" did not detract from troop discipline, nor as a result fighting power. That depended to a much greater extent on "other behavioral patterns that are characteristic in homosexually perverted soldiers."[26] Neither Brickenstein as a medical officer nor the regulations themselves defined the boundary between occasional sexual contact and consistent homosexuality; ultimately it was decided on a case-by-case basis. The doctors were given room for discretion, and it was this very woolliness that opened the door to the arbitrary and unjust use of power. It also gave Bundeswehr psychiatrists a great deal of latitude to busy themselves with the subject in the coming decades. (Numerous sources and the memories of the soldiers Brickenstein "examined" cast him as specializing in homosexuals and their psychiatric "assessment" in Bundeswehr hospitals.[27])

Notions varied as to how ZDv 46/1 should be interpreted. In 1970, lawyers from the BMVg's department of administrative and legal affairs wrote that conscripts of "homophilic disposition" who had "already become active in this context, or for whom well-founded indications exist that they will continue to be homosexually active as members of the Bundeswehr," should be assessed as permanently unfit with Error Code 12 VI and not drafted.[28] In doing so, the lawyers relied on the customary distinction between established homosexuality and occasional same-sex activity; in this case the deciding factor seemed to be sexual activity itself, regardless of how often. The paper was initially drafted to help respond to a query at the press department from the gay publication *Das andere Magazin*. The magazine was curious about whether there were regulations for keeping "homophilic" citizens of the Federal Republic out of the Bundeswehr.[29] The lawyers advised the press

---

26 BArch, BW 24/3736: Lt. Col. (MC) Dr. Rudolph Brickenstein, "Probleme der Homosexualität in der Sicht des InSan im BMVg." In: BMVg, InSan: "Beurteilung der Wehrdiensttauglichkeit und Dienstfähigkeit Homosexueller," 1966, sheets 22–34, here 34.

27 Ibid.; see also Brickenstein, "Probleme der Homosexualität im Wehrdienst"; BArch, BW 24/7180: Lt. Col. (MC) Dr. Rudolph Brickenstein, "Neue wehrpsychiatrische und rechtliche Aspekte für den Dienst bei der Bundeswehr bei homosexuellen Verhaltensweisen" (1970, internal document, unpublished); BArch, BW 24/5553: Lt. Col. (MC) Dr. Rudolph Brickenstein, "Sachverständigenreferat aus psychiatrischer Sicht," delivered at a meeting of the BMVg medical advisory board's committee on preventative health and care and military examinations, 18 April 1980. Also available in BW 2/31225.

28 BArch, BW 24/7180: BMVg, VR IV 1, 29 September 1970.

29 Ibid., editors at *Das andere Magazin* to the BMVg, 17 August 1970.

department to exercise "particular caution" in its reply; the possibility could not be ruled out that "a frank announcement that homophiles are not enlisted in the [Bundeswehr] [...] would prompt [conscripts] to identify themselves as homophiles during their entrance exams to avoid military service."[30]

The fear was not unfounded. At a time when the mere suspicion of homosexual tendencies was enough to declare a conscript unfit, "the cleverest of the bunch [...] showed up for their exams with ear clips and high heels," *Der Spiegel* reported in 1984.[31] "Sissy theater" was the common expression used among conscripts.

In 1969, Dr. Brickenstein reported that the number of cases in which soldiers "falsely stated" their homosexuality with the aim of dismissal from the Bundeswehr was on the rise. Entrance regulations had become common knowledge, and there were likely "controlled 'information centers'" that explained to young men "how they had to behave to be deemed homosexual and thus excluded from military service, even under pointed psychiatric evaluation."[32]

The BMVg was also curious as to how many conscripts were trying to avoid conscription by giving false statements about their sexuality. Out of 294,000 draftees born in the year 1946, district draft boards reported twenty-four suspected cases of "purposive statements," with the 1947 cohort showing nearly the same number of instances at twenty-five.[33] This left the number for each year at less than one in 10,000 draftees, making it impossible to speak of a "preponderance of attempted abuse" as medical service leadership put it.[34]

Beyond a wide range of related medical aspects, the medical inspectorate's (Office of the Surgeon General) 1966 work conference also addressed what bearing homosexuality should have in determining draftees' fitness for service. In this case it was not homosexual activity per se that was the deciding factor in determining eligibility so much as the *behavioral patterns* of homosexually perverted soldiers."[35] These sort of "behavioral patterns repeatedly disrupted troop discipline

30 Ibid.
31 "Soldaten als potentielle Sexualpartner," 22. See also Kulke, "Lieber homosexuell als zur Bundeswehr."
32 Brickenstein, "Probleme der Homosexualität im Wehrdienst," 151.
33 BArch, BM 1/6727: BMVg, InSan I 1, 9 October 1970. The figures for birth year 1946 appear previously in: BArch, BW 24/3736: "Über die Erkennung von sexuellen Perversionen bei der Musterung." In: BMVg, InSan: "Beurteilung der Wehrdiensttauglichkeit und Dienstfähigkeit Homosexueller,"1966, sheets 35–40, here 38.
34 BArch, BM 1/6727: BMVg, InSan I 1, 9 October 1970.
35 BArch, BW 24/3736: Surgeon General Dr. Finger, "Einführende Bemerkungen zu BMVg," InSan: "Beurteilung der Wehrdiensttauglichkeit und Dienstfähigkeit Homosexueller," 1966, here sheet 5 (emphasis in original).

and fighting power," doing so "to such an extent that these disruptive influences should be dismissed if and when they are discovered."[36] Brickenstein later backed up his argument, contending that most homosexuals seemed to be "inherently unsure of themselves and anxious."[37] The medical officer even reached for analogies from the animal kingdom, using phrases that are difficult to understand from today's perspective:

> They will also search out like-minded individuals among the troops, often locating them quite quickly by instinct. In order to protect themselves from their environment homosexuals construct nests, as it were, and conspire with one another. They are vulnerable to all kinds of intimidation, however, especially from foreign agents. As a result, they are not infrequently driven to treachery or other criminal acts.[38]

In 1966, such formulations were far from a slip of the tongue. The psychiatrist spoke in similar terms three years later in an essay about homosexual soldiers: "Using undefined messaging channels among themselves they construct interconnected, tension-laden dens," bringing "considerable disruption to masculine self-discipline, as well as classification and subordination within the military hierarchy."[39] Brickenstein had made a forceful case as to the need to muster homosexual men out of military service once before in 1966: "Homosexually perverted men are permanently unfit for military service. If such men are in fact deemed eligible to serve and wrongly enlisted as soldiers, they must, once their perversion is revealed [...] be deemed unfit for assignment and thus for service, and dismissed from the Bundeswehr or placed in retirement."[40] Brickenstein now elaborated on his reasoning in 1969, explaining that "homosexual soldiers are not a disruptive factor in military units because they can only find sexual satisfaction in same-sex intercourse, but because their homosexual tendencies are most often coupled with other characteristics...and lead to patterns of behavior that endanger troop discipline, and thus fighting power."[41]

---

36 Ibid.

37 BArch, BW 24/3736: Lt. Col. (MC) Dr. Rudolph Brickenstein, "Probleme der Homosexualität in der Sicht des InSan im BMVg." In: BMVg, InSan: "Beurteilung der Wehrdiensttauglichkeit und Dienstfähigkeit Homosexueller," 1966, sheets 22–34, here 22.

38 Ibid.

39 Brickenstein, "Probleme der Homosexualität im Wehrdienst," 150.

40 BArch, BW 24/3736: Lt. Col. (MC) Dr. Rudolph Brickenstein, "Probleme der Homosexualität in der Sicht des InSan im BMVg." In: BMVg, InSan: "Beurteilung der Wehrdiensttauglichkeit und Dienstfähigkeit Homosexueller," 1966, sheets 22–34, here 34.

41 Brickenstein, "Probleme der Homosexualität im Wehrdienst," 150.

With this last argument, Brickenstein anticipated a line of reasoning administrative judges would use up through 1999 in dismissing suits brought by homosexual officers and NCOs to dispute their transfer or rejection from career service. Without fail, judges viewed public knowledge of a superior's homosexuality as jeopardizing his authority, and with it troop discipline and fighting power. Brickenstein himself went further; today, his text reads like a veritable litany of prejudice. Gays either came across to other soldiers as "effeminate" or behaved "with exaggerated force," while others stuck out for being timid. Many "hid" behind a "happy family life, but secretly engaged in homosexual activity as soon as they had the opportunity to do so [...] not infrequently, the very attempt many homosexuals make to hide their difference will have a provocative effect on a soldier with normal tendencies, since they then behave in particularly conspicuous ways." This would often lead to "pronounced psychological deformity" that came to dominate "all their aims and endeavors."[42]

Brickenstein's torrent of bias continued; as in other armed forces, for example in the U.S., homosexuals in the Bundeswehr formed "sociological groups of their own, with shared jargon, near unerring recognition of one another and a widespread system of mutual acquaintanceship linked to treason, addiction and criminality."[43]

The regulations rejecting homosexual men as unfit to serve did not meet with the approval of every medical examiner. To some it was incomprehensible why "conscripts should be released from military service simply because of an abnormal tendency. It is unfair to men of normal sexual sentiment and behavior."[44] Other doctors criticized the regulations from the opposite angle, arguing that they "degraded [homosexuals] to second class people, who suffer enough as it is due to their abnormal tendencies."[45]

The committee responsible for overseeing entrance regulations cleared both objections from the table.

Medical examiners were informed that psychological abnormalities, especially of a sexual nature, must be assessed solely at the functional level and not on the basis of personal worldviews [...] It is thus neither about advantage or disadvantage, but a measure of expediency.

---

42 Ibid.
43 Ibid.
44 BArch, BW 24/3736: Lt. Col. (MC) Dr. Rudolph Brickenstein, "Probleme der Homosexualität in der Sicht des InSan im BMVg." In: BMVg, InSan: "Beurteilung der Wehrdiensttauglichkeit und Dienstfähigkeit Homosexueller,"1966, sheets 22–34, here 26.
45 Ibid.

The benefit goes to the Bundeswehr as a whole, the homosexuals themselves and not least to the heterosexual soldiers who enter soldierly community with them as well as taxpayers.[46]

"Under no circumstances," the medical service leadership emphasized in 1970, did the decriminalization of sexual activity between men in 1969 or (as the BMVg saw it) the liberalization that had come about in its wake alter the "military medical aspects." To buttress its position, it pointed to countries that did not prosecute homosexual acts but still observed similar regulations for military service.[47] The earlier version of medical exam regulations thus remained in effect even after §175 had been reformed, up through their revision in 1979.

Fixated homosexuality [must not] be equated with a psychological inability to control one's drives, i.e. mental incapacity in a homosexual context. Rather, the same applies here for homosexuals as for any person with deviations, namely that the demands made of an individual person by living in society [...] are based on [...] the principle of guilt, and thus also on the postulate of a relatively mature person's mental accountability. This includes postulating the ability to inhibit one's drives.[48]

In short, the essay quoted here from *Neue Zeitschrift für Wehrrecht* declared homosexuals to be accountable, or mentally capable and consequently – albeit without saying it directly – subject to criminal and disciplinary codes. Ultimately, this meant that "homosexuals who were accountable and those of diminished accountability [should not] be dismissed from service without further ado," but should not "generally be assigned to positions of leadership" either.[49] With that, *Neue Zeitschrift für Wehrrecht* anticipated in 1970 the eventual line that the BMVg would take in dealing with homosexual soldiers: fit to serve and thus fit for conscription, but unfit for any sort of qualifications as a superior, and thus any chance of a military career.

b.) Psychiatric Evaluation in the Armed Forces

Subject files pertaining to homosexuality within the BMVg archives also relay instances of soldiers assessed as homosexual undergoing psychiatric evaluation in Bundeswehr hospitals (Bundeswehrkrankenhaus, BWK) and their path leading there. In March 1971, for example, two conscripts were admitted as inpatients at BWK Hamburg to have their sexuality examined, one for fifteen days, the other for

---

46 Ibid.
47 BArch, BW 1/73389: BMVg, InSan, 4 September 1970.
48 Schwalm, "Die Streichung des Grundtatbestands," 97.
49 Ibid.

seventeen. Their stay was prompted by a letter the two had written to Defense Minister Helmut Schmidt that read "Complaint against the Bundeswehr!"[50] at the top, although what followed was not a petition for release or protest against discrimination – not by any means. Rather, the authors informed the minister that

> we met about a half year ago [...] since then we've seen each other regularly and also had sexual encounters. We'd now like to ask your opinion on the matter and, if it's possible, for you to help see to it that we're assigned the same room going forward, or at least to the same company so that we can continue our relationship, as we're very close to each other. Please be so kind as to answer this letter promptly.[51]

Instead of Schmidt, army doctors answered the two soldiers; instead of assigning them the same room or company the doctors ordered the soldiers be admitted to the neuro-psychiatric division at the BWK Hamburg. After a good two weeks the "results" came in. From today's perspective it is surprising that reports that go into such detail about the private and sexual lives of young adults were only slightly anonymized while being sent to the BMVg for internal purposes. In their conclusion, the psychiatrists recommended that the one soldier receive early dismissal as unfit to serve under ZDv 46/1 Error Code 12 V, and receive renewed psychiatric evaluation as to his fitness to serve in around two years. The second soldier, on the other hand, was not a "true homosexual" with no restrictions on his ability to serve. The doctors "nonetheless" recommended that the mechanized infantryman (*Panzergrenadier*) be immediately transferred out of his unit, and that the disciplinary and criminal consequences "of any homosexual acts which might occur within or outside the troops" be brought to his attention for the future.[52] The soldiers wrote their letter in February; the infantryman who had not been dismissed received the minister's outstanding reply in late April 1971. His desire to be assigned "a shared room as to deepen your homophilic relations" with his partner failed to recognize that "criminal charges under §175 StGB may have been relaxed in some areas, but under no circumstances does the Bundeswehr [...] promote such activities."[53]

In 1969 Bundeswehr psychiatrist Dr. Brickenstein published a piece in a specialist journal detailing six cases from his work in a Bundeswehr hospital. While anonymized as a matter of course, the frankness and level of detail with which a

---

50 BArch, BW 24/7180: Petition from two mechanized infantrymen to the BMVg, undated, stamped for entry into the BMVg records 15 February 1971.
51 Ibid.
52 BArch, BW 24/7180: Bundeswehrkrankenhaus Hamburg, neuro-psychiatric division to troop physicians, 17 and 19 March 1971.
53 BArch, BW 24/7180: BMVg InSan I 5 to soldier X., 30 April 1971.

doctor publicly disclosed prior intimate and sexual experiences entrusted to him by young, at times very young, people is astonishing from today's perspective.[54] Their reproduction here is limited to the results of the "evaluation" and the implications that were drawn for military service. One conscript seen as a "potentially disruptive force" in the troops had been given early dismissal under Error Code 12 IV. No recommendation for early release, on the other hand, came for a sailor who professed to being gay but did not come across as "convincing" – the troop physician was, however, advised to "keep a closer watch [on the soldier] than others." "Unjustifiable doubts" also persisted about another conscript's story, who was only deemed provisionally unfit under Error Code 12 V and ordered to come in for re-examination in two years. Bundeswehr psychiatrists did not find "the slightest grounds" for homosexuality in the case of a further conscript. The soldier grew "deeply ashamed when he found himself caught in the act of trying to shirk military service in such a manner." Another case resulted in "no grounds for homosexual tendencies" upon "targeted examination," although they could not be ruled out for certain. No doubts existed about a staff sergeant by contrast; the doctors attested to an "authentic homosexual perversion" that left him permanently unfit to serve. The fixed-term soldier was given early dismissal.[55] BMVg subject files contain other (non-anonymized) cases of soldiers whose dismissal the personnel department ruled out due to doubts about their homosexuality upon examination.[56]

A later study carried out in 1985 on behalf of the department of military psychology at the Armed Forces Office analyzed the problems facing homosexual soldiers. It found that while homosexuality did not fundamentally rule out or detract from "a person's fitness or ability to serve as a soldier," "the mere fact of being identified as a homosexual [may] limit his activity as a soldier, even make it impossible."[57] Fears and prejudices would find their way to the fore within military and civilian environments alike, the report continued, with potential reactions ranging from slight distancing to total rejection. There was also the danger of "a homosexual person consciously being provoked or made to look ridiculous." "The homosexual" continued to represent a "unique projective surface" in society, where he was

---

54 Brickenstein, "Probleme der Homosexualität im Wehrdienst." Instances of "onanism and anal intercourse" and the pretentious, pseudo-medical term "Immissio penis in orem" for "oral intercourse" are pedantically counted up on multiple occasions throughout the article.
55 Ibid.
56 BArch, BW 24/7180: BMVg, P III 7-E, 12 June 1964 and BMVg, P II 7-E, 23 April 1968.
57 BArch, BW 2/32553: Armed Forces Office, Dept. I, Military Psychology Section, February 1985: Max Flach, "Sozialpsychologie Stellungnahme zur Homosexualität in den Streitkräften," here 11. Also available in BArch, BW2/531590: BMVg, PII4, AzKL-1-85.

no longer seen as a "single personality" but "part of a discriminated collective."[58] Not only did all this influence the behavior of his peers, but ultimately the "behavior and thoughts of the homosexual person himself."[59]

One man exempt from military service in 1976 described his own experiences with the Bundeswehr's (medical) practices in an interview.[60] He had been before the district draft board once before for a first appointment in the early 1970s but had not felt confident discussing homosexuality with others at age eighteen, and his military service had been deferred anyway in light of his upcoming studies. Now that he had completed his degree (and come out in the meantime), conscription loomed. To get out in front of the matter, in 1976 he took the initiative to apply for re-examination. The man recalled a number of other young men gathered at the draft board offices in Saarbrücken that day "with all sorts of deficiencies both real and invented, mostly back problems." When the others asked what was wrong with him out of curiosity, the man replied that he was homosexual. The admission came as a source of "great embarrassment" and "incredulous surprise" to those assembled in the waiting room. "It'll go on your record if you say that!" When the man gave the doctor the same answer, the same "great embarrassment" descended on the consulting room. Visibly at a loss for words, the medical examiner began to rifle through his documents slowly and aimlessly; "the topic caused him noticeable discomfort." Once he had gotten himself together, the doctor answered: "You'll have to prove it, I'm sending you to the psychiatrist! It'll cost you if you're lying!" Behind his words loomed the threat that if the results came back negative, the young man would be liable to shoulder the costs of the additional psychological examination.

Several days later, a Bundeswehr psychologist started his "examination" by explaining that homosexuality "was not a conscious matter, but a sexual perversion." Unable to determine homosexuality beyond all doubt in his report, the psychologist recommended the young man be admitted to the central Bundeswehr hospital in Koblenz, repeating the threat that he would have to foot the bill in the event of a negative diagnosis. This did not cause the man to feel fear, however, but "a real eagerness to see what the Bundeswehr would do at the hospital to test my homosexuality. In the end, they would have to confirm it." Things did not get that far. Instead of being admitted to the hospital, he was sent to a civilian psychologist for a final evaluation. After the interview the psychologist attested to the man's "completely normal homosexuality." The examinee was so psychologically stable

---

58 BArch, BW 2/32553: Armed Forces Office, Dept. I, Military Psychology Section, February 1985: Max Flach, "Sozialpsychologie Stellungnahme zur Homosexualität in den Streitkräften," here 13.
59 Ibid.
60 Conversation with E. from Cologne, 14 February 2018, also in what follows.

and self-confident in fact that he was able defend himself against exclusion and bullying, leading the doctor to attach a recommendation of fitness to serve to his "diagnosis." Yet the diagnosis of homosexuality on its own was more than enough for the deciding medical examiner for the military to pronounce the man ineligible "with a long face" and withdraw his military service book. The examiner's diagnosis read "inability to perform." Looking back, the eyewitness concluded that he had not suffered from the "Bundeswehr's hostility toward gays" but used it "to his own advantage to avoid having to go to the military. That was good for me."

c.) New Fitness Regulations for 1979

After fitness regulations were revised in 1979, Brickenstein went before the BMVg's medical advisory board in 1980 to explain it was now only young men whose homosexuality "had degenerated into a pronounced sexual deviation, in the sense of a true perversion" who would be ruled unfit for military service.[61]

The new version of ZDv 46/1 assessed homosexuality at three different levels under Error Code 13: "III/13 – Abnormal patterns of sexual behavior; IV/13 – Sexual maladjustment without significant disruption in the ability to adapt, perform, endure stress or enter community; VI/13 – Pronounced sexual deviation with negative impact on entering community."[62]

The new gradations meant that (known) homosexual conscripts were no longer classified under IV or VI, respectively, as provisionally or permanently unfit for military service. Before, only "occasional homosexual contact" had received Grade III ("fit for assignment with restriction"). In principle, every homosexual man now started in this category and had to line up for duty; conscripts "still capable of integrating without difficulty into a male military community despite an abnormal pattern of sexual behavior" were assessed at Grade III, and provisional or general ineligibility was reserved for the exceptions cited above of "disorders" or "deviations."[63] In practice, this meant that the vast majority of young gay men now had to serve out their time in the military. The new regulations were evidently already in use by 1978, at least in individual cases, as a Munich man's letter to the BMVg's

---

61 BArch, BW 24/5553: Lt. Col. (MC) Dr. Rudolph Brickenstein, "Sachverständigenreferat aus psychiatrischer Sicht," delivered at a meeting of the BMVg medical advisory board's committee on preventative health and care and military examinations 18 April 1980. Also available in BW 2/31225.
62 ZDv 46/1, Guidelines for the medical examination of conscripts at muster and upon entering service, accepting and hiring voluntary applicants and dismissing soldiers, BMVg, Bonn 1979, here No. 261. Excerpts of the same text also found in BArch, BW 24/5553, BW 2/32553 and BW 2/31224.
63 BArch, BW 1/304286: BMVg, P II 1, 12 August 1982.

department of military service affairs indicates. He himself had been found unfit to serve in 1976 for homosexuality, but now his partner had received a conscription notice assessing him at Grade III and thus eligible – despite maintaining his homosexuality. During his medical exam the man's partner had it explained to him that homosexuality was "no longer grounds for exemption from military service under the new regulations."[64] "Why are things judged arbitrarily in our country, why can't the same law be applied to everyone?" the man wrote furiously.[65] Looking past the fact that a conscription notice is not a "judgement," the man could not have known about the revised regulations. To him and his partner, it was a display of arbitrary power; his boyfriend was "practically at wits' end." As a solution, the man asked that his partner at least be stationed close to Munich. A handwritten comment on the letter reads "Psychologist [pleads for them to be sent] close to home! Like accommodation for a married couple!"[66] It is unclear whether this was added by the author of the letter or a BMVg employee.

The new regulations similarly thwarted the plans of a young Hamburg man to free himself from his upcoming military service. He stated his homosexual orientation at his medical exam in March 1980, still likely unaware of the new eligibility guidelines. The draft board asked for an expert medical opinion, which assumed "occasional homosexual contact" to be "indisputably present." "Such an inclination" did not rule out military service under ZDv 46/1, however, but should be assessed under "Physical Defect III/13." "At most, the man's ability to enter the community" required evaluation. The conscript took sports at his high school and was "mentally sound and aware," and no "signs of psychological abnormality" were evident. As such, the conscript was eligible for assignment without restriction.

The young man did not give up; his lawyer filed an appeal in administrative court while introducing "expert testimony" from a civilian doctor, which stated that the young man was "not in a position to hide his homosexual tendencies."[67] "As long as discrimination against homosexuals has not been fully eliminated from the Bundeswehr," this meant military service posed "an unreasonable burden [for him], and he a burden for the community, under the conditions."[68] Military district administration responded by questioning the validity of the report and the competence of the civilian doctor alike, stating that the neuro-psychiatric division at BWK

---

64 BArch, BW 24/7180: Mr. X., letter to the BMVg, 5 March 1978.
65 Ibid.
66 Ibid.
67 Muster Division 2 at Military District Administration I, notice of appeal from 28 May 1980 against the decision of the draft board from 10 March 1980.
68 Expert medical testimony, 11 June 1980.

Hamburg alone was fit to ably assess the demands made on a homosexual's ability to live in community.[69] This brought the man's lawyer back in the ring, who contended that in a legal dispute, an "institution maintained by the defendant could hardly be entrusted with preparing a report."[70] Unfortunately, the documents do not reveal the outcome of the court battle.

Responding in February 1979 to a question from Bundestag deputy Herta Däubler-Gmelin, the BMVg took pains to stress that the Bundeswehr did not fundamentally treat homosexuals "any differently from heterosexual citizens."[71] As long as their orientation expressed itself in occasional same-sex activity or "homophilia," the young men were fit for service and would be called up. Conscripts who made explicit mention of their homosexuality or whose sexual orientation otherwise came out would undergo medical examination, and be declared unfit only in cases where psychological disturbances or "sexual perversions with pathological value" were present.[72] The same applied "in principle" for those who applied to the military, whether as fixed-term or career soldiers. In these cases, however, expert medical opinion would be sought as to the applicant's fitness to serve, and a hiring decision made on that basis. The ministry reiterated that "if a homosexual becomes a soldier, he will not fundamentally be treated differently than heterosexual soldiers."[73] That may well have been the case in 1979, but by 1984 at the latest, a set of BMVg orders had clearly established homosexuals as unsuitable for higher-ranking positions, whether as NCOs or officers.[74] If an aspiring NCO's or officer's same-sex preferences came out the candidate would be dismissed,[75] something that no longer applied for conscripts. Still, the Office of the Surgeon General repeatedly intoned that homosexuality was neither a disease nor a "psychological or mental disturbance, but merely a variation on the norm."[76] In 1986 FüS I 4, the department for Leadership Development and Civic Education at the BMVg, came to the conclusion, that "men with a homosexual orientation are fundamentally fit for military service if they are sufficiently able to adapt, perform, endure stress and become part of the community. To such an extent, homosexuality should not be evaluated

---

69 Military District Administration I to Hamburg Administrative Court, 11 August 1980.

70 Law firm F. to Hamburg Administrative Court, 14 November 1980.

71 BArch, BW 1/304284: BMVg, VR I 1, 15 February 1979 as well as BMVg, parliamentary state secretary to MdB Herta Däubler-Gmelin (SPD), 23 February 1979.

72 Ibid.

73 Ibid.

74 BArch, BW 2/31224: BMVg, P II 1, Az 16-02-05/2 (C) R 4/84, 13 March 1984, for greater detail see chapter 4, section 4.

75 See a full account of this in chapter 4.

76 BArch, BW 1/304285: BMVg InSan, 4 September 1985, and elsewhere.

as a disease."[77] All surviving internal papers from the BMVg repeat this clear position verbatim.

In mid-January 1984, with the Wörner–Kießling affair at its height, the Bundestag took up the question of homosexual men's fitness for military service. Parliamentary State Secretary Würzbach answered for the BMVg, quoting from the mustering regulations: Exclusion from, or early termination of, military service was possible only in cases of a restricted "ability to integrate" or "enter" a "male military community."[78] Deputy Norbert Gansel of the SPD found the expression "male community" not "entirely lacking in same-sex eros," which "may give rise to perpetual self-questioning."[79] In reference to the criteria of "integrating into a male community," SPD deputy Heide Simonis asked the secretary "how exactly [he] would assess women who were supposed to go into the Bundeswehr in that case?"[80] Asking in 1984, Simonis had already laid her finger on the argumentative weak point that would bring restrictions against gays to the point of absurdity when the military opened fully to women in 2000. Würzbach countered that he had cited the "ability to become part of the community"; "wherever this kind of tendency [homosexuality] is present in particularly extreme form, expressing itself in a forceful and possibly uncontrollable urge to act in the direction of that tendency [...] then the ability to enter the community has been disturbed, regardless of the arena."[81] CDU representative Gerhard Pfeffermann immortalized himself in the parliamentary transcript for interjecting that "breast-grabbers would disturb the Bundeswehr, too!"[82] Waltraut Schoppe from the Greens asked the secretary for greater detail regarding such "extreme forms of homosexuality and deviancy." Würzbach demurred, referring for individual cases to "expert physicians, with the possible aid of psychologists" (along to shouts of "Or Mrs. Schoppe!" from the CDU/CSU).[83]

In 1993 *Der Spiegel* issued a new report that homosexual conscripts were being drafted and "could not buy themselves a 'free ticket out' by referring to their preferences."[84] That same year the director of the Bundeswehr Institute of Social Sciences (SOWI), Professor Bernhard Fleckenstein, lectured on Germany's position regarding "homosexuality and military service" at the University of Hull in Great

---

77 BArch, BW 2/31224: BMVg, FüS I 4, July 1986.
78 German Bundestag, 10th legislative period, 47th Session, 19 January 1984, typed transcript, 3374.
79 Ibid., 3376.
80 Ibid.
81 Ibid.
82 Ibid.
83 Ibid.
84 "Versiegelte Briefe," 54.

Britain, reporting that "homosexual men are subject to conscription like everyone else, and eligible for service provided that they are found physically and psychologically fit during their entrance examinations."[85] This explained why young men were asked as to "possible homosexual tendencies" during their medicals. "According to reports, most homosexual recruits reveal their orientation when the medical examiner brings it up for discussion."[86] The doctor would then decide alongside a military psychologist whether the young man was "able to enter the community," in other words "to integrate into a male military community without drawing undue attention as a homosexual."[87] If there were doubts, he would be rejected for service as "mentally unfit" under fitness class T5.[88] Rejection for service was "the rule" in fact; medical examiners pursued a "markedly 'conservative' policy when it came to assessing homosexuals' fitness to serve. All sides are manifestly satisfied with the solution." It lay "in the interests of those affected," who now had to do community service in place of basic military service, but also aligned "with the interests of troop commanders, who did not want them in their units because then they would not [have to] fear any troubles with homosexual soldiers."[89] Fleckenstein stressed that nobody – aside from the doctor and a military psychologist when necessary – was told how the medical examination was conducted or why the results came about.

One man deemed unfit for service in 1992 reported his own experience with Bundeswehr policy; when asked by the medical examiner about any disqualifications for military service, he mentioned membership in a gay/lesbian youth group. This led to a psychological examination where after just a few minutes' conversation the older psychologist demurred, "but you aren't at all fit for military service." When the report was submitted the young man received notification of ineligibility (T5).[90]

---

85 Fleckenstein's study only appeared in English under the title "Homosexuality and Military Service in Germany"; the German original, dated 24 February 1993, went to the BMVg and can be found in BArch, BW 2/32553; this and the following quotes from there.

86 Fleckenstein, "Homosexuality and Military Service in Germany."

87 Ibid.

88 ZDv 46/1, 1979.

89 Fleckenstein, "Homosexuality and Military Service in Germany."

90 Telephone conversation with W., 4 January 2018.

3. Calls for Tolerance within the Ranks

The Office of the Surgeon General had painted a different picture of homosexuals'
everyday life in the service in March 1983, issuing a call for tolerance among soldiers in phrases that cannot be found in any other BMVg paper before that date.
Going forward, troops should be "properly" informed about homosexual behavior
as part of their medical training. Aimed primarily at young conscripts, the straight-
forward language leaves little room for doubt and is worth reproducing:

1. Generally speaking, homosexual behavior is not a pathological form of behavior [...]
2. In specific situations, heterosexual men can also exhibit homosexual behavior, for
   example with loss of inhibition due to alcohol consumption or in sexual atmospheres [...]
4. Homosexually oriented behavior does not force one to lead an unrestrained sexual life
   anymore than does heterosexual behavior. Therefore, the behavior of soldiers with a
   homosexual orientation, who often do not differ from soldiers of heterosexual orienta
   tion in any other aspect of their personality, need not impinge on the moral sensibilities
   of their comrades [...]
6. Tolerance [...] can be learned [...]
7. Both homosexually and heterosexually oriented soldiers must learn the view that neither
   group is made of "better people."[91]

The paper was based on a 1982 report written for the BMVg by Professor Otto
Schrappe, the director of the psychiatric clinic at Würzburg University. In the case
of the cited recommendations, the medical service adopted the language of the
doctor's report verbatim.[92] Another paper assembled four months later by medical
service leadership reads similarly, at times redeploying the same language to set
out guidelines for troop physicians' care of homosexual soldiers. The paper was
novel in rejecting the "blanket term of homosexual" which, it contended, simplified
the matter and supposed "homosexual behavior to be the expression of a uniform
underlying condition."[93] The "issue of homosexuality in the troops" had to be made
more matter-of-fact and destigmatized. Troop doctors should resolve conflicts as
they arise and help to avoid "any escalation." To do so, "doctor–patient relationship[s] based on trust" that took "a differentiated view of each individual case" had
to be worked out with homosexual soldiers.[94] Yet when the inspectorate submitted

---

91 BArch, BW 1/531590: BMVg, InSan II 4, 15 March 1983.
92 Dr. Otto Schrappe, "Gutachten für den Bundesminister der Verteidigung," 16 August 1982. (The
author holds a copy.)
93 BArch, BW 1/531590: BMVg, InSan I 1, 4 July 1983, a copy is also available in BArch, BW 2/31225:
BMVg, InSan I 1, 21 August 1984.
94 BArch, BW 1/531590: BMVg, InSan I 1, 4 July 1983.

a draft of the paper to three sections at the personnel department for cosignature, one declined, reasoning that the draft "did not take sufficient account of the specific interests of the armed forces."[95] In particular, the paper neglected the repercussions a same-sex predisposition would have "on the continued personnel management of longer-serving soldiers."[96] A hand-written question mark by the objective avoiding "any escalation of conflict" hints at what concretely was bothering the staff at personnel.[97] (To be sure: The restrictions threatening gay officers and NCOs in positions of leadership represented an escalation, albeit one on the part of the service.[98]) In 1984 the Office of the Surgeon General resubmitted the paper for cosignature, unchanged and this time to all nineteen (!) sections.[99] The author was not able to confirm the further fate of the paper with certainty.

Similar wording appears in a set of draft orders for handling all matters pertaining to homosexuality put out by FüS I 4 in 1986. Written in the form of a G1 memo (a personnel paper drafted at the general staff level), the proposal that was put to the chief of defense and to the defense minister echoed verbatim the calls for tolerance that the medical services leadership had made in 1983. "Drawing an inference about a person's integrity based on their sexual orientation is [...] generally inadmissible. Neither homosexual nor heterosexual soldiers are 'better people' to begin with."[100] (These sentences were also taken from Professor Schrappe's report for the BMVg in 1982.) "Just like other soldiers," those with a same-sex orientation stood under the precepts "but also the protection of comradeship [as set out under §12 of the SG]."[101] A homosexual disposition forced "one to lead an unrestrained sexual life just as little as did heterosexual behavior" (again taken from Schrappe's report). "In every other aspect of their personality," soldiers of homosexual orientation "rarely differ from heterosexually oriented soldiers."[102] These formulations likely were not the reason why the draft was rejected; the proposed memo was even more contentious on other points about how homosexuals should be treated. Newly minted Chief of Defense Admiral Dieter Wellershoff decided to put the draft on ice, seeing "no need for action at the moment."[103]

---

95 BArch, BW 1/531590: BMVg, P II 1, 1 August 1983.

96 Ibid.

97 Ibid.

98 For a full account see chapter 4.

99 BArch, BW 2/31225: BMVg, InSan I 1, 21 August 1984.

100 BArch, BW 2/31225: BMVg, FüS I 4 to the minister via parliamentary state secretary 22 October 1986, annex, identical to BArch, BW 2/31224: BMVg, FüS I 4, July 1986.

101 Ibid.

102 Ibid.

103 BArch, BW 2/31225: BMVg, handwritten note about a conversation with chief of defense, 4

When asked in 1985 by a young man exactly how "one" was supposed to act if "it came out that one was gay" during military service, a member of the legal department replied that he could "rest assured his superiors would treat him in accordance with the law."[104] The BMVg employee added that the soldier's "superiors would respect his dignity, honor and other rights, and protect him from harm and disadvantage." If this were not "to work out in the individual case," the soldier had "an array of practical and legal possibilities" at his disposal.[105]

4. Excursus: "A Knife's Edge." HIV and AIDS in Bundeswehr Policy in the 1980s

AIDS was a central topic of discussion within the press, public sphere and society of the 1980s. Often tinged with hysteria, the conversations were in part brought on by the great uncertainty that initially presided over the illness, its transmission and its spread. In light of the tremendous prospects for stemming the disease that have opened in the meantime, the feverish debates of the 1980s may be cause for amazement from today's perspective. From a contemporary vantage point, however, things looked different.[106] Today it is clear beyond any shadow of a doubt that HIV and AIDS does not only affect men who have sex with men. Nor can it be dismissed out of hand that in the 1980s, countless homosexual men were infected with HIV, fell sick with AIDS and died. Simply omitting or narrowing the context in retrospect would give a false view of the era's vehement discussions as to how to prevent HIV and AIDS. Contextualizing AIDS and homosexuality is not a simple matter, but is indispensable for any honest reappraisal of the topic.

In September 1985 *Der Spiegel* reported on AIDS testing in the Bundeswehr under the headline "A Knife's Edge."[107] The Bundeswehr was reportedly considering "whether starting next year, all recruits should be made to take an AIDS test. In doing so Bonn would be following in the steps of the U.S. Department of Defense,

---

November 1986, StAL, FüS I, 4 November 1986, as well as FüS I 4, 10 November 1986. See chapter 4 for a full account of the G1 draft and its rejection.

104 BArch, BW 1/531593: BMVg, VR II 7 to Mr. T., Bremen, 13 January 1985.

105 Ibid.

106 A large body of research exists on the history and perception of HIV/AIDS, among others Tümmers, AIDS. For a detailed account of the Bundestag debates on HIV/AIDS see Ebner, *Religion im Parlament*, 265–72. The author is aware that merely mentioning HIV/AIDS in direct connection with a study on homosexuals risks the accusation of feeding prejudices – especially against gay men – by linking the two subjects.

107 "Ein schmaler Grat."

which stipulated that all new recruits receive AIDS tests as of 1 October of this year [1985]." The policy came about "primarily for reasons of expense," as "each case of AIDS saddled the army with up to \$100,000 in care costs."[108]

> What's the point of that, mass [HIV-]antibody tests in the Bundeswehr? [...] Is that why there's increased talk of homosexuals and drug addicts as the "risk groups" they want to focus on in examinations? Are we as gay soldiers being threatened with yet another invention of the bloody chamber of stigmatization and discrimination? Exclusion and isolation as the inevitable consequence of a positive test result allegedly to guarantee the safety of active troops? Can I still go to my troop doctor with an untroubled conscience? Where is the medical confidentiality in that?[109]

This outraged letter from a military captain in response to the article went unpublished. The officer did not leave the matter with a letter to *Der Spiegel*. A few days later a significantly longer letter, albeit carrying the same central message and intention, was sent out to the Minister of Defense and to seventeen other recipients, including the Surgeon General of the Bundeswehr, the parliamentary commissioner for the armed forces, the chairmen of the German Armed Forces Soldiers' Professional Association, the party chairmen in the Bundestag and other members of parliament. Building on his letter to *Der Spiegel*, the captain warned that the policy "would amount to total screening for the entirety of the male youth population eligible for conscription." Alluding to the public controversy surrounding supposed plans to screen for AIDS among the population at large, the captain condemned the military's reported plans as a preliminary step to introducing compulsory HIV tests in general "through the back door," and without an applicable law being passed in parliament. Bothering the captain more greatly still was what the Bundeswehr might do with positive test results. Dismissing conscripts who tested positive for HIV would "hardly meet with resistance." Yet the Bundeswehr also employed fixed-term and career soldiers, and if they were to be removed "from active duty allegedly for their own protection, it would mean exclusion, isolation, loneliness [...] isn't that how those sick with plague were dealt with in the Middle Ages?!"[110] What was more, the officer could report from personal experience that doctor–patient confidentiality was observed in the Bundeswehr "only to a limited extent." Sooner or later, ranking officers and fellow soldiers alike would find out why a soldier had been found fit for service with restriction, or simply unfit, with "stigmatization and discrimination" following in tow. The captain was not against

---

108 Ibid.
109 Unpublished letter from Captain P. to *Der Spiegel*, 10 September 1985.
110 Ibid.

taking precautions or shedding light on the matter; anyone who wanted to take a test should be allowed to do so, but voluntarily and anonymously. The captain appealed to Minister of Defense Wörner "to lead the way" in curbing the disease, but to avoid anything that might bring "renewed stigmatization and discrimination" against homosexuals, as the Bundeswehr's duty of care mandated.[111]

Of the recipients, one response came from the chairman of the CDU/CSU's Defense policy working group. Signing the letter personally, Willy Wimmer assured the captain that the party faction consistently adhered to the principles of the constitution in its work and would request that the BMVg remain "as committed as ever to these principles" regarding the concerns raised.[112] The Deputy Surgeon General of the Bundeswehr responded in detail, explaining there was no mandatory examination planned for specific groups of people. "A list of names of those carrying antibodies or the illness is neither permissible nor intended."[113]

Based on its communications with informants at the BMVg and the Bundeswehr, the GDR's Main Directorate for Reconnaissance noted in 1987 that the Bundeswehr leadership had detected "highly worrisome developments in the illness AIDS."[114] "In contrast to earlier findings, the disease profile is not limited to the identified risk groups [...] Moreover, it should be assumed that a substantially higher portion of those infected will get sick and die than was thought last year."[115] An intensive informational campaign was underway, with all Bundeswehr units being shown the film "AIDS – The Deadly Epidemic" and troop physicians holding educational sessions and discussions. Serological testing for HIV was performed during recruitment screenings and upon acceptance into fixed-term or career service, with voluntary testing open to all members of the armed forces. The following year, in 1988, the GDR foreign intelligence service noted that the Bundeswehr continued to focus on voluntary testing as well as "comprehensive education to influence sexual behavior, in particular each individual's responsibility for himself and others."[116] Here GDR intelligence correctly reproduced the BMVg's position on HIV and AIDS in the Bundeswehr.

In 1988, HIV and AIDS were repeatedly topics of discussion in the Chiefs of Service Council (Militärischer Führungsrat, MFR). The Surgeon General provided

---

111 Ibid.
112 MdB Willy Wimmer responding to Captain P., 30 September 1985.
113 BMVg, Deputy Surgeon General to Captain P., 14 October 1985.
114 BStU, MfS, ZAIG 6016, Bl. 59–70: MfS, HVA, "Militärpolitische Informationsübersichten" 5/87, strictly confidential, here sheets 68–9.
115 Ibid.
116 BStU, MfS, ZAIG 6017, Bl. 176–187: MfS, HVA, "Militärpolitische Informationsübersichten," 10/88, strictly confidential, here sheet 183.

advance information that "global experience [showed there was] [...] at present no doubt that the special conditions of military service, especially including living together in confined quarters, did not in and of themselves lead to a greater risk of infection by HIV."[117] There was no risk of HIV infection in the line of duty. Nor was any "additional" risk of HIV transmission present in the Bundeswehr's first aid service "if the prescribed safety precautions are observed."[118] As of April 1988, every newly enlisted soldier would be offered a voluntary HIV test in the course of having their blood type determined. By the end of February 1988, 100 soldiers had tested positive for HIV, double the number from the previous year. Five soldiers fit the clinical image of AIDS. Council participants asked on multiple occasions about the risk soldiers ran of infection, especially when it came to overly tight living quarters, aboard ship for example, and whether the course of the disease could be accelerated by the burdens of service.[119]

Apparently as a result of the leadership council's meeting, the Office of the Surgeon General of the Bundeswehr drafted an "express letter" intended to inform all offices via a general address distribution list about issues "related to HIV infections and related illnesses." The paper opened with three principles: "By the current state of knowledge, those who are infected with HIV but *do not* show signs of illness are fundamentally fit to serve. On principle, an HIV test may only be conducted with the express consent of the person to be tested. The result of a voluntary HIV test is subject to medical confidentiality in every respect."[120]

More specifically, a voluntary HIV test should be performed if possible while testing for a recruit's blood type, yet must not make up an essential part of the examination itself. Every soldier would be offered personal consultation with the troop physician before testing. The findings could only be disclosed by a doctor who simultaneously provided "appropriate" counselling. Test results were subject to medical confidentiality "in every respect," with the same applying to non-medical personnel. The number of those within medical service facilities made privy to the results must "be limited to what is absolutely necessary."[121] In the event of a positive test result, the solder was free to release doctors from their confidentiality clause; this was a prerequisite if non-symptomatic HIV infection was to be

---

117 BArch, BH 1/29162: BMVg InspSan, 17 February 1988, as an annex to the MFR meeting transcript from 14 March 1988.

118 Ibid.

119 BArch, N 818/59: Estate of Admiral Dieter Wellershoff, transcript from MFR meeting on 1 March 1988.

120 BArch, BH 1/29162: BMVg, InSan I 1, 19 April 1988, as a draft for cosignature from February 1988.

121 Ibid.

taken into account for personnel decisions, especially regarding future assignment. Conversely, that meant that one's HIV status would not be taken into account if medical confidentiality was not waived. HIV positive soldiers showing no signs of illness could still apply to be discharged from the terms of their service. §55 (3) SG provided the legal basis in the event that remaining within the contract would pose a "special hardship." Here too, waiving one's right to medical confidentiality was the prerequisite. The same course of action would be taken with symptomatic HIV infections "as with other illnesses": Without naming the diagnosis, the troop doctor would pass on the soldier's limited fitness for assignment or ineligibility to his immediate superior, and the soldier's future eligibility determined on that basis. In this instance as well, discharge due to "special hardship" was possible.[122]

The draft met with critique when medical services circulated it for co-signature, such as from the Surgeon General of the Bundeswehr, who warned against overburdening troop physicians by requiring in-person consultations to go along with the tests. Anyone familiar with the day-to-day life of a troop physician could not keep them from their actual duties "with such an extensive (and ultimately unrealizable) extra task."[123] Far in excess of 100,000 HIV tests had been performed up to that point (March 1988) without a single basic conscript testing positive (every positive test result had come from older soldiers). The surgeon general also voiced his "utmost concern" about the guideline authorizing a physician to pass along knowledge of an HIV infection to the "relevant authorities and/or at risk persons" in the event that the physician possessed "assured knowledge" that the conduct of an HIV-positive soldier "posed a serious risk to the health and life of others that could not be averted by other appropriate measures."[124] Who were the "relevant authorities"? A soldier's immediate superiors, the health services, the state attorney "or all of them combined?" And who were these "'at risk persons'? Sexual partners? Bunk mates?"[125] The passage demanded much greater precision. The surgeon general took the advice in part, naming health services and the soldier's disciplinary superior as possible "relevant authorities" in the final version. The passage added further that the physician should consult with his superiors in

---

122 BArch, BH 1/29162: BMVg, InSan I 1, 19 April 1988, draft for cosignature from February 1988. Reading out the results of a positive HIV test, the draft continued, might put the person in question under severe mental and psychological strain, even achieving a "pathological value." In such cases the soldier's immediate disciplinary superior should be advised as to his restricted fitness for assignment or ineligibility.
123 BArch, BH 1/29162: Army Surgeon General, 10 March 1988.
124 Ibid.
125 Ibid.

case of doubt.[126] To return to the surgeon general's critique, "all was quiet on the 'AIDS Front'" in the troops he had seen up to that point. "In no way [should that] be traced back to disinterest." Physicians and commanding officers alike acted with "a sense of proportion and responsibility" and avoided "overreacting."[127] The 1990 film "Had I Known" and a flyer bearing the slogan "Soldiers do it safer" were also serving the goal of educating young soldiers about HIV and AIDS.[128]

Bavarian Minister of the Interior Peter Gauweiler (CSU) was also dissatisfied with the armed forces' regulations concerning HIV/AIDS. Gauweiler had already made public postures demanding strict general measures against those with HIV – for everyone, mind you, not simply soldiers. In a letter to Minister of Defense Rupert Scholz of the CDU and fellow CSU member Alfred Biehle (the chair of the Bundestag Defense Committee), Gauweiler "regretted" the voluntary nature of the HIV tests that the express letter had established in April 1988, and picked up on a recommendation by the "Select Committee on AIDS" at the BMVg's military medical advisory board in February 1988 to make HIV tests mandatory during medical examinations and upon acceptance for fixed-term or career service.[129] Scholz responded that no legal "means [existed] for singling out soldiers as a social group and subjecting them to a mandatory HIV test."[130]

Beginning in 1988, one small group of soldiers did undergo a de facto mandatory test. The U.S. armed forces required proof of a negative HIV test for all German soldiers sent to the U.S. for training, a policy that primarily affected air force pilots and members of the navy. With the requirement set to take effect in March 1988, in late 1987 a dispute broke out between the U.S. Embassy and Hardthöhe, the BMVg's seat in Bonn. The Office of Defense Cooperation dismissed the "medical and judicial concerns" raised by the BMVg, and the Americans would not agree to extending the start date to the end of May 1988.[131] The only option remaining for the surgeon

---

126 BArch, BH 1/29162: BMVg InSan I 1, 19 April 1988.

127 Ibid.: Army Surgeon General, 10 March 1988. Army Staff added a handwritten note with the Army's numbers for HIV and AIDS. As of 20 September 1988, four soldiers had died from the effects of AIDS, eight soldiers were ill and seventy-one of the Army's soldiers were infected with HIV. BArch, BH 1/29162: BMVg, FüH I 1, 20 September 1988, marked "Classified – For Official Use Only" (available as of 1 January 2019).

128 The film was presented by the Office of the Surgeon General in October 1990. BArch, BH 1/29162: BMVg, InSan I 1, 8 Oct 1990; the flyer was published by BMVg, InSan I 1, a copy is available in BArch, BH 1/29162.

129 Kohrs, "AIDS-Spezialist Gauweiler sorgt sich um die Bundeswehr," a copy is available in BArch, BH 1/29162.

130 Ibid.

131 BArch, BH 1/29162: U.S. Embassy Bonn, Office of Defense Cooperation to the BMVg, 24 November 1987; ibid., BMVg, InspSan to the Minister via the Secretary of State, 22 December 1987.

general was to propose the defense minister immediately implement HIV testing for all military and civilian personnel scheduled for training in the U.S. "on a voluntary basis," with all personnel notified that refusing the test "could jeopardize" their training abroad.[132] So as not to discriminate against soldiers who were HIV positive, testing would occur as a part of the general examination determining eligibility for foreign assignment. Going forward, an "appropriate rate of attrition" should be planned for when pre-selecting personnel for training in the U.S.[133] Reports about the HIV tests surfaced in the press, where it came to light that the Germans were not the only ones subject to U.S. demands.[134] The Dutch government also gave in, as the "training opportunities in the U.S. were indispensable."[135]

In 1990 the attaché to the British Minister of Defence registered interest in Bundeswehr policies regarding soldiers infected with HIV or sick from AIDS,[136] while in 1992 the U.S. Department of the Army was curious to ask the German Army attaché in Washington whether "possible differences [existed] in the clinical profile of homosexual soldiers" in comparison to "other soldiers, in the case of AIDS [and] HIV for example."[137] In 1993, the director of SOWI reported that it was not possible yet to determine beyond all doubt whether or not "the topic of AIDS had increased reservations toward homosexuals as an at-risk group." There were "however suspicions about a growing fear of contact."[138]

Throughout the first two decades of the Bundeswehr, homosexual men who either openly declared themselves to be gay or were identified as such during medical examinations were consistently rejected for military service. Throughout the 1980s and 1990s, homosexual men could expect to perform basic military service, but could not consider a career. In spite of all the draft regulations and obstacles, the red lights and "fear of contact," homosexuals have served throughout the entire history of the Bundeswehr from its inception on and from the highest levels down, largely in hiding but serving nonetheless. Their memories and experiences make up a central pillar of this study, and are considered in the following chapter.

---

132 BArch, BH 1/29162: BMVg, InspSan to the minister via the secretary of state, 15 January 1988.
133 Ibid.
134 See e.g. Kohrs, "AIDS-Spezialist Gauweiler sorgt sich um die Bundeswehr."
135 "Den Haag gibt wegen AIDS nach," a copy is available in BArch, BH 1/29162.
136 BArch, BW 1/546375; BMVg, InSan I 1 to the British defence attaché in Bonn, 21 August 1990, a copy is available in BArch, BW 1/531592.
137 BArch, BW 2/31224: Embassy of the Federal Republic of Germany Washington D.C., Army attaché, 11 December 1992.
138 Fleckenstein, "Homosexuality and Military Service in Germany."

II Among Comrades: Life as a Homosexual Soldier through the Lens of Individual Memory and Experience

Military culture rests on the unquestioned assumption of heterosexuality and heteronormativity.[1]

In 1999, a gay staff sergeant was interviewed for the magazine *Focus* about his experiences among the troops. Asked "how [he] responded to homophobic comments during [his] time in the service," he replied that when he confronted comrades as to "why they made fun of minorities" what came back was "mostly hot air." Soldiers would verbally abuse fellow soldiers for their homosexuality, calling them "ass-fuckers" or "gay sows who belonged in the psychiatric unit, not the Bundeswehr." Superiors intervened "all too rarely, unfortunately." The problem, the sergeant continued, was "intolerant and ossified leadership in the Bundeswehr and Ministry of Defense." "They would have preferred having only heterosexuals in the Bundeswehr. The prevailing opinion was that gay soldiers had authority issues and would see sexual partners in subordinates."[2]

Speaking in 2016, one sociologist professed to know that "anti-gay and misogynist turns of phrase [still] play a widespread role in everyday life in the military. Homophobic speech is not perceived as a form of discrimination, but a constitutive element of training."[3] And in 1970 a physician at division level found that "one part of homosexuals [were] good soldiers," one part demanded to be released from military service and a third "undoubtedly" suffered difficulties amid the "male society of the Bundeswehr." He cited one homosexual soldier as evidence with what were (allegedly) the soldier's own words: "You try taking a shower with three cute girls."[4] With the comparison, the doctor was apparently looking to illustrate one of the everyday dilemmas homosexual soldiers encountered.

In 1980 Dr. Rudolf Brickenstein, a Bundeswehr psychiatrist who had positioned himself as (or at least claimed to be) *the* specialist in treating homosexual soldiers, delivered a presentation on the daily challenges homosexuals faced in military

---

1 Botsch, *Soldatsein*, 207.
2 "Schwule in die Bundeswehr."
3 Botsch, *Soldatsein*, 214–15.
4 BArch, BW 24/7180: Division physician for the 6th Mechanized Infantry Division to the BMVg, 2 April 1970.

service.[5] "Living in tight quarters with their comrades [presented] a truly great burden" for some; in "tempting situations" it was often difficult for them "to keep to themselves." They rarely knew how to proceed "when roommates pressured them to share their own sexual experiences with girlfriends after a weekend off. Such men are usually quite sensitive, they fear that their homosexuality will be discovered and then they'll be shunned or made a laughing stock."

The question, Brickenstein continued, was whether the instructions given by troop physicians and unit leaders were in fact "working in the direction of the heterosexual majority showing greater tolerance to the homosexual minority." A "certain percentage of soldiers" exhibited tolerance while a further portion was "indifferent," "yet the overwhelming number of soldiers of all ranks [...] holds the position 'These gays are simply awful. We don't even want to give them our hand, because we don't know where they just had it.' This phrase is taken as representative of many and comes from a colonel at the Ministry of Defense, incidentally." Brickenstein reported coming across "mostly highly qualified fixed-term and career soldiers who had so quieted their homosexual desires that they did not have any run-ins with disciplinary or criminal law, but experienced difficulties while serving nevertheless." He had found

> especially sensitive soldiers, often with artistic ambitions, who set everything on keeping their homosexual orientation and activities hidden from their comrades, subordinates and superiors. Yet they live with the perpetual fear that it will come out after all, for example if other soldiers see them in the company of their boyfriends or visiting certain locales, or because they do not report back on heterosexual adventures like the other soldiers.

The contemporary account tallies with those of many former, and some active-duty, soldiers interviewed for this study. One lieutenant colonel, for example, reported that as a young lieutenant he would not visit the gay scene in the large city nearest to him but travel farther afield to rule out the danger of being seen by comrades.[6]

Brickenstein also drew from clinical experience in 1980 to relay the case of a captain who had kept his homosexuality secret from comrades – until, that is, he met someone "who completely turned [his] life around and gave it a new meaning." The career soldier applied for demotion to fixed-term service, at first without listing homosexuality as a reason. When his application was denied he appealed, this time

---

5 BArch, BW 24/5553: Lt. Col. (MC) Dr. Rudolph Brickenstein, "Sachverständigenreferat aus psychiatrischer Sicht" delivered at a meeting of the BMVg medical advisory board's committee on preventative health and care and military examinations 18 April 1980 (the following quotes from the same source). Also available in BW 2/31225.
6 Interview with Lieutenant Colonel D., Berlin, 12 February 2018.

disclosing his sexual orientation. This too was rebuffed. The rejected appeal was forwarded to him via every department, leading to nasty commentary from several comrades. The captain fell into a severe depression.[7] Anyone who thought Bricken-stein might be demonstrating empathy for homosexual soldiers in the problems they faced was disabused of the notion just a few sentences later: "Here too, the question arises as to whether it is possible, desirable or permissible to instruct the military environment in a form of tolerance that is often alien to its nature, with such education sometimes perceived by heterosexuals as impinging on their digni-ty."[8] Note that it is the human dignity of heterosexuals which is of concern here, not the discriminated homosexual minority (an absurd train of thought compared to today's standards, though equally so in 1980).

Brickenstein also reported on a counter-model to the "timid" officer living "with the perpetual fear" of discovery, and that was a group of fixed-term and career soldiers who "openly and unreservedly" admitted their homosexuality and demanded equal rights and treatment from their military environs. Their candor left them invulnerable to blackmail; they demanded they be allowed access to clas-sified material, and that they should not encounter any difficulties in pursuing a military career. Brickenstein characterized the position of these officers as being that "it has to be just as easy for a homosexual to become a three-star general as a heterosexual. It simply is not true that a homosexual superior lets himself be led more forcefully by personal inclinations and antipathies in handing out assign-ments than a heterosexual officer."[9] This was in 1980, mind you, long before the BMVg would hear the exact same argumentation from a gay soldiers' interest group in the 1990s.

1991 saw simultaneous publication of the article "Gay and in the service?!" in military periodicals *Heer*, *Luftwaffe* and *Blaue Jungs*. The piece sought by the editors' own admission "to break with taboo and prompt debate," answering the question "Gays in the military – are they even there?" with a succinct "Of course they are."[10] "The vast majority" would keep their sexual orientation concealed in service, for "many reasons." "Most gays take up the constant charade for fear of being discriminated against and isolated if they do not." The article quoted sol-diers directly, one with the comment that "gay jokes, moronic prejudices and

---

7 BArch, BW 24/5553: Lt. Col. (MC) Dr. Rudolph Brickenstein, "Sachverständigenreferat aus psychi-atrischer Sicht," delivered at a meeting of the BMVg medical advisory board's committee on pre-ventative health and care and military examinations 18 April 1980. Also available in BW 2/31225. A summarized account is given in: Lindner, "Homosexuelle in der Institution Bundeswehr," 225.
8 Ibid.
9 Ibid.
10 Haubrich, "Schwul und beim Bund?!" 34.

crowing about one's sexual prowess do not exactly encourage you to come out as gay." Another countered, saying he had "hardly experienced anything of the sort on staff duty in *Abi-Quartal*."[11] The author of the article, by all accounts a conscript himself, made out two tendencies: "The more educated people are, the more tolerant they are toward gays," while the "'manlier' someone felt himself to be, the more decisively he rejected them." The author found the Bundeswehr to have made a crucial misstep on this count, for instead of urging greater tolerance on the part of the discriminating majority, it blamed the victim. "Would you admonish a soldier teased by his comrades for short-sightedness and thick lenses to wear glasses in secret?!" the article quoted another soldier as saying, before summing up the general dilemma gays in the military faced: "If you confess openly you're considered a potential risk; if you hide, you're considered liable to blackmail and a threat to security." One soldier introduced as Mark had the final word: "I really don't understand the Bundeswehr. By treating gays as deviant and dangerous, those very prejudices, and with them the problems, become entrenched."[12]

Section FüS I 4 in the defense ministry responded directly to the public criticism three months later. "Mark's" view was incorrect by mistaking the cause for the effect; to understand the Bundeswehr's behavior toward homosexual soldiers, the "social reality," or society's stance on the matter, had to be taken into account. The "prejudices and dislike" that existed among the majority of the population exerted an influence on the "behavior and sensibilities" of individual actors toward homosexuals, ranging from "slight distancing" to "complete rejection."[13] This created a risk that "homosexuals would be deliberately provoked or made a laughing stock." As a force of conscripts, the Bundeswehr was "impacted to a special degree by the positions, attitudes and judgements in society that work their impact on a young man for close to eighteen years before he enters the Bundeswehr [...] The social reality vis-a-vis homosexuality is a factor for the Bundeswehr in terms of its reputation, acceptance and operational readiness."[14] Only with changes in society's overall attitude toward homosexuality, the ministry informed its soldiers, would the Bundeswehr would follow suit.

Heer, Luftwaffe and *Blaue Jungs* were journals all directed primarily at young soldiers and conscripts, and the piece focused on problems specific to them. Nine-

---

11 The *Abi-Quartal* was a colloquial term for new draftees who were called up every year on July 1 after completing their Abitur, or high school examinations.
12 All quotes from Haubrich, "Schwul und beim Bund?!" 34–35.
13 Statement issued by the BMVg office FüS I 4 in "Reaktionen und Stellungnahme zum Thema 'Schwul und beim Bund?!'." The statement is also available in BArch, BW 2/31224: BMVg, FüS I 4 to FüS I 3, 4 November 1991.
14 Ibid.

teen or twenty years old on average, most who were homosexual would still be in the process of coming out, or just before doing so. Did serving in the Bundeswehr speed up the process? "On the contrary – all the pressure disturbed [it] in my case," came one soldier's reply. "The internal pressure grew and grew, I only made it through the last three months using sedatives." The "natural solution" was switching to a barracks close to home, which helped one soldier a great deal. "There I could go home at night and be with my boyfriend. That made it no problem for me to keep the two separate and act 'inconspicuously' on duty."[15] The soldier's account is in line with the memories of other former conscripts interviewed for this study; most were stationed close to home after basic training, where after work they could return to their normal lives with boyfriends or partners without it impacting their military service.

Three months after "Gay and in the service?!" was published the magazine editors picked up the hot potato again, this time publishing letters from readers which had reached them. One NCO lauded the editorial board for its courage in broaching the topic: "[It was] at least a start to dispense with all the generally idiotic prejudice." Being gay himself, he wrote that "it's fine if somebody knows, but I'm not just going to let everybody in on it." The NCO hoped that "at some point" it would be "possible to say 'I'm gay,' even in the service."[16] The editors quoted praise from another soldier whose eyes had "grown wider than ever before" when he spotted the headline while leafing through the magazine. It was "a fantastic piece." For him fitness to serve in positions of leadership did not depend on sexual predisposition, which made denying it legally "pure discrimination."

> The opposite is true. A considerable number of the soldiers I know to be gay are among the best. Dismissing these soldiers wouldn't just be a loss for the Bundeswehr. It wouldn't just mean affirming prejudice. It would also be taking their purpose in life from them. For me, as for most gay soldiers, being a soldier means more than simply pursuing a career.[17]

A lieutenant colonel also wrote in. "Well then! The taboo has been broken, the existence of homosexuals in the Bundeswehr is no longer being denied [...] The sexual

---

15 Haubrich, "Schwul und beim Bund?!" 35.

16 Reactions and statements on the article "Schwul und beim Bund?!" As with many other letters to the editor, the BMVg kept the NCO's letter for its files unredacted with a service address (BArch, BW 2/38355: BMVg, FüS I 4). Evidently the editors at the troop magazine forwarded them to the ministry (on request?).

17 Ibid. Copy of a letter to the editor (anonymous) in BArch, BW 2/38355: BMVg, FüS I 4.

revolution of the 70s, the gay struggle for tolerance and freedom – has any of this gone on in the Bundeswehr?"[18]

"Sooner or (rather) later," changing notions of morality, marriage and family, love and sexuality would also overtake the Bundeswehr. For the time being things still looked different – conscripts were "very young and immature," and even if they were homosexual themselves "they either were not concerned yet with their own coming-out and all the problems associated with it, or were far too preoccupied." Officers and NCOs were "on the treadmill" and conformed to the expectations of their social surroundings.[19] Comparing the reprinted excerpts with the full range of letters archived at the BMVg revealed that the magazines' editors did a good job in selecting the overarching concerns and key passages for publication.

Praise for the courage of the author and editors also came from Michael Lindner, an early leader in the struggle for the gay soldiers' rights.[20] Lindner, a former captain and company commander who was given early retirement after being declared unfit for service due to health challenges, wrote that he and other officers had been "truly astonished" by the piece. "What it means to be allowed to read something like this in official magazines can only be fully appreciated by someone who has experienced how the Bundeswehr as an institution has worn people down and broken them in this respect." Even at the time of Lindner's writing, with the article's appearance in troop publications, "a handful of tragic developments had [again] come into view." Clearly writing with a view to homosexual officers he knew personally, Lindner described the "callousness" with which they were treated. "They have to leave the Bundeswehr," one lieutenant colonel had said.

Lindner also wrote to the article's author, Wolfgang Haubrich, directly.[21] Haubrich had "hit the bullseye smack dab in the middle" with his piece; "many cannot believe that it could have been printed at all and still consider it a 'mistake' [...] But it also took courage for whoever approved it, and hopefully they will not get too much grief now." Lindner wrote that the article would help people with a same-sex orientation "find their place in society sooner." For many comrades, the author had taken up the role of "fate" with his article.

---

18 Ibid. Copy of a complete letter to the editor (anonymous), also in BArch, BW 2/38355: BMVg, FüS I 4.

19 Ibid.

20 Letter from Ret. Captain Michael Lindner to the editors of troop periodicals *Heer*, *Luftwaffe* and *Blaue Jungs*, 8 January 1992. A copy is available in BArch, BW 2/38355: BMVg, FüS I 4.

21 Ret. Captain Michael Lindner in a letter to the author Wolfgang Haubrich, 6 January 1992, copy in BArch, BW 2/38355: BMVg, FüS I 4.

> Then there are the discussions ranging throughout the barracks and canteens, which are now forcing everyone, even those who do not see themselves as impacted by it, to think again [...] The fact that a young heterosexual conscript has brought about something that should have been done long ago by the armed forces command staffs leaves one speechless. But it was already clear beforehand, and it does not only apply to this army, that rigid military structures simply cannot do without the intelligence of conscripts.[22]

The 1991 article was not the first of its kind to appear in a periodical intended for soldiers. JS magazine had broken with conventions once before in 1986, publishing a one-page report on "men in the shadows."[23] The article devoted words of great empathy to the group in question:

> It is often precisely during their time in the Bundeswehr that young conscripts detect signs of their same-sex orientation. Knowing their surroundings reject the tendency, at first they try to repress it. They are often still quite aways off from homosexual experiences, let alone self-acceptance. Superiors rarely suspect that a personal struggle of the sort even exists, and are generally helpless if they do come into contact with it. Help in emerging from seclusion and hypocrisy related to sexual orientation is just about the last thing a soldier can, or does expect from his superior. Everyone in the barracks brags about their sexual escapades with the ladies on returning from the weekend. The homosexual conscript – around twenty years old, still unsure of himself – can hardly put up with it, cannot keep up [...] he may even hang a picture of a girl in his locker.[24]

1. Memories of Rejection and Tolerance

Eyewitness interviews provided an indispensable mainstay for this study. All interviews required critical evaluation as sources; memories of events dating back thirty, forty or even fifty years in the past are inflected by subsequent experience and may have evolved over time. Recollections and perspectives that were perforce subjective could only be verified in a handful of instances. The author has done just that, however, as far as was possible and within a justifiable period of time, managing in the process to identify a number of inaccurate statements and stories

---

22 Ibid.

23 Wickel, "Männer im Schatten." Next to the article the editors printed a text box with a number for the "Pink Telephone" service of the gay counseling center "Rosa Hilfe," and offered to send contact information for regional "homosexual and church" groups upon request ("mailed impartially, recipient addresses will be destroyed immediately.")

24 Ibid. These sentences did not come from Wickel. Rather, he copied them verbatim, with some omissions, from an essay published in 1985 by Michael Lindner. See Lindner, "Homosexuelle in der Institution Bundeswehr," 222–23.

and rule them out for further use. Eyewitness memories that could not be confirmed were evaluated on the basis of their plausibility. One challenge throughout consisted in setting written and oral sources into meaningful dialogue with one another wherever possible, juxtaposing them and weaving them together to depict the facts of the matter.

Everyone was subject to medical examination prior to entering military service. Down to the last, all those interviewed affirmed that they were not addressed about their possible homosexuality. Surprisingly for an era whose regulations still declared homosexuals generally unfit for service, it seems the topic did not come up.[25]

Interviewees also unanimously recalled not having the time or energy to spare on any grandiose sexual thoughts of comrades during the first weeks and months of service; basic training had been "far too stressful."[26] Following basic training the range of recollections expands. Most homosexual conscripts were stationed close to home and would return there every day after duty and continue living with their boyfriends or partners as accustomed, without it affecting their service. Gay soldiers who were not stationed close to home were likewise able to leave the barracks any night they were not on duty; there was no need to keep a look out for sexual partners among comrades as they could follow private whims and fancies "outside."

Speaking before the Bundestag in 1984, Parliamentary State Secretary Peter Kurz Würzbach himself referred to the opportunities soldiers had to go about their private lives undisturbed beyond the barracks gate. "Differently from previous armed forces [...] every evening around five, five-thirty or six o'clock the barracks gate practically stands ajar, unless one has a specific assignment, of which there are not very many [...] The majority of soldiers can head out into their garrison city, wherever they like."[27]

One conscript who entered the air force in 1973 did not recall his homosexuality "ever being an issue," either during basic training or later on. He had not "entered the service to get to know men, but actually to learn something." When he "noticed the tendency, it made [him] unhappy." Nobody had known about his

---

25 One former soldier did not recall being asked his sexual orientation or bringing it up when he underwent inspection at his local draft board in 1971. That had been just fine by him; he wanted to go into the service. Under no circumstances did he want to be found unfit based on his orientation – "I was living in a small town," he said, "I wanted to get out, live a little." Interview with K., Cologne, 9 April 2019.

26 For example, eyewitness interview with K., Cologne, 9 April 2019.

27 German Bundestag, 10th legislative period, 47th Session, 19 January 1984, typed transcript, 3378.

sexual orientation, however, so he "wasn't ever teased about it either." In general homosexuality had been a taboo subject, "you weren't allowed to show that you were different."[28]

Another interviewee who served as a conscript in Schleswig-Holstein from 1959 to 1960 brought a heterosexual perspective to bear.[29]

> Something wasn't right. The office NCO received me with a warm hand squeeze. It didn't take me long to work out that he was homosexual. Gaby, the secretary told me so as well. Somehow they had searched me out using my passport picture, maybe seen me at some point. The staff sergeant and the new first sergeant were obviously buddies and the staff sergeant wanted to do the [first sergeant] a favor, who wanted to do one in turn for the desk sergeant.

After basic training the interviewee had thus been assigned to the office. There the "desk sergeant" (sergeant on staff duty) had left him and his coworkers "in peace."

> Everyone knew he was homosexual. That's just how it was. Nobody bothered about it any further [...] One time though during winter maneuvers in Münsingen, he couldn't keep hold of himself. I had to spend the night together with him in a big bucket truck. There were two benches. For sleeping. One each. That night he came over to me and said 'Now let's have a quick fuck for once' [...] I said [to him] 'If you so much as touch me I'll make a woman out of you!'[30] That settled the matter. He didn't try anything ever again.

There were two gay privates first class in the same company.

> They drove trucks. Everyone knew that they got along together. They were proper lads and comrades, we had sympathy for them more than anything. There were never any mean words. Even in the common shower with twenty-five men, nothing more than the usual obscenities between soldiers. I personally found all the antics about soldiers' homosexuality in the media and Bundeswehr administration pathetic. They should just be left alone. It's not like you have to go bed with them.

Another witness recalled almost exclusively positive experiences of tolerance looking back on his time in the Bundeswehr in the early 1970s. Drafted into the light infantry in 1971, then reenlisting a year later as a fixed-term soldier and candidate for NCO in the reserve, following basic training the interviewee had been assigned to a support company in Hessen where he had been quite open about his

---

28 Interview with M., Hagen, 19 February 2019.
29 Email from Roland S. to the author, 25 July 2017.
30 In plain English, he was threatening to cut off the gay man's penis and/or testicles without saying it directly.

orientation.[31] All twelve soldiers in the unit he led were aware of his homosexuality, he "never hid it." There were other homosexual soldiers in his company, too – he "took a look around and spotted others."[32] The interviewee, K., could think back to numerous homosexual encounters with soldiers within his own company and others in the battalion, and stated expressly that he had never witnessed homosexual comrades experiencing discrimination. Not even homophobic slurs – otherwise a regular feature of soldiers' speech patterns – had been heard within the company. The eyewitness accounted for the uncommonly broad acceptance with the large percentage of happy-go-lucky Rhinelanders in his company ("We had a more relaxed view of everything") and homosexuality's taboo status. "Even in a company as tolerant as my own, homosexuality wasn't discussed openly. We just went ahead with it, though we didn't talk about it with other, non-gay soldiers. Homosexuality didn't exist as a topic, it was taboo, which was exactly why it could be pursued without a big fuss." The company sergeant major had also had a considerable hand in creating the tolerant environment; speaking with reference to a handful of the soldiers in his company who were open about their homosexuality, the sergeant major had said it was all the same to him what they did in bed, the main thing was that service was completed properly. The soldiers would not want to know what he got up to in bed with his wife either, he added.

Two years after finishing his first fixed term as soldier and leaving the army, the eyewitness was reassigned to his old company for a fixed term before being promoted to NCO in 1975 – all despite the fact that his sexual orientation was an open secret, even generally known about within the company and battalion. He recalled the next four years as being almost entirely positive, with only a single negative incident sticking out. At the barracks mess hall, the NCO had once had an "unpleasant encounter with a group of sapper engineers also stationed in the barracks." He no longer had the exact exchange of words in mind, but as he went to sit at the engineers' table they had more or less replied there was no room for gays at the table. A number of soldiers from the NCO's own company came to his side, voicing their support. One thing led to the next, and in the end fists flew. A report

---

31 Interview with K., Cologne, 9 April 2019. The following sketch of his time in the service is based on this conversation alone, and ultimately could not be verified. Only the parts deemed plausible are reproduced in what follows.

32 "All the gay soldiers knew each other," K. added. "You could also tell someone was gay by the uniform. We always wore our uniforms tight up against our bodies, and would order one size down in field tunics and pants for our dressing at the uniform store. 'But won't you have to be able to move in your pants!?,'" the ladies in the store asked in shock. We had other priorities than comfort: "That'll be just fine!"

to both companies' superiors followed, and all involved parties had to report to the company chief.

None of the soldiers gave the actual reason for the fight when questioned, however – the insulting words spoken to the homosexual NCO by the sappers. This let the company head rule the incident a common fight between two companies and branches of service, and file it away.

On the whole, the eyewitness, who retired after his term of service was up with the rank staff sergeant in 1978, had "never experienced discrimination in over six years in the Bundeswehr, nothing, not a thing – no insults, no punishment, not even nasty words (aside from the incident in the mess hall with the sappers, though that did not have any other negative consequences). I have nothing bad to say about the Bundeswehr."[33]

Other service members were similarly able to think back to comrades' tolerance, albeit less during the 1970s than in the 1990s. One first sergeant in the reserve for example recalled meeting his first boyfriend during basic military service – not in the army, but at the same time – after entering the Bundeswehr "not entirely of my own free will" in 1994.

> It was obviously all quite confusing to me at first, so there was no possibility of coming out; I had to get clear with myself first. Fortunately, I was in a six-bed room at the time and there were only two of us. My roommate was really fantastic. He could see my insecurity and helped me a great deal in making peace with myself. When my boyfriend would come to visit me in the barracks over the weekends (you had to ask the company sergeant for permission and pay a fee, but otherwise no other questions were asked), my roommate didn't have any problems with my boyfriend being in the room. For a long time the three of us were really close friends.[34]

Many former heterosexual soldiers agreed in retrospect that "being gay" was taboo, and never discussed openly as a topic. "It wasn't allowed to exist so it didn't, apart from some talk behind closed doors."[35] Others characterized fellow soldiers' approach as "if someone wasn't married, all it meant was he wasn't married" – but homosexuality was a forbidden topic.

---

33 Interview with K., Cologne, 9 April 2019.
34 Email from Sergeant First Class in the Reserve S., 5 April 2018.
35 For example, Hagen S., interview, 19 January 2018.

a.) Tolerance and Intolerance within the Ranks

Regulations notwithstanding, far greater tolerance did in fact prevail among the troops in the 1990s. One fixed-term soldier (with a final rank of sergeant first class in the reserve) who entered service in 1994 had "a great deal to thank [the Bundeswehr] for, and never had any bad experiences."[36] Another officer who eventually rose to the rank of general shared a surprisingly early example of tolerance from within the ranks when he found himself confronted with a "very particular" problem as a company leader in 1967.[37] The company sergeant and spokesperson for the enlisted troops had come to him about F., a gay private who was "causing trouble." Ordinarily there were not any problems with the soldier or his orientation, either in the barracks or the platoon. The "trouble" began, the delegation reported, when he drank alcohol; the highly athletic and muscular private would tend to become sexually aggressive toward weaker comrades, running the risk of abusing them sexually. No crimes had been committed as of yet, but there was a real danger. A rapid solution had to be found, with a priority on shielding the soldiers from bodily harm. Aside from his alcohol-induced bouts, the private was considered a valuable soldier – "square" and "stalwart" in the parlance of the day – "nobody who saw him would suspect he was homosexually inclined."

The company leader weighed his options. Simply instituting disciplinary procedures or forwarding the matter on to a military or public prosecutor would have placed a heavy weight on the private's future. §175 was still in effect in 1967, on top of which came suspicions of attempted sexual abuse. "I wanted to spare the man from becoming a pariah," the witness recalled. He considered evaluation by a troop physician or medical expert with the aim of determining the private ineligible for service, but that would go down in the man's file – also a serious liability for his professional future. Together, the company commander, sergeant and troop spokesman came to a pragmatic "internal" solution. "To protect him from himself, and the other soldiers from him," they agreed that whenever the private consumed alcohol or felt that "his hormones were starting to go haywire" he was to report to the NCO on duty. He would then be locked in a storage room in the basement, where a cot was set up especially for him. This sort of consensual detention played out repeatedly over the next months. The arrangement obviously was not kept a secret within the company, and even today the company head is surprised that the solution found the backing of every soldier who knew about it. Nobody reported "upstairs." The private was able to complete his military service without

---

36 Email from Sergeant First Class in the Reserve S. 5 April 2018.
37 Eyewitness interview (kept anonymous upon request).

serious incident and return to civilian life without any entries in his personnel file. The company commander himself was left with creeping doubts as to whether the man's tendency toward aggressive homosexual behavior when drinking would not cause him problems in the future. A pragmatic solution had been found for the man's time in the Bundeswehr, but the commander had been plagued by the thought of having committed a breach of duty in solving the issue internally. "I would have had trouble had it come out."[38]

The episode reveals that it was not uncommon for problems within everyday life in the military to be resolved "without spilling ink," i.e. outside regulations and without reporting to superiors. The notion that more often than not problems were sorted out "among ourselves" formed a part of companies' self-image at the time – the fact that no soldier made a report serves to express their membership in a tight-knit, sworn collective.

Still, homosexual incidents were generally regarded as a matter serious enough for "internal" solutions like the kind described above to remain the exception to the rule. In 1960 or 1961, for example, one lieutenant and platoon commander ran up against a lack of understanding from surrounding soldiers and superiors during a training course. In this case it was not his sexual aggression that "drew attention" but something else: more than once while showering after sports, the lieutenant had not been able to suppress fully his sexual arousal around other classmates. Others had noticed it at least, and reported him. "From one day to the next" and without notice, the lieutenant was dismissed.[39]

A staff sergeant was "withdrawn" from his unit just as quickly in 1966 when (however and for whatever reason) he drew attention as a homosexual. "We assumed he had initially been suspended from service and later dismissed," an eyewitness recalled, at the time a battery commander in Bavaria. The staff sergeant had been a "tall, attractive young man"; "nobody would have thought that of him."[40]

In 1967 disciplinary proceedings against a first lieutenant ended in the second instance with the officer's dismissal from service. The officer was charged among other things with multiple counts of masturbating together with an NCO in his battalion.[41] An otherwise "classic" case was made noteworthy by the two having known each other from before their time in the Bundeswehr – they were continu-

---

38 Ibid.

39 Interview with a retired major general (a classmate of the lieutenant in 1960–61), Potsdam, 15 May 2018.

40 Email from Albrecht G. to the author, 10 November 2017.

41 For a more detailed account with supporting court documents see chapter 3, section 4.

ing, both in the barracks and at home, something they had known from younger days. Yet now they were separated by military rank, with all the associated regulations and expectations. The NCO was quickly dismissed without trial or further notice under §55 (5) SG.

A chance contact with an eyewitness revealed that the same case nearly cost another officer his career in the Bundeswehr. In his youth the contact had belonged to the same scouts group as the two convicted officers. After graduating high school, the now officer cadet revealed to his parents that there had been "something" to the rumors of sexual activities in the group, largely initiated by the troop leader. The cadet himself had never been affected.[42] His father made the "matter" public, further alerting his son's company head and battalion commander to the facts when his son entered service in 1965. "My father had been an officer on the Wehrmacht general staff and was probably thinking 'reporting makes you free.'" It ended with the cadet also being brought under investigation by the state prosecutor's office for violating §175, although the inquiry was suspended without any results. Yet the mere suspicion of homosexuality continued to weigh heavily on the aspiring officer. His father's report forced him "to live out the coming years constantly under the traumatizing stigma" of his superiors' suspicions. In 1966 the officer candidate was even forced to undergo a painstaking ten-day "examination" at the psychiatric ward of a Bundeswehr hospital, an experience that was just as disturbing when recalled more than fifty years later.

Despite "credible assurances that he felt no homosexual tendencies of any sort and had also had girl friends," the cadet could not rid himself of the stigma of homosexuality. It later jeopardized his appointment as a career officer; once again his father was called in before the commander of the army officers' school, and the young officer had to assure everybody that he really was not homosexual but involved with women – this was in the late 1960s, mind you, not the 1950s. The commander himself had received the father's words about the unresolved suspicions of his son's homosexuality with astonishing equanimity, even nonchalance: "There'll be ass-fuckers from time to time." To the mind of the experienced general, it was no reason to destroy the young officer's career. The lieutenant was accepted into a military career.

In a separate series of events from the 1980s, one officer came across a tolerant classmate while enrolled in a course at the army officers' school in Hannover. The course itself consisted of young officer cadets studying alongside longer-serving or older lieutenants who had already graduated from (or prematurely dropped out of) studies at Bundeswehr universities, and were now completing their officers'

---

42 Eyewitness conversation (anonymized), 19 June 2018.

course after switching career tracks. A young cadet in the class at the time recalled an untoward nighttime encounter after a party, in which one of the older lieutenants had entered the cadet's room as he already lay in bed, sat down close beside him and made "explicit sexual advances," though they were purely verbal and did not involve any kind of touching. The surprised cadet had refused the advances, upon which the lieutenant stood up and left the room, though not without asking the cadet to look past what happened as a comrade, and "not give him away." The cadet promised to do so as much and (until his conversation with the author) never let slip a single word about the incident.[43]

A present-day lieutenant colonel assigned to lead a platoon for a signals training company in 1989–90 recalled having "at least" one gay conscript in his unit. Once at a party, some of the other soldiers had made joking insinuations as to the soldier's sexual orientation. "The soldier took it all quite easily, though; he was fully accepted as a member of the platoon as far as I can recall. I didn't pursue the matter any further as platoon leader, much less report it. And why should I have?"[44]

A former navy officer who is not gay himself recalled serving aboard a high-speed patrol boat in the mid 1990s with a signal man whose homosexuality had been an open secret among the crew.[45] Everybody on board had known, though the man had not experienced any recognizable difficulties because of it. The same officer had witnessed other scenes of tolerance before: When a navy cadet came out during his time at Bundeswehr University Hamburg in the early 1990s it had not caused a stir or led to any discernible career setbacks. "Nobody gave a damn," as the eyewitness phrased it. A separate incident from the early 1980s did ruffle feathers by contrast, if the memory of another eyewitness served him correctly.[46] During exercises for an armored reconnaissance battalion a conspicuously long silence fell on a radio exchange with a forward observer in a combat vehicle. Perturbed, the commander drove to the forward position, where he found the two crewmen having sex in the vehicle. The soldiers may have taken their *Hotchkiss*, the type of armored vehicle, as a call to arms, the eyewitness commented sardonically. The commander did not find it as amusing and took measures in response. The NCO was immediately dismissed under §55 (5) SG but not the other soldier, a conscript "who certainly would have liked that." He was transferred instead to another battalion and made to complete the rest of his service there.

---

43 Eyewitness interview with a lieutenant colonel, Potsdam, 22 January 2018.
44 Email from Lieutenant Colonel B., 24 January 2017.
45 Interview with J. from Freiburg, 30 May 2018.
46 Interview by phone with R., 23 May 2018.

A heterosexual major still in active service today recalled two different episodes.[47] In 1995 a walk-through bed inspection of a company in basic training had revealed an object sticking out from beneath one conscript's flattened bedspread. It turned out to be a sex toy. The dildo had not been planted there as a joke by one of the other soldiers though, but belonged to the conscript himself. While the soldier had thus been outed in front of everyone, he had not suffered any sort of discrimination "aside from stupid phrases." This ultimately tallies with the regulatory landscape considered in the preceding chapter, whereby conscripts in basic service generally did not have to fear any consequences in the event they were identified as homosexual.

The eyewitness encountered the same topic the following year. A conscript serving in a small subunit assigned to him had an uncle who as a first sergeant was both his nephew's unit commander and immediate superior. The two had a troubled family relationship, not least because the nephew's homosexuality was a thorn in the uncle's side. The first sergeant would often speak openly and with great contempt about his nephew's sexual tendencies, taking out "words from the deepest part of the gutter" in doing so. While every soldier in the company thus knew about the private's sexual orientation, he did not experience any discrimination aside from the insults coming from his uncle and superior. Only once had the eyewitness overheard a derogatory and insulting comment, coming from an older, longer-serving nonrated soldier. The eyewitness took the man to task and forbade him from making similar comments, citing the duty to camaraderie enshrined in §12 SG.

On his second-to-last day in service, after turning in his uniform and equipment, the private took the liberty of sending a clear signal: Instead of normal civilian clothes, he spent the rest of the day going about the barracks in women's clothing and heavy makeup. When the eyewitness asked him whether "he also went around like that in private," the private responded in the negative. He had borrowed the clothing and makeup from a girlfriend of his to send an indisputable sign of protest against his uncle's intolerance. The eyewitness looked back critically on the fact that nobody in the company, including himself as a staff member in the battalion, had put a stop to the sergeant's insults, much less brought disciplinary

---

47 Interview with a major, Potsdam, 18 January 2018, and in what follows. A former master sergeant recalled a very similar story. During an inspection in 1991 he had discovered lubricant and a sex toy in a conscript's locker that revealed him to be homosexual. The reactions from the conscript's roommates and the members of his platoon had ranged from "dismissive to insulting." There is little need to reproduce the terms used here. Interview with Ret. Master Sergeant W., Ulm, 29 March 2018.

action against him. Yet "twenty years ago it was another Bundeswehr. Life is lived in forward and understood in reverse."

Another heterosexual officer in the armed forces during the 1990s was witness to both tolerance and intolerance:[48] One chief of inspection at a school for troops "had the general reputation of being homosexual, without it ever being said out loud or brought up by him." The rumors had led to "an unpleasant situation for the [inspection chief] and his comrades" during an excursion into the Alps. When dividing up rooms on an overnight stay in a mountain hut, the lone officer equal in rank to the inspection chief fought shy of rooming with the latter, speaking in terms that were unambiguous to all present. After a protracted back-and-forth, another officer declared himself willing to share the room, initially drawing equally unambiguous comments from the others for his troubles. To the observer, "the embarrassing behavior violated the duty to camaraderie as well as the honor of the officer trailed by the rumors." At the other end of the witnesses' recollections stands a memory of a battalion in Baden-Württemberg, where a homosexual relationship between a company chief and a young sergeant in the same company had been an open secret. The company chief, a married father, had taken "astonishingly little trouble to keep his liaison with the sergeant a secret." Neither the battalion commander nor any other superior had intervened so far as the witness knew, although the commander must have been aware.

Another former soldier (also heterosexual) could only think back to experiences of tolerance in his unit.[49] Drafted into the Bundeswehr in the summer of 1989, entering the service had led "to a wealth of new encounters, among them the topic of sexuality." His home unit had been the first place he met someone who was open about their homosexuality. He was not aware of any action taken against the soldier. "The general approach seemed to be quite easy-going instead. While magazines in the vein of *Playboy* were usually consumed in most places, he would have issues of *Playgirl* lying open beside his bed just as often. I remember him as a good pal and a faithful, reliable manager at the fueling station in our transport group."

During his first foreign deployment in 1998, as a reservist for the Stabilisation Force (SFOR) in Bosnia's Rajlovac, the same eyewitness had another comrade who openly admitted his homosexuality, which "hadn't seemed to pose any difficulties for him as a Cologne native and carnival participant." The eyewitness could not think of any sanctions or consequences in this case either, nor any other problems despite the close living and working quarters. "There was no lack of caprice from

---

48 Interview with Lieutenant Colonel K., 14 December 2018.
49 Email from Frank W. to the author, 3 April 2018.

leadership and sanctions for plenty of cases during my time in the service, but never any regarding sexuality or sexual tendencies from what I can recall."

A present-day master sergeant who first entered the Bundeswehr as a basic conscript in 1996 had conflicting experiences to report.[50] Before being called up, the eighteen-year-old had bet his gay circle of friends he would make it into "the toughest branch of the service," which for him were the paratroopers. He won the bet, but during what was in fact a truly demanding basic training, had been forced to put up with terms of abuse and open rejection from his instructor and group leader on account of his "quite obvious homosexuality." ("I was somewhat feminine at the time, so the soldiers quickly spotted what was going on.") Forced to take a position in the mud during one drill, his superior had loudly said "There she is, a fag in the shit." "The NCO had it in for me," the master sergeant concluded. Yet basic training also brought with it the experience of true camaraderie. "My roommates stuck by me. If others had gone after me like the group leader did, I would have quit." This sense of solidarity encouraged him to extend his military service before it ended and become an NCO. He no longer disclosed his same-sex orientation at subsequent posts, however, "otherwise I wouldn't have become what I became." He embarked upon a full military career in 2003.

Throughout the interviews, acceptance into career service emerged repeatedly as a landmark after which soldiers were more open about their homosexuality. After entering career service as a staff sergeant in 1996–97, one officer since retired in the rank of master sergeant took it upon himself to inform his new superiors of his homosexuality whenever he was transferred.[51] None had ever had a "problem" with it; no sort of issue ever arose from his homosexuality while in service. "All my superiors were proper and fair with me." He had already shared an apartment with his boyfriend in Sonthofen years before, "a small town of little importance where everybody knows each other, especially the soldiers stationed there." While this led him to assume that his living situation was also known about at the military school there, he had never been approached about it, nor encountered any other difficulties throughout many years in service.

A former officer (quoted at greater length in chapter 4 below) recalled his own openness with his sexual orientation as a first lieutenant, initially in Brandenburg an der Havel and later in Berlin.[52] This had not led to any run-ins with fellow soldiers or superiors in his case either – on the contrary, he found "a lot of encouragement." Encouragement was certainly something the first lieutenant stood in need

50 Interview with Master Sergeant H., 29 March 2018.
51 Interview with Ret. Master Sergeant S., Freiburg, 21 June 2017.
52 For a more detailed account see chapter 4, section 9.c.

of at the time; starting in 1997 the officer became enmeshed in a battle with the Ministry of Defense and the personnel office after demanding a dialogue from civilian and military leadership at the Bundeswehr about homosexual soldiers' rights. A single incident stuck out – after an officer's party in Brandenburg an der Havel, a high-ranking comrade had tried to "talk him into having sex, putting him under a great deal of pressure." When his efforts did not meet with success, the same officer had attempted to foment negative opinion within the battalion toward homosexuality in general, and the lieutenant in particular.[53]

Tolerance for its own sake was not the only reason that homosexuality might be tacitly accepted among the troops, as one former staff officer pointed out.[54] The officer, himself not gay, often saw "simple human inertia" at work instead. "As long as service operations weren't disrupted you looked the other way." When asked who he meant by "you," the witness replied superiors with disciplinary power (disciplinary authority in today's language), specifically company chiefs. A disciplinary procedure always meant a lot of paper work.

> That sort of incident couldn't be resolved by normal straightforward educational measures ('Write an essay, two pages size A4!'). So, company chiefs kept their eyes shut as long as they were able. Most only got involved when service operations were disrupted, and in that case "bowing sooner to necessity than their own impulses"[55] [...]
>
> The NCOs, platoon leaders and sergeants all stuck to the same script. Less because of the extra work though, and more out of a combination of indifference and tolerance based on a sense of solidarity. The lower-ranking superiors would only report to the boss if service operations were disrupted or the obvious could no longer be overlooked.

As a recruit in 1973, the former officer had been witness to one such disruption to daily routine during basic training. One evening an NCO had run "stark naked across the company floor over to the phone in the sergeant on duty's room to ring for medical assistance." The naked soldier was coming from the room of a first sergeant who had been injured during sex; in great concern and evident panic, the NCO had neglected even to throw on his trunks. Rumors had long circulated within the company about the relationship between the first sergeant and the NCO from the orderly room, "though never anything concrete." There was now something very concrete following the nighttime incident, forcing the company commander to act. The eyewitness could not say anything for sure about the consequences for either party involved. The first sergeant kept his assignment as a platoon com-

---

53 Email from Erich Schmid, 5 December 2017.

54 Interview with a retired lieutenant colonel, Bonn, 20 February 2019.

55 Paraphrasing Schiller, *The Bride of Messina* (1803).

mander but the NCO was never seen in the orderly's room again; whether transferred or dismissed it was no longer recalled.

At least during the 1990s, many soldiers experienced far greater tolerance among troops than what the personnel guidelines stipulated. One company chief's homosexuality had been an open secret within the company in the mid 1990s, but "you didn't talk to the chief *about* something like that."[56] It could be added here that you might well talk about the chief.

A former battery commander (himself not homosexual) recalled his predecessor's homosexuality as being an "open secret, but not an issue" within the battery during the late 1990s, not even in hindsight. The "regency" of the allegedly homosexual chief "didn't have any negative effects, at any rate."[57] A senior NCO in the same battery had a different recollection of the internal conversations.[58] When the preceding battery commander had come out to the battery unit leaders at their first meeting, it elicited "highly differentiated" reactions. Three out of the twelve NCOs, battery sergeant major included, had reacted with open disapproval with phrases like "Well then, we don't have to do anything at all now. He can't tell us anything!" Behind this and similar statements stood a loss of authority for the chief, a situation that may also have threatened discipline within the unit. (This was exactly the sort of scenario that the BMVg and administrative courts were constantly invoking, and which was used to justify the assumption that homosexuals were not fit to lead.) All the other unit leaders, among them the battery staff sergeant, "didn't respond with approval but remained neutral" and kept their loyalty to the chief. The battery staff sergeant in particular "didn't have any sympathy for the commander's homosexuality" but saw it as his responsibility to remain loyal and maintain discipline within the battery.

The case is noteworthy not merely for the warring loyalties among battery NCOs, but principally for the fact that against personnel policy, the chief stayed in office. Nobody reported "upstairs," not even the few NCOs who ventured dismissive reactions. Such a report, as numerous parallel instances from the 1990s show, would have forced the commander and thus the personnel office to enforce the regulations and remove the chief.[59]

One officer, since retired, recalled that his sexual orientation became known to his roommate and three other soldiers during an officers' training course in 1990–91. His roommate was also gay and had introduced him to a number of bars

56 Interview with Ret. Master Sergeant R., 7 February 2018.
57 Interview with Lieutenant Colonel N., 23 February 2018.
58 Interview with Ret. Master Sergeant R., 7 February 2018.
59 See chapter 4 for greater detail.

in Munich, though the two did not have any sort of relationship or sexual contact. Another officer, gay himself, had also known of the interviewee's homosexuality during his time as a young platoon commander in a light infantry battalion in 1991–92. There had not been any sexual contact in this case, either.[60]

A young man who entered the air force as an officer candidate in 1992 experienced his own coming-out at the officers' school in Fürstenfeldbruck.[61] He recalled that "coming out" was not an accurate term, however; it had to be kept a secret at school, otherwise he would have risked cutting his professional life short before it had properly begun. Nobody was allowed to know except for one person – his first partner. The two shared a lecture class; a friendship developed out of a sense of camaraderie – and out of friendship, love. They spent the weekends together, but took care that their relationship went unnoticed during the week at school. Discretion held top priority. Leading a double life at the officers' school had been a "handicap" that cost effort. Looking back self-critically at a bygone era, the former candidate confessed he had been unable to act freely, treading cautiously and acting self-consciously around other soldiers, and unwillingly drawing a line between himself and others. The two men initially stayed together after training in Fürstenfeldbruck before their professional paths, and soon their private lives, diverged.

Lesbian soldiers who served in the medical corps in the 1990s also spoke of widespread tolerance within the ranks. The fact that a troop doctor lived with her partner in the small nearby city was an open secret at work, for example. From time to time sexist, oafish or at the very least unthinking comments would of course be made. Once a missing jack during the card game *Doppelkopf* elicited the comment "Our doctor doesn't play like that with jacks anyway." (Throughout her first assignments as troop physician she had consistently been the first woman the soldiers had seen in uniform holding the position, an unfamiliar sight reflected in their referring to her as "Ms. Doctor.") The casual term of address gave her momentary pause, though she did not find it negative, much less insulting. Other comments that stick out in her memory include "We know in your case that you didn't sleep your way to the top," or "Our doctor will never be deployed, she's from the other team." The words of one colonel stayed with her as well, though: "Doctor, if someone picks on you because you're with a woman just let me know and I'll smash his face in!"[62] The physician is still active in the Bundeswehr, and confirmed that she had never experienced any problems in service due to her sexual orientation.

---

60 Email from Erich S. to the author, 5 December 2017.
61 Interview with K., Munich, 18 May 2018.
62 Eyewitness interview, 28 November 2019.

A female NCO who served from 1994 to 2008 could not report on any problems or discrimination either, although she had not "really been open" about her sexuality in the service and only came out to those "in the same or a similar situation," i.e. other lesbian and gay soldiers. Still, "a lot of people knew about it. I didn't hide myself away, though I didn't communicate openly about it either."[63] Even when falsely accused of interfering in a colleague's marriage after serving abroad, she did not cite her orientation as an exonerating circumstance. (The NCO's friendship with another doctor on assignment had been misinterpreted by other soldiers and shared with the doctor's wife. The wife then filed a complaint, leading to the eye-witness being interviewed by superiors.) The reasons for her continued reticence, even after 2000, came less out of concern for herself than a gay male soldier in her unit with whom she had a close-knit friendship. The two were seen as tight companions, and at the time she thought that if her sexual orientation came out it would immediately lead others to draw conclusions about her friend. She wanted to "protect" him. "Among men it was always something else, difficult." Whenever she was asked about a husband, she spoke of a "de facto spouse," not answering with the masculine in German but in gender neutral terms, as was typical in the Bundeswehr. Using the term among soldiers was a clear signal that other homosexual soldiers, male and female, would have immediately understood.

b.)   Bundeswehr Campus Memories

From the accounts of the officers interviewed for this study, the pressure to dissemble and hide tapered off significantly with their transfer out of the troops and into the Bundeswehr's university system as cadets or young officers. Recollections from their time as students thus deserve special consideration.

Amid the freedom of student life and the breadth of opportunity that the university towns of Hamburg and Munich offered, many, if not all, student officers eventually relaxed regardless of orientation, with a number who were homosexual quickly ceasing to hide it in the 1990s. The contrast between one's relative freedom as a student and the ongoing rules and regulations – a dynamic that was at play in every aspect of life at Bundeswehr universities and was moreover entirely intentional – was reflected in part by how aspiring officers were treated. Any number of interviewees recalled increasing openness about their sexual orientation over the course of their studies, allowing gay students to get to know one another in the process.

---

63 Interview, Ret. Sergeant First Class Martina Riedel, Hamburg 23 January 2020.

One former candidate described Munich's gay life as "like being rescued" after he was transferred to the Bundeswehr University there in 1991.[64] For the preceding fifteen months in training for the navy he had done everything in his power to ensure that homosexuality "didn't come up" as a topic. Munich was the first place "he finally found his way to himself" and managed to develop what had previously been a rather indistinct sense of self. The aspiring officer came from a conservative family; his father had also been a soldier. His son's admission came as a "shock" to both parents, leading the father to seek out a military pastor in his distress.

Another former officer recalled exploring the "unknown freedoms" of Munich during his time as a student in the early 1990s, a city known even at the time for its large and worldly gay scene.[65] Time and again it happened that he would chance upon other students in clubs. They knew others in turn, eventually giving rise to a circle of more than twenty officer candidates and officers. Affairs and partnerships also developed naturally between the men, with many couples who met in the 1990s in Neubiberg (the town where the university was located) still together more than twenty years later, in 2018. The men made up a "tightly sworn circle" at university. They all shared the same problem – if the higher-ups at the university found out about their sexual orientation, it meant the end of their careers in the armed forces. Yet even this scenario did not scare at least some student officers from taking an active part in university life. A number ran as representatives to the student advisory council, soon making up the majority as one recalled. Their involvement in campus life went further to include arranging celebrations, parties and concerts – and appointing a "gay envoy" to the council.[66]

Another officer studying in Neubiberg at the time recalled that as he had started to come out to a "select" cohort, rumors also spread about him on campus, though he neither confirmed or denied them.[67]

> People could think whatever they wanted. Nobody ever talked to me directly about it though, even other gay students. Homosexuality began to be talked about more and more often at university after 1994. In seminars, committees, publications and among soldiers too, of course. A liberal attitude took hold that was palpable, especially among younger soldiers but also our superiors.

The occasional "piece of gossip or cliché" might have gone around campus, but he had never detected "hostility, or even simple avoidance."

---

64 Interview with L., Munich, 7 June 2019.

65 Interview with K., Munich, 18 May 2018.

66 A fuller account comes later in this chapter.

67 Email from Erich S. to the author, 5 December 2017.

One officer studying at the Bundeswehr University Hamburg in 1992 or 1993, himself not homosexual, recalled another student, a lieutenant, coming out in public at a meeting with the head of the (military) student division.[68] The head, a navy captain, was the highest-ranking military man at the university and had responded dryly to the public confession with a "Hrm, aha!" The incident quickly made the rounds. The lieutenant was a paratrooper, and "the idiotic jokes about gay paratroopers [meant that] a number of other paratroopers at school likely saw themselves forced to draw a clear line between themselves and their comrade." Overall, the officer said, "the incident didn't entail anything further to my knowledge. But I didn't bother myself any more about the subject either."

Two further witnesses had opposite experiences to share from the late 1990s, a time at which there were still restrictions in place on officers identified as homosexual. The first had no negative responses or consequences for his subsequent career in the military on which to report; openly homosexual since his studies, he went on to enter career service and soon became battalion commander. The second witness did not experience any negative reactions from his superiors, either – not at first.[69] It was only as his course of study drew to a close and his transfer into the troops approached that his earlier admission became an obstacle. He was informed that under the current regulations (which remained in effect up to 2000), he could not be assigned to lead or train soldiers, nor was he eligible for a military career.

The full story? When he first entered the service in 1993 as an NCO candidate in the navy before eventually switching to the career track of an officer, the witness had had to sort out his sexuality for himself and did not see any "compelling ties to the service." Then he had met his partner while studying in Hamburg (who was not at the university himself). By this point the cadet had long since accepted his homosexuality and now decided for the first time to confide in his immediate superiors. While his trust would later turn out have been misplaced, his superiors initially seemed to warrant the confidence. When the leadership changed in 1998, the now senior cadet went to tell his departing superior himself before the new one took over. The captain prefaced their conversation with the words "If what you want to tell me is what I think it is, you'd really better not!" If he did, the captain would have to "get some paperwork ready" and make a report "upstairs," and it would end with the officer candidate being removed from his course, bringing about a change to the career track of a senior NCO and a reduction in service time. The cadet was spared all this; he took the advice and kept silent. It then turned out his predecessor

---

68 Email from Lieutenant Colonel B. to the author, 24 January 2017.
69 Here and for the following set of recollections, interview with Navy Commander Alexander Schüttpelz, Berlin, 24 January 2019.

appraised his new superior of the situation, despite claims to the contrary. The new captain spoke openly with the cadet about his homosexuality, stressing that he did not have any problems "with it" and that there would not be any official reports "upstairs."

Yet as his course drew near its end the captain asked to speak with the student, by now a second lieutenant. He did not want to see the student in his office, however, but for a walk in the park. On their walk the captain explained that he had "a problem" – he had to give the lieutenant an evaluation, and had doubts as to whether the lieutenant would be able to assert himself as a troop leader, something he intended to express clearly in the review. The captain was as good as his word. The lieutenant filed a complaint against the assessment but it was turned down, and he returned to the navy from his studies bearing a document that attested to insufficient powers of enforcement. It was only years later and at the intercession of later commanders that the interviewee, today a commander (navy), made the leap to career soldier.

The two conflicting, nearly contemporaneous accounts reveal once again that it ultimately came down to superiors' individual behavior. One went strictly by the book; another struck a more tolerant and liberal tone. Back among the troops the second officer stayed true to himself, remaining open about his homosexuality. "Open, but not aggressive," the commander emphasized. He needed to discuss his sexuality only on rare occasions as hardly anyone asked about it, although he confided in a handful of close colleagues. As so often in life there had still been rumors, and when the lieutenant encountered them in a course in 2001 he decided to seize the initiative. The next morning he spoke up in the lecture hall: Yes, he was gay and no, he did not want people talking about him behind his back. Classmates had "reacted in one part by knocking approvingly on the tables, and in another with icy silence and 'sour looks'," though there had not been any explicit retorts or grievances. Later, the class teacher conducted confidential one-on-one conversations with everyone in the class to get a better picture. In doing so he found that the class did not seem to have any problems with one of their fellow students being gay. Yet the teacher did not speak with the lieutenant himself – he had not seen any need to, given what in his mind was a positive situation in the classroom. Shortly before departing, the lieutenant asked the lecturer for feedback. The latter replied that he did not see any need for action at the moment (concerning his future career as a navy officer), while also advising the lieutenant that "he wouldn't have it easy in the navy" as an openly gay man, especially aboard ship, and that he should "reflect carefully" on whether he wanted to go to sea. The lieutenant did.

The comparatively free and informal nature of life and service at the Bundeswehr universities meant the otherwise taboo topic of homosexuality was handled more loosely than in the troops. One relatively early example from 1979 came in the form of a piece written for a student publication on the Munich campus.[70] The article quoted four anonymized sources at length, all of whom were studying to become officers. "You're in the Bundeswehr? There must be a lot of great stuff to get up to there, right!?" one officer was repeatedly asked by other gay men who were not in the service. For his part, the officer could only "respond with a pained smile." Yes, the Bundeswehr was a "male society," but one "painfully bent on its heterosexual self-image." Another interviewee reported that not a single superior knew he was gay. "I'm almost positive not one of them suspects it. There is one other soldier who knows. He's very tolerant and discrete." None of the four interviewees counted on the tolerance of other soldiers; it would be "highly risky." One of them considered the tolerance among officers to be low, although he himself had different experiences. Here, the student newspaper implicitly pointed to the gap between the experience of tolerance and the anticipation or fear of rejection. "I cannot just jump in and brag about the great guy I met on Saturday when the others are talking on Monday." The "ghettoization and tight living quarters in Neubiberg" did not always afford the necessary privacy. Still, things were much better at Bundeswehr University Munich than they would have been in a town or small city. They could not count on being able to convince personnel leadership that their partner should come along if they were transferred to the minute town of Hammelburg in Bavaria after their studies, for example.

The same officer voiced his fear of disclosing he was in the Bundeswehr when he went out in Munich, "however well guys in uniform went down in the gay scene." In fact, "if someone in a green uniform came into a gay bar, you could be sure he wasn't in the service." Practically all homosexuals lived in fear, the student newspaper concluded, speaking not only with reference to the armed forces but society as a whole. "He lives constantly under disguise, ducking for cover as quick as a flash when need be. Sometimes even when it's not necessary." Overcautiousness and fear characterized the four officers' behavior. "I make an effort to be discrete [...] I have to exercise greater self-control [...] I can't watch after a beautiful man walking through the barracks for as long as my comrades would watch after a beautiful woman." A regular meet-up among gay students in the dining hall should actually be part of "a real university," but that sort of thing would not be quick in coming. Nor would a "gay action group [...] be so quick" in coming to the Bundeswehr.[71] The article was published in 1979; fifteen years on, exactly that sort of group came into being, formed mainly by students from the Bundeswehr universities – the Federal

---

70 ATÜ "Homosexuelle an der HSBw." A copy is available in BArch 24/14249 and BW 24/32089.
71 All quotes from "Homosexuelle an der HSBw."

Working Group of Gay Soldiers (Bundesweiter Arbeitskreis schwuler Soldaten, BASS).[72]

c.) "Gays in the Military": A 1994 Article in *Junge Soldaten*

> In truth, all he wants is to be just the way he is. In truth, he loves his work and is fully engaged. In truth, he wants nothing less than to appear in the newspaper. But Michael Müller has a problem – one he doesn't see as a problem to begin with, in truth. Michael Müller is gay and in the Bundeswehr – and those two still don't go together easily, even twenty years after Paragraph 175 was revised.[73]

Staff Surgeon Michael Müller's name and picture had now been printed in *JS*, a magazine published by the Protestant military chaplaincy for "people in the service." The article quoted Müller both directly and indirectly:

> Michael Müller has been a fixed-term soldier in the Bundeswehr for twelve years now. "I was naive at first, thinking what could happen to me as a gay man?" [...] "It's no problem, sexual orientation has nothing to do with medical officers," came the first written responses from the defense ministry in Hardthöhe. Yet when Müller wouldn't let up with his petitions and inquiries, Hardthöhe's policy of excommunicating gays fell on him as well. He now learned that the position of troop physician was out of the question for him, and that his acceptance into a full career had also been ruled out. Müller knew long ahead of time what the reasoning was, because it has been the same for decades. "A gay commander might abuse his position"; the "general rejection of homosexuality undermines the authority of a gay commander"; "it would jeopardize discipline and operational readiness" [...] Since then Michael Müller has worked [...] as a laboratory physician under the motto that it is "undesirable [for him] to treat fellow soldiers" [...] Personally, Müller hasn't ever had problems with superiors or subordinates [...] Even his conversations in Bonn met with understanding. "Person to person they are more tolerant than I thought they would be." But understanding is of little use to him, as it changes nothing about the basic stance of not promoting gays in the military [...] "My superior is a woman. But nobody considers her liable to seduce someone."

By referring to women in positions of authority (at the time in 1994 women were still limited to serving in the medical and music corps), both Müller and the article's author anticipated the line of argumentation that would bring an end to restrictions against gays in 2000. Things had not progressed that far yet, however:

> "Seduction," "creating dependency in subordinates," "sexual practices" – the buzzword of homosexuality seems to conjure up little else for Bundeswehr officials than sex games in the

---

72 See chapter 4 for a full account.
73 Here and what follows, Spiewak, "Schwule beim Bund."

shower and intercourse in the dorms. "As with heteros, a gay man's life doesn't consist of sex 24 hours a day," as Michael Müller says [...] "There are gay service members in every rank, in every garrison."

The name and picture of another officer who studied at the Bundeswehr University Hamburg featured in the same issue (though without his rank listed).

"The Bundeswehr usually goes about bragging how it's a mirror to society. Why should it be any different on this point?" asks Oliver Dembski [...] Only a handful of gay soldiers openly profess their true love out of fear of mockery and sanctions. Most lead a double life. "From 9 to 5 they're hetero, after that they're gay," in Oliver's words. The split in identity leads to grotesque games of hide-and-seek. One's partner becomes "a friend" or "girlfriend"; a picture of a naked girl hangs in the locker for disguise. Many keep altogether silent about their personal lives. "Gays are good actors," Oliver says [...] The official line from Hardthöhe does its best to encourage this sort of double-dealing, for only those who admit their homosexuality are barred from positions of leadership. Anyone who disguises himself in proper Bundeswehr fashion remains eligible. "They force us into a dark corner, so that every gay soldier is subject to the whims of his superior," Michael Müller says.

Müller and Dembski now sought to change that. "The two are no longer willing to accept the degrading self-denial [...] 'We want to show gays in the Bundeswehr that nobody has to keep their problems to themselves.'" That had been the motivation in making their names, photographs and telephone numbers public. The magazine encouraged other readers to contact the two.

That readership included the Ministry of Defense, which retained a copy for its archives featuring a handwritten note at the end that read:

1. The article is factually incorrect and one-sided;
2. The article claims a 'problem' for a very small minority, which is not in fact a problem in the Bundeswehr;
3. The Protestant Minister's Office for the Bundeswehr is being kept apprised on an ongoing basis as to reader reactions and the content of their letters;
4. It will be decided on this basis whether the BMVg will issue a statement in *JS*.[74]

Prospective officers who had been studying at the Bundeswehr universities in 1994 were still able to recall how important the article had been for them and their process of coming out. Students from Munich contacted the staff surgeon and Hamburg student whose names and photos had appeared in the article and a network sprang up; the *Junge Soldaten* article provided an initial spark.[75] What

---

74 BArch, BW 2/38335: BMVg, handwritten note in the files of Section FüS I 4 from 12 April 1994.
75 For example, interview with L., Munich, 7 June 2019.

up to that point had been smaller circles of personal acquaintances and friends within the two universities coalesced into a national group, the "Federal Working Group of Gay Soldiers."[76] Group members sought to advance a common cause and achieve visibility as gay soldiers. One step in this direction came a good year after the article appeared in *JS*, when in 1995 the post of "gay envoy" was established for Bundeswehr University Munich.

d.) The "Gay Envoy" to the Bundeswehr University Munich

The story behind the "gay envoy" at Munich also turns up in the BMVg archives. The event which led to the "incident" was a newspaper report in *Junge Freiheit* shortly before Christmas 1995: The Bundeswehr university had "finally succeeded in bridging the gap to contemporary trends at civilian universities," with the "clientele" of the "gay envoy" at Neubiberg encompassing fifteen student officers to date.[77] News reached the desk of the chief of defense after a retired major general brought it up in a letter to the BMVg. The head of the student division for military affairs at the university subsequently detailed the facts of the matter. In March 1995, the council had set up a small administrative section that functioned as a counseling center for any questions student officers or officer candidates might have regarding homosexuality in the Bundeswehr, while also serving as a point of contact for similar centers in Munich. Up to that point, the chairman of the student advisory council had attended to the work himself on the side. Clearly looking to forestall any unwanted conclusions, the colonel emphasized that no "inferences could be drawn about the representative's homosexuality" based on his work portfolio, while the current "gay envoy" similarly occupied the post "for the function alone."[78] The figure of fifteen students mentioned by *Junge Freiheit* had not been released externally, he continued. The council was (and is) composed of chosen representatives from among the students and officer candidates and had acted within the framework of student self-government; it had not overstepped any bounds or disregarded any regulations in setting up the administrative section – only an "expedient preliminary discussion" with him, the student division head, had been missing. This omission notwithstanding, the colonel gave his wholehearted support

---

76 For a full account see chapter 4.
77 "Bundeswehrunis: Spiegelbilder der Gesellschaft," a copy is preserved in the BMVg archives, BArch, BW 2/38355.
78 BArch, BW 2/38355: Bundeswehr University Munich, student advisory council chair, 22 January 1996.

to the post of "gay envoy." It could only be expected that "out of more than two thousand young men, a need to talk or receive counseling around the topic of homosexuality would arise among those who were potentially affected."[79]

The "gay envoy" at Neubiberg kept the BMVg busy throughout the winter of 1996. The ministry's legal staff affirmed that no breach of official duty which "justified intervention" had occurred, even if "the designation 'gay envoy' certainly seems provocative, and designating an 'equality envoy' that represented other minority interests as well would be preferable."[80] FüS I 4, the ministry desk for leadership development and civic education, saw no legal grounds to object, nor did military leadership at the university regard any intervention on the part of superiors as necessary. For their part, both the commander of the Armed Forces Office as the university's direct superior and his legal advisor viewed banning the "gay envoy" as a distinct possibility. Yet FüS I 4 warned against it; military involvement might "wake sleeping dogs and lead to unwelcome publicity," "even in the event that watertight legal options could be found." The matter had not aroused any media interest to date beyond *Junge Freiheit*, and had not harmed the reputation of the Bundeswehr. Instead, FüS I 4 recommended that the ministry "accept the way things stand with composure."[81]

Staff departmental leaders on the Armed Forces Staff took up the matter in early March 1996; the minutes record the chief of staff "considering it unnecessary to install gay representatives at Bundeswehr educational institutions."[82] After consulting with the deputy chief of defense, responsible among other things for the universities, the legal staff was going over the matter "with a fine tooth comb" – there was no need for the Armed Forces Staff to take action.[83] The deputy chief of defense had inserted a further note to let the whole matter "rest."[84]

One eyewitness similarly recalled the commander at the university, a colonel, having "no problem whatsoever" with establishing a gay envoy when he found out, even advising the informal predecessor organization to BASS.[85] The account was

---

79 Ibid.
80 BArch, BW 2/38355: BMVg, VR I 1, 14 February 1995 (correct date: 14 February 1996).
81 BArch, BW 2/38355: BMVg, FüS I 4, 22 February 1996.
82 Ibid., BMVg, staff officer at FüS chief of staff, short protocol for StAL conversation 5 March 1996.
83 Ibid., BMVg, staff officer at FüS chief of staff, 8 March 1996.
84 Ibid., BMVg, note on consulting with deputy chief of defense, with handwritten comment "completed 9/3."
85 For example, in an email from Erich Schmid to the author, 5 December 2017. From 1993 to 1996 Schmid was a member of his faculty's departmental council, a member of the student council and deputy representative for his year. Between September 1994 and September 1995 Schmid also served as the chairman of the student advisory council and edited the university newspaper *Campus*.

confirmed by another student involved with the student council at the same time; he also recalled an "emissary" sent by the defense ministry who appealed to the council to abolish the post of "gay envoy," or at least rechristen it. The final title for the post was "representative for drugs, gambling problems and homosexuality,"[86] turning what had begun as an optimistic step toward greater openness into a catch-all position. Meanwhile, out beyond the relative freedom of campus life, most homosexuals in the armed forces continued to shy away from opening up about their sexuality throughout the 1990s.

2. Forced Mimesis: Concealment, Repression, Denial

Even if entrance regulations had allowed, indeed required, gays to perform basic military service since 1979, in practice soldiers would "desperately conceal" their homosexuality, *Stern* magazine wrote in January 1984.[87] The article quoted one officer candidate who had been in service for fifteen months. The cadet had invented a girlfriend, complete with a picture to pass around to other soldiers at the barracks, the bar or officers' club. "I put on an act for them and tell them about I what did with my boyfriend as though it had been with a girlfriend [...] You have to have a girlfriend, then you're normal among them." *Stern* summarized the fear of exposure as often leading to "over-accommodation and feelings of inferiority." "The higher his rank, the more difficult life becomes for a homosexual soldier, and the greater the pretense, the self-denial." This was supported by quoting a major whose "private life doesn't fit with what [he does] professionally." Asked whether he felt his homosexuality "conflicted with it," the major's reply was brief: "Yes." The thirty-six-year-old could not imagine living with a boyfriend, "because that doesn't really happen either." He got "sexual satisfaction from occasional 'escapades' with anonymous partners." *Stern* also quoted an active general to prove its point:

> The fifty-year-old [...] succeeded in keeping up appearances before comrades and superiors. He's married, living happily with his wife and children he didn't father. "Sometimes I have no idea who I'm even putting this charade on for," he said in the interview, "at times I'm really quite desperate. I know that it isn't becoming of a general. But it's not becoming of a general to be gay either, is it? There's a deep-seated feeling of unworthiness that gnaws away at you. Not because you're actually unworthy or inferior. No, it's because the damned moral code stipulates it."

---

86 Interview with K., Munich, 18 May 2018.
87 Krause, "Da spiel' ich denen eine Komödie vor."

As with all quotations from officers who were allegedly interviewed, today these statements can no longer be verified for their authenticity. *Stern* quoted the general as resigning himself to the conclusion that it was "nonsense to want to start a discussion about homosexuality in the Bundeswehr with my position and rank."

The letter of one homosexual soldier seeking assistance already mentioned in the introduction was reproduced in a 1984 issue of *Der Spiegel* and reached retired Captain Michael Lindner, by then a public figure. Lindner quoted from the letter at length in his own writing in 1985.[88]

> Who am I supposed to, who can I talk to? My only choice is to admit that I'm "different" or to adapt, to keep quiet, constantly at risk of being "exposed" as gay by one wrong statement, one false move. I'm forced to deny my personality; I suffer from the constant charade, feel like I'm being watched [...] I have to keep myself under control 24 hours a day. It's terribly difficult for me to constantly be shuttling between two conflicting worlds; the "free" world on the weekends and the narrow world of the barracks [...] So, I'm simply afraid, scared of being found out. That's why I withdraw, avoid all close contact with other soldiers, block out conversation. I'm all alone in a large "community."

Many shared quite similar recollections. One lieutenant colonel, who has since retired, explicitly asked the author not to let the "non-operational aspects of extreme psychic burden" from the era go unmentioned: "Concealment, double 'identities,' permanent fear of being discovered and the professional repercussions, the danger of harassment and bullying by fellow soldiers, 'professional lies' in one's private life, different private and professional codes of behavior."[89]

One witness, himself not homosexual, recalled a former classmate who had been remarkably open about his orientation at school since he was fifteen. When he began basic service in 1998, however, he resolved to "hide" his homosexuality in the barracks and serve out his ten months "without attracting attention." Otherwise quite self-possessed as a gay man, in the barracks he did not want to be recognized as such. The act reached the point to where he put up pictures of naked pin-up girls in his locker.[90]

One remarkable series of events from 1978 or 1979 points to the even greater pressure homosexual officers could come under at times, some of whom even resorted to breaking the law to escape it in extreme cases. A lieutenant colonel at the time had asked the whereabouts of a close acquaintance of his, an officer

---

88 Lindner, "Homosexuelle in der Institution Bundeswehr," 223, quoted subsequently in Wickel, "In einer Männergesellschaft nicht hinnehmbar."
89 Email from Lieutenant Colonel D., 13 October 2018.
90 Interview with K., Potsdam, 22 October 2019.

who shared his rank of S2. The officer was responsible for military security in the battalion and had not been seen in service for days. The battalion commander responded drily that the first lieutenant in question had deserted – the commander had received a postcard from Morocco informing him that the lieutenant would not be returning for the foreseeable future.[91] When the perplexed lieutenant colonel asked the reason why, the commander replied that the S2 officer had "likely gotten wind that he was being investigated for illicit sexual acts with dependents." So far as the eyewitness knew, the first lieutenant was being investigated for *consensual sexual activity* with an NCO directly subordinate to him. MAD had also stepped in before the officer deserted due to the highly sensitive nature of the battalion's range of duties and the officer's position, which held security implications.

As the witness told it, the first lieutenant returned to Germany ten years later, "right on time, after the statute of limitations was reached."[92] Here he was incorrect – the story could unmistakably be mapped onto a ruling handed down by the military service court in Koblenz from April 1979. The deserting officer returned to Germany after just two and a half months in Morocco, at which point a local court sentenced him to four months on probation for unauthorized absence. The military court imposed a heftier penalty, dismissing him from service.[93] The officer stood accused of four relatively minor counts of attempted homosexual advances and touching subordinate soldiers or others, which had been rebuffed in each case. The court found an aggravating circumstance in the fact that the first lieutenant had not returned to the barracks from vacation in early May after disciplinary proceedings had been opened in April 1978, but instead left for Morocco for a spell. Speaking before the court, the first lieutenant explained that he had wanted to gain "clarity about [his] position" in the upcoming disciplinary proceedings, and to "get some solid ground under his feet again."[94]

A lieutenant colonel currently active in the military reported having "made a secret of his homosexuality for decades in both his professional and personal environments," and of being at odds with his orientation, not acting on it for a long

---

91 Interview with a retired lieutenant colonel, Bonn, 20 February 2019. As a side note, the eyewitness recalled the battalion commander giving a surprisingly relaxed impression despite the incident. The commander explained that the deserter was currently on assignment at a training course, so the matter lay in the hands of the school commander. The school commander did not fail to report to Army Office that 16.6% of the course had deserted, prompting a flurry of phone calls between the office and the school. The explanation was as simple as it was typical of the Bundeswehr – reports were requested in percentages, and the course only had six students.
92 Interview with a retired lieutenant colonel, Bonn, 20 February 2019.
93 BArch, Pers 12/45192: Ruling at Military Service Court Center, 1st Division, 11 April 1979.
94 Ibid.

time.[95] He had not applied for career service at first, unsure of whether and how he "could hide or even suppress" his sexual orientation over the lifelong career he was thinking to spend in the military. In the words of the officer, "I was cowardly. Fear eats the soul. But at some point the wall gets too low and the water too high, and it spills over." Gradually, the officer found his way through the chasm between service and sexuality, and adapted. It was only after the officer decided to enter career service after all and was accepted, thus shoring up his professional future, that he first ventured out into the gay scene, more specifically a gay sauna. The officer's story confirms a recognizable pattern from other interviews, of acceptance into career service serving as a milestone after which soldiers were more open about their homosexuality.

Even if a homosexual soldier did escape notice, a study commissioned in 1985 by the armed forces' military psychology branch argued that a "male community" like the Bundeswehr would always expect its members to pass muster in "heterosexual trials" if they wanted "to earn the group's respect."[96] A soldier identified as homosexual, on the other hand, would come under constant "pressure of legitimation," always having to prove that "he had not entered the Bundeswehr because he saw better options for his sexual tendencies there."[97]

a.) The Paradigm of "Military Masculinity"

The everyday experiences of homosexual soldiers have also been considered in the social sciences. Alongside interviews with a number of heterosexual soldiers, in 2014 Kerstin Botsch spoke with three gay soldiers in active service: a twenty-four-year-old studying at a Bundeswehr university to become an officer in the air force, a forty-year-old senior NCO in the army and a thirty-one-year-old whose military branch and rank went unnamed.[98] Over the course of her interviews Botsch ascertained that despite the decrees and regulations bringing an official end to discrimi-

---

95 Eyewitness interview (anonymized), Berlin, 17 December 2017.
96 BArch, BW 2/32553: Armed Forces Office, Dept. I, Military Psychology Section, February 1985: Max Flach, "Sozialpsychologie Stellungnahme zur Homosexualität in den Streitkräften," 15–16. Also available in BArch, BW2/531590: BMVg, PII4, AzKL-1-85.
97 Homosexual individuals developed various "compensatory mechanisms" in order to withstand the constant and excessive psycho-social pressure: "Hyper- or hypoactivity," "avoidance behavior," "adopting roles (authoritarian, distanced)," "an exaggerated sense of ambition related to self" and "somatization of unprocessed motivational energy, i.e. diversion to organ systems resulting in psychosomatic disturbances (e.g. migraines, stomach ulcers, heart trouble)," ibid.
98 Botsch, *Soldatsein*, 339–40. A sample of individual interviews.

nation against homosexual soldiers in 2000, homosexuality itself continued to be a taboo subject well into 2004, even if homophobia had shifted to other forms of discrimination. Speaking about homosexuality in the present day (2014) represented a "discursive limit." Just like their heterosexual comrades, soldiers with a same-sex orientation would "use the paradigm of militarized masculinity as their point of reference."[99] "Whatever is manly," Botsch continued, "cannot be homosexual. This logic of homosexuality's imputed lack of compatibility with the military is also plain to see in the distance adopted from homosexuality."[100] Military homosexuality thus filled "military requirements for masculinity exactly, since adapting to the models of military masculinity and normalization played such a central role in the institution."[101] By looking to the "paradigm of militarized masculinity," Botsch and other social scientists saw homosexuals enacting a form of "mimesis," "assimilation" or "presentation," taking their cues from "social situations and actions that expressed institutional and individual norms without the actors necessarily being aware of it."[102]

Mimesis for Botsch "brings (at least) two worlds in reference to each other – the first world is assumed to exist (although it can also be fictional, ideal, or made up of interpretations), while the second, mimetic world exists in a real sense of physical sensation. The difference between the two worlds is perceived as a threat."[103] The threat emerges above all in "sexualized" moments or situations "in which physical proximity and nudity are a present possibility, e.g. on foreign deployment or in the shower." "Showering demands controlling or habituating one's glance in a way that presupposes practical knowledge (in this case about modes of behavior when showering)." One of the homosexual soldiers Botsch interviewed is quoted with the words "Yes, you look around [...] during sports for example it's obviously critical because you don't know how to look, and in the shower of course it's really dumb [...] you cannot attract attention."[104] Within an academic context, Botsch translates individual experiences that other homosexuals have certainly either shared or can relate into a distinction between "seeing and being seen."

> In this light, the interviewees are placed under constant possible surveillance by the all-seeing gaze of their comrades [...] The potency of this potential surveillance is internalized and

---

99 Ibid., 208–9.
100 Ibid., 245.
101 Ibid., 249.
102 Gebauer and Wulf, "Soziale Mimesis," 75. Similarly in Botsch, *Soldatsein*, 252.
103 Botsch, *Soldatsein*, 254.
104 Ibid., 254–55.

incorporated by Soldier U – self-monitoring replaces the actual or imagined possibility of surveillance.[105]

Botsch wisely conducted all her interviews well after the Bundeswehr had fully opened to homosexuals in 2000. Yet they continue to offer important insights into the behavioral patterns of gay and lesbian soldiers. In the preceding era, the adaptive forms of behavior Botsch describes and analyzes would likely have been much more pronounced.

In the end, the forms of behavior gay soldiers imposed on themselves wound up reflecting other soldiers' prejudices and clichés. Looking back on his early days in the Bundeswehr, one homosexual officer said he had never been a "permanent fixture in the shower," picking up on a popular phrase.[106] Sexualized situations, "an everyday part of life in the military" that was "at odds with the desexualized demands" of ministerial orders and regulations, were particularly sensitive.[107]

> Among homosocial male communities, an emotional connection arises through latent homoeroticism [...] Homosexuality cannot, however, follow from homoeroticism [...] Still, within homosocial communities sexual practices strengthen bonding among the men [...] Paradoxically, as long as they are set within a heterosexual context, practices like group masturbation do not threaten the narrow line between homosocial and homosexual, and homosocial and homoerotic [...] Consuming pornography together while masturbating can without doubt be seen as a homoerotic act that can only take place within the safety of a heterosexual group of men. Masculinity is also staged via shedding emotional and physical inhibitions. Not just drinking games, but ritual masturbation demonstrate a form of going beyond one's borders, and setting the individual within the collective.[108]

Within these intimate circles there also sat (unidentified) gay soldiers. Games like these presented a particular tightrope walk for them, a "forced activity." Retreating from the circles would be "precarious, because your heterosexuality would come into question." Focusing too intently on other soldiers as they masturbated would be just as precarious.[109]

Botsch's sociological work and interviews on this specific account tally with what a former soldier in the navy told the author for the present study. Called up to serve in 1995, he spent several months aboard a ship in the Persian Gulf. Shortly before the end of his time there two sailors had been dismissed on account of their

---

105 Ibid., 256.
106 Interview with Lieutenant Colonel P., Berlin, 17 December 2017.
107 Botsch, *Soldatsein*, 257.
108 Ibid., 257–59.
109 Ibid., 260.

homosexuality, according to rumors on board. A seaman at the time, the soldier had kept his own homosexuality to himself, and his behavior totally inconspicuous so as not to jeopardize his deployment in the Gulf. A number of situations he recalled matched those in Botsch's study. In the crew's sleeping quarters, nightly porno films and communal masturbation sessions among those present (usually six to ten men; the shift system for guard duty meant the twelve men quartered in the room were never all present) had been the rule. Mutual touching had also been common practice without it being seen as homosexual. "Everyone present took care not to be identified or seen as being gay," although the eyewitness had noticed some of his comrades "looking less at the screen with the porno as they masturbated and [instead] directing their gaze stealthily, but still recognizably, to the excited soldier next to them."[110] Aside from the nightly masturbation sessions, the interviewee did not have any further sexual, let alone explicitly homosexual, contact on board.

Had he been spotted as gay, it would not merely have signaled certain exclusion from the intimate nighttime gatherings, but probably a premature end to his deployment in the Persian Gulf as well. On board, homosexuality was considered a "criterion for exclusion," which meant coming out was out of the question. Instead, much in Botsch's terms, the private consciously placed every action on board "under constant possible surveillance by the all-seeing gaze of [his] comrades," adapting himself and unconsciously choosing a strategy of mimesis.[111] Here the eyewitnesses' experience match the social scientist's findings neatly:

> The homoeroticism inherent in these types of practices can be labelled heterosexual by disregarding or negating homosexuals, or homosexuality itself. The presence of homosexuals would reveal the line that has been drawn and destroy it. Male homosexuality is not just avoided as a topic, it is not only communicated about in a certain forms (e.g. in jokes), but is also subject to taboos that relate [...] to action.[112]

Eyewitness experiences likewise strongly corroborate Botsch's general findings. Conversations about private matters or "partners" would feature "mimetic elements," with homosexual soldiers adopting the speaking or thinking patterns of their (heterosexual) comrades, and making themselves similar, a habit that "includes constantly disavowing and keeping silent about one's own partner and leading a double life."[113] (The assertion that homosexual soldiers led a "double

---

110 Interview with S., Freiburg, 15 June 2017.
111 Botsch, *Soldatsein* 261.
112 Ibid., 261.
113 Ibid., 262.

life" can be found in BMVg documents from 1966 on.[114]) Botsch draws the conclusion that social mimesis may be seen as necessary for homosexuals to pursue their everyday life in a military setting.[115]

A majority of interviewees stressed that, prior to the year 2000, they either kept their sexual orientation a secret or at least did not "broadcast it."[116] A present-day master sergeant who initially entered service as a conscript and was later accepted as an NCO recalled that his own homosexuality had been an open secret at his post. He had also had sexual experiences with other enlisted men (themselves heterosexual, in fact) and NCOs in his unit. The secret to his "success"? "You simply have to be able to keep your mouth shut."[117] His transition to career soldier in 1998 similarly went off without a hitch despite the secret.

Another officer had similarly "kept his mouth shut" after completing his degree.[118] Back in the navy, he returned to being extremely circumspect about his homosexuality; his external image mattered a great deal to him as a young officer, a position of authority aboard ship. Specifically, he was afraid of being seen walking hand-in-hand with his partner around town, a distinct possibility with a crew of three hundred. Out of five young officers aboard ship, three were gay, something the eyewitness, today a commander in the navy, only discovered years later. He regretted not having known at the time – "if we had [...] we could have protected and supported each other." He became increasingly easy-going about his sexual orientation in subsequent assignments on land, and today it is a "lived normalcy" for him and his husband.

One captain recalled his time as a sergeant and platoon leader of a training company in 1985, where young officer candidates were also set to gain their first leadership experiences within the ranks.[119] Based on a shared schedule for time off and weekends as fellow superiors, the sergeant struck up a friendship with one of the candidates that eventually turned into a sexual relationship. When the cadet's father (himself a staff officer in the Bundeswehr) caught wind of his son's relationship with the sergeant he threatened to report the two, and thus see to it their careers ended. As it stood, the sergeant, who was carrying on an illicit sexual rela-

114 BArch, BW 24/3736: "Erfahrungen bei der Entdeckung homosexueller Verhaltensweisen von Soldaten." In BMVg, InSan: "Beurteilung der Wehrdiensttauglichkeit und Dienstfähigkeit Homosexueller," 1966, sheets 56–63, here 59.
115 Botsch, *Soldatsein*, 264.
116 In the words of Ret. Master Sergeant W., Ulm, 29 March 2018 and Master Sergeant R., Potsdam, 5 January 2018.
117 Master Sergeant R., Potsdam, 5 January 2018.
118 Interview with L., Munich, 7 June 2019.
119 Interview with Captain H., 12 June 2018.

tionship with a direct subordinate, would in all likelihood have had disciplinary proceedings instituted against him. The cadet likely would not have had any disciplinary procedure to fear for his part, although his father's report would have brought an immediate end to his time in the Bundeswehr. As a known homosexual, he would be subject to immediate dismissal as an officer candidate under the current regulations. The son yielded to his father's threats and cut off contact with his sergeant and friend; his assignment within the ranks had ended anyway and he returned to training school.

Thirty-five years later the former sergeant, by now a specialist officer, chanced upon his former company sergeant major, now retired. The former "sarge" still easily recalled the cadet and replied, when the latter mentioned in passing he had married a man, "ah ha, so he did have a 'good gut instinct'." The retired sergeant told him he had once suspected the young cadet's homosexuality at the time but never brought it up. The eyewitness learned that things could turn out differently as well when he came out to his family in 1998 and met with curt rejection from his conservative parents. When he left the next year on foreign assignment, his mother reportedly told his sister that "hopefully a bullet gets him." (This sadly recalls Magnus Hirschfeld's testimony from World War I. At the request of an officer who had been dismissed for his homosexuality, Hirschfeld spoke with the officer's mother to gently explain her son's impending return from the war. The mother had replied she would have preferred Hirschfeld "bring the news that [her] son had died."[120]

Eyewitnesses provided vivid and compelling accounts about the great pressure under which they suffered as homosexual NCOs and officers, in some cases for years, in others decades. The daily, unrelenting obligation to betray themselves or risk their professional future swayed above them like the sword of Damocles. Many moved between service and their private lives "as between completely divided worlds, one the world of the barracks, the other past the barracks gate."[121] Maintaining a strict divide between the two and keeping one's private life separate from the service was essential to keeping or advancing one's career as a soldier. As the threat of §175 had done before, this inflicted a psychological burden in a number of cases, even depression. The number of cases of suicide that had homosexuality as their actual background is impossible to determine in retrospect.

---

120 Hirschfeld, *Von einst bis jetzt*, 152–53.
121 As described in an interview with Master Sergeant H. in Berlin, 2 July 2018.

b.) Suicide or Marriage?

In the throes of deep depression, the later French general Hubert Lyautey found himself faced with a decision in 1909: commit suicide or get married? He opted for marriage, choosing the widow of a captain he knew.[122] Lyuatey's career only properly took off after the wedding, landing him atop the French military as Minister of War during World War I, and later as a Marshal of France. Lyuatey is a prominent example of matrimony serving as an effective shield against the potential stigma of one's homosexuality becoming public knowledge. In actual fact Lyautey was astonishingly "open [about his homosexuality], regularly seducing the best and brightest of his lieutenants as part of their military education."[123] In getting married, however, Lyautey acceded to the social conventions demanded for a truly great career. All the mockery behind closed doors notwithstanding, Lyautey achieved the greatest military honors France had to offer, with the nation according the marshal a grave of honor at Les Invalides in Paris.[124]

Soldiers are particularly adept at camouflage. Officers seeking safety in the port of marriage appear repeatedly throughout history, as they do in literature. Thus does Max René Hesse's character Ernst Partenau, a gay first lieutenant in the 1929 novel named for its protagonist, seek the classical escape route of marriage. When Partenau's passion for a cadet is revealed before the assembled officer corps, the lieutenant tells his superior that he intends to "call upon" a lady from the area. The elderly captain has known Partenau longer – and better – and makes "an embarrassed, unhappy expression." Hesse has the captain rub salt in the wound in describing the purported escape marriage offers.

> So, you're ready then, to get up before the baroness and her clan, before the regiment, and fail at the courtship dance, fail completely, and for the sake of the boy, all for the sake of the boy [...] you'll pull yourself together, even if it is while burning in seething oil. After four weeks' vacation [...] the boy will be in another regiment. You'll marry Baroness Streifelt, or try to [...] You've got your family, a couple boys, and all the other intoxicating and magical potions now taste stale and tepid [...] all that matters is your agreement that I arrange everything silently

---

122 Biographical writing on Lyautey freely gives away the fact that he "did not have sexual relations with his wife." Quoted here from a series of biographical sketches of well-known homosexuals.

123 Hussey, *The French Intifada*, 281–82.

124 Prime Minister Georges Clemenceau was said to have described the general and former war minister as an "admirable and courageous fellow who always had nuts below his backside. Unfortunately, they were rarely his own." ("Ca, c'est un homme admirable et courageux, qui a des coulles au cul. Dommage que ce ne sort pas souvent des siennes.") Hussey, 282.

with [Colonel] Mafai. Shake on it [...] And that's how it will be Ernst, you can rely on it. You won't be let down.[125]

Both the personnel records kept by military service courts for individual military members charged with homosexual activity and the higher instance of military service senates contain a striking number of references to the accused either getting married in the meantime, or becoming engaged and intending to marry soon.

Oftentimes, and especially in the case of appeal proceedings, the incident in question would be separated from the disciplinary proceedings by at least a year, sometimes several, giving anyone suspected of homosexuality ample time to seek out the relative safety of marriage. In many respects, matrimony seemed a safe way to mitigate the social ignominy of one's same-sex orientation drawing notice and having it put on trial. Many such men married in the conviction that "it definitely offered the best protection" against persecution by the police and the courts, not to mention social exclusion.[126] Current research indicates that matrimony was also seen as a way out in the early days of the Federal Republic; the threat of punishment loomed large over the lives of these men. "Even after liberalization, many still were not able to work out a free form of sexual expression since they had not been able to do so for many years, usually formative [...] Some men who married for cover likely still carry a guilty conscience today toward their (former) wives."[127]

Untangling the deciding causes behind a suicide after the fact is possible only in certain instances; when a note is left behind, for example. The Bundeswehr does not keep tabs on potential motives in its statistics on suicide, making it impossible to draw any reliable statistical conclusions about the relationship between a soldier's suicide and potential homosexuality. What the author has been able to do here is reconstruct a handful of cases based on eyewitness accounts.

In a case discussed at greater length at the end of the present chapter, the restrictions against a company chief and his partner of many years, a conscript serving in the company, ended with the conscript's attempted suicide in 1981. The

---

125 Hesse, *Partenau*, 240, 243–44.

126 Such at least was the opinion of Hans. G, a policeman initially sentenced to death for homosexuality in 1943 then shipped to the Neuengamme concentration camp when his sentence was delayed. Having survived the camp, he saw marriage as the best protection against renewed persecution after 1945 and "had to live through many unhappy years of marriage." Eyewitness report from Hans G. in Stümke and Finkler, *Rosa Winkel, Rosa Listen*, 301–6, here 306. Another Wehrmacht soldier convicted of "illicit sexual acts" and sent to serve in a penal battalion also married after the war. "There was no way that could go well," he recalled. "I myself found out years later just how miserable it could be." Eyewitness report Harry Pauly in *Rosa Winkel, Rosa Listen*, 312–16, here 313.

127 Bormuth, *"Ein Mann, der mit einem anderen Mann Unzucht treibt,"* 53.

conscript reproached himself bitterly for what had happened, taking the blame for the trouble his partner had run into. The suicide attempt was discovered in time, and the young man's life was saved.[128]

A later surgeon general recalled that during his time as a paramedic team leader for the Richthofen fighter squadron in Wittmund during the mid-sixties, an enlisted man hanged himself.[129] While going through the soldier's locker, they found a number of unsent love letters to a lieutenant colonel in the fighter squadron. "The two soldiers clearly had a relationship." The squadron's wing commander questioned the lieutenant colonel, eventually reaching the decision "[you] cannot stay here!" The lieutenant colonel was transferred to another base. "With that the matter was cleaned up quickly and straightforwardly, that's how things were handled at the time."[130] As far as the witness could recall, it "had never occurred" to the wing commander, a highly decorated fighter pilot in World War II, to open disciplinary proceedings against the lieutenant colonel for his homosexuality, let alone call in the public prosecutor (at the time homosexual activity was still subject to punishment under §175). The eyewitness could not say whether personnel staff was informed about the backdrop to the lieutenant colonel's transfer.

In November 1967, a twenty-two-year-old petty officer tried to end his life by cutting his wrists after being discovered naked in bed with a seaman apprentice who was his direct subordinate during evening inspection.[131]

As early as 1908, one army insider was reporting on homosexuality, or rather its rejection as a possible cause for soldiers committing suicide. Writing in the inaugural issue of the *Zeitschrift für Sexualwissenschaften* (Periodical for the Sexual Sciences) with reference to reports of five suicides, a "judicial employee" (likely from Magnus Hirschfeld's institute) complained that:

> In the last month alone, between 20 November and 20 December that is, the German Army lost at least three officers to the notorious §175: Captain S. in M. to suicide, according to the 20 November *Berliner Tageblatt*, and, according to the *Täglicher Rundschau* of recent days, two lieutenants to court-martial conviction in Neiße and the first guard division [...] It may be due to chance that this month was been particularly busy. On the other hand, anyone sharing the tendency will have checked himself in the past few months and many a case will not have gone public, so that one may assume a monthly average of three such instances [...] It has cost

---

128 For a full account see section 4 e, this chapter.
129 Interview with Ret. Surgeon General Dr. Horst Hennig, Cologne, 14 February 2018.
130 The wing commander had also been considerate enough to select a base close by to the lieutenant colonel's current one, so that he wouldn't have to change his private place of residence. Interview with Dr. Horst Hennig.
131 For a full account see chapter 3, section 3, below.

NCOs, soldiers, state officials, and other respectable citizens much more, but can be estimated all the less.[132]

Partially contradicting the forced "mimesis" of concealment and denial is the notion that homosexuals make ideal soldiers, and was there was no lack of gay soldiers who saw themselves in this light. As one officer candidate who entered the air force in 1992 put it, "gays were and are the ideal soldiers after all, no kids, no family obligations of their own, eligible for transfer anywhere and therefore particularly well suited for foreign deployment. It was dumb of the Bundeswehr not to use this potential, but reject it."[133]

3. "The Ideal Soldier"? Self-Assurance through Alexander, Caesar and Prince Eugene

When he ran into other soldiers in the 1980s who welcomed the Bundeswehr's restrictions against homosexuals, one eyewitness had automatically replied that Prince Eugene himself had been gay. "We'd all be Turks today if they had demoted him."[134] Another former soldier recalled that referring to Prince Eugene of Savoy and his battlefield triumphs against the Ottomans had managed to "'pacify' even right-wing comrades."[135] Born François-Eugène de Savoie-Carignan in Paris in 1663, the prince has surfaced repeatedly in the accounts of homosexual soldiers seeking to affirm their sense of self. Speaking on Austrian national public radio in the midst of the Wörner–Kießling affair in 1984, one Austrian doctor recalled a medical exam during which an officer had told him that his homosexuality was not a problem at all, "because Prince Eugene was one too after all."[136] Ever since his victories in the Turkish wars and the War of the Spanish Succession, Prince Eugene has been lauded as one of history's greatest military commanders. Rumors about the warlord's private life abounded during his lifetime; unmarried and without children, he operated under the principle that "for a man of war, a woman is obstructive furniture."[137] Vienna scarcely lowered its voice when it spoke of the "Mars without a Venus."[138] Numerous contemporary reports point to Eugene's

---

132 Leexow, *Armee und Homosexualität*, 104–5.

133 Interview with K., Munich, 18 May 2018.

134 Eyewitness recollection of S., Freiburg, 17 August 2017.

135 Email from Lars R., 4 May 2018.

136 Hecht, "Gay ORF?!" 18, cited in Schwartz, *Homosexuelle, Seilschaften, Verrat*, 296.

137 Schulz, "Der Multikulti-Prinz."

138 Ibid. Meanwhile, the phrase "Mars without a Venus" shows up in practically every biograph-

homosexuality, a trail of gossip that leads back to the rumor mills of seventeenth century Paris and has lasted centuries in the prince's case. In the early twentieth century he was taken up (today one might say "outed") by the incipient gay emancipation movement as one of the most famous cases in the history of homosexuality – by Magnus Hirschfeld in 1914 and before that by Albert Moll in 1910.[139] In 1910, even the most scoffed at, marginalized, persecuted and often ridiculed of gay soldiers could take heart from Prince Eugene's example. Just as little as all the talk swirling about Eugene had been able to diminish the awe with which his talent for war, industry and aesthetic sensibilities was regarded during his own lifetime, his outing as a homosexual could not undermine his revived status as a twentieth-century hero. In this the prince shared a similar fate to Frederick II or, farther back in the past, Alexander the Great, King Nicomedes, Caesar, and the Roman emperors Titus and Trajan.[140] The examples of Prince Eugene and Frederick the Great chosen by Hirschfeld and other early campaigners for homosexual self-esteem would also have been due in no small part to their uninterrupted popularity. The homosexual Reichswehr lieutenant in Max René Hesse's novel similarly cites the established canon of Alexander, Caesar and Frederick of Prussia in looking to shore up his own love for men.

> Alexander was believed to be the son of Jupiter Amon, but you don't hear anything about women around him, only [male] companions. Rarely, only very rarely does a man who fulfills the promise of his younger self [to become a fighter] belong to someone as King Nicomedes did to Caesar [...] You don't see a single woman around Frederick the Great from the day he takes command.[141]

---

ical sketch of Prince Eugene, often accompanied by new and imaginative ways of paraphrasing something that is never directly expressed, but still plain to see. "There was no Eugenia for this Eugenio. A Mars without a Venus." Roos, "Der bittre Ritter."

139 Hirschfeld, *Die Homosexualität des Mannes und des Weibes*, 661–62; Moll, *Berühmte Homosexuelle*, 36. Hirschfeld in turn quotes Vehse, *Geschichte des östreichischen Hofs* (published 1852). On page 259, Vehse writes that Prince Eugene was known as a "passive pederast" in Paris at the time, and alternatively dubbed "Madame Simone" (the name of a prostitute who was known citywide) and "Madame Consienc." Hirschfeld took up Vehse's account of the age-old Parisian rumors, making them truly public for the first time. This led Konrad Kramar and George Mayhofer to ask in a 2013 book "whether he's been outed." The authors quoted Liselotte von der Pfalz by way of an answer. "He [Eugene] doesn'nt trouble himself with women, a couple of lovely pages are more his thing." Ultimately, however, gay relationships were widespread among the young French nobility. For a full account see Kramar and Mayrhofer, *Prinz Eugen*, both quotes on p. 87.

140 All names can be found in Hirschfeld's 1914 work, *Die Homosexualität des Mannes und des Weibes*, 650–73.

141 Hesse, *Partenau*, 93–94. Amon, or Amun, was an ancient Egyptian god of war. He corresponded to the Greek father of the gods Zeus, and the Roman war of God Jupiter. Nicomedes IV of Bithynia

The first lieutenant's words convey an elite sensibility that was not entirely unfamiliar among officers, gay officers included. Or was it precisely among gays that such thinking was widespread? Throughout history, homosexuals' sense of being different, the marginalization and dismissal they have felt from mainstream society has in some cases (though by no means every case!) led to an internal sense of superiority, or a higher calling. This form of elitism has found expression among homosexual painters, sculptors, authors and other artists, politicians and not least – perhaps especially – soldiers. The shared thought behind the conviction was that dispensing with the distractions of marriage and a swarm of children enabled one to commit fully to one's artistic talents, affairs of state or the art of warfare.[142] Nor is it uncommon to find examples of homosexual officers and sergeants from the more recent past who were convinced that a total lack of family distraction enabled them to look after their troops in their care or, if they harbored greater ambitions, to immerse themselves in studying the high arts of strategy. Ultimately the former Bundeswehr soldier who cited Prince Eugene's military accomplishments was not doing so merely as a way of criticizing current restrictions. Subliminally, a steady note of self-assurance came through in recourse to "gay heroes" of the past; one is not, or was not a worse soldier for loving men and may even – like Eugene himself – have been a better soldier on that very account.

In 1908 Karl Franz von Leexow, mentioned in chapter 1 above, responded negatively to his rhetorical question of whether "homosexuality [harmed] a race's military efficiency." Among other sources, he supported his claim with numerous quotations from a work that had come out the year before, *Die dorische Knabenliebe (Dorian pederasty)* by Erich Bethe. The ancient Athenian Pausanias had once proclaimed that "the strongest army will be the one made up entirely of lovers," while Plutarch contended that "lovers are unparalleled fighters, and never once has the enemy broken through a couple or come back out from between them in one piece," as history showed: "Man beside man, the lovers of the Sacred Band of Thebes covered the battlefield of Chaeronea."[143]

Surprising similarities appear in the relationship between knights and squires during what is often superficially referred to as the "dark ages" of medieval Europe. Reports of love affairs between knight and squire came especially from particularly strict orders of religious knights. Squires were allowed to bear arms and fight

---

(reigned ca. 94 to 74 BCE) and Caesar were rumored at the time to have a homosexual relationship, though it is not confirmed.

142 Ibid., 188–189.

143 Eric Bethe, *Die dorische Knabenliebe: Ihre Ethik und ihre Idee* (published 1907), cited in Leexow, *Armee und Homosexualität*, 30.

starting around age fourteen, but the most important charge was caring for their knight. Engaging on an endangered knight's behalf was tied in one part to a sense of camaraderie, as it later came to be called, but was also generally an expression of the love between the two, including physical love. It is love itself that is regularly described as the deciding factor in European knights' victories on the field, a clear parallel to antiquity. The sources hardly permit much more than speculation about went on beneath the armor. Squireship lasted up through age eighteen, at which point the squire could himself become a knight. If he did not have the means to finance his own knighthood, he would either stay on with the knight or look for another to serve.[144]

Leexow goes on to list Alexander, Caesar and Emperor Trajan as heroes of antiquity rumored to be homosexual. "He, the victor over Dacia, the Euphrates, Arabia, did not let a tendency toward his own sex prevent him from developing the most outstanding abilities as a soldier."[145] While the book does not lack for what might go by namedropping or "outing" today, the author does qualify the rumors, writing that "we don't know whether Frederick the Great really had homoerotic sentiments."[146]

The same line of argumentation appears in a letter "personally" addressed to Defense Minister Wörner in February 1984, in which a Hamburg doctor writes that "it isn't uncommon for homosexual officers to make for particularly adept and conscientious troop leaders."[147] The immediate point of departure for the note was the scandal surrounding the (heterosexual) General Kießling's provisional suspension from duty. Speaking about the Kießling affair before the Bundestag, Antje Vollmer of the Green Party referred to "great and renowned armies" whose chieftains and soldiers had "practiced what in this case [i.e. the Bundeswehr] is viewed as a security risk and a potential disruption to a male community of soldiers."[148] Parliamentary State Secretary Würzbach replied for the BMVg that both he and "many of us here [are] familiar with great figures in a variety of fields – literature, art, in administrative leadership and certainly in the military as well – with similar dis-

---

144 Email from Ret. Major General Hans Uwe Ullrich from 11 January 2021. Ullricht has conducted extensive research into chivalry in the Middle Ages.

145 Leexow, *Armee und Homosexualität*, 39–41, here 41.

146 Ibid. The anonymous author, whose sympathies lay with Prussia and the German National People's Party, was clearly loathe to cast a dent on the proud figure, and made do without the hero in his argumentation.

147 BArch, BW 1/378197: Letter from Dr. S., Hamburg, to the BMVg, Manfred Wörner, 25 February 1984.

148 German Bundestag, 10th legislative period, 47th Session, 19 Jan 1984, typed transcript, 3378.

positions. But in this case, I'm not talking about those chieftains you mentioned but the normal, everyday routine in our barracks."[149]

In 1997, Alexander the Great found renewed relevance for the Bundeswehr and its gay soldiers. Under the title "Alexander the Great wouldn't even make field sergeant today," an article in *Neue Deutschland* denounced "Rühe's Army" as "one of the most anti-gay institutions in Germany."[150] Five years before journalists had looked to the "many examples of homosexuals fit to serve throughout human history" in criticizing a 1992 ruling against homosexual soldiers at the Federal Administrative Court, "from Julius Caesar to the Spartans, the legendary Amazons to 'Old Fritz,' the Prussian king Frederick II rumored to be homosexual."[151]

Leexow's observation of and conversations with homosexuals in the Prussian Army who were carrying on more or less secret love affairs similarly led him to conclude in the early twentieth century (1908) that homosexuals made more ideal soldiers than did heterosexuals.

> Homosexuality seems to me to increase among the higher posts, despite the persecution to which the invert is subjected. This gives pause for thought. It likely comes from the fact that even today, intimate friendship makes one particularly well-suited to being a soldier [...] While those with a normal sexuality see from the very beginning a straight line before them, the homosexual is by his very condition given to brood, and much thinking deepens the spirit. No traps threaten the normal soldier, only the invert must keep a watch out to steer his ship through life's perilous junctures. Even under other conditions, this lets one see clearly. And the homosexual officer is an artist. There is something that drives him to embellish the drab monotony of service, to elevate it and give it a human warmth, and I am certain that more is achieved through such work than through drills and dully cramming in the required exercises. While the normal soldier performs his service for service's sake, the homoerotic soldier performs it out of love. It is often touching to see the care with which the superior enfolds his subordinates, how he encourages the apprehensive, instructs the clumsy, restrains the careless, supports the weak. A short while back one officer went mad with grief after his orderly drowned while bathing the officer's horse. But such love – please don't take the word in its sensual sense – also breeds affection within the ranks, an emotional bond encircles their hearts and binds them more tightly than mere camaraderie or oaths sworn. When the author once asked a homosocial non-commissioned officer whether sexual things that inverted

---

149 Ibid.

150 At the time, Volker Rühe was federal minister of defense. Heilig, "Alexander der Große wäre heute nicht mal Feldwebel."

151 Schwartz, *Homosexuelle, Seilschaften, Verrat*, 283. Schwartz gives the example of an article by Andrea Theyssen, "Heißer Tip," which appeared in *Abendzeitung* on 1 July 1992. For more on press criticism regarding the ruling at the Federal Administrative Court's 2nd Military Service Senate on 30 July 1991, see chapter 3, section 9.c.

officers may have committed while drunk weren't easily divulged by the enlisted men, he responded with words heavy in meaning: "But we wouldn't betray the best."[152]

Shifting attention from the Prussian Army to the Bundeswehr turns up similar, nearly identical accounts. Former officers were almost unanimous in recalling the broad acceptance they found among the troops as company head or platoon leader, or at least felt they did. Such was the case with a senior NCO who once "allowed himself a slip-up" while overseeing a sergeant training course. After a night of heavy drinking at a class party he had clearly "come on" to one of his soldiers, probably trying to kiss him as well. When the incident came up for discussion over the following days, the eyewitness had been left wanting to quit the service "out of shame." "You always have to be able to look yourself in the mirror." Yet his course participants, fellow instructors and commanding officer all reacted quite differently than feared. Nobody brought the events at the party out against him; to the contrary, everyone encouraged him not to leave the service. The interviewee drew the personal conclusion from this formative experience that it always depends on the individual, his standing and accomplishments in the service, but most of all on his character. In that case, even a misstep would be overlooked out of a sense of camaraderie.[153]

Subordinate soldiers' acceptance of homosexuality does not just emerge subjectively in the memories of commanding (homosexual) officers, but shows up in written testimonies as well. A brief 1981 report in *Stern* about Captain Lindner's intention to retire due to illness (a case discussed at length elsewhere) elicited a number of letters to the editors at the magazine, including two from soldiers Lindner had led.[154] One NCO in the reserve wrote with a big "tip of the cap" that he had served under Lindner and could only endorse him with "hymns of praise." "It's regrettable that a highly praised superior [is being] 'ousted' here."[155] As a "non-gay" but "an understanding person," he wished the captain all the best. An officer candidate in the reserve who had served in Lindner's platoon as a conscript during 1970–71 was equally full of praise: "You were tough as nails, but fair with a great deal of heart! In many matters you were our model! For all of us, down to the least gunner, you were the best!"[156]

When a lieutenant was relieved of leading a platoon in an air force security squadron due to his sexual orientation in 1998, the enlisted men under his

---

152 Leexow, *Armee und Homosexualität*, 109–11; also cited in Hirschfeld, *Von einst bis jetzt*, 150.
153 Interview with Master Sergeant R., Potsdam 5 January 2018.
154 Claussen, "Schwule werden abgesägt."
155 Letter from Wolfgang S., Eutin, to *Stern*, 25 June 1981.
156 Letter from Wolfgang J., Itzehoe, undated. Stamp of receipt at *Stern* 1 July 1981.

command spoke out, with twenty-one men in the platoon signing a letter to their commander. The lieutenant, the letter read, had "always led his platoon as one might expect a platoon leader to do."[157]

Soldiers often only found out many years later, and then by chance, that former comrades from the 1980s or 1990s were homosexual, comrades "of whom they never would have thought it."[158] In many cases it had been the most athletic or "toughest" soldiers in the company. Looking back, eyewitnesses wondered "what life together and camaraderie would have looked like back then if soldiers could have been more free and open with their sexuality."[159]

Soldiers' testimony and their memories of time spent in the Bundeswehr recall similar arguments from the time of the German Empire. Leexow quotes an acquaintance who had served in the foreign legion, whose transhistorical argument culminates in the following plea:

> The homosexual is an especially good soldier, the born careerist. He is especially courageous and given to sacrifice, full of thinking discipline. In no way does that contradict the feminine impression that many give. A troop which has many homosexuals has a much greater communal feeling of camaraderie [...] An officer whose heterosexuality is so strongly pronounced that intimate proximity to another man is revolting is not suited for training young soldiers.[160]

Leexow rhetorically asks whether "it mustn't now lie within the endeavors of a great modern power to harness forces that lie fallow, such as those of homosexuality, and to ennoble them?"[161] Writing in 1922 Hirschfeld reached for the heights of pathos, quoting from "Ich hatt' einen Kameraden" (a popular mourning melody which he termed "a song for old friends"): "But to many it meant more, and to some it meant all."[162]

---

157 BArch, BW 1/502107, sheets 65–118: Constitutional complaint of First Lieutenant Stecher from 23 December 1998, here sheet 107, annex 8: Letter from the enlisted men of Platoon II / Air Force Base Battalion 3, 1 April 1998.

158 Interview with Master Sergeant H., Berlin, 2 July 2018.

159 Ibid.

160 Leexow, Armee und Homosexualität, 97.

161 Ibid., 66.

162 Hirschfeld, Von einst bis jetzt, 151.

4. Five Military Lives in Personal Recollections

The current chapter concludes by sketching the working lives of five soldiers in their entirety: That of a private released from his fixed-term contract after less than two years in the service; a captain who took early retirement due to health reasons; another captain who was demoted from career to fixed-term service at his own request; and a first sergeant and lieutenant colonel, both of whom completed out their service under normal conditions.

a.) "It was as if my world collapsed." A Private is Forced Out

As a young Hamburg man living in the Rhineland, Dierk Koch, volunteered for the navy in 1962, gladly anticipating his entry into the service in April 1963 for the new set of responsibilities and professional perspective it would bring. "My hopes and dreams of becoming a proper sailor in the navy were within reach."[163] Yet just a year and a half into service, in November 1964, his future career came to an abrupt, unwelcome end. The beginning of the end lay months previously, with the sexual advances of a petty officer second class. The officer had offered to support Koch after the latter failed a training course; when Koch, a seaman apprentice had encountered tentative physical contact on his first visit to the officer's room, he initially resisted.

> But then [...] maybe because it had been in me for a long time, I gave into the pressure and took comfort in his physicality. It went on like that for several days, and I enjoyed it. After a petty fight I accused him of having used the promise of help only as a lure, and having no real interest in my professional future [...] From then on, I refused, while he sent me very clear signs that he was my superior in rank. The rift deepened. I confided in my company leader and asked for a transfer. At the time I had no idea that he would report my revelation to the naval personnel command.[164]

Koch's transfer request was granted. After successfully completing his course at the end of September 1964 he applied to serve on one of the "large traveling units," and received call-up papers to serve on the frigate *Emden*. There were rumors circulat-

---

163 Dierk Koch, from an unpublished manuscript of his life experiences with the working title "My unforgotten friends" ("Meine unvergessenen Freunde").
164 Ibid. Also from an interview the author conducted with Dierk Koch in Hamburg on 22 February 2018. *Bild* magazine also took up the topic in late August 2019, publishing an extensive interview with Koch: Scheck and Utess, "Was wir damals gemacht haben, war kein Verbrechen."

ing within naval circles that the *Emden* would accompany the training vessel *Gorch Fock* that October on its visit to the 1964 Olympic Games in far-off Tokyo, Japan.[165] Yet the *Emden* set sail without Koch; the apprentice's earlier report had caught up with him.

> It must have been early October when I was ordered to the garrison commander. There I was told short and sweet that the naval personnel command had decided to rescind my orders to report to the *Emden*. 'We can't send a soldier tied up in a matter like that out into the world.' I was very disappointed, my dream had burst like a soap bubble. I was supposed to continue my service in the typing pool of a training company. Several weeks later, on a Wednesday, I was ordered to report again. Without any warning it was revealed to me that I had been demoted to plain sailor and discharged dishonorably from the navy. I was to quit my post effective immediately and leave the barracks as a civilian by that coming Friday at noon [...] It was as if my world collapsed, inside of me things must have looked black and empty [...] My mind was a muddle of confusion and conflict. Where should I go? Come Friday at twelve noon I would be without home or any means of surviving![166]

The leader of the naval personnel command had reached the decision to discharge the seaman apprentice on 12 November 1964; it took effect three days later on 15 November.[167] The dismissal could not proceed quickly enough for the service; it did not even wait until the end of the month but settled the matter overnight so to speak, without notice. The entries in Koch's military service book attest to his summary dismissal with official seal and signature.

> Only one week after my last home leave, which usually came every four weeks, I was back at my parent's door [...] near Düsseldorf. My family greeted me in astonishment, 'Why are you back already, and without telling us?' I replied reluctantly that I had left the navy and wouldn't be returning. I asked my father, who had served as a naval officer during the war, for a private conversation. 'If it's that important, we'll go to the garden.' There, among the blooming dahlias and roses, I revealed that I 'had gotten involved in a homosexual encounter and been demoted and discharged dishonorably from the navy.' I was met with a deep and at the same time gentle look, and a friendly pat on the back of the head. 'Then we'll have to see about finding a job for you. And by the way – we shouldn't tell mom about any of this.' I loved my father at that moment! I couldn't have guessed what his reaction would be. It was one of great human decency and warmth.[168]

---

165 Email from Dierk Koch to the author on 6 September 2019, and a phone interview on 7 September 2019.

166 Ibid. Also available in excerpt form in Scheck and Utess, "Was wir damals gemacht haben, war kein Verbrechen."

167 BMVg, R II 1, 1 August 2018, Decision on the dismissed private's application for restitution, as well as entries in Koch's military service book.

168 Koch, "Meine unvergessenen Freunde."

The apprentice immediately petitioned against his release, which was later rejected on 8 October 1965, after nearly eleven months.[169] Be that as it may, research has shown that Dierk Koch did not miss out on his hoped-for trip to Tokyo after all, because such a trip never took place; no record of it exists either in academic literature or naval archives.[170]

The seaman apprentice's dismissal and accompanying loss in rank did not mean the matter had ended for the navy, however. Rather, it passed the case on to the public prosecutor, so that in 1965 the young man found himself back in Cuxhaven local court.[171]

b.) "Remain a Soldier or Become a Human." A Captain Remembers

I turned 17 in June 1961. With that, everything became clear. On July 3 I volunteered for the service [...] It was a Monday and we were welcomed with lentil stew [...] The question of sexuality didn't come up, not in the least. I didn't have any interest in women though it didn't bother me, and as for homosexuals, you really only heard about them when they were convicted, and everything was probably justified on that account [...] The NCO corps was always having some kind of party or another [...] Even those who weren't married brought women along, of course. Somehow it was always a problem for me. On the one hand I didn't have the slightest interest in women, and on the other there was so much snickering it got on my nerves. I would make an excuse not to go to the parties if I could manage it in one way or the other [...] Apologies had to be more explicit when I became an officer. In summer 1967 we had to take our annual leave during a fixed period as officer candidates. I wasn't ready and asked a comrade of mine – slender, blond, blue-eyed – if he knew where he wanted to go. We quickly decided on Spain, with an auto and tent. On one of the very first nights Jürgen asked [...] if I was homosexual. Crystal clear, straight out. That caught me unprepared [...] I denied it with total indignation. How could he even come up with something like that? We'd both masturbate in the tent though, half in secret, it was never talked about. Neither of us wanted to be openly gay. At the end of the trip he said 'If you rat me out it's all over.' His concern was understandable but unfounded, all I wanted myself was to get out of the situation. Later, 1970, after the first criminal code reforms, I visited him in Frankfurt; he had long since been released from the Bundeswehr and was studying. It was like before, but without any fear [...] *so this is sexuality*, the thought flashed across my mind [...] I was twenty-six the first time I shacked up with a guy. It was indescribably beautiful [...] 1971 was probably the most important year of my life thus far [...] That was also the year I met Torsten [...] Torsten was an officer candidate

---

169 BMVg, R II 1, 1 August 2018, Decision on the dismissed private's application for restitution.

170 Alongside the *Karlsruhe*, the *Emden* set sail for the Mediterranean on 12 September 1974, stopped over in La Valetta Malta between September 19 and 24, then returned to its home port on 30 September 1964. No further trips abroad are documented for the year 1964, and thus no trips to Japan. See Hildebrand, Röhr and Steinmetz, *Die deutschen Kriegsschiffe*, 61.

171 For a full account see chapter 3, section 11.

from another battalion housed in the same barracks where I had an apartment as a lieutenant colonel [...] Meeting him shook me to my core. He wasn't afraid of gays at all, unheard of at the time for a twenty-year-old [...] He met his current wife in 1973. She, not he, made the decision. In 1976 she married him. Throughout all those years we had been able to maintain a precarious state of equilibrium. We had somehow come to terms – until this woman showed up [...] It was Torsten who finally left me certain that I could no longer run away from my being gay. Remain a soldier or become a human – that was the immediate question.[172]

In 1973, a platoon leader set to take over a company the following year, the fate of then lieutenant colonel Michael Lindner rested on the edge of this stark question. Lindner decided to remain a soldier despite his homosexuality, becoming a captain and company leader in Albersdorf's ABC Defense Battalion 610.

When I went to discuss my situation with my commander, he told me to my face that as far as he was concerned, homosexuals were perverse. He was my direct superior. You don't get to choose your commander [...] Finally, in 1977 a new commander arrived who knew and appreciated me. My assignment as leader was extended [...] Yet my mood grew worse and worse, without clear reasons for it at the time [...] The prospect of an entire lifetime of hiding, of giving up on freedom itself, exposing myself to abuse and blackmail made me ill [...] Soon I could hardly sleep, I was overtaken by nightmares.[173]

In January 1980 he was admitted at his own request to the neurology and psychiatry department at the Bundeswehr hospital in Hamburg, where he met the unit head, Dr. Brickenstein.

They sent all the gays to him in the hopes of being free of them. But he would often send them back, saying he didn't see any problem. He explained to me that the Bundeswehr was the most progressive in the entirety of NATO. He had seen to that himself. The thing about not being promoted was an issue of course. But that wasn't something he was responsible for [...] On 4 February 1980 I was dismissed from the Bundeswehr hospital as fully fit for service and went back to my company [...] joined the [current] exercises and was right back in it [...] Psychically too it was going better for me now, just like that, the pressure had completely gone. So, you could lead a company as a homosexual.[174]

A few weeks later Captain Lindner read about a ruling at the Federal Administrative Court that found that homosexual tendencies made a soldier unfit to serve

---

172 Lindner, "Nicht mehr mein Weg," 89–94. A more complete account exists in another unpublished manuscript of Lindner's from 1985, "Das halbe Leben halb gelebt" ("A half life half-lived," the author has a copy in his possession).
173 Lindner, "Nicht mehr mein Weg," 95.
174 Lindner, "Nicht mehr mein Weg," 98–99.

as a commanding officer.[175] As a company chief at the time, Lindner recalled that learning of the decision had been devastating: "I didn't know whether I was even allowed to be company head as a homosexual."[176] The judgment came as a "shock" to him, rattling his already fragile self-confidence as a homosexual officer, and his trust in the military to an even greater extent. As it was, the regular end of his time as company head was scheduled for April 1980.

> Three days before [...] the commander had me called in. I had to remain until further notice. I found out the reason why from another source – at a going-away party my intended successor [...] had gotten involved a homosexual "situation" of his own and it had gotten out, and was now no longer fit to serve as company head.[177]

(What comes across as a tall-tale was in fact possible to research and verify with court decisions from Military Service Court South in Ulm.[178] The captain who had been designated to succeed Lindner was discharged from the service.) Months later, in July 1980, Captain Lindner took up an assignment on a Hamburg brigade staff. Lindner was subsequently declared unfit for service in September 1980 with the return of his psychological difficulties, and received an illness certificate. Two years later at age thirty-eight, the captain was given retirement on 30 September 1982 due to illness under §44 (3) and (4) of the SG, for "depressive neurosis, homosexuality and psychopathy," as *Der Spiegel* reported.[179] "The continual game of hide-and-seek and the fear of rubbing someone up the wrong way made the officer a case for the psychiatrists. Three reports with conflicting results sealed an early end to a story-book career," the article continued.[180] Lindner himself recalled that:

> The formal act of retiring, having my dismissal certificate handed to me, took place in an ice-cold atmosphere. A single word would have been too much. The whole thing barely lasted a minute, and I was back outside. No cognac, no coffee, no word of thanks, no farewell. Even if they hadn't brought any fault upon themselves, the rules of camaraderie didn't apply for homosexuals.[181]

---

175 Federal Administrative Court, 1st Military Service Senate, ruling from 25 October 1979, Az.: BVerwG, 1 WB 113/78. For a complete account see chapter 4, section 2.
176 Interview with Michael Lindner, Hamburg, February 2017. The quote itself comes from "'Berufliches': Michael Lindner," 176.
177 Lindner, "Nicht mehr mein Weg," 99.
178 Ruling by Military Service Court South, 1st Division on 7 October 1980, Az S 1-VL 10/80. For a full account see chapter 3, section 9.
179 BArch, BW 1/503302: BMVg, PSZ III 6, 29 June 2001; ibid., BMVg, PSZ I 8, 20 June 2002; also mentioned in "Soldaten als potentielle Sexualpartner," 22.
180 "Soldaten als potentielle Sexualpartner," 22.
181 Lindner, "Nicht mehr mein Weg," 101.

Even before he left active service but especially after, Captain Lindner directed all his focus and energy on changing the way homosexual soldiers were treated. It is no exaggeration to say that for a time it became his chief mission, his purpose in life.[182]

c.)   Trailed by Rumors: Thirteen Years as an Officer

The memories of one officer given early dismissal in 1992 illustrate both the havoc that contemporary regulations wreaked on military members' career hopes as well as the broad discretionary powers given to personnel management. The officer joined light infantry as an officer candidate in 1979, entered career service in 1987 and achieved the rank of captain and company head before requesting demotion to fixed-term soldier in 1992, with the end of his military career following shortly thereafter. He described leaving the Bundeswehr after thirteen years as a "traumatic experience" for him.[183]

Flashback to 1980, when the cadet entered the former Bundeswehr academy in Hamburg at age twenty, still in the process of searching for his own sexuality. "From the perspective of a young man in search of his sexuality," the Bundeswehr's well-known restrictions on homosexuality were "highly problematic." At the time it became clear to him that he would not be able to live out his homosexuality openly "without great risk to his career prospects."

After his studies the officer was initially assigned to lead a platoon, where there was talk of his possible homosexuality. Yet after a minor incident that on its own is hardly worth the mention, his position in the platoon and the company rapidly deteriorated, leading to disciplinary measures for the young lieutenant and his removal as platoon leader. The officer's sterling service record led the battalion commander to refrain from passing the matter on to the discharge authorities, potentially exposing him to censure by a military service court. The lieutenant "got off with a slap on the wrist," as he conceded; he was transferred, and the incident forgotten. The officer was subsequently promoted to lieutenant colonel, and years later assigned to lead a company.

His time as company commander also came accompanied by rumors about his homosexuality, all without a single specific incriminating incident (or so the retired

---

182 See chapter 4 for a full version.
183 Interview with W. in Hamburg, 4 April 2019. The following sketch of his service is based exclusively on the interview, and ultimately couldn't be verified. Only the parts deemed plausible by the author have been reproduced here.

captain maintained; his account could not be verified). Ultimately, the rumors led once again to the escalation of an incident that on its own was harmless. The precipitating event was a blood drive in the barracks. The battalion commander purposefully arranged to go to the donation point with the officer (and others) to observe whether the company chief's blood donation went off without a hitch. In response to the troop physician's routine question about any trips abroad, the company head mentioned a recent vacation to Kenya, with the result that he did not have any blood taken. The commander, however, interpreted the incident as confirming the rumors about the company chief's homosexuality. The soldiers in his company for their part came up with their own reasons as to why the blood donation had rejected him, bringing his suspected homosexuality back into the conversation. (Sexually active homosexuals are considered a high-risk group to this day and are not supposed to give blood due to the anticipated risk of HIV, a regulation or recommendation that has long been criticized by homosexual associations and their supporters.) The commander took action, petitioning personnel leadership to dismiss the captain from his post. The captain was initially transferred to the brigade staff; his career prospects "looked bleak." When he asked his personnel manager and the manager's superior to give him a "fair chance," the section head replied that the captain should note that he was not being unfair. And after receiving excellent marks on subsequent assignments and superior grades in basic training at the Bundeswehr Command and Staff College, the personnel office did in fact assign him to lead another company. This second assignment brought the captain to the paratroopers, a period he considered his best years spent in the military in retrospect. The winning streak came to end however when he was not approved for general staff officers' training; his personnel manager had not so much as presented him at the selection committee. In 1992, primarily out of disappointment at no longer being able to achieve his career goals, he requested demotion to fixed-term service, and with it an end to his time in the service. He was dismissed from the Bundeswehr at the end of September 1992 as desired, along with the mass of conscripts in his company.

d.) "Your Reputation May Precede You." A Staff Sergeant Looks Back

In 1996, with twelve years in the service now at an end, a staff sergeant drafted a thirteen-page single-spaced report on his experience in the military and sent it to the parliamentary commissioner for the armed forces.[184] The sergeant recorded all

---

184 BArch, BW 2/38355: Reserve Staff Sergeant K. to the parliamentary commissioner for the armed forces, 15 August 1996.

sorts of experiences and occurrences, in one part pertaining to his sexual orientation. At no point in time had it been "an issue" for him "'to take hold of' another soldier." He had been drafted in 1984, a time when the majority of young gay men preferred civilian service "for any number of understandable reasons." He himself had wanted to "fulfill his duty to society of serving the fatherland" and not "just loaf about as a draft-dodger."

Neither at his medical inspection nor his fitness or assignment exams had he been asked about his sexual orientation (or "sexual self-determination," as he phrased it consistently throughout the report).[185] Nor for that matter had anyone asked during basic training or in his first unit, a mechanized infantry company, initially leading to his reassignment as a normal enlisted soldier occurring without issue. Every once in a while "two soldiers might share a bed for the night" in his company, but it had not ever been a "big topic for conversation" or "any cause for issue." Instead, a "so-what mentality" had prevailed. A "good-looking" roommate had once asked the sergeant outright if he was "interesting" to the sergeant, who in turn acted "as though I hadn't understood." This came both "out of conviction" and his upcoming reassignment and training as a driving instructor.

The following years as a sergeant and driving instructor also passed by without incident, with soldiers never demanding to know anything about his private life – until 1992. One March evening at the NCO club, another driving instructor asked the sergeant "somewhat in passing" if it was true that he was gay. The sergeant did not deny it, instead replying "'What of it?' What followed was aggravating, to put it mildly [...] At any rate I noticed right away that something was up [...] there was 'something afoot'." The sergeant was questioned by his superior, who he had to assure "more than once" "that he'd never had anything to do with even a single student driver." His boss had also demanded he "keep his hands off anyone where there might be a connection to the (Bundeswehr) uniform."

From this point on the sergeant was only assigned office duty, no longer used as a driving instructor. His disappointment was great enough that he considered an early end to his service. Driving instructors were in demand but his superior wanted to hear "nothing at all" about thoughts of the sergeant transferring to another driving group; "your reputation might precede you." With good cause, he found himself asking whether "it no longer mattered from one day to the next that for years I'd been able to show the best training and exam results in that driver training group?" Another staff sergeant and driving instructor each admitted their homosexuality to him, but only in confidence. They had no intention of publicly

---

185 An exclamation point lies next to this passage on the photocopy of the report sent to the BMVg, which was taken into the ministry's files.

admitting it, with his own experiences "clearly [serving as] enough deterrent." On the second to last day of a course in 1993, one student driver had come to the sergeant and told him they "were on the same wavelength." He did not react – "What else could I have done in my situation at the time? [...] The topic being taboo made open conversation impossible." The student came back on the following, final day of the course: "You understood correctly yesterday, staff sergeant sir!" Again, the sergeant did not react. "If the 'pressure' (which the Bundeswehr itself created) hadn't been there, we might have had a conversation at least [...] without any second guesses!" As it was, the "situation" forced him "to leave the driving school area immediately after work [that day]." Reading the sergeant's report, one cannot help but think of the words of another eyewitness cited in this study: Fear eats the soul.

In 1993, the sergeant was transferred after all and became a subunit leader of four conscripts. He recalled wondering, "did my disciplinary superior really have that much trust in me?" After three days he called the four soldiers together, speaking "in plain language. 'You know what they say about me. But I'm not looking to satisfy any personal needs with you,' was the message in brief." At no point in time did he encounter problems managing to enforce even difficult commands. With the "highly beneficial, especially psychological support" of his disciplinary superior, he finally succeeded "in dealing much more openly with [himself], which had been both impossible and unthinkable in driving school, unfortunately [...] When I reported to my superior that I was leaving in January 1994, he expressed his deep regret that [my] planned reassignment hadn't come about."

e.) "Then All Hell Broke Loose." A Company Commander Is Discharged

He assumed command of his first company at the age of twenty-seven and by 1981, at the age of thirty-one, the first lieutenant was serving his third turn as company head. He was recognized among colleagues and the soldiers in his company alike for his accomplishments and leadership qualities, while exceptional assessments gave cause to hope for a bright future ahead. Then suddenly, none of it mattered anymore – the captain was gay. "All hell broke loose" when it came out, as he recalled.[186] It was not that he had disclosed his sexual orientation, much less made any public demonstration of it, but rather a cruel chain of coincidence that brought his private life to the attention of the military. In 1981 the officer's long-term partner was drafted into the service, and after basic training sent to serve

---

186 Interview with Ret. Lieutenant Colonel N., 20 July 2018.

as an orderly in the officers' club of a barracks. Within the chain of command, the orderly just so happened to be assigned to the very company the captain led, making him the direct disciplinary superior to his life partner. The captain did not see any way of preventing his partner's assignment to his company without raising questions, so he opted for a strategy of "Grin and bear it!" Everything would turn out alright. On the horizon however, storm clouds were already gathering.

The relationship between the men had drawn notice and gone on file before the younger of the two was called up. Before Christmas 1980 the two had taken a road trip to West Berlin, taking the prescribed transit highway through GDR territory. When they reached the checkpoint at the Drewitz border crossing, the uniformed border patrol units of the Stasi took the opportunity, common at the time, to engage the captain, who would have been recognized as a military officer at the latest upon his exiting the GDR. "Good day, captain sir!" The border guard's attention came to rest on a gay travel guide for West Berlin that lay open in the car. "What's that then?" the guard asked. Now seeing himself at risk of being approached by the GDR intelligence service he had reported the incident to MAD; the officer did not see any threats to his professional career with his partner not yet in the service. His sole concern lay with preventing possible compromise by an enemy intelligence service, and by reporting the incident to MAD he was certain of having done his duty. Nor did any negative consequences come about at first; neither MAD nor personnel leadership contacted him. "I was naive, I thought my relationship with Ralf wouldn't be an issue in the service. I had been with him long before he became a soldier, after all." Shortly after the events at the Inner German border, however, the issue become a problem, starting behind closed doors at MAD. As the captain later found out, upon evaluating his report MAD had passed on news of the relationship directly to divisional headquarters, upon which the battalion commander and brigade commander had intervened on the captain's behalf.[187]

The battalion commander remembered the captain as an especially effective leader who "could really get things done." He had asked division to wait on measures until he returned from vacation (he was set to leave the following day for two weeks). Upon his return, his deputy informed him that the company chief had already been removed from his post – and the service. The battalion commander was "seriously worked-up" that such a course of action had been decided over his head as the company chief's superior. Practically nobody in the company knew why their chief had been removed. The soldiers evidently believed the explanation they received during roll-call, that their former head was urgently needed at division staff to prepare for an exercise. The soldiers did, by contrast, learn the

---

187 Ibid.

reason for the removal of the captain's successor just a few weeks later. During an overnight stay on training grounds, the new company head had made physical advances on his driver against the latter's will in the commander's vehicle. The battalion commander decided to remove the new head at once and forward the case to the disciplinary prosecutor. The division immediately took the case up. Through inquiries at the personnel office, the battalion commander learned that the captain had "already been known in this regard." This led him in turn to file an official complaint about the brigade, as to "how [personnel leadership] could make such a man chief," all the more so in a company that had recently had a similar, albeit "incomparably less dramatic case." He never received an answer.[188]

The brigade commander for his part had told the divisional commander "but nothing actually happened,"[189] upon which he received a phone call from the commanding general of the corps asking "whether he was one too," seeing as how he was defending the captain. If these subsequent memories are accurate (they could not be verified), it would be a further indication that soldiers and officers in the troops could at times show greater tolerance than higher-ranking generals, BMVg jurists or higher command posts.

The battalion and brigade commanders' interventions changed nothing; in August 1981 the division decided to immediately remove the captain from his post as company chief and transfer him to a division staff. This was merely on paper, however, as at the same time the captain was provisionally released from service, forbidden to wear his uniform or enter the barracks, and had half of his salary withheld. The company chief had to be relieved of command quickly but methodically; it was essential to maintain the impression of a "proper" transition for company soldiers to prevent any additional disquiet from surfacing. Once they had lined up as they did every morning, the soldiers and NCOs of the company were thus surprised one day to learn from the deputy battalion commander that their former company head had been transferred to division staff for pressing responsibilities effective immediately. It was only with difficulty that appearances could be kept up for the "parade of lies," in the words of the captain. "A mood reigned over the grounds like at a burial."[190]

The captain's petition to repeal the disciplinary measures – his termination as company chief, provisional removal from service, prohibition on wearing a uniform, and retention of half of his salary—was denied by the division commander.

---

188 Phone interview with Ret. Colonel R., 21 September 2020.
189 Interview with Ret. Lieutenant Colonel N., 20 July 2018, and in what follows.
190 Ibid.

> By order dated 10 July 1981 disciplinary proceedings were instituted against you for standing suspected of having had a homosexual relationship with an infantryman under your command. You yourself confirmed this suspicion upon questioning on 7 July 1981, not only admitting to the existence of a same-sex relationship since 1977 with [...] but also to feeling homosexual tendencies starting eight or nine years ago.[191]

The officer's younger partner Ralf was likewise immediately transferred to serve in another barracks' NCO club. He reproached himself bitterly for what had happened, taking the blame for the difficulties his partner had run into. The only way out that Ralf saw lay in suicide. The attempt on his own life was discovered in time and he survived, after which he was given early release. (The men's relationship did not survive the turmoil, although the two remain close friends today.)

Aside from holding serious concerns about his partner, the captain was drawn into a legal battle against the Bundeswehr. "It was a stressful time," the officer recalled. He saw himself as being in the right and never once thought of giving up. He had been naive before; now he was fighting, though on his own behalf and "not out of some sort of principle, and definitely not as a champion for the homosexual movement."[192]

In his capacity as a disciplinary prosecutor, the division's legal advisor brought proceedings before the military service court with the stated aim of removing the captain from service. The captain explained his point of view in a letter to Military Service Court South in Ulm:

> I was furthermore of the view that it could not be of interest to the service how an officer behaved at home within his own four walls, and what form of sexual activity he undertook, all the more so as it represents an essential feature of the free development of personality guaranteed in the constitution. I was unaware of any culpable breach of duty – on the contrary, I was of the opinion that I had demonstrated an exceptional sense of duty by immediately informing military counterintelligence of the series of events that occurred while returning from a trip to Berlin on the stretch between Berlin-Hirschberg, even if doing so revealed my homosexual contact with X. I was so convinced of being in the right that I even testified to continuing to have sexual intercourse with [...] after he became a soldier. I made this statement deliberately in order to demarcate my legal options and know as well that the Bundeswehr tolerates my actions on the basis of our laws.[193]

By today's standards and regulations, the captain had not done anything wrong; his position that "it could not be of interest to the service how an officer behaved at home within his own four walls, and what form of sexual activity he undertook"

---

191 BArch, Pers 12/45130: Commander of the 10th Panzer Division, 19 August 1981.
192 Interview with Ret. Lieutenant Colonel N., 20 July 2018.
193 BArch, Pers 12/45130: Captain N. to Military Service Court South, 25 August 1981.

entirely matches the altered regulatory landscape after 2000. Unfortunately for the captain, he was about twenty years ahead of his time. In 1981 there was only one way the Bundeswehr knew how to react when it discovered the captain's relations with the soldier: temporary suspension and disciplinary proceedings seeking his removal. No heed was paid to the fact that the officer and soldier had known each other privately for years before the latter's conscription into the Bundeswehr, and according to investigation files, had a "relationship akin to marriage." The captain mentioned explicitly, and in his view consistently, that his intimate relationship to Ralf predated Ralf's entry into the service on 1 April 1981. As such, it "did not constitute a breach of duty under the jurisprudence with which I am familiar, as homosexual contact with non-members of the Bundeswehr does not violate service obligations."[194]

The division commander, and the investigating disciplinary prosecutor after him disregarded this prehistory, concentrating solely on the relationship between subordinate and immediate superior that had existed since May 1981. So convinced was the captain of the legality of his view that private was private, he initially declared himself unprepared to break off contact with his partner when first questioned by the disciplinary prosecutor. Taking heed of the sharp response his statement elicited and the regulatory situation, he subsequently stated his willingness to break off contact with Ralf through to the end of his military service, and that he had not been sexually active with his partner since the latter was called up. Through his attorney, the captain agreed to be assigned elsewhere on staff rather than as company commander going forward. As the lawyer phrased it, "although the claimant's heart lies with his soldiers as a former officer in the troops, he would for better or worse toe the line with a decision to that effect."[195]

It was no use; the gears of the Bundeswehr judiciary were already in motion. In September 1981 Military Service Court South in Ulm rejected the captain's petition to repeal his provisional removal from service and the ban on wearing a uniform. The ruling stated that the captain had, "during his first examination, admitted to the conduct he was charged with, then just a few days later stated that he would not break off his homosexual relationship to mechanized infantryman X." Under established case law, the military service senates viewed "homosexual conduct on the part of superiors with subordinates [as] such a serious breach of duty that the person concerned can no longer be left in service but had to be removed."[196]

---

194 Ibid.
195 BArch, Pers 12/45130: Lawyer's letter to Military Service Court South, 26 August 1981.
196 Ibid., Ruling at Military Service Court South, 1st Division 22 September 1981.

The court ruled on the merits of the case two months later. The military judges in Ulm did not follow the disciplinary prosecutor's request to remove the captain from service but decided instead on a reduction in rank to first lieutenant. The court considered it proven that the soldier had continued a homosexual relationship with his partner, here referred to as a witness, that began years before the latter entered the Bundeswehr as a conscript. The chamber considered this a deliberate breach of duty to respectful and trustworthy behavior outside of service (§17 (2) Line 2 SG), and therefore a breach of duty under §23 (1) SG, for which the soldier was under increased liability as a superior under §10 (1) SG.

> A company commander who maintains a homosexual relationship with an enlisted soldier commits a serious breach of duty. Nor have the shifts in attitude toward homosexuality among parts of the population or the liberalization in criminal law in this area done anything to change this. Same-sex activity between members of the armed forces is intolerable. A commanding officer who acts in this way makes himself dependent on his partner, undermines his own authority and erodes discipline to a high degree; his reputation suffers considerable harm and he offers a point of attack for enemy intelligence services. As a rule, this means the relationship of trust between the service and the soldier concerned is totally destroyed. Particularly incriminating the soldier in this case is the fact that he continued same-sex relations with Witness B. even after the witness had transferred into his company, making him the witnesses' direct superior.[197]

Yet weighty factors also spoke in favor of the captain. The relationship had not begun with him as a member of the Bundeswehr, which meant he could "only be accused of not immediately breaking off the relationship once his partner entered the Bundeswehr." In addition, the officer had never attempted "to pursue any kind of homosexual contact with other Bundeswehr service members."

> Beyond that the soldier was an irreproachable leader and received above-average assessments. Nor did his misconduct come out within the battalion, such that the court does not view it as essential for the soldier to be removed from service. He has however disqualified himself from his service rank of captain with the position of company chief, such that it seems appropriate to demote him to the rank of first lieutenant.[198]

Both parties appealed the decision, the defense aiming for acquittal, the military disciplinary lawyer still with the goal of removing the soldier from service. The captain's future now lay in the hands of the judges at the Federal Administrative

---

[197] Ruling at Military Service Court South, 1st Division, 17 November 1981, AZ: 1 VL 15/81.
[198] Ibid.

Court, whose second military service senate acquitted him on all charges of breach of duty in May 1982.

Formally, the judges grounded their acquittal on the fact that the men's statements not to have had sex with each other while the younger partner was in the service could not be refuted. Both had stood steadfastly behind the claim every time they were questioned and in court. Yet only sexual relationships between superiors and subordinates were of interest where disciplinary law was concerned, not an otherwise platonic form of friendship or love.

> The soldiers' appeal brought success. The senate was unable to rule out any final doubts as to whether the soldier was guilty of the breach of duty with which he was charged in the letter of accusation. The letter of accusation charged the soldier [...] with having maintained a homosexual relationship with mechanized infantryman X., who came under his direct command in May 1981. The accusation turned expressly on a homosexual love affair, not for example a homoerotic relationship in the sense of mental and psychological devotion or fulfillment, such that in order to reach a conviction it had to be shown for the soldier that sexual activity between him and X. had occurred within the period of time in question. Ultimately this went unproven [...] Under these circumstances and in accordance with the principle *in dubio pro reo*, the senate had to assume the most favorable set of facts for the soldier that could not be ruled out, namely that no (more) sexual activity occurred between him and infantryman X. in the alleged timeframe. This meant the soldier was not guilty of a breach of duty as laid out in the letter of accusation, so that the contested decision had to be revoked and the soldier acquitted. Consequently, the military disciplinary prosecutor's appeal seeking heightened measures was turned down.[199]

In their decision the judges also pointed to the fact that during the appeals process, the captain "had not left behind an impression of wanting to engage in a fight over homosexual issues beyond relations with [[...] his partner]. Nor do the soldier's assessments show any sign of a lack of realism on his part."[200]

Herein presumably lay one of the reasons for what was an astonishing ruling by comparison to many others. Beyond the obstinate denial of both men and the principal of "when in doubt, for the accused," the captain's clear disavowal of any sort of combative argumentation on behalf of homosexual rights may have proved decisive for the judges. By explicitly setting his own concrete case off against the plight of homosexual soldiers in general, he gave the judges an opportunity to decide in favor of the accused in this single instance without it setting legal precedent. A campaign over legal principals as conducted by so many other officers both

---

199 Ruling at Federal Administrative Court: BVerwG, 2nd Military Service Senate, 11 May 1982, Az 2 WD 4/82.
200 Ibid.

before and after him would in all probability have sent the captain packing. By adopting a shrewd defense strategy instead, the officer and his attorney succeeded.

The captain reentered service just one week after acquittal, no longer serving in his old company but on a brigade staff. While everyone knew there knew the story, he experienced a great deal of support from colleagues. His work in the brigade's G3 division consisted in preparing for military exercises and maneuvers, with a similar assignment following on division staff.[201] Throughout, the obstacle remained that he was still denied security clearance for documents classified as confidential or secret. The captain filed a petition against this measure as well, this time unsuccessfully, although it was not particularly harmful to his work on the staff.[202] The captain received the division's badge of honor upon retiring, though not directly from the divisional commander but his deputy – "you already know the reasons why."[203]

His next assignment was managing a lecture hall at a service branch school; the officer that Bundeswehr jurists and generals had wanted to throw out of the armed forces five years before was now charged with leading and training young officer candidates. He stayed on for four years. The responsibility of training future officers ranks as one of the preeminent assignments an officer can receive; personnel leadership had entrusted the captain with the task, placing the young candidates in his care despite a dossier thick with the years-long legal battle surrounding his homosexuality, or, put another way, his fitness as a superior. His following assignment was as a deputy battalion commander, after which he was given command of a battalion as lieutenant colonel. Each subsequent assignment stood in opposition to ministerial orders, which explicitly ruled out using homosexual officers and NCOs in leadership positions. (Incidentally the officer was not aware of this particular decree throughout his career, first learning about it during his interview for this study in 2018. He was all the more surprised that the leadership positions had been conferred on him.)

The saga seems once again to confirm the truth that there is always an exception to the rule. Neither personnel management nor his superiors seem to have viewed this particular officer's sexual orientation as any obstacle to senior leadership roles; evidently his personality profile and track record were convincing enough. The case also demonstrates that in the end, there was always a way to assign outwardly homosexual soldiers to leadership or training roles if nothing spoke against it in that specific instance. How many decisions and careers followed

---

201 Interview with Ret. Lieutenant Colonel N., 20 July 2018.
202 For a full account see chapter 5.
203 Interview with Ret. Lieutenant Colonel N., 20 July 2018.

a similar course remains to be seen; such cases distinguish themselves precisely for not being linked to homosexuality on paper. It was a lucky strike for historical research that this particular set of unhappy circumstances (from the officer's perspective) left traces in court records, which could be researched and later confirmed by interview. Today, the retired lieutenant colonel looks back on a "excellent career as an officer," recalling his 1981 removal as company chief and the years-long legal struggle without rancor. "I'm not angry with the service. I didn't suffer any lasting damage from what happened."[204]

The NCOs and officers interviewed for this study reported clearly and credibly about the great pressure under which they stood for years or decades as homosexuals in the Bundeswehr. At the same time, many eyewitnesses recalled experiencing a great deal more tolerance within the ranks than what the regulations actually permitted. During the 1990s in particular, any number of officers and NCOs whose homosexuality was an open secret served as superiors, at all levels of leadership.

---

204 Ibid.

III Illicit Acts? Male Homosexuality in Criminal and Disciplinary Law

Homosexual behavior cannot be tolerated within the line of duty.[1]

From 1872 on, Paragraph 175 (§175) of the Imperial Penal Code made "illicit sexual acts against nature between persons of the male sex or by people with animals" punishable by law.[2] In its jurisprudence, the imperial courts limited applying the paragraph to anal intercourse and "intercourse-like acts." Female homosexuality was never criminalized. In 1935 the National Socialists drastically expanded and amplified the threat and reach of punishment under what became two paragraphs.

1. §175 after 1949 in West Germany

After 1949, West Germany preserved the law in its more severe form from the National Socialist era, thus its relevance for this study.

§175 StGB
(1) A man who commits illicit sexual acts with another man, or allows himself to be misused for illicit sexual acts by a man, shall be punished with imprisonment.
(2) If an involved party was not yet twenty-one years old at the time of the crime the court may refrain from punishment in particularly minor instances.

§175a StGB
Penal servitude of up to ten years, and in mitigating circumstances imprisonment of not less than three months shall apply to:
1. a man who by violence or threat of present violence to life or limb compels another man to commit illicit sexual acts or to allow himself to be abused for illicit sexual acts;
2. a man who, by abusing a relationship of dependency established by service, employment or subordination, induces another man to commit illicit sexual acts with him or to allow himself to be abused for illicit sexual acts;

---

1 This guiding principle can be found in scores of disciplinary rulings, as for example in the decision of the 8th Division of Military Service Court Center from 8 October 1990, reproduced in BArch, BW 1/531592: BVerwG, 2 WD 5.91: Federal Administrative Court, 2nd Military Service Senate, decision from 30 July 1991.
2 The Imperial Penal Code took effect 1 January 1872; the original text is available at https://www.deutschestextarchiv.de/book/view/unknown_strafgesetzbuch_1870?p=56 (last accessed 31 Mar 2021).

3. a man over twenty-one years of age who seduces a male person under twenty-one years to commit illicit sexual acts with him or to allow himself to be abused for illicit sexual acts;

4. a man who commits illicit sexual acts or allows himself to be abused as a regular source of income, or offers to do so.[3]

According to the 12 May 1969 edition of *Der Spiegel*, §175 was the only law strengthened during the National Socialist era still in effect twenty-four years later.[4] "For the homosexual minority, the legal end of National Socialism came about only twenty-four years after the collapse of the Third Reich."[5] Aside from threatening increased prison terms, replacing the term "illicit sexual acts against nature" (*widernatürliche Unzucht*) with the much broader "illicit sexual acts" (*Unzucht*) proved decisive. The change in wording had grave consequences as it made all sexual activity between men criminal, no longer anal intercourse alone. Masturbating in the presence of another man without any touching involved, even simply looking at another man with "lustful intent" was sufficient. "Illicit acts *with* another occurs whenever one uses the body of another man as a means of arousal or satisfying sexual desire," reads one commentary from 1942. "It is not necessary for physical contact to have taken place or even been intended."[6]

Between 1949 and 1969, close to 50,000 men were sentenced under §175 in West Germany, preceded by preliminary investigations – of which there were, for example, just under 100,000 between 1953 and 1965.[7] Those detained during the era report authentically on being treated like "serious criminals" while in policy custody and awaiting trial. "We were equated with serious offenders like murderers and whoever else."[8]

The first decades of the Federal Republic were generally a period of "strict sexual morality"; sexuality was hardly ever discussed in public, rarely even in

---

3 Article 6 of the law for altering the Criminal Code from 28 June 1935, RGBl. I, p. 839; the wording is available at https://lexetius.com/StGB/175,6 (last accessed 31 Mar 2021). For a detailed account of the legal history of the cited paragraphs under National Socialism, see Burgi and Wolff, *Rechtsgutachten*, 17–22.
4 "Späte Milde," 57.
5 Stümke, *Homosexuelle in Deutschland*, 132.
6 Commentary from 1942 on the use of the term *Unzucht* in §175, found in Stümke and Finkler, *Rosa Winkel, Rosa Listen*, 216. See also Schomers, *Coming-out*, 67.
7 Rampp, Johnson and Wilms, "'Die seit Jahrzehnten belastende Schmach fällt von mir ab'," 1145.
8 Günter Landschreiber, taken into custody in Gelnhausen in Hessen during the 1960s after he was reported by the mother of his ex-partner, speaking on the television documentary "Schwulen Paragraph," broadcast on hr-fernsehen 10 October 2019 at 11.15 p.m.

private. It fit the contemporary conception of morality that legal proceedings concerning homosexuality could be, and often likely were, kept outside the public eye.[9]

§175 in particular reflected the convictions of mainstream society. In a representative survey conducted by the Allensbach Institute in February 1969, 46% of West Germans came out against the slated decriminalization of homosexuality between grown men, 36% were for it, 18% were undecided.[10] It was "against popular opinion" and "against one of the most tenaciously held prejudices of German citizens'," *Der Spiegel* wrote, that the Bundestag and the government pushed through the revision of §175.[11]

One report in *Die Zeit* from 1964 did not mince its words as to the state of homosexuals in West Germany. "Our society makes life miserable for this group, homosexuals. Today, sanctions born from the spirit of bygone centuries that no longer went unquestioned even when they were first put to writ still encourage the machinations of informants, denouncers and blackmailers."[12]

The ultimate goal of prosecuting homosexual acts was likely to "enforce the normalization" of gay men in the direction of "mainstream sexuality."[13] "As with the ban on the death penalty, lawmakers had to bring better knowledge and insight to bear over and against one of Germany's most tenaciously held prejudices," *Der Spiegel* wrote in its usual blunt style. It was "parliamentary decision against popular opinion."[14] Federal Minister of Justice Horst Ehmke, appointed to spearhead the law's revision by dint of office, came out with a more or less public apology that simple homosexuality's imminent decriminalization in no way signaled a "decline in moral value judgements,"[15] much less "moral approbation."[16] To conservative

---

9 Bormuth, *"Ein Mann, der mit einem anderen Mann Unzucht treibt,"* 53.

10 "Späte Milde," 55.

11 Ibid.

12 Cited in Stümke and Finkler, *Rosa Winkel, Rosa Listen*, 379. A useful overview of the situation of homosexual women and men in the Federal Republic is provided in Könne, "Gleichberechtigte Mitmenschen?" and in Wolfert, *Homosexuellenpolitik in der jungen Bundesrepublik*. See Pretzel and Weiß, *Ohnmacht und Aufbegehren* for a collected series of wide-ranging essays.

13 This is Michael Schwartz's argument in his introductory talk at a symposium on justice and homosexuality at the Judicial Academy of North Rhine-Westphalia in Recklinghausen on December 18 and 19, 2017.

14 "Späte Milde," 55. For a comprehensive account of Bundestag debates surrounding "morality and custom" and the controversial decriminalization of homosexual acts, see Ebner, *Religion im Parlament*, 95–142 and 185–210.

15 See Schwartz, "Entkriminalisierung und Öffentlichkeit," 85, as well as in a subsequent talk given at the Judicial Academy of North Rhine-Westphalia in Recklinghausen on December 18 and 19, 2017.

16 First mentioned in Stümke and Finkler, *Rosa Winkel, Rosa Listen*, 354.

jurist Walter Becker, "same-sex activity" continued to constitute a clear violation of "the law of custom as defined in the Basic Law" even after it was struck from criminal law.[17]

In 2000, the Bundestag unanimously adopted a resolution acknowledging that "the human dignity of homosexual citizens was violated by the threat of punishment that continued to exist after 1945."[18] In June 2018, speaking with reference to the persecution and prosecution homosexuals were forced to endure in the first decades of the Federal Republic, German President Frank-Walter Steinmeier asked their "pardon on account of all the pain and injustice that went on, and for the long silence that followed." "The German state inflicted serious harm on all these people," Steinmeier continued; those who were "arrested, convicted and locked up" on the basis of §175 "were still forced to hide, still exposed, still risking their economic existence."[19] A report considering legal rehabilitation for men convicted under §175 found that conviction "inflicted harm to freedom, body and spirit while also imposing heavy social burdens, ranging from losing one's job or apartment and exclusion from broad parts of society to losing one's rights as a citizen."[20] If the convict happened to be a soldier, the criminal verdict was followed by a disciplinary hearing and sentencing in a military service court, which up through to the end of the 1960s generally meant removal from service.

Such was the verdict service judges reached in one case cited at the very outset of this study – the sergeant observed having sex with a private in the bathroom of the barracks canteen one Saturday in December 1962. In February 1964, a military service court ordered Sergeant K. to be removed from service and demoted him to private first class, ruling that "the nature, gravity and effects of the drunken acts [constitute] such a gross breach of duty that the accused is no longer acceptable for service in the Bundeswehr."[21] Court records are silent as to the fate of

---

17 Schwartz, "Entkriminalisierung und Öffentlichkeit," 85.

18 German Bundestag, Bundestag document 14/4894, 4.

19 *Die Zeit*, "Steinmeier bittet Homosexuelle um Vergebung"; *Süddeutsche Zeitung*, "Steinmeier bittet Lesben und Schwulen um Vergebung." In the words of one eyewitness who was impacted, "That's exactly how it was!" A letter from Michael Lindner in Hamburg to the author on 20 July 2019.

20 Burgi and Wolff, *Rechtsgutachten*, 11.

21 Taken from the court opinion of Military Service Court C1 from 20 February 1964, cited in the Federal Disciplinary Court on 25 August 1964, I WD 69/64. The full text of military service senate decisions are accessible online for viewing and research at https://www.wolterskluwer-online.de/, along with nearly all judgements passed down at the Federal Administrative Court, and prior to that at the Federal Disciplinary Court. Unless otherwise stated, all decisions at the Federal Administrative Court and its military service senates reproduced here come from this online resource. The author would like to thank Lieutenant Colonel Michael Peter for directing him to the site and his assistance with research.

the private. He was likely dismissed according to the guidelines of the day, which allowed without a hitch for conscripts ruled unfit or fixed-term soldiers still within the first four years of their service to be discharged immediately and unaccompanied by disciplinary procedure.[22] The sergeant appealed the decision. Not only did the 1st Military Service Senate at the Federal Disciplinary Court reject the sergeant's appeal, it canceled his transitional allowance (he had since departed regularly from the armed forces) as well as any professional development funding usually provided to give soldiers a start in their civilian careers. The senate struck a decidedly sharper tone in its opinion than had the first court.

> Illicit sexual acts between men, as the accused [...] and Private Sch. Committed with each other further demonstrate serious aggravating circumstances [...] On top of this comes the fact that the crime occurred within the barracks in which the accused was by all accounts Sch.'s commanding officer [...] The image that the accused presented as non-commissioned officer and superior was extremely objectionable [...] The accused accordingly lost so much by way of authority, reputation and trust that the service could no longer be expected to continue its relationship of employment with him.[23]

Soldiers in particular suffered grave social consequences in addition to "civilian" conviction by a criminal court, simultaneously losing their place of work; their place of residence if they lived in the barracks, as was customary among young soldiers at the time; and not least their social world, which often revolved entirely around their company and comrades. The return home might easily be met with stigmatization or social exclusion from rural or small-town society, often making it necessary to strike out somewhere new as a stranger.

2. A World War Veteran Comes Undone

Among the careers §175 brought down was that of a highly decorated World War II veteran with high aspirations in the Federal Republic. What might have been a "bright" future came to an abrupt end around 1 a.m. on a Saturday night in April 1958, at a parking lot in downtown Cologne.

The subsequent inditement filed by the public prosecutor's office in Cologne presents the following series of events: According to his statement, one night after

---

22 Under the Conscript Act in effect after 21 July 1965, conscripts could be dismissed from service due to physical or mental unfitness (§29 (2) in the earlier version). Thanks to Governmental Director Guido Gutzeit for this reference.

23 Federal Disciplinary Court ruling from 25 August 1964, I WD 69/64.

work a police sergeant passed by a public parking lot, where he spotted a lone car parked. The light burning in the Mercedes struck him as suspicious; he approached the car and shone a pocket flashlight into the car's interior. "The two men were apparently so taken up in their activity that they did not notice the light from his pocket lamp [...] both were shocked and aghast."[24]

The sergeant filed a criminal report. By the Monday after the fateful night, the staff officer had been brought in for questioning by the disciplinary prosecutor responsible for his unit. He vehemently disputed "any sort of mutual illicit touching." A former comrade of the accused from World War II who himself later rose to lieutenant general in the Bundeswehr could still easily recall the unhappy incident:

> He [Bernd] was gay. He went to Cologne. And then he went to a local bar where gays met. He comes out, gets into his car with a lover, and behind him a policeman peeks through the rear window and sees all the fun. Well, and there you have it. He asked me, "My god, what do I do now?" I advised him to turn at once to [a higher-ranking officer he knew] [...] we brought in a legal adviser – but long story short, Bernd had to go. He wasn't allowed to set foot in the base any longer and asked me to get his things in order.[25]

In late June 1958, right before the trial was set to begin in local court, the officer requested release from the armed forces "since he no longer felt equal to the demands made of an officer." The president of the Federal Republic granted the request effective August 1958. The celebrated officer now turned his back on Germany, fleeing abroad to build a new existence for himself in a place where he was known and prized as a war hero, anything but a "hundred and seventy-fiver."

The trial began in Cologne in July 1958; in March 1959 the civilian defendant was ordered to pay a fine of 300 DM in lieu of a sentence of thirty days in prison, which the officer forfeited per se.[26] The very possibility of the defendant's conviction under §175 owed directly to the Federal Republic having retained the paragraph in 1949 as it had been strengthened by the National Socialists, a fact that now also proved the war hero's undoing. In December 1958 the Cologne court issued an arrest warrant for the fugitive officer. Criminal proceedings against the defendant were ultimately dropped for the time being "because he had evaded prosecution [...] by emigrating."

---

24 BArch, Pers 1/60262: Police chief constable's testimony as cited in the ruling at Military Service Court F, 2nd Division, Az F 2-Vla 11/59 on 5 December 1962.

25 From the transcript of an interview with a retired Lieutenant General conducted on 13 January 2004 by Dr. Kurz Braatz, quoted with his friendly permission. The first name used in the quote has been changed by the author.

26 BArch, Pers 1/60262: Cologne Local Court, 31 DS 309/58, decided 9 March 1959.

Both the armed forces and the criminal justice system might have let the matter rest at that. The disciplinary prosecutor, however, had no intention that the discharge authorities hold off on disciplinary proceedings. In 1960, two years after the incident in the parking lot, the prosecutor had a written inditement delivered to the now officer in the reserve via the consulate of the Federal Republic in the officer's new country of residence.

In January 1961 the presiding military service court decided to discontinue disciplinary proceedings. The disciplinary prosecutor appealed the decision. In July 1962, four years now after the incident, proceedings were reinstated. The 2nd Division of Military Service Court F in Stuttgart initially found that the ruling reached at Cologne local court against the man in the car with the staff officer did not bind the court, as it was not issued against the latter. The disciplinary judges resolved to hear their own evidence instead, calling the other parties to the crime and the police sergeant in to testify. The transcript of the Stuttgart proceedings is an astonishing document compared with nearly every other surviving court record involving similar cases which the author has been able to look over. What strikes one is the judges' effort to take note of any potential doubts regarding the policeman's description of events, and call his memory into question. "So many doubts [remained] [...] that proof of mutual homosexual activity appears not to have been fully established." For the policeman, the court's attack against his credibility as a witness may well have come as an entirely unfamiliar, novel experience. The sense of good will that prevails toward the defendant throughout the entire trial, on the other hand, is not matched by any other military service court proceedings examined by the author to date. It certainly is not wild speculation to assume that the defendant's wartime distinctions and his standing as a "war hero" impressed the judges and predisposed them to leniency. In weighing the pros and cons, the judges came to the decision that since "the consummation of illicit acts between men [had not] been fully proven," the defendant's removal from service would not have entered the realm of thought if the defendant had not quit himself. At most a reduction in rank to first lieutenant, as had also been requested by the disciplinary prosecutor, was appropriate. Yet the military service court in Stuttgart rejected this proposal as well, letting the rationale for its surprising leniency show clearly:

> The defendant acquired and earned his service rank in the war through courageous, extraordinary dedication. He staked his life in aerial warfare for years and has been highly decorated. He has shown above-average dedication in the Bundeswehr as well, and he has never failed in office but served consistently as a model [...] The defendant lives far abroad [...] There's much to suggest that it would require a serious incident to call him up. Depriving

the defendant of his service rank in this case – in whole or in part – would be too harsh and inappropriate a punishment for his crime and level of guilt.[27]

Further proceedings were suspended. The staff officer's case shows that in looking at restrictions against homosexual soldiers, it is essential to look beyond rulings in civil or military court, or formal measures such as military discharge. In this instance, a former Wehrmacht officer still esteemed for his record in World War II had both his career and his professional and civilian existence destroyed – all without a criminal sentence, military court ruling or a decision to remove him from service. In anticipating the impending legal proceedings, he quit the service himself.

3. Punishing Consensual Sexual Activity Between Soldiers Under §175 StGB (up to 1969)

In January 1964, the 2nd Military Service Senate at the Federal Disciplinary Court heard the case of a sergeant. The September before in 1963, Husum local court had sentenced the thirty-two-year-old, married man under §175 to a fine for "illicit same-sex acts, in particular mutual masturbation" on at least nine occasions. By the court's account, the man had had sex with other men in public toilets, though it had not gone beyond forms of joint or reciprocal satisfaction by hand. (In this case too, the very possibility of convicting the man under §175 was owed directly to the Federal Republic's upholding of the paragraph in its more severe form from the National Socialist era.)

Here too there followed a ruling in military court demoting the reservist sergeant, who had since departed regularly from the service, to private first class. The disciplinary prosecutor for the military objected; the decision was too lenient for his liking. The Federal Disciplinary Court heightened the sentence by revoking the man's benefit claims for time in the service. The senate spoke out sharply against the man and any sort of homosexual activity in its ruling.

> Under current Senate jurisprudence, homosexual misconduct by a soldier must be met with strict disciplinary action, as such behavior greatly jeopardizes soldiers' sense of community, camaraderie and troop cleanliness [...] The accused may not have committed indecent acts against other soldiers, but he did involve himself repeatedly with homosexual men over a

---

27 BArch, Pers 1/60262: Cologne Local Court, 31 DS 309/58, decided 9 March 1959.

period of two years, first as an NCO and later as a sergeant and at times in uniform, thereby bringing severe damage as much to his own official reputation as that of the Bundeswehr.[28]

Speaking in favor of the accused was his statement that "he acquired his homosexual tendency after being seduced by a soldier in the navy at age fourteen." This circumstance "likely admits greater leniency in assessing his conduct, but even so the overall circumstances would not have allowed the accused to remain in service if his term had not yet expired."[29]

This final passage in particular reveals a traditional view of homosexuality not as something that is part and parcel of human nature but, as with a psychological "abnormality" or an illness, something that was triggered by infection from outside.

The court's choice in wording that the sergeant "greatly eopardize[ed] [...] troop cleanliness" is also telling. Whether consciously or unconsciously, the view comes to the fore here that homosexuality was something unclean, dirty. The topos of "cleanliness" surfaces in numerous court opinions throughout the Fifties and Sixties. In one decision from 1964, military judges noted seemingly in passing, but conspicuously nevertheless, that "without washing before, [the two men] then lay down beside each other on the bed beneath the same quilt."[30] Of the NCO who had been observed having sex with a private in the canteen bathroom in December 1962, the disciplinary judges wrote that his behavior was "highly detrimental to troop cleanliness, internal order and discipline."[31]

It would be too narrow to conceive of phrases like "purifying" or "troop cleanliness" as applying especially or exclusively to homosexual activity, even if many regarded it as something dirty at the time, including many jurists. Purifying disciplinary measures, as they came to be called, were imposed for many other kinds of offenses as well. It was (and today remains) a common form of expression among jurists.

The 2nd Military Service Senate heard a nearly identical case in January 1965, again involving a sergeant. "A man with such a tendency," the court wrote in its decision, "poses a threat to soldiers' sense of community, camaraderie and troop cleanliness. The accused would have to be removed if he were still in service."[32] The man stood accused of "six counts [...] of illicit sexual acts, in particular mutual

---

28 Federal Disciplinary Court, 2nd Military Service Senate, 6 Aug 1964, Az II WD 35/64, found on www.jurion.de.
29 Ibid.
30 Ruling at Military Service Court A on 14 May 1964, cited in BVerwG, I (II), WD 129/64: Federal Disciplinary Court, 2nd Military Service Senate, decided 10 June 1964, found on www.jurion.de.
31 Ruling BVerwG, 25 August 1964, I WD 69/64.
32 Ibid.

masturbation" as a civilian in 1963, again mostly in public toilets. The local court imposed a sentence of one month on probation for violating §175 in six instances. The military service court concurred with the local court's ruling and ordered the accused to be removed from service.[33] When the defendant appealed, having since departed the armed forces under normal circumstances, the military service senate rejected his petition and increased the sentence by revoking both the man's benefit claims for his time in the service and his right to vocational assistance with a new civilian career.

Even if comparisons are odious, striking parallels do emerge between the military service court rulings and those of the Wehrmacht judiciary from twenty to twenty-five years prior, as is shown in what follows.

4. Courts Martial from 1899 to 1945 and Parallels with Rulings in Military Service Court Rulings

On 25 September 1942, the field court martial for the eighth anti-aircraft division in Bremen sentenced a twenty-one-year-old private "in the name of the German people" to three weeks' close arrest "on two counts of illicit acts contrary to nature." A similar decision and rationale might have come from one of the Bundeswehr's service courts in 1962. The parallels began with the formal procedure and working methods of the court alone, regardless of the case being heard. As with military service courts, the accused sat before three judges: a career judge (in 1942 holding the rank of General Staff Prosecutor for the Air Force) as well as two honorary members – an officer and a soldier holding the same service rank as the accused (private first class in the present case). The judges considered it established fact that two years before at the age of nineteen, the private had in his native Westphalia "committed illicit acts with another man and allowed himself to be misused for illicit acts on two instances."[34] Amid the parallels, one important difference is worth pointing out: Bundeswehr service courts could only impose disciplinary measures, whereas the courts martial of the Wehrmacht were able to hand down criminal sentences. Not only did the 1942 field court martial issue the private a disciplinary

---

33 BVerwG, II (I), WD 121/64: Federal Disciplinary Court, 2nd Military Service Senate, decided 15 January 1965. The decision includes references to and quotes from the initial court ruling at Military Service Court F on 30 April 1964, found on www.jurion.de.

34 North Rhine-Westphalia State Archives, Westphalia inventory, Q 222/957-960, Bochum public prosecutor's office. The file contains the decision by the field court martial for the 8th anti-aircraft division, K.St.L. 992/1942 from 29 September 1942. Thanks to Frank Ahland for this as well as the following sources.

sentence; it immediately pronounced criminal judgement over him in place of a (civilian) local court. In the Wehrmacht, as in the Reichswehr and other previous German armies (and today in many armed forces the world over), active soldiers stood exclusively under military jurisdiction. That included crimes committed as civilians or even, as here, those predating their conscription.

Like their counterparts in the Bundeswehr, Wehrmacht jurists also drew a neat distinction between those who had been seduced and were in fact "normally disposed" (deemed "casual offenders," or *Gelegenheitstäter* by Wehrmacht jurists) on the one hand, and "habitual offenders" or *Hangtätern* on the other (another term from the Wehrmacht archives; Bundeswehr jurists preferred the expression "homosexually inclined"). One of the latter, a dancer from Düsseldorf drafted into the Wehrmacht, appeared in court in January 1945. The sentencing court in Paderborn for the field court martial presided over by the commanding general and officer of Luftgau VI sentenced the private to one year and six months in prison for "illicit acts contrary to nature" committed not while on duty but in his home town. "The accused associates with homosexual circles. In the conviction of the court-martial, the accused is therefore to be regarded as a habitual offender."[35]

A court decision from 1899 has also been preserved against a *Vizefeldwebel* in the Prussian Army (the equivalent of a sergeant in the Bundeswehr) from Company 10 of Regiment 56. Sentenced to six months in prison "for illicit acts contrary to nature with base degradation," the officer sat out his prison term at the Wesel citadel.[36] The convict left the military without a military attestation or a civilian pension voucher, likely making it much harder for him to get a start in civilian life. Military service senates took a similar tack when they revoked the benefit claims and vocational assistance measures Bundeswehr soldiers had earned through their time in the service.

Until §175 and §175a StGB were revised, military superiors also routinely referred cases of consensual sexual activity to criminal investigators or public prosecutors. It was a policy that a major at Bonn's Federal Ministry of Defense and his partner V., a civilian employee also working at Hardthöhe were forced to experience in 1965 when their relationship was reported upstairs by V.'s colleagues. Details about the relationship came from V. himself, who had likely confided somewhat too freely in his coworkers. A wide-ranging disciplinary investigation file opens with a comment from November 1965 that "for some time, colleagues have watched on

---

35 North Rhine-Westphalia State Archives, Westphalia inventory, Q 926/11618, Werl Penitentiary, Arrest Files for Hermann S., 1944–1945. Field court martial ruling by the commanding general and officer of Luftgau VI, Sentencing Division I K.st. Paderborn, L 173/44, VL 814/44.
36 Witten City Archives, "Witten-Alt" inventory, 2.25b.330, dossier on Robert M.

uneasily at the relationship between V., a twenty-seven staff employee, and Major S., who was forty-four."[37] The investigation ran its course, with the BMVg passing the matter on to criminal investigations in Bonn. Neither of the men withstood interrogation. Each began to accuse the other order to secure a more lenient punishment for himself; only in this way could investigators have found out for themselves what had gone on behind bedroom doors without any further witnesses. Ultimately, both the investigators and the court became convinced that even if the sexual activity itself had been consensual, the major had plainly seduced the much younger and more inexperienced, somewhat I staff employee.

In February 1966 Bonn local court ordered the major to pay a fine of 2,000 DM, a large sum of money at the time, in lieu of a two-month prison sentence.[38] The BMVg suggested to the major that he apply for his own dismissal, and in April 1966 the president of the Federal Republic recognized "a career soldier's request for dismissal from service at his own wishes." Yet even now the BMVg did not let up on the major, now chastised and staring into a professional abyss. "After consulting with P II 5, disciplinary proceedings against S. will be continued, since they've already been introduced."[39] In June 1967 the military service court in Düsseldorf demoted the reservist major to private first class.[40]

In 1965, military reports passed along to criminal investigators saw a lieutenant back before local court; the officer had been talked into sex by a private first class during military exercises. (There were also cases in which lower-ranking soldiers seduced their superiors.) While massaging the lieutenant in his room after sports one day the private grazed the officer's genitals, who then removed his gym shorts. The private then pleasured the lieutenant with his hand.

> Both men were sexually aroused. When [Private First Class] R. also undressed, then lay down in bed next to the accused [the lieutenant] and tried to take hold of his member again and kiss him, the accused directed him to leave the bed. Private R. resisted at first, saying that it would be an unforgettable night. When the accused [the Lieutenant] now explained to him that he had received a training in one-on-one combat and would use force if R. did not leave, [the private] got out of the bed and got dressed. He [the private] demanded a pistol with a single round of live ammunition, since he wanted to shoot himself. The accused talked him out of it, upon which Private R. came to the decision to report himself.[41]

---

37 BArch, BW 1/12819: BMVg, S II 7, Az 06-26 from 29 November 1965.
38 Ibid., Order of punishment from Bonn Local Court, 45 Cs 56-57/66 from 25 February 1966.
39 Ibid., BMVg, handwritten note from 26 May 1966 without listing the department responsible.
40 Ibid., Disciplinary prosecutor for Military Service Court A, 3rd Division for Military District Command III, AZ 25-01-30-01 1/66 from 7 July 1967.
41 BVerwG, II WD 44/66: Federal Disciplinary Court, 2nd Military Service Senate, decided 12 January 1967. The decision refers to the ruling at Ahlen local court (Westphalia) which took effect 16

Speaking in his room over the course of a good two hours, the lieutenant tried to calm the private down, pointing out the consequences that reporting to the authorities would entail for both of them. It was all in vain. Around five o'clock that morning the private reported to the officer on duty that he was guilty of a misdemeanor under §175, adding the lieutenant as a witness.

The commander of the seventh mechanized infantry division in Unna initiated disciplinary action against both men, suspending them pending final conclusion of legal proceedings in the matter. The private was quickly given immediate dismissal from the Bundeswehr under §55 (5) SG.

In February 1966, a local criminal court in Westphalia's Ahlen sentenced the reservist lieutenant and former private to pay a fine of 150 DM each in lieu of fifteen days in prison for violating §330a StGB (drunkenness) in conjunction with §175. Later that year in July during the internal military disciplinary trial, Military Disciplinary Service Court E convicted the lieutenant of a breach of duty, demoting him to the lowest service rank in mechanized infantry. The officer appealed and was vindicated, at least in part. In January 1967, after a trial that remained closed to the public, the 2nd Military Service Senate at the Federal Disciplinary Court decided to reduce the lieutenant's rank to that of a non-commissioned officer of the reserve. The officer "had only been the passive participant in the illicit activity that resulted from the drunken atmosphere. He had turned down more serious illicit acts, and finally put an end to them." The senate regarded the incident as a "one-time lapse that was out of character for an otherwise morally stable man."[42] With that the judges were able to leave him with the reserve rank of NCO, and thus the functions of a superior.

A second set of appeal proceedings decided on in 1967 involved a first lieutenant on active duty contesting his dismissal from service. The lieutenant had previously been convicted by a juvenile court of "two counts of illicit sexual acts between men under §175, one case ongoing" and ordered to pay two fines of 350 DM and 140 DM. When the defendant appealed the decision, the 1st criminal division in regional court suspended proceedings at the state's expense and with the consent of the public prosecutor, "since the culpability of the perpetrator was minor and no public interest in prosecution" existed any longer. This was not the opinion the disciplinary prosecutor, however, who continued to take an official "interest in prosecution."

February 1966, as well as the initial ruling at Military Service Court E on 27 July 1966. Found on www.jurion.de.

42 Ibid.

Aside from pursuing homosexual activity outside of the line of duty while camping with adolescents from his scouting troop, the first lieutenant stood accused of repeated joint and mutual masturbation sessions with an NCO in his battalion. The noteworthy aspect of this seemingly "classic" case was that the first lieutenant and NCO had known each other before the Bundeswehr, from the very same scouting troop where the court found "illicit same-sex activity, especially masturbation" to be nearly standard practice. ("Activity of the sort was nothing out of the ordinary in the troop."[43]) During their time together in the service, the two now secretly continued in the barracks what had been a familiar routine in earlier days. It was just that now they stood separated by degrees of rank, with a directive governing superior–subordinate relations and how officers were expected to behave in the barracks, both in general and especially toward subordinates. The NCO was quickly dismissed without trial or further notice under §55 (5) SG. As for the first lieutenant, a military service court ordered his removal from service and demoted him to the lowest rank in the reserve. When he appealed, the presiding military service senate upheld his removal but left him with the rank of private first class in the reserve. The trial before regional court had already

> *failed* to show that the accused had induced the non-commissioned officer to commit illicit sexual acts with him by abusing his position as an officer. No abuse of a superior–subordinate relationship occurred [...] [NCO] F. was seduced, he himself had performed illicit acts of this sort with other men, he was a willing victim [...] The accused F. was aware of the activity, it was not anything extraordinary for him, he even enjoyed it by his own account.[44]

Still, the first lieutenant could not be allowed to remain in active service. Even consensual sex between soldiers constituted a breach of duty in multiple respects when it took place in the barracks and, moreover, involved a superior and subordinate. The officer had "violated his duty to respectable behavior (§17 (2) SG),[45] his duty to camaraderie (§12 SG) and his duty to provision of care (§10 (3) SG), all under the increased liability of a soldier holding a superior position (§10 (1) SG)."[46]

---

43 BVerwG, II WD 60/67: Federal Administrative Court, 2nd Military Service Senate decided 15 December 1967, with references to the rulings at Juvenile Court H on 1 November 1966, Regional Court G. on 23 December 1966, Military Service Court B on 13 June 1967. Found on www.jurion.de.
44 Ibid.
45 §17 (2) of the Soldier's Act demanded that every soldier "behave in a way that doesn't seriously detract from the reputation of the Bundeswehr or the respect and trust that his official position requires, including while off duty and away from official living quarters and facilities."
46 BVerwG, II WD 60/67: Federal Administrative Court, 2nd Military Service Senate decided 15 December 1967, with references to the rulings at Juvenile Court H on 1 November 1966, Regional Court G. on 23 December 1966 as well as Military Service Court B on 13 June 1967.

Unlike the military service court before it, the senate found itself disposed to assume a less serious case, "though the defendant could not be left holding any service rank that would legally confer superior functions on him. Leaving [him with] the rank of private first class in the reserve therefore seemed appropriate."[47]

The following year, in 1968, service court judges in Kiel saw no cause for leniency in the case of a petty officer second class, nor were they swayed by the defense lawyer's reference to alcohol consumption. Rather, the officer had "deliberately approached his subordinate and repeatedly induced [him] to homosexual activity." The judges viewed it as an aggravating circumstance that the incidents had played out in service quarters. "The nature and severity" of the violations "in their broad range" had further convinced the court of a "manifest tendency" in the petty officer, making him seem unfit for continuing to serve in the Bundeswehr. Differently than in the case of the sergeant described previously, service court judges found no excuse for suspicions of homosexuality in 1968. The decision from Kiel ordered the officer's removal from service and demoted him to private in the reserve.[48]

The backstory went as follows: In October 1967, after a night spent drinking together in the petty officer's room, the twenty-two-year-old had talked his direct subordinate, a private, into having sex with him, albeit not against the latter's will. The two remained sexually active in the weeks to come, each time more or less drunk but always consensually. They were found out in November, when an on-duty officer discovered them sleeping naked in bed together on a night patrol of the living quarters. The next day the petty officer tried to take his own life by slitting his wrists. Itzehoe regional court sentenced him to nine months in prison for "crimes" under §174 StGB (sexual abuse of wards) in conjunction with "crimes" under §175 and §175a StGB, though the sentence was suspended on probation against a fine of 600 DM. Both paragraphs were applied in this instance because the accused, as a man over the age of twenty-one, had had intercourse with a man under the age of twenty-one who had had been further been entrusted in the officer's care as his direct subordinate.[49] The defendant did not appeal either this decision or that of the military court and the probationary sentence, including both the fine and removal from service, became final.

In 1966, Hamburg criminal investigations took up the case of a petty officer in the navy, after a policeman had caught him engaged in intimacies with the officer of a Brazilian trading ship by the Bismarck Monument just north of the city port around 2 a.m. New Year's Day. Speaking for the transcript with an irksome love of

---

47 Ibid.
48 BArch, Pers 12/45954: Ruling at Military Service Court A, 1st Division on 8 October 1968.
49 Ibid., Ruling of the youth division of Itzehoe regional court on 26 July 1968.

detail, the police master reported his observations to criminal investigations, and later the military service court.

> The area is often frequented by homosexuals who pursue their tendencies there. The accused and the Brazilian drew the attention of the witness [...] who initially got his service dog into position before approaching the pair from the opposite side. At about three steps' distance he shone the flashlight he had brought with him on the couple, and was able to observe the Brazilian embracing the accused with both arms and kissing him on the mouth. The accused was simultaneously holding the Brazilian's aroused member with both hands as it stuck out of his pants and rubbing it. The fly of the accused also stood open. The witness was not able to observe whether the member of the accused was hanging or sticking out. The accused and his partner allowed themselves to be taken to the nearby police station in St. Pauli without resisting.[50]

The petty officer explained that he had gone to St. Pauli looking for sex with a prostitute he knew, but had not found her. He had spent the rest of New Year's Eve in and out of Hamburg's bars, eventually encountering the Brazilian at the public bathroom by the Steintor. The officer had then thought to accompany the Brazilian for part of the way back to his ship, toward Altona. How he had wound up at the traffic circle in front of the Bismarck Monument engaged in sexual activity, the officer could not say. He knew in any event that the Brazilian had been the one to initiate the "advances." It was the first time the officer had gotten "mixed up" in something of the sort; he had not ever "taken part in same-sex activity," though he had had sex with more than forty women.

The lead public prosecutor discontinued the investigations being pursued under §175 StGB.[51] Military service judges, for their part, stressed that criminal proceedings being suspended did not stand in the way of "punishment" by the Bundeswehr judiciary. (In doing so, they abandoned a principle that was otherwise consistently upheld, namely that Bundeswehr jurists were not there to punish, but only to impose disciplinary sanctions.) The petty officer, "disappointed [...] at not having found the girl, succumbed to the Brazilian's rough advances"; he had never engaged in same-sex activity before and had excellent marks in the service. What was more, the sex had occurred in a public place, at the traffic circle in front of the Bismarck Monument, "and not in the bushes or other places where homosexuals usually withdraw." The only thing the judges did find "concerning" was that the accused had let himself get involved in "this type" of sex on a public square, yet this alone could not justify his removal from service. A very lenient ruling came

---

50 BArch, Pers 12/45777: Military Service Court A, 1st Division, decided 23 August 1966.
51 Ibid., Nolle prosequi by the lead public prosecutor at Hamburg Regional Court, 4 March 1966.

out of the court's deliberations, demonstrating a remarkable degree of goodwill toward the accused in comparison to other decisions in similar cases. The officer was demoted by one rank in seniority and a further year's delay in reinstatement to the next rank (i.e. his former rank of seniority).[52] The officer's lawyer had clearly handled the case adeptly; only on the rarest of occasions throughout the 1960s did an NCO or sergeant emerge unscathed from the Bundeswehr judiciary for proven homosexual activity. Put in headline form, the case might have read "Dastardly Brazilian seduces innocent and unwitting German NCO."

5. Psychiatric Evaluations as a Means of Adjudication

Throughout the 1950s and 1960s, psychiatric evaluation presented an entirely common way of determining homosexual tendencies in the court system, as with the case of a staff sergeant in 1967. The sergeant had become involved with a stranger in a public urinal when a police official, whether coincidentally or not, made an inspection of the facility and caught the two "red-handed." Stuttgart local court imposed a fine of 150 DM on the sergeant for violating §175 StGB; a military service court then sentenced the sergeant to be removed from service and reduced his rank to plain sergeant.

In fixing the disciplinary measure, the military service court found that while the staff sergeant could not be shown to have engaged in same-sex activity while on duty, it was "to be feared that here too [while on duty] he would slip up at some point, all the more so as the past life of the accused shows that sexual deviancy is not foreign to his nature." Nor was his misconduct based on seduction, but his own impulses. "As such, the trust in him carrying out his official duties in accordance to regulation has been irrevocably destroyed, as his tendency could also bring harm to the troops from an intelligence standpoint."[53] The sergeant appealed. The 1st Military Service Senate repealed the initial sentence, demoting the accused instead to private first class. This allowed him to remain in active service, even if with the rank of a common soldier. The decision was based on a series of psychiatric evaluations, the last involving a full thirteen-day stay at a hospital. The resulting report certified the sergeant with a "latent homosexual drive as a partial symptom of neu-

---

52 Ibid.

53 BVerwG, I WD 33/66: Federal Administrative Court, 1st Military Service Senate, decided 20 October 1967. The decision refers to the order of punishment by Stuttgart Local Court on 29 March 1965, and quotes from the ruling at Military Service Court D on 25 April 1966. Found on www.jurion.de.

rosis,"[54] allowing the senate to refrain from removing the sergeant from service, unlike the initial measure.

A military prosecutor requested a similar psychiatric evaluation for a petty officer second class in 1968. That February while at a party with friends, the officer had "laid his right arm over the shoulder [of a private], kissing him on the mouth and cheek, and licking his cheeks." It was not the "delighted" private who had reported the incident but other soldiers, which their superior then reviewed before passing it on to the Flensburg public prosecutor. An investigation for suspected violation of §175 StGB was suspended that April due to lack of evidence. The petty officer had previously spent two weeks in the neuro-psychiatric department of the Bundeswehr Hospital in Hamburg, where he received a "thorough physical examination and psychiatric as well as psychological review."[55] The court records contain the doctor's report, which does not shy away from intimate details about the officer's sexual activities from adolescence on. The Bundeswehr psychologist found "a truly low level of" intelligence, "certain tendencies in the direction of homoeroticism" and "homoerotic patterns of behavior under the influence of alcohol," but no signs of a "homosexual tendency."[56] The military service court in Kiel heard the case later that year in July, after which it discontinued proceedings based on the psychiatric report.[57]

Such reports remained common through the 1970s as a way to determine homosexual tendencies, and into the 1980s on isolated occasions. They were also employed to rule out those same tendencies, as in the 1974 case of a senior staff physician (equal in rank to major). One Thursday morning another soldier, an acquaintance of the physician, had seen the latter hugging and kissing a "good-looking young man" on the street, "including a French kiss and taking hold of his companion's genitals above his pants" (taken from the witness statement). The witness reported what he had observed to his superiors who then took disciplinary action, one part of which included four weeks (!) of inpatient observation at the neuro-psychiatric division of a Bundeswehr hospital. The resulting psychological report concluded that "the conditions for early retirement laid out under §44 (3) SG have not been met due to lack of demonstrable homosexuality [on the part of the senior staff physician]." The one filing the report, incidentally, also held the rank of senior staff physician. His words, paired with those of the defense lawyer concerning his

---

54 Ibid.

55 BArch, Pers 12/45936: Report from the neuro-psychiatric division at BWK Hamburg to the legal advisor at WKB Kiel, 1 April 1968.

56 Ibid.

57 Ibid., Ruling at Military Service Court A, 1st Division on 12 July 1968.

client's alcohol consumption prior to the event, allowed the military service judges to view the incident "not as an expression of homosexuality, but simply excess of alcohol," albeit one which "had given the impression of a homosexual tendency." The judges imposed a one-year ban on the physician's promotion.[58]

Another staff sergeant was made to undergo psychiatric evaluation in a Bundeswehr hospital in 1967. He had not drawn any attention in the line of duty previously, but was then "caught" engaging in homosexual activities in his private life – most recently, and probably decisively for his fate, in a public toilet. Police investigators began a meticulous search for earlier crimes, uncovering numerous homosexual "offenses" that reached back to 1963 in the process. The local court sentenced the man to eight months in prison on nine counts of illicit sexual acts with men, suspended to three years' probation in exchange for a fine of 800 DM. The commander of the staff sergeant's armored battalion opened a disciplinary investigation into the same matter, shipping the sergeant off to the neuro-psychiatric division at a Bundeswehr hospital in the interests of obtaining an "expert opinion." The doctors there found him "permanently unfit for assignment due to inability to perform." Army personnel command placed the staff sergeant in retirement as unfit to serve under §44 (3) Clause 1 SG. With that it was "case closed" for the troops; not so, however, for the military disciplinary prosecutor or the military service judges, who stripped him of his retirement pension for official misconduct in 1968.[59] To put it plainly, the Bundeswehr judiciary was removing the material basis for the retirement into which it had forced the staff sergeant.

The sergeant's lawyer filed an appeal, arguing that his client's homosexual tendencies "had been recognized as an illness through the administrative act of placing him in retirement," one to which the disciplinary court was also bound. The service senate judges rejected this line of reasoning, replying that retirement had come about "from an inability to serve derived from [the accused's] tendency," whereas the "cause for disciplinary action [...] is not a soldier's same-sex tendencies but their enactment." Nor in this instance did the judges at the Federal Administrative Court accept the lawyer's accusation of double jeopardy (protected against by the constitution); career sanctions were not imposed under general criminal

---

58 Ruling at the 12th Division of Military Service Court North on 16 September 1975, mentioned in BVerwG, II WD 57/75: Federal Administrative Court, 2nd Military Service Senate, decided 29 April 1976. Found on www.jurion.de.

59 BVerwG, II WD 59/68: Federal Administrative Court, 2nd Military Service Senate, decided 10 June 1969. Includes references to the rulings at Rheine Local Court on 25 July 1967 and a military service court on 24 July 1968. Found on www.jurion.de, as well as what follows.

law "but were typical of disciplinary action, which falls under disciplinary law, not criminal law."

From a strictly legal point of view, disciplinary action was not the same thing as punishment per se. Bundeswehr jurists placed value on the proper designation of "disciplinary measures."[60] The constitutional ban on double jeopardy would have precluded disciplinary action after conviction by a local or regional court.

Generally speaking, the mere existence of §175 StGB, when paired with the punishment it threatened, prevented homosexual men in the Federal Republic from living a life that was in keeping with their nature, and restricted them in expressing their sexuality and way of loving. Their experience was one of standing outside a mainstream society that was hostile to them, and of persecution at the hands of the state and its judicial system.

In a rare case of extremes, in 1969 three gay men from Rhineland-Pfalz, among them a conscript, chose the most radical path for rejecting society and its norms when they murdered four innocent soldiers guarding a munitions depot in Saarland. The case garnered a great deal of public attention at the time, with the homosexuality of the perpetrators playing a star role in the media interest.

6. Excursus: The 1969 Murder of Four Soldiers

20 January 1969, 3 a.m., paratroopers on watch at a munitions depot in Saarland's Lebach are surprised in the middle of an otherwise peaceful night by an insidious attack on the guardroom. Private Dieter Horn, Private First Class Arno Bales and Sergeant Erwin Poth are shot in their sleep, Private Ewald Marx later succumbs to his wounds. A further soldier survives with severe wounds. The two perpetrators make off with three G3s, two P1s, and a thousand rounds of ammunition.

MAD, the police and the public prosecutor's office initially assumed a politically inspired – i.e. radical leftist – attack on the Bundeswehr in the ensuing investigation. The highly active Außerparlamentarische Opposition (APO) came under suspicion; another possibility was a group from the communist underground seeking to arm itself for guerrilla warfare in the event of war with the Eastern Bloc. Military counterintelligence analysis even entertained the notion of Bundeswehr sympathizers or members of the armed forces looking to show up serious security gaps in guard details as a possible background to the assault, before dismissing the

---

60 In the old version of the Military Disciplinary Code, disciplinary measures decided in court, or "gerichtliche Disziplinarmaßnahmen" as they are called today in Germany (see §58 of the disciplinary code), were designated "disciplinary punishments," or "Disziplinarstrafen."

explanation as highly unlikely and focusing instead on the radical left. The case was not solved by MAD however, but by the ZDF TV show "Aktenzeichen XY [...] ungelöst" [File Reference XY [...] unsolved] and a fortune teller in Remagen who had previously been blackmailed by the criminals.[61] The actual motive took both police and MAD by surprise. The culprit turned out to be a young man who until December 1968 had served as a conscript in Paratrooper Battalion 261 in Lebach. Working alongside his boyfriend, the conscript had planned the attack on the munitions depot, which was familiar to him from his time as a conscript, in order to secure weapons and ammunition to rob banks. The conscript had stolen a P38 pistol during a military exercise in Baumholder with the same purpose in mind; his partner had taken another pistol from the evidence room at Landau local court, where he worked as a legal secretary. Another friend had been involved in the planning as well, a conscript working at the Bundeswehr hospital in Koblenz at the time of the crime. The ultimate motive was the three friends' desire to finance a life together in South America or the South Pacific, far away from the hostility they felt from German society.[62] As the trial played out before Saarbrücken regional court in the summer of 1970, media attention came repeatedly to rest on the sexual orientation of the three accused. In one report the trial observer for *Der Spiegel*, Gerhard Mauz, set fictitious words of understanding in the mouth of the regional court president regarding the specific problems faced by a minority that up until the year before had been subject to legal persecution.

> "Mr. Fuchs," Mr. Tholl might say, "you have formed a disposition toward Ditz and especially Wenzel that one generally calls homosexual. A prejudice exists against this disposition – it is called 'deviant,' even today" [...] "It might be possible to recognize the path by which you found your way to one another, to join together against a world from which you feel barbarically excluded and irrevocably judged."[63]

In August 1970 the Saarbrücken court sentenced the two men to lifelong sentences for murder, and gave the Koblenz conscript six years in prison for aiding and abetting a murder. For one of the two main criminals, a "lifelong" sentence meant release

---

61 One of the blackmailers employed the same pseudonym with the female fortune-teller as in his subsequent letter of confession to the attack in Lebach. The fortune-teller had taken down the license plate of the blackmailer at the time. When she heard and saw the distinctive name on television, she informed the police, and the license plate number quickly lead to the criminals. For more see the TV documentary "Der Soldatenmord: Die Schüsse von Lebach," a part of the series "Die großen Kriminalfälle," first broadcast 6 February 2001 on ARD.

62 Storkmann, "20. January 1969."

63 Mauz, "Warum so und später anders...?"

in 1993 after twenty-three years, as was common practice. The second, seventy-five as of 2018, has declined to submit a petition for release for thirty years now and still sits in prison.[64] Such an appalling and senseless act was not and cannot be justified by the persecution of homosexuality at the time; all the same, it was the same-sex orientation of the culprits, their service in their Bundeswehr and the potency of §175 that held the center of media interest.

7.   "Lex Bundeswehr?" The BMVg and the Decriminalization of Male Homosexuality in 1969

In 1969, West Germany declared sexual activity between consenting adult men (those over twenty-one at the time) exempt from punishment. Jurists spoke of "simple homosexuality" in distinguishing it from more serious cases, which continued to be punishable.

§175 StGB Illicit Sexual Acts between Men
(1) A term of imprisonment of up to five years shall apply to:
   1. a man over eighteen years of age who commits illicit sexual acts with another man under twenty-one years, or who allows himself to be abused for illicit sexual acts;
   2. a man who abuses a relationship of dependency established by service, employment, or subordination by inducing another man to commit illicit sexual acts with him, or who allows himself to be abused for illicit sexual acts;
   3. a man who commits illicit sexual acts or allows himself to be abused as a regular source of income, or offers to do so.
(2) In the case of Paragraph 1 No. 2, the attempt is punishable.
(3) The court may refrain from punishment where a party was not yet twenty-one years of age at the time of the crime.[65]

The 1969 reforms reached far beyond §175 and addressed the previous prohibition on adultery and "procurement in the sense of exchanging partners."[66] Yet both publicly and behind closed doors, a serious debate emerged, especially regarding the future of the "homosexual paragraph." In private, conservative jurists and politicians sought to avert what they feared would be a "worst-case scenario" for discipline and order in the Bundeswehr, one in which men ages twenty-one and up

---

64 Meyer, "Lebacher Soldaten-Morde."
65 Burgi and Wolff, *Rechtsgutachten*, the current phrasing since 1 April 1970. In the version from 1 September 1969, for "term of imprisonment" simply read "prison."
66 BArch, BW 1/187212: Bundestag legal affairs committee, resolutions of the criminal law division, 19 September 1968.

would be allowed to engage in sexual intercourse without fear of reprisal, even in close quarters or group situations as found in the Bundeswehr or the Federal Border Police. The problem had been "discussed in detail" both in the special committee at the Bundestag and the "Grand Criminal Law Commission," with BMVg jurists playing an important role in the background. By 1958, with §175 StGB already on shaky ground and reform anticipated, conservatives – here taken in a double sense to mean adhering to a current in partisan politics but also traditional values and inherited social structures – had envisioned a new paragraph to protect against the "clearance" of sex between men in the Bundeswehr and Federal Border Police. The second paragraph of the new §222 StGB would read: "Men who live together in an association or group and commit sexual acts with each other shall also be punished"[67] – a law specially conceived for the Bundeswehr and the border police. §222 was never introduced, though it "would have been decidedly better," as one jurist lamented in *Neue Zeitschrift für Wehrrecht* in 1970.[68]

A peek behind the curtains at the work of the criminal law subcommittee within the Bundestag Committee on Legal Affairs reveals that the specific "age of consent" of twenty-one was worked out with a view toward Bundeswehr fears about "impairments to military order and a resulting decrease in the fighting power of the Bundeswehr."[69] Sources show the lengths to which the BMVg went in pushing for regulations specific to the armed forces. Strictly speaking it was military leadership, and Chief of Defense Ulrich de Maizière to be exact, who spoke out vehemently in favor of keeping homosexual behavior between soldiers a criminal act. At the time leadership sought no less than a law created specifically for soldiers, even if it was not supposed to look that way.

The BMVg lawyer charged with the affair acquiesced to demands that he advocate for special regulations regarding soldiers during the committee session, "certain reservations regarding criminal law dogma notwithstanding." In legalese it was not special regulations that were spoken about here but "expanded protection for soldiers under criminal law." Concretely, the BMVg called for the "protection of criminal law" to be upheld for those under twenty-one years of age, subordinates and those within enclosed military facilities.[70] The Federal Ministry of Justice rejected the proposal as "too far-reaching," but declared itself willing to accept it

---

67 Schwalm, "Die Streichung des Grundtatbestands," 85.
68 Ibid.
69 Burgi and Wolff, *Rechtsgutachten*, 33. For the political and judicial debates surrounding the 1969 reform of §175 StGB during the 1960s and 1970s and their impact on the armed forces, also see Brühöfener, "Contested Masculinities."
70 BArch, BW 1/187212: BMVg, VR II 7, 17 January 1969, as well in the following. (Emphasis in the original).

if the BMVg lawyer were able convince the legal affairs committee in the Bundestag. The decision now lay before parliament and thus in the hands of lawmakers, where it belonged. 16 January 1969 was the pivotal day. Shortly before the session was set to begin, a brigadier general approached the BMVg lawyer. The general had spoken with the chief of defense; the lawyer would have to exact even greater "protection under criminal law" for soldiers. General de Maizière now demanded that "*every* homosexual act by a soldier be punishable in every instance, no matter when, where, or with whom." At the same time, de Maizière had explicitly stipulated this could not result in a "Lex Bundeswehr." Yet the one was not possible with the other. The BMVg lawyer himself called it a "practically unachievable demand," tantamount to preserving a law (§175 StGB) upon whose repeal the committee was "resolutely (unanimously!) determined."

A memorandum put out directly before the meeting by the senior department head for all non-military offices at the BMVg similarly lamented the chief of defense's "much farther-reaching" demands.[71] Neither he nor his legal department had been informed ahead of time. During the morning session, the BMVg representative presented the committee with wording for a new version of §175 StGB that was in keeping with the BMVg's initial set of wishes; according to the report, the committee members responded "quite open-mindedly."[72]

During the midday pause, the lawyer then drafted a new version of §175a to include the sweeping demands of the chief of defense.

A term of imprisonment of up to three years shall apply to anyone who
1. as a Bundeswehr soldier
2. as a law enforcement official of the Federal Border Police or the riot police or
3. as a member of the Civil Defense Corps, or while performing alternative service, commits illicit sexual acts with another man or allows himself to be abused for illicit sexual acts, insofar as the crime is not punishable under §175.[73]

On paper one finds the comment "worked out due to request from mil., in line with the Engl. and Swiss solution." Presumably the introduction of the Federal Border Police, riot police and Civil Defense Corps represented an attempt to blur the impression of creating a law created specifically for soldiers. The new proposal had the effect of "chilling somewhat the committee's visible readiness from that

---

71 BArch, BW 1/187212: BMVg, Head of Department III, 17 January 1969.
72 Ibid., BMVg, VR II 7, 17 January 1969.
73 BArch, BW 1/187212, sheet 49: BMVg, VR II 7, suggested formulation, solution No. 1, undated, as well in the following. The draft used the term "penal servitude," later it was emended by hand to "term of imprisonment."

morning to accommodate the interests of the Bundeswehr."[74] Even that account was glossed over. With his heightened demands, de Maizière had minimized the chances of his ministry's previous, more moderate proposal succeeding; the legal affairs committee now looked on any sort of law particular to soldiers with skepticism.

Thus, the drastic stipulations backfired, figuratively speaking. With the "military side" still holding tight to its maximal demands,[75] Minister Schröder of the CDU decided against them, charging the lawyers in his own ministry with advocating only for the original, more moderate request. Two elements for a crime should "unconditionally" be brought to bear, namely, "a.) active and passive parties must both be soldiers; b.) the crime must have a material or spatial relationship to military service."[76] With that de Maizière's demand that *any* homosexual activity by a soldier be made punishable, including with civilians, was off the table.

The defense ministry's lawyers ultimately came up short in the behind-the-scenes struggle, unable to hold even the final line of defense regarding a "material or spatial relationship to military service." The BMVg was able to notch a minor victory in retaining a ban against homosexual activity for those under twenty-one, an age limit that was fixed not least in deference to the interests of the Bundeswehr. The age group that continued to stand under threat of punishment represented those eligible for military conscript. In reality, the age limit led "to the objectively unjustifiable result that men of the same age who kept up a homosexual relationship until their eighteenth year went unpunished, became subject to punishment between eighteen and twenty-one, then again became exempt from punishment after that."[77]

Within specialist circles as at *Neue Zeitschrift für Wehrrecht*, jurists picked the reform of §175 StGB to pieces ("not exactly the lawmaker's finest work") while considering the implications for the armed forces. The fact that it was the Bundeswehr that had called for the age-limit did nothing to alter the "imbalance in the new regulation."[78] Still, the author wrote, all the accusations of a "Lex Bundeswehr" missed the mark; the reform did not stipulate any special regulations for communities or groups, nor did the age limits and special protection afforded to relationships of

---

74 Ibid., BMVg, VR II 7, 17 January 1969.

75 Ibid., BMVg, Head of Department III, 17 January 1969.

76 Ibid., BMVg, Minister's office, 17 January 1969 (with handwritten notes from Defense Minister Schröder), also in VR II 7, 22 January 1969.

77 BArch, BM 1/6727, Bundesrat: Motion by the State of Baden-Württemberg for the Bundesrat session on 23 October 1970. This was the justification used by the state government in Stuttgart to motion that the Bundesrat replace "twenty-one" with "eighteen" in §175 (1) No. 1.

78 Schwalm, "Die Streichung des Grundtatbestands," 83. In what follows as well.

service, employment or subordination apply to the armed forces alone, but generally.[79] So had a law been created specifically for the Bundeswehr or not? Perhaps not in letter, but in intention it was beyond doubt.

Reference to the age limit of twenty-one being introduced at the Bundeswehr's request in 1969 also appears in the defense ministry's written internal correspondence from the following year. The Air Staff for example expressed great satisfaction

> that young adults and those dependent on a relationship of service or subordination continue to find protection from homosexual assault in the new version of the statutory provision. It especially takes into account the justified demands that the Bundeswehr has made on account of the specific nature of a soldier's life. The exceptional aspects of the military context have not changed in this respect compared to the past. Protection under criminal law thus continues to be a requirement. In my view it cannot be replaced by status law or disciplinary measures, especially because they are not as comprehensive in their effects as legal regulation.[80]

The BMVg was not able to prevent the revamping of sexual offense law in 1969. Yet, as seen here with air force leadership, it was satisfied to see that at least conscripts between the ages of eighteen and twenty-one-years-old would continue to enjoy protection from "homosexual assault" under the law and – in the event they desired each other – to know they were subject to it.

How would the armed forces deal with the newfound liberality in criminal law within its ranks? Military criminal courts did not exist in West Germany after 1945, and for good reason.[81] Even before the reform took place, BMVg lawyers recognized that the new, more liberal laws governing sex offenses would impact disciplinary measures; a form of behavior that is no longer punishable under criminal law also loses "weight" as a breach of duty or misdemeanor. There would be cases that could now "no longer in any way" be seen as a service violation. Jurists warned that doing away with the criminality of simple homosexuality would cause "considerable problems" for the Bundeswehr's administration of justice by 1968.[82]

---

79 Ibid. Schwalm coined the phrase "Lex Bundeswehr" for the new version of §175 StGB in his 1970 essay. As shown above, Chief of Defense de Maizière had already used the phrase in January 1969, albeit in an internal document (BArch, BW 1/187212: BMVg, VR II 7, 17 January 1969). It is doubtful that Schwalm was aware of the usage, and more likely that he came up with the term, which comes to mind quite quickly on its own. The term has been used repeatedly since, as in Brühöfener, "Contested Masculinities," 303.
80 BArch, BM 1/6727: BMVg, FüL II 6, 7 October 1970.
81 A military criminal code has existed in the Federal Republic since 1957, however; the law applies to punishable crimes committed by Bundeswehr soldiers.
82 BArch, BW 1/187212, disciplinary prosecutor for the Bundeswehr, 27 September 1968.

The age limit was eventually lowered to eighteen in 1973, brought on by the age of legal adulthood being lowered generally.

8. "Civilian Courts' Lax Handling of Homosexuality": Disciplinary Rulings against Consensual Sex after Criminal Reform

Jurists in the BMVg's administrative and legal affairs department did not regard a more liberal "moral criminal code"[83] as fundamentally impacting how homosexual activity would be assessed under service law, writing in 1970 that the catalog of duties enshrined in the Legal Status of Military Personnel Act (Soldier's Act) operated independently alongside the stipulations of criminal law, and thus "was not directly affected" by any changes. This meant same-sex activity could still constitute a violation of duty "even in the event that" the crime no longer stood under "threat of criminal punishment." The lawyers stated it even more clearly: Same-sex activity "by soldiers with other soldiers, but also with third parties [!]" was fundamentally to be regarded as a serious breach of duty.[84]

In August 1969 the BMVg sent out an advisory about the new legal situation to every commander and head of office so as "to avoid confusion." The note observed that the "catalog of duties" laid out in the Soldier's Act stood independently alongside the provisions of substantive criminal law as a matter of course, given the different aims that criminal and disciplinary law pursued. The liberalization of the "moral criminal code" had "no fundamental impact" on service law: same-sex activity among soldiers would continue to be regarded as a breach of duty even if it was no longer punishable as a criminal act.[85] BMVg lawyers drafted a list of scenarios to assist with applying the service law going forward.

1. The crime *fulfills* the elements of an offense under the *new version of §175 StGB.*
2. The crime *does not fulfill* the elements of an offense under the *new version of §175 StGB,* but involves same-sex activity
   a.) between a soldier and another soldier, another member of the Bundeswehr, or with a third party inside military installations or facilities;
   b.) between a soldier and another soldier or member of the Bundeswehr outside of military installations or facilities, especially those between a superior and a subordinate, a soldier of a higher-ranking service groupand a member of a lower-ranking service

---

83 The original German term is "Sittenstrafrecht."
84 BArch, BW 24/7180: BMVg, VR IV 1, 29 September 1970.
85 BArch, BW 2/31225: BMVg, FüS I 3, Az 16-02-02, 7 August 1969.

group, an older man and a sig-nificantly younger man, or a soldier and another
soldier or member of the Bundeswehr who belong to the same unit or service post;

c.) between a soldier engaged in official duties and an outside third party outside of
military installations or facilities;

d.) between a soldier with an outside third party outside military installa-tions or facili
ties in cases other than those named in a.) and c.), if the crime or its discovery affects
official interests.[86]

With that, the commanders and office heads had it in black on white: They were
able, in fact were obligated, to bring disciplinary action against soldiers for any
kind of sex involving other soldiers or civilian member of the Bundeswehr, even if
that were to occur "outside military installations," be it in one's hometown apartment or a hotel. Yet even sex outside the barracks with a man who did not belong
to the armed forces was subject to disciplinary action if the soldier involved was
on official duty, or, barring that, if "the crime or its discovery [affected] official
interests."

Still, proceeding by process of elimination, BMVg officials and lawyers had for
the first time opened the door to no longer regarding consensual sex outside of
the barracks with a non-member of the armed forces a breach of duty. In doing so,
however, they drafted a paragraph that could be interpreted at will, and applied to
any case involving sex between men – as soon as it was discovered, that is. This had
always been the case, as without an act's discovery there would be no cause for the
Bundeswehr to begin an investigation. "For soldiers, discovery of the crime and the
perpetrator's membership in the Bundeswehr routinely results in a considerable
loss of authority and trustworthiness, disruption to troops' internal composition,
their order, discipline, and sense of camaraderie, and damage to the reputation
of the Bundeswehr."[87] Fundamentally, the lawyers in Bonn wrote, the changes in
criminal law did not matter to them; as far as soldiers were concerned, practically
every form of homosexual activity would still be subject to disciplinary action. The
parents of conscripts would "rightly" expect the Bundeswehr to keep the official
realm and, "as far as possible the extra-official realm [!] free of homosexual relationships."[88]

In 1993, the commanding officer for Military District Command III (an area
corresponding to the state of North Rhine-Westphalia), General Major Manfred
Würfel, was still wondering aloud in *Der Spiegel* "How can I make it clear to my

---

86 Ibid., original emphases.
87 BArch, BW 24/7180: BMVg, VR IV 1, 29 September 1970. The same wording can be found in
BArch, BW 24/7180: BMVg, FüS I 1, 9 September 1970.
88 Ibid.

people that I cannot tolerate homosexuality in my units [...] when it's no longer punishable in society at large?"[89] By the article's account, the general was "at loggerheads with civil jurisdiction" and "feared for troop discipline if the lax treatment of the male homosexual community at the hands of the civilian courts spread within the 'tightly confined quarters' of his own 'male community'" –this was in 1993, mind you.

The Federal Administrative Court for its part had been ruling since 1970 that homosexual conduct no longer represented a breach of duty, provided it occurred outside of service and was not tied to official responsibilities in any particular way. That year saw a ruling on the appeal of a petty officer second class previously convicted in disciplinary court; as the first trial involving a soldier's homosexual activity since the reform of §175, the decision had a bearing on future precedent.

The legal reforms that decriminalized homosexual activity between adults took effect on 1 September 1969, and immediately began to work in favor of the petty officer. Just four days before, at the proverbial final buzzer, Military Service Court F had ordered him removed from service, simultaneously reducing his rank to private first class. The officer stood accused of carrying on homosexual relationships in private as well as attempted advances on fellow soldiers, a charge which proved untenable when the service court heard evidence. Actions taken in the purely private sphere were all that remained, some reaching back to 1963, long before the officer had entered the service. The court decided nonetheless that a service violation had occurred and imposed the harshest possible disciplinary measures – in other words, a ruling that was entirely in keeping with the previous hard line.[90] When the officer appealed, the judges on the military service senate cleared the initial ruling from the table. To date, disciplinary action had always involved cases where the behavior was at the same time criminal. For the first time now, that no longer applied. The judges considered it immaterial that the behavior itself occurred before 1 September 1969, as the accused had not been punished by a criminal court before 1 September and thus could no longer be punished per §2 (2) StGB.[91]

As §17 (2) SG stated, however, conduct did not necessarily have to be criminal to be in breach of duty. "As such, the depenalization of simple homosexuality does

---

89 "'Versiegelte Briefe'."

90 Ruling by the 6th Division of Military Service Court F on 28 August 1969, mentioned in BVerwG, II WD 73/69: Federal Administrative Court, 2nd Military Service Senate, decided 10 June 1970. Found on www.jurion.de.

91 BVerwG, II WD 73/69: Federal Administrative Court, 2nd Military Service Senate, decided 10 June 1970.

not mean that homosexuality has lost its disciplinary import in general." Still, in this case it had, as

> the situation is different in cases of the present type, which concern events that took place outside the Bundeswehr and without any ties to the official realm. Henceforth, such behavior cannot be recognized either as damaging to the Bundeswehr's reputation or unworthy of respect regarding the soldier concerned. The end of simple homosexuality as a crime rests on the notion that a liberal society must tolerate behavior that may well deviate from the norm, but fundamentally belongs to people's private sphere. The senate is well aware of the fact that general appraisal has not changed at the same time as the legal system. Continuing with the previous form of rejection – itself subject to changes in perception anyway – cannot, however, be granted disciplinary relevance; in this regard the concept of tolerance holds greater relevance.[92]

All this meant the petty officer should be acquitted. The records leave it uncertain as to whether his acquittal subsequently offered him a way forward in the navy. He had already been admitted once before in late 1968 to the neuro-psychiatric department of a Bundeswehr hospital "on suspicion of a homosexual disposition." Upon evaluation, physicians determined that "he was homosexually predisposed and thus permanently unfit for assignment." Efforts by the officer's superior to remove the officer as unfit to serve under §55 (2) SG were discontinued after disciplinary court proceedings began. Court records, however, remain silent on whether – with disciplinary proceedings now ended in acquittal – the "medical card" would be played again in order to "be rid" of the petty officer.

Independently of how the officer fared personally, the judges were well aware that their ruling was breaking new legal ground, and would have a signaling effect. The revision of §175 could not stop at the doors of the military service courts. The decision circulated in specialist judicial journals, drawing commentary and summary of its key message: "Homosexual activity outside of the Bundeswehr and without any connection to the official line of duty, no longer punishable as of 1 September 1969, is in any event not a breach of duty if the same-sex relationships have not been carried out in an offensive or – as necessitated by particular circumstances – conspicuous manner."[93]

With the 1970 ruling, military service senates recognized case law that had been adopted by disciplinary senates for civilian public servants five years previously. In 1965, the Federal Disciplinary Court ruled that disciplinary action could only be taken against a state employee based on his homosexuality "if his conduct

---

92 Ibid.
93 *Neue Zeitschrift für Wehrrecht* (1971): 31.

at work or in public was liable to give offense."[94] Four years before criminal law reform, the highest disciplinary court thus provided a way for civil servants known to be homosexual to remain in service, assuming they did not "arouse public indignation." Concretely, this meant that homosexual state employees were finally able to be private in private. If they were to give cause for "offense," on the other hand, it would diminish the reputation of the civil service and thus the state – another parallel to the careful legal protection afforded to the "reputation of the Bundeswehr."

> Independently of changes in its status under criminal law as expressed in the repeal of the earlier version of §175 StGB, same-sex activity between members of the Bundeswehr is and remains intolerable for a male community as tightly quartered as the army. It is not only that [such activity] diminishes moral cleanliness, nor that the unit's reputation and public perception of the Bundeswehr in general are damaged. Graver still is the risk of a disruption in internal order, which must be sustained by discipline and authority.[95]

It was in these no uncertain terms that the judges on the 2nd Military Service Senate at the Federal Administrative Court ruled against a sergeant first class in 1970. The sergeant was charged with carrying on consensual sexual activity, even a love affair with a young private in his battery, i.e. one of the companies in his artillery troop. Throughout 1967 other soldiers in the battery had repeatedly observed the two "conspicuously tumbled about with each other," stroking and kissing each other lovingly. The soldiers filing the report subsequently served as key witnesses against the defendants, who disputed the charges. The state prosecutor opened an investigation into the sergeant and private for suspicion of sexual crimes under §174 or 175 StGB,

> yet sufficient suspicion of a criminal act could not be demonstrated. It was predominately "battery talk," soldiers swapping rumors that did not stand up upon closer inspection [...] More serious seems the witness statement [of Sergeant B.] that upon entering the room of the accused he had [...] seen [the accused] and R. in a tight embrace, kissing each other. These statements were also disputed by both accused. There is no doubt as to the veracity of the witness Sergeant B.'s statement. A simple kiss between men, however, is not generally regarded as illicit under jurisprudence or legal doctrine [...] differently from what is termed a French kiss. Under BGH 1/298 a kiss – particular aberrations notwithstanding – is *not* an illicit sexual act. Since Witness B. saw the two defendants only very briefly upon opening the door to the room, these kind of aggravating circumstances against them cannot be proven; French kissing for example would hardly have been possible to identify.[96]

---

94 Gollner, "Disziplinarsanktionen gegenüber Homosexuellen im öffentlichen Dienst," 106–7.
95 BVerwG, 25 June 1970, II WD 18/69, ruling of the Second Military Service Senate at the Federal Administrative Court on 25 June 1970. Found on www.jurion.de.
96 Here and in the following: Nolle prosequi from State Attorney T. dated 2 July 1968, cited in the

The Bundeswehr's own disciplinary justice system, however, brooked no doubts in favor of the accused. The first division of Military Service Court D found the sergeant guilty of breach of duty and ordered his discharge. The sergeant appealed, to no avail. In 1970, the Second Military Service Senate at the Federal Administrative Court upheld the initial verdict against the sergeant's love for the private, holding the observations of a range of witnesses for both to be credible and sound. The senate was convinced that "all the touching had been an expression of homoerotic relationships."

> The external order and internal composition of a military unit demand at all times that the unit remain free of injurious ties of this sort. To such an extent a soldier, but especially a superior, must impose discipline and restraint on himself; above all else he must serve as an example of poise and commitment to duty to younger comrades, and a guarantor of respect for the dignity and honor of fellow soldiers. In this the accused has lapsed, losing his authority as a superior and destroying his employer's trust in him.

By way of postscript, the court records mention in passing that the two men continued their "close friendship" even after the private's time as a conscript had come to an end and the sergeant was first suspended, then dismissed.

a.) "Otherwise Normal." A 1970 Ruling on a Staff Sergeant and Five Other Soldiers

1970 saw a further case of consensual sexual activity between soldiers in the barracks tried in a service court. That April, the court ruled that "same sex activity within a confined male community is inimical to the inner composition of troops and their discipline to a high degree," and that it continued to constitute a serious violation of duty even with legal reform. Before the judges stood a staff sergeant, a mature man serving as a fixed-term soldier, the married father of a school-age child who between 1968 and 1969 had repeatedly had consensual sex with another staff sergeant in his unit. The case was tried in local court before the criminal law reforms had gone through; the defendant had been ordered to pay a fine of 210 DM in lieu of two weeks imprisonment for crimes under §175 StGB. The staff sergeant was not alone – a total of six soldiers who were sexually active with each other had been discovered within the company. Three of the soldiers also received fines in the local court proceedings; another was sentenced to three weeks in prison,

---

ruling of the 2nd Military Service Senate at Federal Administrative Court, II WD 18/69, 25 June 1970 (emphasis in original).

apparently without probation; while the sixth, a staff sergeant regarded as a repeat offender, was given three months in prison on nine criminal counts under §175 StGB.[97]

Four of the soldiers involved were dismissed swiftly and without delay from the Bundeswehr via the administrative route, under §55 (5) SG. The remaining two, a lieutenant and the staff sergeant, had disciplinary proceedings initiated against them; both had been in the service more than four years, blocking simplified dismissal under §55 (5) SG. Disciplinary proceedings against the lieutenant ended with an eight-month pay reduction by one-twentieth. The leniency of the verdict came about from the judges' assumption that the lieutenant had acted in a state of full intoxication. The staff sergeant, on the other hand, could not show having consumed a considerable amount of alcohol before sex. This absence of what the judges viewed as an exonerating factor led them to consider him at least latently, and at times actually, interested in same-sex activity, or "an otherwise normal and plain casual offender" in their phrasing. The service court deemed his activities a serious breach of duty. "Anyone who, like the defendant, engages so unreservedly in homosexual activity with a [soldier] of equal service rank makes himself untenable as a superior." A demotion in rank to private first class followed.[98] The fact that the staff sergeant was not dismissed in 1970 reveals that the previous years' legal reforms were also having a moderating effect on the Bundeswehr. Previously, NCOs had as a rule been dismissed for similar, even less concentrated sexual activity.

Later that year in December 1970 the 1st Military Service Senate at the Federal Administrative Court again upheld the new liberal line, this time repealing an initial court decision to remove a staff sergeant from service. The sergeant had on separate occasions directed different (and willing) young men to sleep with his wife in front of him. While they had intercourse with his wife, he would then touch the men intimately. The scene repeated itself nightly, at times involving other young men and always to the delight of all those involved, until a neighbor complained about the nocturnal disturbances to the police. The "lively threesomes" (the judges found the more sober term "triplet intercourse") entered the purview of the law. Kempten regional court sentenced the sergeant to one year without probation for "attempted aggravated illicit homosexual acts in conjunction with continued aggra-

---

97 Ruling at Ellwangen Local Court on 21 April 1969, found in BVerwG, II WD 67/70. Ruling in appeal proceedings before the 2nd Military Service Senate at the Federal Administrative Court on 12 November 1970. Found on www.jurion.de.

98 Ruling of the 1st Division of Military Service Court D on 28 April 1970, found in BVerwG, II WD 67/70, ruling in appeal proceedings before the 2nd Military Service Senate at the Federal Administrative Court on 12 November 1970.

vated procurement" – for consensual sex in his own bedroom.[99] The verdict did not stand. During appeal proceedings, the regional court shifted the ruling slightly but significantly to "continued aggravated procurement with illicit homosexual acts" and commuted the prison sentence to a fine.

In its own disciplinary proceedings that same year, a military service court ruled that the sergeant should be removed from service.[100] This harsh verdict was not upheld either. The military service senate overturned the decision, and in its ruling lay out baseline considerations for disciplinary action against private sexual conduct: "As with any other off duty transgression in the private sexual realm, [soldiers engaging in homosexual activity] constituted a violation of duty only if the transgression affects the official realm by disrupting military order."[101] As the wording and meaning of §17 (2) SG made clear, the duty to maintain respect and trust was "not an end in itself." Nor was the ban on conduct detrimental to respect or trust meant "to make the soldiers of the Bundeswehr into a sort of moral model for the rest of the population – such an aim would likely be condemned to failure from the outset for an army of conscripts the size of the Bundeswehr." Barring a "spatial or personal connection with service," a breach of duty would be present only in cases of exception, "if the action is particularly reprehensible."[102] A much lesser form of disciplinary action that was exclusively financial in nature was now taken in place of removal from service.

The winds of change that had begun to course through society in 1968, including at the Federal Administrative Court, could again be felt in the leniency of the 1970 verdict. New names now stood beneath the rulings of the military service senates; new judges bringing new ideas with them to the courts. With such a mild verdict, those judges now drew a clear line between what held official relevance and what had to remain private. Inconsequential sex games in one's own bedroom, even if they did raise eyebrows or unleash secret fantasies, were generally a private matter. The sexual revolution had changed minds, the judges' included – a process to which the verdict from Kempten regional court, which commuted an initial sentence of one year in prison without probation to a small fine, can attest. It was not the somewhat curious nature of the case at hand that proved the deciding factor but rather that, once again, the highest disciplinary court had ruled that non-crim-

---

99 BArch, Pers 12/45043, with references to the ruling at Kempten Local Court, 7 July 1969.

100 Rulings at Kempten Local Court on 18 September 1969 and Military Service Court D on 4 March 1970, mentioned in BVerwG, I WD 4/70: Federal Administrative Court, 1st Military Service Senate, decided 3 December 1970. Found on www.jurion.de.

101 BVerwG, I WD 4/70: Federal Administrative Court, 1st Military Service Senate, decided 3 December 1970.

102 Ibid.

inal homosexual activity or relationships pursued by soldiers outside the line of duty no longer constituted a violation. This principle was subsequently upheld by every ruling in administrative court.

b.) Private Is Private – or Is It?

The question of the day was how the line of duty should be demarcated. In taking disciplinary action, the necessary link to the official realm was obvious in the case of a soldier who had sexually molested or even assaulted another soldier, just as consensual sexual activity between soldiers while in a barracks continued to represent a violation of duty. The "defining criteria for the scope of duty should be whether a soldier is party to the homosexual activity."[103] But what was to be made of consensual sex between soldiers when it occurred fully in private, away from the barracks and after hours? A more recent legal report found that as of 2000 the Federal Administrative Court still had not settled the matter.[104] To give one concrete example of the issue at hand: Was it a breach of duty if two men met in one's apartment for sex, and it came out that both were soldiers during a cigarette afterwards?

There were no such doubts when it came to existing superior–subordinate relationships – in that case, sexual activity was punished as a breach of duty even when it was pursued in private, or outside barracks gates. Military service courts used a fine-edged ruler in doing so: Even an abstract relationship of subordination sufficed according to the directive governing superior–subordinate relations, a situation that led to officers and NCOs being reprimanded for sexual relationships with lower-ranking soldiers from other units but who were in their barracks. In individual instances, the possibility of soldiers from separately stationed battalions but the same regiment or brigade meeting during joint exercises was enough to establish a relationship of subordination in the eyes of the court. In 1980 for example, the 2nd Military Service Senate at the Federal Administrative Court upheld a verdict against two soldiers from different units within the same regiment who had met purely by chance and then had sex with each other; the ruling even referred to the two companies' being stationed 100 km away from each other.[105] It

---

103 BArch, BW 1/502107: Report from Doctor of Law Armin Steinkamm, Bundeswehr University Munich, 25 January 2000, here p. 2.
104 Ibid.
105 Federal Administrative Court, 2nd Military Service Senate, BVerwG, 2 WD 80/79, decided 2 September 1980. Found on www.jurion.de and mentioned in 1985 in Lindner, "Homosexuelle in der Institution Bundeswehr," 213. For a full account of the verdict, see chapter 3, section 8.c.

was necessary to establish a given act's ties to service in order to find it in breach of duty; the question of how to do so lay in the hands of the disciplinary courts, with judges given a great deal of discretionary authority. Over the course of the coming three decades, they came to interpret the line of duty more and more narrowly; conversely, more and more cases of private sexual activity escaped disciplinary sanction (or, as Bundeswehr lawyers liked to call it, "valuation").

Responding in 1979 to a query from Bundestag deputy Herta Däubler-Gmelin, the Ministry of Defense stressed that no special principles were brought to bear in the "disciplinary valuation" of homosexual activity compared with other sexual activity, with adultery cited as a concrete example.[106] Only in instances where that activity stood in close spatial or personal proximity to the line of duty, thus disrupting military order, could disciplinary action result. That was the case if the activity occurred within service quarters or on official property, the ministry continued, or if the other partner was a soldier or otherwise belonged to the Bundeswehr.[107] Considering the implications somewhat more carefully here, this (once again) classified consensual sex between two soldiers who did *not* know each other from service as a violation of duty. To take back up with the scenario, if during their cigarette the two men discovered that they both happened to be soldiers, both could attest to a violation. Yet here too, there was no judge without a plaintiff, and that included military service courts. Gay soldiers nonetheless remained uncertain as to whether they were committing a breach of duty or not in having sex with other soldiers, whether at home or elsewhere.

A G1 memo written by FüS I 4 put out in 1986 looked to bring some order to the chaos surrounding disciplinary action for sexual activities that soldiers engaged in off duty and outside the barracks. The proposal put to the chief of defense and Minister of Defense sought to regulate *all* issues pertaining to homosexuality, sketching concrete hypothetical cases to cover every situation conceivable. The section concerning disciplinary measures made any and all homosexual activity involving subordinates or lower-ranking soldiers a breach of duty, "regardless of whether it is performed on or off duty, in or outside of service quarters, and against their will or with their consent."[108] Note here the use of the term "lower-ranking" as opposed to subordinate, for instance. Under the somewhat complicated regulations governing superior–subordinate relations, a higher rank hardly means the soldier is also

---

106 BArch, BW 1/304284: BMVg, VR I 1, 15 February 1979, also BMVg, parliamentary state secretary to MdB Herta Däubler-Gmelin (SPD), 23 February 1979.
107 Ibid.
108 BArch, BW 2/31225: BMVg, FüS I 4 to the minister via the parliamentary state secretary, 22 October 1986, annex, identical to BArch, BW 2/31224: BMVg, FüS I 4, July 1986.

a superior. Yet a man in this position would also be guilty of violating his duty, at least in theory. Concretely, this would have meant that aside from the obvious case of sexual acts carried out against subordinates' will, a soldier would be guilty of a breach of duty if – to stay with the previous image – it had come out during "the cigarette after" consensual sex between men in one or the other's private residence that both were soldiers but held different ranks. Given the low probability that both men held the same rank, the great majority of these private, often chance encounters would fall under a breach of duty.

The BMVg draft also foresaw classifying homosexual activity between soldiers and/or the civilian staff of the Bundeswehr that "diminished respectability or trustworthiness" as a breach of duty not only when it occurred in service quarters, but while off duty and outside the barracks as well. While the specific meaning and interpretation of the clause was left open, the actual phrasing would have opened the door to prosecuting private sexual encounters between men who both happened to be in the military, even as civilian employees. Finally, in keeping with current ruling practice at military service courts, homosexual activity with "outsiders," or people without any connection to the Bundeswehr, would also have been regarded as a breach of duty if "committed in an offensive or – brought on by the particular circumstances – conspicuous manner."[109] That included all crimes under the criminal code. The draft was never put into practice, likely to the benefit of gay soldiers on these points at least. The new regulations would have resulted in any number of new potential violations. Instead, military service courts continued to operate on a case-by-case basis.

Consensual sex between soldiers, even while off duty, outside the barracks and involving soldiers from different units, continued to be classified as a breach of duty after 1970 when it involved an officer or NCO who had intercourse with a soldier he knew to be of lower rank. The Federal Administrative Court elaborated on this rule in 1980, using as an example the case of a sergeant first class who had been accused of having sex with a private from another barracks. The case also demonstrates that the line dividing sexual assault from consensual acts could not always be drawn free of doubt. Often, it was one word against another. Where did consensual sex end and assault begin? In 1979 this question, which holds renewed, or rather continued relevance today (in the "Me Too" movement, for example), stood at the center of the evidence heard against the sergeant.

---

109 Ibid.

c.)   A Mild Verdict against a First Sergeant from 1980

A first sergeant spent his 1978 summer vacation at home. One night on his way back from a club around 2 a.m., he met a private also dressed in civilian clothing who asked whether he was going to the barracks. The accused replied in the negative, but showed himself willing to take the private part of the way there. It is important to know in classifying the case that the two did not know each other from the line of duty, and had never met before. They served at different locations, but in the same regiment – a fact that would eventually prove relevant during sentencing. After a night spent consuming a significant amount of alcohol at the sergeant's apartment, the two wound up having sex when they woke up later that morning. The private left the sergeant's apartment around noon, not before enjoying another beer together. Back at the barracks he lay down to sleep, exhausted and hungover. His absence from service had not go unnoticed; he was woken by his superior informing him that he could expect disciplinary consequences for his conduct, which had drawn attention on multiple previous occasions.

Ordered before the battery commander, the private did not know how else to help his cause other than report on the morning's events in the sergeant's apartment – and to cast it as sexual assault, evidently in the hopes of greater leniency. His calculations were correct, initially at least; no disciplinary action was taken and instead the sergeant became the central focus. The sergeant was initially banned from showing up to service and later given provisional suspension, with half of his pay docked. The public prosecutor opened an investigation against him on suspicion of insult, bodily harm and sexual coercion, but discontinued proceedings in March 1979 when no evidence of criminal activity could be shown. The credibility of the lone witness in the case, the private, seemed too much in doubt to the prosecutor.[110]

With that the Bundeswehr might have filed the case away – if the disciplinary prosecutor for the military had not opted to proceed, that is. In September 1979, fourteen months after the incident in question, a military service court ruled the "behavior of which the soldier was accused in the inditement proven, considering it a willful violation of his duties to uphold respectability and trust outside the scope of duty (§17 (2) Clause 2 SG) and camaraderie (§12 SG), and thus a breach of

---

110 Nolle prosequi from the public prosecutor at Itzehoe Regional Court from 13 March 1979, mentioned in the 2nd Military Service Senate of the Federal Administrative Court, BVerwG, 2 WD 80/79, decided 2 September 1980.

duty (§23 (1) SG), committed under the increased liability of a soldier in the position of a superior (§10 (1) SG)."[111] The court found further that:

> due to their potentially grave consequences, homosexual acts by non-commissioned officers toward subordinates should be considered an especially grave form of misconduct. The associated loss in esteem and authority for the superior may be adverse to discipline and ultimately affect troops' operational readiness. [By acting in such a way] a superior puts himself in the hands of his subordinates in a certain sense, and may lose the independence and freedom necessary to act in roles of leadership.[112]

Given such a forceful opinion, the leniency of the verdict itself came as a surprise: a ten-percent reduction in salary for one year. The judges found that the first sergeant had never abused his position as a superior, nor was the private his subordinate. The sergeant also served in another location. Nothing harmful, in particular no loss in authority, had resulted in the line of duty. "The matter" had, it was true, become public knowledge within the officer corps, "but had not caused a sensation." What was more, "the incident" had not played out in a military installation but a private apartment.

When the military prosecutor appealed, the case landed before the 2nd Military Service Senate. The case files and appeals decision show the lengths to which the Munich judges went to clear up what had transpired in the sergeant's bed, practically dissecting the series of events. To make a long story short here, too, the judges did not believe the sergeant's testimony that the caresses had begun with the private, nor did they think much of the private's account that he had been forced into sex against his will. "The senate is convinced that the truth lies in between the two accounts [...] In the conviction of the senate, both sought sexual satisfaction by mutual agreement in this sense."[113]

Even if the case involved consensual sex outside both the confines of the barracks and a superior–subordinate relationship, it was clear to the senate that the sergeant had committed a breach of duty. The connection to the line of duty arose from the circumstance that the sexual partner was another soldier, a conscript, who may not have been in the same unit but was in the same regiment nonetheless.

> It casts serious doubt on the trustworthiness of a soldier in the position of a superior when he – be it with his partner's consent – engages in same-sex relations with another soldier.

---

111 Ruling by the 6th Division of Military Service Court North on 6 September 1979, cited in Federal Administrative Court, 2nd Military Service Senate, BVerwG, 2 WD 80/79, decided 2 September 1980.
112 Ibid.
113 Federal Administrative Court, 2nd Military Service Senate, BVerwG, 2 WD 80/79, decided 2 September 1980. A copy is available in BArch, BW 1/546379.

His superiors have no guarantee that he can be assigned to train young conscripts without one day looking for a similar kind of contact within the more immediate scope of his unit or subunit, thus provoking all the negative effects on troop discipline and cohesion.[114]

Still, the judges saw an array of mitigating factors in the case: The lack of a concrete superior–subordinate relationship for one, and especially their assumption that the sex had been consensual, contrary to the private's testimony. Complicating matters was "the particular intensity of the same-sex activity, such as rarely comes before military service senates as the subject of evaluation." They overruled the decision, increasing the sentence to a three-year ban on promotion.[115] The significance of the verdict beyond the case itself lay in concretizing the landmark 1970 decision as to how private and consensual homosexual acts between soldiers should be assessed in a disciplinary context, at least where officers and NCOs were involved. As a rule, they would continue to be seen as service violations.[116]

Postscript: After the state prosecutor halted his investigation, the first sergeant continued to serve as usual in his unit; a few weeks after the military service court's ruling he was formally recognized by his battery commander for exemplary performance of duty.[117]

d.) "A Deviation in Impulse under the Disinhibiting Effects of Alcohol"

Another sexual encounter from 1988, this time between a senior staff physician and a private first class during a stay on military training grounds, clearly was not a case of assault but a consensual act. The military prosecutor nonetheless spotted a serious breach of duty, both on account of the different service ranks as well as the site of sexual activity being within service quarters. They had also been observed by other soldiers, a classic case of being "caught in the act." Here it was not the deed itself that occupied the court's attention when it took evidence, which stood uncontested, but the task of differentiating between a "genuine" homosexual orientation and a mere "deviation" in feeling. What proved to be a clever defense strategy ended up shielding the senior staff surgeon from demotion. A first court did

---

114 Ibid.
115 Ibid.
116 The decision received mention as early as 1985 due to its fundamental significance in Lindner, "Homosexuelle in der Institution Bundeswehr," 213; later it was also mentioned in BW 1/546379 and BW 1/502107 in a report from Doctor of Law Armin Steinkamm, Bundeswehr University Munich, 25 January 2000.
117 As is mentioned in the later ruling by the military service senate.

initially demote the officer by one rank to staff surgeon. The judges considered it a mitigating factor that no direct superior–subordinate relationship existed between the soldiers but only one based on rank. Nor was the reservist private "some young conscript, but a grown man of thirty-two years who voluntarily and with his full approval got mixed up in homosexual activity with the [other] soldier."[118]

It was decisive for the judges that an expert psychological report had not detected a "marked tendency toward homosexuality" in the accused; "the homosexual actions could [instead] be traced back exclusively to a deviation in impulse under the disinhibiting effects of alcohol."[119]

The officer clearly had a good lawyer; in his grounds for appeal, the lawyer insisted that his client's same-sex activity was "not a serious breach of duty as he stood under the heavy influence of alcohol, and thus succumbed to a deviant impulse." The judges at the Federal Administrative Court concurred. First, however, the judges delved into the fundamentals, underscoring and upholding previous assessments of "homosexual misconduct by soldiers" that could not be tolerated within the line of duty.

> Troop cohesion would be severely disrupted if homosexual relationships between individual soldiers, with all their emotional implications, were to be tolerated. Homosexual activity between superiors and subordinates is all the more intolerable as it not only weakens the superior's authority but subordinates' readiness to obey [while also leaving] the superior susceptible to blackmail, which is inimical to performing one's official duties and coexisting within the ranks. It is for this reason that if a superior's personality is characterized by a tendency toward homosexuality and corresponding activity within the line of duty, removal from service must be the standard measure of punishment applied.[120]

Over the following ten years this excerpt was redeployed word for word in a multitude of statements by the federal government and its departments for defense and justice, serving consistently as confirmation by a supreme court of the restrictions that had been retained against homosexual superiors.[121] Yet at the time, the judges

---

118 Ruling by the 4th division of Military Service Court Center on 14 October 1987, cited in BVerwG, 2 WD 6/88: Federal Administrative Court, 2nd Military Service Senate, decided 7 June 1988. Found on www.jurion.de.

119 Ibid.

120 BVerwG, 2 WD 6/88: Federal Administrative Court, 2nd Military Service Senate, decided 7 June 1988.

121 See for example BArch, BW 2/31224: BMVg, VR I 5 to FüS I 4, 16 December 1992; BW 1/546379, BMJ, "Bericht für den Rechtausschuss des Bundestages zur Lage von Menschen mit gleichgeschlechtlicher Orientierung," 15 October 1997.

viewed the case in a different light, replacing the initial verdict of demotion with a more lenient sentence of a three-year ban on promotion.[122]

Soldiers who engaged in homosexual activity while on-duty or within military installations – in the present case on military training grounds – could thus hope for leniency from disciplinary judges, even in the event one was a superior and the other of lower rank. Yet those hopes were justified only if it was not a "genuine" homosexual tendency that was identified but merely a "deviant impulse," ideally under the influence of alcohol. A "deviant impulse" in a state of drunkenness existing as "substantial mitigating factor" is something that can only be found in the papers of the BMVg's legal division. "Cleansing measures," i.e. demotion in rank and removal from service, could be overlooked entirely even in the case of "insistent homosexual advances" if these came "merely" from "the disinhibiting effects of alcohol."[123]

The jurist Georg Schwalm had already explicitly pointed out the necessary legal distinction in the military between "real, i.e. fixed" and "false" homosexuality in 1970, as well as possible "impairments in the capacity to inhibit" homosexual activity, "e.g. alcohol consumption, prolonged isolation in a male community," which could provide grounds for mental incapacity in the legal sense.[124]

9. Sexual Assaults Perpetrated by Homosexual Soldiers

Records also reveal numerous cases of sexual assault by NCOs and officers against lower-ranking, largely younger soldiers. Public and media attention has focused almost entirely on women as the victims of sexual assault, with men, especially soldiers, finding close to no consideration as victims. To date, crimes of the sort seem to have remained entirely off the radar of the media, academic scholarship and the public.[125] The *New York Times* broke with the tradition in September 2019, reporting that some 100,000 men in the U.S. armed forces had experienced sexual assault in recent decades; in 2018 alone the number was close to 7,500 men. By comparison, that same year the Pentagon recorded 13,000 cases of female soldiers falling subject to sexual assault. The challenge facing both the investigating authorities

---

122 BVerwG, 2 WD 6/88: Federal Administrative Court, 2nd Military Service Senate, decided 7 June 1988.
123 BArch, BW 2/31224: BMVg, VR I 5 to FüS I 4, 16 December 1992.
124 Schwalm, "Die Streichung des Grundtatbestands," 88.
125 In 2018 Élise Féron cracked open the taboo with a groundbreaking study of sexual violence against men in war and civil war: Féron, *Wartime Sexual Violence against Men.*

and the statistics themselves was that only one in five male soldiers reported their assault.[126] According to the *New York Times* article, the Pentagon had first started gathering numbers about male victims of sexual assault in 2006; before then, the US Department of Defense had been certain it was exclusively an issue for women. Assaults either were not reported in the first place, or were not pursued.[127]

Within the Bundeswehr as well, court rulings and disciplinary action reveal more than a handful of isolated instances in which men fell victim to sexual assault, even sexually motivated violence, during their time as soldiers. These and similar cases were (and to this day remain) obviously punishable under disciplinary law and criminal law where applicable, independently of the question of homosexuality. In early January 2000, a paper put out by the Bundeswehr's personnel department once again reached the conclusion that homosexual activity should not be evaluated any differently than heterosexual activity in a disciplinary setting.[128] Sexual assault does not necessarily involve a purely sexual motivation; it can also serve as a demonstration, or rather an abuse of power. In what follows, several select examples from an alarmingly long list will be discussed.

> "Here, I'll show you." And before the witness knew it, the accused had removed his erect penis from his trousers. When the witness asked what exactly that was supposed to mean, the accused replied "Why don't you show me yours so we can compare them."[129]

The witness referred to here in the Rendsburg court's decision was a private first class, the accused a staff sergeant. When the private refused the sergeant's demands the latter insisted "Don't make such a fuss!" and grabbed between the soldier's legs at his genitals, at which point the soldier invented an excuse to leave the room. It came to light in conversation with another soldier that a different private had experienced a similar attempt by the same sergeant a week before, though he had quickly extracted himself from the situation. In its 1957 decision, the mixed bench in Rendsburg settled on a fine of 300 DM.[130] In subsequent disciplinary proceed-

---

126 The male victims, most younger than twenty-four, were of low military rank. According to the Pentagon, more than half of the assaults were committed by men. Quoting the original article from the *New York Times*, *Der Spiegel* reported 30% of the men stating that the perpetrators had been female, while 13% of the cases had involved multiple perpetrators of both sexes. For the article in *Der Spiegel* see "'New York Times': Zehntausende Männer im US-Militär sollen Opfer sexueller Übergriffe geworden sein." The original article came under the headline "More than 100,000 men have been sexually assaulted."
127 Phillips, "More than 100,000 men have been sexually assaulted."
128 BArch, BW 1/502107, no pagination, BMVg, PSZ III 1, 5 January 2000.
129 BArch, Pers 12/45377: Ruling at Rendsburg Court on 22 November 1957.
130 Ibid.

ings, the military service court in Kiel ruled that the sergeant be removed from service.[131] In 1959, the military service senate at the Federal Disciplinary Court denied the appeal of the accused.[132]

That same year the Federal Disciplinary Court had also denied a senior NCO's appeal against an initial court ruling to remove him from service. A mixed bench court in Hamburg found that the accused had either touched or attempted to touch the genitalia of five different soldiers under his command, in some cases repeatedly, and sentenced him to a total of nine months in prison on five criminal counts under §174 StGB in conjunction with a misdemeanor under §175 StGB. Military Service Court C subsequently ordered the NCO's removal from service based on the findings in criminal court. "The Bundeswehr has to guarantee the public that every effort is being made to protect young soldiers from harassment and seductions of this sort. The Bundeswehr also holds a responsibility toward the parents of young soldiers in this regard, especially conscripts."[133]

A court ruling against a staff sergeant from 1961 reads similarly. The sergeant had repeatedly kissed a young conscript, "partly with his tongue," and "tried in vain to perform anal intercourse on him." A week later he exhibited the same behavior toward another young soldier. The mixed bench sentenced the accused to three months in prison. When the public prosecutor's office appealed, the superior criminal division at regional court raised the sentence to a total of five months in prison for two counts of treating a subordinate in a degrading manner, one in conjunction with illicit sexual acts between men. The sentence was suspended on probation. Meanwhile, the military service court ordered the defendant's removal from service, granting him 50 percent of his pension for one year. When the military prosecutor appealed, the court's decision was modified so that the entire allowance fell by the wayside.[134]

Sources also document a serious case from 1962 in Flensburg. A naval commander and the head of a ship was accused of three attempts of aggravated illicit sexual acts, the majority with soldiers under his command, and three further counts of completed illicit sex. The commander was taken into temporary custody,

---

131 BArch, Pers 12/45377: Military Service Court A, 1st Division, decided 20 June 1958.

132 Ibid., Military Service Senate at the Federal Disciplinary Court, WD 12/58, decided 28 January 1959.

133 BVerwG, WD 5/59: Federal Disciplinary Court, Military Service Senate, ruling on 11 March 1959, referring to and quoting from the initial court ruling at the 1st Division of Military Service Court C on 16 December 1958. Found on www.jurion.de.

134 BVerwG, WD 8/62: Federal Disciplinary Court, Military Service Senate, ruling on 9 May 1962, referring to and quoting from the initial court ruling at Military Service Court C on 15 November 1961. Found on www.jurion.de.

which changed the following day to detention awaiting trial. The regional commander concurred with the state prosecutor's office in Flensburg that "in order to protect the reputation of the Bundeswehr," only a brief press report should be released, reading "On 28 August 1962 an officer stationed in Flensburg was arrested on suspicion of crimes against §175 and 175a StGB." The high rank of the accused (something that could not be gleaned from the skimpy press report) brought the case to the attention of the Kiel state chancellery via the lead attorney general and the ministry of justice.[135] The BMVg opened investigations under disciplinary law in November 1962, with the ongoing criminal investigation taking precedence.[136] In April 1962 Flensburg Regional Court sentenced the ship commander to a term of one year in prison.[137] With the sentence the staff officer automatically lost his status as a career soldier, his service rank and his entitlement to a pension, and disciplinary proceedings were suspended.[138]

The sheer number of cases in which the military service senates went beyond initial court rulings also merits attention, as with proceedings in 1964 against a captain: Brought in on two counts of attempted advances against soldiers in his company, the captain was initially given a very lenient sentence of an eighteen-month reduction in pay by one-tenth by the military service court in Kiel. On two separate occasions after an evening spent drinking together in his private apartment the officer had grown insistent, looking to caress and kiss the soldiers. Both times the soldiers had quickly left the apartment, before going on to report the incident. A third instance came to light in the course of the investigation. The military judges did not mince words in their ruling: "An officer and career soldier who draws suspicion from young soldiers, and gossip about holding homosexual tendencies and having made advances in that direction, deserves a punishment suitable to have a lasting deterrent effect."[139]

The judges opted nonetheless for mild disciplinary action. A real homosexual tendency could not be demonstrated. What was more, the captain had been blocked by the ongoing disciplinary proceedings from repeating a staff officer's course he had failed once before, and was already facing an early end to his time in the service. The senior public prosecutor's office in Kiel ultimately rejected the facts of the case, classifying the advances as an insult and ordering the captain to pay a

---

135 BArch, BW 1/12609: Commander of Territorial Defense Staff I A Flensburg, Az 13-00-21, 29 August 1962, Special Incident: Here the arrest of FKpt [...], first interim report.

136 BArch, BW 1/12609: BMVg, P III 5-H, H 313/62, from 29 November 1962.

137 BArch, BW 1/12609: Ruling at Flensburg Regional Court, Az 6 KLE 2/62 (I 1475/62), 3 April 1963.

138 BArch, BW 1/12609: BMVg, P III 5-H, 18 October 1963.

139 BArch, Pers 12/45631: Ruling at Military Service Court A, 1st Division, 11 June 1964.

fine of 100 DM. While the military prosecutor may have been helpless against the forbearance shown by the public prosecutor, he was still able to appeal the leniency shown in military court. The military service senate repealed the first court's decision in a harsh critique, ordering immediate removal from service.[140]

A petty officer first class was dismissed under similar circumstances when he became sexually aggressive toward a petty officer second class enrolled in a course he was overseeing. One night around 11 p.m., as the course participant lay awake in bed, the officer had entered his room under the influence of alcohol and touched the student directly on his genitals. He then invited him to come have a beer or two in his room, where the two proceeded to have oral intercourse. The events did not remain under the cover of night; the chief of inspection struck up a disciplinary investigation and passed the case on to the public prosecutor's office. Niebüll local court sentenced the first class petty officer to one month arrest for illicit acts with a man under §175 StGB, which was suspended in return for a fine of 400 DM. The court acquitted the officer of the more serious charges of sexual coercion and abusing a relationship of dependency under §175a StGB. While a direct relationship between superior and subordinate did exist, it had not mattered to the student at the time of the offense. "To him what mattered was that he would get a bottle of beer." The student also admitted to letting himself enjoy the "illicit acts."[141]

Disciplinary action followed after the criminal case, resulting in the petty officer's removal from service. The judges deemed it particularly serious that the accused "took the sailor's genitals in his mouth." The military had to heed "cleanliness in the moral realm, not simply among soldiers per se," but especially from higher-ranking soldiers in positions of leadership where subordinates were involved. The loss of confidence in the petty officer weighed so heavily that it was unreasonable for him to continue in service.[142]

A case against a staff sergeant from 1966 also resulted in a harsher verdict at the military service senate than the first court. Between 1963 and 1964 the officer had on three separate occasions grabbed the genitals of rank-and-file soldiers. The judges grounded their decision in clear and basic terms: "Both the military itself as well as the general public must under all circumstances be able to rely on the fact that longer-serving soldiers will not assault young conscripts in a homosexual manner."[143] The final attempt ended with a private and another soldier setting

140 BArch, Pers 12/45631: Ruling at 2nd Military Service Senate at the Federal Disciplinary Court, II (I), WD 125/64 on 9 March 1965.

141 BArch, Pers 12/45897: Ruling at Niebüll Local Court on 26 June 1967.

142 Ibid., Ruling at Military Service Court A., 1st Division on 16 November 1967.

143 BVerwG, II WD 19/66: Federal Disciplinary Court, 2nd Military Service Senate ruling on 26 July

about the staff sergeant with their fists and locking him in his room. A mixed bench in Neuburg (Donau) granted the two soldiers acquittal during main proceedings. The court then ordered the sergeant to pay a fine of 210 DM for the "continuing offense of physical insult." Remarkably, the criminal court denied that the elements for a crime had been satisfied either under §175 or §175a. The elements of §175a Number 2 StGB required that "the perpetrator uses a relationship of dependency to induce another person to perform or tolerate illicit sexual acts." On its own, the existence of a relationship of dependency between the parties to the offense would not necessarily lead to such a situation arising. Nor did the Neuburg jurors' find "any sort of pressure present whatsoever." In main proceedings the military service court halved the amount of time that the staff sergeant, since departed regularly from the armed forces, was entitled to a transitional allowance. The court did, however, let him keep his rank and thus his position as a superior, unlike many other cases. Evidently the judges did not see the accused as having a "genuine" same-sex orientation; the staff sergeant successfully referenced his marriage and five children in contending that he could not be homosexual. All the leniency was too much for the military prosecutor. The sentence was increased upon appeal and the reservist staff sergeant was demoted to private first class.[144]

At times, judges' method of measuring specific sexual acts in their time and place against the provisions governing superior–subordinate relationships could lead to curious phrases, as when finding that a staff sergeant "was not the superior of former Medical Orderly S. at the time he was masturbating in front of him."[145] This sentence came down as part of a 1987 decision by Military Service Court South against a sergeant arraigned on five counts of sexual assault against soldiers in his company. After hearing detailed evidence, the judges acquitted the accused on three of five counts. They considered the other two counts proven and demoted the staff sergeant by one rank. Civilian proceedings in the same matter had already

---

1966, referring to court rulings at Neuburg (Donau) on 26 January 1965 and Military Service Court D on 29 November 1965. Found on www.jurion.de. Practically the same wording can be found in the ruling at the 2nd Division of Military Service Court C on 10 July 1968 as cited in BVerwG, I WD 54/68: Federal Administrative Court, 1st Military Service Senate, decided 12 February 1969, supplemented with the warning that such acts would not have a "lasting influence" on the "moral development" of conscripts. Found on www.jurion.de.

144 BVerwG, II WD 19/66: Federal Disciplinary Court, 2nd Military Service Senate, ruling on 26 July 1966, referring to court rulings at Neuburg (Donau) on 26 January 1965 and Military Service Court D on 29 November 1965. Found on www.jurion.de.

145 Ruling at the 4th Division of Military Service Court South on 9 July 1987, cited in BVerwG, 2 WD 69/87: Federal Administrative Court, 2nd Military Service Senate, decided 11 November 1988. Found on www.jurion.de.

been suspended on the condition the defendant pay a fine of 500 DM. The service court judges based the relative leniency of their ruling on the "considerable time" that had elapsed since the offenses were committed; a "favorable social prognosis due to familial relations being reestablished"; and, as cited above, the absence of a specific superior–subordinate relationship at the time of either offense. Given that the offense had not since been spoken about in the line of duty, "a court disciplinary measure of reduction to the rank of sergeant it is essential, but also sufficient, taking into account a general preventative perspective on disciplining violations of duty."[146]

The military prosecutor appealed with the aim of having the staff sergeant removed from service, and succeeded. The military service senate discussed the allegations anew, with an attention to detail that is rarely on display in similar rulings. Yet the judges also identified mitigating factors; the accused was married and had never drawn attention to himself before "in a homosexual respect."

> It had to be assumed in favor of the soldier therefore that his willingness to engage in same-sex activity existed only in latent form and, at least in part, only appeared as a deviant impulse under the influence of alcohol. Yet a disposition of this sort is more easily controlled than a genuine inclination toward homosexuality, and generally allows for more favorable future prognosis.[147]

Still, in determining the scope of disciplinary action, the judges found themselves faced with a formal legal issue.

> In light of the significant extenuating circumstances surrounding the offense itself, removal from service would not have been a foregone conclusion. The cleansing measure of demotion in rank would, however, have been unavoidable. Yet the demotion in rank from staff sergeant to sergeant imposed by the military service division was inappropriate to the nature and severity of the violation. The senate no longer considers the soldier fit to remain a superior in the rank of senior non-commissioned officer. If, however, a senior non-commissioned officer's reduction to the rank of enlisted soldier or even non-commissioned officer is appropriate to the nature and severity of such violation, it can only lead to removal from service if it involves a career soldier who may only be demoted to sergeant (§57 (1) Clause 1, WDO [Military Disciplinary Code].[148]

---

146 Ibid.
147 Ibid.
148 Ibid.

In short, the staff sergeant fell victim to the traps and snares of disciplinary law. The special clause in the Military Disciplinary Code left the judges with no option but to order his removal from service.

a.) Parallels to Rulings in Imperial Navy Courts of Honor

As with the Bundeswehr, consensual sex between superiors and subordinates in the Imperial Navy constituted both a breach of official duty as well as a criminal act under §175. The federal archives house court of honor documents from Baltic Navy command, for example, including one 1883 ruling against a lieutenant in the navy released from service for "crimes against morality and illicit acts" with subordinates from the officer corps.[149] Ten years later, records show a decision reached against a lieutenant commander for "illicit sexual acts against nature" with a cadet: "Dismissal without adornment/without honorable farewell."[150] The sources withhold comment on whether the case involved consensual sex or sexual assault, though it was ultimately of little importance anyway, as both were punishable and insulting forms of conduct.

In 1904 a court of honor admonished a lieutenant after he had drunkenly ordered an NCO to his room then commanded him to let his pants down and show his genitals.[151] The officer got off with an extremely light punishment, managing to credibly present a case that he did not harbor any homosexual ambitions and had merely wanted to inspect the NCO for possible venereal diseases. An additional, and likely deciding factor assisting him before the court was his drunkenness at the time of the offense. In this case, the judges overlooked the fact that the defense strategy lacked internal cohesive force on this point – an uninhibited state of drunkenness hardly aligns with a circumspect, solicitous intention to prevent the spread of venereal disease. The latter was likely merely an assertion made to shield himself, albeit one which was then believed. The important point was that the officer was not a "homosexual by inclination." Bundeswehr service court judges would in all likelihood have come to a similar decision.

---

149 BArch, RM 31/1857, Baltic Sea Naval Station [of the Imperial Navy], Headquarters, ruling of the court of honor from 3 August 1883. The author would like to thank Commander Dr. Christian Jentzsch of the ZMSBw for directing him to this source. For a fuller account of courts of honor, see Jentzsch, *Vom Kadetten bis zum Admiral*.
150 BArch, RM 31/1857, Court of honor ruling from 4 November 1893.
151 BArch, RM 31/1857, Court of honor ruling from 26 January 1904.

b.) Disciplinary Action after Acquittal in Criminal Proceedings

Sources also record many instances in which soldiers are found guilty of homosexual activity by a military service senate after first being acquitted on the same charge in criminal court. This does not mean that the senate decisions were erroneous, however. Criminal proceedings hold different legal interests than disciplinary proceedings. The same matter might be unthinkable for punishment under criminal law and still represent a violation of duty, a situation that was not always easy to communicate to the parties involved.

Such was the case with a staff sergeant who had been an officer cadet for a time in the mid Sixties. Acquitted in three instances of "committing illicit sexual acts with a man" by a first criminal court, a second court then acquitted him of the final remaining count on appeal. He was charged in every instance with having touched fellow soldiers on their genitals with sexual intent, at times unclothed while in the bathroom or washroom, at others above their uniform trousers. The soldiers put up resistance in every case, one with the words that the accused "probably didn't have enough going on with girls." A mixed bench found that none of the acts of lesser duration and intensity met the elements of a crime under §175, leaving only "an attempt at illicit sexual acts under §175 StGB, which is not punishable." The staff sergeant petitioned for release from the Bundeswehr even before appeal proceedings (and acquittal) at regional court. A military service court found the now reservist sergeant guilty of deliberate breach of duty on all counts, but did not consider demotion a fit measure and suspended the process. The decision was subsequently overruled at the Federal Disciplinary Court when the military prosecutor appealed and the sergeant was demoted to the rank of private first class.[152]

To clear up any potential false impressions: It was not officers and non-commissioned officers alone who appeared before disciplinary judges for infractions related to homosexuality. Enlisted soldiers showed up as well, as for example in 1966 with a private and NCO candidate for repeatedly attempting to touch fellow soldiers' genitals, whether in the bathroom or through the flies in their uniforms. The soldiers had repelled his advances in every instance. After a first criminal court partially acquitted him, his appeal at regional court cleared him of attempted aggravated same-sex acts when a "will to seduce [was] not demonstrated." Nor were the elements of a crime under §175 StGB "present, as in every instance the accused was immediately pushed away by the two witnesses, and attempts at illicit same-

---

152 BVerwG, II WD 8/66: Federal Disciplinary Court, 2nd Military Service Senate, ruling on 21 April 1966, referring to rulings at K. court on 10 October 1963, K. regional court on 1 October 1964 and Military Service Court E on 20 September 1965. Found on www.jurion.de.

sex activity do not stand under threat of punishment."[153] For its part, the military service court considered the established behavior "defamatory and morally objectionable" and held the accused "guilty of having violated his duty to respectable behavior (§17 (2) SG) and camaraderie (§12 SG)." The disciplinary judges viewed it as an aggravating circumstance under §10 (1) SG that in one case the private had been the ranking officer among all the soldiers in his unit as the NCO on duty. The court demoted the private, who had already been reduced to a rank-and-file career track and departed from the military regularly after completing his two-year service obligation, to an airman in the reserve.[154]

As a side note, the court took note of the fact that the former soldier was due to marry a few days after his trial in the service senate. In reviewing the personal circumstances of the accused, which always precede court rulings, it is striking that the vast majority of cases involve men who are married and often fathers already, or who get engaged and start planning for marriage shortly before the proceedings. As discussed in chapter 2, marriage represented a common path to escape the stigmatization of homosexuality, not merely for homosexual soldiers but any number of people of same-sex orientation in society at large.

c.) Drunkenness as a Mitigating Factor

Numerous other rulings at military service courts reveal that being under the influence of alcohol was generally viewed as a mitigating circumstance during sentencing, with the serious charge of homosexual activity often dismissed in favor of the much less serious charge of full intoxication. One decision from 1962 underscores the point in exemplary fashion. Drunk from his visit to a bar that night, a staff sergeant drove his own car back to the barracks, a private from his unit in the passenger seat. When the private nodded off to sleep, the NCO opened his fly and played with his exposed genitals. "After [Private] F. woke up and pushed the accused away, [the accused] continued driving, but shortly before the Bundeswehr barracks stopped again and tried to open the fly of the sleeping [private]. The private now energetically resisted the harassment from the accused, upon which the latter drove into the barracks."[155]

---

153 BVerwG, II WD 27/66: Federal Disciplinary Court, 2nd Military Service Senate, ruling on 13 December 1966, referring to the rulings at P. court on 15 July 1965 as well as Military Service Court B on 13 April 1966. Found on www.jurion.de.
154 Ibid.
155 BVerwG, II WD 35/63: Federal Disciplinary Court, 2nd Military Service Senate, ruling on 14 Oc-

For his actions, a regional court initially sentenced the accused "to three weeks in prison and two weeks' arrest" for crimes under §175 StGB and misdemeanors under vehicle licensing regulations as well as traffic law.[156] On 14 December 1962, the military service court demoted the staff sergeant to plain sergeant, a ruling with which the military service senate would take issue during appeal proceedings two years later. As in so many other cases, the first verdict interpreted the defendant's drunkenness in his favor; it was what "explained" the sergeant's assault on the sleeping private and precluded "genuine" homosexuality. This interpretation led the service court to an astonishingly light sentence which left the accused in the rank of sergeant and non-commissioned officer, and thus in a supervisory role. In a word, being drunk at the wheel was regarded as a much less serious infraction than a "genuine" homosexual disposition. A short while later the demoted sergeant let himself go again, drawing two further accusations of attempted sexual advances on other sergeants. This time the military service court demoted him to private first class.[157] The Federal Disciplinary Court later rejected the military prosecutor's appeal against what he considered to be overly lenient decisions in the first instance.

Substantial alcohol consumption subsequently "spared" many soldiers their departure from the armed forces, again in spite of sex offenses against lower-ranking soldiers directly within their official orbit. This was the case with another staff sergeant in 1967: On two separate occasions after a party with other soldiers, the NCO entered a private's room later that night as the private lay in bed, took hold of his penis and fumbled with it. Other soldiers took note and reported the incident. A disciplinary investigation was opened and the NCO's superiors passed the case on to the public prosecutor's office; the elements for a crime under §175 and §175a may have been met, after all. Yet for the mixed bench in Wuppertal, the drunkenness of the accused put sentencing him under §175 out of the question even if those elements had been satisfied. Instead, the court ordered him either to a pay a fine or spend thirty days in prison for full intoxication.[158] The accused's drunkenness was similarly viewed as a mitigating circumstance during proceedings at the military service court, which imposed the least reduction in rank possible, to plain sergeant. This was feasible because the judges did not see any evidence for the accused

tober 1964, referring to the initial ruling at the military service court on 14 December 1962. Found on www.jurion.de.

156 Ibid.

157 Ibid., with references to the later ruling by the military service court on 27 January 1964.

158 BVerwG, II WD 39/68: BVerwG, 2nd Military Service Senate, ruling on 5 December 1968, with references to the court decision in Wuppertal on 2 February 1968 as well as Military Service Court E on 24 July 1968. Found on www.jurion.de.

actually holding same-sex tendencies. Had this not been the case the staff sergeant would not have been able to reckon with clemency at all, as shown by numerous other rulings. Yet the decision was too lenient for the military prosecutor. On his appeal the service senate demoted the sergeant a further rank to private first class, although not on account of his possible homosexuality ("the accused has not previously appeared in a homosexual context") but his "intemperate drinking."[159]

Cologne local court heard a case that was similar down to many details the year before, in 1966. After a night of drinking a staff sergeant had entered the enlisted soldiers' quarters, laid down in bed next to a sleeping private and agitated the man's penis – until the private woke up that is, and put an "energetic" end to the business. The judges in Cologne had their doubts as to whether the staff sergeant had been fully intoxicated, but applied the principle of *in dubio pro reo*, sentencing him for full intoxication under §330a StGB instead of §175 and issuing a fine of 300 DM.[160] The Bundeswehr judiciary concurred with the local court's assessment – the accused had "never drawn attention in this context," leading the court to assume not a drive toward homosexuality but "one-time misconduct that was out of character." The service court demoted the sergeant to private first class.[161]

Drunkenness similarly demolished a sergeant's inhibitions one Monday evening in October 1979, while eventually also bringing him a lenient sentence. The judge ruled out any homosexual ambitions on the part of the accused, who in his intoxication had merely "given a bad impression of seeking same-sex satisfaction from subordinates."[162] Weighing heavily against the sergeant was a culpable violation of the duty to behave in a respectable and trustworthy manner, brought on by excessive alcohol consumption. Weighing in his favor the judges saw a "certain lack of contact" and "frailty"; this and other problems "may be wrapped up with each other in an inextricable knot of cause and effect." In the end the judges showed a great, even startling degree of clemency, banning the sergeant's eligibility for promotion for two and a half years and reducing his pay by one-twentieth for a year but not demoting him. The sergeant had already been transferred to another company by the time proceedings began. He was most likely pleased with the mild sentence, and neither side appealed.[163]

A staff sergeant also got off lightly in a case from 1987. One night the sergeant had assaulted a nonrated soldier from his platoon while in his lodgings, using phys-

---

159 Ibid.
160 BArch, Pers 12/45828: Ruling at Cologne Local Court on 4 March 1966.
161 Ibid. Military Service Court A, Division 1a, decided 17 August 1966.
162 BArch, Pers 12/45309: Military Service Court Center, 5th Division, decided 26 June 1980.
163 Ibid.

ical force to make him engage in passive oral intercourse and demanding that the gunner also engage in active oral intercourse. The soldier managed to free himself from the sergeant's grasp and flee. The military service court merely demoted the staff sergeant to plain sergeant. A similar incident would doubtless incur much more severe disciplinary action by today's standards; it is doubtful whether the ranking officer would be able to remain in service. Not so in 1987. The service court saw "no cause" "to assume a tendency toward homosexuality as marking the personality of a soldier who has not previously drawn attention in a homosexual respect, and thus to raise the question of his removal from service."[164] Here too, the judges proceeded under the premise that it was merely a "deviant impulse" brought on by alcohol, leading them to the conclusion that "despite serious homosexual activity against the will of the witness," the staff sergeant was still tenable as a senior NCO.[165]

It casts serious doubt on the trustworthiness of a soldier in a position of leadership when he engages in same-sex activity with another soldier in military installations, even if with the latter's consent. Behavior of this sort between a superior and a subordinate is liable to create a relationship of dependency that is not merely injurious to discipline but leaves the superior susceptible to blackmail. Common soldiers, who as a general rule are required to live in barracks, must also not be exposed to the risk of being made an object of sexual desire against their will by their superiors.[166] These unambiguous, basic phrases could be found in an appeals decision taken against a sergeant first class in 1990.

Three years earlier (such was the length of the disciplinary proceedings), the sergeant had had sexual intercourse with a nonrated soldier at his service post. One evening he and the private had emptied a bottle of vodka; the local court ruling then reads that the sergeant performed anal intercourse on the private without a condom. The private later disclosed what had happened to a comrade, and reported to the medical station. The private's disclosure turned into an investigation on charges of sexual abuse of those incapable to resist (§179 StGB). At the start of work the next day police led the sergeant away in handcuffs. The chief had the soldiers line up then, visibly affected, informed them of what had happened. Among the soldiers there circulated a rumor that the sergeant had either offered

---

164 Decision of the 8th Division of Military Service Court North on 18 August 1987, cited in BVerwG, 2 WD 63/67: Federal Administrative Court, 2nd Military Service Senate, decided 8 June 1988. A copy is available in BArch, BW 1/531591.
165 Ibid.
166 BArch, BW 1/531592: Ruling at the 8th Division of Military Service Court Center on 8 October 1990, cited in BVerwG, 2 WD 5/91: Federal Administrative Court, 2nd Military Service Senate, decided 30 July 1991.

the private money for sex or paid him.[167] In 1988 local court cleared the sergeant of charges under §179 StGB when they could not be substantiated beyond doubt.[168]

The military prosecutor continued with his investigation, and in 1990 the case came before military service court. In the proceedings the judges were bound to the sergeant's acquittal from the criminal trial; German jurists speak of a *Sperr-wirkung*, a ban that only allows subsequent disciplinary proceedings to consider facts that do not fulfill the elements of a criminal act. Among other things, it meant the charge of anal intercourse against the private's will could no longer be considered in reaching a verdict. While the judges still concluded that a serious violation of duty had occurred, a "series of mitigating factors," the accused's considerable intake of alcohol chief among them, meant they could look past a demotion in rank. In the end a near two-year ban was placed on the sergeant's promotion.[169] In this case as well, the judges saw drunkenness as an exonerating circumstance.

The military prosecutor appealed the ruling. Going by the current case law in the military service court, the accused should have been removed from service, but at the very least demoted. In light of "such weighty and intensive homosexual activity" the soldier could not be "credited" with an alcohol-induced lack of inhibition, all the more so as the private himself had not taken any sort of initiative toward homosexual activity.[170] (Note here the revealing use of alcohol consumption as a "credit.")

Yet the military service senate too recognized a series of extenuating circumstances in favor of the accused, the most important being an expert report that had been unable to determine any "homosexual tendency" in the accused. "The soldier's homosexual activity sprang instead from a deviant impulse under the dis-inhibiting effects of alcohol," and should consequently be seen as a "slip-up." The sergeant had also not "proceeded in brutal fashion," which meant "no instance of 'rape' was present." By today's standards, the court's assessment and formulations appear as incomprehensible as the mild disciplinary measures. "Having considered all the incriminating and exonerating factors, the senate was of the opinion that the

---

167 Interview with H., Bruck an der Großglocknerstraße, 2 August 2018. H. was a soldier in the unit at the time.
168 BArch, BW 1/531592: Ruling at L. Local Court on 6 June 1988, cited in BVerwG, 2 WD 5/91: Federal Administrative Court, 2nd Military Service Senate, decided 30 July 1991.
169 BArch, BW 1/531592: Ruling at the 8th Division of Military Service Court Center on 8 October 1990, cited in BVerwG, 2 WD 5/91: Federal Administrative Court, 2nd Military Service Senate, decided 30 July 1991.
170 BArch, BW 1/531592, Military prosecutor grounds for appeal, cited in BVerwG, 2 WD 5/91: Federal Administrative Court, 2nd Military Service Senate, decided 30 July 1991.

soldier, despite certain concerns, should be allowed to remain in the service rank group of senior NCO. As such, demotion to plain sergeant was appropriate."[171]

Recall that what was being tried in this instance was homosexual intercourse performed on a rank-and-file soldier and direct subordinate against the soldier's will, or at least without his consent. For the soldier who had been penetrated involuntarily, it must have been totally irrelevant whether his superior was a "genuine" homosexual or had abused him out of a "deviant impulse" under the influence of alcohol. Yet the disciplinary judges' were not primarily concerned with redress for a victim of sexual assault. Rather, they were taken up almost exclusively with maintaining troop order and discipline. In their eyes, a perpetrator who purported to be "merely" "stray" or drunken posed a significantly smaller risk to troops than if he showed a "genuine" inclination toward homosexuality. At the same time, the leniency shown to casual offenders – ideally operating under the influence of alcohol – that crops up repeatedly in disciplinary court rulings lacks internal logic. Even given the interest in maintaining troop order and discipline, intoxicated, "stray" instances of sexual assault against soldiers posed no less of a risk than if those same acts were committed by "genuine homosexuals." Someone who had harassed or assaulted others, even if he did so while drunk, could still become a repeat offender. Under sober consideration, it even seems quite a bit more likely that a person who gravitates toward excessive alcohol consumption will on more than a single occasion lose control over themselves and their "feelings" and come to harass or attack other soldiers. Yet almost without fail, the Bundeswehr jurists reserved their harshest disciplinary measures for offenders who had been identified as "genuine" homosexuals.

The verdict against the sergeant first class found its way into the press, where it came in for harsh criticism. "Love between men jeopardizes the Bundeswehr: BVG upholds a verdict against anal intercourse in service," read one headline in *taz*.[172] In June 1992 *Berliner Tageszeitung* reported in tabloid fashion: "Sex verdict from administrative court: Soldiers can't love men." Yet the editors evidently could not decide what to decry, the verdict or the act itself. The judges determined that rape had not occurred "because the subordinate was not will-less," even if it was due to alcohol and fatigue that he had not resisted anal intercourse. The paper found the sergeant had "gotten off lightly," only being demoted to plain sergeant. The "dis-

---

171 BArch, BW 1/531592, BVerwG, 2 WD 5/91: Federal Administrative Court, 2nd Military Service Senate, decided 30 July 1991, extensively quoted and commented on in *Neue Zeitschrift für Wehrrecht*, 2/1992, 78–79.

172 "Männerliebe gefährdet die Bundeswehr," cited in Schwartz, *Homosexuelle, Seilschaften, Verrat*.

inhibiting effects of alcohol" had proved decisive in court, as had the sergeant's "above-average service" and "clean record to date."[173] The paper took up the ruling a second time in an opinion column entitled "Bundeswehr = Middle Ages?" that contained a diatribe against the armed forces. All people were equal the column noted, although this principle clearly did not apply in the Bundeswehr. There was no other way to make sense of the verdict "against love between men."

> If a private loves a female medic, nothing happens. If a major sleeps with his secretary, nothing happens. If a captain finds his delight in a female army physician then again, nothing happens. But when a homosexual first sergeant has sex with a subordinate, he's tossed out of the army dishonorably, or at least demoted. Like in the Middle Ages. Does the army really need this sort of gay-bashing? Aren't we finally in a position to at least tolerate minorities?[174]

What was being tried and decided on again here? Sexual intercourse performed on a rank-and-file soldier and direct subordinate against the soldier's will, or at least without his consent. The commentary in the *Berliner Tageszeitung* leaves a very strange impression if one keeps the crime front and center. As justified as concerns about ending restrictions on gays in the army may have been, they were just as out of place in this setting; the editors chose the wrong case from which to launch a moral inditement of the Bundeswehr. It made (and continues to make) a large difference whether a private loves a female medic or a superior assails his subordinate and, as in the present case, at the very least physically penetrates him without his consent – rapes him, in other words. In 2022, the instance would be subject to disciplinary punishment as a matter of course, potentially criminal punishment. It was not that the offender, which is what the sergeant must now be designated, fell victim to the Bundeswehr's rumored homophobia – on the contrary, he got off "lightly," as the paper noted rightly. The disciplinary judges sought out anything and everything that spoke in favor of his exoneration, found it, and added it to the scales. Taking the sergeant's punishment as evidence for "gay bashing" and "medievalism" on the part of the Bundeswehr fully missed the mark.

The miraculous, exonerating side-effects of alcohol were not limited only to trials conducted against soldiers; other academic research has come to similar conclusions.[175] Excessive alcohol consumption did not provide *carte blanche* in every case, however. Service court judges were capable of reaching other, harsher verdicts as well.

---

173 "Soldaten dürfen keine Männer lieben."
174 Küthe, "Bundeswehr = Mittelalter."
175 Bormuth, *"Ein Mann, der mit einem anderen Mann Unzucht treibt,"* 51.

In 1980 a lawyer claimed drunkenness in defending a staff sergeant against six counts of attempted sexual assault before the central service court in Koblenz. The nocturnal attacks against the subordinate soldiers in question already lay years in the past. The soldiers had resisted the sergeant's advances down to the last, with one private threatening that he and his buddies would "give him what he needed when the time came."[176] In November 1976, the same private reported the attack to an on-duty NCO; the ensuing investigation unearthed an entire series of similar but unreported incidents reaching back to 1973. The soldiers explained their silence either with reference to a good working relationship with the accused, or fears of damaging an application to become an NCO.

The case highlights what is likely the large number of sexual assaults against soldiers that have gone unreported and unpunished, whether out of a mistaken understanding of camaraderie, fear of reprisal or threats by a ranking officer. Only one in every five soldiers reports their assault.[177] In the case of the staff sergeant, the disciplinary investigation uncovered multiple false official reports, financial irregularities and one especially curious incident: One night around midnight while at a discotheque, the sergeant had promoted two pilots in his unit to privates, doing so without any legal basis and what was more while in West Berlin, where the Bundeswehr did not exist at the time due to the Allied right of control. (The accused did not let it rest with the midnight disco ceremony, but registered it in their military ID cards with his signature.) The military service court punished the long list of violations, including sexual assault, with removal from service.

Prior alcohol consumption was not enough either to dispose the judges at Military Service Court South in Ulm toward leniency in 1980. The court was faced with deciding on the fate of a captain who had wrecked his own professional path shortly before he was set to take over a company. The inditement listed five instances in which the captain, who worked in an officers' club, was said to have approached orderlies with sexual intent on two evenings, in December 1978 and again in March 1980. The ruling pedantically listed the quantities of beer, wine spritzers ("composed of 1/8 liter wine and 1/8 liter of sour sparkling water"), mixed drinks ("Asbach with Cola"), schnapps and cognac that had been consumed prior to the advances. Once drunk, the captain had touched multiple orderlies in the area around their upper thighs, also trying unsuccessfully to open their uniform trousers. The soldiers had avoided the contact. One soldier later testified that while

---

176 BArch, Pers 12/45181, Ruling at Military Service Court Center, 1st Division, 31 March 1980.

177 Years later in 2006, the *New York Times* and in turn *Der Spiegel* would draw attention to the problem facing investigating authorities and the statistics (Phillips, "More than 100,000 men have been sexually assaulted"). See the beginning of chapter 3, section 9.

he "kept pushing [the captain's hand] away," he had not "dared" to do any more "for fear of professional repercussions."[178] In both instances, later that night the officer had come up to the rooms where the soldiers were sleeping and tried to touch them. The soldiers once again repelled the attempts, one fending the captain off with a punch. An expert attested to the defendant's reduced culpability as a result of heavy alcohol consumption. The court followed the report, but the "mitigating causes" were not enough for them to refrain from strict disciplinary measures. "A captain who assaults common soldiers between the ages of nineteen and twenty-one on repeated occasion diminishes the trust his employer has in his cleanliness and respectability so gravely, that as a general rule he is no longer tenable in the Bundeswehr."[179]

The Bundeswehr, the court opinion continued, further owed it to soldiers' parents "to do everything in its power to protect their often quite young and inexperienced sons from homosexual attacks by superiors."[180] There is nothing more to add to the opinion, which even today remains completely justified, regardless of sexual orientation. Yet the verdict stands out in its severity compared with similar, even significantly more serious cases of sexual assault; after all, the reasons it cites read like many others that ended in more lenient disciplinary measures. The risk of a repeat incident is mentioned explicitly and may well have been the deciding factor. As a "latent homosexual," the officer ran a risk of committing another assault after drinking – a risk the Bundeswehr was not prepared to accept.

Military service judges in Münster had another, highly similar case to rule on in 1983. The letter of inditement charged another captain and company leader with seven detailed counts of sexual assault against rank-and-file soldiers in his company within the space of half a year. When the fifth soldier listed in the letter reported what had happened to his spokesperson in March 1982, the spokesperson replied having heard similar reports before, and that it was a "precarious situation." The situation was indeed precarious; that same night the captain assaulted two other soldiers. According to the verdict, the company sergeant and spokespeople for the troops and NCOs had searched for a way to report the incidents "without one of themselves coming to harm."[181] Just how difficult it was for them to report

---

178 Ruling at Military Service Court South, 1st Division on 7 October 1980, AZ S 1–VL 10/80.
179 Ibid.
180 Ibid.
181 BArch, BW 1/531591, ruling at the 14th Division of Military Service Court North on 21 July 1983. The assault occurred in a barracks named after Prussian War Minister General Karl von Einem. Von Einem himself emerged as advocating a particularly hard line against homosexual officers (for a full account see this work, chapter "Early Days: Homosexuality's Reception in Previous German Armed Forces").

their boss can be seen from the chronology alone: After three incidents on the same evening in March, the captain was not banned from performing his duties until early July. The military service court heard the case in June 1983 and came to an unambiguous conclusion. Young conscripts had to be able to expect "not to be abandoned to the personal desires of their superiors."[182] The liberalization in sex offenses pertaining to homosexuality cited by the defense had no standing in the Bundeswehr. This was an unhappy turn of phrase, as the decriminalization of simple homosexuality obviously applied to soldiers and the armed forces as well. The Bundeswehr neither had nor has a separate criminal justice system. Yet it does have its own internal disciplinary laws, and this is certainly what the judges meant. Most importantly though, a loosening in the laws governing sex offenses could not serve as an excuse for sexual assault, hence the verdict: The captain should be removed from service.[183] His lawyer appealed, to no avail. While the military service senate saw exonerating factors in the captain's exceptional service record and consumption of alcohol beforehand, "these causes for leniency were not sufficient to refrain from the utmost disciplinary measures in light of the nature and severity of his transgressions."[184] The judges allowed the captain retain his rank in the reserve nonetheless.

In 1984, the German Bundestag took up the subject of how to protect young conscripts from "same-sex seduction" in the barracks. In response to a question from a CDU deputy that the transcript notes met with "laughter from the SPD and the Greens,"[185] Parliamentary State Secretary Würzbach (also CDU) argued:

> Experiencing one or the other reaction just now, this is to my mind a very serious matter (applause from the CDU/CSU). For how would one of us, one of you, one of the parents of a conscript react if they were forced to learn that a conscript had a non-commissioned officer, an officer, a superior who was trying in one way or another to establish a relationship of dependency [...] in this capacity?

In the subsequent course of debate, Würzbach was explicit about the fact that "such [consensual, homosexual] activity [between adults] is not subject to punishment by law, there's no argument about that, no two opinions."

---

182 Ibid.

183 Ibid.

184 BArch, BW 1/531591, BVerwG, 2 WD 57/83: Federal Administrative Court, 2nd Military Service Senate, decided 25 July 1984.

185 German Bundestag, 10th legislative period, 47th Session, 19 Jan 1984, typed transcript, 3378. In what follows as well.

d.) "Why Are You Only Reporting This Incident More than Half a Year Later?" Investigations into Navy Officers

Asked in December 1989 by the investigating officer why he was only reporting the incident now, with more than half a year gone by, a private replied that the topic had caused him embarrassment, especially as he did not know whether the examination of his genitalia had been "lawful or unlawful."[186] A petty officer second class answered the same question by explaining his assumption that the alleged "hygienic exam" was normal procedure – it was not until November 1989 that he heard from other soldiers who received similar "examinations." The circle of those sharing the experience quickly expanded until at last a petty officer at the base medical station inquired whether such an exam was permitted. The chief medic's ears perked up; no, they were not. The NCO spokesperson filed a report in December. One witness statement has a seaman saying that he had not found out other crew members had been "examined" until the day before, leading him to make his own report.

The investigations brought four other cases to light. One petty officer second class explained his failure to report on account of taking the officer's behavior for a "gaffe," that and the embarrassing nature of the goings-on. Another petty officer second class the officer in question had pursued with particular doggedness over a longer period of time, and had finally given in on one occasion, told the investigator he was happy that "the matter was out now."[187] The very day before his deposition, the accused had warned the petty officer against reporting anything with the words "You'll see what you get from that!"[188] The accused officer was detached from the crew and given a staff assignment. The investigating officer filed to open disciplinary proceedings, as simple disciplinary action did not seem sufficient.[189] At the same time, the commander leading the investigation passed the case on to the public prosecutor's office on suspicion of abuse of authority for improper ends (a crime under §32 of the Military Criminal Code).

In early February 1990 the fleet commander temporarily suspended the officer from service and forbade him from wearing his uniform. In the course of the military prosecutor's investigation three witnesses added details to their initial state-

---

186 BArch, Pers 12/46028, Military Service Court North, 10th Division, Case files Az N10 VL 9/90, transcript of a witness examination, 12 December 1989.

187 Ibid., transcript of a witness examination, 13 December 1989.

188 Ibid.

189 BArch, Pers 12/46028, Military Service Court North, 10th Division, case files Az N10 VL 9/90, Request to initiate disciplinary proceedings, 18 December 1989.

ments, further incriminating the accused. The incomplete nature of their first statements, they explained, owed to the great deal of shame they felt; what had happened was still "extraordinarily embarrassing."[190] "Aboard a warship nobody dares to contradict a superior just like that."[191] The main hearing was conducted in closed court before Military Service Court North in Hamburg in June 1990, and upheld the charges brought concerning the supposed "hygienic examination" of seven soldiers, involving touching in the genital area, mutual sexual contact with a direct subordinate, and a further attempt at sexual contact that had been rebuffed. There was no doubt in the court's mind that the officer had exploited his position and abused his authority to achieve his ends; in certain cases he had ordered the soldiers to him via the ship loudspeaker system. "A soldier who violates the human rights of his subordinates so grossly is no longer tenable for the armed forces."[192] The court decided to remove the career officer from service; he never appealed.

Disciplinary judges' ability to impose drastic measures is also shown in another case from the 1990s that can only be sketched here in the abstract, given its relative proximity to the present and the prominent position of the accused. Over a period of just under two years, a high-ranking commander repeatedly sought out intimate contact with a nonrated soldier under his direct command. In a detailed letter of accusation, the military prosecutor charged the commander among other things with four concrete counts of sexually motivated attempts and actual instances of touching the soldier's genital area. The soldier had resisted in every case except one, to which he had agreed and participated actively in. In hearing the evidence, the court determined that the initiative lay entirely with the soldier in this particular instance, holding it in favor of the accused.[193]

The case of the love-drunk commander recalls similar incidents in the annals of armies and fleets past, which often found their way into literature. In Max René Hesse's novel *Partenau*, a first lieutenant from the Reichswehr whose passion for a cadet sets him on the road to ruin confesses to his company commander that "I can't live without the boy anymore. I have to hear the boy, see him [...] It's the most potent, the most bewitching drink life has on offer. That's the magic. I can't

---

190 "I was embarrassed during the [initial] round of questioning to state it so clearly." BArch, Pers, 12/46028, Fleet Disciplinary Prosecutor for Military Service Court North, witness interviews from 14 March 1990.

191 Ibid., Fleet Disciplinary Prosecutor for Military Service Court North, witness interviews from 19 March 1990.

192 Ibid., Military Service Court North, 10th Division, decided 27 June 1990.

193 10th Division of Military Service Court North, ruling on 16 January 1998, cited in BVerwG, 2 WD 15/98: Federal Administrative Court, 2nd Military Service Senate, decided 23 February 1999. Found on www.jurion.de.

[...]"[194] Similar, if more modern words of passion could be found coming from the commander as he stood before the military service court in 1998. He had been "crazy about the private, emotionally."[195] In the novel the company commander advises, or rather impels his first lieutenant to marry a lady from the area as a way out. Such an arrangement was neither possible or permissible in the Bundeswehr of the 1990s. A common soldier had been pursued by his commanding officer for months; the evidence pointed toward repeated sexual harassment of a subordinate, not some innocent love dream; nor was it the only accusation. Further charges of "seven separate, documented instances of sexual harassment against three non-rated soldiers belonging to his own crew, in part completed, in part attempted" weighed heavily against the commander. The accused had repeatedly visited the common soldiers' sleeping quarters aboard ship and tried to touch their genitals as they slept.

The judges found the senior officer guilty and sentenced him to be removed from service. The court that heard the appeal considered the allegations to be proven and upheld the first decision, issuing an unambiguous ruling:

> Article 1 (1) of the Basic Law makes a person's dignity inviolable. Respecting and protecting it is the duty of all state power. This dictate cannot be approached differently inside the armed forces than it is outside them. It also provides the basis for the military constitution of the Federal Republic of Germany (§6 SG), even demanding particular observance in the military realm. Homosexual advances, intrusions and activity regularly constitute dishonorable treatment of one's comrades, and thus undermine the sense of camaraderie upon which the cohesion of the Bundeswehr is essentially based as per §12 (1) SG; destroys the superior's authority; and diminishes subordinates' readiness to obey.

"Through his overall misconduct, [the senior officer] has inflicted lasting damage to his reputation as a superior and suffered considerable loss of authority." The unrest had damaged the internal cohesion of the area under his command and jeopardized operational readiness, and thus ultimately fighting power.

It gives the author of this study pause to consider here how it was that such a high-ranking officer's behavior – which had not escaped notice within the scope of his authority – could go on for nearly two years without anybody intervening. One possible answer lies in the officer's high standing and range of authority. The court opinion mentions among other things that the soldiers who were subject to

---

194 Hesse, *Partenau*, 242–43.
195 Here and in what follows, 10th Division of Military Service Court North, ruling on 16 January 1998, cited in BVerwG, 2 WD 15/98: Federal Administrative Court, 2nd Military Service Senate, decided 23 February 1999.

the nocturnal assaults had "expressed confidence" in the officer in the presence of his deputy "and requested he not be [released] from his command post 'because he was actually a good commander.'"

This in turn recalls a previously discussed treatise about homosexuality in the military from 1908 written by an "expert on the field" under the pseudonym Karl Franz von Leexow. When asked "whether sexual things that inverted officers may have committed while drunk were not easily divulged by the enlisted men," an NCO replied, "But we wouldn't betray the best."[196]

A legal journal had the following to say about the judgement in 1999: "A soldier who as ship commander and disciplinary superior shows a definite tendency toward homosexuality through homosexual activities toward his subordinates has become untenable in the troops and must be removed from service."[197]

10. Statistics in Summary

The sources only give reliable statistical surveys on the number of soldiers punished in criminal and/or disciplinary court for homosexual acts in isolated instances, limited by time, place and organizational branch.

a.) 1956 to 1966

In 1966, a colonel from the personnel department at the BMVg reported the Bundeswehr as having brought disciplinary proceedings against thirty-six officers for homosexual activity between the years 1956 and 1965. He did not note how the proceedings ended. His department noted a further 182 disciplinary cases against NCOs and common soldiers in 1964 and 1965 for incidents of the same kind.[198] Given a total personnel count of 450,000 soldiers, such numbers were cause "neither for alarm nor concern."[199] One medical officer considered such a low number for disciplinary proceedings of the sort "impressive" given that an estimated four percent of the total male population was homosexual, and questioned "whether the other

---

196 Leexow, *Armee und Homosexualität*, 109–11. Also cited in Hirschfeld, *Von einst bis jetzt*, 150.

197 Neue Zeitschrift für Verwaltungsrecht – Rechtsprechungs-Report Verwaltungsrecht (NVwZ-RR), 11+12/1999, 513–14.

198 The paper doesn't mention whether these involved only court (i.e. criminal) cases or only disciplinary proceedings, or both.

199 Here and in what follows, BArch, BW 24/3736: BMVg, InSan: "Arbeitstagung zur Beurteilung der Wehrdiensttauglichkeit und Dienstfähigkeit Homosexueller," 1966, here sheet 94.

homosexual soldiers who had not been found out would otherwise perform their duties inconspicuously." A psychologist involved with the topic sought to explain away the seeming contradiction by conjecturing that the assumption of four percent was wrong. Entrance examinations would find "consistent homosexuality in significantly fewer men." The explanation that immediately suggests itself from today's perspective – that the majority of men with homosexual tendencies would have behaved inconspicuously during their military service – seemed unlikely, even impossible, to the professor in 1966, as it was "impossible for the majority of consistent homosexuals."

An internal Navy statistic from 1963 reveals fifty-six soldiers sentenced for violations under §175 StGB, four the following year, and another thirteen in 1965.[200] The annual fluctuations are noteworthy, as is the comparatively high number of convictions for 1963. The paper ventures one explanation for the surprising figure: the inclusion of sexual acts or "silly games" among comrades where no consistent homosexuality was present. The Navy jurist argued that the cases should "in all fairness" be removed from the statistics, citing the example of a seaman on a coast guard ship who "tried to see for himself whether two comrades he suspected were homosexually inclined" and became sexually involved supposedly for that reason alone. Yet "all three soldiers weighed down the statistics," just like four other Navy soldiers in Wilhelmshaven who "had hired themselves out for dollars to an English sailor while inebriated and [let] themselves be abused." Though none were homosexually inclined, all four soldiers were sentenced under §175 StGB.[201] The Navy further explained the number of convictions dropping as significantly as it had in the following years on account of its policy of removing soldiers from service. "Word had gotten round" that Navy headquarters was "generous" in its dismissal policies where instances of homosexuality were suspected. Not a few soldiers made use of this to exit the Navy.[202] Unspoken, this probably meant to say that if one were no longer a soldier, any subsequent convictions would no longer weigh on the statistics.

In 1963 the Navy had an overall personnel strength of 26,000, putting the share of soldiers convicted under §175 StGB at 0.2%. In 1965, with a total staff size of 31,000, that number was 0.04%. These calculations supported jurists' contention in 1966 that "there was no sign in the Navy [...] that homosexuality threatened to

---

200 In each of the three years, sources note four acquittals or proceedings being suspended. BArch, BW 24/3736: "Erfahrungen mit homosexuellen Soldaten in der Marine." In: BMVg, InSan: "Beurteilung der Wehrdiensttauglichkeit und Dienstfähigkeit Homosexueller," 1966, sheets 64–77, here 73.
201 Ibid., 76.
202 Ibid., 70.

assume worrisome proportions."[203] The Navy lawyer stressed the strict line he and his colleagues pursued in punishing incidents of the sort, heedless of the negligible percentages. Today one might speak of a "zero tolerance strategy"; in 1966, that sounded as follows:

> It is simply a matter of keeping relationships between men free from sexual influences. Experience has shown that it is especially easy for those who are homosexually inclined and susceptible to come into contact during longer stays aboard ship as a result of the close living quarters, in many cases leading to a relationship of sexual dependence (nesting). These relationships of unfreedom and dependency, which may also form between superiors and subordinates, not only destroy camaraderie within the close-knit living community aboard ship but also a sense of manly self-control [Manneszucht], in the truest sense of the term.[204]

The lawyer cited the example of a minehunter aboard which multiple soldiers had taken advantage of a petty officer's homosexual tendencies to "free themselves from watch duty in exchange for relevant favors."[205] While it did not occur to the lawyer in this case to pass the incident, which had occurred while on duty or within the line of duty, on to the public prosecutor's office, he did bemoan the inconsistency of soldiers and superiors alike in reporting. Over the course of his investigations as a military prosecutor he had seen "the great reluctance of some soldiers to report a comrade's attempted homosexual advances out of a false understanding of camaraderie."[206] Higher-ranking superiors similarly often shied away from passing incidents on to the public prosecutor. The lawyer estimated the number of unreported cases in the Navy at around 25%, whereas in the civilian sphere this number amounts to around 99% for offenses under §175 StGB.[207]

Numbers from 1964 also exist for Military District I, which included all the branches of the armed forces for the states of Schleswig-Holstein and Hamburg. Nine soldiers were sentenced under §175 and another five under §175a StGB.[208]

BMVg lawyers further created an overview of the number of soldiers convicted for sexual offenses in 1965 and 1966 in the course of the debate surrounding the reform of §175. Thirty-eight soldiers were convicted under §175 in 1965 (two officers, four NCOs and thirty-two nonrated soldiers) and eight acquitted, while one had his case suspended. Six additional convictions (four NCOs and two nonrated

---

203 Ibid., 76.
204 Ibid., 65.
205 Ibid.
206 Ibid., 74.
207 Ibid.
208 Ibid., 56–63, in this case 57.

soldiers) and two acquittals came under §175a StGB (aggravated illicit sexual acts between men). 1966 saw thirty-nine convictions (one officer, ten NCOs and twenty-eight nonrated soldiers), three acquittals and two suspended cases under §175; and eight convictions (five NCOs and three nonrated soldiers) and one acquittal under §175a.[209] Deviating slightly, the numbers for 1965 and 1966 show an average of around forty-five convictions annually.

Even if criminal courts acquitted them by law, gay soldiers still stood under the threat of the Bundeswehr's internal disciplinary mechanisms. The Navy jurist commented on this in 1966, noting that "the Navy has taken strict disciplinary measures in every instance of immoral behavior between men, drawing professional legal consequences in the case of regular acquittal during criminal proceedings, or their suspension on account of the trivial nature [of the case]."[210] The jurist grew more concrete: Both the "active participant" as well as the "other who let himself be misused for illicit acts" would be dismissed; what was more, this was "regardless of whether it could be proved that the offenders had homosexual tendencies or not."[211]

b.)   1976 to 1991–92

Here too, the information sources provide about internal Bundeswehr measures or court disciplinary action is sporadic and limited to narrow windows of time. Reliable figures exist for the period between 1981 and 1992. In advance of a Bundestag Defense Committee meeting, in September 1982 the BMVg requested the numbers as they stood within each branch of the armed forces. The Navy had "no identified or reported cases of homosexuality" for 1981 and two cases for the first half year of 1982. "Overall, however, the problem of 'homosexuality' does not exist in the Navy."[212] The air force reported one conscript sentenced under §175 StGB in 1981 for homosexual activity with a minor. Legal personnel measures for 1980 and 1981 included one dismissal under §55 (5) SG, another under §29 (1) of the Compulsory Military Service Act and two further cases of disciplinary action in the

---

209 BArch, BW 1/187212, "Abgeurteilte Soldaten nach §§172, 175, 175a und 175b 1965/1966," no author, no date.
210 BArch, BW 24/3736: "Erfahrungen mit homosexuellen Soldaten in der Marine," in BMVg, InSan: "Beurteilung der Wehrdiensttauglichkeit und Dienstfähigkeit Homosexueller," 1966, sheets 64–77, here 67.
211 Ibid.
212 BArch, BW 2/31225: BMVg FüM I 3, 4 August 1982.

form of twenty-one days' and seven days' arrest, respectively.[213] Army Staff had no numbers to report, but once again took the opportunity to put fundamental principles to writ.[214]

In October 1991 the BMVg requested statistical data from the three military service courts about convictions from the past ten years related to "homosexuality in the armed forces," as the subject heading read.[215] Between 1981 and 1991 Military Service Court North in Münster/Westphalia registered twenty-eight cases, with another three added in handwriting for 1992. In 1981 a captain serving as company commander and two sergeants first class had been convicted in disciplinary proceedings. The company commander was charged with misconduct against two common soldiers in his unit; the resulting disciplinary action took the form of a two-year ban on promotion and a one-year reduction in pay by one-twentieth, quite a light punishment by comparison. One company sergeant had sexually assaulted a total of seven soldiers in his company and was demoted by two ranks to plain sergeant. The other had also been brought in on seven counts of sexual assault, in this case against soldiers in his platoon, direct subordinates of his. He was banned from promotion for two years and had his pay reduced by one-tenth for a year – again, a light punishment. The statistics do not reveal the specific charges on which the captain and sergeant first class were arraigned.

1982 likewise saw the conviction of three company commanders, among them a captain who was removed from service for showing sexual aggression toward seven soldiers in his company. One major was demoted to the rank of captain based on one incident, while another major received a pay cut and was banned from promotion for four years. In 1984 a sergeant was demoted to the rank of private first class for nine counts of sexual assault against soldiers in his barracks who were not his immediate subordinates. That same year, another sergeant was charged with assaulting six soldiers who stood directly beneath him in his position as a mess sergeant for the officers' club at the barracks. Disciplinary action banned him from promotion for four years and reduced his pay by one-tenth for a year. The BMVg

---

213 Ibid.

214 "Homosexuals' deviant sexual behavior cannot be tolerated within the purview of the army in the event that it disrupts the camaraderie and cohesion of the military community [...] and troop discipline. So long as homoerotic tendencies are limited to the extra-official private sphere, they [...] will be tolerated." BArch, BW 2/31225: BMVg, FüH I 3, 6 August 1982.

215 The precipitating event for the request was an inquiry the BMVg received from the British defence attaché in Bonn on 9 September 1991. The BMVg's reply came on 5 November 1991, asking for the attaché's understanding as to the delay; the requested numbers first had to be asked for at the military service courts. BMVg, VR I 5 to the British defence attaché, 5 November 1991, BArch, BW 1/531592.

overview includes one case already discussed at length, that of an officer dismissed from service in 1990 for assaulting seven members on his crew. One company commander in the rank of major was acquitted of the charges against him in 1984, as was a sergeant in 1987.[216] The acquittals do not indicate consensual sex, however, which itself constituted an official violation. The leniency in the disciplinary measures mentioned above sooner point to consensual contact.

The number of soldiers that were sexually assaulted in each case deserves attention; as a rule, these were not isolated events. Multiple soldiers were attacked in nearly every instance, seven at a time on multiple occasions and as many as nine in one case. These numbers in turn point out another difficulty: The first victims apparently did not report the incident, possibly covering it up completely, whether out of uncertainty, shame or some other reason. This in turn enabled the superior to renew or repeat his attacks before any report came to be, along with the ensuing investigations and potential disciplinary measures. It was usually the latest offense in a series that (finally) drew attention, which then brought similar previous, as yet unreported incidents to light. The common reticence to "blow the whistle" held a variety of motivations, and suggests a high number of unreported cases; we have already seen a Navy jurist pointing out soldiers' and superiors' inconsistent reporting in 1966. The number of (homo)sexually motivated attacks was in all likelihood significantly higher than the number of cases heard in military service courts. Coming on top of all the reports that are presumably missing were cases that resulted in the immediate dismissal of the accused under §55 (5) SG, and therefore were not included in the statistics.

Military Service Court Center in Koblenz heard nineteen cases for the period between 1981 and 1991, fourteen of which resulted in disciplinary action, four in acquittal and one in trial suspension. The highest-ranking soldiers convicted were a major and a senior staff physician, who were demoted to captain and staff physician respectively. The harshest disciplinary action was taken against a company commander in 1982, and again in 1990 against a platoon commander in the rank of staff sergeant – both were removed from service. The captain had assaulted two privates in the company he was leading, the staff sergeant an airman in his platoon.[217]

Military Service Court South in Ulm reported nine cases during the same period of time, with five completed and one ongoing for 1992 added in writing.

---

216 BArch, BW 1/531592, President of Military Service Court North, Az 25-01-30, to BMVg, VR I 5, dated 17 October 1991.
217 BArch, BW 1/531592, Military Service Court Center Headquarters, Az 25-01-10 to BMVg, VR I 5, dated 14 October 1991.

Differentiated by rank, seven of the accused were captains, one a first lieutenant, five were staff sergeants and one a sergeant. In terms of their relative position, five had assaulted soldiers directly under their command, two had otherwise been in a position of authority and three of the accused were superiors based on rank. The cases reported for 1992 were not differentiated in the same way. Three of the captains and the first lieutenant had been dismissed from service. Another captain was acquitted in 1982. The remaining disciplinary measures either took the form of demotion in rank, promotion bans or a reduction in pay.[218]

Comparing the three service courts shows thirty-one sets of disciplinary measures taken in the north and fourteen each in the central and southern courts. The greater number for Military Service Court North in Münster is ultimately traceable to the larger area for which it was responsible, and thus the considerably higher number of units under its jurisdiction. The areas for which the Koblenz and Ulm courts held responsibility were much smaller, making it impossible to draw any definite conclusions about the comparative frequency of reporting between north and south, or the harshness or clemency with which the courts treated those cases that were reported.

It may also be of some interest to break the reports down by military branch. Court statistics do not differentiate according to army, air force and navy, nor do rank designations allow for distinguishing between the army and air force. The navy, however, does stand out with its own service ranks. Out of a total of thirty-one convictions Military Service Court North lists five disciplinary court actions taken against navy officers, petty officers and crew members. Given the limited number of naval personnel stationed in the area under the jurisdictions of the two southern courts, it is unsurprising that neither lists any disciplinary actions against Navy members. Out of sixty-three total cases tried in the armed forces between 1981 and 1992, five involved the Navy, with four ending in final disciplinary action. That makes up 8% of cases, surprisingly close to an exact match for the navy's share of personnel in the Bundeswehr at large, just under 9%.[219] Contrary to certain assumptions or prejudices, the Navy was thus right in line statistically speaking, i.e. it had no more or fewer cases onboard ship than what was average for any other branch.

The BMVg summarized the reports, breaking down fifty-five decisions at military service courts between the years 1981 and 1991 into nine removals from service, eighteen demotions in rank, eight temporary bans on promotion, two

---

218 BArch, BW 1/531592, President of Military Service Court South, Az 25-01-35/06-2 to BMVg, VR I 5, dated 22 October 1991.

219 In 1985 the Bundeswehr had a total of 495,000 soldiers, 39,000 of which were in the Navy. See Federal Ministry of Defense, *Weißbuch 1985*, 238 and 240.

reductions in pay and ten combined punishments of a ban on promotion and reduction in pay. Seven trials had ended in acquittal, one in suspension. Nineteen officers were tried, thirty senior NCOs and six junior NCOs.[220] Each year an average of close to five soldiers were sentenced to disciplinary measures.

A handwritten update added an additional eight cases for 1992 (one against an officer, five against senior NCOs and two against junior NCOs). Five had ended in disciplinary action – two demotions in rank and three bans on promotion – one set of proceedings had been suspended and two others were ongoing.[221] 1992 upheld the average calculated for the previous ten years of five court disciplinary actions per year. In summarizing the results, the director at the Bundeswehr Institute of Social Sciences commented that the annual number of "only 5.2" was "extraordinarily small," concluding that "within day-to-day service operations, homosexuality [is] more of an academic topic."[222]

The BMVg had calculated a similar annual average of five disciplinary court actions taken against homosexual activity in 1979 for the years previous.[223] (Presumably it was disciplinary actions decided on by military service courts that were meant here, involving cases of both sexual assault and consensual sex.) The Ministry of Defense also shed some light on the number of soldiers convicted under §175 and §176 StGB: twenty-one in 1975, eighteen in 1976 and fifteen in 1977.[224] These numbers included cases of both non-consensual and consensual sex, two fundamentally different scenarios that nonetheless both represented a violation of official duty in the thinking of the day. This makes the statistics from those years ill-fit to uncover the number of cases involving consensual homosexual activity that may be entitled to rehabilitation.

---

220 As of 31 October 1991, BArch, BW 1/531592: BMVg, FüS I 1 on 3 March 1993; also available in BW 24/14249 and BW 2/31224: BMVg, VR I 5 to FüS I 4, 16 December 1992 in the annex.

221 BArch, BW 1/531592: BMVg, FüS I 1, 3 March 1993, also available in BW 1/32553: BMVg, VR I 5, March 1993 and FüS I 4, 3 February 1993.

222 Fleckenstein, "Homosexuality and Military Service in Germany." In a similar vein and appearing nearly at the same time is the article in *Der Spiegel*, "Versiegelte Briefe."

223 BArch, BW 1/304284: BMVg, VR I 1, 15 February 1979, as well as BMVg, parliamentary state secretary to Deputy Herta Däubler-Gmelin (SPD), 23 February 1979.

224 BArch, BW 1/304284: BMVg, VR I 1, 15 February 1979. In evaluating these numbers, it is important to keep in mind that after its reform, §175 StGB no longer punished homosexual activity between men as such, but only when it involved minors under eighteen. §176 dealt with sexual activity involving children under fourteen.

11. Immediate Dismissal under §55 (5) of the Legal Status of Military Personnel Act

Service court documents have for the most part been preserved in their entirety, as have appeal rulings at military service senate. Between them, the sources offer a detailed and multifaceted picture of the cases tried before the two courts. In contrast, dismissals under §55 (5) of the Legal Status of Military Personnel Act (hereinafter: Soldier's Act; in German: Soldatengesetz, SG) constitute a blind spot. In the event of a breach of duty or serious threat to military discipline, the clause allows (to this day) for the possibility of rapidly dismissing a soldier still in the first four years of his service in a simplified procedure, without a disciplinary court hearing.[225] A range of violations qualify under the clause; by no means is it limited to cases of homosexuality. Dismissal under §55 (5) was a routine matter in military life, usually at the instigation of platoon leaders and company commanders who knew their soldiers. As a rule, the decision was made by the division personnel office.[226]

In cases where the simple legal route of rapid dismissal under the clause existed, the impact of §55 (5) was to remove the need for a long, drawn-out trial before the military service courts – one whose outcome moreover was not guaranteed. Dismissal under the clause did not (nor does it today) require that the underlying violation of duty lead to removal in a court disciplinary hearing; it was a personnel decision, not a disciplinary action. Immediate dismissal under §55 (5) should also be distinguished from dismissal due to "unsuitability" under §55 (4) SG, both in terminology and substance. In 1984 the Bundeswehr personnel office referred explicitly to §55 (5) "for cases in which a fixed-term soldier is reprimanded or criminally convicted for homosexual acts [to order] his discharge during the first four years of service, if remaining in service would pose a serious risk to military discipline or the reputation of the Bundeswehr (§55 (5) SG)."[227]

The G1 memo draft discussed above from 1986 that sought to regulate all matters pertaining to homosexuality also included mention of dismissal within the first four years of service under §55 (5).[228]

---

225 http://www.gesetze-im-internet.de/sg/__55.html. Last accessed 31 March 2021.

226 Interview with a retired major general, Potsdam, 15 May 2018.

227 BMVg, P II 1, Az 16-02-05/2 (C) R 4/84 from 13 March 1984; nearly identical wording in BArch, BW 2/32553: BMVg, FüS I 4, 3 February 1993.

228 BArch, BW 2/31225: BMVg, FüS I 4 to the minister via the parliamentary state secretary, 22 October 1986, annex. Identical to BArch, BW 2/31224: BMVg, FüS I 4, July 1986.

Documents related to dismissal proceedings became part of soldiers' personnel files, subject to destruction after a set period of time under data protection law. Today, this means that only isolated, rather coincidental references to dismissal via that particular route exist.

One set involves a captain whose case has already been considered in detail. When he seduced a lieutenant in 1965 while massaging him after sports, the captain was quickly discharged under §55 (5). In another case that has also been looked at from 1969, disciplinary proceedings were opened against six soldiers, with four quickly dismissed from the Bundeswehr under §55 (5). The remaining two had their cases heard before court; they had done more than four years in service and simplified dismissal was no longer possible.

Chance finds and eyewitness interviews allowed a few other cases to be identified. In a previously described case from 1966 in which a first lieutenant and an NCO continued a consensual sexual relationship from their youth, a former officer filled in what could not be found in the court acts, namely that the NCO had been dismissed under §55 (5).[229]

The only instance of statistical surveys for this kind of dismissal comes in a 1966 report from a Navy jurist, according to which Navy headquarters dismissed one sergeant and three common soldiers under §55 (5) in 1964. The Navy dismissed seven rank-and-file soldiers under the same clause the following year; another set of dismissal proceedings had yet to be completed due to one soldier's appeal. Another three nonrated soldiers were dismissed for homosexual activity based on other legal provisions, namely §55 (2) SG for inability to serve and §54 (1) SG for unsuitability for fixed-term service at the end of a six-month probationary period.[230] (§54 (1) SG governs the end of service once a set period of service has finished, in this case a "semi-annual review.") All the dismissals involved soldiers serving a fixed term. In 1965, another four conscripts were dismissed under §29 (1) No. 5 of the Compulsory Military Service Act.[231]

In an interview for *Der Spiegel* in 1993, BMVg spokesperson First Lieutenant Ulrich Twrsnick explained that "no injunction to prosecute or witch burning" existed in the Bundeswehr.[232] The service was not interested in what soldiers "do off duty," nor did the BMVg see "any problems" if soldiers with the same service

---

229 Interview (anonymous), 19 June 2018.

230 BArch, BW 24/3736: "Erfahrungen mit homosexuellen Soldaten in der Marine." In BMVg, InSan: "Beurteilung der Wehrdiensttauglichkeit und Dienstfähigkeit Homosexueller," 1966, sheets 64–77, here 73.

231 Ibid.

232 "Versiegelte Briefe," 54.

rank "'were caught engaged in homosexual practices [...]' Both are doing it voluntarily, both are eighteen and there's no relationship of dependence." It would be a different situation, Twrsnick continued, "if three or four, say, began to terrorize a bedroom."[233] The press officer's statement that soldiers caught engaged in homosexual acts would not pose a problem allows one to infer that no disciplinary investigation would follow even if soldiers were discovered engaged in sexual activity in service accommodations or while on duty. Wisely, this applied only to common soldiers and, unmentioned here, only for conscripts. Twrsnick's words could also be read in reverse: If it was not common soldiers but sergeants, staff sergeants or officers who were "caught," there would be trouble.

Trouble was exactly what two sergeants ran into in 1994. An S2 officer responsible for military security in the battalion at the time, today a first lieutenant, recalled their immediate dismissal.

> I learned that both sergeants had been dismissed before their four-year commitment expired due to sexual activity while on duty. At the time I was extremely angry about how the two men had been treated and asked them in my office why they had not appealed their dismissal [...] Both soldiers told me that they "would let the matter rest." Their time in the service would have been over soon anyway, and they did not want to take any further action.[234]

In the period that followed, company members were mocked by other units as "the pink company." "Yet I think I wasn't the only one for whom the two soldiers' dismissal went too far. To my knowledge it wasn't talked about among the officers. But the commander at the time didn't like to allow conversations about official decisions anyway." Stationed in Baden-Württemberg at the time, the witness added that even back then he had been of the opinion "that a dismissal like that wouldn't have occurred in northern Germany."

In this respect the officer was likely mistaken. The same regulations obviously applied in northern Germany as well. Still, it depended on the person whether or not a company head turned around and reported what he had been told "upstairs," and a commander then initiated dismissal proceedings. There was room for discretion. In classifying the disciplinary measures taken against the two sergeants, it should again be pointed out that any sort of sexual activity was prohibited within official quarters and facilities. That included while off duty, and obviously even more so while on duty, as the sergeants were when they were found out. The same

---

233 "Versiegelte Briefe," 49.
234 Email from Lieutenant Colonel B. to the author, 24 January 2017, and in what follows.

applied for heterosexuals without exception.[235] In early January 2000, a personnel department section reemphasized that the disciplinary relevance of homosexual activity should ultimately be assessed the same as heterosexual activity.[236] (In 2004, revised departmental orders for "Handling Sexuality in the Bundeswehr" loosened the clauses governing "sexual activity" for free time spent in the barracks as well.[237])

A further case of immediate dismissal was possible to reconstruct based on the personal memories and documents of Dierk Koch, a seaman apprentice in the Navy whose brief stint in the military is discussed at length in chapter 2. When he came under professional and sexual pressure from his direct superior, a petty officer second class, the seaman confided in the head of his company and requested a transfer.[238] Searching the federal archives for documents related either to Koch's dismissal or the petty officer's own proved unsuccessful.[239] To date only a small portion of the substantial archival material has been made accessible, unfortunately, leaving a subsequent find entirely possible. Original documents in the possession of the former seaman were partially able to fill existing gaps. It is nevertheless likely that the petty officer in the story was dismissed under §55 (5) SG without a hearing in service court. Internal Navy statistics for crimes under §175 StGB contain a minor reference, with the year 1964 listing three common soldiers and one NCO dismissed under §55 (5) SG.[240] Aside from the seaman apprentice the petty officer could absolutely have been among those dismissed.

Yet the seaman's demotion in rank and dismissal from service did not mean the matter was finished for the Navy. Rather, Navy lawyers brought the public prosecutor on board, so to speak. In 1965, the young man found himself back before Cuxhaven local court, with the petty officer sitting next to him in the dock. As Koch recalls, the judged showed a clear liberal bent and excused himself before the two accused for having to sentence them under §175 StGB, albeit only to a fine of 100 DM for Koch and a somewhat higher fine (500 DM in Koch's memory) for the

---

235 For a full account see Lutze, "Sexuelle Beziehungen und die Truppe."

236 BArch, BW 1/502107, no pagination: BMVg, PSZ III 1, May 1 2000.

237 For a full account, see chapter 4, section 7.

238 See chapter 2, section 4.a.

239 An inspection instigated at Koch's request to the BMVg proved similarly unsuccessful on account of incomplete documentation "due to the passage of time." The personnel files that had been preserved were located, as was the private's health card, but they don't contain any mention of homosexuality or its justifying immediate dismissal. BMVg, P II 1 to Dierk Koch, 26 February 2019.

240 BArch, BW 24/3736: "Erfahrungen mit homsexuellen Soldaten in der Marine." In BMVg, InSan: "Beurteilung der Wehrdiensttauglichkeit und Dienstfähigkeit Homosexueller," 1966, sheets 64–77, here 73.

petty officer.[241] The judge was bound to the applicable laws, and he could not rule for acquittal in favor of the accused as the facts of the case were undisputed. He was only able to use his discretion in deciding the extent of punishment so as to impose the absolute minimum. The verdict in Cuxhaven thus takes its place among the handful of symbolic guilty verdicts against gay men that progressive judges would hand down from time to time, although these tended to remain the exception.[242]

12. The Matter of Rehabilitation

In 2017, at Dierk Koch's request, the verdict reached in 1965 by Cuxhaven local court was rescinded.[243] In June of 2017, the Bundestag passed the Act to Criminally Rehabilitate Persons Who Have Been Convicted of Performing Consensual Homosexual Acts After 8 May 1945 (StrRehaHomG). The law took effect on 22 July 2017, rendering null and void criminal decisions and court orders issued for consensual homosexual activity under the previous versions of §175 and §175a StGB in West Germany, or §151 in the East German criminal code.

> By today's standards, the ban on consensual homosexual activity under criminal law and the resulting prosecution contravene the Basic Law and human rights to a special degree. It is the goal of the [present] law to remove the stigma of punishment based on those convictions with which affected parties have had to live until now.[244]

"It is a delayed act of justice. But it is never too late for justice," then Federal Minister of Justice Heiko Maas said while addressing the act's adoption in parliament. "The state greatly incriminated itself with §175 StGB by making the lives of innumerable people more difficult. The law caused unimaginable suffering. This law allows us to rehabilitate the victims. Convicted homosexuals no longer have to live with the stigma of conviction."[245]

---

241 Interview with Dierk Koch, Hamburg, on 22 February 2018, and an email from Dierk Koch to the author on 6 September 2019, as well as a further interview by phone on 7 September 2019. Also mentioned in Scheck and Utess, "Was wir damals gemacht haben, war kein Verbrechen."
242 In 1961, the press reported on a "three mark sentence": in an appellate hearing on 22 July 1961 the Hamburg District Court sentenced two men to a fine of three marks each for consensual sex.
243 Decision of the Stade public prosecutor's office, 19 September 2017.
244 Statement by the Federal Office of Justice
245 Statement to the press by the Federal Ministry of Justice and Consumer Protection on 21 July 2017. https://www.bundesregierung.de/breg-de/aktuelles/pressekonferenzen/regierungspressekon ferenz-vom-9-maerz-2018-848296 (last accessed 16 April 2018).

Dierk Koch saw it the same way. "The disgrace of having a criminal record that has weighed on me for decades now has fallen by the wayside [...] The conclusion of this process makes me proud and happy!"[246] Koch puts it even more plainly in an interview with *Bild*: "I've turned seventy-seven in the meantime. I didn't want to die a criminal. What we did back then wasn't a crime."[247] Koch's loss in rank and dismissal from the Navy, by contrast, were neither repealed nor canceled. Nor for that matter have any other cases of disciplinary action (or rather punishment) or dismissal from the Bundeswehr cited in this study received judicial reappraisal – not to mention the numerous instances of disciplinary measures or dismissal not considered here. Their legal force, and even more so their impact, live on in the memories of those who have been affected. The Federal Ministry of Defense had to take its own steps toward repeal or some other form of settlement. This is neither to advocate for the repeal of disciplinary action taken against cases of sexual assault nor to minimize those cases. Yet instances of disciplinary punishment or dismissal on account of consensual sexual activity between soldiers were still awaiting reappraisal, or at least some sort of gesture from the armed forces – up until 2020. That year, based in part on the research results published in this study, former Minister of Defense Annegret Kramp-Karrenbauer introduced a legal initiative to repeal the same disciplinary measures and verdicts under discussion here. At the same time, Kramp-Karrenbauer complied with the wish for a gesture shared by many who had suffered injustice: She requested official pardon.

To return to Koch, however: In 2019 the BMVg came back with a very different answer to his specific case. Even if archival finds did turn up evidence of dismissal due to homosexuality, the current laws did not offer him a chance for formal rehabilitation. The law on rehabilitation that had passed (StrRehaHomG) only targeted criminal verdicts, and had already been accomplished in the former seaman apprentice's case. "We are aware that this is not a satisfactory state of affairs for the impacted parties. Based on the prevailing laws and orders during your service period, it is understandable that homosexual soldiers feared discrimination [during military service]. This is truly regrettable."[248] It is worth noting here that gay soldiers not only had to "fear" discrimination but actively experienced and suffered from it as well. From Koch's point of view, the BMVg's phrasing in this case is unsatisfactory, to say the least.

The Working Group for Homosexual Members of the Bundeswehr persisted on the issue in a letter from April 2018, specifically calling on the defense minister to

---

246 Koch, "Meine unvergessenen Freunde."
247 Scheck and Utess, "Was wir damals gemacht haben, war kein Verbrechen."
248 BMVg, P II, 1 to Dierk Koch, 26 February 2019.

annul "verdicts reached against soldiers of all ranks [by military service courts] on the basis of consensual homosexual activity alone." To do so, the letter pushed for the existing law on criminal rehabilitation to be updated and expanded to include rulings in military service courts.[249]

The ministry responded that same month, underscoring the "great esteem" in which it and "especially the minister personally" held the working group's engagement "on behalf of homosexual members of the Bundeswehr." Yet the ministry demurred when it came to annulling service court decisions and financially compensating those who were left at a professional disadvantage. The argument used then is repeated today. The criminal rehabilitation act could not be applied to disciplinary rulings; such an act would require a new legal basis. The ministry had already approached the justice ministry to this end with a request to consider amending the law to include disciplinary rulings. To date, however, the justice ministry had replied in the negative. The rehabilitation act (StrRehaHomG) served "solely to remove the stigma of punishment suffered as a result of a criminal conviction [...] Other legal consequences resulting from conviction, especially when professional in nature (such as the lost of professional status or any consequences from a conviction under disciplinary law) were explicitly excluded."[250] While the justice ministry "in no way [failed to recognize] that affected parties were also subject to considerable discrimination and suffered disadvantages," it was exactly those disadvantages that "did not inhere in the stigma of criminal conviction that alone holds relevance for StrRehaHomG." As of 2018, the justice ministry thus had no intention of expanding the law to "bodies of evidence outside criminal law" such as military service court rulings. Despite the justice ministry's position, the BMVg noted that its legal department would "keep an eye on the matter and explore other possibilities."[251]

Specialist legal journals came out in support of the BMVg's position. The rehabilitation act expressly did not touch on past disciplinary measures but served "solely to remove the stigma of punishment suffered from prior conviction."[252] It was emphasized explicitly that jurisprudence did not find any unconstitutionality present in the convictions.[253] In 2019 a first ray of light seemed to appear as the Federal Ministry of Justice began to consider "in the meantime [...] whether also

---

249 Letter from the Working Group for Homosexual Members of the Bundeswehr to the Minister of Defense, 16 April 2018.
250 BMVg, R I 5 to the Working Group for Homosexual Members of the Bundeswehr, 16 August 2018.
251 Ibid.
252 Rampp, Johnson and Wilms, "Die seit Jahrzehnten belastende Schmach fällt von mir ab," 1146.
253 See also the decisions at BVerfG from 1957 and 1973, already discussed at length in this study.

to provide for persons who were not criminally convicted but were persecuted for their homosexuality in other ways."[254]

In closing, one farther-reaching thought: Anyone sentenced to longer than one year in prison automatically loses the legal status of a soldier. If this sort of conviction against homosexual soldiers were repealed by the criminal rehabilitation act, what implications would that hold for service law? Would that mean a loss of legal status under §48 and §54 (2) SG as well? Would the armed forces then have to make payments to fixed-term soldiers, say, even career soldiers to make up for missed salary? This remains a theoretical question at present.[255] The research at hand did not turn up any cases where soldiers were sentenced to such a long prison term for consensual, same-sex activity. Any number of dismissals reviewed to date were without doubt based on convictions under §175 StGB and will have to be annulled now, but they all lay well under a year imprisonment. Cases uncovered so far in which fixed-term or career soldiers lost their legal status as soldiers for prison terms over one year exclusively followed on rulings that dealt with severe cases of sexual assault, which were expressly excluded from the rehabilitation act.

The convictions that Lüneberg regional court handed down to Sergeant K. and Private S. discussed at the outset of the chapter similarly fall under the category of rulings under §175 StGB in need of rehabilitation. The sergeant's subsequent conviction by a military service senate occurred under disciplinary law, not criminal law. Additional, new steps were required to annul this and other rulings. This in turn paved the way for new legislation in 2020, with the Bundestag set to take up the "Act to Rehabilitate Persons Who Have Been Professionally Disadvantaged For Performing Consensual Homosexual Acts, For Their Homosexual Orientation, Or For Their Sexual Identity" in April and May 2021.

---

254 BMVg, P II 1 to Dierk Koch, 26 February 2019. The guidelines for compensating this group as well took effect on 13 March 2019.

255 As BMVg, R I 5 explained to the author, the questioned had already been answered. §1 (5) StRehaHomG provides that the repeal of criminal convictions would have no legal effect outside the scope of the act, excluding "resuscitation" of a service position that had ended in criminal conviction. BMVg, R I 5, 27 April 2020.

IV Unfit to Command?

Homosexual tendencies of this nature rule out a soldier's fitness to serve in a position of leadership.[1]

Up until the year 2000, the severe stigma associated with homosexuality in the Bundeswehr persisted beneath the threshold of disciplinary action as well, regularly entailing serious consequences for military service. "Outing" oneself invariably meant the end of one's career. As jurists from the Bundeswehr's department of administrative and legal affairs wrote in 1970 – or one year after the reform of the criminal code – the legal system demanded "that a soldier with a homophilic disposition also observe his military service obligations and curb his inclinations."[2] Now, it stands as a matter of course that a soldier would have to fulfill his service obligations and "curb" whatever sexual inclinations might arise while on duty. This in turn coincided with the Bundeswehr's own express interest in "stifling homosexual dependencies, tensions, petty jealousies, cliques and nesting in the military," all well-trodden stereotypes about homosexuals continually being updated to fit the latest fashion.[3] Yet the lawyers did not simply seem to have the line of duty in mind, but evidently meant the soldier's conduct overall, including in private. Conscripts' parents would "rightfully" expect the Bundeswehr to keep the official realm "free from homosexual relationships" and, as far as was possible, "the extra-official realm as well [!]."[4] The jurists went on to note that "a soldier's homophilic *tendencies* are irrelevant to service law as long as he does not act in a like manner."[5] When asked whether Bundeswehr members "whose homophilic disposition became known" would have to reckon with career roadblocks or even dismissal,[6] the lawyers replied "no, so long as they do not pursue their tendency and do not engage in homosexual activity."[7] Here too, there was not any limitation as to the line of duty.

By today's standards, recommending sexual abstinence in order to avoid repercussions may sound like satire. At the time, though, it was bitter reality. Up through

---

1 Federal Administrative Court, 1st Military Service Senate, ruling on 25 October 1979, Az.: BVerwG, 1 WB 113/78. Found on www.jurion.de.
2 BArch, BW 24/7180: BMVg, VR IV 1, 29 September 1970.
3 Ibid.
4 Ibid. Identical wording in BArch, BW 24/7180: BMVg, FüS I 1, 9 September 1970.
5 Ibid., emphasis in original.
6 BArch, BW 24/7180: Editors of *Das andere Magazin* to the BMVg, 17 August 1970.
7 Ibid., BMVg, VR IV 1, 29 September 1970.

the 1950s and 60s, abstinence served as a tried and tested way of working around one's homosexuality. Ultimately, it recalls the celibacy demanded by the Catholic Church of its priests, monks and bishops (which naturally applied, and does still for any form of sexuality.) In later decades the military no longer demanded private abstinence but "merely" silence when it came to homosexuality. This too resembles the practices of Christian churches; the Protestant Church previously, and today the Catholic Church.[8] An army is not a church, however, the officer corps is not clergy and a lieutenant is not a priest voluntarily submitting himself to celibacy. In 1984, legal sociologist Rüdiger Lautmann was already criticizing the Bundeswehr alongside the school system and church ministry for continuing to threaten homosexuals with the "an employment ban and attempts at intimidation" and "controlling their appearance both on and off-duty."[9]

In 1972 a reservist officer took up the fight against the Bundeswehr's contempt for openly gay service members. Perhaps that was what it took – an engaged member in the reserve – to make the initial push just under three years after male homosexuality was decriminalized. Fixed-term and career soldiers ran a different sort of risk of jeopardizing their professional existence in taking such a step.

1. "Unresolvable by Us." A Reserve Lieutenant against the Ministry of Defense, 1972

The precipitating event for what would eventually turn into a years-long legal battle was a commonplace letter. In June 1972 Defense District Command 355 in Gelsenkirchen "invited" Mr. Rainer Plein, a lieutenant in the reserve, "to call in the coming days [...] with a view to the announcement of your promotion. Please bring your military pass with you."[10] After a second request the recipient replied, writing that he was the "founder of the Homosexuality Activist Group (HSM Münster) and

---

8 For a comprehensive account of the Protestant Church's handling of homosexuality see Fitschen, *Liebe zwischen Männern?* On the controversy surrounding homosexuality among Catholic clergy, and especially within the Vatican see Martel, *Sodom*, as well as Drobinski, "Römisches Doppelleben." Drobinski summarizes Martel's argument, writing "The more harshly one damns gays, the sooner he is one himself, the more rigidly he judges, the higher the likelihood that he is leading a double life." Many homosexuals in the clergy and especially the Vatican had "made themselves at home in the old system of keeping silent and [carrying on] a double life."

9 Lautmann, *Der Zwang zur Tugend*, 197–98.

10 Defense District Command 355, S1, 12 June 1972 (The author holds possession of a copy of the letter.)

was himself homosexual." He would not accept his certificate of promotion as long as his "situation and position in the Bundeswehr [had not] been fully clarified."[11]

With that, Plein had thrown down the gauntlet. The personnel worker in Gelsenkirchen must have initially been taken aback, and forwarded the matter to the head office in Cologne. The head of Gelsenkirchen Defense district command added in writing "Baseline issue, unresolvable by us. S1: Prepare the file with attachments for forwarding to PersABw!"[12] Plein heard next from Section San I 3 that he had "raised an issue of principals,"[13] meaning the Federal Ministry of Defense would have to be called in. In his letter to the BMVg, the head of the Bundeswehr personnel office stressed that "new regulations brought on by criminal law reform notwithstanding," he considered it "indefensible that an officer in the reserve with this sort of tendency" and a mindset as made clear from his activities in the homosexual movement should serve "as a superior with young soldiers as his subordinates."[14] A letter from the head of the personnel office – pointing out that as a reservist, Plein was still subject to military surveillance regardless of declaring his homosexuality – prompted a lengthy response from Plein, where he first made his true, revolutionary sociopolitical concerns known.

> I'm inclined to believe that if you make me first lieutenant – and the certificate of promotion has been ready for some time now, waiting only on my acceptance – that I have the right to pose critical questions. This promotion brings with it increased demands on me. It follows only too naturally from this that I have to ask in my situation as a homosexual what position the Bundeswehr takes regarding this fact about my personality [...] I see a contradiction when on the one hand homosexuals are disqualified during entrance examinations by being certified with an "inability to perform" and thus absolutely unfit to serve, yet another person receives further promotion, to the rank of officer no less [...] Once more – two months have gone by, after all – I request an unambiguous and clear statement regarding my question.[15]

The BMVg reacted, informing Plein that he "was not intended for the time being" to be called in for further military exercises, which meant there was "no space at

---

11 Reserve Lieutenant Rainer Plein, addressed with "To be forward to the responsible Bundeswehr office," 13 August 1972. A copy is available in BArch, BW 24/7180.

12 Ibid., as well as Defense District Command 355 to Bundeswehr Central Personnel Office, 22 August 1972, BArch, BW 24/7180.

13 Bundeswehr Central Personnel Office, San I 3, 30 August 1972. The letter was signed by a chief of veterinarian staff, plainly angering Plein still further, who jotted down "responsible for pigs?"

14 BArch, BW 24/7180: Office head for Bundeswehr Central Personnel Office to the BMVg, P II 1, 4 September 1972.

15 Reserve Lieutenant Rainer Plein to the office head of the Bundeswehr Central Personnel Office, 9 October 1972. Emphasis in the original.

present" for his promotion to first lieutenant in the reserve.[16] Plein appealed, the appeal was denied. A subsequent letter to the reserve lieutenant from the defense department's lawyers offered a fundamental take on the situation.

> Even without medical examination, it must be assumed that your case is one of consistent homosexuality, manifesting itself in same-sex activities. This likely makes you unfit for military service. Men who are consistent homosexuals are a disruptive factor in the military sphere [...] The military sphere is negatively impacted, as such a disposition is most often linked to other properties, and homosexual activity [is linked] to other forms of behavior inappropriate to the military, which jeopardize troop discipline and fighting power. This applies especially in cases where homosexuals are called to serve as superiors in the troops, and to set an example of model behavior for their subordinates (§10 (1) SG).[17]

This was the "unambiguous and clear statement" that Plein had sought. As could hardly be expected otherwise, the statement came out against him and others in a situation like his. Plein filed a complaint before Münster Administrative Court, demanding "to be promoted to first lieutenant, even as a homosexual. The reasons given for not promoting me do not stand up to rigorous scientific examination in any way, and are injurious and discriminatory against my person in the highest degree."[18] In a statement to the court, the lawyers in Bonn responded that there was no discrimination against the plaintiff taking place. Rather, it was in keeping "with experience that homosexual men put troop discipline and fighting power at risk within the military sphere." It would bring "serious cause for concern if homosexuals had to serve as superiors in the troops, and at the same time set an example of model behavior to their subordinates." Also, it had not been ruled out "in light of the plaintiff's conspicuous tendency" that "same-sex activity was not occurring within the military sphere."[19] The lawyers also cited an increased risk of grooming by other intelligence services.

Münster Administrative Court rejected the plaintiff's appeal, following the BMVg's argumentation, if not in every point. "Increased risk of contact with other intelligence services and potential blackmailing [scenarios] could hardly be expected if the soldier openly admits to his homosexuality." The judges also viewed the BMVg's contention about "forms of behavior inappropriate to the military [that] endanger troop discipline and fighting power" as "wanting explanation and clarification," only to waive it in the next sentence: "The court has nonetheless not

---

16 BMVg, P II 1, 23 November 1972 and BMVg, P II 3, 12 December 1972.
17 BMVg, VR I 1, 20 February 1973.
18 Rainer Plein to Münster Administrative Court, 23 March 1973.
19 BMVg, P II 7 to Münster Administrative Court, 16 July 1973.

considered a discussion that goes into individual details necessary," because the BMVg's considerations were "capable of supporting the contested decisions." The key sentences in the ruling point beyond the troops and toward general attitudes within the broader population.

> Notwithstanding the fact that criminal law has largely restricted the criminality of homosexual acts between men, one must count on a considerable measure of reserve toward homosexuals among the general population. In light of these circumstances, the assumption on the part of the defendant [the BMVg] that this same reserve could be counted on to a particular degree among soldiers and non-commissioned officers, making it seem unassured that the plaintiff would hold a sufficient degree of authority as a first lieutenant in the reserve, is not objectionable.[20]

Still, casting its eye toward the future the Münster court spied a bright spot on the horizon, identifying a noticeable "trend toward tolerance" within public opinion and the population's attitude toward homosexuals. Be that as it may, it "was not being decided here" whether or not the current ruling might continue to apply in the future "upon the trend's continued existence."[21]

North Rhine-Westphalia Superior Administrative Court also followed the BMVg in rejecting Plein's appeal. The Bonn lawyers had sharpened their argument before the second appeals decision, writing that "the defendant's promotion to first lieutenant would, in light of his homosexuality, not only have substantially diminished his authority but also the trust troops must place in superiors, as well as military order itself."

The lawyers had even stronger words: "Superiors with the defendant's disposition encounter flat-out rejection in the troops. Forms of insubordination not only cannot be ruled out, they must be expected with certainty. Within the ranks, homosexuality is considered unmanly at best, something that the legal reforms cannot do anything to alter – not at least for the time being."[22]

The judges at superior court likewise stressed the considerable reserve shown toward homosexuals among the population "and thus among soldiers as well." The potential impairment of troop discipline and fighting power was a "cogent reason for differentiating, i.e. for not recognizing [the plaintiff's] fitness to serve as a superior, and thus as an officer in the Bundeswehr." The judges ruled further that "it does not matter whether [the plaintiff] has engaged in some form of homosexual activity previously while in the line of military duty and thus given cause

---

20 Ruling at Münster Administrative Court, 10 June 1974, Az 4 K 338/73.
21 Ibid.
22 Ruling at North Rhine-Westphalia Superior Administrative Court on 4 September 1975.

for offense, because the defendant has rightly proceeded solely on the basis of his consistent homosexual tendencies." General value standards, and specifically the principal of equal treatment would not be violated. "It is plain to see that different conditions apply for consistently homosexual men than for heterosexual soldiers in a community composed exclusively of men, as with certain sections of the Bundeswehr specified for defensive combat operations." The Bundeswehr also could not wait to see whether a particular soldier did in fact endanger troops' discipline and fighting power, "or in other words 'let chance dictate.'"[23]

The final act in Reservist Lieutenant Plein's legal dispute with the Federal Republic was staged at the Federal Administrative Court, where his appeal against the superior administrative court's previous decision was rejected.[24] The BMVg had prevailed in all instances; the officer had lost the battle and the war.

In evaluating the legal course of action, it should be kept in mind that the reservist officer played an early role in the emerging homosexual movement as a founder of the Münster activist group. He used the unexpected opportunity that presented itself in the original letter from defense district command to involve the Bundeswehr in a battle of principles against discrimination against gays and lesbians. Coming as a complete surprise to the armed forces, the otherwise routine procedure of promoting an officer in the reserve turned into a politically charged issue with potentially far-reaching effects. Plein could have accepted or rejected the promotion without further ado, but it was not about the promotion for him, it was about principal. Personnel management at defense district command understood this and referred the case to the defense ministry, which then took up the gauntlet before taking off the gloves, so to speak. By now it was much more than the promotion of a reserve that was at stake in the controversy. The administrative court rulings subsequently generated in the Plein trials established the principle that gays should not be seen as fit to serve as instructors or superiors in the military. For the first time, the BMVg was forced to take a legal position on homosexual soldiers' fitness for service in leadership roles and defend it in court.

The judges' ruling did not escape criticism from within their own ranks. Erhard Denninger, a law professor from Frankfurt am Main, objected that the military service senate had only noted the "abstract risk" that homosexual orientation might "carry into" the realm of service, but discounted the "risk" in the specific case of the plaintiff. This meant the assumed risk of "a possible impairment in troop discipline and fighting power" was sufficient to "deny the ability to serve as an officer generally." Instead of creating an "individualized ruling to forecast suitability" the

---

23 All quotes ibid.
24 Ruling at BVerwG, 16 February 1976, Az VI B 83.75.

Bundeswehr had made a "general statement on unfitness," thus violating the ban on discrimination under Article 3 of the Basic Law.[25]

In November 1976 Rainer Plein died by his own hand. *Stern* magazine reported on the story in 1984, linking the suicide to the final court ruling.[26] A close associate of Plein's rejected the suspicion voiced here and elsewhere that the suicide was closely tied to his losses in court.[27] The principles that were formulated during the proceedings against Plein endured for over twenty-five years.[28]

Change must often be instigated outright; Rainer Plein provided an initial impetus. It was only after (many) courageous souls had stood up and demanded their rights that the pressure to change truly arose. The second impetus came from another lieutenant, this time from within the ranks themselves.

2. "Jeopardizing Discipline and Fighting Power." The 1977 Case of a Lieutenant

Discovery of homosexual tendencies in a superior by subordinates, the Federal Administrative Court wrote in 1979, can bring disruption to service, weakening troops' fighting power and ultimately impairing the Bundeswehr's defense mandate, which took constitutional priority. The ruling came in response to a complaint filed by a lieutenant who had written to the BMVg about his homosexuality in April 1977.

> I hereby inform you of my homosexuality. It is not possible for me to pretend any longer, nor do I see any reason why I ought to. Every acquaintance in my private life knows about it and accepts me. I've only ever had positive experiences with admitting my homosexuality up to now. I did not acknowledge it in some spectacular fashion but tried to present my tendency

---

25 Denninger, "Entscheidungen Öffentliches Recht," 444–46.

26 "Following the final ruling at Federal Administrative Court, he took his own life in 1976." Krause, "Da spiel' ich denen eine Komödie vor."

27 "Many posited a close link between the Bundeswehr's crusade and the suicide; in my personal view (and source material only I have access to), the Bundeswehr was only a part of the picture." Email from Sigmar Fischer to the author on 19 March 2018. On Rainer Plein's life and the debate surrounding a street being named for him see Heß, "Der ungeliebte Aktivist"; Fischer, "Er organisierte Deutschlands erste Schwulendemo: Gedenken an Rainer Plein." For a fuller account see Fischer, "Bewegung zwischen Richtungsstreit und Stagnation." A draft resolution to name a street after Plein was initially rejected by majority vote of the district council for Münster city center in 2013, but then accepted in 2017. Since then, the city has had a street named Rainer-Plein-Weg.

28 This is Günther Gollner's argument in "Disziplinarsanktionen gegenüber Homosexuellen im öffentlichen Dienst," 116.

as something self-evident. Even in cases where I've shared it with one comrade or another, they've taken it in stride. My tendency has not had any negative impacts on my service up to now, nor can I picture any. My decision to report my homosexuality was influenced in part by the fact that I want to engage publicly to make equal rights for homosexuals a reality, so before you find out about my homosexuality through other sources, I'm telling you myself.[29]

The lieutenant built on his first announcement with two more letters in May 1977 stressing "his goal to break down prejudices against homosexuality in the Bundeswehr."

To date he had not seen any of the dangers to service operations that allegedly came from homosexual officers, nor did other homosexual officers he knew have any negative impacts to report on their own activity in the service. The time had come to dismantle discrimination against homosexuality in the Bundeswehr, and accept it just as heterosexuality was.[30]

In March 1978, the BMVg personnel department conducted the staff review requested by the lieutenant, informing him that his same-sex orientation precluded both fitness for and assignment to positions of leadership, as well as continued measures of support and promotion. He was advised further to apply for dismissal under §55 (3) SG. ("A fixed-term soldier is to be discharged at his request if remaining in the service would mean particular hardship for him due to personal, especially domestic, professional or economic reasons."[31]) The lieutenant declined, instead filing a complaint against the announced ban on his advancement and promotion in which he argued that his superiors were committing a breach of duty by denying his eligibility to serve as an officer based on his sexual orientation. He had been trained and qualified as an officer but was not being deployed as such, nor was he receiving support for further training. This was a contestable decision that could not be justified based on the alleged threat homosexuals in positions of leadership posed to young conscripts. No such threat existed in the present case. Assuming the existence of such a threat implicitly accused homosexual officers of undisciplined behavior without any justification, and could not be demonstrated empirically. His own situation was much closer in nature to that of women serving in the Bundeswehr medical corps. His transfer to a permanent student position on special assignment in the Army Office was not only unusual but unlawful. At the same time, the BMVg was failing to live up to its contractual obligation to continue the lieutenant's training at the Army's officer academy and his service branch

---

29 Quoted in the ruling at the Federal Administrative Court, 1st Military Service Senate, 25 October 1979, Az.: BVerwG, 1 WB 113/78.

30 Ibid.

31 http://www.gesetze-im-internet.de/sg/__55.html (last accessed 31 March 2021).

school. By contrast he, the plaintiff, had not violated his own official duties to date, even by reporting his homosexuality. The BMVg asked the court to deny the petition. The 1st Military Service Senate in turn ruled that:

1. The motion is admissible [...]
2. The motion is however, unfounded [...] The reason for the BMVg's contested decision was the petitioner's report that he was homosexually inclined. Homosexual tendencies of this sort exclude a soldier from being fit to serve as a superior.[32]

Be that as it may, determining whether a soldier was in breach of duty if he partook in homosexual activity outside the line of duty should be distinguished from the question of whether a homosexual soldier was qualified to serve as a superior and receive further professional support.

> Independently of the concrete risk, which depends on the person of the soldier in question, the very circumstance of a superior's homosexual tendencies becoming known to his subordinates can bring lasting disturbances to service operations. Modes of conduct that would be viewed as normal or common in heterosexuals may, in the case of someone with a homosexual orientation, take on a significance in the eyes of subordinates that can lead to gossip, suspicion or rejection of the superior, and to difficulties in giving and receiving orders. The BMVg need not close its eyes to this possibility with respect to Article 3 GG.[33]

This meant that the principle of equality embodied in Article 3 of the Basic Law did not apply in full for homosexuals in the armed forces. Nor was the Bundeswehr required to stand up to the prejudice that existed against homosexuals among the troops by "asserting homosexual soldiers' presumptive claim to equal treatment against general opinion." Doing so "would weaken troop fighting power due to the unavoidable official difficulties that would result, thus impairing the Bundeswehr' defense mandate, which in turn holds constitutional priority." Rather, "even after the criminality of 'simple' male homosexuality had been abolished," the BMVg could still "take into account that in such a tightly bound male community as the Bundeswehr, homosexuals were still largely not accepted as before."[34] The court did not accept the lieutenant's analogy of female medical officers, who "were not subject to a loss in authority due to their heterosexual orientation." The military

---

32 Federal Administrative Court, 1st Military Service Senate, ruling on 25 October 1979, Az.: BVerwG, 1 WB 113/78.

33 Ibid., excerpts quoted in *Stern*, 19 January 1984 in Krause, "Da spiel' ich denen eine Komödie vor."

34 Federal Administrative Court, 1st Military Service Senate, ruling on 25 October 1979, Az.: BVerwG, 1 WB 113/78; also quoted in *Stern* on 19 January 1984.

service senate ruling was reprinted and commented on in specialist journals, especially given the limited view it took of the principle of equality in Article 3 of the Basic Law.[35]

Similar to the Münster reservist officer five years before him, the lieutenant now found himself drawn into a battle over legal principles on behalf of homosexual rights. He persisted in his case against the Bundeswehr purely by formal means, turning directly to the Ministry of Defense when personnel leadership ignored his letters at first. When the ministry did not respond to his grievances in time either, he followed up with further complaints. A full year passed before the BMVg acceded to the lieutenant's request for a staff review. There he was not surprised to learn of the Bundeswehr's position regarding homosexual soldiers in supervisory roles; herein lay the cause for the legal action he was pursuing in such a dogged and targeted fashion. It was no longer his continued assignment as lieutenant with a foreseeable end to his time in the service that was at stake.

One can at least attach a question mark as to where the lieutenant's motivation lay in exposing himself in such a way. It can be gleaned from the administrative court ruling that he still had the remainder of his time in the troops to serve out after being released from his course of studies in the Bundeswehr university system. If the lieutenant's only concern had been to continue with regular training and assignment, he could have done so without making his sexual orientation known. This allows speculation as to whether all the announcements, legal complaints and court action merely represented an attempt to improve the lot of open homosexuals in the Bundeswehr, or whether they also harbored the notion of early dismissal back into civilian life as a self-outed homosexual. Whatever the lieutenant's ultimate motives, the dispute ended in a landmark ruling, similarly to the 1976 proceedings. The lieutenant's openly stated intention of "engaging publicly to make equal rights for homosexuals a reality" made it all the easier for the BMVg and the court to reject his claim. In their ruling the administrative judges wrote that "such strident display of his own homosexuality would only multiply the likelihood and scope of difficulties within the line of duty."[36]

The two rulings from the Federal Administrative Court provided a north star for all subsequent court decisions until 1999. They were regularly invoked up through 2000 by the BMVg as a way of justifying restrictive practices, as in its 1995 response to a young man's questions, submitted via the parliamentary commis-

---

35 See for example *Neue Juristische Wochenschrift* 21 (1980): 1178.

36 Federal Administrative Court, 1st Military Service Senate, ruling on 25 October 1979, Az.: BVerwG, 1 WB 113/78.

sioner for the armed forces. The legal department quoted the 1979 ruling verbatim, although without identifying it as such.

> Independently of this concrete risk, which depends on the person of the soldier in question, the very circumstance of a superior's homosexual tendencies becoming known to his subordinates can bring lasting disturbances to service operations. Modes of conduct that would be viewed as normal or common in heterosexuals may, in the case of someone with a homosexual orientation, take on a significance in the eyes of subordinates that can lead to gossip, suspicion or rejection of the superior, and to difficulties in giving and receiving orders. The BMVg need not close its eyes to this possibility with respect to Article 3 GG.[37]

The Bundeswehr took care to ensure that troops were also made aware of the 1979 ruling. To that end an early, longer article appeared in 1981 in the magazine *Truppenpraxis*, bearing the conspicuous title "Current Legal Cases: Homosexual Tendencies within a Military Superior." The article concluded that

> Homosexual tendencies within a military superior – specifically an officer – preclude his suitability for promotion because those tendencies are liable to encumber the exact sort of close-knit official and person-to-person points of contact that are necessary in the military. Nothing else applies concerning an officer's fitness for assignment as a superior or further promotion.[38]

Civilian publications were clearer still in their translation of the verdict and its implications: "Homosexual tendencies rule out a soldier's fitness for assignment as a superior."[39] With the *Truppenpraxis* article, homosexual soldiers now had it in writing that their only chance in the Bundeswehr was to continue concealing their orientation and private lives. One of them was Captain Michael Lindner, company commander in ABC Defense Battalion 610.

---

37 BArch, BW 1/531593: BMVg, VR II 7, to Mr. T., Bremen, 13 January 1995.
38 Weidinger, "Homosexuelle Neigungen eines militärischen Vorgesetzten."
39 *Neue Juristische Wochenschrift* 21 (1980): 1178. The name of Michael Kühnen should also be remembered here, a lieutenant who studied at the Bundeswehr University Hamburg and was dismissed as a fixed-term soldier in 1977 not for his homosexual orientation, but due to right-wing extremist political activity. Later, he achieved dubious fame as "Germany's most prominent right extremist," as the *taz* put it in 1991. Wolfgang Gast, "Neonazi Michael Kühnen gestorben," *taz*, 26 April 1991.

3. A Subject for Debate in Parliament: The Case of Captain Lindner, 1981

The ruling came as a "shock" for Captain Lindner, rattling his already fragile sense of self-confidence as a homosexual officer and overall confidence in the service, and ultimately leading to psychological problems, increasingly strident declarations and dismissal for reasons of health.[40] Declared medically unfit for service since 1980, the captain was retired due to illness on 30 September 1982 under §44 (3) and (4) SG.[41] Lindner's struggle for gay rights in the military, both in general and on his own behalf, encompassed innumerable petitions and complaints filed against his superiors and the BMVg, written publications, and open lectures.[42] In doing so the captain could not hope for any support from the German Armed Forces Association (Deutscher Bundeswehrverband); a 1982 attempt to win the association chairmen over for the cause of homosexual soldiers, let alone interest them, had failed. The subject had never come up before at either district or general meetings – the "overwhelming majority of soldiers" was "not attached [to the topic] in the way you might have expected." It "was not a subject for the Bundeswehr" if one wanted to "avoid arguments," association chairman Colonel Volland informed Lindner, it was "rather a negative stance that was adopted" in this case. It was the same old story: "Integrating homosexual soldiers would necessarily lead to unrest within the ranks."[43] The office of the parliamentary commissioner for the armed forces had already replied to a previous petition from Lindner in 1980 by rehashing the ministry argument about "endangering discipline and fighting power."[44]

Lindner did not lose heart, laboring to make sure that homosexuality ultimately remained a topic on the desks, and thus in the minds of officers, government officials and lawyers alike. His letters, proposals and informational pieces, as well as his legal complaints and action, take up any number of thick folders in multiple BMVg offices.[45] In July 1981, already declared medically unfit but still in

---

40 For a full account see chapter 2.

41 BArch, BW 1/503302: BMVg, PSZ III 6, 29 June 2001; ibid., BMVg, PSZ I 8, 20 June 2002. Also mentioned in "Soldaten als potentielle Sexualpartner," 22.

42 On 17 June 1982, for example, Lindner addressed "The fate of homosexuals in the Bundeswehr" at the Martin Luther King House in Hamburg – and then again on 9 February 1984 at Hamburg's Magnus Hirschfeld Center, an initiative he cofounded – regarding the current scandal surrounding General Kießling.

43 Federal Chairman of the German Bundeswehr Association to Captain Lindner, 21 July 1982.

44 Office of the Parliamentary Commissioner for the Armed Forces to Captain Lindner, 9 September 1980.

45 To cite just a few examples, on 22 September 1981 Lindner wrote to BMVg, Org. 1; that same day

active service, Lindner informed the BMVg that he was planning an international press conference in Bonn for that October. The topic would be "Human rights and dignity in the Federal Republic of Germany – On the example of homosexuals in the German armed forces."[46]

The captain's case also engrossed the German Bundestag in 1981 after Lindner won Hamburg deputy Helga Schuchardt (FDP) over to his cause. In an inquiry to the defense ministry, Schuchardt asked "how the federal government accounts for the contradiction that homosexual men are fundamentally fit for military service and longer periods of voluntary service, yet denies their suitability for leadership positions despite scientific consensus that homosexuality is not an illness but merely one variety of sexual behavior?"[47]

As was customary for this sort of question-and-answer period, a prewritten answer was read aloud to the plenary session word for word before debate about the inquiry and its response began (a format that has come in for frequent criticism).[48] Parliamentary State Secretary Wilfried Penner of the SPD answered for the BMVg in 1981, contending that the government did not see any contradiction in the juxtaposition; the two sets of facts were not comparable. When it came to military eligibility, it was the person's ability to integrate that was of defining importance. Being suitable for leadership roles, on the other hand, depended on whether a "person is capable of exercising the corresponding degree of authority in that role."[49] This latter question had been answered in the negative, in accordance with court rulings at the highest instance. Schuchardt responded with a "practical question": If homosexuals were not able to take on leadership roles, how likely did the state secretary consider it that those soldiers would be susceptible to blackmail, "precisely because they had denied their homosexuality?"[50] The state secretary

---

about another matter to BMVg, P II 1; on 30 September 1982 to the editorial board at the magazine *Truppenpraxis*, and again to FüS at the BMVg on 20 January 1983 under the letterhead "Independent Homosexual Alternatives, Public Affairs," from Hamburg. All archived in BArch, BW 2/31224.

46 BArch, BW 2/31224, letter from Captain Michael Lindner to the Federal Ministry of Defense on 29 July 1981.

47 German Bundestag, 9th legislative period, 45th Session, 24 June 1981, typed transcript, 2541.

48 In an interview with Roger Willemsen for *Die Zeit* (Die Zeit 17, 16 April 2014), former Bundestag President Norbert Lammert criticized the period as "the weakest part of the German parliamentary system," "unpresentable" and "politically meaningless in its current format". Willemsen is the author of a satirical book about the course of daily debate in the Bundestag entitled *Das hohe Haus* (The high house). "There were no ministers on the government bench, only the state secretary [...] the opposition had already handed its written questions in. And then the state secretary read a prewritten answer out loud." Quoted in Graw, "Echter Schlagabtausch oder höfisches Ritual?"

49 German Bundestag, 9th legislative period, 45th Session, 24 June 1981, typed transcript, 2541.

50 Ibid.

countered that he had limited himself to the issue of authority in his answer. When Schuchardt then asked what the basis was for the supposition that homosexual soldiers or superiors had no authority, Penner tersely responded, "certain life experience."

Deputy Ralph Herberholz (SPD) continued the line of questioning, asking whether "the ability to display authority depends on an individual's sexual behavior?" Penner replied that he "did not mean to be understood in that way." What mattered, he continued, was whether certain sexual behavior became known about, eliciting then party colleague Karl-Heinz Hansen to interject "Aha, so it's nineteenth-century hypocrisy then!"[51] A question from Deputy Schuchardt followed as to whether the government shared the opinion that its treatment of homosexual soldiers was not reconcilable with the legal reforms of §175 StGB from 1969 and 1973. Penner replied that "the reforms concerning §175 StGB hold no direct bearing on whether or not homosexual soldiers are fit for positions of authority. Fitness can also be denied in cases where neither a criminal act nor disciplinary misconduct is present."

The FDP deputy was not done yet, and returned to the question of authority. "Do not the risks of being discovered tempt those affected to hypocrisy? Do not you believe that people who are prone to hypocrisy can no longer be the first to hold authority?" (*Der Spiegel* picked up Schuchardt's veiled accusation in an article that year, writing that the FDP deputy had charged the defense ministry with "practically inciting homosexual soldiers to hypocrisy."[52]) Dr. Penner responded that "the difficulties in which the group of people under discussion find themselves are sufficiently known about." It had not been possible up until now to look beyond the security precautions he had described, although it was possible that society would continue to evolve. When Schuchardt asked hopefully whether she might draw from this a certain chance to expedite the defense ministry's process of forming an opinion on the matter, the state secretary sidestepped the issue. He did not believe that it was a matter of the BMVg forming an opinion, "at any rate I would not want to restrict the developments to this establishment alone. I believe it's a matter of society as a whole forming an opinion."[53] At this point, Deputy Herberholz asked

---

51 Here and in what follows, ibid., 2542. At the time proceedings were underway to expel Karl-Heinz Hansen from the SPD due to his harsh critique of counter-armament, specifically for claiming that Chancellor Schmidt's defense policies were "a sort of secret diplomacy against his own people."

52 "'Berufliches': Michael Lindner," 176.

53 German Bundestag, 9th legislative period, 45th Session, 24 June 1981, typed transcript, 2542.

the parliamentary state secretary and fellow party member a question that immediately showed the visible discrepancies in the BMVg's position.

> State Secretary sir, you have just said that only when a certain form of sexual behavior
> becomes known about does one lose the ability to exercise authority. Am I to assume then that
> sexual behavior unknown to the BMVg basically guarantees the ability to exercise authority
> where this matter is concerned? If you affirm this, then how is it that the BMVg actually deter-
> mines sexual behavior if people do not exactly go around shouting it from the rooftops?[54]

In this instance, all Secretary Penner could do was assure the representatives in
parliament that the BMVg did not make inquires about sexual tendencies. Conservative SPD member Lothar Löffler sprang to the secretary's defense, using a follow-up question to articulate the position that sexual behavior was not something
that could be fixed by defense ministry decree but a broader social issue. Penner
concurred readily, replying that that matched his view. Claus Jäger of the CDU then
provided the finale to the debate, tiresomely dressing up in the form of a question his own announcement that "in securing suitable growth in leadership, [the
Bundeswehr] has quite a different set of concerns weighing at present then the
impact of the reform of §175 on soldiers' ability to lead." Penner did not pick up the
ball from the opposition, responding that "Unlike you, I'm of the opinion that from
time to time, when appropriate, it is perfectly becoming for parliament to make
visible discrimination against different groups of people." The transcript records
applause from the SPD and FDP and interjections from the CDU/CSU that "that was
not at all what he asked!"[55]

Nineteen years later in 2000, *Der Spiegel* asked Wilfried Penner, now parliamentary commissioner for the armed forces, about his previous position on homosexual soldiers in positions of authority. He replied that "even at the time he had
not felt right" about his statements before the Bundestag. He had changed his
opinion in the meantime, and "the younger generation views it much more casu-
ally anyway."[56]

In 1979 at the request of Bundestag representative Hertha Däubler-Gmelin,
the BMVg's legal department filed a summary of the regulations concerning the
"assignment and career advancement of homosexual soldiers." Signed by Parliamentary State Secretary Andreas von Bülow, the document began by stressing that
a homosexual soldier was "as a matter of principle not treated any differently than

---

54 Ibid., 2543.
55 All quotes ibid.
56 "Im Kosovo noch lange benötigt."

heterosexual soldiers," and that it would only be different "if the soldier's homosexual activity impacts the official line of duty."[57] At any rate, "whether the soldier can continue to advance, remain in his official post or should receive a different assignment [...] or whether there is a possibility of dismissal" would be decided based on individual circumstances. A soldier's homosexuality being known about within the service meant it was no longer a private matter but had now made its way into the official realm. It meant that the soldier was unfit for a higher assignment and the greater supervisory powers it would entail. As a rule, the soldier's advancement was no longer possible.

A closer look at the phrasing reveals differences to corresponding statements from the 1980s and 1990s. Unlike later communications, there was no mention of homosexual soldiers' general ineligibility to serve as superiors or military instructors in 1979. Nor, in contrast to subsequent regulations, was there any reference to mandatory dismissal from positions of authority, as with the case of Lieutenant Winfried Stecher in 1998.[58] In the 1979 paper, transfer, and thus removal from one's official post was required only in the event that the "respectability and trustworthiness" of the soldier in question had been diminished. This formulation would certainly have allowed platoon leaders like Lieutenant Stecher and others whose homosexual orientation had no impact on their official duties to remain in their posts. This in turn intimates what other source comparisons reveal: Throughout the 1980s and 1990s the Ministry of Defense took a decidedly harsher stance against homosexual superiors, maintaining this strict line undeterred up to the new millennium. Two ministry papers from the early 1980s proved decisive markers along the way.

4. Policy Papers, from 1982 and 1984

An officer or non-commissioned officer who states his homosexual tendencies must reckon with no longer being promoted or entrusted with higher-order tasks. Furthermore, he can no longer remain in the troops in the service post of direct superior (e.g. as a group leader, a platoon leader, company head or commander). He will receive an assignment in which he is no longer the direct superior of predominately younger soldiers.[59]

---

57 BArch, BW 1/304284: BMVg, VR I 1, 15 February 1979. See also BMVg, parliamentary state secretary to Representative Herta Däubler-Gmelin (SPD), 23 February 1979, as in what follows.

58 See below in section 9 e of this chapter for a more detailed account.

59 BArch, BW 2/31224: BMVg, P II 1, Az 16-02-05/2 (C) R 4/84, 13 March 1984. A copy is also available in BArch, BW 2/38355, and verbatim in a BMVg previous response to a letter from a petty officer 2nd class in early February 1984, i.e. at the height at the of the Kießling affair. BArch, BW 1/378197: BMVg, P II 1 to Petty Officer, 2nd Class G., 8 March 1984.

Issued by Section II 1 of the BMVg personnel department on 13 March 1984, the quoted regulations came in a circular letter intended and subsequently used as guidelines for department employees. Though the date suggests otherwise, the policy paper was not created in the wake of the Wörner–Kießling affair. The exact same wording can be found in another paper from the same section two years before in August 1982, which among other things discusses gay officers' "reduced ability to assert themselves" and the need to "protect military subordinates against ranking homosexual officers."[60] In the view of the personnel unit, it was not merely conscripts and their parents but "broad segments of the population" that "would show no understanding for soldiers being exposed to the influence of superiors with deviant behavior." For young prospective officers who were gay, their unsuitability for positions of authority meant the end of their careers before they had begun. A young cadet admitting his homosexuality would lead to dismissal in a simplified procedure as "unfit to serve as officer," with §55 (4) SG providing the legal basis in this case.[61] (A staff officer today recalls one incident from his officer training in 1995, when his then partner had planned a weekend visit to the school in which he was enrolled. Following protocol as he did, the private (and officer candidate) requested permission for the overnight stay from his superior. The course leader asked him what his relationship to the man was. All of a sudden, the entire future career of the prospective officer hung in the balance. Without knowing the personnel guidelines himself, the officer cadet instinctively sensed the danger that lay in an honest answer and opted for an untruth, replying that the visitor was an old friend from school. The course leader was satisfied, and the cadet's partner came to visit that weekend. Officer training continued, the eyewitness became on officer and today is a lieutenant colonel.)

Even if, as in this case, an officer candidate behaved "inconspicuously" and succeeded in making the rank of lieutenant, he was still liable to be shown the door – both lieutenants and younger lieutenant colonels could be dismissed up to

---

60 BArch, BW 1/304286: BMVg, P II 1, 12 August 1982.

61 Ibid. "A fixed-term soldier may be dismissed during the first four years of his service if he no longer meets the demands his career track will make of him. An officer cadet who is unqualified to be an officer, a medical officer cadet unqualified to be a medical officer, a military music officer cadet unqualified to be a military music officer, a sergeant cadet unqualified to be a sergeant and a non-commissioned officer cadet unqualified to be a non-commissioned officer shall be discharged without prejudice to the first sentence of this paragraph." If the party concerned has previously been a fixed-term non-commissioned officer or enlisted soldier prior to his admission to the career of officer or sergeant, he shall not be discharged but "restored [to his former status], provided he still has a service rank that corresponds to that career track." See http://www.gesetze-im-internet. de/sg/_55.html (last accessed 31 March 2021).

the end of their third year under §46 (4) SG for "lacking qualification as a career soldier."[62]

A closer inspection of the sources leaves it unclear as to whether this regulation affected all officers or only career soldiers. The personnel division took the latter view in 1990, writing that the differences in regulation between fixed-term and career soldiers were "hardly satisfying."[63] A previous paper by the legal department from 1979, on the other hand, had explicitly limited the measure to lieutenants in career service.[64] However, the policy of dismissing homosexual officer candidates as unsuitable applied indisputably for all prospective officers.[65]

The BMVg's excommunication policies did not only affect gay officers and officer candidates, but reached conscripts hoping to continue voluntary service in the rank-and-file as well. The justification cited in the latter case was that "NCOs are largely recruited for the Bundeswehr from this career group," and homosexuals were not qualified to serve as NCOs.[66] Privates or privates first class also did not stand any chance of remaining in the Bundeswehr even without the intention to apply for NCO, as "longer-serving rank-and-file soldiers still obtain a position of trust in their units or formations even without admission to the career group of NCO."[67]

Even a soldier with a sterling assessment record stood zero chance of lengthening his contract or being appointed to career service if his homosexuality became known, justified in terms of the restricted number of assignments available to him.[68] Since the Plein proceedings in 1972, Bundeswehr leadership had settled on the following point: Homosexual superiors lacked the requisite trust of the soldiers under their command.

> Underlying the view of the BMVg is the experience that due to the broad rejection of homosexual forms of behavior within the ranks, superiors with homosexual tendencies are unable

---

62 BArch, BW 2/31224: BMVg, P II 1, Az 16-02-05/2 (C) R 4/84, 13 March 1984. A copy is also available in BArch, BW 2/38355. See also BArch, BW 2/32553: BMVg, FüS I 4, 3 February 1993.

63 BArch, BW 2/31224: BMVg, P II 1, 2 March 1990.

64 BArch, BW 1/304284: BMVg, VR I 1, 15 February 1979, as well as BMVg parliamentary state secretary to MdB Herta Däubler-Gmelin (SPD), 23 February 1979.

65 Ibid.

66 BArch, BW 2/31224: BMVg, P II 1, Az 16-02-05/2 (C) R 4/84, 13 March 1984, verbatim previously in BArch, BW 1/304286: BMVg, P II 1, 12 August 1982 and in the BMVg response to a letter from a petty officer 2nd class in early February 1984, i.e. at the height at the of the Kießling affair. BArch, BW 1/378197: BMVg, P II 1 to Petty Officer, 2nd Class G., 8 March 1984.

67 Ibid.

68 These are the retrospective findings on §37 SG, which governed appointments of career or fixed-term soldiers, in Walz, Eichen and Sohm, *Kommentar zum Soldatengesetz*, 647–48.

to hold their ground without suffering a severe loss in their official authority. As the career groups of NCOs and officers consist of a series of assignments that are predominately carried out within the ranks, superiors with a same-sex orientation cannot be entitled to expect treatment equal to soldiers with normal sexual tendencies – especially when it comes to official promotion.[69]

The same argumentation was now extended even to longer-serving privates first class and lance corporals. Homosexual soldiers' alleged unfitness to serve as superiors thus also justified their exclusion from lower career groups down to the rank-and-file, a line of reasoning that was unconvincing even at the time but provided effective cover for itself. It made no difference that by far not every nonrated soldier wanted to become an NCO, and not every NCO or officer wanted to enter career service. In the end, the disadvantages mutually sustained each other from different vantage points and the circle closed in on itself, leaving soldiers who identified outwardly as homosexual without any career prospects in the Bundeswehr.

A BMVg spokesperson made no secret of this policy speaking to *Der Spiegel* in 1993. Anyone who announced his homosexuality when applying to be an officer cadet would be turned away "as fundamentally unfit for the officer and NCO career groups." Bundeswehr leadership viewed "soldiers with deviant sexual behavior as a 'potential target for foreign services'," the article continued, going on to cite the well-known case of the Austrian colonel Alfred Redl. The BMVg spokesperson pointed to the "the topic's polarization in broader social discourse" as a further reason for restrictions.[70]

Günther Gollner had already warned the Bundeswehr against its reliance on disciplinary measures in 1977, in one of the first academic publications on discrimination against homosexuals in professional life. It would be better instead "if they settled issues related to homosexuality at the level of personnel leadership. Matters that no longer lead to removal from service but a transfer at most will soon no longer create a stir, and what does not create a stir is hardly capable of diminishing someone's reputation."[71]

This was exactly how the BMVg and the Bundeswehr were already proceeding. Yet Gollner turned out to be mistaken in his assumption that personnel measures like transfers would not create a stir.

Where exactly do you draw this inhuman attitude from, of regarding every homosexual officer or NCO as unfit a priori for leadership responsibilities? [...] From Alexander the Great and Gaius Julius Caesar on down to Prussia's Frederick the Great, their homosexual tenden-

---

69 BArch, BW 2/31224: BMVg, P II 1, Az 16-02-05/2 (C) R 4/84, 13 March 1984.
70 "Versiegelte Briefe," 51.
71 Gollner, "Disziplinarsanktionen gegenüber Homosexuellen im öffentlichen Dienst," 116.

cies are common knowledge. You would hardly want to insinuate that these men had difficulties in giving orders and receiving compliance. Your automatism in immediately viewing
gay superiors as unfit to serve can only be based on your prejudices and/or your homophobia
[...] As a homosexual soldier and officer, I find your statements discriminating in the highest
degree, because they are stigmatizing. Up until now I had believed that the defense ministry
had woken up, at least by the end of the Kießling affair, and finally set aside past relics of vil-
ifying homosexuals from the era of the Nazi dictatorship. It pains me greatly to have learned
the opposite from you.[72]

This was a captain's 1985 rejoinder after the BMVg responded to his question about
the treatment of homosexual superiors. The BMVg's letter had "sent a 'cold shiver'
down the spine, to say the least."[73] The captain issued a clear challenge two weeks
after receiving the reply, personally forwarding news of his own homosexuality
along with a request for a career prognosis through his superiors to the BMVg personnel department.[74] The department responded within days, listing the entire
menu of restrictions. Going by the current personnel guidelines, the only "career
prognosis" was its end, or in the words of the personnel officers and lawyers, "no
leadership assignments, no further advancement or promotion." Four days after
the captain's direct superior received the letter, the captain was removed from his
post as the area leader of a telecommunications sector.

The press also took up the case, with *taz* publishing an article in August 1986
that bore the headline "Unacceptable in male society."[75] "Hostility toward homosexuals" lived on in the military even after the Wörner–Kießling affair, with "gays
[...] forced into mendacious and secretive behavior by every means." The captain's
status as a career soldier was changed to that of a fixed-term soldier with a term
of twelve years; he would leave the Bundeswehr "in just under a year," in summer
1987.[76] Yet the change in status could only occur with the captain's consent, as soldiers of any rank identified as homosexual generally had not been subject to immediate dismissal since the 1970s (as long as they had not implicated themselves in

---

72 Letter from Captain P. to the BMVg head of information security from 8 October 1985. (The
author has a copy of this and the following letter from 21 October 1985 in his possession. Thanks to
Michael Lindner of Hamburg for supplying them.)
73 Ibid.
74 Letter from Captain P. to the BMVg, P IV 5 from 21 October 1985, with copies sent to the legal
advisor of the chief of defense, the parliamentary commissioner for the armed forces, the board
chairman at the German Bundeswehr Association, the Bundestag Defense Committee and the defense policy working groups at the CDU/CSU, SPD and FDP, among others. Excerpts also quoted
in BArch, BW 2/31224: Military Service Court North, 12th Division, ruling, Az N 12 BL a 3/86 on
16 December 1986.
75 Wickel, "In einer Männergesellschaft nicht hinnehmbar."
76 Ibid.

any other sort of official misconduct). The same went for career soldiers who had completed their third year of service as it did for fixed-term officers, NCOs and non-rated soldiers who had completed their fourth year of service. The BMVg had again ruled out premature retirement for the "person concerned" in its decree from March 1984, at least so long as no evidence of inability to serve was present, "something toward which homosexual orientation [did] not count."[77] The year before, in 1983, the personal department had ascertained that "early retirement that did not rest on inability to serve or a court ruling" was not possible in the case of an officer "at present."[78] Ten years later a BMVg division again found that homosexuality was "not grounds for dismissal for reasons of health [sic]."[79] The Bundeswehr was far more progressive on this point in the late 1970s than other NATO forces, many of which continued to dismiss homosexuals without exception into the 1990s, even up through 2000.[80]

The BMVg made no attempt to hide the matter from the media, for better or worse. In 1993 *Der Spiegel* quoted a ministry spokesperson as saying that "homosexual soldiers who were already officers or NCOs will remain in the Bundeswehr if no extraordinary circumstances arose. They will, however, only be assigned to posts that hold no leadership responsibility."[81]

The August 1982 paper did not simply look to justify the current restrictions against homosexual superiors, officers and officer cadets. The author, a member of the personnel department, also cast an eye toward future developments for which the Bundeswehr had to be prepared, in his view. The document's candid and undogmatic reflections are surprising in how closely they anticipate the changes that would come about in 2000, and deserve to be acknowledged and recounted here.

Society's increasingly liberal views on homosexual behavior, the author wrote, may bring changes in jurisprudence "if it is not possible to set forth compelling reasons to rule out introducing this liberalization to the armed forces."[82] This made it "necessary to develop ideas amenable to the armed forces in a timely fashion that will also allow superiors with a same-sex orientation to continue to advance officially through access to higher-rated service positions." The paper was also ahead of its time in reckoning that the armed forces would open further to women. In that case, it was an open question whether case law would still accept the argument

---

77 BArch, BW 2/31224: BMVg, P II 1, Az 16-02-05/2 (C) R 4/84, 13 March 1984. A copy is also available in BArch, BW 2/38355.
78 BArch, BW 1/304286: BMVg, P II 1, 12 August 1982.
79 BArch, BW 2/32553: BMVg, FüS I 4, 3 February 1993, also in BW 24/14249.
80 See chapter 7 for a full account.
81 "Versiegelte Briefe," 49.
82 BArch, BW 1/304286: BMVg, P II 1, 12 August 1982. Also in what follows.

that "a homosexually inclined superior is constantly exposed to the risk of seeing potential sexual partners in his subordinates, and being influenced by sexual motivations in his behavior toward subordinates." Logically, it followed that the same "would also have to apply for heterosexually inclined male or female superiors toward subordinates of the respective opposite sex."[83]

Every subsequent official position and reply from the BMVg on the subject of homosexuality repeated the 1984 orders verbatim. BMVg department InSan I 1 did however build on the guiding principle in 1990 by noting that if someone applied for career or fixed-term service without disclosing his (homo)sexual orientation, he would be accepted based on qualification and need.[84] ("Qualification and need" were and remain a standard formula in the Bundeswehr for any statement dealing with hiring or subsequent personnel decisions.) Fixed-term soldiers were acceptable as career soldiers. In short, "as with heterosexual soldiers, an entirely normal military career stood open to this group" one sentence began – before going on to qualify – "insofar as their sexual orientation does not in some way become known to the service." The phrase "in some way" deserves attention here, as it specifically implied revelations that were not only offered freely by soldiers themselves but chance discoveries, as in the course of MAD reviews or by targeted denunciation. This relativized the promise of an "entirely normal military career." Yet in practice, nothing changed. As ever, the sword of Damocles continued to swing above the heads of gay officers and NCOs, capable of coming down on them at any time, without any say or possibility of redress. Nearly all the eyewitnesses interviewed by the author gave impactful accounts of how aware they were of the constant risk, the tremendous psychological burden and the limitations it imposed, including on their private lives.

Looking back, the BMVg emphasized in 2016 that "No ministerial orders were issued to all personnel posts in the Bundeswehr."[85] Was this a defensive, even a false statement to downplay earlier papers that were unflattering from the present perspective? It was not. The BMVg personnel department had explicitly emphasized previously in January 2000 that no "ministerial orders for personnel oversight over homosexual soldiers" had been sent out to all personnel posts. Rather, the 1984 letter from division P II 1, internally dubbed the "Westhoff paper" after its author, had only been circulated to the personnel offices at the joint staff of the armed forces and central personnel posts. These formalities notwithstanding, the

---

83 Ibid.
84 Here and in what follows, BArch, BW 1/546375: BMVg, InSan I 1 to the British defense attaché in Bonn, 21 August 1990.
85 BMVg, P II 1, Az 16-02-5/2 from 22 August 2016.

paper reflected the "principles that apply to date [January 2000]." Ministry-wide orders had consciously been avoided in 1984, with the view being that "the presumably smaller percentage of homosexual soldiers compared to the overall population does not justify it." The number of legal remedies (read complaints and inditements) to which the ministry had to attend was minor, "if labor intensive."[86]

The personnel department did draft a centralized decree in advance of the 1998 Bundestag elections that explicitly contained "no trends toward softening" but instead couched current practices in clean-cut legal formulations, i.e. which would have locked the restrictions in place. The armed forces suggested instead letting the orders quietly vanish into the drawer "for reasons of expediency." (Soldiers like to speak in this context about "Filing Unit P," – "P" for paper basket.) The reason for their concern was another "media field-day."[87] What was more, at the time the chairman of the German Bundeswehr Association had promised to cover the legal costs "up to the final instance" of an air force lieutenant then protesting his transfer based on his homosexuality.[88] This led the ministry to assume that the association's representatives in the joint spokesperson committee, the principal body representing soldiers' interests at the BMVg, would object to new, restrictive orders.[89] The old policies thus remained in place without being put to writ or confirmation coming through the established channels.

In March of 1984 the BMVg went public with the regulations even before they were circulated among the personnel department. And it did so not just anywhere but on the most important stage in German politics, during a plenary session of the Bundestag. In mid-January 1984, as the Wörner–Kießling affair reached fever pitch, parliament took up the topic of the Bundeswehr's treatment of homosexual soldiers in Bonn. Deputy for the Greens Wolfgang Ehmke inquired among other things about the legal basis for dismissing homosexual soldiers and superiors. BMVg Parliamentary State Secretary Würzbach responded by quoting from the personnel guidelines, which were distributed shortly thereafter. Under §55 (5) SG, a fixed-term soldier could be dismissed from the Bundeswehr during his first four years of service "if remaining in his post would seriously endanger military order or the reputation of the Bundeswehr." That included cases in which fixed-term soldiers came under disciplinary action or were criminally convicted for homosexual activity. §55 (4) SG stipulated that an officer candidate unfit to become an officer should be dismissed. "Here too, homosexual activity could be grounds for such mea-

---

86 BArch, BW 1/502107: BMVg, PSZ III 1, 5 January 2000.

87 Ibid.

88 See chapter 4, section 9.e, and chapter 6, section 2.

89 BArch, BW 1/502107: BMVg, PSZ III 1, 5 January 2000.

sures in specific cases. The same applied for lieutenants up until the end of their third year as officers under §46 (4) SG."[90] Moreover, a military service court could order both fixed-term and career soldier to be removed from service under §63 of the Military Disciplinary Code in the event of serious disciplinary misconduct, "e.g. same-sex relations with a subordinate." Würzbach's remarks reflected the legal situation with great precision, meaning that parliamentarians and the press – and with them the public – knew about the BMVg's guiding practices by January 1984 at the latest. SPD deputy Dietrich Sperling's followed up by asking whether that meant "a soldier who openly confesses his homosexuality and wishes to become an officer has an incomparably more difficult time getting promoted and becoming a superior than someone who openly discusses his heroics with women, and must endure much more invasive investigation of his fitness to serve than the other who openly and permissively lives out his virility as a heterosexual." "Colleague, sir, I can confirm this," came the state secretary's reply.[91]

The state secretary stressed the fact that "no initiatives had been developed at the Bundeswehr to learn about soldiers' homosexual tendencies," in line with the "respect the service held for the soldier's entitlement to the protection of his private sphere." For these reasons there had been "no systematic registration of cases in which same-sex behavior by soldiers had led to dismissal or removal from service by court order."[92]

In the course of the lengthy debate, which even today is worth reading, State Secretary Würzbach laid out a further aspect that seemed important to him: A duty of care existed toward homosexual soldiers, especially "if they showed extreme tendencies," since it had come to pass "that other soldiers would make fun of them, yank their chain, encourage or force them to behave in certain ways [...] press-gang or blackmail them." This explained why "certain measures within an organization such as the armed forces are [were] required."[93]

Norbert Gansel of the SPD later asked whether he could summarize the state secretary's position as being that "in the Bundeswehr, a soldier who is homosexual but has neither incriminated himself under general criminal law nor abused his official position and otherwise lives among ordered relations is not discriminated against in any way." "Yes," Würzbach replied "as I relate that to the service and superiors." Würzbach then added that "in human practice" discrimination by

---

90 German Bundestag, 10th legislative period, 47th Session, 19 Jan 1984, typed transcript, 3377.
91 Ibid., 3379.
92 Ibid., 3377.
93 Ibid., 3378.

fellow soldiers "could not be ruled out and, as experience teaches us, tends to set in."[94]

One idea advanced in the personnel office's paper came in for special criticism from the armed forces: Creating service posts specifically for homosexually oriented soldiers. "Establishing and demarcating service posts for this group would as a matter of course lead to heterosexual soldiers also being assigned to those posts, who could potentially find this unacceptable."[95] There was no need for action in general; the rulings at the Supreme Administrative Court were sufficient. In 1987 FüS I 4, the personnel section responsible for leadership development and civic education, cited another reason to stay as far away from the topic as possible: "Homosexuals are among the high-risk groups when it comes to the immunodeficiency disease AIDS, bringing a new dimension to the issue that in light of the political disputes requires proceeding with the utmost caution."[96]

Given the circumstances, and since no new findings were expected, FüS I 4 saw no need for a meeting. Section P II 1 could "not provide endorsement" and insisted on one.

> I admittedly share your view that the subject requires the utmost caution, and likewise your concerns about establishing dedicated positions, or even the potential consequences of holding a position dedicated especially to the group of people in question. I'm not able to share your view that the supreme court rulings are enough to enable providers to decide appropriately in individual cases.[97]

What was more, homosexuals, including soldiers, would open up "more and more frequently about their tendencies." Interested parties would increasingly make it an obligation to protect minorities. In saying so, the personnel office was not interested in revising its position so much as fortifying it yet again for the foreseeable judicial and political disputes.

> In my opinion, the current line should be maintained. In all likelihood, this will result in increased complaints and court proceedings as well as activity within parliamentary politics and on the behalf of the interested parties. I thus see coordinating between users and providers as indispensable.[98]

---

94 Ibid., 3379.
95 BArch, BW 2/31224: BMVg, FüS I 4 to P II 1, 2 September 1987.
96 Ibid.
97 BArch, BW 2/31224: BMVg, P II 1 to FüS I 4, 7 October 1987.
98 Ibid.

(In the world of the Bundeswehr, Bedarfsträger or "users" meant the armed forces, while *Bedarfsdecker* or "providers" meant personnel leadership.) The meeting resulted in the following arrangement:

1. Advancement (training for advantageous assignments, transfer to similar service posts and subsequent promotions) is generally ruled out. Cases that arise will be considered on this basis. Exceptions are possible only within narrowly defined bounds.
2. There will be no tagging of service posts for which homosexually oriented soldiers would come under consideration.
3. A regulation (ministry decree, G1 Note) will not be issued.[99]

Decisions dating back thirty or forty years neither can nor should be measured (exclusively) against today's standards. The armed forces' line of reasoning at the time was entirely plausible from their point of view: The prejudices that existed among the broader population toward homosexual men would find reflection in the minds of its soldiers. In doing so, BMVg lawyers generally had their eyes trained on conscripts and younger fixed-term soldiers who would carry societal reservations with them into the Bundeswehr, although those same reservations certainly existed among all ages and ranks in the armed forces. In the estimation of the Bundeswehr, reservations like these could trigger a loss in authority in superiors who were known to be homosexual. The following line of argumentation has been described repeatedly; the BMVg lawyers derived it from the constitution, elaborating a highly abstract but legally effective justification for the restrictions. With the arguments they believed themselves forearmed for the possible and increasingly likely scenario of a complaint before the Federal Constitutional Court (Bundesverfassungsgericht, BVerfG). By the ministry's logic, the judges at the Karlsruhe court would then have to weigh and decide between the constitutional mandate to defend the country and the foreseeable argument of the constitutional ban on discrimination. The Bundeswehr's legal staff spied a favorable hand for itself in that case. Yet their arguments had a weak spot: The evidence for, let alone the plausibility of their causal chain was lacking. Did homosexual superiors jeopardize the combat readiness of the armed forces in actual fact? Ultimately, the reservations about homosexuals playing out in the minds of the lawyers and employees of the BMVg reflected the norms and values of society at large.

This sort of assessment may still have been current in the 1960s, the 1970s and the early 1980s. Yet with each new decade, gay (and lesbian) life paths met with increasing tolerance and acceptance. This was the very trend, already visible on the

---

99 BArch, BW 2/31224: BMVg, P II 1, note from the meeting on 22 October 1987. A copy is available in BArch, BW 2/31225.

horizon in 1973, that the Münster administrative judges had anticipated with their ruling as a window onto the future.

The BMVg was already pointing out the connection between developments in the Bundeswehr and in society by 1993; speaking to *Der Spiegel* with a view toward further "shifts in society's moral conception," the ministry spokesperson would not rule out the possibility "of homosexuality someday no longer being a problematic topic in officers' circles."[100]

5. Excursus: "Teachers' Fear of Outing Themselves."

It was not just soldiers whose careers threatened to come to an end if their homosexuality came out, but nearly anyone in public service. "Even if you don't violate any existing laws as a homosexual in the public service, you still hold no guarantee of being left in peace, not by a long shot," one writer lamented in 1981. "Professional bans on homosexuals are seldom acknowledged in public, because most of those affected keep silent as to the actual reasons for not being hired or their dismissal out of fear of their surroundings and justified concern for their further career path."[101]

One case from 1974 did draw notice, involving a lawyer working in the cultural ministry for Saarland's state government, whose "homosexual relationships" had exposed him to "potential public or secret extortion." Demoralized, the government councilor had quit the service, as *Der Spiegel* reported.[102] The list of teachers dismissed for their sexual orientation is also long.[103] Much longer would be the never-compiled list all the men who were rejected for the civil service and/or government posts from the outset due to their sexual orientation. "If you won't go so far as to openly justify it based on the homosexuality of the person, there are usually other ways and means to be free of the candidate."[104]

As with criminal law, civil service law in the Federal Republic followed the well-trod paths of previous decades, following the principle in effect since the turn of the twentieth century that "no homosexual can remain in service, much less enter it".[105]

---

100 "Versiegelte Briefe," 54.

101 Stümke and Finkler, *Rosa Winkel, Rosa Listen*, 375

102 *Rosa Winkel, Rosa Listen*, 376–77.

103 For more see Gollner, "Disziplinarsanktionen gegenüber Homosexuellen im öffentlichen Dienst," 117–124.

104 Stümke and Finkler, *Rosa Winkel, Rosa Listen*, 377.

105 Gollner, "Disziplinarsanktionen gegenüber Homosexuellen im öffentlichen Dienst," 106

Special standards applied (and still do) to teachers who had either received tenure or held permanent salaried positions. In 1979, the disciplinary tribunal at Düsseldorf Administrative Court ordered a teacher from North Rhine-Westphalia to be removed from his post in the civil service. A regional court had previously sentenced the teacher to pay a fine for crimes against §175 StGB (the newer version) after the judges became convinced he had repeatedly engaged in consensual homosexual activity with a fifteen- and sixteen-year-old. The disciplinary judges for the state of North Rhine-Westphalia certified that the accused had "failed in the core area of his duties as a teacher," and as such was no longer tenable.[106] The teacher, who had been provisionally removed from service in the meantime, filed an appeal against the ruling that was subsequently denied by the disciplinary senate at North Rhine-Westphalia Superior Administrative Court.[107]

In 2019, a former teacher from Berlin looked back on the difficult situation gay teachers still faced in the 1970s in an article for *Der Tagesspiegel* entitled "Teachers' fear of outing themselves." "Before, homosexuality in schools was absolutely taboo, you didn't talk about it. When we became active and visible with the gay movement in the early Seventies, there were professional bans and discrimination at the work place."[108]

6. "I'll Just Say I'm Gay Then." Attempts to Shorten the Length of Service

The number of qualified or outstanding officers and NCOs who declined to apply for fixed-term or career service due to restrictions against homosexuals cannot be reckoned. The Bundeswehr rejected them, their potential went unrealized. The author himself can recall many such instances of longer-serving comrades, highly rated officers among them, from his own officer training starting in 1995, and after 1997 as a student at the Bundeswehr University in Hamburg. The armed forces lost highly qualified leaders forever as a result of its policies.

Quite a few officers and NCOs used the fact that the service uniformly denied identified or self-ascribed homosexuals' ability to serve in positions of leadership to their own particular advantage. From the very beginnings of the Bundeswehr there have been soldiers who sought to exit the military for the free economy as quickly

---

106 Disciplinary division at Düsseldorf Administrative Court, Az 15-0-12/79, ruling on 28 June 1979.
107 Disciplinary Senate at North Rhine-Westphalia Superior Administrative Court, Az V-11/79, ruling on 7 October 1980.
108 »Die Angst der Lehrer, sich zu outen«.

as possible after completing a degree at one of the Bundeswehr universities. For top graduates from technical or economics courses, offers of well-paid jobs at private companies beckoned in place of the sometimes harsh realities of military life. The issue was that the Bundeswehr did not make it all that easy for officers to leave once they had successfully completed their degree, insisting that they now fulfill the agreed upon period of service. Some tried to get around it by filing as war resistors, although the approval procedure generally showed limited prospects for success. To others it seemed more promising to identify themselves as homosexuals, and thus set the mechanism of automatic dismissal into motion. "I'll just say that I'm gay then" was one option. Former officers recall that any number of officers dismissed from the armed forces in this way had not actually been homosexual. A person's sexual tendencies obviously could (and can) not be "verified," at least not without violating the basic standards of human dignity. In the final instance, the regulations were clear: more or less credible report of a same-sex orientation was enough. The officers turned the Bundeswehr's own weapons against it.

One officer in this category had studied mechanical engineering at the Air Force Technical Academy. In 1972, now a captain and career soldier in his final year at a civilian technical college paid for by the service, he filed a petition for release due to inability to serve under §44 (3) SG on account of his homosexuality. The personnel department at the BMVg denied the motion.[109] The officer's appeal to the BMVg was similarly denied on the grounds that while homosexuality could constitute unfitness to serve under §44 (3) SG in principle, not "every homosexual tendency sufficed, but only one heightened to a sexual perversion." That was not the case with the petitioner, who up to that point in his service had understood how to "curb his tendencies to the extent that they did not cross the threshold of military service or criminal law."[110] The captain made a renewed effort, this time under §46 (3) SG due to special hardship. The Bundeswehr granted this request, but demanded the captain repay all his training expenses to the tune of around 38,000 DM. The former officer filed suit. Bremen Administrative Court accepted the lawsuit and ruled the payment request, which in the meantime had been lowered to around 13,000 DM, unlawful. In their rationale, the Bremen judges took the BMVg's going line of argumentation as to why gay men were unfit for leadership positions and turned it against the armed forces (and thus the taxpayer) to impose a burden, in this case financial:

---

109 BArch, BW 24/7180: BMVg, P IV 4, 23 May 1972.
110 BArch, BW 24/7180: BMVg, VR I 1, 4 July 1972.

Were the plaintiff to remain in service, it would have meant a disproportionately heavy burden for him. Despite the liberalizations that have taken effect in the meantime – and leaving open for now whether it is justifiable or not – homosexuals still come across as out of place in the Bundeswehr's male society. This makes it plain to see that the plaintiff would have had to count on his homosexual tendency posing all kinds of difficulties if it came out in the Bundeswehr. His career path as an officer too would also have been [...] diminished, as same-sex tendencies preclude [...] a soldier's suitability positions of authority [...] It would have been unreasonable therefore for the plaintiff to remain in career service.[111]

The BMVg's demand to pay back educational expenses would similarly represent a special hardship for the plaintiff.[112] The lawyers for the BMVg decided against appeal and embraced, or perhaps put up with, the judgement. Four expert reports confirmed the former officers' homosexuality as "heightened to a sexual perversion," the court's ruling on special hardship was "unshakeable."[113]

Still, the service did not make departure all that easy. The sources preserve one case from 1988 involving a lieutenant. The officer, who had signed on for a period of six years in the service, was removed from his course of study at Bundeswehr university after failing his preliminary diploma examination and transferred to serve out the remainder of his time in the troops. The lieutenant sought to avoid what clearly seemed to him unfavorable career prospects by filing for release due to inability to serve under §55 (2) SG, on grounds of homosexuality. The personnel division at the BMVg turned down the lieutenant's first application; a Bundeswehr hospital had found him fully eligible for military service, and under the guidelines of ZDv 14/5 no illness or inability to serve that would justify dismissal under §55 (2) SG was in evidence.[114] The officer's attorney filed an appeal. His client was homosexual, something he had felt more and more strongly over the past years and to which he now openly confessed. Independently of whether or not homosexuality should be viewed as a disease in the strict medical sense, it presented an obstacle to his client in fulfilling his service duties. In this case the lawyer flipped the familiar restrictions against homosexual superiors around to use them as ammunition against the BMVg on behalf of his client.

My client's tendency brings him into continual conflict when performing his service within the ranks. On the one hand he knows that officers and nonrated troops learning of his tendency could lead to difficulties. In view of the vast discrepancies in society's attitudes toward homosexuality, it could only be feared that a number of officers would lose their trust in my client, while a number of NCOs and enlisted men would lose respect. For this reason, up to

---

111 BArch, BW 1/304284, ruling at Bremen Administrative Court, Az 3 A 342/79 from 24 July 1980.
112 Ibid.
113 BArch, BW 1/304284: BMVg P II 8, 2 December 1980.
114 BArch, BW 2/31224: BMVg, P III 5, Notice of appeal, addressee and date redacted.

now my client has endeavored to prevent his tendency from becoming known about within his unit [...] At the same time, serving in the Bundeswehr rests on a sense of camaraderie and life together in extremely tight quarters. It is nearly unbearable for my client to constantly have to keep up pretenses under these circumstances. Homosexuality is an obstacle to my client in fulfilling his role as an officer, and ultimately may diminish troop fighting power. My client has already been forced to give up all leadership responsibilities.[115]

In concluding, the lawyer asked whether it was true that homosexuality was cause for dismissal under §55 (2) SG for career soldiers, but not for fixed-term soldiers, which would constitute an utterly incomprehensible instance of unequal treatment if so.[116] Ultimately, the lawyer had merely written down the ministry's well-known arguments and returned to sender. The BMVg's lawyer remained unconvinced.

The fact that you can no longer be employed in the essential functions commonly associated with an officer in the rank of lieutenant owes exclusively to the homosexual tendency you have disclosed. Yet according to medical report results [the tendency] holds no value as an illness, and thus cannot be understood as a "physical affliction" in the sense of §55 (2) SG. Nor does the tendency satisfy the element of a "weakness in physical or mental forces" in the legal sense. Your disclosed homosexual tendency thus establishes a lack of suitability of a different kind than the one that could lead to dismissal for inability to serve. Lawmakers have refrained – not least in the interests of protecting soldiers – from granting the service the possibility of dismissal ex officio in the event of any kind of unsuitability.[117]

The jurists in Bonn did, however, hint at another way out of the Bundeswehr for the lieutenant. Upon request, "cases involving a homosexual tendency" frequently met the conditions for dismissal due to special hardship under §55 (3) SG. It could not be reviewed whether the elements were present in the petitioner's case, as he had only filed for dismissal for inability to serve under §55 (2) SG. Nor did any regulations providing for a career soldier's dismissal on grounds of homosexuality exist under §55 (2) SG.[118]

There seem to have been different views within the BMVg regarding this last statement, to put it cautiously. In direct reference to the lieutenant's complaint, in March 1990 the personnel office observed that lieutenants serving as career soldiers could be dismissed for homosexuality under §46 (4), but an equivalent regulation for fixed-term officers was lacking. The discrepancy was "hardly satisfactory."

---

115 BArch, BW 2/31224, the lawyer for a lieutenant, complaint and grounds for complaint, sender and date redacted.
116 Ibid. By way of explanation, §55 (2) SG only applies to fixed-term soldiers.
117 BArch, BW 2/31224: BMVg, VR I 5. Notice of appeal, addressee and date redacted.
118 Ibid.

The office repeated its internal suggestion to allow the petitioner dismissal under §55 (3) SG, applying a "broad interpretation" to the concept of "special hardship."[119]

The lieutenant did not file for dismissal due to special hardship, however, but continued serving in the troops, specifically on a regimental staff. After a year or so he requested assignment as a platoon leader and instructor, which the personnel office denied him with reference to the officer's homosexuality being on record. Again the lieutenant filed a complaint. The case ultimately reached the Federal Administrative Court, and it is this circumstance alone that research has to thank for the coming to light of the lieutenant's earlier request for dismissal due to inability to serve. Under normal conditions, procedures that touch on personal or medical matters can no longer be found in the available source material. As always in its rulings, the court began its ruling with a detailed account of the plaintiff's service history, allowing it to be recounted here.[120]

7. "Homosexuality and Military Service in Germany." A SOWI Study from 1993

In 1993 a study on "Homosexuality and Military Service in Germany" by the Bundeswehr Institute of Social Sciences (SOWI) came out, based in part on a survey it conducted on the "sexual morality" of conscripts. (SOWI was responsible at the time for surveying soldiers about a wide range of topics, work that the ZMSBw continues today.) In 1992, the institute asked 433 soldiers from western Germany and 882 from the five "new states" of eastern Germany (as they were commonly referred to at the time) to anonymously state their opinion about cohabitation without marriage, prostitution, abortion and homosexuality. Close to 32% of the young soldiers in the west and 28% in the east found homosexuality "acceptable." 20% in both east and west found it "unacceptable." Ten percent in the west and 13% in the east viewed it as "negative," while 35% and 42% rated it "very negative," respectively.[121] Young soldiers from the east showed a clearer rejection of homosexuality, with those in the west tending toward greater acceptance.

Evaluating the differences between two groups in a Germany that had been reunited just two years before raises methodological questions that were left unaddressed in the SOWI study, chief among them the division into east and west. At

---

119 BArch, BW 2/31224: BMVg, P II 1, 2 March 1990.
120 BVerwG, 1 WB 61/90: Federal Administrative Court, 1st Military Service Senate, ruling from 8 November 1990. Found on www.jurion.de.
121 Fleckenstein, "Homosexuality and Military Service in Germany."

How basic military conscripts perceive homosexuality in east and west 1992

West   East

28   28

36

42

14   20

22   10

☐ Acceptable   ☐ Unacceptable   ☐ Negative   ■ Very Negative

Source: Fleckenstein, Homosexuality and Military Service in Germany (numbers given as percentages).   ©ZMSBw 09583-02

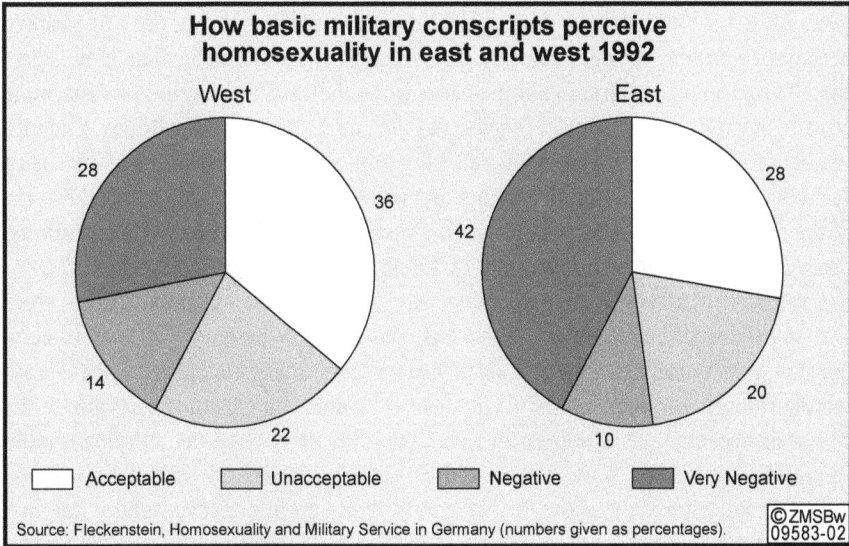

the time the survey was conducted, many soldiers from eastern Germany were serving in barracks in the West; on Sundays they would travel by car or train from Saxony or Mecklenburg to Lower Saxony or Schleswig-Holstein, to return home the following Friday afternoon. Anyone scanning the barracks parking lots of Baden-Württemberg, Hessen or Lower Saxony could not fail to notice the number of east German license plates, which were often in the clear majority. If barracks location was a deciding factor in classifying the soldiers as coming from the west or east, a great number of soldiers of East German origin and socialization would thus have fallen under "West." In this case the values for western Germany would have been much more strongly influenced by East German socialization than vice versa. The collected data would hold greater validity if, on the other hand, one's place of birth or residence was the deciding factor in the east-west classification. Yet even a quick glance at the graphic depiction of the survey results when divided by geography reveals the similarity between the two – the differences between east and west were not that serious after all. If the geographical division is done away with, the indisputable finding remains that two-thirds of all young men performing basic military service looked on homosexuality as either "unacceptable," "negative" or "very negative."[122]

These results were subsequently used throughout the 1990s by the BMVg, the armed forces themselves, the legal profession and administrative court judges

---

122 "Homosexuality and Military Service in Germany," Table 2.

alike when they attributed a gay superior's anticipated loss in authority to a lack of acceptance among younger soldiers. This disapproval of homosexuals, now scientifically proven, came first in a line of reasoning that was then used to substantiate risks to discipline and order in the units as well as their combat readiness, and ultimately to justify restrictions against placing homosexuals in positions of authority. The survey data and familiar conclusions were last cited in January 2000 as part of the federal government's response to questions from the Federal Constitutional Court concerning the action brought by First Lieutenant Winfried Stecher.[123]

While the survey data may have kept aging, the conclusions drawn from it remained unchanged. In the late 1990s the ministry debated whether to commission a new study including a survey of soldiers; there was general agreement among the offices involved about the need for a sociological study to evaluate the "issue of acceptance." The question was whether or not the commission should remain in-house with SOWI or sourced externally. In 1999 the staff departmental leader at FüS I postponed the decision until the Federal Constitutional Court had ruled in First Lieutenant Stecher's case.[124] This meant that in 2000 the BMVg had been relying on the same survey results since 1992.

In 1993, SOWI Director Professor Bernhard Fleckenstein drew on the survey for a paper on the German position regarding homosexuality and military service in the UK city of Hull. Even now the German military continued to be a "male society in tightly confined quarters," Fleckenstein argued, echoing General Major Manfred Würfel's contention from that February.[125] Military personnel policy was "geared toward preventing any problems that might arise for communal life in the troops due to homosexually oriented soldiers from occurring in the first place."[126] Concretely, Fleckenstein lectured on policies concerning the treatment of homosexual officers and NCOs that this study has already considered in some detail.

The presentation also raised the sharp critique coming from "interest groups" who faulted the Bundeswehr with lagging "far behind the current state of social development" and "leading the charge in social intolerance." In their eyes, jurisprudence had to date been in violation of the constitutional principle of equality, proceeding along lines that amounted to "discrimination against homosexual sol-

---

123 BArch, BW 1/502107, no pagination. BMVg, State Secretary, draft response to Federal Constitutional Court, Az 2 BvR 2276/98, undated, here p. 4.
124 BArch, BW 1/502107, no pagination: BMVg, PSZ III 1, 5 January 2000.
125 Fleckenstein, "Homosexuality and Military Service in Germany," p. 2 and Table 2. The major general's quote comes from the *Der Spiegel* article "Versiegelte Briefe."
126 "Homosexuality and Military Service in Germany." The German original is available in BArch, BW 2/32553.

diers that went so far as destroying their professional existence."[127] Fleckenstein took an opposing stance:

> Notwithstanding the political sloganeering so typical of press releases, the question that lies at the heart of the matter is whether military personnel leadership will continue to be left with discretionary powers of its own in evaluating the fitness of its leaders and instructors. The primary mission of personnel management is a strong and capable Bundeswehr. This aim takes constitutional priority. Based on real-life observation, Bundeswehr leadership cannot close its eyes to the fact that homosexual soldiers – especially those in positions of authority – still fail to gain acceptance in the armed forces without complication.[128]

The Minister of Defense was also not obliged in the current legal landscape "to actively implement homosexually oriented soldiers' (purported) claim to equal treatment against prevailing opinion – and thus potentially at the cost of troops' ability to function." The service also had a "duty of care toward the other 98% of men in the armed forces at least who were heterosexual." A younger soldier had put it to the SOWI director as follows: "I respect the intimate realm of my comrades; I also have a right to be spared the intimate realm of others."[129]

8. Case by Case, or Blanket Rejection?

In a statement about the SOWI paper, Section I 1 in the BMVg's legal department stressed from the outset that homosexual soldiers were unquestionably given promotion or assignment in accordance with their suitability. "It is true, however, that despite changing opinions within certain sections of society, the sort of suitability required [...] for higher-value assignments cannot unreservedly be affirmed for homosexual soldiers after considering their individual case."[130] The sources give contradictory answers as to the policy of individual case inspections; not only did the positions shift over a longer period of time, but different departments and sections within the ministry in Hardthöhe took opposing standpoints nearly simultaneously. In 1993, for example, Section VR I 5 gave prominence to a policy of "considering the individual case when it comes to homosexual soldiers."[131] Just a few

---

127 "Homosexuality and Military Service in Germany," 8. In the paper Fleckenstein quotes from a press release by the Gay Federation in Germany from 27 January 1993.
128 "Homosexuality and Military Service in Germany."
129 Ibid., 9.
130 BArch, BW 2/32553: BMVg, VR I 1, 2 March 1993.
131 Ibid., BMVg, VR I 5, 29 March 1993.

weeks before, the spokesperson for the Ministry of Defense himself had confirmed to the press that homosexual soldiers were not "uniformly discriminated against" but instead received "case-by-case examination" when leadership positions were involved.[132] Yet another paper put out at nearly the same time by Section FüS I 4 includes no mention of individual case examinations when "detaching" homosexual superiors from positions as leaders, instructors or educators.[133] The same section had put out a position paper three years before in 1990 that explicitly rejected "any exceptions" to denying homosexuals assignment as commanding officers or instructors.[134]

A great deal of official commentary from the section records the same unambiguous position, as with a 1986 G1 memo draft regulating all matters pertaining to homosexuality. The memo states that "an officer or non-commissioned officer whose homosexual tendencies become known can no longer remain in his service post as a leading figure in the troops. He must be given an assignment in which he is no longer in a position of authority over predominately younger soldiers."[135] The clarity of phrases like "can no longer" or "must" allowed no room for interpretation or possibility for decision on a case-by-case basis. The policies of dismissing officer cadets under §55 (4) SG and officers up through the third year of their service under §46 (4) SG likewise show up in the paper in unaltered form.

The G1 draft was never implemented; Chief of Defense Wellershoff decided to shelve the matter instead. According to him, there was "no need to act at present," and he considered the "time and place inappropriate."[136] In a nutshell, "[if done, it would be done] as inconspicuously as possible *but not, under any circumstances, now!*"[137] Exactly one year later in November 1987, the personnel department again decided against the need for regulations in the form of a ministry decree or G1 memo. "Treatment on a case-by-case basis was both possible and sufficient" due to the limited caseload, and the problem also had to be approached "carefully" as "regulation could be perceived as revealing and discriminating."[138]

---

132 Ministry of Defense: The number does not come close – No "blanket" discrimination against homosexuals, 27 January 1993, 10:22 a.m., BArch, BW 24/14249.

133 BArch, BW 2/32553: BMVg, FüS I 4, 3 February 1993.

134 BArch, BW 2/31224: BMVg, FüS I 4 to P II 5, 25 June 1990.

135 BArch, BW 2/31225: BMVg, FüS I 4 to minister via the parliamentary state secretary, 22 October 1986, annex, identical to BArch, BW 2/31224: BMVg, FüS I 4, July 1986.

136 Ibid., BMVg, FüS I 4, 10 November 1986; Ibid., BMVg, StAL FüS I, handwritten note from a conversation with the chief of defense, 4 November 1986.

137 Ibid., BMVg, a further handwritten note on a conversation with the chief of defense, 4 November 1986 (emphasis in original).

138 Ibid., BMVg, P II 1, 23 November 1987.

"Homosexual soldiers' 'fitness' for positions of authority has been denied by a court of the highest instance," soldiers and the interested public were able to read in a 1991 article that appeared in the military magazines *Heer, Luftwaffe, and Blaue Jungs.*[139] "An official position could be abused, while soldiers' lack of acceptance could jeopardize authority, which in turn could disrupt service operations and weaken discipline and fighting power" wrote the author, succinctly summarizing the arguments advanced by the administrative courts and the BMVg before clearly articulating the crucial point: "What matters in any case is that it is possible, not that it is actually so."[140]

The year before in 1990, FüS I 4 had argued that society had a right to "impeccable superiors," continuing to represent the "baseline position that homosexual soldiers should be removed from assignment as superiors and instructors without exception, and kept at a remove from such assignments."[141] In doing so, the section was plainly rejecting calls for decisions on a case-by-case basis that surface from time to time in the internal papers of the BMVg (including within Section FüS I 4), as well as in published opinions from the 1980s and 1990s.

Come September 1994, on the other hand, FüS I 4 was touting case-by-case decisions as the path of the future in a letter to a staff surgeon who eventually petitioned successfully for acceptance as a career soldier.

> On its own, homosexuality cannot be grounds for exclusion from a particular assignment; it is neither a health disorder nor a general criminal offense, nor does it necessarily restrict one's ability to carry out his duties. Yet it is plain to see that problems and situations of conflict can arise between superiors or soldiers slated for positions of authority in the Bundeswehr who have acknowledged their homosexual inclinations on the one hand, and the heterosexual majority on the other, which is why the Bundeswehr insists on the need for individual assessment in such instances.[142]

January 2000 saw a renewed effort within FüS I 4 to abandon the restrictive policy of blanket exclusion in favor of case-by-case examination, though it was all in vain.[143] "Other sections have pointed out that this essentially meant aban-

---

139 Haubrich, "Schwul und beim Bund?!" Chapter 1 has already discussed the article in detail.
140 Ibid.
141 BArch, BW 2/31224: BMVg, FüS I 4 to P II 5, 25 June 1990.
142 BArch, BW 2/38357: BMVg, FüS I 4, 15 September 1994. The letter would continue to hold sway in the future, with Hamburg Administrative Court citing it in its ruling on 26 November 1997 (AZ 12 VG 5657/95, a copy is available in BArch, BW 2/38353). In 1999, Federal Constitutional Court President Jutta Limbach also requested the paper from Defense Minister Scharping in the course of an action brought by a first lieutenant. BArch, BW 2/38357: President of the Federal Constitutional Court to Defense Minister Scharping, 15 July 1999.
143 BArch, BW 2/38358: BMVg, FüS I 4 to the chief of defense, 14 January 2000.

doning the current position. The representatives of the [service branches] were not prepared for that."[144] One former staff officer active at all levels of personnel leadership, including the ministry, explained that the matter had been decided on "uniformly and without case-by-case examination."[145] "Military leadership wanted calm to prevail in the troops; when there were individual cases to decide on, they were settled according to current ministerial orders." There were the orders from 1984 to fall back on, after all. The personnel department at the BMVg, the officer continued, had operated under the premise that homosexuals had to be "removed" immediately from the troops; when he had asked in turn why that was the case, the legal staff from Section P I 1 cited their (alleged) susceptibility to blackmail and "the protection" of young conscripts. From his own vantage point in personnel leadership, the eyewitness recalled finding the treatment of homosexual officers "completely impossible" even in the 1990s. "I never understood it. A group, a minority had been sought out and uniformly excluded."[146] Suggested language worked out for the chief of defense by FüS I 4 in January 2000 once again ruled out any sort of case-by-case decision-making.[147]

All in all, no cogent ministry line on the matter is evident. At times the policy of case-by-case assessment is highlighted, at others it is strictly ruled out. It seems as though referring to case-by-case assessments was itself decided case by case, and depended on the individual stance of whichever section employee or head was responsible for the issue at hand. The contradictory positions allow for multiple interpretations; what is striking, however, is that case-by-case assessment is highlighted for the most part in ministry statements that were directed externally, with unilateral rejection only coming in internal papers. This in turn permits two conclusions:

(1) The BMVg's position was never established internally in a binding manner but adjusted either according to fit the need in the present case or the views of the officer responsible, with military command adopting the harshest stance.

(2) The BMVg's position hardened over the course of the 1990s under pressure from the military side of the institution; later in the decade the ministry opted for a general and strict rejection of case-by-case assessment, which had been envisaged in 1993 and occasionally before then.

---

144 Ibid., as well as an undated draft from FüS I 4.
145 Interview with Ret. Colonel Dieter Ohm in Meckenheim, 17 April 2019.
146 Ibid.
147 BArch, BW 2/38358: BMVg, FüS I 4, recommended wording for the chief of defense for the Military Leadership Council on 19 January 2000, TOP 3.

The exception proves the rule, as the saying goes. The archives themselves proved no exception in this regard, revealing case-by-case decisions as to how gay officers should be treated. One personnel division note from 1990 concerning an air force captain, for example, reads: "Contrary to my previous view, in this particular instance I am now prepared to rescind my fundamental concerns against [the captain's] attending GL FBS C, and thus against his subsequent potential assignment to staff officer."[148]

In this case the officer had let his homosexuality be known in 1979; three weeks later the personnel officer had knowingly assigned him to a position of disciplinary authority and promoted him to captain three years later, in 1982. "Taking into account Federal Administrative Court jurisprudence [...] and personnel leadership practices to date, the service would have had to tell the soldier that his homosexual tendencies ruled out any chance at further promotion," the BMVg personnel employee admonished. "In that case the soldier would still have had the chance to reorient himself professionally at twenty-nine years old." Instead, the officer had been installed as a disciplinary superior and promoted. "This must have given him the impression that the service did not attach any fundamental importance to his tendencies in continuing his military career. Accordingly, he refrained from looking around for career alternatives."[149]

It was not until four years later during a staff appraisal meeting in 1983 that the officer found out he "wasn't under consideration" for further advancement. The fault lay entirely with the service; the officer had trusted in the personnel decisions. Conserving the soldier's trust in the service's decisions weighed more heavily for the BMVg than sticking to its principals on how homosexuals were treated. In addition, there was no particular interest in adhering to those principals, as the captain's homosexuality was known about "only by a very narrow circle." A great deal spoke in favor of his case.

> Three years' probation as a disciplinary superior, a minimum of eleven years (since his disclosure) of proven and inconspicuous service as a troop leader and teaching officer; support and positive behavioral forecasts from multiple disciplinary superiors [...]; discrimination due to disclosure at his own initiative; without it he would likely already be staff officer. Due to these factors [...] P II 1 no longer maintains its original view and recommends allowing the soldier to attend the course.[150]

---

148 BArch, BW 2/31224: BMVg, P II 1, 2 March 1990. FBS C is the basic continued training course for captains offered at the command and staff college in Hamburg, and is required for promotion to staff officer (Major and up).
149 Ibid.
150 Ibid.

Before the decision came out in his favor, the BMVg had initially voted against the captain attending the course in 1989.[151] Without Basic Training Course C at the command and staff college, the captain would have spent the rest of his time in the service in the same rank, signaling the end of his career despite an excellent track record – and all due to his sexual orientation. Official correspondence preserved in other files shows that deciding whether or not to admit the captain to the command and staff college had already been a source of controversy at the BMVg in 1986, when the legal staff of Section VR I 1 declined to cosign a rejection worked out by the personnel section in charge of the matter. The document was faulted with failing to consider the case at hand; the officer had been promoted to captain in 1982 "with knowledge of his tendency." Neither the captain's superiors nor personnel leadership had expressed any concerns about his attending the college at the time.[152] Four years later, the jurists' earlier arguments now persuaded personnel management to agree to the captain's attendance.

Any other officer's attendance at Basic Training Course C represented a foregone conclusion, an absolute necessity. Admitting a homosexual captain to the course, on the other hand, took multiple ministry offices and four years to consider and decide. The captain swallowed the (initially) negative response, replying in writing that he did not intend to seek legal redress. "That doesn't mean that I would be in agreement."[153] The reasoning behind the officer's atypical decision to forego legal means reveals a deep and principled, but also unquestioning trust in the lawfulness of the military's decisions, even if they did elicit personal "unease."

> If the decision is correct, then ultimately there is no basis for disputing it – aside from a potentially subjective feeling, under the circumstances [...] If the decision were unlawful, even legally questionable, why would it be issued in the first place [...]? Why, then, have this established in administrative court proceedings? To my mind the process of clarification – whatever legal process is involved – is something for the office deciding on the matter before it does so.

Reading these lines, one cannot help but picture a somewhat naive officer with an aversion to conflict and a blind trust in his employer. Yet he does finally go on to pull himself together and find fault with the ministry's position. "Lacking fitness for a position of authority and a lacking fitness for promotion is supported by every

---

151 Ibid., BMVg decision by P IV 3, 2 January 1989.
152 BArch, BW 2/31225; BMVg, VR I 1, 5 December 1986.
153 BArch, BW 2/31224, Captain S. to his commander, 31 January 1989. The following quotes from the same source.

contingency and assumption imaginable, but not by facts." The captain then laid out his counterargument in full for his commander.

> What is an open question for me – though I am party to the affair – is whether bringing to bear every unfavorable *possibility* and negative assumption conceivable, as necessary as that may be for personnel planning, allows one to disregard the facts (insofar as admitting to such a tendency is not already worse than any court conviction); whether "sound public sentiment" can be sufficient cause to neglect legal claims and the preservation/protection of one's personality rights; whether people with a homosexual orientation do have an *actual* claim to "equal treatment" after all; whether a sovereign authority would in fact – at all times! – have to preserve and protect the rights of the individual in its (administrative) actions, including potentially against "broad acceptance."[154]

The captain then posed the question of all questions, marking the constitutional crux of all administrative court decisions to date: "Can it really be that under the constitution, immutable and inalienable rights and constitutional principles no longer apply before the defense mandate?" With this, the captain had clearly identified the weak point in the argumentation of the service and its legal staff in 1989, ten years before the Federal Constitutional Court agreed to hear a first lieutenant's constitutional complaint or the European Court of Human Rights found the British armed forces in breach of the European Convention on Human Rights. In 1989 however the captain left it with a letter to his commander, explicitly forgoing the legal option. Instead of confrontation he extended a hand to personnel leadership, writing "I will make every effort not to generalize my conclusions unduly. It pains me to have caused the personnel department and my superiors more work than others with my tendencies." It remains to be seen whether or not the captain's concession in turn increased personnel leadership's readiness to concede. As described above, in 1990 the BMVg reversed its January 1989 decision. Ministry documents on the matter are silent as to whether the captain subsequently attended the leadership course and continued to receive regular promotion and assignment, though a great deal speaks for that being the case. Be that as it may, the significance the chronicle holds for this study lies in the fact that Hardthöhe did actually consider a case on its individual merits and decided accordingly – if only after four years' of back and forth between various sections.

---

154 "Non-acceptance" was likely meant here instead of "broad acceptance."

9. Internal and Political Pressure for Change

"The defendant is obliged to accept the plaintiff in the capacity of a career soldier."[155] Here the defendant was the BMVg, the plaintiff a staff surgeon at a Bundeswehr hospital, and Hamburg Administrative Court the ruling body.

a.) "Completely Detached from the Individual's Personality." A Medical Officer's Years-Long Struggle for Gay Rights in the Military

Before appealing directly to the Minister of Defense and the parliamentary commissioner for the armed forces in 1991, Michael Müller had in his own words campaigned for years (since 1987) "openly and vigorously" for the interests of homosexuals in the Bundeswehr.[156] Hardthöhe replied in October 1991 that in the case of potential fixed-term or career soldiers, prior disclosure of one's homosexual orientation eliminated the option of career service. This was not a "negative valuation or assessment of the individual personality," however.[157] Rather, the "matter of homosexuality in the armed forces must be analyzed in the context of the social reality of German society, completely detached from the individual personality of the homosexual officer." As in the preceding two decades, in 1991 the BMVg continued to emphasize the potential threat that coming out as homosexual posed to troop discipline and potentially combat readiness, a risk which had to be headed off "early on by having appropriate measures in place from the outset." The same "naturally" applied for troop physicians in the event that "soldiers who personally rejected the physician now known to be homosexual led to deficits in maintaining health, and thus impaired operational readiness in the armed forces." At the same time, proceeding in this way "[served] to protect the homosexual superior."[158]

---

155 Hamburg Administrative Court, ruling on 26 November 1997, Az 12 VG 5657/97. A copy is available in BArch, BW 2/38353.
156 BArch, BW 2/38353: Staff Surgeon Michael Müller to the minister of defense, 10 July 1991; reference to his petition to the parliamentary commissioner for the armed forces from the same day in ibid., parliamentary commissioner to the BMVg, 26 August 1991.
157 BArch, BW 2/38353: BMVg, FüS I 4 to Staff Surgeon Müller, 29 October 1991. Also cited in Hamburg Administrative Court's ruling on 26 November 1997, Az 12 VG 5657/97. A copy is available in BArch, BW 2/38353.
158 All quotes ibid. Müller declared the answer unsatisfactory, prompting further letters to the Chief of Defense and Surgeon General of the Bundeswehr in early 1992. BArch, BW 2/38353: Staff Surgeon Michael Müller to General Klaus Naumann and Surgeon General Dr. Desch, 7 January 1992.

Staff Surgeon Müller drew the implications from the unambiguous rejection and filed for early release from service in 1993, using the possibility afforded under the Military Personnel Strength Act as a formal basis. The doctor explained that he could no longer endure the BMVg's contradictions: On the one hand he had served as an instructor and superior for years now, all without any detectable shift in the ministry's baseline position. This meant that going forward he would continue to be subject "to the whims of his superiors." The staff physician's direct superior at the Bundeswehr hospital supported his subordinate's request for early departure. "Based on his outstanding service record," the physician concerned should have been "approved for unrestricted advancement and corresponding prospects." Since neither this nor a "timely individual case inspection" had come about, it followed that the doctor should be released per his wish. Yet the medical officer was not released; simply put, there was a severe shortage of laboratory physicians and he was "urgently needed."[159]

When he received written proof of his indispensable service on the ministry's own letterhead, Müller turned the tables and applied for career service. His application was denied, his complaints rebuffed. With that the officer had showed up the BMVg's contradictions in the most blatant form imaginable, giving him ammunition for his legal fight. The German Bundeswehr Association pledged to cover his legal costs.[160] The doctor arrived in court well-armed – and prevailed.

In January 1994 the physician wrote again to the ministry, this time documenting the Bundeswehr's treatment of homosexuality over the course of forty-three pages. Deftly tying various strands into a cogent argument, he succeeded in making even plainer show of the contradictions in the ministry's line of reasoning. Recipients of the polemic included the chief of defense, the chiefs of the services and the surgeon general; five BMVg sections; the office heads for the army, navy and air force; the parliamentary commissioner for the armed forces; the Bundestag Defense Committee; and all four parties in the Bundestag. Müller began by stating that he had worked since 1987 for "equal rights and conditions for homosexual soldiers in the assessment of their [military] eligibility, fitness for service and assignment."[161] A letter exchange from 1987 confirms that as a senior officer candidate in

---

159 BMVg, decision on Staff Surgeon Michael Müller, 2 February 1994 (copy sent in a personal correspondence).

160 The action brought before Federal Administrative Court cost 4,775 DM, for example. A letter from the German Bundeswehr Association, 12 May 1999.

161 BArch, BW 2/38353: Staff Surgeon Müller to Chief of Defense General Klaus Naumann 20 January 1994 and verbatim in BArch, BH 1/29162: Staff Surgeon Müller to the Chief of the Army, 20 January 1994. Army Staff commented in writing under the sentence "while in service? With official means?" A duplicate letter to a different addressee at the BMVg is in BArch, BW 1/502107.

the Navy at the time, Müller had in fact asked how the BMVg would assess homosexuals' fitness to serve as officers and superiors before going on to challenge the familiar positions of the ministry repeatedly and eventually coming out himself.[162]

Looking back on his motivations at the time, Müller cited a desire for the same standards of measurement to be applied to him as for others, without his sexual orientation being taken into consideration. All he had really wanted was to be treated "fairly and justly." This was what had led him to fight first and foremost on his own behalf and, unlike others, never hold pretensions of a messianic fight for the rights of all homosexuals in the Bundeswehr. He turned down every media offer – of which there were a number – to appear on talk shows, including on television. Throughout the course of his dispute with the BMVg he enjoyed the support of his superiors in the medical corps, including its surgeon generals.[163]

Hardthöhe responded in April 1994, writing that the BMVg's actions were lawful and had not violated the principle of equal treatment under Article 3 of the constitution. It drew on the SOWI survey from two years previous to do so, according to which half of conscripts viewed homosexuality as "negative" or "very negative." The ministry's practices were in keeping with the constitution in the sense that homosexual soldiers were not uniformly dismissed, nor excluded from every kind of assignment. The staff surgeon responded with another twenty-three page letter essentially laying out the apparent contradiction: The BMVg generally did not consider homosexuals fit for service as superiors or instructors, yet at the same time the Bundeswehr had employed him as an instructor and superior for years.[164] Section FüS I 4 wrote back for the ministry that homosexuality "per se was not grounds for exclusion from a particular assignment," nor was it "a health disorder or a criminal offense," nor again did it necessarily "limit an ability to perform one's duties."[165] What was called for rather were case-by-case examinations "based on the criteria of performance, qualification and professional competence." While the fitness of known homosexual soldiers could not "regularly be affirmed without restriction," "a favorable assignment decision was possible" in the event that inspection "dispelled fitness concerns." In considering individual cases, "homosex-

---

162 Interview with Dr. Michael Müller, Berlin, 1 August 2019, and letters from Senior Navy Cadet Michael Müller to the BMVg on 2 February 1987, 19 March 1987 and 22 April 1987, as well as replies from BMVg P II 1 on 9 March 1987 and 7 April 1987, and from BMVg P V 6 on 10 July 1987.
163 Interview with Dr. Michael Müller, Berlin, 1 August 2019.
164 BArch, BW 2/38357: BMVg reply on 12 April 1994 and Staff Surgeon Müller's response to the BMVg, the chief of defense, and eleven other addressees on 12 June 1994. A copy is also available in BArch, BW 2/38353 (Copies in BArch, BW 2/38353 and in BW 1/502107).
165 BArch, BW 1/502107, no pagination: BMVg, FüS I 4, 15 September 1994, cited in a ruling at Hamburg Administrative Court on 26 November 1997, Az 12 VG 5657/97.

ual soldiers' constitutional right to equal treatment and the armed forces' interest in an unrestricted ability to serve had to be weighed against each other."[166]

This was the first time that the BMVg had conceded "homosexual soldiers' constitutional right to equal treatment" and opened the door to case-by-case examinations that might, if they ended positively, grant access to assignments that had previously been closed off. In reality, the armed forces, personnel leadership and the Ministry of Defense all steadily refused to consider cases on an individual basis throughout the late Nineties, persisting with a general and abstract line of reasoning about potential loss of authority. The FüS I 4 document from September 1994 appears to be an outlier in this context, sticking out from an otherwise steady stream of unambiguous rejections. Evidently the reply had not been discussed or coordinated with other sections and legal staff. Be that as it may, the written proof of the need for case-by-case decisions would later prove useful to the plaintiff in Hamburg Administrative Court.

The BMVg legal staff relied on their standard repertoire of arguments before the judges in Hamburg, albeit adapted to the physician's specific case. The lawsuit could not succeed, they argued, if only because that the plaintiff had made his continued willingness to serve contingent on conditions that the Bundeswehr was not able to satisfy, namely fundamental changes to the armed forces' personnel policy by granting equal treatment to homosexual and heterosexual medical officers. To this extent an "open difference of opinion" stood between the plaintiff and the accused. The plaintiff was not "suitable without restriction" for assignment as a career officer because "he 'was neither inclined nor capable' to control his sexual preferences and tendencies to the degree required for permanent assignment as a medical officer."[167]

The judges found reason to object; ruling now in 1997, they determined instead that the refusal issued to the plaintiff was unlawful and violated his rights. He was entitled to be taken on as a career soldier, for which he indisputably fulfilled the preconditions. It simply "was not acceptable to deny a soldier's fitness to enter career service solely on the basis of his stated homosexuality, if his service record did not offer the slightest indication that the soldier concerned might lack the requisite fitness." Such was the case at present.[168]

---

166 Ibid.
167 BArch, BW 2/38353: BMVg response to the complaint, quoted in Hamburg Administrative Court in its ruling on 26 November 1997, Az 12 VG 5657/97.
168 BArch, BW 2/38353: Hamburg Administrative Court, ruling on 26 November 1997, Az 12 VG 5657/97.

Did the ruling represent the turning point sought by the plaintiff? No. Even now, nothing changed. The BMVg was able to retreat behind the fact that the case concerned a lab doctor at a Bundeswehr hospital and could not be applied to the troops.[169] Lower Saxony Superior Administrative Court concurred with BMVg opinion in a suit brought by a staff sergeant similarly seeking appointment to career service, ruling that the Hamburg verdict could not be applied to other suits that revolved around whether homosexual soldiers were fit to be used as instructors.[170]

Seeking to prevent a landmark decision on the case at the Federal Administrative Court, the lawyers in Hardthöhe did everything within their power to limit the impact of the Hamburg ruling. The Hamburg court explicitly left a direct path open for a leap-frog appeal which the BMVg then took, bringing the case before the high tribunal. The lawyers in Bonn must have gauged their chances a second time before withdrawing; the ministry announced it would now accept the plaintiff as a career soldier. This meant the suit was dropped,[171] and a landmark decision where the stars were misaligned for the BMVg was avoided.[172] Still committed to the goal of "fair, just and equal" treatment, the staff surgeon and his lawyer now sought to have Federal Administrative Court resolve whether any restrictions would be set on future assignments in career service – Müller made acceptance of his letter of appointment contingent on exclusion of these restrictions.[173] Acting consistently he did then in fact decline it, explaining that his future assignments would continue to come under restriction. The Federal Administrative Court would not go along, however. "Changing the object of the proceedings from a matter of principle regarding acceptance [to career service] to the question of future assignment" was not possible on appeal.[174]

---

169 See for example the BMVg's application to dismiss the suit, cited in Lüneburg Administrative Court in its ruling on 3 June 1999, Az 1 A 141/97, p. 3.

170 Lüneburg Superior Administrative Court, ruling on 16 December 1998, Az 2 M 4436/98. For a detailed account see *Neue Zeitschrift für Verwaltungsrecht Rechtsprechungs-Report* 11/12 (1999): 772–773.

171 The Associated Press entitled their report "Suit by homosexual Bundeswehr soldiers finished. Federal Constitutional Court sees no reason for proceedings after acceptance." AP report from 15 January 1999, a copy is available in BArch, BW 1/502107 and BW 2/38353.

172 The observation that "a landmark decision potentially ruling against the BMVg could thus be avoided" can be found in BArch, BW 2/38353: BMVg, FüS I 1, 19 January 1999.

173 BArch, BW 2/38353: BMVg, FüS I 1, 19 January 1999.

174 AP report from 15 January 1999, copy in BArch, BW 1/502107 and BW 2/38353. For a retrospective account of the affair see BArch, BW 1/503302: BMVg, PSZ I 8, 20 June 2002.

The disputed 1997 verdict from Hamburg thus did not have any resounding impact on other legal disputes. It remained unique, the exceptional case of a medical officer at a Bundeswehr hospital. In its subsequent rulings on other cases, the Federal Administrative Court stuck by the old restrictive line.

For his part, Staff Surgeon Dr. Müller did not leave it at position papers and letters to the Ministry of Defense but made a further effort to connect with other soldiers and show strength in unity. It was with this goal in mind that his name and picture appeared in *JS*, a magazine put out by the protestant military chaplaincy, in an article entitled "Gays in the Military."[175] Müller's plan had the desired effect, with the article providing an initial spark. Out of what to date had only been small circles of personal acquaintances and friends between the two Bundeswehr universities there now emerged a national network of gay soldiers, resulting in the Federal Working Group of Gay Soldiers, or BASS.

b.)   The Federal Working Group of Gay Soldiers

A photocopy stored in the federal archives of a January 2000 press report in the *Berliner Morgenpost* about the "Federal Working Group of Gay Soldiers" contains the handwritten remark "FüS I: Is this working group known to us?"[176] The ministry had known about the circle since 1995 as it turned out, although there was more. The group of gay soldiers had actively sought contact with the BMVg since 1996, writing repeatedly to the defense minister and military leadership with offers to talk.

What eventually became a national network started out through personal contacts, the kind of democratic organization often referred to as "grassroots" in the U.S. and Great Britain. In keeping with German naming standards, the movement of gay soldiers dubbed itself the *Bundesweiter Arbeitskreis schwuler Soldaten*, abbreviated to BASS. More than "twenty gay and lesbian soldiers both former and active" attended a first informal meeting in January 1996 in Munich.[177] The following year, BASS recorded sixty-three new members.[178] The initial impetus, one of the founders recalled, came from networks of gay officers that had arisen independently

---

175 Spiewak, "Schwule beim Bund." The article is discussed at length in chapter 2.
176 BArch, BW 2/38354: BMVg, FüS I 4, photocopy of the article "Schwulenfeindliche Studie nicht von der Bundeswehr."
177 Press briefing by the Federal Working Group of Gay Soldiers, 4 February 1996. A copy is available in BArch, BW 2/38354.
178 Statement to the press by the Federal Working Group of Gay Soldiers, 27 January 1997. A copy is available in BArch, BW 2/38354.

at the two Bundeswehr universities in Munich and Hamburg in the 1990s before growing quickly. Initially it had more been a way of spending free time together and swapping experiences, with the activities first taking an increasingly political bent after 1995. At the end of that year the two circles met in Hamburg; in the meantime another small group of soldiers impacted by personnel measures had formed around Staff Surgeon Michael Müller. Out of this informal core a series of regular regional meetings took shape in Munich, Berlin, Hamburg, Cologne and Kiel, finally coalescing into a founding meeting on the premises of a gay counseling service in Cologne. The group soon had soldiers representing every career group and region joining. It principally drew public visibility through street parties and parades, also by distributing informational fliers and actions.[179] BASS took on the typical organizational form of an association, hosting general meetings and featuring a speaker's council, with Dr. Müller serving as the first chair and initial driving force behind the network. Müller was succeeded by Major Bernhard Rogge in 1997 when the former stepped down due to a heavy professional workload. The group took aim at "exposing and combatting discrimination based on sexual orientation. Tolerance and acceptance should be ordered."[180] The path to this led via "constructive engagement with the responsible Bundeswehr offices," "political lobbying," and as large a media presence as possible.[181] The ministry itself viewed the association's goals in the narrower light of equal rights and treatment for homosexuals in personnel decisions.[182] Based on conversations with its former members, Jens Schadendorf characterized BASS primarily as "an informal network for swapping experiences with somewhat vague goals."[183]

---

179 Summarized from an email from Erich Schmid to the author, 5 December 2017.

180 Press briefing by the Federal Working Group of Gay Soldiers, 4 February 1996. A copy is available in BArch, BW 2/38354.

181 Statement to the press by the Federal Working Group of Gay Soldiers, 27 January 1997. A copy is available in 2/38354. BASS had the media's attention since its founding. *Magnus* magazine, which aimed at a gay target audience, issued a full report in April 1996, quoting from the same press release. "The somewhat stiff sounding words from the press statement, which shouldn't be changed, have their cause. The topic is explosive and Bonn is trying by every means possible to keep it out of the headlines, so the general public can only be spoken to in carefully formulated statements at first. In this complicated situation, BASS is trying to bring something into movement, cause for wonder in and of itself in light of all the bureaucratic stones laid in their path." Glade, "In Reih und Glied!" 10–11. Division FüS I 4 at the BMVg kept a copy of the article for its archives, BArch, BW 2/38355.

182 BArch, BW 2/38354: BMVg, FüS I 4, 1 February 2000.

183 Schadendorf continued that over the "few years of its existence it had quickly and steadily shrunk in size" and "later disbanded almost unnoticed." Schadendorf, *Der Regenbogen-Faktor*, 71.

To Dr. Müller's mind, the aim of the organization had been to bring interests together, not to confront the ministry. The group had "not been seditious,"[184] even if the BMVg saw things differently. Former BASS members recounted two different currents within the group: One did not want to put pressure on the ministry but offer it "a way out that would save face," while others argued for applying exactly this kind of pressure, whether through legal action, holding court in the media and public, or bringing politicians onboard. The organization ultimately opted for a combination of the two. The organization disbanded in 2001 once equal treatment before the law had been achieved, although that same day some members decided to found a new representative body. The new organization, the Working Group for Homosexual Members of the Bundeswehr (AHsAB), got its start in 2002. Led by its first chair, Alexander Schüttpelz, the group avoided any further confrontation with BMVg, looking instead to play the role of a partner in dialog to the ministry.[185]

The group's struggle for equal rights also played out within the armed forces themselves, with BASS offering counseling, assistance and support to lesbian and gay soldiers and military administrators "in all matters of discrimination based on their sexual identity."[186] The group also publicly advertised its regional and federal meetings in the German Bundeswehr Association magazine *Die Bundeswehr*.[187]

The speakers council wrote multiple letters to the Minister of Defense, chief of defense and chiefs of the servies on BASS letterhead, censuring the BMVg's manner of determining suitability and fitness for assignment for "discriminating against loyal and duty-conscious soldiers [in a way that was] no longer acceptable."[188] The supreme court case law the ministry cited "time and again" in upholding its position could be shown to still draw on judgements from the 1960s, prior to reform of the "shameful" §175 StGB. German society's growing acceptance and tolerance of homosexuals over the past two decades had found as good as no reflection in the Bundeswehr to date.

> Fear of discovery leaves its imprint on a large number of Bundeswehr members, a number of whom are serving in leadership positions – even within the BMVg itself [...] Assessments with

---

184 Interview with Dr. Michael Müller, Berlin, 1 August 2019.

185 Interview with Navy Commander Alexander Schüttpelz, Berlin, 24 January 2019. For more on the AHsAB based on conversations with activist members, see Schadendorf, *Der Regenbogen-Faktor*, 73–74.

186 BASS press statement 27 January 1997, BArch, BW 2/38354.

187 See for example an invitation to a regional meeting on 18 June 1999 in Berlin, and ten days later in Cologne. Printed in *Die Bundeswehr*, 6/1999, 29.

188 BArch, BW 2/38353: BASS to Defense Minister Rühe, 27 January 1997, signed Major Bernhard Rogge. A copy is also available in BArch, BW 2/38354.

marks that are far above average are rendered obsolete the instant that the personnel department or branch headquarters receives news of homosexuality. Why then go to the trouble of case-by-case inspection? Or does case-by-case inspection not exist in the first place?[189]

BASS also received support from the Gay Federation in Germany (SVD), which helped in drawing up and printing flyers, among other things.[190] In 1993, the SVD sent its national spokesperson and eventual Bundestag representative Volker Beck to advocate on the soldiers' behalf before Defense Minister Volker Rühe. Nine years after the Wörner–Kießling affair, Beck now looked to call attention to "what continued now to be an unbearable situation for gays in the Bundeswehr."

> The claim that soldiers are citizens in uniform, the guiding principle for an Army in a democratic state, has not been redeemed so long as gay citizens in the Bundeswehr continue to be treated differently than their heterosexual counterparts based on their sexual identity when it comes to promotions or receiving security clearance [...] We consider the soldiers and conscripts of the Bundeswehr intelligent and democratically minded enough to "expect them to accept" gay instructors and superiors as well. The Bundeswehr's current practices amount to capitulating before prejudice.[191]

Beck demanded that Rühe "finally [grant] equal rights to gay conscripts, soldiers and officers."

Soldiers regularly paid a high price for their activities in BASS, usually with the end of their professional path forward in the armed forces. Letters sent to the Minister of Defense, individual branch chiefs or personnel office represented a decisive step out of the private realm and into the public world of the service, bringing legal consequences for one's career. Anyone who resolved to do so while knowing the consequences was an activist in the best sense of the term, a person who was no longer fighting for his or her own future alone but setting it on the line with the broader aim of breaking down discrimination. One former company head and founding member of BASS interviewed by the author had not gone public as other officers had, and had kept cover instead, recalling that "everything had to be kept strictly separate from service."[192]

Most of the officers who were active in BASS departed the service regularly, and many today hold positions of leadership in the broader economy. Others stayed

---

189 Ibid.
190 In its written exchange with the BMVg, BASS also gave the SVD's address in Berlin-Brandenburg.
191 BArch, BW 2/38355: Gay Federation in Germany to Defense Minister Rühe, 27 January 1993, signed by the group's federal spokesperson, Volker Beck.
192 Interview with Lieutenant Colonel D. in Berlin, 31 March 2017 and 12 February 2018.

on in the armed forces to become career soldiers, keeping their sexual orientation to themselves outside the protected circle of like-minded peers and steering clear of attention. Today, as of 2020, the first officer to attend BASS' first meetings in 1996 has since gone on to achieve the rank of full Colonel/Captain at Sea. Yet those who took up the struggle for homosexual rights against the BMVg, whether publicly or internally, still looked out on bleak professional prospects in 1996. They became anathema to the service, as the following case of an officer in a mechanized infantry unit shows.

c.) A Letter to the Minister and Its Consequences: A First Lieutenant's Career Comes to an End

In 1998, a report in *Berliner Zeitung* announced the case of a young officer who had been removed from assignment as a platoon leader and transferred to a post on staff the year before.

> First Lieutenant Erich Schmid is no longer able to train recruits. Despite good marks in service, the twenty-seven-year-old fixed-term soldier, a former platoon leader in a mechanized infantry battalion from Brandenburg, was moved to a desk job by his superiors. In addition, the Bundeswehr will not accept the highly promising officer for career service. The reason? Erich Schmid is gay. Homosexuals are not fit to serve as instructors or for leadership positions, according to the Ministry of Defense. Erich Schmid had a brilliant career before him.[193]

The personnel measures that brought an end to Schmid's military career were triggered by letters sent by the officer in 1996 to the Minister of Defense, the chief of defense and the chiefs of the services. Writing on BASS letterhead, the first lieutenant protested the fact that the BMVg's handling of its homosexual soldiers could "no longer be reconciled with current constitutional norms." A "prejudice-free debate" and "constructive dialogue" were "urgently required."[194] None of the addresees ever responded.[195] BMVg files contain a response from FüS I 4 written on

---

193 Bruhns, "Homosexualität wird bei Outing zum 'Eignungsmangel'."
194 A letter from BASS to Minister Rühe and Chief of Defense Hartmut Bagger signed by First Lieutenant Erich Schmid on 21 October 1996 in BArch, BW 2/38354. An identical copy of the letter to Chief of the Army Lieutenant General Helmut Willmann is available in BArch, B 2/38358 and is also cited in ruling BVerwG, 1st Military Service Senate, Court opinion, WB 48.97 on 18 November 1997.
195 Interview with Erich Schmid, Berlin, 5 December 2017. Schmid's letter to the chief of the Army has on it a number of handwritten notes, including "Who is this? Stationed where?" "Please arrange legal review," "no offer to talk from our end" as well as "if necessary no reply." BArch, BW 2/38358.

behalf of all the recipients, stating that the Bundeswehr's position was in line with the current legal situation and consistent with the Basic Law, or constitution. It was not based on prejudice nor did it constitute discrimination, as charged. This meant there were no grounds for a change in position, "obviating the need for further discussion."[196] The chief personnel office replied in place of the minister and chiefs of the services and invited the officer in for a staff review. Yet instead of the "constructive dialogue" the first lieutenant was hoping for, the personnel manager now revealed to him that his career was at an end.

"Despite a partial shift in social perception," homosexuality "continued as before to signal a lack of fitness in the view of personnel management." With this in mind, the first lieutenant could expect to be removed as a platoon leader and assigned to a post without leadership responsibilities. He would not receive any other leadership responsibilities for the duration of his time in the service, nor "contrary to original intent [would he] be taken on as a career soldier with his lack of fitness now becoming known."[197] (Strictly speaking, career service was not "intended" but a firm offer. As a conscript in 1989, the officer candidate testing center had made Schmid a binding offer of acceptance for career service without further selection procedures after successfully completing an officer's training course and his course of study.[198] BMVg notes confirm this version of the story; the chief personnel office had given its word in 1990.[199]) According to another note from the personnel section, the first lieutenant had insisted that he continue to serve as mechanized infantry platoon leader, and company commander over the mid-range. For its part, the section insisted on transferring him to a "service post without leadership responsibility at the earliest possible convenience."[200]

Schmid recalled that personnel leadership had instructed his commander and company head to ask whether he was the author of the letter, which he confirmed. "I revealed to them at the same time that I had written as someone affected [by the matter]. Both reacted with great composure." His superiors had been somewhat

---

196 BArch, BW 2/38358: BMVg, FüS I 4 to BASS c/o SVD Berlin Brandenburg, 28 November 1996.
197 BMVg, P III 2: Note on staff review meeting from 7 January 1997, copy available in BArch, BW 2/38358. Copies of all relevant papers and written exchanges concerning First Lieutenant Schmid's case are available in BArch, BW 2/38358. They confirm the course(s) of action detailed in the military service senate's ruling in November 1997.
198 Interview with Erich Schmid, Berlin, 5 December 2017.
199 BArch, BW 2/38358: BMVg, PSZ III 6, 12 April 2000.
200 Ibid., BMVg, P III 2: Note on staff review meeting from 7 January 1997. Schmid's formal rejection for career service came via letter, BMVg, P III 2 on 6 June 1997 (available as a copy in ibid.). The letter referred explicitly to the fact that he had "stated his homosexual tendencies," and thus did not meet the conditions for acceptance, since he was unfit for assignment without restriction.

surprised by the harsh response from personnel leadership. "From the very first moment, personnel leadership at Hardthöhe showed consistent refusal and went about implementing the letter of the law unconditionally."[201] The first lieutenant appealed the decision, following regulation by turning first to his direct superior, the company head. Outside of official channels he also petitioned the parliamentary commissioner for the armed forces in the Bundestag. Schmid wrote that his removal as platoon leader "obviously came about in connection with my openness about my homosexuality."[202] This represented "colossal discrimination" on the part of the ministry. His homosexuality had been known about for over five months now, and had at no point resulted in a loss of authority or "respect," or in any way interfered with service operations.[203] When that April his company head forbid him from signing documents as his deputy, the first lieutenant appealed directly to the BMVg. "What other surprises do I have to reckon with still? Will there be a 'mudfight' or 'salami slicing tactics' to deal with?"[204]

In July 1997 personnel leadership transferred Schmid onto the staff of Light Infantry Battalion 1 in Berlin, though not without giving his new commander advance notice as to the cause being the lieutenant's homosexuality. Schmid's current battalion commander wrote an "unsolicited opinion" protesting the transfer, noting that he "had not managed to find any lack of fitness [in the first lieutenant]; on the contrary, within a short time he had proven his capability as a leader, instructor and educator among conscripts."[205]

The former officer still recalled the support of his commander and all the company heads at the time.[206] Once his letter to the BMVg became an official matter and his commander and company head had asked him about it, word about his homosexuality "got around the battalion very quickly." Schmid and his company head agreed to actively inform the battalion officer corps and the company NCO corps, which naturally lead to just about everyone in the barracks finding out instantaneously. It had been a similar situation in the light infantry battalion in Berlin, all the more so as his transfer had come "preceded by his forcible outing by personnel leadership," as Schmid described it. Given the situation, Schmid brought his life partner along "completely as a matter of course" to events where other offi-

---

201 Email from Erich Schmid to the author, 5 December 2017, and in what follows.
202 First Lieutenant Schmid, service complaints on 12 March 1997 and 17 March 1997 and to the parliamentary commissioner on 18 March 1997, available as copies in BArch, BW 2/38358.
203 Ibid.
204 First Lieutenant Schmid, complaint to the BMVg P II 5, 23 April 1997. Available as a copy in BArch, BW 2/38358.
205 Cited in BVerwG, 1st Military Service Senate, Court opinion, WB 48.97 on 18 November 1997.
206 Here and the following: Email from Erich Schmid to the author, 5 December 2017.

cers and NCOs brought their own (female) partners. While assigned to the Berlin staff he had with a single exception only ever experienced "proactive" and "energetic, at times even unsolicited, support through assessments and written statements" in his disputes with personnel leadership.

The first lieutenant protested his transfer and the revelation of his orientation to his new commander, and petitioned that his transfer orders to Berlin be revoked:

> The BMVg's view that career and fixed-term soldiers with a same-sex orientation cannot be deployed as immediate superiors with training and leadership duties is outdated. Changes in society and everyday military life have disproved the notion that a superior disclosing his homosexuality jeopardizes his authority, and thus troop combat readiness. [Schmid's] homosexuality was also known about within the ranks after all, without this leading to any impairment of authority. What is more, it is discriminatory to insinuate that superiors with a same-sex orientation would see a sexual partner in every subordinate [...] Moreover the division leader informing the commander of [Schmid's] homosexuality over the phone [...] constitutes a massive invasion of privacy, since sexual orientation is an essential component of private life, and therefore must not be made the subject of personnel measures.[207]

Looking back from a distance of more than twenty years, the former officer drew the conclusion that

> unlike most of the others who had run afoul of this before me and gone all the way to the highest courts, I had something at my side that they did not: a firm commitment of acceptance [as a career soldier] that stood shortly before redemption, and which in fact only I could turn down, not the BMVg [...] The idea was that if there was ever a chance to succeed, it was in this form. Knowing the price, signing at the bottom of the letter to the minister in 1996 was the highest possible level of commitment.[208]

The BMVg filed for the lieutenant's appeal to be decided at the Federal Administrative Court, seeking its rejection:

> The claimant's lack of fitness arises from his homosexual tendency. A different baseline assessment does not follow on the claimant's argument that there are no identifiable circumstances

---

207 Cited in BVerwG, 1st Military Service Senate, Court opinion, WB 48.97 on 18 November 1997.
208 Email from Erich Schmid to the author, 15 November 2018, as well as a follow-up. To Schmid's mind all the soldiers who had gone to court before him went with a disadvantage: "Their homosexuality was used to insinuate a lack of fitness before they tried for a switch in career or status. My case was different. The service had already confirmed my fitness and qualifications. All I had to do was pull the trigger. If I did that, the service would have to revise a decision that had been confirmed multiple times. A new constellation. That was why I went on the offensive with the letter. Ready to bring legal action up to the highest office and to take political action in the highest circles." Email from Erich Schmid to the author, 5 December 2017.

present in his particular situation to justify the assumption of a loss in authority. At odds with changing social views on homosexuality and increasing tolerance among segments of the population, there still exists a not-inconsiderable risk that nonetheless persistent stereotypical ideas about the conduct of men with homosexual inclinations would be transferred onto the claimant, severely calling his authority into question without his being able to influence it...Informing the commander about the background for the claimant's transfer as his future superior was also lawful. The fact of a homosexual tendency is not an exclusively private matter, but also a matter of fitness and assignment, meaning his next disciplinary superior had to be informed.[209]

By way of response, the lieutenant argued in a supplementary opinion piece to the ministry that it

> failed to recognize that attitudes about sexual behavior are evolving. While taboos continued to exist in the sexual realm, homosexuality or same-sex attraction was not one of them. If the BMVg nevertheless buried him beneath "a bundle of measures" on account of his homosexuality, it would be ignoring societal developments from the past two decades.[210]

None of the soldiers in either the non-commissioned officer training course or the general basic training course he had led indicated a "problem" with his person or his homosexuality, the lieutenant stressed. Quite the opposite; they admired "his conviction and asked how they might support him."[211]

The Federal Administrative Court dismissed the lieutenant's appeal submitted by the BMVg for deliberation as "partly inadmissible, partly unfounded." The claimant's transfer was lawful and did not violate his rights. The court had repeatedly found in the past "that it was not legally objectionable not to assign homosexually inclined soldiers as troop instructors." The same held true for the present case.

> Even if the way in which homosexual tendencies are viewed has continued to change in segments of society and increasing tolerance is to be noted in this regard, a general level of tolerance existing among soldiers in training, especially conscripts, to an extent that would make the BMVg's calculations seem improper cannot be assumed. It cannot be ruled out for one part of young conscripts or their family members that they would show no sympathy for soldiers with homosexual inclinations being assigned as permanent or temporary instructors, and thus educators. Even with the greater tolerance shown today toward those who are homosexually inclined, behavior which is seen as normal and common among heterosexuals, when coming from a homosexually inclined soldier, might still acquire a significance in the eyes of subordinates that led to gossip, suspicion or the instructor's rejection, and thus difficulties in the service realm. To this extent it is not decisive that no cause for complaint or other

---

209 Cited in BVerwG, 1st Military Service Senate, Court opinion, WB 48.97 on 18 November 1997.
210 Ibid.
211 Ibid.

objection regarding the claimant's homosexuality arose during his previous assignment as a platoon leader, as stated. What is alone decisive for the claimant's future assignments is the fact of his homosexuality now being known about within the ranks.[212]

It is striking how closely the key phrases in the ruling mirror others from the 1970s and 1980s. The judges seem to have been trapped in the same time capsule as the politicians, civil servants, jurists and BMVg officers.

The Supreme Administrative Court ruled further that the revelation of the plaintiff's homosexuality by the division head at BMVg personnel headquarters did not constitute a service measure directed against him. The telephone conversation between the division head and the plaintiff's future commander had rather been a "a purely internal affair without other effects."[213]

The ruling against the first lieutenant reverberated in the media. In April 1998 *Süddeutsche Zeitung* lead with an article entitled "Gay officer not allowed to be a boss."[214] *Berliner Zeitung* consulted a BMVg spokesperson, quoting his response: A superior would lose his authority if subordinates were to learn of his inclination; soldiers had been known to refuse the commands of gay officers. The spokesperson could not cite specific instances but said that in this way, a gay officer could indirectly contribute to the death of comrades in the field. "How would we explain that to the ones left behind?" Still, the spokesperson conceded "inconsistencies" in the Bundeswehr's stance. "As long as we do not know anything about it, homosexuality does not constitute a lack of fitness."[215] Love between men was only a problem if the Bundeswehr found out.

For his part, *Berliner Zeitung* quoted First Lieutenant Schmid as saying "I'll go to the Federal Constitutional Court if need be to sue for my acceptance [as a career soldier]."[216] A constitutional appeal was already in preparation, he said, before another lieutenant's trip to the BVerfG in 2000 led to the BMVg relenting.[217] A legal opinion sought out from Professor Armin Steinkamm in advance of Schmid's upcoming constitutional complaint had "urgently" advised the ministry "to avoid what would most likely be a defeat in Karlsruhe."[218]

---

212 BVerwG, 1st Military Service Senate, Court opinion, WB 48.97 from 18 November 1997; also reprinted under the title "Keine gleichgeschlechtlich veranlagten Soldaten als Ausbilder."
213 Ibid.
214 Müller-Jentsch, "Schwuler Offizier darf nicht Chef sein." Filed in BMVg archives under BArch, BW 2/38353.
215 Bruhns, "Homosexualität wird bei Outing zum 'Eignungsmangel'."
216 Ibid.
217 See chapter 7 for a full account.
218 Email from Erich Schmid to the author, 15 November 2018. See chapter 6 for a complete account of Professor Armin Steinkamm's report from January 2000.

The same article quoted Colonel Bernhard Gertz, chair of the German Bundeswehr Association, who told *Berliner Zeitung* that the Bundeswehr had to play the role of "breaking down prejudice, not locking it in place." "If a superior does his job well, it's all the same to soldiers who he sleeps with." Still, as of 1998 Gertz saw the lieutenant as "hardly standing a chance" under current case law. "Yet that could change soon," the piece concluded. "In late 1997 a gay fixed-term soldier in northern Germany succeeded in petitioning to enter career service. The Bundeswehr filed for appeal, and the case now lies before the superior administrative court in Berlin." The article quoted a spokesperson for Minister of Defense Rühe as saying that "if the court decides differently, we'll orient ourselves by that."[219]

Likely triggered by the newspaper reports about First Lieutenant Schmid, in summer 1998 the subject of homosexual soldiers took to television for the first time, with a BMVg spokesperson reiterating his institution's well-known position for a morning talkshow on ZDF. The chair of the German Bundeswehr Association contradicted him live on-air: "With all due respect," the ministry's position was "sheer and utter nonsense."[220] Gertz continued that "the way somebody arranges his sexual life can only be seen as relevant to security by someone who is still thinking in the categories of the Cold War. What matters is the kind of personality a superior has; if it is convincing, it's all the same to the soldiers who he sleeps with."[221]

The association also provided legal support to members who were petitioning against transfer or dismissal based solely on their sexual orientation,[222] including the costs of a lawyer for Winfried Stecher's constitutional complaint in Karlsruhe when the first lieutenant's insurance did not cover it.[223] Internally, the BMVg noted that the association chair had promised to bear the lieutenant's legal costs "up to the final instance." This led the division responsible at BMVg to conclude that the association's representatives in the joint spokesperson committee would balk at new, restrictive orders.[224] (This led the BMVg to quash internally the draft for the orders that had been sketched.) Upon more questions from the media, the German Bundeswehr Association stated in 1999 that the employment principals of "suit-

---

219 Bruhns, "Homosexualität wird bei Outing zum 'Eignungsmangel'."
220 Ten days later, the exchange on 16 July 1998 between BMVg armed forces staff spokesperson Joint Staff Lieutenant Colonel Kaatz and Colonel Gertz was reprinted in the weekly magazine *Bundeswehr aktuell* on 27 July 1998.
221 Ibid.
222 *Rosa Rauschen*, "Schwule bei der Bundeswehr."
223 Interview with Winfried Stecher, Hamburg, 25 January 2018.
224 BArch, BW 1/502107, no pagination: BMVg, PSZ III 1, 5 January 2000.

ability, qualification and performance" had to be applied for all soldiers. Sexual orientation did not appear in the list of criteria.[225]

By way of epilogue, from July 1997 up to the end of his tour of duty in 2002, Erich Schmid remained on the same battalion staff in different posts. In 1999 he was promoted to captain, further proof that as the new millennium approached a general ban on promotion for officers identified as homosexual no longer existed.

Schmid also appealed blockage of his entry into career service at Berlin Administrative Court. In January 2000 the judges requested an official statement from the BMVg, explicitly mentioning the European Court of Human Rights' September 1999 ruling against the British armed forces and its practice of dismissing homosexual soldiers.[226] Schmid's suit did not advance any farther; in 2000 the BMVg offered him an out-of-court settlement.[227]

Boldly declaring oneself to be homosexual was not the only way to set the restrictive gears in motion – far from it. As a series of events in 1996–1997 shows, spontaneous and unguarded comments also sufficed. A chief petty officer became ensnared in the machinery of "personnel measures" when he asked his personnel manager during a routine staff interview to keep his partner's interests in mind with a planned transfer; the two had formed a tight bond and were living together. "This highly personal information, intended only for my personnel manager, was now used against me," the officer wrote in a letter to the Bundestag Defense Committee.[228]

> The monumental Bundeswehr, which especially in the moments of political upheaval in 1990–91 presented itself as just and trustworthy and acted accordingly, is now tottering and has elicited a deep crisis of trust in me regarding the constitutionality of its personnel policy.[229]

In a further letter of complaint to the BMVg the officer denounced the attempt "to litigate my [homosexual] inclination, which I had no choice over." It was "unjust." The service had to accept the laws of nature, not turn them into a liability.[230]

What was the background to the episode? Immediately after the officer's confidential talk with his personnel manager at Navy headquarters, his disclosure had

---

225 *Rosa Rauschen*, "Schwule bei der Bundeswehr."
226 BArch, BW 2/38358: BMVg, PSZ III 6, 12 April 2000. See chapter 6 for a full account of the European ruling.
227 See chapter 6.
228 BArch, BW 2/38358: Chief Petty Officer F. to the Bundestag Defense Committee, 10 September 1997.
229 Ibid.
230 BArch, BW 2/38358: Chief Petty Officer F. to the BMVg, 19 June 1997.

sent all the familiar bureaucratic wheels spinning. The officer was now "fit only with restriction," and could not "be installed as a direct superior in the position of a commander, instructor or educator." He would also be removed from his current course immediately.[231] The soldier filed numerous complaints, including one to Parliamentary Commissioner for the Armed Forces Claire Marienfeld, contending that the Bundeswehr's actions violated the principle of equality set out in Article 3 of the constitution. He felt he had been "branded a 'second-class' person," and that it played "no role how good or bad a soldier he was." It was "high time to recognize that the 'problem of homosexuality' existed in the Bundeswehr as well."[232]

The commissioner's office replied that the decision taken by Navy headquarters "had been confirmed in its legality by court decision in numerous comparable cases."[233] This meant personnel management's method of proceeding had not been "inappropriate for the matter." What was more, the soldier had revealed his sexual disposition "without needing to do so." The measures had been taken "to avoid possible reactions within your milieu – rejection, provocation, exposure to teasing – from the outset, and thus to rule out risking a loss in authority and impairing discipline." The office of the commissioner then turned to the underlying principles in the officer's case: The Bundeswehr had an obligation to remain mindful of the broader antipathy to homosexuality that still existed within society. "It cannot be the mission of the Bundeswehr to become a vanguard for society's acceptance of homosexuality."[234] The defense ministry similarly turned back the officer's complaints.[235]

A spectacular series of events from 1999 showed that rash statements could cost soldiers their careers even while they were on holiday. While watching "Summer Special '99 – Hot Vacation," an RTL II show filmed on Mykonos, a captain at a Bundeswehr hospital recognized two of his soldiers. The head of a paramedic training company, one of the soldiers the captain spotted on the show was a staff sergeant in training in his company. The captain reported to the hospital director that the two soldiers had admitted to being gay on TV and "candidly [described] the possibilities that Mykonos offered for their orientation." This made the staff sergeant "subject to attack" and "untenable" for his intended assignment as an

---

231 BArch, BW 2/38358: Navy Headquarters, note from 29 October 1996.

232 BArch, BW 2/38358: Chief Petty Officer F. to parliamentary commissioner for the armed forces, 3 December 1996.

233 Parliamentary commissioner for the armed forces to Chief Petty Officer F., 9 January 1997.

234 Ibid.

235 BArch, BW 2/38358: BMVg, P II 7, to Chief Petty Officer F., 12 July 1997. It could not be established whether the soldier continued to pursue the matter through legal action. No record of a court decision has turned up to date.

instructor and platoon leader.[236] It took just two days for the hospital to petition personnel to change the sergeant's planned assignment "in order to maintain discipline and out of concern for the soldier"; he was "no longer tenable" as an instructor and platoon leader. In making its request, the hospital stated explicitly that the sergeant's sexual preferences had "not previously come to light in any form whatsoever in the service realm."[237] The staff sergeant appealed the same day, objecting that his authority had never been called into question. "I have kept and will in the future keep my service and private lives strictly separate."[238]

d.) "In the Name of the People: The Plaintiff Is Legally Entitled to Be Accepted for Career Service."

Other soldiers pursued a legal route in fighting for their rights as well. In 1998, media attention fell on a staff sergeant from a mechanized reconnaissance unit. The case dated back three years to 1995, when MAD discovered the man's sexual orientation during a routine security check and reported it. Throughout his entire career in the service the sergeant had not come out as homosexual at work, nor drawn notice or been outed as such. Now, however, his "limited fitness for career development" was certified in reference to his sexual orientation, leaving him unfit for career service.[239]

In 1997 the BMVg rejected his complaint.[240] The sergeant then filed suit, contending that his fundamental rights to equal treatment, freedom to choose a profession and equal access to public office had been violated. It was "constitutionally problematic to read a lack of acceptance among subordinates that was merely asserted or supposed into the term 'fitness'."[241] The Ministry of Defense applied to have the suit dismissed, arguing that

---

236 BArch, BW 2/38357: Report from 8 September 1999 (Further details have been avoided to protect those involved).

237 Ibid., Request to Army Headquarters on 10 September 1999.

238 Ibid., Complaint from 10 September 1999. Neither the outcome of appeal proceedings nor subsequent personnel measures could be determined.

239 Ibid., BMVg, PSZ III 6, 12 April 2000. Focus magazine also ran a piece entitled "Gays in the Bundeswehr." See chapter 5 for MAD's role in this particular case.

240 BArch, BW 2/38358: BMVg, PSZ III 6, 12 April 2000.

241 Grounds for complaint from 11 September 1997, quoted in Lüneburg Administrative Court, decided 3 June 1999, Az 1 A 141/97. A copy is available in BArch, 2/38357.

a homosexual soldier's fitness for assignment to positions of leadership [...] raises fundamental doubts even in the abstract, without that depending on whether official duties have been observed to date. The abstract risk of a loss of authority exists independently of whether the social attitude toward homosexuality has changed among large segments of the population.[242]

The way the judges from the first court were leaning could already be gleaned from the temporary order they issued to the Ministry of Defense on 7 September 1998 to leave the staff sergeant in service past his upcoming regular departure on 30 September 1998, pending conclusion of the lawsuit.[243] When the BMVg then petitioned to have the decision repealed by the next highest instance,[244] the sergeant was dismissed after his service ended.

The main proceedings still had not been decided on, however, and in June 1999 the Lüneberg judges from the first court ruled clearly in favor of the plaintiff, unwilling to be cowed by the edicts of the superior court. "In the name of the people [...] The action is admissible and well-founded. The plaintiff has a legal right to be accepted for career service."[245] The court opinion lambasted the service's position as violating the plaintiff's fundamental rights. The Basic Law, or really its interpretation by the Federal Constitutional Court, had placed a person's sexuality under the constitutional protection of the free development of personality guaranteed in Article 2 as part of the private sphere, in conjunction with the inviolable dignity of man guaranteed in Article 1. It would thus contravene the Basic Law "to tie the plaintiff solely and exclusively to his sexual identity, which is completely inconspicuous both in and out of service, at his expense."[246]

The link to homosexuality as "the sole remaining reason for rejection" constituted a violation of Articles 1 and 2 of the Basic Law, as well as the prohibition against arbitrariness under Article 3. "Within the scope of the free and democratic constitutional order established under the Basic Law, with its emphasis on human dignity," a soldier "cannot have his suitability denied and consequently be sidelined, ostracized or discriminated against on the basis of inconspicuous sexuality alone." This violated the plaintiff's right to dignity as a person "with a form of sexuality that happened to be different (than is characteristic of the majority of peo-

---

242 BMVg application, ibid.
243 Lüneburg Administrative Court, ruling on 7 September 1998, Az 1 B 53/98.
244 Lower Saxony Superior Administrative Court ruling on 16 December 1998, Az 2 M 4436/98. In detail, see *Neue Zeitschrift für Verwaltungsrecht Rechtsprechungs-Report*, 11/12 (1999): 772–773.
245 Lüneburg Administrative Court, ruling on 3 June 1999, Az 1 A 141/97. A copy is available in BArch, BW 2/38357.
246 Ibid.

ple)."[247] The judges confronted the ministry with its own orders from 1994, which stated that "on its own, homosexuality cannot be grounds for exclusion," as well that the Bundeswehr decided on a case-by-case basis.[248] The "possibility of a loss in authority first arises independently of [...] sexual preference – whether homosexual, lesbian, or heterosexual – when the superior [...] does not understand how manage his sexuality."[249] As evidence the judges cited cases of sexual harassment involving an inspection chief's pursuit of female soldiers and a regiment commander pursuing a female civilian employee. In the plaintiff's case, a "'risk' that was not even tangibly present but only feared generally" could not be inferred to his detriment. Rather, the BMVg had "itself conceded that the plaintiff had to date managed his official duties particularly well."[250]

The judges in Lüneberg put a hole in the wall of the administrative courts' "cemented case rulings" against homosexual soldiers. The alarm bells were sounding at Hardthöhe as the personnel department convened,[251] though it was not a crisis session yet – that would not come until six months later. *Focus* magazine reported a "triumph in court: The thirty-year-old became the first gay soldier to bring the force to its knees."[252] The ministry was not "kneeling," however, but appealed the decision at Lower Saxony Superior Administrative Court (also seated in Lüneberg). The first decision from June 1999 had not entered force of law yet. Nor was a decision ever reached – another lawsuit overtook the pending appeal.[253]

e.)   A Lieutenant Is Removed as Platoon Leader, 1998

Twenty-nine-year-old Winfried Stecher had every reason to be satisfied. His career as a Bundeswehr instructor was both challenging and fulfilling. He was valued by superiors and subordinates alike. He was even designated a model soldier. All gone and done for. A superior

---

247 Ibid.

248 BMVg FüS I 4, from 15 September 1994, Az 35-04-00.

249 A copy of the ruling contains the handwritten remark "false argumentation" next to this sentence, presumably from the BMVg. Lüneburg Administrative Court, ruling on 3 June 1999, Az 1 A 141/97. A copy is available in BArch, BW 2/38357.

250 Lüneburg Administrative Court, ruling on 3 June 1999, Az.: 1 A 141/97. A copy is available in BArch, BW 2/38357.

251 The four sections in the personnel department were invited to the meeting, as was the policy division at legal affairs and FüS I 4. BArch, BW 2/38357: BMVg, PSZ III 6, 1 January 1999.

252 "Schwule in die Bundeswehr."

253 For a full account see chapter 6.

asked Stecher whether he was homosexual. His "Yes sir" went down in the personnel files; Stecher wound up behind a desk.[254]

Even as a cadet at Air Force Officers' School, former classmates recalled Winfried Stecher showing true leadership qualities. A staff sergeant with significant experience training troops, Stecher joined the officer's career track the undisputed informal leader of his class. It was not simply prior experience that made Stecher the classic "alpha" but his personality alone – a true leader, as another former student put it. Everyone had been positive Stecher would continue on his way through the air force to a successful career. Things turned out differently. Those who knew him at officers' school and in the troops recalled Winfried Stecher as a soldier with all his heart and soul, someone whose entire life was in his career. Stecher had planted both feet firmly on the ground of serving as an officer, and it was *his* Bundeswehr that pulled it out from under him.

Beginning in 1996 Lieutenant Stecher first built up, then led an anti-aircraft platoon at an air force base battalion. In February 1998 an otherwise outstanding record of achievement was turned on its head when, as reported in *FAZ*, a MAD communication revealed the lieutenant's sexual orientation.[255] Confronted about it directly by his squadron chief, the lieutenant confirmed his homosexuality; he had lived with his dedicated partner for a long time. He again replied in the affirmative when the battalion commander asked him the same question.[256] Looking back, Stecher recalled that his superiors were interested "primarily in his life partner's rank, and even more in his military branch." Their interest grew out of the directive governing superior–subordinate relations: If Lieutenant Stecher's partner was an NCO or a nonrated soldier in the air force, or even worse from his own barracks, the regulations would have taken hold, making Lieutenant Stecher guilty of a breach of duty. His superiors were palpably relieved to hear his partner was a petty officer in the Navy.[257] The battalion commander then spoke with soldiers from the anti-aircraft unit; none of the soldiers reported any problems with their platoon leader's homosexuality, instead they voiced their trust in him and spoke out against a possible transfer.[258] Some men within the platoon went further, taking the initia-

---

254 *Rosa Rauschen*, "Schwule bei der Bundeswehr."

255 For a detailed account of MAD's role in this particular case, see chapter 5.

256 BArch, BW 1/502107, sheets 65–118: Constitutional complaint of First Lieutenant Stecher from 23 December 1998, case facts, here sheet 69.

257 Interview with Winfried Stecher, Hamburg, 25 January 2018.

258 Ibid., as well as BArch, BW 1/502107, sheets 114–115, Annex 12: Kdr ObjSBtlLw to Lieutenant Stecher, 20 April 1998.

tive to write a letter to the commander which twenty-one then signed, speaking out for a second time against their leader's planned dismissal.

> Lieutenant Stecher has at all times led his platoon in the way one would expect of a platoon leader [...] If [his] transfer is intended as a way of protecting subordinates we see no need, as there have not been any incidents in the past that might have pointed to his homosexuality. If it turns out to be the case that Lieutenant Stecher is transferred after all because he kept quiet about his homosexuality, we would like to give some food for thought that in our view, the private and official sides of a superior should be kept clearly separate from one another. In our view the way in which Lieutenant Stecher is being dealt with is highly discriminatory.[259]

Stecher himself could not think back to any negative reactions from within his squadron either; he had experienced "unconditional support and encouragement." One incident stayed with him in particular, where an enlisted man from another platoon, "heavily tattooed and generally [considered] the toughest of the bunch" came up to him and said: "If anyone says anything to you, he'll have me to deal with!"[260] On 20 April 1998, the battalion commander informed the Bundeswehr personnel office of Stecher's case in writing via the division commander. He also wrote to Stecher, informing him that after "thorough investigation and seeking legal expertise" he had to report the facts of the matter "due to the prevailing legal position in the BMVg." The personnel office would "decide on further measures or consequences."[261] The battalion commander stressed that he had passed along the words of the enlisted men and troop spokespersons in favor of the lieutenant's remaining, and that he himself did not expect "any homosexual advances from your end toward the soldiers in your platoon" nor see any susceptibility to extortion.[262] In fact, the battalion commander had recommended that the personnel office consider

> whether a more liberal view was advisable and the claimant remaining at his post [...] might be taken into consideration. The reservations that the Federal Ministry of Defense commonly holds against homosexuals in positions of authority do not apply in the claimant's case. He continues to find acceptance despite his homosexual tendencies and holds the trust of his

---

259 BArch, BW 1/502107, sheets 65–118: Constitutional complaint of First Lieutenant Stecher from 23 December 1998, here sheet 107, Annex 8: Letter from the enlisted men of Platoon II / Air Force Base Battalion 3, 1 April 1998.
260 Interview with Winfried Stecher of Hamburg, 25 January 2018.
261 BArch, BW 1/502107, sheets 65–118: Constitutional complaint of First Lieutenant Stecher from 23 December 1998, here sheets 114–115, Annex 12: Kdr ObjSBtlLw to Lieutenant Stecher, 20 April 1998.
262 Ibid.

subordinates. The troops could and would positively support his retention. The superiors (squadron chief and commander) could and would take responsibility for the situation.[263]

The squadron sergeant also intervened on Lieutenant Stecher's behalf to the parliamentary commissioner, describing him as an "irreproachable, model officer" distinguished by his "engagement, thirst for action and exemplary leadership."[264] All of it – the recommendation of the battalion commander to which the division commander added his name, as well as the letter from the sergeant – came to nought.

The squadron chief's report to the battalion commander set off a chain reaction that ended in regulations taking hold at the personal office. The battalion commander would still likely have been able to achieve an "internal" solution proportional to the case at hand; he was already well on the way to doing so by questioning the "impacted" squadron soldiers himself, before then opting for the path, all too common in the military, of reporting upstairs. "Reporting frees you and grieves the boss" is an old soldiers' saying.

The stone set in motion by the squadron chief's initial report soon turned into an avalanche that ultimately flattened the already derelict edifice of restrictions in place against homosexual soldiers. Yet laying the "blame" at the feet of the squadron boss alone would miss the mark. The entire premise upon which the Bundeswehr, the BMVg, MAD and personnel leadership based its treatment of homosexuality was unhappy, to say the least; sooner or later it had to end in a serious conflict like the one surrounding Lieutenant Stecher. The personnel office decided to transfer the lieutenant to squadron staff. Yet then, in July 1998, he was promoted to first lieutenant, in another sign that the ban on promoting officers identified as homosexual either no longer existed by the late 1990s, or was not applied.

The personnel office's decision met with "outrage, more than anyone from the conscripts in his platoon." "As a loyal subordinate I have to back the decision, but I see lasting damage to motivation and internal cohesion."[265] The squadron spokesperson wrote to the parliamentary commissioner with a similar message:

> I might have wished that the BMVg [personnel department] would refrain from these measures, as it was not necessary from the point of view of all those directly involved [...] Not simply among those directly affected but a wider circle of soldiers, there is an impression that the current views of the BMVg mean the soldier is being ostracized without due consider-

---

263 Kdr OBjSBtlLw to PersABw, 20 April 1998, cited in Federal Administrative Court, 1st Military Service Senate in its ruling on 19 November 1998, BVerwG, 1 WB 54.98.

264 BArch, BW 1/502107, sheets 65–118: Constitutional Complaint of Lieutenant Stecher from 23 December 1998, here sheet 107, Annex 9: Letter from Squadron Sergeant 3./ObjSBtlLw to the parliamentary commissioner for the armed forces, 22 May 1998.

265 Ibid.

ation of his past accomplishments or personal circumstances [...] It seems that homosexually inclined soldiers are ultimately treated according to the same means and schema, without truly taking the opinions and recommendations of the responsible disciplinary superiors into account, and especially those of spokespersons [...] The number of homosexually inclined soldiers both male and female is likely not insignificant. Yet the restrictive position of the service means that only a few cases reach the public; the majority of those in question do not admit to their tendencies due to the negative consequences. I would like now [...] to request that you [...] look after this matter. It seems requisite given the considerable differences that exist between the general level of social acceptance of this group of persons and that within personnel management, one which can no longer be justified given the general shift within society.[266]

Stecher appealed his transfer before Federal Administrative Court. In stating the reason for appeal, the lieutenant's lawyer noted that differently from previously decided cases, her client had

kept his homosexuality strictly separate from his official duties as a part of his private sphere. His soldiers expressed confidence in him as a platoon leader and officer while knowing of his homosexuality, and wanted to keep him on as a superior. No security concerns were present, as his admission left him unsusceptible to blackmail. His authority has also always been accepted within the line of duty.

The lawyer continued that it was "unlawful not to use homosexually inclined soldiers as troop instructors as a matter of principle. There has been a fundamental shift in general attitudes toward homosexual tendencies. There is no life experience to show that young conscripts show a lesser degree of acceptance."[267] The BMVg, ensconced in its time capsule, responded with the same arguments it had been using for decades: "Homosexuals, meanwhile, are not suitable without reservation as military superiors, since their homosexuality becoming known could have the loss of official authority in their position as a consequence. The BMVg could not accept a potential threat to the armed forces' combat readiness resulting from this."[268]

Responding directly to the first lieutenant's arguments, the lawyers in Bonn countered that it could not be "ruled out that ideas still in existence about the behavior of homosexuals would also be applied to him, even if he did not provide

---

266 Ibid., Annex 11: Spokesperson letter from Air Force Base Battalion 3 to the parliamentary commissioner for the armed forces, 4 August 1998.
267 Grounds for petition, cited in Federal Administrative Court, 1st Military Service Senate, ruling on 19 November 1998, BVerwG, 1 WB 54.98.
268 BMVg statement, quoted in ibid.

any objective cause. The acceptance that exists among superiors and subordinates at present does not refute this prognosis."[269]

In November 1998 the judges at the first military service senate ruled against the first lieutenant, finding his application "admissible" but "unfounded." The transfer order was "lawful and did not violate the plaintiff's rights." A soldier had "no claim on assignment to a particular location or area." The senate had "repeatedly found that it was not legally objectionable not to employ homosexually inclined soldiers as instructors in the troops," most recently in November 1997.[270]

> The sole deciding factor for the plaintiff's future assignment is the fact that his homosexual tendency has become known within the ranks. This alone means that it is no longer limited to the private sphere but has encroached on the official realm of the Bundeswehr. It changes nothing that the plaintiff has not sought explicitly to disclose his tendency outwardly but separate it from the official realm as a part of his private life. Its knowledge within the official realm has made it a part of that realm. Nor does the BMVg's determination of suitability violate the duty to camaraderie under §12 SG [...] The plaintiff is not being considered generally unfit as a soldier or comrade, but only as a troop instructor.[271]

The judges also rejected the plaintiff's reference to female soldiers, who at the time had begun to serve in a limited number of areas within the armed forces. Women serving as superiors "could not be compared" to men with a homosexual orientation, as it was not "the risk of sexual advances" that was at issue "but the view of the BMVg that men with homosexual tendencies were still broadly rejected by heterosexual men." There was a danger this would result in "an unacceptable loss of authority."[272] (One woman in uniform at the time recalled how indignant she had been upon learning in the press about Lieutenant Stecher's treatment. She had thought to send an inquiry to the defense minister and ask for clarification as to why on the one hand homosexual soldiers, herself included, were allowed to serve while homosexual superiors were discriminated against. It had run contrary to her sense of justice, the physician recalled, although she did not quit the service over the matter.[273])

The judges at the Federal Administrative Court thus continued to stand by the side of the Ministry of Defense in 1998. The lieutenant now took his case to the

---

269 Ibid.
270 Ruling at Federal Administrative Court, 1st Military Service Senate, 19 November 1998, BVerwG, 1 WB 54.98.
271 Ibid.
272 Ibid.
273 Eyewitness interview, 28 November 2019.

Federal Constitutional Court (Bundesverfassungsgericht, BVerfG), ultimately bring-ing the entire, decades-old edifice of argumentation crashing down around itself. Yet the armed forces had already lost or scared off any number of well qualified soldiers, NCOs, officers and potential candidates simply because they were homo-sexual. That was the price the Bundeswehr paid – or perhaps the actual aim of its efforts.

Homosexual men continued to opt for a soldier's life despite knowing the restrictions. From time to time at public presentations, an audience member has uncomprehendingly asked the author how homosexuals could even think of joining the Bundeswehr as career soldiers and voluntarily expose themselves to such a "homophobic milieu." Yet why would a woman or man who wanted to pursue the path of a soldier, whether it was because they were convinced of the Bundeswehr's mission or simply because they wanted to become a soldier, give up on their dreams simply because of their sexual orientation? Setting this wish aside from the very beginning based on the restrictions would be tantamount to giving up on, or discriminating against oneself. One author on a gay website spoke to his own changing opinions in a 1999 article about the BMVg's defensive legal action against homosexual officers.

> At eighteen, I could have wished that the Bundeswehr was as intolerant as the Venezuelan Army and sent gay conscripts home. I would even have outed myself for that. But there are also gay people who want to become soldiers. And I can't entirely understand why they shouldn't be allowed to. Maybe the generals are picturing a bunch of shrieking queens throw-ing cotton balls at tanks. What do I know. And the Bundeswehr isn't exactly known for being a progressive part of society.[274]

The eyewitnesses the author interviewed for this study still speak about First Lieu-tenants Erich Schmid and Winfried Stecher in high regard. "They were the first young officers to lift their heads above cover."[275] It should always be remembered in this context that Air Force Lieutenant Stecher was outed against his will. In his mind this left him with no choice but to go to war in court and the media – and with firm resolve.

---

274 *Rosa Rauschen*, "Schwule bei der Bundeswehr."
275 E.g. interview with Lieutenant Colonel D. of Berlin, 12 February 2018.

f.)   Political Pressure

Whether through direct inquiries to the BMVg or indirectly via the parliamentary commissioner, members of parliament repeatedly sought to bring about a change in the ministry's position, or at least maintain pressure. Although they did not succeed in their efforts, the questions coming from the Bundestag forced the officers and civil servants at Hardthöhe to deal with the topic on a recurring basis. Every new solicitation would start the wheels of bureaucracy; draft responses were composed, other ministry sections brought on to sign. The sheer number of inquiries solicited by the Bundestag and the political parties is astonishing; the phrasing in the BMVg's answers less so, nearly always sounding the same. This makes it pointless to reproduce the replies from Hardthöhe here, which echo each other nearly verbatim. What is of interest and relevance here, however, are the names of those who took an early interest in homosexual soldiers' rights, or at least asked the BMVg about their treatment. They include Herta Däubler-Gmelin (SPD) in 1978;[276] Helga Schuchardt (FDP) in 1981;[277] Wolfgang Ehmke (The Greens) in 1984;[278] Andreas von Bülow (SPD) in 1985;[279] Herbert Rusche (The Greens) in 1986;[280] Jutta Oesterle-Schwerin (The Greens) in 1988;[281] Vera Wollenberger (Alliance 90/The Greens at the time) in 1993;[282] Wolf-Michael Catenhusen (SPD) in 1995;[283] Günther Nolting (FDP, regarding a first lieutenant's removal from the head of a mechanized infantry

---

276 BArch, BW 1/304284: BMVg, Office of the Parliamentary State Secretary, 21 December 1978 as well as BMVg, parliamentary state secretary to Deputy Herta Däubler-Gmelin (SPD), 23 February 1979.

277 For more on Schuchardt see chapter 4, section 3.

278 BArch, BW 2/31224: BMVg response to Deputy Wolfgang Emke's inquiry during question period in the Bundestag on 18 and 19 January 1984. Also available in BW 1/546375.

279 BArch, BW 2/31225: Deputy Andreas von Bülow to the BMVg, State Secretary Würzbach, 28 May 1985.

280 BArch, BW 2/31224: Response of the federal government on 16 December 1986 to the minor inquiry from Deputy Herbert Rusche and the Green Party faction, document 10/6333.

281 BArch, BW 2/31224: Deputy Jutta Oesterle-Schwerin to the Parliamentary Commissioner for the Armed Forces on 28 June 1988; Parliamentary Commissioner to the Chief of Defense regarding the same topic on 15 July 1988; BMVg FüS I 4, 11 October 1988, Draft response for the Chief of Defense to the inquiry from the Parliamentary Commissioner (also in BW 2/32553), ibid., Supporting input from BMVg P II 1 to FüS I 4, 9 August 1988; additionally BW 2/31224: Major inquiry into homosexuals' right to informational self-determination, Bundestag document 11/2586, likewise from 1988.

282 BArch, BW 2/32553: BMVg, Parliament and Cabinet Division, 15 February 1993.

283 BArch, BW 2/38355: Wolf-Michael Catenhusen to Minister of Defense Volker Rühe, 13 September 1995.

platoon in 1997);[284] Peter Zumkley (SPD) in 1998;[285] Gabriele Iwersen in 1999 (SPD, regarding First Lieutenant Stecher, who was stationed in her electoral district in East Frisia);[286] Hildebrecht Braun (FDP, who also took the side of the forcibly transferred lieutenant in 1999);[287] Volker Beck (Alliance 90/The Greens) in 1999 and at other points;[288] and Christina Schenk (PDS), also in 1999.[289] In 1995 Ruprecht Polenz of the CDU raised concerns as the directly elected deputy for Münster about problems arising from discrepancies in the treatment of homosexuals within the joint German–Dutch corps stationed there.[290] Finally, in 1997 Deputy Heinrich Graf von Einsiedel (PDS) opened a minor inquiry into "Violence and discrimination against gays in the Bundeswehr."[291]

The FDP proved especially reliable in its support of gay and lesbian soldiers; as early as 1993 the party's youth organization submitted a petition at the national congress.

> Even today, homosexuals continue to experience discrimination in many areas of life. This is especially pronounced in the Bundeswehr. While gay men have to perform basic military service like any other, fixed-term and career soldiers as well as reservists are blocked from rising in the Bundeswehr if their homosexuality is made public. Homosexual soldiers in the Bundeswehr have their fitness to serve as superiors denied without having their individual cases inspected, even without sexual activity occurring during service [...] The FDP calls on its caucus in parliament to effect a change in the internal regulations at the Federal Ministry of Defense. Moreover, the FDP calls for a clarifying amendment to [§] 3 of the Soldatengesetz. "Sexual orientation" should be included explicitly in the catalog of prohibited forms of discrimination.[292]

---

284 BArch, BW 2/38358: Deputy Günther Nolting to the BMVg, 28 February 1997. A detailed account of the first lieutenant's dismissal and his transfer to a staff position is given above.

285 In June 1998, in conversation with Lieutenant General Olboeter. BArch, BW 2/38358: BMVg, StAl FüS I, 11 August 1998.

286 BArch, BW 2/38357: Deputy Gabriele Iwersen, comment from 26 January 1999.

287 Ibid., Deputy Hildebrecht Braun to the Defense Committee chairs, 23 June 1999.

288 See for example Deputy Volker Beck to Minister of Defense Scharping, 2 June 1999.

289 BArch, BW 2/38358: Deputy Christina Schenk (PDS), minor inquiry to the federal government, 1 October 1999 (corrected by hand to 5 October 1999), Bundestag document 14/1750. Deputy Schenk had already directed a catalog of questions to the BMVg in June 1999. BArch, BW 2/38357: Deputy Christina Schenk, 8 June 1999.

290 BArch, BW 2/38353: Deputy Ruprecht Polenz to Minister of Defense Volker Rühe on 29 November 1995. See chapter 7 on the subject of the German–Dutch corps.

291 BArch, BW 2/38358: German Bundestag, 13th legislative period, minor inquiry from Deputy Heinrich Graf von Einsiedel and the PDS group, Document 13/8676, see also http://dipbt.bundestag.de/doc/btd/13/089/1308950.pdf (last accessed 16 May 2019).

292 BArch, BW 2/38355: Federal executive board for the Young Liberals, Application No. 16 for the FDP party congress in Münster 11–13 June 1993.

With the group's consent, the petition was referred to the party's federal committee on peace and security policy "for in-depth consultation." Nine months' time (March 1994) did not witness the birth of any form of resolution, though the topic was still being discussed in committee. The BMVg characterized it as a "businesslike follow-up from the federal party congress."[293] Between the lines that read: "No cause for alarm, the topic will get buried in committee."

The FDP's youth chapter stuck to the topic, issuing a dramatic call in 1997 to "stop the employment ban for gays in the Bundeswehr now!"[294] Differently than in 1993–94, both the national party and its parliamentary caucus now responded to the demands of its youth. In July 1997 the difficulties homosexual soldiers encountered in making a career occupied the top slot on the agenda of the FDP's parliamentary working group on security policy, which directed sixteen questions to the BMVg.[295] The Liberals continued to pursue the matter after that as well, bringing an inquiry before the Bundestag in October 1999: "The German Bundestag calls on the federal government to guarantee that soldiers are not discriminated against on the basis of their sexual orientation within the working operations of the Federal Ministry of Defense."[296]

10. Silent Acceptance?

In January 2000, shortly before a BMVg meeting scheduled in light of the multiple petitions, a division at personnel department summarized the regulatory landscape and the ministry's practices to date. Nothing had changed since 1984: "Despite the shift in society's views of homosexuality [...] the *assignment restrictions* associated with soldiers with a homosexual disposition continue to constitute a fundamental

---

293 Ibid., BMVg, Parliament and Cabinet Division, 22 February 1994, including a draft agenda for the federal committee on peace and security policy session on 11–12 March 1994.

294 Young Liberals, 17 August 1998. A copy is available in the files of the BMVg in BArch, BW 2/38358.

295 BArch, BW 2/38358: Fax from Deputy Günter Nolting to the BMVg, 17 June 1997, in advance of a meeting of the FDP parliamentary working group on security policy on 23 June 1997. The FDP also inquired as to practices within other NATO armed forces, prompting a series of queries to military attachés. For more see chapter 7.

296 German Bundestag, 14th legislative period, Document 14/1870, inquiry from Deputy Hildebrecht Braun (Augsburg), Günter Nolting, Jörg van Essen, other members of parliament and the FDP caucus: "Bekämpfung jeder Art von Diskriminierung in der Bundeswehr," 27 October 1999, http://dipbt.bundestag.de/doc/btd/14/018/1401870.pdf (last accessed 16 May 2019). See chapter 6 for a full account.

lack of fitness. This applies for male and female soldiers alike."[297] This was the first time that the BMVg formulated a position on lesbian soldiers in writing.

The same restrictions applied for lesbians as for their male counterparts: They could not be installed as troop leaders or instructors (the specific positions named were platoon leader, company head and battalion commander); in "certain elevated *troop assignments with a special scope of duty*" such as company sergeant; or posts demanding an "especially close relationship of trust," as for example an Army doctor. "Soldiers who are assigned to such 'critical' posts in ignorance of their homosexual disposition will be *transferred out* upon discovery of their circumstances." The justification was the same danger of a loss in authority that had been cited for over twenty-five years, and with it

> the *jeopardization of troop combat-readiness* [...] It does not matter in this context how the disposition comes to light. Nor does it matter if it is accepted by subordinates in the individual case. Enduring acceptance – especially on deployment – cannot be relied on for reasons of personnel exchange, and because behavior from a homosexual superior that is itself innocuous may be misinterpreted without the superior being able to control it.

Former BMVg State Secretary Peter Wichert noted in retrospect that the Bundeswehr being an Army of conscripts "complicated things somewhat." The armed forces did not only draw on high-school graduates or tolerant people from large cities but "men from the countryside" with socially conservative views who were far less tolerant and open-minded then others. It was critical to avoid dissatisfaction, even unrest within the ranks.[298] Wichert emphasized to the author that "differently from today, where applicants are carefully screened, the Bundeswehr's highly cursory examinations [at the time] did not allow it to detect xenophobia, racism, homophobia, etc." There was a significant risk of misconduct toward homosexual soldiers, much greater than today. "The Bundeswehr would have come under heavier public criticism than any other institution," to Wichert's thinking.[299] It had always been the aim of the military leadership to protect the institution of the Bundeswehr from harm.[300]

Numerous interviews with gay soldiers who have since retired confirm that, at least in the 1990s, tolerance in the troops was often much greater than the regulations actually allowed for. An officer or sergeant who had been identified as gay

---

297 Here and in what follows, BArch, BW 1/502107, no pagination.: BMVg, PSZ III 1, 5 January 2000 (original emphases)
298 Interview with Ret. State Secretary Peter Wichert, Bad Münstereifel, 10 April 2019.
299 Email from Ret. State Secretary Peter Wichert to the author, 26 April 2019.
300 Interview with Ret. State Secretary Peter Wichert, Bad Münstereifel, 10 April 2019.

could not technically remain at his post, yet in practice there were any number whose homosexuality existed as an open secret in the barracks, and who continued to serve in positions of authority. Looking back, Wichert saw it in the same way: The reality had clearly differed from what the regulations, or "regulatory maxims," called for, with different "action maxims" prevailing among the troops instead, and "silent acceptance" serving as the going practice.[301] In speaking of "action maxims," Wichert claims a form of tolerance for the armed forces.

There is evidence to support his view, as one written exchange from 1995 attests. The Bundeswehr, wrote section FüS I 4, must "respect the constitutional rights of the individual citizen to develop his personality within our legal system."[302] This "naturally [applied] to soldiers as well, insofar as service operations and combat readiness are not impaired."[303] These unambiguous terms were directed to Mr. S. from the vicinity of Hannover. (Today one might label him a "concerned citizen" with slight irony.) In 1995 that concern revolved around the Bundeswehr's approach to homosexuality.

> For some months now I have seen how a Bundeswehr captain in my circle of acquaintances carries on a same-sex relationship with another man. This is done with complete separation between the two spheres, i.e. the professional and private. What bothers me, born in 1950 and brought up somewhat old-fashioned, is the fact that a German officer who is undoubtedly in command over many soldiers subordinate to him should have such a lifestyle.[304]

In its response the FüS I 4 thanked the man for his letter, initially striking an obliging tone. Even if society's attitude toward homosexuality had changed in recent decades, he "was almost certainly not alone [in his rejection] of the behavior he described." The Bundeswehr "naturally had to consider" this attitude in how it dealt with homosexual soldiers. Yet then the argumentation shifts. It cites the constitutionally enshrined right to the free development of personality as quoted above, before drawing the clear conclusion that "as long as this officer's behavior [did not have] any impact on his service," it was not subject "to any service assessment."[305] So long as private matters remained private and did not encroach on one's office, the BMVg saw no need to act. It did so only when someone turned "activist," in Wichert's words, i.e. made a demonstrative show of his own homosexuality to actively campaign against personnel management, or even went public

---

301 Ibid.
302 BArch, BW 2/38355: BMVg, FüS I 4 to Wolfgang S., 24 October 1995.
303 Ibid.
304 Ibid., Wolfgang S. to the BMVg, 11 October 1995.
305 Ibid., BMVg, FüS I 4 to Wolfgang S., 24 October 1995.

on behalf of all homosexuals. In that case the personnel office, and if necessary the ministry, would decide strictly according to the "regulatory maxims." "We could not allow the rules to be broken in a way that was obvious to everyone."[306]

The question of whether something can be talked about or not was (and remains) the decisive gauge for acceptance in society. The same applies within the armed forces. Openly admitting one's homosexuality was the major step along the path that would lead to the regulations taking hold. Anyone who outed himself sent up red flags for personnel leadership. As long as homosexual officers and NCOs simply went about their lives without shouting it out from the proverbial rooftops, they could make their way through the armed forces, even up to the highest echelon, with surprising ease.

A career in the military did come at a price, though: The pressure of having to conceal and dissemble at work did not let up at the end of the day or the barracks gate, but reached deep into the private realm and family life. Soldiers who were never able to speak about their weekends or vacations unselfconsciously, even within the free and easy milieu of fellow soldiers, who had to take care either not to mention a life partner or always replace "he" with "she" carried a tremendous burden throughout their lives and service. That burden often took a heavy toll, leading to mental illness in some soldiers; in 1999 *Die Zeit* was still forcibly criticizing the "psychological self-mutilation that the Bundeswehr inflicts on its soldiers."[307] Nearly twenty years previous in 1981, FDP deputy Helga Schuchardt had accused the defense ministry of "practically inciting homosexual soldiers to hypocrisy."[308]

In 1996 gay magazine *Magnus* spoke with a fixed-term soldier introduced as Franz. Franz did not see "any contradiction between being gay and being a soldier," and could not understand men "who rejected the Bundeswehr based solely on their being gay. These people don't seem to possess any other characteristics aside from their sexuality."[309]

Many gay soldiers wished for a more open and unencumbered life, free of secrecy. On the other hand, obviously not every homosexual or bisexual man wanted to make his intimate life public. Many held no intention of revealing their sexual preferences to their families or friends, much less their employer, preferring instead to live out their desires discreetly, even anonymously. If they were soldiers,

---

306 Interview with Ret. State Secretary Peter Wichert, Bad Münstereifel, 10 April 2019.
307 "Helden wie wir."
308 *Der Spiegel*, "'Berufliches': Michael Lindner," 176.
309 Glade, "In Reih und Glied!" The BMVg retained a copy of the article for its archives, BArch, BW 2/38355.

the service's expectations for them not to let on about their homosexuality was more than acceptable; the discretion demanded of them fully matched with their own life plans. Every man and woman has an obvious right to his or her privacy, applying in particular to one's intimate affairs. Many men and women have also lived by the principle of maintaining a strict division between their professional and private lives. The Military Counterintelligence Service (Militärischer Abschirm-dienst, MAD), on the other hand, did not draw an explicit distinction between the professional and the personal, and classified sexual behavior along with suscepti-bility to blackmail as potential security risks in need of investigation.

V   Under Suspicion: Homosexuality as a Security Risk

> As with any other soldier, a homosexual disposition in a general can lead to security concerns if it gives rise to the possibility of extortion. A homosexual disposition in and of itself does not constitute a security risk.[1]

Even if homosexuality did not come up explicitly in the security review question-naires of the Bundeswehr's Military Counterintelligence Service (MAD), the service would quickly come across soldiers' sexual tendencies in the course of researching their personal backgrounds. The way in which the service handled such sensitive information formed a central research interest in the present work.

It is in the nature of secret services to keep their movements or documents hidden. Every secret service shields its internal workings, methods, technical capa-bilities and especially its sources from overly inquisitive eyes. The same applied for MAD, making even a brief glimpse behind the scenes all the more revealing.[2]

1.   "Personnel Security Risks": Security Review Guidelines

In its assessments, counterintelligence drew a fundamental distinction between "feature relevant" and "incident relevant." Soldiers were not explicitly asked about their sexual orientation during security reviews; there was nowhere for them to state or check it off in the long questionnaires they had to fill out. Former MAD employees emphasized the fact that same-sex orientation was not an attribute that was screened for, and thus was not "feature relevant." A soldier was denied security clearance only when issues that touched on criminal law arose, sex with minors for

---

1 BArch, BW 2/31224: BMVg, P II 1, Az 16-02-05/2 (C) R 4/84, 13 March 1984. A copy is also available in in BArch, BW 2/38355.
2 This chapter, as with this study overall, only drew on sources that weren't categorized as clas-sified documents. Documents marked "Classified – For Official Use Only" were only reviewed if more than thirty years had elapsed. Helmut Hammerich also goes into MAD's security clearances in a detailed history of the organization, but does so somewhat generally and with a great deal of statistical information. The work doesn't consider the concrete process of conducting security reviews, much less cast an eye toward the aspect of sexual orientation, with only a single reference to a case from the fall of 1981. Hammerich, *"Stets am Feind!"* 240–60.

example. In that case, knowledge that was "incident relevant" had come into play.[3] One such incident came from within MAD's own ranks in 1967.

Any MAD employees who had to conceal their same-sex preferences were at particular risk of grooming by enemy intelligence services. One of the few cases that reached the press involved Petty Officer 2nd Class Walter Gant. The naval officer served at MAD's Group IV in Mainz, and came under police investigation in 1967 for crimes related to §175 StGB. To avoid a subpoena for questioning by Mainz's criminal investigations unit, that December he fled to the GDR. The petty officer had deserted, but that was not all. He passed along his internal knowledge of MAD to the GDR's Ministry for State Security, and went on East German television as a propagandist.[4] The normally well-informed *FAZ* reported on the MAD employee's flight in April 1968, and it did not fail to mention the reason for his flight: a criminal investigation under §175 StGB.[5] Gant did not hold out long in the GDR, however, filing three applications to return to the Federal Republic in 1973 alone. After they were rejected, Gant used his post in the GDR merchant marine to jump ship in Denmark and return to West Germany, where he found the Mainz police waiting for him. Gant was sentenced to three years in prison for "aggravated illicit sexual acts with men."[6]

a.) "Enemy of the State"?

Incidents with a bearing on security are highly complex affairs, often involving not a single isolated motive but a "bundle," as one BMVg employee phrased it in a 1966 report entitled "Sexual perversions as factors threatening security."[7] Nonetheless, based on "our experience in the intelligence service" and having evaluated some 200 security-related incidents, "sexual perversions tended to [take on] a privileged role" within this context, with homosexuality posing a "pivotal threat to security" even more than "exhibitionism/pornography," "hypersexuality/indecency with

---

3 Phone interview with Ret. Sergeant S., 27 March 2017. S. was active in MAD for over ten years beginning in 1990, including as an interviewer and assessor for ongoing security reviews.
4 BArch (MAD Archives), BW 31/1203: Final Report on Chief Petty Officer Gant, 9 July 1974. Thanks to Lieutenant Colonel Dr. Helmut Hammerich of the ZMSBw for the reference. For a detailed account of Officer Gant, see Hammerich, *"Stets am Feind!"* 352–354.
5 *Frankfurter Allgemeine Zeitung*, "Der Fluchtgrund des MAD-Manns."
6 BArch (MAD Archives), BW 31/1203: Final Report on Chief Petty Officer Gant, 9 July 1974.
7 BArch, BW 24/3736: "Sexuelle Perversionen als sicherheitsgefährdende Faktoren." In BMVg, InSan: "Beurteilung der Wehrdiensttauglichkeit und Dienstfähigkeit Homosexueller," 1966, sheets 78–81, here 78–79.

minors" and "sodomy." Pressing forward despite the absence of any sufficiently reliable studies to substantiate such a connection, the presenter posited a "positive correlation between homosexuality and criminality." What was more, "we tend toward the view that homosexuality is overwhelmingly associated with other unfitting forms of behavior."[8] The "we" in this instance would have referred to the presenter, as well as the psychologists working for an intelligence service that went unnamed.

Specific security concerns included homosexuals' criminal coercion, wrongly referred to in the report as blackmail. Homosexuals' ostracization, their feelings of shame and fear of possible reprisal laid the foundation for their coercion, which opposing intelligence services exploited "wantonly" along with other, similar factors. What was more, "the homosexual [...] [tended toward] disingenuousness, aggression toward those with a different nature, [and] feelings of hatred."[9] A psychologist picked up on the torrent of prejudices, reporting homosexuals had a stronger "penchant for perverted tendencies" than "feelings of responsibility toward one's ethical obligation to the state." It was not just homosexuals who ran the risk of coercion, but their families. The decisive step in safeguarding against the possibility was recognizing the "danger spots"[10] – in other words, a person's homosexual disposition if they were employed in a security field.

The psychologist speaking for the secret service at the BMVg conference certainly was not alone in his estimation. A Bundeswehr psychiatrist followed a similar, if much less drastic, line of argumentation in 1969 – this time not behind closed doors but in a journal. Soldiers who engaged in homosexual conduct gave "the agents of other powers the opportunity to coerce them into betrayal by threatening to reveal their homosexual activities."[11] Senior Field Physician Dr. Brickenstein went on to explain that "homosexuals do not turn into traitors because they are asocial or criminal by nature, but because when faced with choosing between shame and punishment or betrayal, these often insecure and fearful men, lacking self-confidence, tend to go with the latter."[12] Brickenstein's article comes across as much more mild and understanding than the position of his secret service colleague three years prior. As always, the lessons drawn were the same: Homosexuals were unfit to serve as superiors and especially to handle confidential documents, as they were at perpetual risk of blackmail and betrayal. This echoed a common ste-

---

8 Ibid.
9 Ibid., 80.
10 Ibid.
11 Brickenstein, "Probleme der Homosexualität im Wehrdienst," 150.
12 Ibid.

reotype echoed in countless states and eras that was constantly retrofitted to match the latest fashion.[13] Historically, suspicions concerning the "homosexual enemy of the state" have run deep within secret services.[14]

In the U.S., self-stylized "communist hunter" Senator Joseph McCarthy also took homosexuals into his scope in the early 1950s. For McCarthy and his team investigating "un-American" machinations in the government, armed forces and society, homosexuals stood directly alongside purported or actual leftists as a security threat. Especially in the State Department, those suspected of homosexuality fell subject to McCarthy's maneuvers and those of his chief assistant, Roy Cohn.[15] The irony here was that Cohn, who was surprisingly young for his post, was himself gay. Cohn brought his close friend G. David Schine into his office and thus to McCarthy's side, despite Schine's just having turned twenty-five and holding no qualifications. When Schine was drafted Cohn tried to get his friend out of the Army, putting pressure on the military brass with the force of his investigations. This triggered a direct confrontation with the Army which brought about McCarthy's rapid downfall, and ultimately the end of his political career. Even at the time rumors circulated alleging the homosexuality of the senator and the two good-looking young men at his side; at least for Roy Cohn, it can be assumed as a foregone conclusion.[16]

b.) 1971: "Abnormal Tendencies in the Sexual Realm"

The underlying issue sketched briefly here regarding homosexuality was not specific to MAD alone; the positions found consistent reflection in the security clearance guidelines enacted for all federal employees in 1971. It was not BMVg or MAD, but the Federal Ministry of the Interior that was responsible for the guidelines, which applied to every governmental department.

Among other "security risks that lie within the person of the employee," point 7.3 of the guidelines lists:

---

13 For a broad historical arc, from the Eulenburg scandal in 1907–08 and Colonel Redl to the alleged "secret homosexual clubs and spy groups" during the Cold War, see Schwartz, *Homosexuelle, Seilschaften, Verrat.*

14 For more see Nieden, "Der homosexuelle Staatsfeind."

15 For more see Marquez, "Persecution of Homosexuals in the McCarthy Hearings."

16 "Mr. Cohn, Mr. Schine and Senator McCarthy, all bachelors at the time, were themselves the targets of what some called 'reverse McCarthyism.' There were snickering suggestions that the three men were homosexuals, and attacks such as that by the playwright Lillian Hellman who called them 'Bonnie, Bonnie and Clyde.'" Krebs, "Roy Cohn."

a.) serious mental or psychological disorders
b.) abnormal tendencies in the sexual realm
c.) Alcoholism or drug addiction[17]

"Abnormal tendencies in the sexual realm" was listed again as a security risk in the BMVg's catalog of special security threats under Appendix C 1 No. 3 (again as b.) of ZDv 2/30.

In 1980, at a working conference for the BMVg's medical advisory board, governmental director Arthur Waldmann cast some light on the set of practices that had developed within the secret services out of the terse wording of the guidelines. When determining whether a security threat was present in a given case, employees let three questions guide their work:

– Does a potential for "kompromat" exist? ("Kompromat" means evidence or knowledge that was fit to compromise a person when divulged to third parties)
– Can a relationship of dependency based on homosexual activity be ruled out?
– Is it certain that unauthorized sharing of a subject's homosexual disposition will not lead to their disregard or ostracization within society, service or their circle of colleagues, even if and despite the fact that the disposition is known to MAD and immediate superiors?[18]

Another member of MAD, Lieutenant Colonel Oskar Schröder, added subsequently that recruitment by means of kompromat "assumed the candidate's fear of disclosure, revelation and discrimination. It [...] generally precludes a relationship of trust from developing between the lead officer and agents."[19] More than by way of footnote, three years later both Colonel Schröder and Waldmann would play a key role in resolving the Wörner–Kießling affair.

Bundeswehr psychiatrist Dr. Brickenstein, mentioned repeatedly in this study as specializing in cases of homosexuality, also spoke from experience at the meeting. On the topic of blackmail Brickenstein reported that cases of "severe coercion" were "not all that rare" among homosexual superiors, whatever that might have meant in specific numbers. "Their susceptibility to blackmail as superiors alone means they cannot be entrusted with secrets. I have ample experience in this

---

17 Federal Ministry of the Interior: Guidelines for the security clearance process for federal employees from 15 January 1971, point 7. Available in BArch, BW 1/378197: BMVg, Abt. KS to Secretary of State Dr. Rühl, 25 January 1984.
18 BArch, BW 24/5553: Governmental Director Arthur Waldmann, "Sachverständigenreferat aus sicherheitsmäßiger Sicht," at a meeting of the BMVg medical advisory board's committee on preventative health and care and military examinations, 18 April 1980. Also available in BArch, BW 2/31225.
19 Ibid.

regard."[20] Brickenstein gave the example of a staff officer: "Thirty-eight years old, a top staff position, dazzling qualifications, married, three children – revealed to his superior that he had been blackmailed into paying off his homosexual partner, who had threatened to make his homosexual activity public if he did not, marking the end of his career." His superior had thanked him for his candor and assured him he would not have any professional repercussions to fear. Yet it was now no longer the officer but his deputy who was now brought into confidential or secret negotiations. Eventually the officer was advised to transfer. He was initially "welcomed" at other posts given his qualifications, but rejected without fail "upon inquiries as to why his previous post had wanted to detach itself from the officer." The officer fell into a deep depression and had to retire due to inability to serve. Later, he succumbed to alcohol.[21]

Writing in 1970, one year after reform of the criminal code, the lawyers at the BMVg's administrative and legal department affairs department found that "liberalization of the criminal law on morality cannot obscure the fact that the majority of the population continues to disapprove of homosexual activity morally, and that homosexuals, knowing this, shy away from their tendencies becoming known." This in turn provided "points of departure for the Bundeswehr to be spied on by intelligence agencies."[22]

Ten years later, MAD now found that relaxing criminal and service law had significantly lessened homosexuals' risk of being compromised ("service law" likely meant the restricted application of disciplinary law to homosexual activity conducted in private).[23] Nonetheless, there was "solid intelligence" that "enemy intelligence services sought contact with homosexually inclined members of the Bundeswehr." These agents tended to be homosexual themselves, and sought to establish a "relationship of dependency based on homosexual activity."[24]

Waldmann reported in 1980 that "in nearly every [known and reviewed] instance" of homosexuality in soldiers, MAD had either been forced to deny or

---

20 BArch, BW 24/5553: Lt. Col. (MC) Dr. Rudolph Brickenstein, "Sachverständigenreferat aus psychiatrischer Sicht," delivered at a meeting of the BMVg medical advisory board's committee on preventative health and care and military examinations, 18 April 1980. Also available in BW 2/31225. Summarized in 1985 in Lindner, "Homosexuelle in der Institution Bundeswehr."
21 BArch, BW 24/5553: Lt. Col. (MC) Dr. Rudolph Brickenstein, "Sachverständigenreferat."
22 BArch, BW 24/7180: BMVg, VR IV 1, 29 September 1970.
23 See chapter 3 for greater detail.
24 BArch, BW 24/5553: Governmental Director Arthur Waldmann, "Sachverständigenreferat aus sicherheitsmäßiger Sicht," at a meeting of the BMVg medical advisory board's committee on preventative health and care and military examinations, 18 April 1980. Also available in BArch, BW 2/31225.

revoke their security clearance, a practice supported by the Federal Administrative Court.[25]

> Fulfilling the defense mandate can only be safeguarded by granting access to classified information exclusively to soldiers for whom no type of security concerns exist. The resulting need to review Bundeswehr members for security concerns is taken as a precautionary measure intended to preclude security risks. Security concerns arise whenever the soldier in question is viewed as a potential target by foreign services.[26]

The result meant homosexual soldiers' exclusion from nearly every elevated or higher-ranking service post. The BMVg had already described the effects in 1973 with reference to Rainer Plein's case: "Without level 1 security clearance, an officer can, aside from exceptions, only receive limited assignments within the area corresponding to his rank. Limitations of this sort on an officer's ability to serve are fundamentally unacceptable."[27]

Waldmann was frank in admitting the "considerable" consequences of the measures. For both career and fixed-term soldiers with more than four years in the service, it often meant

> removal from their current post and subsequent transfer away from their current place of service; removal from [...] a course of instruction; ineligibility for promotion in the future, since no longer fully fit for assignment; assignment to a post that is not security-sensitive, which may mean that a lieutenant colonel is assigned to an A 11 [captain's] service post until retirement, or that a captain is no longer promoted despite qualifications.[28]

The explicit mention of restrictions placed on fixed-term soldiers with more than four years in the service was an important one. For soldiers who had served a shorter period of time, the consequences of having their security clearance denied or revoked were graver still: They would be released under §55 (5) SG in the event

---

25 A security clearance, or *Sicherheitsbescheid*, confirms the results of a security review and, depending on the level of clearance, provides the basis for access to secret or top secret documents. This makes holding it a requirement for many important posts.

26 BVerwG, 2 WB 60/79: Federal Administrative Court, 1st Military Service Senate, ruling on 12 January 1983, found on www.jurion.de.

27 BMVg, P II 7, to Münster Administrative Court, 16 July 1973. The author holds a copy in his possession.

28 BArch, BW 24/5553: Governmental Director Arthur Waldmann, "Sachverständigenreferat aus sicherheitsmäßiger Sicht," at a meeting of the BMVg medical advisory board's committee on preventative health and care and military examinations, 18 April 1980. Also available in BArch, BW 2/31225.

that "the homosexual relations also constituted a breach of duty." Extending one's period of service was not possible, as a valid security clearance was required to do so.[29]

In short, the MAD representative described a bleak, nearly hopeless landscape for homosexuals serving in the armed forces, bluntly describing their depressing reality and the pressures to which they were exposed. The governmental director did see one small ray of hope, noting that security concerns could be put aside in the event that a person was involved "as it were in a steady living arrangement" with his partner and could "demonstrate" this. The conditions in this case were to include the partner in the security check and for the check to conclude "without adverse findings," no discernible negative impact on the official realm and an "obligation to report a new partner to MAD in case of separation."[30]

On this point as well, Waldmann was surprisingly critical of the approach taken by his service. The "issue," as he described it, lay in reconciling Articles 1 and 2 of the Basic Law (a person's dignity and his right to the free development of his personality). The "particular (coercive) situation" in which homosexuals in the Bundeswehr found themselves left it "an open question" whether the information MAD demanded was "still compatible with our legal system." Yet what at first glance came across as unexpected criticism and sympathy for homosexuals' predicament was then immediately used against them. In the event that the requested information were to be classified as unlawful, "security risks identified for any homosexual in the Bundeswehr would [necessarily] lead to nonretractable security concerns," bringing denial or revocation of their security clearance with all the attendant consequences.[31]

The BMVg had drawn the very same conclusions the year before in 1979 in responding to Bundestag deputy Hertha Däubler-Gmelin. "As a general rule," a soldier whose homosexuality became known had his security clearance withdrawn "because there is a risk that he would be more easily blackmailed by opposing intelligence services." Withdrawal of a security clearance in turn "considerably" restricted the range of assignments for which the soldier was eligible.[32]

A BMVg paper from several years later in August 1982 left it open as to whether a soldier who voluntarily disclosed his same-sex "disposition" should be seen as a security risk, finding that "in such cases the risk of blackmail by an intelligence

---

29 Ibid.
30 Ibid.
31 Ibid.
32 BArch, BW 1/304284: BMVg, VR I 1, 15 February 1979, as well as BMVg, parliamentary state secretary to Deputy Herta Däubler-Gmelin (SPD), 23 February 1979.

service should be considered low."[33] This assessment, which came from the personnel department rather than the legal department that supervised MAD and was responsible for questions of the sort, was rather ahead of its time, anticipating as it did the eventual amendment to the guidelines. Under the version in effect at the time, any sort of "abnormal tendency in the sexual realm" was still considered a security risk. This meant the regulations governing security checks, or rather their application in the real-world, ignored the fact that homosexuality between adults had been decriminalized in 1969. "Is no one brought up short?" asked the *Nürnberger Nachrichten* in the wake of the Wörner–Kießling affair in January 1984. "Has not this society long since taken some credit perhaps for classifying homosexuality as 'different' but at least no longer as 'abnormal'?"[34] Setting the regulations within the broader context of how the armed forces handled homosexuality, the editors at the Nuremberg paper called on the Bundeswehr "finally to dismantle the taboo surrounding homosexuality."[35] It was not until 1983 – fourteen years after the 1969 changes – that the armed services revised the guidelines to at least partially mirror the evolution in criminal law.

c.) 1988: "Sexual Conduct That Can Lead to Blackmail"

A revised draft of the guidelines came out in November 1983, which among other "criminal acts" that constituted "personnel security risks," like alcoholism or drug addiction, listed "sexual behavior that can lead to extortion" under §5 (2).[36] The proposed change in phrasing was more than a mere formality. The draft effectively meant that a soldier who openly admitted to his homosexuality was no longer relevant to MAD in matters of security. Cases in which soldiers or civil servants kept their homosexual or bisexual orientation from their families, spouses, friends and most importantly the service itself were another question; here MAD spotted a potential risk of contact and subsequent blackmail by enemy intelligence services. The threat of blackmail existed anytime the external image on offer did not match the underlying reality, independently of sexual orientation. If the constructed image was material, even indispensable to one's career, the threat of its destruc-

---

33 BArch, BW1/304286: BMVg, P II 1, 12 August 1982.

34 Fh, "Das Tabu: Bundeswehr und Homosexualität," cited in Schwartz, *Homosexuelle, Seilschaften, Verrat,* 302.

35 Cited in Schwartz, *Homosexuelle, Seilschaften, Verrat,* 303.

36 BArch, BW 1/378197: Federal Ministry of the Interior: Guidelines for the security clearance process at federal agencies, draft as of 10 November 1983.

tion by the revelation of facts to the contrary took on existential importance – the greater a person's interest in keeping up appearances, the greater his susceptibility to extortion.

The timing of the guidelines' revision is worth noting. One source gives the date of the draft as 10 November 1983, about two months after the MAD office in Düsseldorf began its investigations into General Kießling's involvement in Cologne's gay scene.[37] It remains an open question whether a causal link also existed in the striking temporal proximity, or whether the investigation simply happened to run in parallel to revisions that were anyway already under consideration.

When the planned revisions were announced in 1984, they were viewed in public as a consequence (and lesson) drawn from the Wörner–Kießling affair. There was more – the FDP, at the time part of the governing coalition, took ownership of the push toward new regulations, announcing in that July that "at the initiative of the FDP, [the new guidelines] would be written so as not to discriminate against minorities. The focus should fall instead on general life circumstances that may lead to blackmail. The target of assessment [...] should be the specific case at hand."[38] The author of this study was not able to determine whether the impetus behind the scenes came from the FDP-led Ministry of Justice. Sources do date the revised draft back to November 1983, however, meaning that it could not have been due to the public uproar surrounding the scandal. The FDP at any rate managed to communicate the context in clever fashion, and to its own benefit. They went further, interjecting during the fierce Bundestag debates of January 1984 to remind former Federal Chancellor Brandt it had been under his watch as chancellor that the security guidelines now under such heavy criticism had taken effect in 1971.[39]

As the scandal surrounding General Kießling culminated in January 1984, the BMVg section responsible for supervising MAD laid out the new position explicitly in a commentary to State Secretary Lothar Rühl:

> Sexual behavior should only be regarded as a "personnel security risk" *if it can lead to blackmail.* While this viewpoint has also been observed up until now, the new version is likely to result in fewer cases of security concerns being brought up when assessing homosexual conduct, for example. (It must be kept in mind, however, that heterosexual behavior and cases of sodomy can also lead to susceptibility to blackmail [...])[40]

---

37 See section 3 in this chapter for a full account.
38 Cs, "FDP setzt sich mit rechtstaatlichen Forderungen durch" in *Die neue Bonner Depesche*, July 1984, cited in Schwartz, *Homosexuelle, Seilschaften, Verrat*, 315.
39 Schwartz, *Homosexuelle, Seilschaften, Verrat*, 317.
40 BArch, BW 1/378197: BMVg, Abt. KS to Parliamentary State Secretary Dr. Rühl, 25 January 1984 (original emphasis).

The BMVg desk stressed that "sexual behavior that can lead to blackmail" occupied fifth place out of a total of ten characteristics in the new regulations, whereas "abnormal tendencies in the sexual realm" had previously ranked second out of nine. This in turn presented the conclusion "that the significance of such behavior should not (any longer) be regarded as 'extraordinary'."[41]

Rühl's extensive handwritten commentary reveals the extent of his skepticism toward the new regulations, which he notes might become "a burden for us," i.e. the BMVg and its subordinates, "out of all proportion to the real security risks and the effort involved."[42] In essence the new version should "only eliminate discrimination against homosexual inclinations," yet the updated formulation regarding "sexual behavior that can lead to blackmail" would now also bring heterosexual behavior into the fold. Within the federal administration, the Bundeswehr and the BMVg would bear the full brunt of the revisions. "We have around 700,000 employees, the vast majority of whom should be considered sexually normal."[43] "For those with normal sexual behavior, 'susceptibility to blackmail'" was linked to extramarital intercourse. Here State Secretary Rühl saw a "Pandora's box" being opened and "a real problem in the security provisions' relationship to the essence and concept of personal freedoms, and safeguarding the private sphere in our liberal constitutional state."[44] In this the secretary did not err. Yet the very tension he was problematizing, between security interests on the one hand and personal freedoms and the private sphere on the other hand, was inherent in the work of the secret services, and remains so today. It was also precisely the sort of encroachment that homosexuals had been forced to endure on their private and intimate lives. It was now with regard to heterosexuals, those deemed "sexually normal," that it struck BMVg leadership as an issue, likely for the first time. It is possible that the adage about peoples' tune changing once things get personal applies here as well.

The new guidelines were put into place, reservations of the state secretary notwithstanding, though not in 1984. A ruling at the Federal Administrative Court in April 1985 was still citing the previous wording of the security risks inherent in an "abnormal tendency in the sexual realm" as the applicable regulation.[45] In October 1985, the responsible information security officer at the BMVg noted that along with other data protection regulations, the Federal Constitutional Court's

---

41 Ibid.

42 Ibid., handwritten notes from Parliamentary State Secretary Dr. Rühl on the document BMVg, Abt. KS to State Secretary Dr. Rühl, 25 January 1984.

43 Ibid.

44 Ibid.

45 BArch, BW 2/31224 and BW 2/31225, BVerwG, 1st Military Senate, Az 1 WB 152/84 from 11 April 1985.

landmark decision on the controversial topic of the December 1983 census had also delayed the revised regulations for security screenings.[46] It now seemed that the new regulations could take hold only once the Constitutional Protection Act had been amended.[47] One paper from the Federal Ministry of the Interior has the new guidelines taking effect on 1 May 1988.[48] Under §4 (2) of the new version, a security risk was "only then" assumed in the presence of circumstances that substantiated "a heightened risk of attempts at grooming or solicitation by foreign intelligence services" and possible blackmail.[49] The BMVg division responsible for overseeing MAD viewed it in the same light: On its own, the "abstract circumstance" of homosexuality "was not enough to raise security concerns."[50] The wording in a set of internal Bundeswehr publications from 1991 gives one indication of the broad scope of discretionary powers at MAD's disposal. As anyone interested in soldiers or the Bundeswehr could read in *Heer*, *Luftwaffe* and *Blaue Jungs*, "What is decisive in any case is that it might be possible – not that it actually is the case. The same applies for security clearances being downgraded or revoked in the event of 'security concerns'."[51] "Many gays are even understanding of this. But this makes somebody who has intercourse with prostitutes just as 'susceptible to blackmail' in their eyes [...] as someone who is a known right-extremist or drinker."[52]

In 1983, the 1st Military Service Senate at the Federal Administrative Court ruled that denying security clearances was warranted in the event of same-sex activity which held relevance under criminal law, due to the associated potential for compromise. The judges left it "explicitly" open, however, as to whether a same-sex disposition in and of itself was sufficient grounds for rejection.[53]

Every internal BMVg paper that has been preserved echoes this position verbatim, as with the 1986 G1 memo draft seeking to regulate all matters pertaining to homosexuality. "Homosexuality is not generally regarded in the Bundeswehr as a

---

46 Federal Constitutional Court, BVerfG, ruling on 15 December 1983, Az. 1 BvR 209, 269, 362, 420, 440, 484/83.

47 BMVg, Security Information Officer, Org 6, to Captain P., 4 October 1985. The author owns a copy of the document.

48 BArch, BW 2/31224: Federal Ministry of the Interior, Section O I 4, 6 December 1988, draft response to the major inquiry from Deputy Ms. Oesterle-Schwerin, Bundestag printed material 11/2586, annex.

49 BArch, BW 1/546375: BMVg Org 6, 14 November 1991.

50 Ibid.

51 Haubrich, "Schwul und beim Bund?!"

52 Ibid.

53 BVerwG, 1st Military Service Senate, ruling on 12 January 1983; see also BArch, BW 1/502107: Report from Doctor of Law Armin Steinkamm, Bundeswehr University Munich, 25 January 2000, here p. 2. See the following for a detailed account of the military service senate's ruling.

security risk. It is not an abnormal tendency in the sexual realm that is viewed as a security risk, but rather sexual behavior that can lead to blackmail. A finding to this effect is only permissible after review and assessment on an individual basis."[54] An initial draft composed by the same department three months previously had envisioned much more detailed regulations:

> Deciding whether a risk to military security is present in the soldier's person must be made by the Bundeswehr authorities appointed for this purpose, taking into account and with appreciation for the specific military concerns involved. Yet the decision by the responsible military post as to whether or not a soldier represents a security risk must not be unreasonable or arbitrary in its effects on the rights of the person concerned; it must always be based on the individual case, and not the result of improper generalization.[55]

The planned G1 memo was never adopted, either in its long or short form. There was little point anyway where assessing security risks were concerned, as it was the regulations under ZDv 2/30 and departmental guidelines for security reviews that were decisive.

2. Security Reviews in Practice

We owe an unusual and rare glimpse behind the scenes of MAD security screenings to a first lieutenant's legal complaint after his security clearance was denied in 1977. Two years prior, both the lieutenant's level 1 and 2 security clearances had been revoked when "it was discovered in the course of investigations against civilians that the claimant had carried on homosexual relations, including with minors."

The lieutenant now applied to have both security clearances reinstated, a motion that was turned down by the Bundeswehr Security Office (Amt für Sicherheit der Bundeswehr, ASBw). The petitioner appealed this decision in writing as well, which was in turn rejected by the Bundeswehr deputy chief of defense. In the appeal, the lieutenant argued that he was wrongly being seen as a security risk.

---

54 BArch, BW 2/31225: BMVg, FüS I 4 to the minister via the parliamentary state secretary, 22 October 1986, annex. Identical to BArch, BW 2/31224: BMVg, FüS I 4, July 1986. The formulation followed the wording of a suggestion by the BMVg's head of information security. BArch, BW 1/378197: BMVg Org – Security Information Officer, 18 June 1986.

55 BArch, BW 2/31224: BMVg, FüS I 4, July 1986, adopted again in BW 1/378197: BMVg Org – Security Information Officer, 18 June 1986.

His homophilic tendencies are known, which removes his susceptibility to blackmail. He has had no homophilic contact for over two years now, nor does he intend to resume. He takes his career as a soldier seriously and wishes to continue it. Potential blackmail attempts could be deflected by immediately reporting any grooming attempts to the responsible authorities.[56]

The BMVg also rejected his appeal, on the grounds that the claimant "continued to represent a security risk."

The claimant's statement that he has not had any homosexual contact for two years is of no decisive importance because the tendency in question continues to exist. The fact that this tendency is known about within the official sphere may diminish the possibility of compromise, but does not preclude it.[57]

The lieutenant applied for a decision at the Federal Administrative Court, and it is this circumstance that research has to thank today for the fact that the proceedings can be accessed like any other administrative court decision. The first lieutenant opened his argument before the court by arguing it was "incorrect that an abnormal tendency in the sexual realm was present in his case." He could not accept such an "assessment by non-experts." Reports obtained previously from Bundeswehr neurologists and psychiatrists had already confirmed his ability to serve as an officer.

He had never brought his tendency with him into the official line of duty. It was a private matter; it did not affect the interests of the Bundeswehr. He would be able to deflect any attempts at grooming or compromise by an intelligence agency with composure. He will report any attempts at grooming.[58]

In its response, the BMVg insisted that the claimant continued to pose a security risk.

The deficit in trusting and comradely contact that necessarily results from a homosexual tendency leads to officers with such a tendency being forced into circles that stand at a distance from the Bundeswehr. Such officers are not shown the requisite trust by their comrades. It

---

56 Plaintiff's grounds for complaint from 18 August 1978, cited in: BVerwG, 2 WB 60/79: Federal Administrative Court, 1st Military Service Senate, ruling on 12 January 1983, found on www.jurion.de.
57 BMVg notice of rejection from 6 October 1978, cited. in: BVerwG, 2 WB 60/79: Federal Administrative Court, 1st Military Service Senate, ruling on 12 January 1983.
58 BVerwG, 2 WB 60/79: Federal Administrative Court, 1st Military Service Senate, ruling on 12 January 1983.

would be seen as inappropriate if these officers were granted security clearances like everyone else and given access to classified material.[59]

In plain language, the BMVg's position amounted to nothing less than assessing even openly gay soldiers as a security risk. The previous mantra about the risk of blackmail was not applied, as it was not an issue for gays who were open about their orientation. Instead, in the Federal Administrative Court the BMVg now declared all homosexual officers outsiders, unworthy as it were of being put on the same tier as others – i.e. soldiers with "normal sexuality" – when it came to matters of security. As much as this line of reasoning reveals, it does not show up in other publicly accessible sources.

The judges at the court broke through the back-and-forth in unorthodox fashion, looking to set the matter back on factual grounds by instructing MAD and the ASBw to conduct a new security check on the lieutenant, obviously without informing him before. MAD opened an investigation into the gay scene in a nearby city, and found what it was looking for: The first lieutenant was contacting "hustlers he would seek out in local bars and other hangouts," potentially including minors. His "extensive sexual activity" ("nearly every night") made it likely that "the hustlers and a wide swath of the scene were aware of his affiliation with the Bundeswehr and of his status as a career officer."[60]

Based on these discoveries, in 1982 the ASBw decided that the lieutenant's security clearances still could not be reissued. This was a clear win on points for MAD, as the officer had stated repeatedly in his appeals that he had refrained from all homosexual activity since 1976, and broken off with all previous contacts.

At least on the surface, the lieutenant did not give any impression of being swayed by the results of the MAD investigation, and attempted to regain the argumentative high ground.

2. The affirmation that my behavior is supposed to pose a heightened security risk must be categorically denied, as infiltration of homosexual circles by [male] agents of enemy intelligence services is conducted on a much smaller scale than is the case with female agents. How is it that an unmarried man (heterosexual) [who frequently exchanges partners] is not classified as just as great a security risk by the ASBw and BMVg?

3. Nor can susceptibility to blackmail be spoken of in this case, as my tendencies are already known about at the responsible Bundeswehr authorities [...]

6.b) [...] How does one justify having a perpetual security risk, since I would hardly be able to change or cast aside my homosexual disposition by the end of my service?[61]

---

59 Written statement from the BMVg from 15 March 1979, ibid.

60 ASBw decision from 16 July 1982, ibid.

61 Written statement from the plaintiff on 30 August 1982, ibid.

The lieutenant then brought the career and assignment disadvantages threatening soldiers known to be homosexual to bear on his argument, tying them to his own unalterable homosexual orientation and thus the unalterable fact of a continued security risk. He closed by citing Articles 1 and 3 of the Basic Law: "7. I feel discriminated against in all of this. I feel my human dignity has been violated (Art. 1 GG) and that Article 3 of the Basic Law has not been observed."[62]

The administrative court judges did not find the lieutenant's arguments persuasive. His petition was unfounded; the claimant was not entitled to receive a security clearance. As they explained,

> deciding whether a risk to military security is present in the soldier's person must be made by the Bundeswehr authorities appointed for this purpose, taking into account and with appreciation for the specific military concerns involved. As with all questions of fitness, they are limited legally as to the scope their review can take [...] It can be left aside in the present case whether or not the claimant's homosexual disposition constitutes an abnormal tendency in the sense determined by letter b. [of ZDv 2/30 Annex C 1 No. 3], and must therefore be considered a security risk from the outset. The claimant has not been able to contest the fact in any case that his shifting sexual contacts have included men under the age of eighteen, and thus that he has made himself liable to prosecution under §175 (1) of the Criminal Code (letter i.). This leaves him considerably more vulnerable to compromise than a man engaged in homosexual practices that are not punishable by law. In the case of unstable personalities or highly unfavorable circumstances, even the threat of criminal proceedings based on criminal forms of sexual behavior can, when seen objectively, provide opposing services with a point of departure. It is not objectionable if the risk the claimant poses is not dispelled in the eyes of the ASBw and BMVg by the claimant's declaration that he would immediately report any such attempts by enemy services. For one thing, given the right circumstances such contacts may only become recognizable to the claimant once entrapment has already occurred, or the claimant may find himself in a psychological state that does not (or does not any longer) permit him to behave in the way imagined at present.[63]

In concluding, the judges stressed that "the claimant is not unreasonably or arbitrarily affected by having his security clearances denied. The negative decision is based on objective conditions and does not constitute a targeted discrimination against the claimant and his disposition."[64]

As a part of the expanded screenings required for level 3 security clearance, MAD would question personal references of the person under review. Former MAD employees recall that sexual orientation and tendencies were routinely asked after in connection with the candidate's private life, always with the aim of identifying

---

62 Ibid.
63 Ibid.
64 Ibid.

potentially compromising material, i.e. weak points that other intelligence services might use to then try to initiate contact with or blackmail the person. By no means did this have to entail homosexuality; it might also include womanizing, visiting swinger's clubs with a spouse, etc. While no references were interviewed in the simplified procedures for level 1 and 2 security clearances, if the candidate's homosexuality came out in conversation with MAD, either from the person themselves or by other means, MAD would as a matter of routine again screen for potential "kompromat" (evidence or knowledge that was fit to compromise a person when divulged to third parties). The service saw this as a possibility in cases where the candidate was not "out" in private. MAD interviewers from the era recall it as usually being enough for the service to rule out the possibility of blackmail if the soldier was open in private about his homosexuality, even if they were not in the official realms.

Other eyewitness confirm that MAD actively investigated soldiers whose alleged homosexuality had become "conspicuous." In the second half of the 1970s one company head, a captain in Albersdorf's ABC Defense Battalion 610 not yet out at the time, recalls asking a MAD employee how the office actually handled cases of homosexuality after the latter had sought him out on another topic. Evidently on the basis of this question alone, two MAD employees later called on the S2 officer in the Albersdorf battalion, asking for information about the captain and his private life.[65] After the captain's homosexuality became public knowledge by 1979 at the latest, the G2 staff officer responsible for matters of security in the 6th Mechanized Infantry Division heading the battalion went to the battalion commander and recommended the captain's security clearance be revoked. The commander turned down the recommendation and informed the captain of the G2's request.[66]

A master sergeant who was himself relatively open about his homosexuality during his time in service recalled that a sergeant in his company, himself homosexual, had once identified himself as an (alleged) MAD informant and attempted to sound him out about a captain in another post who was reportedly gay.[67] An isolated incident?

The notion that homosexuals were susceptible to blackmail as such was not completely unfounded, as a look back into the not-so-distant past reveals. In a

---

65 Interview with Michael Lindner, Hamburg, on 7 and 14 February 2017. The facts of the matter were confirmed over the phone on 20 April 2017 by the S2 officer at the time.
66 The conversation between the G2 officer and the battalion commander evidently took place on 25 February 1980. Interview with Michael Lindner, Hamburg, on 7 and 14 February 2017.
67 Interview with S., Freiburg, 21 June 2017. The alleged MAD informant expressly denied having done so to the author.

series of 1922–23 articles on the history of the gay movement, Magnus Hirschfeld presents an unsparing account of blackmail in a chapter on the topic:

> Just one generation ago, nearly every urning [an expression Hirschfeld used for homosexual men] had his blackmailer, attached to him like the parasite that lives in and from a living creature. Like a mortal threat, the confidant of a weak moment accompanied the urning throughout his life. There were well-to-do homosexuals who included a substantial line item in their yearly budgets from the outset under the name "blackmail expenses," albeit usually under a different title. Much more revealing is the fact that when the Berlin office of criminal investigations was divided into different departments, the blackmail squad was merged with the homosexual squad to form a single unit, a connection that continues into the present day and has proven highly practical.[68]

Hirschfeld did not fail to identify the root cause of the extortionism, which was society's rejection of homosexuality, and in particular its criminal prosecution. The author quoted the former head of the blackmail and homosexual department at Berlin criminal investigations in this regard, who found that "what set Paragraph [175] apart from all the others was really that it was only of value to the extortionist."[69] Throughout the Federal Republic of the 1950s and 1960s the situation remained the same; a former police officer sentenced to death for homosexuality prior to 1945 who barely survived the war in the Neuengamme concentration camp recalled that in 1946 a former lover tried to blackmail him. "It was loathsome [...] thank God I held out."[70]

Codifying homosexuals as a threat to security was perceived in the media of the day as coinciding with a broad social consensus. "Whenever murder, manslaughter, blackmail or betrayal of one's country is reported on in connection with homosexuality [...] the majority sees its own views confirmed," *Der Spiegel* found in 1969.[71]

MAD also became involved in a case described previously, where by an unhappy twist of fate a man was transferred into the company led by his partner, a captain.[72] After the two were identified as gay by East German security when crossing the border into West Berlin, the captain had reported the incident to MAD so as to forestall any possibility of compromise by enemy intelligence. Since his partner was not yet a soldier at the time, the officer did not see any potential risks for his professional future. Yet as the officer would later find out, after evaluating his report MAD had reported his relationship with a direct subordinate to the division,

---

68 Hirschfeld, *Von einst bis jetzt*, 23.
69 Ibid., 29.
70 Interview with Hans G. in Stümke and Finkler, *Rosa Winkel, Rosa Listen*, 301–6, here 306.
71 "Späte Milde," 58.
72 See chapter 4, section 4.e.

with the consequences that ensued.[73] By August 1981, three days before division ordered the captain to be removed immediately as company head and provisionally removed from service, MAD revoked his level 1 and 2 security clearances. At the time, ASBw justified the measures with "security concerns as defined in Annex C 1 to ZDv 2/30."[74]

After acquittal in the second instance by the 1st Military Service Senate, the captain reentered service in June 1982, albeit no longer in his old company but on brigade staff. This was followed by his assignment to the G3 department at division staff, which among other things is responsible for planning exercises and maneuvers. Yet he continued to be denied access to documents classified as confidential or secret throughout, an obstacle that MAD justified on account of his homosexuality. The armored brigade had already petitioned military counterintelligence in June 1982 for the captain to receive a supplemental review with the express aim of reinstating his level 1 security clearance. This lowest level of clearance entitles the holder access to documents categorized as "classified material-confidential" and is practically indispensable for work in the G3 department. The ASBw initially rejected the application, though in April 1983 it decided to reinstate the captain's level 1 clearance after all. In the meantime the captain had decided to go higher up the chain and seek a level 2 clearance from the deputy chief of defense, an appeal that was rejected in October 1983. The BMVg turned down a further appeal in August 1984, at which point the captain sought a decision before the Federal Administrative Court.

In court the officer argued he had already furnished proof of his sense of responsibility in 1980 by immediately reporting the incident on the GDR border, and therefore would not represent a "potential target for enemy intelligence services" in the future. By having his level 2 security clearance withheld, a career soldier "is practically excluded from further promotion"; "such a drastic measure" was "unwarranted" in his case.[75]

The BMVg shored up its own line of argumentation with reference to the regulations stipulated under ZDv 2/30, which cited an "abnormal tendency in the sexual realm" as a heightened security risk in Annex C 1 No. 3 b. This threshold expressly did not "require any sexual pathological disturbance, [but rather] any form of homosexual activity was sufficient, as a mode of sexual conduct that deviates

---

73 Ibid.

74 ASBw, 4 August 1981, cited in: BArch, BW 2/31224 as well as BW 2/31225: Ruling at BVerwG, 1st Military Service Sente, Az 1 WB 152/84 on 11 April 1985.

75 Plaintiff's statement, cited in BArch, BW 2/31224: Ruling at BVerwG, 1st Military Service Senate, Az 1 WB 152/84 from 11 April 1985.

from the practices and opinions of the majority."[76] "As a general rule," the soldier had a special interest in keeping circumstances secret which might result in his being compromised "due to the feared drawbacks if [those circumstances] became known."[77] With this, the BMVg's legal staff had laid its finger on the great dilemma facing homosexual soldiers – leaving aside, of course, the notion of resolving it by prompting a change in those "feared drawbacks." Instead, the jurists concentrated on whether or not the claimant's sexuality continued to pose a security risk, leading in the end to a legal battle over the formulations included in a specially commissioned medical report by a Bundeswehr psychiatrist regarding the captain's sexuality and their interpretation. The lawyers from Hardthöhe also did not accept the captain's argument that he had demonstrated a sense of responsibility in reporting to MAD. On the contrary, the captain had initially tried to conceal his homosexual relationship, stating that his partner was in fact a family relation. The claimant also continued to "deny" an "abnormal tendency in the sexual realm as defined in ZDv 2/30 Annex C 1 Sentence 1 in connection with No. 3 b."[78] What was more, the BMVg saw an "increased risk" in the GDR authorities now knowing about the captain's orientation.

The 1st Military Service Senate ruled that the captain's motion was admissible but unfounded. The petitioner was not "entitled" to a security clearance. The judges turned to the broader context in their decision by citing the defense mandate enshrined in the constitution, much as they had when ordering the transfer of soldiers identified as homosexual or declaring them no longer fit for service. "Fulfilling the defense mandate can only be safeguarded by granting access to classified information exclusively to soldiers for whom no type of security concerns exist. The resulting need to review [...] for security concerns is taken as a precautionary measure [...] Security concerns arise whenever the soldier in question is viewed as a potential target of foreign services."[79]

At present it could be "left aside whether or not the claimant's homosexual disposition constitutes an abnormal tendency as defined by letter b. [under ZDv 2/30 Annex C 1 No. 3], and must therefore be considered a security risk from the outset." The ASBw and BMVg's shared assumption of the claimant posing a security risk was not legal grounds for objection, nor was their refusal to consider those concerns allayed by a soldier stating that he would immediately report any relevant attempts

---

76 BArch, BW 2/31224: Response to the motion by the BMVg.
77 Ibid.
78 Ibid.
79 BArch, BW 2/31224: Ruling at BVerwG, 1st Military Service Senate, Az 1 WB 152/84 on 11 April 1985.

by enemy services. "Under the right circumstances, such contacts may only become recognizable to the claimant once entrapment has already occurred, or the claimant may find himself in a psychological state that does not (or does not any longer) permit him to behave in the way imagined at present."[80]

The judges found no "legal error" in the captain's being denied a level 2 security clearance, as he would not be "unreasonably or arbitrarily affected." The decision was based on "objective conditions," and did not constitute "targeted discrimination against the claimant and his disposition."[81]

The judges provided a detailed litany of rationales taken from military service senate rulings on disciplinary issues and personnel measures against homosexual soldiers (drawing in particular from the ruling on 25 October 1979, which has already been analyzed elsewhere).[82] They then went on to clarify that whether or not a soldier committed a breach of duty by pursuing homosexual activity outside of service should be kept separate from whether a security risk was present or not.

> Up into the present day, the prevailing negative view of homosexuality in the Bundeswehr has hardly changed. This explains why a homosexually inclined soldier will generally make an effort not to reveal himself as such. If his disposition does become known about at his assigned post, he will be forced to reckon with the difficulties laid out in greater detail in the ruling of 25 October 1979. And it is precisely here where the risk of blackmail sets in. It is not simply potential or actual sexual partners, not simply his subordinates who are liable to pose a threat, but anyone who is aware of his disposition – and not only for those of particularly frail constitution. If [the blackmailer] reveals what he knows, it often entails highly consequential, at times existential problems for the person concerned. Susceptibility to blackmail can provide enemy intelligence services with a point of departure [...] The Senate does not thereby overlook the possibility of cases in the Bundeswehr for which a substantially lower risk of blackmail exists because the homosexual soldier has consciously and emphatically admitted to his disposition.[83]

The explicit mention of the October 1979 ruling in this instance is noteworthy. In the ruling the judges had based their decision against a lieutenant on the significant reservations that continued to exist among the citizenry, and thus among soldiers, despite homosexuality's decriminalization. By this logic, actual or anticipated rejec-

---

80 Ibid. Nearly identical in wording to a previous ruling from the 1st Military Service Senate on 12 January 1983, BVerwG, 2 WB 60/79.

81 BArch, BW 2/31224: Ruling at BVerwG, 1st Military Service Senate, Az 1 WB 152/84 on 11 April 1985.

82 Ruling at BVerwG, 1 WB 113/78, on 25 October 1978, see chapter 4, section 2.

83 BArch, BW 2/31224: Ruling at BVerwG, 1st Military Service Senate, Az 1 WB 152/84 on 11 April 1985.

tion from one's fellow soldiers became yet another reason to hide one's true orientation, in addition to the stance of the service.

The same reservations that had justified personnel measures against the lieutenant as a gay superior now served to block the captain's security clearance. What the military service senate effectively put in writing in 1985 was that a virtually impenetrable thicket of restrictions existed for homosexual superiors: The manifold sanctions threatened by the Bundeswehr, paired with the reservations and rejection they would receive from fellow soldiers, made it necessary for soldiers to conceal and deny their sexuality. Yet doing so left them potentially subject to blackmail, and thus a security risk in the eyes of MAD.

To return to the case at hand, however: It was not until 1989, or four years later, that a report from the head doctor of a Bundeswehr hospital reopened the door to the captain receiving a security clearance. The doctor, who in 1994 went on to become the famously resolute first female Surgeon General of the Bundeswehr, emphasized in her assessment that homosexuality did not harbor any potential for blackmail when lived out in the open, and thus did not pose a security risk. MAD ultimately used this to grant the captain access to documents classified as secret.[84]

In 1986 Military Service Court North in Kiel had to rule on a captain's motion to protest the revocation of his access to "top secret" classified material. The court found the captain's commander had made an error in judgement, laying out their rationale in unusually clear terms that bear repeating at length:

> An error in judgement should be assumed for cases where a measure [...] leads to a serious violation of the constitutional prohibition on excessiveness [the principle of proportionality]. In this case the commander has justified [...] his decision exclusively on the grounds that the claimant is homosexually inclined. He possessed no other sort of [...] knowledge that this meant a security risk was present. The opposite was the case. The claimant had made his disposition known to his superior. With the revelation, he has eliminated discernable points of departure for a conceivable blackmail threat impacting the security of the Bundeswehr [...] Moreover, the measure brought about a considerable intrusion into the legal sphere of the petitioner without the existence of a reason material to security concerns. Admittedly it is not the mission of the Bundeswehr to settle social tensions and development within its domain [...] However this cannot lead to a situation in which unreasonable intrusions are tolerated in order to fulfill the defense mandate, especially when there is no identifiable security risk. Reducing authorization from "top secret" to "secret" on the sole grounds that the petitioner is a homosexual without any further findings touching on security constitutes a serious intrusion on a person's identity and a soldier's career in the service. It must therefore be concluded that the measure reached by the commander [...] was an error in judgement.[85]

---

84 Interview with Ret. Lieutenant Colonel N., 20 July 2018.
85 BArch, BW 2/31224: Military Service Court North, 12th Division, ruling, Az N 12 BL a 3/86 on 16 December 1986. A copy is available in BArch, BW 1/531591.

The claimant in this case was a captain and career soldier who had been assigned a sensitive post as the head of a communications center. In October 1985 he had informed the personnel department at the BMVg that he had homosexual tendencies "through official channels," i.e. via his direct superior the regiment commander, and requested a career prognosis. That November the regiment commander filed for MAD to revoke the captain's level 2 security clearance, at the same time reducing the captain's access from "top secret" to "secret" by his own decree.[86]

In December 1985 the captain was dispatched to the other side of Germany to serve in a higher-ranking position on staff headquarters, then transferred in March 1986 to a post at a higher learning institute. The captain filed a complaint "about his superiors' discriminatory behavior once they had found out about his homosexual disposition," referring specifically to comments made by his regiment commander during his personnel interview.

> To his mind, sexuality had been intended by nature to guarantee the preservation of the species. As such, men and women belonged together – not least before God. Everything else was at the most a cultural phenomenon and thus "unnatural." What was more, sexuality in general and homosexuality in particular was a purely private matter for him, not something you could take out in public.[87]

In the end the colonel had ruled out the possibility of assigning the claimant any further positions on site, because his homosexuality was common knowledge and the "talk of the town." He, the colonel, "had a regiment to lead and had to heed public opinion."[88]

As quoted at length above, the military service court in Kiel actually upheld the petitioner's complaint, ruling his commander's decision to reduce the captain's authorization from "top secret" to "secret" unlawful. This addressed just one of many objections, however – the captain's petition also sought decisions regarding his dismissal as commander of the communications center, as well as his subsequent commandeering and transfer. The court referred the case to the military service senate at the Federal Administrative Court, citing its own range of jurisdiction. For

---

86 Authorization to view "top secret" material is equivalent to a level 3 security clearance. It remains unclear why the captain evidently only had a level 2 clearance but was still authorized as "top secret." It is possible that he had been granted temporary authorization in the course of his review to qualify for level 3.

87 Complaint from the Captain to Air Force Operation Command on 8 November 1985, cited in BArch, BW 2/31224: Military Service Court North, 12th Division, ruling, Az N 12 BL a 3/86 on 16 December 1986. A copy is available in BW 1/531591.

88 Ibid.

its part, the service senate found the complaint brought against the commander's request for MAD to revoke the captain's level 2 security clearance inadmissible; such a petition would be justified "under certain circumstances" only if the security clearance had in fact been revoked. The court similarly found the complaint leveled against the commander's comments during the personnel interview to be inadmissible, regarding them not as service related "but a private opinion uttered in an official context. This sort of private opinion may well be [...] subject to complaint from the standpoint of §12 SG. It cannot, however, be challenged in the context of court proceedings initiated upon petition."[89]

It had all started out with a conversation between the captain and a MAD officer in May 1985 about the "highly disagreeable 'Kießling affair'," as the captain recalled. When the captain asked the MAD man's take on homosexuals in the Bundeswehr, the latter had responded that "people like that were unacceptable in a male society like the Bundeswehr, especially as officers."[90] He, the captain, had been "truly taken aback by the extremely discriminatory position toward homosexuals." When he followed up by asking "whether [the MAD officer] would want to universally dismiss all homosexuals from the Bundeswehr provided he was able to find them," the captain remembered the officer's "Yes." Horrified and incensed about what he had heard, the captain decided to write directly to Defense Minister Wörner: "I am asking you whether you endorse the MAD officer's statements."[91] The captain went on to detail the constraints homosexual soldiers came up against, albeit without revealing that he was himself gay.

> Regarding susceptibility to blackmail and the associated security risks, it is certainly interesting to reflect for a moment as to why many homosexuals do not seek to make their tendencies public. As a general rule it is the fear of professional, and thus social consequences. Is not it up to you as the highest ranking authority to lead by setting a good example and nip any possible forms of discrimination under your jurisdiction in the bud?[92]

The ministry's answer came in early October. The BMVg's security officer rehashed the ministry's well-known positions on homosexuals in positions of authority in painstaking detail. At the center of his own field of responsibility, the officer wrote to the captain, the decision about "whether a military security risk lay in the person

---

89 BArch, BW 2/31224, Military Service Court North, 12th Division, Ruling, 12 Az N 12 BL a 3/86 on 16 December 1986. A copy is available in BW 1/531591.
90 Letter from Captain P. to the minister of defense on 15 May 1985. The author holds possession of a copy.
91 Ibid.
92 Ibid.

of the soldier had to be made under consideration and in appreciation of specific military interests." In doing so, those responsible were "legally limited as to the scope their review can take." The decision should "be neither unreasonable nor arbitrary in its effects on the rights of the person in question," "always based on the individual case" and "not the result of improper generalization." In his response, the security officer repeated word for word the position taken by the BMVg and the administrative courts so oft before.[93]

"MAD cannot leave off gay hunt" blared a *taz* headline from May 1988 in large letters, followed by the teaser: "Gay sergeant in the Bundeswehr forcibly transferred for the second time / Security officer believes homosexuality makes one susceptible to blackmail and becomes a security risk, even if openly admitted."[94] Using the officer's real name, the piece recounted the case of a sergeant at an air force communications center who had his clearance "for the strictest secrecy level 2" revoked in August 1986 and was subsequently transferred to another post "where there was apparently less to hide." According to taz, he was given the reason that "in keeping with the sexual conduct determined, [he could not] warrant that he would handle the contents of classified information [...] in accordance with the regulations on maintaining secrecy."[95] Nor could the possibility of blackmail be ruled out, even though the sergeant had long since made his homosexuality known.

The sergeant himself took quite a different view of the matter. He sought protection against his transfer from the Federal Administrative Court, only to be denied. The court ruled that provided there was an official need, a superior could decide about a soldier's transfer at will. The plaintiff's transfer was neither disproportionate nor did it constitute an error in judgement.[96] The sergeant also filed a motion against his security clearance being revoked at Military Service Court South in Karlsruhe; this time he was vindicated.[97] His clearance was reinstated, or as *taz* put it, "the soldier again gained access to overheard radio conversations from the East."[98] Still,

---

93 BMVg, Security Information Officer, Org 6 to Captain P., 4 October 1985. The author holds possession of a copy.

94 Thomas, "MAD kann Schwulen-Hatz nicht lassen." A copy is available in BArch, BW 2/31224.

95 Ibid.

96 BVerwG, 1st Military Service Senate, Az 1 WB 11/87, 18 March 1987. A copy is available in BArch, BW 1/531591.

97 Military Service Court South, 4th Division, Az S 4-BLa 1/87, ruling on 27 August 1987. A copy is available in BArch, BW 1/546375 und BW 2/31224.

98 Thomas, "MAD kann Schwulen-Hatz nicht lassen."

the notion that a gay man should still have access to secret classified material evidently vexed the security officer at Hardthöhe so greatly that in February – scarcely six months after the ruling in Karlsruhe – [...] he gave orders for the game to begin all over again. Once again, the twenty-five-year-old had the magic slip of paper taken away from him [...] Inquiries by MAD had brought to light that "in addition to a long-term partnership [the soldier] had sought out a number of different short-term relationships in Trier's gay scene." The whole world knew about [X.]'s homosexuality, leading Hardthöhe to the conviction that he was liable to black-mail and a security risk – and all because he wanted to protect his partner. "The claimant is willing to refrain from anything that might detract from his partner's professional develop-ment or further knowledge of their partnership – and acts accordingly."[99]

Several days after the piece came out Südwestfunk radio picked up the story, broad-casting a detailed report on its popular SWF 3 program along the lines of the *taz* article and including an interview with the staff sergeant.[100] Multiple sections within the BMVg kept after the media trail, maintaining a fastidious archive. Unfor-tunately, ministry documents do not reveal the outcome of the renewed efforts to revoke the sergeant's security clearance, though they do show the military service court verdict mentioned in *taz*. The newspaper had told the story in hyperbolic but accurate fashion: The court ruled that taking away the captain's security clearance, and thus his access to classified material, was unlawful and the decision should be repealed. The judges failed to see any blackmail potential or security risks in the sergeant, who was open about his homosexuality.[101] The ruling left the chief of the air force unable to reject the sergeant's motion against his transfer, and had to reverse the decision.[102]

MAD showed greater caution and restraint on other occasions, as with one case which can only be sketched here due to the involved parties' privacy rights. In September 1981, MAD received confidential information from a criminal inves-tigations department that a high-ranking staff officer was sexually involved with a young male prostitute. Right around the same time, a separate MAD office received a similar, but much more highly-charged account of the goings-on from the officer's wife. When MAD confronted the officer, he denied having homosexual tendencies in general, and his wife's reproaches in particular.[103] Given the serious nature of

---

99 Ibid.

100 Broadcast on SWF 3 at 8:40 am (broadcast script in BArch, BW 1/546375 and BW 2/31224).

101 Military Service Court South, 4th Division, Az S 4-BLa 1/87, decided 27 August 1987. A copy is available in BArch, BW 1/546375 and BW 2/31224.

102 BMVg, Chief of the Air Force, 20 November 1987. Copies are available in BArch, BW 1/546375 and BW 2/31224.

103 BArch, N 724/42: MAD office, 5 December 1984. A former high-ranking MAD officer confirmed the facts of the case in an email to the author on 15 January 2017.

the accusations, which went straight to the heart of family life, the state prosecutor brought charges against the officer in the first half of 1982, with the BMVg initiating parallel disciplinary proceedings on the same matter. Later that year, local court halted proceedings against a large fine.[104] The disciplinary action was brought to an end in early 1983 at the behest of the deputy chief of defense "despite continuing suspicions," when "a serious loss in [the staff officer's] respectability and trustworthiness could not be established with final certainty."[105] As a result, MAD decided that the officer did not represent a security risk, that no vulnerable points existed where enemy intelligence might make an approach, and that the staff officer should continue to receive access to top secret documents.

In 1984, MAD again received information alleging the staff officer's homosexuality. The office found that repealing a security clearance required evidence with a "likelihood verging on certainty." "To this extent suppositions are not sufficient."[106] Any further investigation of the officer would have to be conducted "applying means of intelligence," yet those were impossible out of legal considerations. What was more, the officer under scrutiny had not drawn any attention for homosexual tendencies throughout his entire military career. In weighing the matter, the service came to the decision that the state of the investigation at present did not justify declaring the presence of a security risk, and the officer again retained his security clearance.[107] In this case MAD acted according to the Latin legal principle *in dubio pro reo* ("when in doubt, for the accused"). It is possible that the high rank of the officer entered the calculus here, as did the ripple effects of the General Kießling affair, which lay only a few months in the past. Multiple former MAD employees interviewed for this study concurred that the service "burned its finger" on the Kießling affair and afterwards would only handle the subject of homosexuality "with kid gloves" or – if it was "in any way defensible" – not at all.

Numerous homosexual soldiers interviewed for this study corroborated this version when asked whether they ran into trouble with MAD. Of those who replied in the affirmative, some faced considerable difficulties and disadvantages in the service (see the case studies later in this chapter). Erich Schmid – introduced last chapter in the context of his removal from command of a platoon after writing a letter to the defense minister and the chief of defense on BASS letterhead – reported

---

104 Nolle prosequi from local court, mentioned in BVerwG, 21 WB 73/83: Federal Administrative Court, 1st Military Service Senate, ruling on 29 May 1984.
105 Nolle prosequi for disciplinary proceedings, cited in BVerwG, 21 WB 73/83: Federal Administrative Court, 1st Military Service Senate, decided 29 May 1984.
106 BArch, N 724/42: MAD office, 5 December 1984.
107 Ibid.

that MAD had also been active during his dispute with the BMVg and the personnel office. For a short while between May and August 1998, MAD had "observed" his residential surroundings and leisure activities on multiple weekends, posing questions to neighbors on multiple occasions. The public presence of BASS in the weeks surrounding Christopher Street Day in Berlin, Cologne, Munich and Hamburg, as well as the group's member meetings, similarly drew MAD's attention.[108] (It should be noted that the author was not able to verify these memories, which were not part of a routine security review but linked to a dispute between the first lieutenant, BASS and the BMVg that was partially carried out in public.)

Yet the vast majority of those interviewed did not recall any problems with MAD, some simply because they lacked a steady partner and did not have to list one in the forms and thus "out" themselves, others because they only underwent security reviews after 2000. One lieutenant colonel thus recalled that he had not been required to list a life partner because he did not have one, although MAD had not asked about his sexual orientation, either.[109] A former master sergeant recalled he had not had to apply for a level 2 security clearance until 2000, after the service had changed its position on homosexuality. When a MAD employee did come to speak with him, the sergeant recalled he had cheekily asked whether MAD knew at least which man he was with at the moment. "Well then, you're up to date," the former sergeant had replied when the employee gave the right name.[110]

Many other interviewees could similarly attest to never running into difficulties with MAD on account of their homosexuality. Another former master sergeant still recalled with some surprise that the service had not made an issue of it even after he first began to list his partner during security checks in 2006, effectively allowing MAD to determine in retrospect that his earlier statements had been false (since 1991 at any rate).[111]

Another eyewitness since retired as a high-ranking staff officer could not recall any issues with MAD either, even when the service discovered in 1999 that the officer did in fact live with his partner, contradicting the statements he had made during a security review. A long conversation with two men from MAD had followed in his office. The officer explained that while several people knew about it within the line of duty, he saw "no discernible reason" "to insist on making a

---

108 Email from Erich Schmid to the author, 5 December 2017.
109 Interview (anonymized), Berlin, 17 December 2017. Nearly identical to the recollections of Master Sergeant R. of Potsdam, 5 January 2018.
110 Interview with Ret. Master Sergeant W., 29 March 2018.
111 Interview with Ret. Master Sergeant S. of Freiburg, 21 June 2017.

private affair public."[112] When asked whether he would be willing to inform his superiors and personnel manager (the MAD men had indicated the officer's potential susceptibility to blackmail if he kept it a secret in service), the officer repeated his "basic standpoint" that he could not figure out why he should "aggressively" reveal his "normal living circumstances" or sexual orientation. He would not lie if asked of course, but he failed to see why it would be necessary to go to his superiors. In the end he agreed to inform his superiors and report back to MAD afterward. He reconsidered over the next several days, however; when he informed MAD of this, the office requested that the officer at least refill out the security statement and Annex C 11 to ZDv 2/30 and list his partner, which he did.

a.) The Principles of "Legality" and "Opportunity"

MAD received countless tips (referred to internally as "Troop Reporting Incident"), both anonymously and from soldiers' circles of friends and acquaintances, 90–95% of which a former colonel in a lead role at MAD described as "nonsense."[113] Within the remaining 5–10% was one anonymous tip that concerned one of MAD's own, an officer who frequently patronized a gay sauna in Cologne. The report was confirmed by on-site verification. The officer was not publicly known to be homosexual, which according to the guidelines meant a security risk. The parties reached a solution: The officer could search out a new post and line of activity, but no longer stay on at MAD. And the new post could not require any sort of security review. Working in conjunction with the Bundeswehr personnel office, the transfer went off quickly and without complications.[114]

Former mid-level MAD employees unanimously emphasized adhering strictly to the "principle of legality": If the Security Review Act did not permit it, it did not happen. There were no "tricks" to get soldiers to confess, or even act in a way that they would not have done on their own. In short, "no smoke, no fire."[115] Another former MAD officer stressed that the service relied exclusively on open questions its during security reviews, never subversive methods.[116]

---

112 Email from a retired colonel to the author on 17 December 2017, as well as a memo from 1999 from the former lieutenant colonel. Also cited in what follows.
113 Interview with Ret. Colonel Heinz Kluss, Wachtberg, 13 February 2018.
114 Ibid.
115 Interview with a captain, Potsdam, 18 January 2018.
116 Interview with Captain H., 12 June 2018.

Another high-ranking MAD officer since retired painted a broader picture, recalling that and that he himself had operated in a "gray zone," with the "principle of opportunity" applying for leadership roles. Consensual arrangements were sought when possible, which included deviating from standard doctrine and regulation or "smearing ointment on the wound," as the officer phrased it.[117] Ultimately, the principle of opportunity meant nothing other than freedom to act within the confines of a given legal framework.

A solution MAD found for an older, high-ranking staff officer in the early 1980s gives one example of this principle in action. The officer had been arrested by police in Cologne after becoming involved in a physical altercation with a young man at the central train station; MAD was brought in after the man's high military rank came out during police questioning. It turned out the young man had been offering sex for money as a hustler, when, as became clear in questioning, the young man was "*his* [i.e. the officer's] hustler." The two had been involved in a long-term sexual relationship, with the officer paying the young man's flat and living expenses in exchange for his supposed "fidelity." When the officer found his partner, who he had believed was his alone, continuing to ply his trade around the train station he flew into a rage and boxed the young man's ears. "The swine is earning some on the side." The threat of the incident becoming public presented a security risk for MAD; the high-ranking staff officer was married, the father of a family and leading a double life. Facing the loss of his security clearance, which would have necessarily meant the loss of his post, MAD worked with the officer to reach a joint solution.[118] The officer would retire several years early; a decision personnel management would "arrange."

b.) Pragmatic Solutions from 1916

Coming up with pragmatic solutions for employees whose homosexuality had come out was not specific to MAD alone; earlier sources relay a very similar instance from 1916. The recently published diary entries of Colonel Walter Nicolai, head of Department IIIb in Supreme Army Command and thus of German intelligence

---

117 Interview with Ret. Colonel Heinz Kluss, Wachtberg, 13 February 2018.
118 Ibid. In his history of MAD, Helmut Hammerich mentions the case of a staff officer who had "come to the attention of a special police unit within the 'hustler scene' around the Cologne train station" in fall 1981. MAD investigations had not uncovered "any sufficiently incriminating material" and thus been unable to determine that a security risk was present. The officer's security clearance had not been revoked. See Hammerich, "*Stets am Feind!*" 274. It remains unclear whether this is the same case, based here on the contemporary witness' account, although it is likely.

in World War I, provide a credible account of a practical resolution that the secret service found when an officer within its own ranks was discovered to be homosexual. Cavalry Captain Hans Freiherr von Gebsattel served on the Western Front as an intelligence officer to Wilhelm, the crown prince of Germany and Prussia. In May 1916 Colonel Nicolai received a request from the cavalry captain's personal secretary asking to be released from his post. The secretary, Reserve Captain von Heimendahl, declined to give his reasons. When the head of intelligence persisted, the captain explained that he had "become a chance witness to the fact that [the cavalry captain] was unhealthily predisposed as defined by §175." This made it "impossible to continue to serve under Cavalry Captain v.G." Colonel Nicolai decided "the opposite would occur," namely that the reserve captain would remain and it was "v.G. who would go."[119] Removing the cavalry captain was not as simple as that, however. The matter was significantly complicated by the friendship that had sprung up in the meantime between the Crown Prince and Freiherr von Gebsattel. The Crown Prince's chief of staff, General Konstantin Schmidt von Knobelsdorff, categorically opposed the cavalry captain's removal from service, or even his post. Colonel Nicolai recorded von Knobelsdorff's reasoning in his diaries.

> The Crown Prince would take it very badly if v.G. were taken from him without any reason given. Naming the reasons would mean the destruction of. v.G.'s existence, which had to be avoided out of consideration for the family and especially the father, as well as the strong reaction this would elicit in both the father and the Crown Prince out of consideration of the fierce battles before Verdun. [Von Knobelsdorff told me] I should have responded to von Heimendahl by saying "Move out, you stool pigeon!" While I can understand the reasons he cites, I find this last opinion incomprehensible. When I think back to the events surrounding Prince Philipp von Eulenburg, whose removal from the emperor's side was set in motion by the Crown Prince himself, I think that my view would match his own, and that Knobelsdorff is not right to let him unknowingly bestow his friendship on someone who is unworthy [...] The first in line of responsibility is the chief of staff for the Crown Prince, however, so at the moment I cannot prevail against him.[120]

From the postscript to this diary entry from 30 May 1916, it can be gleaned that Nicolai was in fact able to bring about the cavalry captain's transfer. That summer, a new post for intelligence officer opened up in Romania; neither Knobelsdorff nor the Crown Prince were involved but presented with a fait accompli by "cabinet decree." When an upset Knobelsdorff came calling, Nicolai informed him of his discovery in the meantime "that similar events had caused v.G. to leave military

---

119 Nicolai, *Geheimdienst und Propaganda im Ersten Weltkrieg*, 255–57. Thanks to Lieutenant Colonel Dr. Christian Stachelbeck of the ZMSBw for the reference.
120 Ibid.

service before the world war."[121] Cavalry General Ludwig Freiherr von Gebsattel, the cavalry captain's father and head of the III Bavarian Army Corps, had come to Nicolai himself previously in October 1915 and told him "his son had already caused him worry and [he] hoped that he would prove his worth."[122]

The captain's transfer to far-off Romania under official pretext might have ended the matter agreeably for the captain and the Army alike without the actual reasons ever coming to the fore. Yet here the captain and the Crown Prince himself both stood in the way, making plain use of the encrypted long distance telephone channels between Romania and the Western Front to keep up personal contact, which now concerned exclusively private matters. The new intelligence officer for the Crown Prince had to encrypt and decode every message, and reported to his boss. Nicolai forbid von Gebsattel from using official telegrams for unofficial personal ends. Gebsattel complained to the new head at Supreme Army Command, Field Marshal Paul von Hindenburg, who in turn demanded an explanation from Nicolai.

> "You will be sure to know why, and would I suppose be so kind as to send me an answer?" The answer was that G. [Gebsattel] had been transferred to a new position. I had no choice but to explain the decision based on what had gone on. He agreed with me and thanked me for my views and the way it was carried out, with condolences for [Gebsattel's] father, who was a friend of his.[123]

Ultimately, a pragmatic solution protecting all those involved had been found before it was torpedoed by the undiscerning persistence of some. As so often when high- or higher-ranking officers were involved, the "principle of opportunity" received preference over the "principle of legality," first with von Gabsettel's transfer to Romania, and more clearly still with Knobelsdorff's opposition to his removal. Under the principle of legality, a captain reporting an "unhealthy disposition under §175" would necessarily have resulted in a criminal investigation.

---

121 Ibid., 257.
122 Ibid., 256.
123 Ibid., 257.

c.) An "Admissible, Requisite and Imperative Measure with a Great Sense of Proportion"

The case of Lieutenant Winfried Stecher has already been considered in some detail; he was relieved of his post as platoon commander in an air force base battalion in 1998 "after military counterintelligence discovered his homosexual tendencies."[124] This study succeeded in reconstructing the events concealed behind this terse clause. In reproducing them, the scholarly pursuit of knowledge had to be weighed against both the involved parties' right to privacy as well as the interests of MAD.

Rumors about the lieutenant's homosexuality had begun to circulate among the air force squadron in 1997. Eventually MAD was informed, and their investigators spoke with the squadron soldiers responsible (in a secondary capacity) for security matters, as well as the squadron chief. They agreed to report any future discoveries about the lieutenant to the service. In a later incident report, MAD assumed that it had been the conversations with the intelligence service that subsequently prompted the squadron boss to question the lieutenant about his homosexuality.

MAD concluded that its staff had taken the "measures necessary" following on from such a report "with a great sense of proportion," thereby adhering to the Security Review Act. Consulting the lieutenant's disciplinary superior had been "admissible, requisite and imperative" as a way of "verifying potentially security-related information with the slightest possible intrusion on the rights of the individual." The report explicitly dismissed the need for any investigation or direct conversation with the lieutenant; the service did not see a risk of blackmail after his "confession of homosexuality" (to the squadron chief), and thus no security threat, meaning there was no need to take action.

In its statement to the Minister of Defense, the personnel department agreed with the section responsible for MAD oversight that the intelligence agency's questions to the squadron chief had been decisive in the chief subsequently asking the lieutenant about his homosexuality. Without making any investigations of its own, MAD had limited its involvement solely to "inquiries about the state of affairs" to the squadron chief.[125]

So what went awry in the lieutenant's case? When asked about the chain of events, MAD staff who were unfamiliar with the specific instance themselves stressed that the service had acted correctly and in accordance with its own rules

---

124 *Frankfurter Allgemeine Zeitung*, "Homosexueller darf nicht ausbilden."
125 BArch, BW 1/502107, no pagination: BMVg, PSZ III 1 to the Minister via the State Secretary, 29 November 1999.

and regulations. Bringing up any tips that came from within the ranks with the relevant disciplinary superior was standard procedure; other soldiers in the squadron were not questioned "to safeguard the interests of the involved party that warranted protection." As a general rule the disciplinary superior, in his position of trust, was the first and only person contacted by MAD in the unit. Counterintelligence had approached the superior merely as a way of verifying sensitive personal information confidentially, and had under no circumstances done so with the aim, much less instructions, to involve the lieutenant's personnel manager. This, however, was precisely what the squadron chief did, passing along the suspicions against his platoon head to the battalion leader. The battalion leader reported to his superior, who turned it over to the personnel office. This put an official file on the desk of the lieutenant's personnel manager that was then treated and decided according to the prevailing ministerial orders. The BMVg's 1984 orders certifying known homosexual officers' lack of fitness to serve as a direct superior or instructor have been closely analyzed elsewhere in this study.[126] In his position Stecher was both, and was now transferred to a position on staff.

Former MAD employees also pointed out the limitations on using collected data stipulated in §21 of the Security Review Act. The section strictly forbade any sharing of personal living circumstances that surfaced during a security review with offices outside of MAD except for security officers at command posts and the BMVg. This, the employees stressed, would have made it unlawful for the personnel office or a commanding officer to receive information about a soldier's homosexuality or other characteristics related to his personality, including indirect information, or to show indiscretion toward other members of the company, the battalion or at higher levels of staff. Safeguarding personal interests that warranted protection took top priority. While every MAD staff member had (and still has) the importance of §21 impressed upon them during training, it was and remains common practice to initially consult with the soldiers' direct disciplinary superior upon receiving a report or otherwise learning of suspicions against a soldier for purposes of verification. Other soldiers from the unit or battalion are not questioned at first "to prevent rumors from circulating." It is for this same reason that MAD generally does not tell the person themselves what the service has learned about him from others; the soldier should not be made to feel unsure by what is being said about him in his company. At the same time, this also makes disciplinary superiors privy to sensitive, sometimes quite delicate information about subordinates they must evaluate every two years. While this could certainly be seen as contradicting the ban on sharing information, it does not violate the limitations §21 establishes for using collected

---

126 See chapter 4, section 4.

data. Speaking with the soldier's superiors, the former MAD interviewers stressed, served as a way to determine the credibility and integrity of reports they received.

Lieutenant Stecher's case shows that even from this constellation, serious problems could easily arise. The squadron chief appears first on the list in the search for a "guilty party"; he had an obligation to treat the information from MAD confidentially and discretely rather than report it "upstairs," in which case the sensitive information would have remained with the squadron chief and MAD. If further substantiating evidence came to light MAD would either have opened or continued a security review, issuing a decision upon completion that did not state the reasons for a security clearance being revoked if it were. The MAD staff consulted for this study made a special point of emphasizing that a disciplinary superior who had been informed about investigations conducted during or prior to a security review should also handle them confidentially, or better still discretely, and definitely not share with personnel management. "Everything had gone wrong" in the case of the air force lieutenant; the squadron chief's report to the battalion commander set off a chain reaction that ultimately meant the regulations took hold at personnel office. Still, it would miss the mark to fault the squadron chief alone. The overall pattern of response to homosexuality at the Bundeswehr, the BMVg, MAD and personnel leadership was set up in such a way that sooner or later it had to end in serious conflict, as it did with the lieutenant.

d.) "It's Nobody's Business Who I Go to Bed With"

In 1998 a staff sergeant took his own case before the public, reporting to *Focus* magazine that when his homosexuality first came out in an official context, his existing offer to enter career service was rescinded.[127] MAD had come across the sergeant's sexual orientation during a routine security review and passed it along; the sergeant had not previously identified himself or ever drawn notice as a homosexual in the service. The ruling at Lüneberg Administrative Court made reference to the security review as the origin of the sergeant's sexual orientation being discovered;[128] *FAZ* similarly held "MAD's investigations" responsible.[129] The former sergeant provided greater insight in his *Focus* interview.

---

127 "Schwule in die Bundeswehr."
128 Lüneburg Administrative Court, ruling from 3 June 1999. Az.: 1 A 141/97, here p. 2.
129 *Frankfurter Allgemeine Zeitung*, "Homosexueller darf nicht ausbilden."

I never openly admitted my homosexuality. It's nobody's business who I go to bed with [...] MAD performed a security check and came sniffing around my personal life, which included talking to acquaintances of mine. One of them said I did not have a girlfriend but a boyfriend. With that I became a security risk to the Bundeswehr, despite excellent [work] assessments. Leadership rejected me for career service even though I already had a written promise of acceptance. But I wo not take this discrimination lying down.[130]

Here too the service's course of action is only given in brief, as research findings had to be weighed against the interests of MAD standing in need of protection. Sources confirm that the sergeant filed for a security review as part of an official require-ment, in the course of which MAD informed the officer of contradictions that arose between his own statements and other interviews the service had conducted as a routine part of its reviews for higher ranks. The "contradictions" pertained to the subject's homosexuality, of which he had not yet informed MAD. By MAD's account, its staff informed the staff sergeant about the standard assessment of unacknowl-edged homosexuality as a potential source of blackmail, and thus a security risk. The investigators had also explained the consequences that any negative results would entail, although they had not discussed any future career impacts – the con-versation had revolved exclusively around the security review itself and MAD's possible assessment of a security risk. After "admission of homosexuality," the service reached the conclusion that no threat of blackmail and with it no security risk now existed, and issued the sergeant a security clearance.

When BMVg leadership asked the personnel department whether MAD had induced the sergeant to declare his homosexuality by assuring him that he stood under no threat of punishment, the department coordinated its response with the division responsible for overseeing the counterintelligence agency. MAD investi-gators had not given the sergeant any assurances that "no disadvantages under career law would threaten if he admitted his disposition." What was more, "at no point had the conversation reached beyond security review proceedings to touch on aspects such as career law."[131] This study was not able to establish with suf-ficient certainty how it was that the sergeant's "admission of homosexuality," as MAD and the BMVg phrased it, then became known to personnel management, and ultimately a barrier to his acceptance for career service. The MAD staff interviewed for this study stated unequivocally that the service had never demanded someone to out themselves in the official sphere – "under no circumstances."[132]

---

130 "Schwule in die Bundeswehr."
131 BArch, BW 1/502107, no pagination. BMVg, PSZ III 1 to the Minister via the State Secretary, 29 November 1999.
132 Among others, an interview with a captain, Potsdam, 18 January 2018.

A former MAD officer who long concealed his own homosexuality reported no fear of discovery or consequence where the service's internal procedures regarding homosexuality as a security risk where concerned. Daily experience as an investigator and interviewer had left him certain "that the service didn't dare tackle the subject."[133] Yet homosexual soldiers in the troops did "of course show deference, even fear of discovery by MAD." To them, the service seemed "all-knowing and omnipresent," even though "MAD also put its pants on just one leg at a time." The topic of how to approach homosexuality "surfaced only briefly at the far margins" of conversation during internal training, and the officer held the impression that MAD "made a long detour around the subject."

The highly sensitive nature of MAD's work placed heightened demands on employees' private lives, making it especially important for them to ward off any potential blackmail threats. Living as a closet homosexual ranked as one such threat, and ultimately brought the officer to cease making a secret altogether of his homosexuality in the late 1990s: One day, a rainbow flag fluttered from the flag pole of his home plot. To anyone in the service who asked him "straight away" whether he was gay he would likewise "straight away" reply in the affirmative. By contrast, anyone who "pussyfooted" about the question – as did his MAD superior, surprisingly – would receive like treatment. In 2003 the officer decided "to come clean with it," reporting to his superior that the rumors about him were true.

Lesbian soldiers were subject to the same guidelines and demands: Right at the beginning of her service in 1991, a prospective troop physician still being assessed for suitability had to decide whether to reveal that she lived with her partner to her post's security officer, thus revealing her sexual orientation. She decided to do so, "dutifully" entering the real information about her life partner on the questionnaire. As the officer read through the form, the prospective doctor openly asked him whether he "had a problem." The master sergeant had been left speechless, his complexion had changed colors. A conversation with the S2 officer followed, as well as three separate visits by MAD employees. The doctor recalled the MAD men's demeanor as "inappropriate, even impertinent, something along the lines of 'I'd lay any woman'."[134] In the end the service decided to give her a security clearance on the condition that the medical officer come out as lesbian to her current disciplinary superior and all future superiors. During their initial conversations the security officer had been content with a sealed envelope containing the officer's required confession of her homosexuality, and explicitly forbade "access to people

---

133 Interview with Captain H., 12 June 2018. In what follows as well.
134 Eyewitness interview, 28 November 2019.

unrelated to the security review."[135] It was left instead "to [the doctor's] discretion" to "inform [future disciplinary superiors] herself in due course and as necessary." After this initial confrontation the doctor never ran into another problem with the service. "They left me in peace." She did as she was ordered and reported to her superior, revealing her homosexuality after being received with a friendly and cheerful "What's up, Doc?" Her superior, a colonel, took it fully in stride: "As long as [she] didn't go around like Hella von Sinnen," he did not have any problem with it.[136]

The doctor stressed for emphasis that she never had any problems with her sexual orientation in the service aside from the initial friction with MAD. Looking back in 2019, she found that "many young soldiers today have no idea what §175 was. They can hardly believe the earlier restrictions against same-sex relationships when they hear about them."[137] Another female sergeant who served from 1994 to 2008 was not able to recall any problems with MAD.[138]

3. A Hurricane Whirls about the Taboo: The General Kießling Affair, 1983–84

A general is given provisional retirement under §50 SG – not an everyday occurrence, but a completely normal procedure nonetheless. On the long list of generals released in this way, one name sticks out: Günter Kießling. The terrific scandal surrounding Kießling's retirement in 1983 is the greatest in the history of the Bundeswehr, and is closely linked to the taboo of homosexuality and its (supposed) security risks. The general defended his honor against false accusations of homosexuality by means of an excellent lawyer, a handful of supporters in the officer corps and especially the media – which in the end achieved, or rather forced, Kießling's restitution by bringing the scandal to public attention. Information and rumors leaked to the public led to an affair that culminated in a show of force by the Ministry of Defense in January 1984, after it found itself so backed into a corner by Kießling's campaign that it threw its full institutional weight behind continuing investigations of the general.

> It was this – not the twentieth "revelation" or twenty-first piece of tacked-on "evidence" – that served as the actual topic of debate on television in those days, where all the talk of open

---

135 The Bundeswehr academy for medical and health services, S2, 6 February 1991.
136 Eyewitness interview, 28 November 2019.
137 Ibid.
138 Interview with Sergeant First Class Martina Riedel, Hamburg, 23 January 2020.

bathrobes, bar stools, fixtures on the scene and seedy company, of a major sense of duty and minor set of tendencies rarely ever approached the crux of the matter: the ability to stigmatize a person one believed could be counted as possessing the existence and type of a fringe group.[139]

Historian Heiner Möllers, a specialist on the Kießling affair, described it succinctly as "essentially revolving around the Bundeswehr's self-image: the notions of civilians in uniform and the much-vaunted [concept of] 'leadership development and civic education'."[140]

It all began with rumors circulating in NATO circles that four-star general Günter Kießling, deputy to the Supreme Allied Commander in Europe, was "homosexually inclined" and had been spurned by his boss, U.S. General Bernhard W. Rogers. Kießling's imputed homosexuality meant further that the highest-ranking German general in NATO was susceptible to blackmail, and thus a security risk.

On 29 July 1983, the Bundeswehr Security Office ordered a security review and commissioned military counterintelligence to investigate the general "on suspicion of homosexuality." Yet the commander of MAD group S in Bonn, the group assigned the task, ordered "no action to be taken whatsoever." The review would have involved one of the highest-ranking generals in the military; the nature of the case meant it should not be assigned without "briefing political and military leadership first." Nor was the task "clearly defined enough, it was lacking in content, even superficial and thus unqualified."[141]

This in turn brought about an investigation into Cologne's gay scene by MAD's Group III in Düsseldorf. But why Cologne? Would not Hamburg have presented the obvious choice, where Kießling had made his home since 1979 in nearby Rendsburg? Or Brussels, with its proximity to NATO headquarters? Or had there been a concrete tip-off? According to the former head of MAD's Düsseldorf unit, retired Colonel Heinz Kluss, the service had settled on Cologne because it had the largest gay

---

139 *Die Zeit*, "Ein kleiner Fall Dreyfus."

140 Möllers, *Die Affäre Kießling*, in this case from the book cover description. Heiner Möllers has rightly pointed to the fact that "differently from many other procurement scandals," in this case it was the "military's image of people that stood at the center of public perception." Aside from a monograph published in 2019, Möllers has composed numerous works of research on the Kießling affair. Analyzing what Möllers calls the "greatest scandal in the Bundeswehr" in detail here would go beyond the framework of the study and distract from its central area(s) of concern. The sketch of the complex affair that follows is supported by (and limited to) the author's own research findings, many of which appeared between 2014 and 2018, as well as new findings that are presented here for the first time. See Storkmann, "Cui bono?" and Storkmann "Der General-Verdacht." On the scandal and especially its future implications for MAD, see Hammerich, *"Stets am Feind!"* 261–83.

141 BArch, Bw 32/5, no pagination. Commander of MAD Group S, note from 30 January 1984.

scene and was regularly frequented by foreign nationals and passers-through.[142] This meant without any concrete information and on the off-chance as it were, MAD had selected a random, if near-by, city and chosen bars to search for clues at will, no matter how well popular they might have been. Be that all as it may, it would still be difficult to classify MAD's course of action as proceeding in "incident-relevant" fashion. Rather, the service opened an investigation even though it had only been presented with "feature-relevant" information, i.e. vague rumors about the generals' homosexuality. At least in the initial stages of a security review, it would seem that the line dividing "feature relevant" from "incident relevant" was not maintained all that strictly, after all.

As the investigating committee in the Bundestag and the press later found out, a master sergeant at MAD now got in touch with a personal contact at criminal investigations in Cologne, who brought in another colleague. This colleague then took a retouched photo of Kießling around to two gay bars: Both owners instantly recognized the man. He was "from the Bundeswehr," his name was Günter or Jürgen, "something with ü anyway."[143] An internal note from MAD reads "Through targeted investigations into the Cologne gay scene [...] the subject of investigation was clearly identified out of a series of photos as 'Günter' from the Bundeswehr."[144] The "subject [had also] clearly been identified as 'Günter from the Bundeswehr'" at a "relevant" local bar that was known as a "disco for young hustlers and criminals." Günter still frequented the club on a monthly basis and consorted with young hustlers in exchange for money.[145] MAD's purported probe of Cologne's gay scene, or rather the probe conducted on its behalf, was announced in eye-catching fashion on a *Spiegel* cover in 1984.[146] Kluss, the head of MAD's Düsseldorf branch, wrote in retrospect that "while this firmed up initial suspicions, all that was involved was a

---

142 This came out of a series of interviews with Ret. Colonel Heinz Kluss by email between 2014 and 2016, as well as an in-person discussion on 13 February 2018. Kluss was the head of MAD's Group III in Düsseldorf from 1981 to 1985.
143 The phrase "something with ü" was frequently bandied about in subsequent press reports about Kießling, turning into something of a catchphrase. See among others Range, "Irgendwas mit ü."
144 Note from MAD office III, Division III-1 E B, Düsseldorf 9 September 1983, reproduced in an unpublished manuscript by Heinz Kluss entitled "Kein Versöhnungsbier in Moskau. Die Affäre Kießling und der Militärische Abschirmdienst. 30 Jahre danach als Lehrstück von einem mitverantwortlichen Akteur ausufernd erzählt" [No make-up beer in Moscow: The Kießling affair and military counterintelligence, a didactic tale told 30 years after the fact by one of those responsible.] First published in fascimile in Storkmann, "Der General-Verdacht," 294–307 and later in Möllers, *Die Affäre Kießling*, 75.
145 Ibid.
146 *Der Spiegel*, 4/1984.

photo. Mix-ups were always a possibility, and mistakes could easily creep in over the telephone – that's known the world over. The credibility of the contacts (bartenders, chance guests) was also dubious."[147]

These doubts are likely what led Kluss to note in a separate field to the right of the form that

> everything within this red-bordered box was considered half-baked information that should remain internal to MAD [...] It is a vague lead that must be followed up on, nothing more [...] That way I was certain I had done everything in my power to protect the general against [sic] indiscretions [...] With the exception of General Behrendt [the head of ASBw, which ranked above MAD], none of our people had learned the name of the 'subject under investigation'."[148]

Brigadier General Behrendt had no choice but to immediately inform the Minister of Defense.

As an aside, in a letter to State Secretary Dr. Günter Ermisch from April 1984 MAD confirmed there had been "insufficient processing within ASBw Department I's field of activity connected to General Kießling's security review." This, along with "continued serious deficiencies in another case that have come to the attention of BMVg leadership," made it necessary from the service's point of view at least to lessen, "if not to avoid the fatal consequences of faulty processing for the Bundeswehr members involved."[149]

a.) "No Fritsch Affairs"

The private notes of Jörg Schönbohm, at the time a colonel on the joint staff serving as adjutant to Minister of Defense Manfred Wörner, shed some light on the conversations and reflections occurring behind closed ministry doors at the time. On 14 September 1983 Schönbohm noted that Brigadier General Helmut Behrendt, in charge of MAD as the head of ASBw, had first met privately with the minister in his office ("subject not mentioned," "something out of the ordinary," the adjutant

---

147 Kluss, "Kein Versöhnungsbier in Moskau," 15. For Kluss' recollections and the MAD memo, see Storkmann, "Cui bono?" and later Möllers, Die Kießling-Affäre, 517–50.
148 Kluss, "Kein Versöhnungsbier in Moskau," 16. For a source history of Kluss' note, see Möllers, *Die Affäre Kießling*, 74–76. The formula, internal to MAD, is only briefly alluded to in the investigative committee's report on the Kießling affair in the Bundestag, with the technical term "source-protected report." See German Bundestag. "Diskussion und Feststellung," 91.
149 MAD, Dept. KS to BMVg StS Dr. Ermisch, 18 April 1984, Az 06-24-00, marked "Classified – For Official Use Only" (declassified as of 1 January 2015). Copy is in possession of the author.

wrote regarding the MAD chief's urgent request for an audience with the minister). When Schönbohm joined the conversation "several minutes after," the minister had appeared "upset."[150]

With Schönbohm now present, Behrendt continued with the minister: "Gen. K. [Kießling] immediately + clearly identified by photo as a regular visitor to 2 gay bars – Günter from the Bw [Bundeswehr]; – appears monthly, buys hustlers for money – no further investigation possible at present to protect the informant + avoid unrest in the scene; wait at least 2 weeks (scene highly criminal)."[151] The colonel noted again at the beginning "BM [Minister of Defense] upset."[152] Behrendt's reference to an "informant" indicates actual ties to the gay scene in Cologne, something that if it were the case would explain why the investigating officers instantly made two "hits" in their search for witnesses. For his part, Colonel Kluss recalled thirty-three years later including a three-week deadline in his report to the MAD chief, to signal to the minister that he had three weeks to find an agreeable solution.[153] In that case Behrendt as the head of the secret services would have added the informant himself in his report to the minister, possibly to lend his presentation greater gravity. Schönbohm's notes communicate the deep doubts that Defense Minister Wörner had concerning the information he was receiving, although the head of the intelligence service dismissed them as groundless. "*When questioned by BM* – mixed identity ruled out + confirmed by police/criminal investigations." Later, one reads "Kluss tasked by Waldmann whether K.'s homo tendencies can be verified,"[154] resulting in "confirmation by Cologne criminal investigations, according to MAD Group III report." Among Schönbohm's notes on a conversation with State Secretary Rühl, one finds "StS [State Secretary] Dr. Rühl asks about police," "certainty of identification," and "Evidence: Officers in criminal investigations."[155]

The notes repeatedly quote Wörner with the words "no Fritsch affairs." While this can be read as an admonition against allowing a scandal similar to the one that enveloped Army Commander in Chief Werner Freiherr von Fritsch when he

---

150 Estate of Ret. Lieutenant General Jörg Schönbohm, presented to the ZMSBw, Research Unit Military History after 1945, provisional call number VJS 07, notes from 14 September 1983. Original emphases.
151 Ibid.
152 Ibid.
153 Email from Heinz Kluss to the author, 23 June 2017.
154 For more on Governmental Director Arthur Waldmann, who played a key role in precipitating the scandal, see his presentation on homosexuality "from a security standpoint" on 18 April 1980, BArch, BW 1/378197.
155 Sketch by the adjutant to the minister of defense on 14 September 1983, from the Schönbohm estate in ZMSBw, provisional call number VJS 07.

was accused of homosexuality in 1938, the comment can also be read as a form of self-assurance that things would not come to that. The complete memo for the meeting, which aside from Wörner, Behrendt and Rühl now brought in Chief of Defense General Wolfgang Altenburg as well as the head of the personnel department, reads "Same presentation of facts from office head as before! Discussion of credibility / possibility of confused identity; conclusion: no doubts as to the certainty of investigation results; suspicion well-founded, but gather more info; avoid indiscretion! *No Fritsch affairs.*"[156]

By Schönbohm's account, Wörner's immediate circle came back repeatedly to the security threats the case presented. The minister tasked the head of ASBw with collecting more information "in conjunction with criminal investigations" and apprising criminal investigations leadership of the explosive nature of the matter. The conversation memo includes multiple warnings from Wörner against indiscretion. In the end it was agreed "the chief of defense will speak with Gen. K + then BM as necessary on the 15th [of September]." The notes under "concluding questions" bear witness once again to Wörner's doubts, only to be dispelled once again by MAD: " – possible intrigue; – possibility of mixed identities ruled out; – police are sure – indiscretions."[157]

The defense minister's closest circle and the chief of defense now turned to the difficult relationship between General Kießling and the supreme NATO commander in Europe, U.S. General Bernhard W. Rogers. "1. Relationship to SACEUR [Supreme Allied Commander Europe]: Breach [in the relationship] known!" as well as potential risks that could arise, beginning again with warnings about "2. Possible indiscretions; Implications for the [...] reputation of NATO, the Bundeswehr; Dr. K. no authority any longer; 3. [...] potential blackmail; 4. Security risk; check / reject any ties that would threaten security." Point number 5, repeated almost as a group mantra, again emphasizes "no Fritsch affairs." [158] Minister Wörner, Chief of Defense Altenburg and MAD chief Behrendt were thus all fully aware of the risk of escalation. "The problem wasn't the [alleged] homosexuality; the problem was the [supposed] security threat," Altenburg stressed in retrospect.[159]

The Minister of Defense acted quickly. In the presence of the chief of defense, on 19 September 1983 he and Kießling agreed to Kießling's early retirement on 31 March of the following year. Kießling set great store by the fact that the deal should not be seen as an "admission of guilt." Wörner reciprocated by ordering a

---

156 Ibid.
157 Ibid.
158 Ibid.
159 Ret. General Wolfgang Altenburg to the author during a phone call on 5 July 2017.

halt to all MAD investigations, including his previous instructions to collect more information.

Then, in a surprise turn, State Secretary Joachim Hiehle, now returned to his desk after months of illness, ordered MAD to resume its investigations in early November 1983. He thus counteracted the minister's initial decision, having convinced Wörner beforehand. As a jurist, Hiehle was of the opinion that a general was not entitled to receive different treatment than any other soldier, rejecting agreements like the one reached by Wörner and Kießling on principle.

The report ASBw presented on 6 December 1983 ultimately repeated its previous findings from September as no new investigations had taken place per Wörner's last instructions, although the report did now (wrongly) list the State Office of Criminal Investigation for North Rhine-Westphalia as a source. Brigadier General Behrendt strongly suggested "not to take the common course of action in continuing to handle the matter," as its discovery by the public "would be detrimental to the reputation of the Federal Republic of Germany in light of General K.'s exposed position and cause great damage." This meant revoking Kießling's security clearance was "not expedient."[160] Just how prescient the MAD chief was with his warning would reveal itself in the ensuing scandal, which brought enormous damage to the standing of the Bundeswehr, the Ministry of Defense and MAD alike. BMVg leadership, however, heeded neither Behrendt's advice nor the timeline it had already agreed upon with the general for his end of service.

On 8 December Wörner decided to place Kießling in early retirement by year's end, without consulting the general and, in a particularly bitter blow, without bestowing military honors. Wörner's rationale remains unknown to this day, although it was likely Hiehle's arguments that carried the day.

> One possible explanation is that the ministry completely misread the reaction that was bound to follow from the opposition and press as surely as the "amen" in church. The accusation they expected was that Wörner was protecting a friend. There was a desire to move Kießling off ship as quickly as possible to head off this criticism. Nobody could have imagined the exact opposite occurring, which was that the media, public and politicians would intervene passionately on behalf of the general, seeing him as the victim of human malice, bureaucratic whims and secret service intrigue.[161]

---

160 The wording from the ASBw report included in the Bundestag committee report on Kießling, 101–03.
161 Kluss, "Kein Versöhnungsbier in Moskau," 27.

On top of this came the fact that many people no longer accepted that homosexuality was worthy of scandal.[162]

On 23 December 1983 Kießling was handed his discharge certificate by Hiehle himself. In exchange he passed along a letter consisting of only two sentences that demanded a set of disciplinary proceedings against himself. "As a reason I give my insistence on clarifying the accusations leveled against me."[163] Kießling further filed a complaint at Cologne Administrative Court in January 1984.[164] Much more important, and ultimately decisive in the matter, was the campaign Kießling waged in the press to aid in the fight for his honor.[165]

Throughout January press reports on Kießling's case dominated newspaper and magazine headlines and the evening news on ARD and ZDF. The attention succeeded in riling up a crowd who had never heard a word about General Kießling before, as seen with a Munich man who wrote the General a personal letter in January 1984.

> I didn't even know you existed before you were in the papers. What they're doing to you smells rotten. I don't give a damn if it's true or not. The reason I'm grumpy is because all of a sudden someone who behaves like the criminal code allows is supposed to be liable to blackmail [...] But there is one thing I don't like about you. Why did you get sick of all of a sudden? Can't you fight?[166]

What the gentleman from Munich could not know was that behind the scenes, Kießling, assisted by his lawyer and by means of targeted leaks to the press, was waging a very skillful, and ultimately successful battle.

b.) Investigation by Any Means

In early January 1984 a new set of investigations was opened, based formally on the disciplinary proceedings Kießling had filed against himself. The start of the

---

162 Schwartz shares the opinion, citing voices in the press during the debate surrounding the Wörner–Kießling affair "who not only took the minister to task for dismissing a general on account of (unproven) homosexuality, but for the associated stigmatization against homosexuals in Germany in general." Schwartz, *Homosexuelle, Seilschaften, Verrat*, 298.

163 BArch, Bw 1/535370, sheet 1.

164 BArch, Bw 1/237515: Files of BMVg Parliamentary State Secretary Peter Kurt Würzbach.

165 For more on the crucial role that the media played in the affair see Möllers, *Die Affäre Kießling* and before that Möllers, "Die Kießling-Affäre."

166 BArch, N 851/82: Kießling estate, Letter from Helmut S. of Munich to General Kießling, 15 January 1984.

investigative report shows an initially undated note from Section P II 5 at the BMVg personnel department that reads "do disciplinary accusations even exist?; – in my opinion [there's] only a security risk!; – check the admissibility of the motion first; – factual clarification only upon order." "Issued on 9 Jan" has been added later.[167] Participating offices included the ES division at BMVg (Special Investigations), P II 5 and FüS II 6, the ASBw, and MAD, as well as the military disciplinary prosecutor and the minister's office itself. The BMVg now threw its full institutional weight behind uncovering "proof" that would incriminate Kießling – and exonerate Wörner. "In this case *all* potential breaches of duty should be pursued, not only those viewed in connection to retirement proceedings."[168]

As the opposition SPD party would later write in its section of the committee report from parliament's investigation of the Kießling affair, the investigations were conducted "with unimaginable scope in every direction conceivable," with the "single discernible aim of finding a belated justification for the unlawful retirement of the general."[169] The SPD especially criticized the fact that

such a thorough illumination of personal relations could not be reconciled [...] with the basic constitutional principles of the Federal Republic of Germany; it violated the precept of respect for and protection of human dignity set out in Article 1 paragraph 1 of the Basic Law, as well as the principle of proportionality rooted in the principle of a state founded on the rule of law.[170]

The general's two chauffeurs had also been "subject to extreme interrogation about their intimate spheres, especially their sexual lives. This sort of questioning cannot be reconciled with the precept of respect for their dignity as people."[171]

The SPD was right; investigative documents since made available reveal that over the course of three days each of the young drivers, a sergeant and a staff sergeant, had undergone hours-long questioning about their own sexual experiences, and specifically any homosexual encounters.[172]

Rumors about Kießling's homosexuality had accompanied the general for years at every station along his career, preceding his arrival at NATO headquarters in the form of what was later inflated as a "dossier," really a set of letters that British General Sir Anthony Farrar-Hockley wrote to SACEUR about the German gener-

---

167 BArch, BW 1/535360, no pagination, before sheet 1.
168 Ibid. Emphasis in original.
169 German Bundestag. "Diskussion und Feststellung," 171–72.
170 Ibid.
171 Ibid., 172–73.
172 Record of interrogation in BArch, BW 1/535370.

al.[173] High-ranking German officers at NATO tried to prevent Kießling's accession to NATO in 1982, appealing unsuccessfully to the deputy leader at the BMVg personnel department with reference to the general's supposed sexual orientation.[174] Rumors were thus already swirling, either unnoticed or ignored by Kießling, when the lid blew off the top of the affair and the scandal ran its course.

Opinion as to the now all-pervasive scandal was divided among the officers in the Bundeswehr.[175] There was no lack of those who considered it possible, even likely that the general was homosexual. He was in any event a "strange old codger," as one lieutenant colonel who served as a young officer under Kießling's command of the 10th Armored Division recalled thirty years later.[176] Those who knew Kießling better were sure that there was nothing to the accusations.[177] Numerous highly personal letters in Kießling's estate from soldiers, NCOs and officers formerly under his command speak to the high regard and respect they held for an erstwhile commander who had now come under such heavy fire. Three examples are cited here as representative: One from a lieutenant colonel serving abroad in Djibouti at the time called the proceedings around Kießling pure "trash." "General, sir, regarding your noble fight against practically East and West I would like to express – speaking as a battle-hardened lieutenant colonel, at any rate – my own moral support from Africa!"[178] A first sergeant from Heidelberg lamented the "disgraceful treatment" and "unbelievably slipshod methods/research from MAD",[179] while two privates first class from Westerburg wrote after Kießling's restitution that it "strengthens their confidence in the principle of a state founded on the rule of law."[180]

One retired brigadier general wrote to Kießling – albeit "without [knowing] the details" or "the background" of the case at hand – based on his experience as a

---

173 See Möllers, *Die Affäre Kießling*, 57–58.

174 Interrogations of Captain J. and Lieutenant Colonel B. on 10 January 1984 and report from BMVg, P II 5 on 16 January 1984, BArch, BW 1/535370. The BMVg redacted the statements before presenting the files to the investigative committee in parliament. First mentioned in 2014 in Storkmann, "Cui bono?" 720. Möller's in-depth research confirms the UK's Sir Farrar-Hockley as the source of the rumors and offers a compelling account of their path to General Rogers and NATO headquarters. See Möllers, *Die Affäre Kießling*, 57–58.

175 See Möllers, *Die Affäre Kießling*.

176 From a personal conversation between the author and a lieutenant colonel well known to him, 2014.

177 Multiple interviews with retired Surgeon General Dr. Horst Hennig, Cologne. Hennig was one of Kießling's oldest and closest friends.

178 BArch, N 851/82: Kießling estate, Letter from Lieutenant Colonel L., Djibouti to General Kießling, 26 January 1984.

179 Ibid., Master Sergeant L., 19 January 1984.

180 Ibid., Privates J. and G., 6 February 1984.

former group commander at MAD and division leader at FüS II, the BMVg department responsible for the intelligence services.

> Intelligence agencies tend to reason on the sixth floor without having evidence on the ground level. Yet this often does not come out, as they have no executive privileges [...] Since MAD has to do something that is completely atypical for armed forces [...] for years it operated under the motto – and keeping in mind the jealousy of each military branch – "Anybody can do MAD" [...] Not exactly a guarantee for effective personnel selection [...] On top of this comes common human weakness. Take somebody who has struggled for decades to justify his and his work colleagues' existence because intelligence-driven sabotage does not occur in peacetime, and otherwise principally tends to look for security risks below the belt for whatever reason [...] the trouble is pre-programmed.[181]

The general was writing to Kießling so that the latter might not "rack his brain over the causes."[182]

At one of a series of informational meetings on the current scandal that the chief of defense ordered for the entire armed forces, a captain "went to the heart the tragedy – to hearty applause from the soldiers present: 'If not even a four-star general's word of honor counts in the Bundeswehr these days, who would believe me in the face of such accusations? I wo not be conducting any more two-person conversations!"[183]

This final recollection came from a retired brigadier general, in a long letter written in 2005 to retired Federal Chancellor Helmut Kohl that chronicled the scandal as the author experienced it from his post in NATO headquarters. His own contact with General Kießling had ceased in late fall of 1983, when Kießling had told him at NATO with great consternation that he was being called back to Germany with no justification whatsoever. Kießling's remark that "there was unfortunately no chance of enduring enemy fire" prompted the witness to make the general "pledge not to take his own life."[184] The brigadier general himself had remained "clueless"; he did not recall any rumors himself, contrary to other reports from NATO headquarters.

---

181 Ibid., letter from a retired brigadier general to General Kießling, 30 March 1985.
182 Ibid. "Ultimately it is all the same whether or not NATO Counter Intelligence exchanged 'information' with MAD, and on whose orders. Either way it remains a huge disgrace for MAD and our commanders in chief which won'nt have to be paid for by those responsible but the many 'gray mice' who pursue their work with courage and dedication." Ibid.
183 Ret. Brigadier General Lorenz Huber to Ret. Federal Chancellor Dr. Helmut Kohl, 8 November 2005. Thanks to Mr. Huber for sharing a copy of the letter with the author.
184 Ibid.

Thirty-five years after the fact, one captain recalled a visit in January 1984 from the commander of the school for replenishment forces in Bremen while attending a course for prospective company commanders. The commander had begun his address by saying that those in the class had a right to know the commander's position on the scandal surrounding General Kießling: He was of the opinion that the defense minister had to resign.[185]

That January the now public scandal was the single most discussed topic among active officers. This included phone conversations that the GDR was listening in on, as revealed in a transcript of a long-distance call by a general who remains unnamed here.

> We've known each other for years now and I told him [Kießling] that I would believe everything he said on his word of honor, which is also the case, and you can definitely rely on it. When he [K.] says that he never set foot in the bar, that he doesn't know it at all, then that's true and they can investigate whatever they want to. He's always been a loner and somewhat eccentric. But I doubted this [accusation] from the very beginning and if he's contesting it now then I have no more doubts whatsoever.[186]

The wiretapped general was convinced it had been Wörner's "immediate advisors" who were the "main culprits," not the minister himself ("He was on vacation, after all"). His interlocutor, a colonel, responded that "accusing a general of being a security risk for the Republic is really crossing the line." The general grew angrier: "The minister says, 'I'm not accusing you of breach of duty. It's just you're a security risk' ([colonel] laughs). There's a government for you." During the conversation, recorded on 13 January, the general already had a solution in mind. If it should turn out that Kießling were innocent, "then of course there had to be a Grand Tattoo and let bygones be bygones, because everybody makes mistakes sometimes."[187] It also happened to be the exact same solution struck upon on February 1 by Kießling's lawyer Konrad Redeker and CDU parliamentary lawyer Paul Mikat, sitting in as the "parliamentarian" for CDU chairman Helmut Kohl (formally not speaking for the federal chancellor): immediate reappointment and transfer to provisional retire-

---

185 Eyewitness memory, Ret. Colonel Professor Winfried Heinemann, Berlin, 9 August 2019.
186 The general's phone call with a colonel (the general's exact ranking is not given here to protect his privacy) was listened in on and recorded by GDR radio reconnaissance, BStU, MfS BV Suhl, Dept. III, No. 2040, sheets 1–2: Wiretap log from GDR radio reconnaissance, recorded on 13 January 1984. The general in question also spoke directly with Kießling on 20 January, assuring the latter of his support. See Möllers, *Die Affäre Kießling*, 174.
187 BStU, MfS BV Suhl, Dept. III, No. 2040, sheets 1–2: Wiretap log from GDR radio reconnaissance, recorded on 13 January 1984.

ment on March 31 with a Grand Tattoo.[188] Things had not come so far yet, however; in the two weeks following the recorded phone call, the scandal was still to take on even more absurd features.

On 19 January 1984, two obscure, self-appointed "informants" from Cologne's gay scene reported to the minister's office. They had offered their services to Wörner, though ultimately they had nothing concrete to report – and still the gears of the rumor-mill continued to turn. The next day Wörner received a visit from Alexander Ziegler, a journalist, writer and actor from Zurich who had held out the prospect of new incriminating material against Kießling in a letter to the minister. Ziegler himself was openly gay. The conversation lasted over two and a half hours, involving the minister (at least for part of the time), his new adjutant Colonel (GS) Klaus Reinhardt (a future four-star general) and the head of the chancellor's office, Waldemar Schreckenberger. Ziegler claimed that Kießling had kept up contact with a "hustler" from Düsseldorf, leading to the unlawful examination of the data of 304 conscripts carrying the same name as the alleged hustler, twenty-two of which were requested from district recruiting offices – with no results.[189]

Ziegler's story about Kießling's trysts quickly made it back to the press, and proved to be the straw that broke the camel's back. The written transcript of Wörner's questions to the obscure witnesses, which have since become accessible, and especially the transcript of an audio recording Ziegler brought to Bonn, may well contain the most bizarre material ever put to writ in the office of a federal minister, including purportedly anatomical details about the general that were practically pornographic in nature.[190] Retired General Gerd Schmückle, one of the predecessors at Kießling's NATO post, accused Wörner of "mobilizing the international hustler-scene."[191] Retired General Altenburg similarly recalls that he had threatened irately to resign as chief of defense in the event that proceedings against Kießling were not brought to an end.[192]

---

188 Möllers, *Die Affäre Kießling*, 230.

189 A young soldier as a supposed male prostitute – the notion recalls an actual series of events from the German Empire, when recruits sold themselves for sex in Berlin's Tiergarten and the parks around Potsdam. See Domeier, "'Moltke als Schimpfwort!'." For a detailed account of the scandal surrounding Eulenburg and Moltke, see Schwartz, *Homosexuelle, Seilschaften, Verrat*, 16–76.

190 Heiner Möllers, who has looked through these and other files himself and published on them, talks about their "obscene" content. He sees Wörner's meeting with Ziegler as the turning point in public coverage in favor of Kießling. Möllers, "Die Kießling Affäre 1984," 539–40.

191 *Der Spiegel*, "Wörner – 'der Lächerlichkeit preisgegeben'."

192 Interview with Ret. General Wolfgang Altenburg, Lübeck-Travemünde, on 11 June and 7 August 2014.

A phone call tapped by GDR foreign intelligence on 27 January showed that Wörner still firmly believed "he had been entirely correct in his handling of the Kießling matter, even if the proceedings carried out at Kießling's own wish had gone completely off the rails."[193] The Ministry for State Security was similarly listening in on the call when Wörner asked likely the most influential man at Axel Springer publishing "to hold off on the press campaign against him [Wörner] at least over the weekend."[194] Wörner continued to debate whether or not to "rehabilitate" the general, griping that Franz Josef Strauß would "move against him."[195] The GDR secret service was also made privy to rumors spreading in Bonn that it was not Kießling but Wörner himself who was homosexual,[196] and that "investigative services in the BRD [Federal Republic]" had made further inquiries in the Cologne gay scene on 27 December 1983 with a photo of Kießling.[197] Kießling himself later commented in an unpublished manuscript entitled "Meine Entlassung" [My Dismissal] that in January 1984, an observation team from MAD had visited the well-known gay bars in Cologne in the hopes of spotting the general there.[198] Other internal documents meanwhile confirm that MAD had been given a new investigative assignment in the Kießling case. Ultimately, when nothing incriminating was found against Kießling despite enormous expenditure, Wörner changed his tune.[199] On 1 February Kießling was reinstated to active service, then retired with full military honors on 31 March 1984.

In the above mentioned letter to former Chancellor Kohl from a brigadier general, the writer faulted General Kießling for accepting the Grand Tattoo, stressing that it had prevented the Bundeswehr from coming to terms with its actions. For the majority of soldiers it had not been about Kießling or Wörner but a "failure of leadership among the Bundeswehr generals, with Kießling as a case study."[200]

---

193 BStU, Mfs HA III 9289, sheets 89–90: HA III, "Source 1," Information No. 0655/1/1, recorded on 27 January 1984, top secret.

194 The call reveals a surprising parallel between Wörner's actions and those of Federal President Christian Wulff in December 2011 when he called *Bild* chief Kai Dieckmann.

195 Ibid. The Ministry for State Security had gathered from phone calls between influential and well-informed figures that Franz Josef Strauß, Alfred Dregger and Friedrich Zimmerman were all under discussion as successors to Wörner. Ibid., sheet 113, information from 27 January 1984, top secret, as well as ibid., sheet 148, information from 30 January 1984, top secret.

196 Ibid., sheet 142, recorded on 30 January 1984, top secret.

197 Ibid., sheet 31, Information No. 0597/1/1-84, recorded on 25 January 1984, top secret.

198 BArch, N 851/156: Kießling estate, unpublished manuscript "Meine Entlassung."

199 Möllers carefully pieces together the series of events occurring in private that led to Wörner's change of heart, especially Chancellor Kohl's spirited intervention.

200 Ret. Brigadier General Lorenz Huber to Ret. Chancellor Dr. Helmut Kohl, 8 November 2005.

For his part, Defense Minister Wörner came up against derision and caustic mockery not only in the press, but from parliament too. Green deputy Joschka Fischer provided the highpoint of parliamentary debate on 8 February 1984. For Fischer it was not the general's early resignation that had shaken him but "the way in which Mr. Wörner and his panicky choir at Hardthöhe have tried to finish off Günter Kießling as a person, both publicly and morally, when they came under political pressure to prove their case." Fischer reserved sharp words for Wörner:

> He let others carry the manure bucket [...] Whether or not Günter Kießling was homosexual, he is now! Whether or not he was liable to blackmail, he is now! Whether or not he was a danger, he is now! This was an attempt to stage a moral execution of a man in public to let a minister in love with the military stay in office.[201]

SPD Chairman Willy Brandt used his own time to speak with great gravitas about the importance of "honor in general" and an "officer's honor in particular." "These [...] terms had been twisted and used [in this affair] until only caricatures remained." In a speech that is again (or still) highly relevant today, Brandt made an appeal to "protect individual citizens against intelligence services, be they German or foreign, that are insufficiently qualified [...] potentially even given to over-zealousness."[202]

The indignation of the homosexual community and its press was largely directed against Ziegler, who was seen as an informer, as in this letter to Kießling from the editors at the magazine *Du und ich.*[203]

> For us, the real scandal consists in the fact that homosexuality can still be used today for private as well as – what is much worse – political intrigue and blackmail attempts. It is totally irrelevant as such whether a case deals with actual or imputed homosexuality. On top of this in your case come the scandalous practices of a secret service operating in the shadows, a visibly overburdened minister and attempts at denunciation by conniving opportunists. As far as we can judge the matter, the majority of homosexual and heterosexual citizens alike don't accept scandalous proceedings of this sort.[204]

For his part, Ziegler himself sought to explain and excuse himself to Kießling. His aim in going to the defense minister with the Düsseldorf hustler's "story" "about his

---

201 German Bundestag, 52th Session, 8 February 1984, 3695–96.

202 Ibid., 3687 and 3690.

203 BArch, N 851/155: Letter from the "gay liberation front" in Cologne to Kießling on 27 January 1984. A copy was sent to Kießling, who kept it for his files.

204 Ibid., Kießling estate, letter from the editors at *Du und ich,* Hannover, to Kießling on 26 January 1984.

intimate relations with a [...] 'top dog' in the Bundeswehr named 'Günther Kießling'" had been "to bring about rapid police clarification of this mysterious information, and thus prevent the informant from potentially going public himself." Ziegler now saw himself the "victim of a large-scale press campaign with the ugliest sort of defamation," and by his own account was "on the verge of a physical and mental breakdown."[205] He took his own life in 1987.

The commotion within the gay community caused by the unexpected media hype surrounding an allegedly gay general and the gay scene in Cologne was on plain view in the small magazine *Gay Journal*, which devoted five full pages to the Bundeswehr scandal in its February 1984 edition.[206]

c.) Protecting the Private Sphere, or Security Interests?

The public debate surrounding the Kießling affair raised previously unasked questions as to whether MAD had the right to pry so deeply into the most private and intimate details of a soldier's life in the first place. That answer, based on the mission of the service, came in the affirmative. As a deputy to the Supreme Allied Commander for NATO in Europe and one of three four-star generals active in West Germany, Kießling held a prominent place within the Bundeswehr, NATO and the public eye itself. By MAD's line of reasoning, the tremendous potential for a fall from grace alone brought considerable security risks in tow. The general also had access to top secret documents, making it seem an absolute necessity to pursue any reports about him. The initial goal of the investigation had been to verify the rumors as discreetly as possible. At the time, the indications of contact with male minors and young men offering sex that turned up in the service's inquiries into the gay scene in Cologne (which later proved false) left all the warning signals flashing.

MAD also saw a significant risk for blackmail because the general had not admitted to being homosexual[207] – with reports of interactions with young men offering sex for money, which was potentially subject to criminal prosecution under §175 StGB, only exacerbating the (assumed) threat.

Yet not everything that is legal is legitimate, especially not where ethical and moral considerations are brought to bear. A core area of private conduct that is

---

205 Ibid., Letter from Ziegler to Kießling, 30 January 1984.
206 *Gay Journal*, February 1984, title page and 4–7, especially 6.
207 Hammerich, on the other hand, views MAD's position that homosexuality was a security threat no matter what the case as a "very particular interpretation" of the security guidelines in effect at the time and a serious dereliction of duty. Hammerich "*Stets am Feind!*" 273–74.

deserving of protection from state interference, in this particular case the military and its intelligence service, must be preserved. A person's choice of partner, and especially his or her private milieu, make up an essential part of private conduct as protected under Germany's Basic Law. From an ethical standpoint, it should not be the target of state action, and thus not "investigations" by intelligence services, a prohibition that obviously only applies as long as the person operates within the prescribed legal framework, i.e. does not commit violations or crimes in his or her private and sexual life.

On the other end of the scales lies MAD's duty to ensure the security of the Bundeswehr. In cases where soldiers or civil servants kept their homosexual or bisexual orientation from families, spouses, circles of friends and most importantly the military itself, MAD spotted a potential danger in enemy intelligence services establishing contact with the person and subsequently subjecting them to blackmail. The threat of blackmail existed anytime the external image on offer did not match the underlying reality, independently of sexual orientation. If the constructed image was material, even indispensable, to one's career, the threat of its destruction by the revelation of facts to the contrary took on existential importance – the greater a person's interest in keeping up appearances, the greater his susceptibility to extortion.[208] The security interests of the Bundeswehr and the state more generally thus stand opposed to the constitutional protections afforded in the private sphere, and the two must be weighed against each other. How far should the state be permitted to interfere in the private lives of its citizens in order to identify potential threats to its interests? To what extent should the Bundeswehr and its intelligence services be permitted to probe soldiers' and civil servants' intimate lives? These questions are by no means passé but retain their urgency today, as shown in the controversies surrounding personal data storage and telecommunications surveillance.

When applied to the proceedings against Kießling in 1983–84, all this meant was that to MAD it was entirely relevant from a security standpoint whether the general was homosexual and visited bars in Cologne. Yet homosexuality between consenting adults had not been a crime since 1969. Did the type of rumors circulating about Kießling constitute a legitimate target of investigation? From MAD's point of view: absolutely – the fact that the general had not admitted to his reputed homosexuality meant he had something to hide. The foundational tragedy of the affair lay in the fact that Kießling was not homosexual with a likelihood bordering

---

208 Schwartz shares this view: "The higher the position occupied by a clandestine homosexual, the more quickly the general suspicion arrived that he could be forced into betraying secrets." Schwartz, *Homosexuelle, Seilschaften, Verrat*, 283.

on certainty, and thus had nothing to reveal or conceal in the first place. Ultimately, the overall thrust of the investigations was absurd; the resulting errors came about practically as a matter of course. Admittedly, this sort of conclusion is only possible with a full knowledge of the facts; hindsight is always twenty-twenty.

What began with a set of rumors, then, set off a volatile chain reaction linked by unhappy coincidence, mistaken identities and decisions, and bad information and a lack of scrutiny, resulting in a scandal that tarred the reputation of the armed forces in West Germany, NATO, the defense minister and especially MAD. Wörner's initial misgivings on 14 September 1983 as to the credibility of MAD's information had proven correct: The man in question was a lookalike, a civilian watchman for the Bundeswehr who was active in Cologne's gay scene and had been mistaken for the general.

What lessons remain to be learned from the scandal? Could the investigating authorities have contented themselves with an inability to confirm suspicions of homosexuality? Hardly. Beginning with the premise that a high-ranking military officer's (unacknowledged) homosexuality automatically entailed a security risk, the matter could not be set aside by "acquittal on lack of evidence" or the principle of "when in doubt, for the accused." So long as all doubt had not been dispelled, the risk potential was there. Adopting such a stance toward homosexuals placed the institutions involved in the Kießling affair in a dilemma that left them open to false suspicions and slander. Regardless of whether the "suspect" was gay or not, how could he have defended himself, refuted inaccurate rumors or proven that he was being mistreated, that his path in life gave no cause for concern?

Every former MAD employee interviewed for this study drew a distinction in the service's work "before and after Kießling." After 1984, the agency only handled the topic of homosexuality "with kid gloves," proceeding strictly according to the letter of the law.[209] MAD had "burned its finger" on the Kießling affair where homosexuality was concerned; it could not be allowed to happen again. This led the service to "prefer to keep its eyes shut when it was responsible [for issues related to homosexuality], instead of making an official business of the delicate topic and potentially providing the opening salvo for a new scandal."[210]

---

[209] One MAD captain stated or example that "In my personal view, the Kießling affair and its reverberations both within and outside the service, and the new position MAD adopted as a result, brought a considerably stronger break than [reunification]." Interview with a captain, Potsdam, 18 January 2018. Another former MAD officer employed the same phrase of "kid gloves" in his interview. Interview with Captain H., 12 June 2018.
[210] Ibid.

d.) "What Will They Do with Me?" The Kießling Affair's Impact on Homosexual Soldiers

The media commotion surrounding General Kießling's investigation suddenly turned the armed forces' treatment of gay soldiers into a hot topic or, as *Der Spiegel* phrased it, "soldiers as potential sexual partners."[211] *Die Zeit* also reported on the Kießling affair in January 1984, tying its own account to a captain's experiences of discrimination in the military to pose the rhetorical question "Homosexuality – A Security Risk?"[212] In a present-day interview that former officer, who had campaigned for equal rights for homosexual soldiers since the mid 1970s, looked back on the Kießling affair as the "thrust that brought my own case back to the attention of the media." On 9 February 1984 the captain gave his own take on the affair to a packed room in Hamburg's Magnus Hirschfeld Center, a center he helped found: "I'm ashamed of my ministry."[213]

The Wörner–Kießling affair was not merely an "affair of state" but had a broad societal impact, one man who was personally affected in 1984 recalled. "I had only a few times throughout my life been treated with hostility for my homosexuality (born in 1954, came out to my family and friends in the early 70s, competitive athlete, strong, brave, not a 'queen'), but during the time of the affair I encountered any number of homophobic comments." The scandal surrounding the general had been "really intense" and increased homophobic sentiment.[214] While out on a walk through Schwabing in northern Munich in January 1984, a group of adolescents had verbally assaulted him and his then partner – an athlete like himself – for being gay. While there was no immediate causal connection linking the media coverage of Kießling to the incident, the steady presence of "gays" in the media during those weeks had likely been the impetus for the words of abuse.[215]

The details surfacing in the press throughout January 1984, as investigations into the general's private life unfolded, also gave officers who had kept their own homosexuality secret cause for fear. One twenty-five-year-old officer at the time who made first lieutenant in January 1984 could still easily recall his apprehension thirty years after the fact. "If they could do that with even the highest general, what will they do with me if they find out?"[216] The lieutenant, now retired, still remem-

---

211 "Soldaten als potentielle Sexualpartner," 22.
212 "Homosexualität – ein Sicherheitsrisiko?"
213 Interview with Michael Lindner, Hamburg, 7 and 14 February 2017.
214 Email from Harry K. to the author, 5 February 2018.
215 Phone interview with Harry K. on 26 February 2018.
216 Interview with Lieutenant Colonel D., Berlin, 31 March 2017 and 12 February 2018. Quoted as well in what follows.

bered the tremendous impact the Kießling affair had on him. He was home for New Years' 1984 at his parents' rural home when he first heard about the "general being dismissed for alleged homosexuality" on television. "I was deeply unsettled but still made a painstaking effort not to give my parents any hint of my insecurity," as his parents did not know about their son's homosexuality. Afterwards, the young officer's fear of discovery drove him to avoid going out to gay bars and clubs in the nearest city. He would drive to cities farther afield for a night out instead, but the fear was such that he was not confident registering under his real name at hotels, and used a pseudonym at reception. Aside from his dread of discovery and the professional consequences, the officer carried a deep fear of MAD with him on his future path in the Bundeswehr. "The Kießling affair defined my entire life as an officer." Even decades later, the officer was not able to muster any faith in MAD's advertisements to "Open yourself up, confide in us!" "I always thought that if I revealed my partner and thus my homosexuality to the service, I would be opening up the trapdoor to the same snake pit that General Kießling fell into." The officer never mentioned his long-term partner during mandatory security reviews until finally taking the leap of faith in 2013, with unexpected results.[217]

The Kießling affair similarly brought home the dangers lurking for homosexual officers in the Bundeswehr to a young cadet, one year after the Navy accepted him as a medical officer candidate. "What was I supposed to do now? I loved the career of a soldier," the eyewitness recalls thinking in 1984. It was the Kießling affair that had made him "grow up," leaving a lasting imprint on his identity as a gay officer.[218] As with the Navy cadet, a retired staff sergeant (in 1984 a conscript still in his first year of service, though with the ambition of becoming an NCO) had followed the affair very closely in the press and drawn his own lessons: "Oh my. If that can happen to a general, I really have to take care here that they don't find out about me."[219] At the time, the BMVg had to publicly deny that it kept lists with the names of (suspected or actual) homosexual soldiers.[220]

The Kießling affair led directly to a letter discussed above that circulated in the BMVg's personnel department in March 1984, outlining how homosexual soldiers should be treated. The letter's causal link to the affair reveals itself in the explicit mention of generals with a homosexual orientation, a reference that otherwise comes across as somewhat unusual and out of place: "Like any other solider, a general with a homosexual disposition can give rise to security concerns where

217 See section 6 of this chapter.
218 Interview with Dr. Michael Müller of Berlin, 1 August 2019.
219 Interview with Ret. Master Sergeant W., 29 March 2018.
220 Deutsche Presse-Agentur press release, 20 January 1984.

susceptibility to blackmail results. On its own, a homosexual tendency does not entail a security risk."[221]

e.) "Can a homo become an officer in the Bundeswehr?" Public Response to the Scandal

The Ministry of Defense received countless letters from citizens over the course of the affair that ran the fall gamut of opinion regarding homosexual soldiers generally and the Bundeswehr's handling of the specific matter at hand.

The *Verband von 1974 e.V.*, "one of the trans-regional associations [operating] in the interests of homosexual and bisexual people" by its own account, took the "events surrounding Dr. G. Kießling" as an opportunity to demand that the Ministry of Justice undertake reforms to the security guidelines. The reform of §175 StGB in 1969 had removed the basis for "relevant" blackmail attempts, an argument that incidentally had been used in favor of the law's revision. Homosexual officers were "only delivered up to extortion attempts because the security guidelines themselves lay the groundwork for them."[222] Those impacted by the regulatory state of affairs were "plunged into the difficult psychological conflict of having to deny their homosexuality if they did not want to run the risk of being dismissed as a security threat, or at the very least [...] no longer being promoted [...] because ultimately no choice remains for an officer who loves his profession" other than to stay silent about his tendencies. The association appealed to the justice minister to alter the security guidelines so that homosexuality would no longer be grounds for dismissal on its own, and "homosexuals might live out their lives as soldiers in the Bundeswehr as well, without having to conceal their identities."[223]

A Hamburg doctor's letter ("personally") to Defense Minister Wörner prompted by the Kießling affair can be encapsulated in the plain phrase "homosexual men are not any more susceptible to blackmail than heterosexual men."[224] The letter found

---

221 BArch, BW 2/31224: BMVg, P II 1, Az 16-02-05/2 (C) R 4/84, 13 March 1984. A copy is also available in BArch, BW 2/38355. The same wording can be found in the BMVg's response to a letter from a petty officer in early February 1984, at the height of the Kießling affair. BArch, BW 1/378197: BMVg, P II 1, to 2nd Class Petty Officer G., 8 March 1984.
222 BArch, BW 2/31224: Letter from Verband von 1974 e.V., Hamburg to Federal Minister of Justice Hans Engelhardt, 5 February 1984. A letter with the same wording was also sent to Federal Minister of the Interior Friedrich Zimmermann. A copy of both is available in BArch, BW 1/378197.
223 Ibid.
224 BArch, BW 1/378197: Letter from Dr. S., Hamburg, to Manfred Wörner of the BMVg, 25 February 1984.

that "except for parts of the Catholic Church," the population's attitude toward gays had largely adapted to the laws (from 1969). The grounds for soldiers' susceptibility to blackmail "now [came] exclusively" from the Bundeswehr's own security guidelines, "which forbid [...] soldiers identified as homosexual from being promoted to officers." The physician called for an immediate change in the guidelines; it had "long been known" that it was much more common for people with secrets to be blackmailed by women, with most cases of espionage developing out of (heterosexual) affairs. The doctor continued that

> the Bundeswehr's position toward homosexuality is characterized by forms of "homophobia" and "hysteria" that are unjustifiable on any grounds. The total cluelessness and lack of expertise within the responsible MAD divisions is evident from the highly unlikely assumption that a general who has proven himself for decades now would search for sexual partners in hustler bars [...] My own experiences on the front during the last war acquainted me with a series of highly qualified commanders who would regularly sleep with their chauffeurs or cleaners without it bringing harm to discipline or security. At the same time, I'm aware of multiple cases in today's Bundeswehr in which capable officers were either driven to suicide or shut out of the Bundeswehr for homosexual activity that occurred privately, outside the troops. The Bundeswehr must begin to rethink things here.[225]

The doctor then laid his finger directly on the contradictions in the BMVg's course of action. "You cannot draft homosexual conscripts into service and at the same time deny them promotion to higher ranks despite their being qualified. Homosexual officers not infrequently make especially well-adapted and conscientious leaders."[226] Hardthöhe took note of the letter, flagging it with a "green cross" for presentation at the ministerial level. This prompted an elaborate process requiring both the chief of defense and the parliamentary state secretary to sign off on a draft response, with State Secretary Günter Ermisch signing off for the defense minister. Ermisch corrected the doctor, noting that the security guidelines criticized in the letter applied for all federal authorities, and the BMVg was not alone responsible. The doctor was also mistaken in his assumption that the guidelines included a ban on promotions. Fundamentally, it had to be observed for the guidelines that a homosexual "inclination" on its own was not grounds for a security risk.[227]

The letters sent into the BMVg often included extreme positions or phrasing, and – differently from today's social media – came with the sender's information and name attached. (Assuming that the information provided was correct, this

---

225 Ibid.
226 Ibid.
227 BArch, BW 1/378197: BMVg, Dr. Ermisch, standing in for the minister of defense, to Dr. S. of Hamburg, undated draft.

would indicate that even senders with extremely hostile views toward gays held no qualms or reservations about giving their full names. This too was a sign of the spirit that still prevailed in 1984.) Writing in response to the scandal in March 1984, Willy M. asked Hardthöhe whether "a homo can become an officer in the Bundeswehr?" He was also curious "whether a relevant investigation is carried out before someone is promoted to officer, and whether there are questionnaires where those concerned have to provide information themselves about the delicate issue?" Finally, he wanted to know "If a homo can't become an officer under the laws of the Bundeswehr, wouldn't you have to give a sworn oath as to whether or not you are one?" He gave the reason for his questions as being "a homosexual's promotion to lieutenant in Hamburg."[228]

Evidently he never heard back from Bonn, because three weeks later he wrote again, "as this matter is quite important, after all." "It could easily be the case that if this lieutenant later entered higher ranks, a debacle similar to Kießling's case might repeat itself."[229]

In response to a 16 January 1984 article in the *Münchner Merkur* with the title "There are at least 65,000 homosexuals in the Bundeswehr," Alfred-Carl G. wanted the Ministry of Defense to know that he

> [found] it absolutely marvelous! Should it actually be the case that there really are 65,000 homosexuals in the Bundeswehr, I urgently suggest the creation of three "Homosexual" divisions [...] Just imagine the striking power the three divisions would have if things got serious! The Bundeswehr captain mentioned in the article, Michael Lindner, who as the paper writes is engaged "in scholarship" on the "topic of soldiers and homosexuality," should be made division commander for one of the A [...] – [...] – Divisions as quickly as possible. Both of my sons happily made it through the Bundeswehr "in one piece." They were evidently spared contact with Captain Michael Lindner. Among the sections of the troops that I served in for nearly six years anyway (Crete/Africa/Italy/Western offensive 1944), Mr. Lindner would have had the living daylights beaten out of him, to put it mildly. A pity no one is prepared to do so now![230]

The section head at FüS I 4 responded for the defense ministry:

> An extremely broad range of opinion on homosexuality prevails in our country; the actual attitudes within the population do not necessarily coincide with the legal landscape. Among other things, this makes it no simple matter for the Bundeswehr to make comprehensible to any one person the conditions under which men with a homosexual orientation are or are not capable of service or the military. You may rest assured, however, that the cohesion of the

---

228 BArch, BW 2/31224: Letter from Willy M. to the federal minister of defense, 31 March 1984.
229 Ibid., Letter from Willy M. to the federal minister of defense, 24 April 1984.
230 Ibid., Letter from Alfred-Carl G. to the federal minister of defense, 15 March 1984.

> military community and a sense of camaraderie among soldiers will remain the deciding and overriding criteria for relevant service regulations.[231]

While the section head was in essence repeating the BMVg's position in the simplest terms possible, it vexes from today's perspective that the ministry did not condemn, or at the very least push back on such sharp personal attacks against a former captain in the military, including advocating the use of physical violence. This omission can again be taken as a sign of the winds that continued to prevail around the topic at the BMVg in 1984. Authors who wrote with the opposite intention received different-sounding answers signed by the same section head.

> Allow me, however, to state with all certainty that homosexual soldiers and/or superiors are fundamentally fit for service provided they are sufficiently able to adapt, perform, endure stress and enter community. Still, discrimination-free integration of homosexual soldiers into the military community will remain a problem to be taken seriously so long as broad circles of the population look on homosexual behavior with condemnation and it stands opposed to general educational goals.[232]

In this response as well the section head correctly repeats the BMVg's position, albeit with a clear difference in focus and choice of wording than in his previous reply. The ministry was flexible in the formulations it used, striking an accommodating stance toward a given author without abandoning the party line. Evidently the stance was so broad as to be able to draft satisfactory answers for contradictory positions; in its intent and phrasing at any rate, the letter Ms. Katharina H. wrote proved opposite to Mr. G's. Ms. H. left no doubt as to her opinion that

> homosexuality is not a criminal offense [...] Given this set of circumstances, how is it that discovery of a man's homosexual tendencies [...] even the mere suspicion of a form of behavior fixed by nature, can be viewed in the Bundeswehr as so defamatory that such a man – should he advance to an office of high rank on account of his abilities – must then be dismissed from the Wehrmacht [sic] without military ceremony even if he has not drawn any criminal attention to himself? After all, anyone in this our land, even a citizen in uniform, can, so long as he does not breach the prescribed borders of decorum and above all the law, be blessed in the pursuit of his fancy![233]

---

231 Ibid., FüS I 4 to Alfred-Carl G., 6 April 1984.

232 Ibid., FüS I 4 to Katharina H., 20 February 1984.

233 Ibid., Letter from Katharina H. to the federal minister of defense, 13 January 1984.

Ms. H.'s motivation in writing the letter as the scandal surrounding General Kießling can be gleaned from its date alone, 13 January 1984. There were "only two 'clean' solutions" from her perspective:

> Either the Bundeswehr recognizes that a homosexual is a man like any other, leaving aside sexual practices that are truly irrelevant for military eligibility – in which case he is worthy of the military not only as a simple soldier but an officer, regardless of rank. Doubtless, there are a number of effeminate types among homosexuals, just as there are always "slouchers" among heterosexuals. But many homosexuals are fine male specimens, and should they wish to serve in the Bundeswehr [...] then there is no reason to deny them rising to the rank of officer if the right sort of soldierly ability is present. Either that, or the liberalization of §175 is officially undone and the Bundeswehr enacts a sort of professional ban on homosexuals.[234]

In offering her sarcastic alternative Ms. H. almost certainly articulated the unspoken wishes held by any number of officers, civil servants and lawyers at the ministry and Bundeswehr. Yet in doing so she also echoed, albeit unwittingly, a position that the BMVg discussed internally in advance of the 1969 reforms. While calls for a separate criminal law for the armed forces (and possibly for rapid response police units) stood little chance of an audience at the time, the BMVg had in fact seriously pursued it as an option.[235]

4. Parliament Debates "Homosexuality as a Security Risk"

Assessing the security risk homosexual soldiers posed surfaced repeatedly for discussion in the Bundestag, including when the chamber took up MAD's treatment of homosexual soldiers in mid-January 1984 with the Kießling affair still at its height. Two questions from Jürgen Reents of the Green Party to the BMVg provided the immediate occasion; Reents asked whether, as reported in the newspapers, the Ministry of Defense had said that "homosexual activity impacting the line of duty cannot be accepted in a male community as closely knit as the Bundeswehr," and that "the discovery of gays in a unit brought about considerable complications and unrest."[236] Parliamentary State Secretary Würzbach of the CDU responded that a "very clear and precise answer" to the question existed in this case: The quotes in

---

234 Ibid.
235 See chapter 3, section 7, for a full account.
236 German Bundestag, 10th legislative period, 47th Session, 19 January 1984, typed transcript, 3372–73.

question had not come from the Ministry of Defense.[237] SPD deputy Dietrich Sperling saw through Würzbach's response:

> State Secretary sir, now that you have described the wording of the quotes cited in the press as inauthentic, if not the spirit, I would like to know whether you share my opinion of the need for the federal government to bring Article 1 of the Basic Law to the attention of a wide array of employees, especially doctors at Bundeswehr hospitals and MAD staff, for them to observe the article and preserve human dignity even where minorities are concerned.[238]

Würzbach countered that while he shared in the "spirit" of the question, he did not consider instruction of the sort necessary as it was "self-evident" "that it was imperative to observe the articles in the Basic Law. I do not find it necessary, referring today to one article and another tomorrow, to specially state that these laws and precepts must be those guiding every individual form of behavior."[239] Würzbach stressed further that no soldier "was dismissed from the Bundeswehr [...] based on a suspicion [...] no matter in what direction." When Antje Vollmer of the Greens interpreted this freely to mean that nobody "would be dismissed from the Bundeswehr on account of homosexuality or other sexual practices," the state secretary found himself compelled to reemphasize his exact wording: Nobody would "be dismissed from the Bundeswehr on account of suspicion – whatever suspicion based on whatever form of behavior that may be."

Vollmer also asked whether "homosexual members of the Bundeswehr are registered as homosexual, and whether suspicions or reports are registered."[240] Würzbach made it clear that no lists were kept, nor were any surveillance measures being conducted. Deputy Wolfgang Ehmke, also of the Greens, wanted to know how the state secretary had arrived at the assumption that "a member of the Bundeswehr [...] is liable to blackmail or is a security risk based on something that is completely legal and lay within the scope of his private life."[241] Würzbach replied that "a soldier, like others, may be liable to blackmail if he wants to conceal something he's done, and if there are people who know what was done and would like it to come out. There are a great number of situations in life where this is the case."[242] It was Deputy Sperling of the SPD who again put his finger on the mark, "gladly" asking "whether – since certain locales are frequented by those with a given ten-

---

237 Ibid., 3373.
238 Ibid.
239 Ibid.
240 Ibid., 3374.
241 Ibid.
242 Ibid., 3375.

dency that hold less interest for others, because visiting them may be grounds for dismissal from the Bundeswehr – whether you might not like to warn soldiers which locales they were better off avoiding."[243]

The allusion to MAD's observation of bars frequented by homosexuals in Cologne was all too clear. Würzbach would not let himself be drawn in, responding that he did not want to anticipate the question period concerning the Kießling case set for the next day. In general, "public locales were an area outside the barracks, outside the immediate scope of official duty." Peter Conradi of the SPD asked pointedly whether homosexuality or contact with homosexuals presented a security risk in the opinion of the Bundeswehr. Würzbach's response: "Not in principle, colleague, sir, though it may."[244] It depended on the individual case. The state secretary responded in greater detail to a follow-up question from another SPD deputy, explaining that there were cases in which the person holding a service post was known to have "this tendency" and openly admitted to it, and in which "there was no reason for him to have anything to hide," thus eliminating the risk of blackmail. Deputy Norbert Gansel of the SPD persisted: "In the Bundeswehr, is it possible for a soldier otherwise living in an orderly relationship as defined by the defense ministry, except that it is on a quasi-marital terms with another man, to become a disciplinary superior, an officer?"[245]

This represented a "borderline case" for Würzbach that "would have to be gone into down to the very last details. There is no general, across-the-board provision providing a template for everything." Another SPD deputy inquired whether it could be gathered from Würzbach's remarks that a high-ranking officer who admitted his homosexuality when asked would not have to fear his security clearance being revoked under any circumstances; the state secretary answered in the negative. It depended on the individual case, "including the post, the person and the circumstances."[246]

Now came Horst Jungmann's turn from the SPD. Citing a paper from the BMVg's medical services scientific advisory board that found homosexuality to be "an abnormal sexual behavior" and mandated "withdrawing security clearances per Bundeswehr security regulations," Jungmann asked whether the state secretary would consider "revising" the board's finding.[247] Würzbach's response was a

---

243 Ibid.
244 Ibid.
245 Ibid., 3376.
246 Ibid.
247 Ibid., 3380. In all likelihood, the deputy was drawing from remarks by high-ranking MAD employees given at an 18 April 1980 meeting of the BMVg medical advisory board's committee on preventative health and care and military examinations. BArch, BW 24/5553 and BW 2/31225.

master class in political evasion; he responded that his statements before the Bundestag "rested on all the binding statements, documents, rules and prescriptions then in effect."[248] The state secretary omitted the decisive part: The position Jungmann had cited was much more than a paper from the scientific advisory board for the BMVg's medical services; at the time, in 1984, it continued to be the operative legal principle guiding security reviews at every federal authority.

Two years later homosexuality as a security risk again made up the business of the day, when Vice President Annemarie Renger (SPD) called up question 39 from Deputy Herbert Rusche (The Greens) during a question period on Thursday, 20 March 1986. "In the opinion of the Federal Ministry of Defense, what form of sexual behavior can lead to blackmail if instead of an 'abnormal disposition in the sexual realm' a security risk is now described as 'sexual behavior that can lead to blackmail,' as reported in the *Tageszeitung Express* on 14 February 1986?"[249] Würzbach looked to fend off the question with a passing reference to the response given by the state secretary for the Federal Ministry of the Interior in preceding question periods – to no avail. Vice President Renger allowed the Green Party deputy a follow up question:

> State Secretary sir, I found it necessary to pose this question to the defense ministry in particular because in 1984 a highly unpleasant scandal, and one which was highly unpleasant for the Bundeswehr as well, took place surrounding the four-star general General Kießling. I would like to hear from you, most of all in connection with my most recent question, whether going forward this sort of scandal will no longer possible in the Bundeswehr.

Würzbach shot back that "every scandal is unpleasant, and one is well advised to do everything to avoid them."

The Kießling affair had been "thoroughly investigated and critically appraised," its origins and course "considered [in detail] from the various sides of the [BMVg]." Würzbach himself had nothing more to add, though the same certainly could not be said for Deputy Rusche, who pressed on. "Does the Bundeswehr share the cited magazine's view that investigations like the one into former four-star General Kiesßling are no longer possible, or if so, then on what grounds?" More specifically, "will it no longer be the practice of MAD to spy on soldiers, their superiors and generals in gay bars or other localities in Bonn or surroundings?" Würzbach countered that he would "forego the opportunity to discuss hypothetical, theoretical possibilities."

---

248 German Bundestag, 10th legislative period, 47th Session, 19 January 1984, typed transcript, 3380.

249 Here and in what follows, German Bundestag, 10th legislative period, 207th Session, 20 March 1986, typed transcript, 15891–93.

Rusche turned to the subject of blackmail, which he described as arising from homosexuals in the Bundeswehr who were forced to keep their orientation a secret, and take care that it did not become public knowledge. "My question to you now is: If a homosexual citizen is open and honest about his homosexuality with his superiors and among the troops at large, is a security risk no longer present?"

Würzbach chose to reply in the odd form of the first person singular: "I can only be blackmailed if I do something that I do not want others to know about. A risk only materializes if a person behaves one way but the public has the impression he was not, that he was doing the opposite." Norbert Mann, likewise of the Greens, followed up by asking

Mr. Würzbach, colleague sir, to repeat the question in plain language: Putting aside for a moment the individual case, which must always be reviewed as a matter of course, is it not now the case under the new version of the guidelines – where it says "sexual behavior that can lead to blackmail" – that homosexual behavior will essentially receive the same treatment as normal sexual behavior, meaning for example that somebody who carries on a relationship with a woman while married poses just as great a security risk as someone who may be homosexual and carries on a relationship with a man, or multiple men?

Würzbach dodged again, continuing to refer to the words of the Ministry of the Interior even after repeated follow-up questions. Willi Tatge from the Greens would not desist, demanding to know whether "a superior who admits his homosexuality will have to expect consequences for his position leading soldiers?"

Speaking from whatever sudden impulse may have taken him, State Secretary Würzbach now became very concrete and spoke at length:

Colleague, sir, that can only be sketched in a simplified manner in the short answer I am held to by the rules of procedure [...] At present, though, I would like to add a consideration despite the prescribed brevity. Just ask for once the many, many fathers and mothers and girlfriends and acquaintances and brothers of conscripted soldiers – I'm deliberately approaching this question obliquely – who we call upon and demand that they spend fifteen months serving in the Bundeswehr, and who have been raised in such a way that as a man, they do not want to be involved with men but want to be with a woman, ask their father, their mother, their brother or friends what they would think if that conscript came home on the weekend and said: My commander has somewhat different tendencies than I do. Ask this question just once from that angle. Now ask that commander's commanding officer whether in individual cases – to mention [individual cases] again – it would not be better not to place this man in charge of other soldiers but, in accordance with his knowledge and abilities, place him in a post from which he neither brings others nor himself into this situation. Case-by-case examination, colleague, sir!

The press had a field day with the state secretary's plain response, taz most of all: "The otherwise lively" state secretary had "struggled for words," answering the Green party's question with "disarming honesty."[250]

"Homosexuality as a security risk in public service" also provided the target of an inquiry from Deputy Jutta Oesterle-Schwerin in January 1988.[251] As usual, the Bundestag took up the inquiry in a plenary session. This time it fell to Carl-Dieter Spranger (CDU) as the Parliamentary State Secretary for the Ministry of the Interior to answer. He reported on the new security guidelines that would take effect that May, clarifying that "circumstances which are public knowledge and to which a person openly admits cannot as a rule be used as a means of blackmail; this generally means they do not constitute a security risk either. This applies fundamentally for the matter of homosexuality alluded to in the question."[252] In addition, unlike the preceding guidelines, the new security guidelines were not classified as confidential material, which meant all federal employees could now find out for themselves what was considered a security risk.[253] Peter Sellin of the Greens wanted to know "how [the secretary] could allay fears that someone who acknowledged his homosexuality would be at a disadvantage when applying for a security-sensitive area?"[254] Spranger made renewed reference to §4 of the guidelines, which "operated under the assumption that circumstances to which a person has freely admitted and can now be made public, from which no drawbacks are to be feared, cannot as a rule be used as a means of blackmail. That's why the provision was made the way it was."[255]

Deputy Oesterle-Schwerin delivered her remaining questions orally:

> Does the federal government share the view that the negative consequences threatening gay men and lesbian women if they admit to their homosexuality (e.g. the loss of security clearances in the case of officers, or professional consequences from admitting one's homosexuality) give rise to a situation where people have to conceal their homosexuality, thereby creating security risks in the first place, and what measures does the federal government plan on taking to allay the fears of the parties affected, and give them the courage to come out as

---

250 Wickel, "In einer Männergesellschaft nicht hinnehmbar."
251 German Bundestag, Document 11/1734, Inquiry from Deputy Jutta Oesterle-Schwerin, January 1988.
252 German Bundestag, 11th legislative period, 57th Session, 3 February 1984, typed transcript, 3939.
253 Ibid.
254 Ibid., 3940.
255 Ibid.

homosexuals or bisexuals by [giving] clear guidelines on avoiding blackmail and unnecessary risks?[256]

Spranger was tight-lipped, and referred to his answer to the first question. Oesterle-Schwerin hit back: "You are making this incredibly easy for yourself. That shows how difficult it is for you to talk about this topic."[257]

When Spranger's next two replies were equally brief and evasive, Oesterle-Schwerin tried to put it more concretely: "How will the federal government remove the enormous pressures of professionals repercussions for coming out as homosexual on the one hand, and fear of being discovered on the other, and what does it plan on doing to spare gays and lesbians from these sort of conflicts?"[258] The secretary refused to be caught up, and once again dodged the question.

Deputy Oesterle-Schwerin would not let go of the issue, and that same year filed a major inquiry into homosexuals' right to informational self-determination, including and specifically with regard to how security guidelines were applied. The Ministry of the Interior, tasked with the response, included a detailed description of how it proceeded with security checks in its preliminary remarks:

> Within the context of personnel security, information about a person's sexual tendencies are relevant to federal intelligence services only to the extent that it *may* constitute a security risk in individual instances. This may not necessarily be the case even in the event that homosexual tendencies are determined. Rather [...] a security risk is only assumed in the presence of circumstances that provide grounds for an increased threat of attempted approaches or solicitation by foreign intelligence services, and in particular concerns regarding susceptibility to blackmail. Underlying this regulation is the notion that general categories cannot be formed for types of sexual behavior that automatically lead to the assumption of a security risk, and that ultimately it must depend instead on considering and weighing the particular circumstances in the individual case [...] On its own, a homosexual tendency that has become public knowledge under no circumstance justifies a person's inclusion in computer files, lists or other forms of records taken by federal intelligence services. In particular, no information on the individual characteristics of a person's sexual behavior is stored in the files [...] "Homosexuality" – as shown here – does not constitute a security risk as defined by federal security authorities.[259]

---

256 Ibid.

257 Ibid., 3941.

258 Ibid.

259 BArch, BW 2/31224: Federal Ministry of the Interior, Section O I 4, 6 December 1988. Draft response to the major inquiry from Deputy Ms. Oesterle-Schwerin, Bundestag document 11/2586, annex.

Prior to issuing the response the ministry circulated a draft for approval to the Federal Office for the Protection of the Constitution, the office of the chancellor and the Federal Ministry of Defense. Among other revisions, the BMVg suggested adding the phrase "*on its own*" to the last sentence, so the final version would read "On its own, 'homosexuality' – as shown here – does not constitute a security risk as defined by federal security authorities."[260] The section suggesting the revision, Org 2, was responsible for overseeing MAD and offered a full explanation of its reasoning: Inserting the phrase "on its own" would make it clear that "in assessing homosexuality as a [potential] security risk, additional special circumstances would have to be present to justify a negative decision on a security clearance." "For the area of the Bundeswehr in which men live together in confined quarters and which depends on a trusting relationship between superiors and subordinates in the military realm that is free of sexuality, it is an obvious choice to refrain from disclosing one's homosexual tendencies, or for disclosure to considerably disturb service operations."[261]

This was what had repeatedly led the military service senates at the Federal Administrative Court to accept level 2 security clearances being revoked or denied in the past.[262]

5. Between Scylla and Charybdis

A "Do not ask!" policy would not have been possible at MAD, where one part of the service's mission consisted (and still consists) in questioning soldiers and then reviewing those statements in the course of its security reviews. For many soldiers under review, MAD's mandatory questionnaires contained a trap from which there was no escape, even if it did not explicitly ask their sexual orientation: a required statement as to one's spouse or life companion. Security Review Act regulations incorporated both these statements, as well as the partner's own family background, into its investigations; if a gay soldier was in a committed relationship he would have to give the actual name of his life partner, and the trap would snap shut. The soldier's duty to answer truthfully forced him to admit to his partner, and thus his own homosexuality. If on the other hand he kept it a secret from MAD, he would (if he were found out) lose credibility in the eyes of the service. Doubts about a soldier's reliability formed another reason to deny him security clearance, while the

---

260 BArch, BW 2/31224: BMVg, Section Org 2 to BMI, Section O I 4, 16 January 1989.
261 Ibid.
262 Ibid.

service also saw him as leaving himself exposed to blackmail attempts by enemy intelligence services.[263]

Captain Michael Lindner, who retired in 1982, described this "fatal situation" in 1985: Admitting one was gay meant no longer receiving promotions or assignments to positions of authority; hushing it up made a person liable to blackmail, and thus a security risk.[264] For Lindner this created a sort of catch-22 that forced homosexual superiors into "constant denial and hide-and-seek," with many leading a double life "so as to at least awaken the impression of 'normality'."[265]

In 1986 *JS*, a magazine put out by the Protestant military chaplaincy, described a similar catch-22 situation for homosexual superiors.[266] Both *JS* and Lindner had struck on an apt phrase. The litany of sanctions threatening homosexual officers, and in part NCOs, made it necessary for them to conceal and deny their sexuality. Yet this left them potentially subject to blackmail and a security risk in the eyes of MAD, opening the door to further consequences if the service acted. The mere knowledge of these sanctions raised the pressure on homosexual soldiers to dissemble or hide to the best of their ability; if it all possible, MAD should be kept in the dark as well. At times this could lead gay soldiers to act quite conspiratorially; avoiding the gay scene in nearby cities for fear of discovery, for example, and traveling farther afield instead. Soldiers sought out discrete, anonymous sexual encounters, leaving them exposed to other risks in the process. It raised the risk to security from MAD's perspective if a soldier was observed behaving conspiratorially during a security check, which then accelerated the vicious cycle. Ultimately it amounted to a self-fulfilling prophecy that left a great deal of work for MAD and an unending fear of discovery for the soldiers who were affected. Like Odysseus himself, homosexual NCOs and officers seemed forced to sail between the sea mon-

---

263 Writing in 2001, Stefan Waeger also found that questions about sexual orientation were no longer asked directly, but there was an explicit question about people with whom the soldier under inspection lived in a marriage-like arrangement. "Non-disclosure of homosexual living arrangements [was] repeatedly classified as an index of blackmail potential and thus a potential security risk [...] In the past legal action against denying or withdrawing a security clearance seemed to hold out little chance of success, as the courts had allowed the deciding military commander significant discretion." Waeger, "Sexuelle Ausrichtung und Führungsverantwortung," chapter 4.1.3.2.

264 Lindner, "Homosexuelle in der Institution Bundeswehr," 212. Schwartz uses similar, if different wording: "Where the Bundeswehr was concerned, the pressure to keep [one's homosexuality] secret made the same institution that generated it view homosexual soldiers – officers in particular and generals most of all – susceptible to blackmail by enemy services and thus extremely dangerous." Schwartz, *Homosexuelle, Seilschaften, Verrat*, 280.

265 Lindner, "Homosexuelle in der Institution Bundeswehr," 212.

266 Wickel, "Männer im Schatten." See chapter 2.

sters of antiquity, Scylla and Charybdis, with MAD acting as the former and the personnel department as the latter.

In 1999 the defense ministry spokesperson himself inadvertently called attention to the hopeless situation that the interplay of MAD and personnel leadership had created for homosexual superiors in the *Frankfurter Allgemeine Zeitung*:

> The Bundeswehr has nothing against homosexuals in principle, the spokesperson reported; conscripts and soldiers are not asked about their sexual tendencies. Yet he admitted that information about sexual tendencies was given weight in the context of MAD's security reviews. A soldier had a "bad hand" if it turned out that he had kept quiet about his homosexual tendencies. This gave rise to a risk of blackmail for soldiers who tried to keep a secret. The spokesperson said that the Bundeswehr regarded homosexuals as unfit for leadership and training positions.[267]

That same year the *Frankfurter Rundschau* quoted the spokesperson as saying "If a security review by lead officers points to signs of homosexuality then MAD will investigate for possible susceptibility to blackmail,"[268] and overall that "a person who conceals his homosexuality is a security risk, while a person who admits his homosexuality may suffer a loss in authority." It remains unclear whether the spokesperson actually used these words or not – if it was the case then he would have succinctly spelled out the entire dilemma facing homosexual soldiers. It was inadvertent, but it was also without empathy; the spokesperson was quoted further as saying "We [the Bundeswehr] do not find these regulations to be discriminatory."[269]

The "problem" was not limited to NCOs and officers in the troops but reached the doors of the ministry in Hardthöhe. Multiple eyewitnesses independently recalled a homosexual staff officer serving in the Minister of Defense's inner sanctum around the turn of the millennium. When the officer came up against the problem of his potential susceptibility to blackmail, and with it the possibility of MAD intervening to block his access to secret or top secret material, he resolved it by submitting written testimony of his homosexuality to be kept in a safe on the ministry's floor. In the event that MAD did get involved or even directly revoked his security clearance, this would allow the officer to produce his admission, answer-

---

267 "Homosexueller darf nicht ausbilden."
268 "Rot und Grün streiten über homosexuelle Bundeswehrsoldaten." The term used by the spokesperson for "lead officers," *Führungsoffizier*, was not used in the Bundeswehr and was an unhappy turn of phrase; the GDR State Ministry for Security used it to refer to the handlers of informal collaborators. The newspaper itself used the term to mean "superior." It is unlikely to assume that a BMVg spokesperson would have used the term in this way.
269 Ibid.

ing and presumably allaying a set of concerns that was entirely justified under the regulations. Knowingly or not, the minister's immediate circles were following the path *Der Spiegel* had indicated before in 1993 as one possible way out of the dilemma between outing oneself and posing a security risk. In individual instances, staff officers would admit to their homosexuality in a sealed letter to forestall black-mail concerns.[270] This proved one route of escape across the billowing sea that lay between the two terrors.

In 2001 Stefan Waeger described the "problem of security reviews for homo-sexual soldiers" objectively as a

> conflict of interest that arose on the one hand out of their obligation to give complete and honest answers in the course of security reviews as part a soldier's duty to honesty, and on the other [from] the fact that the eligibility and assignment restrictions discussed here would come to pass in the event they did openly confess their orientation.[271]

Aside from family reasons, Waeger principally linked soldiers' efforts to conceal their sexual orientation to repercussions in service. Soldiers' "potential suscepti-bility to blackmail thus came out of a situation that the service itself had created through its stance on homosexuals."[272] The BMVg itself fully recognized the "dilemma." One comment from Section FüS I 1 in February 2000 reveals the institu-tion's awareness of the problem with remarkable clarity:

> The current process for security reviews appears problematic from the perspective of leader-ship development and civic education; MAD explains to the soldier that he will only receive the security clearance he seeks for acceptance into career service if he discloses his homosex-uality to his superiors, yet the consequences this report then brings about [...] are the same as being denied a security clearance, namely not being accepted for career service [...] This leaves the soldier in a dilemma from which there is no escape: Either he is a security issue, or is not fit for career service because he is not fit to serve as a superior.[273]

The note contains a later, revealing addition in handwriting: "Meeting with StS [State Secretary] Dr. Wichert on 17 February 2000 resulted in no change in state of affairs. It remains a dilemma."[274]

---

270 "'Versiegelte Briefe'," 54.
271 Waeger, "Sexuelle Ausrichtung und Führungsverantwortung," chapter 4.1.3.2.
272 Ibid.
273 BArch, BW 2/38358: BMVg, FüS I 4, 20 January 2000, emended in writing to 15 February 2000.
274 Ibid., handwritten note from 17 February 2000.

The only way out of the dilemma was a shift in the Bundeswehr's position toward homosexuality. It took the long hoped-for and necessary step in 2000, just a few months after the note was written.

6. New Legal Principles, New Regulations: "Irrelevant to the Security Clearance Process"

The end of restrictions against homosexual officers and NCOs did not also mean an end to MAD's review of possible security-related "insights." As the BMVg section responsible for MAD oversight phrased it in a February 2004 position paper to the parliamentary commissioner for the armed forces,

> the fact that legal principles in general (e.g. the Partnership Act) and regulations in the BMVg's working operations (e.g. no assignment restrictions based on homosexuality) have taken on more liberal forms is irrelevant to the security clearance process to the extent that where security law is concerned, homosexuality [...] is assessed exclusively from the perspective of its potential blackmail risks.[275]

Objectively speaking this was correct; nothing had changed from the office's perspective about the need to rule out blackmail risks based on undisclosed life circumstances. The position paper followed on complaints filed by two soldiers who lived together as a couple, and who in the course of their security reviews now found themselves forced to decide whether or not to disclose their partnership, and with it their sexual orientation. As with so many other homosexual officers and NCOs in decades past, the two found themselves caught between not wanting (or being allowed) to give false statements on the required questionnaire on the one hand, nor to reveal their sexual orientation to the service on the other. As one of the soldiers explained, he did not trust the security officer at his post and did not want his sexual orientation to come out through the form, and thus decided not to list his partner for the time being. Instead, the two men decided to contact MAD directly and request a private conversation.

One of the two soldiers recalled in an eyewitness interview the conversation that had subsequently unfolded with the security officer of a higher command authority and her female colleague. It took place in the basement of a government

---

275 BArch, BW 1/532308: BMVg, Org 6 to the parliamentary commissioner for the armed forces, 16 February 2004. Only material that had not been marked "Classified – For Official Use Only" was drawn on in considering this case as well, as the thirty-year deadline had not yet expired for material that had been classified.

office building, coming across to the man and his partner "like an interrogation room in a film." The two women had insisted that the soldiers had no choice but to come out to their superior and the security officer in their barracks, and that a note would also have to be made in the personnel files. It was the only way to eliminate the threat of blackmail and thus security risks – after which nothing else would stand in the way of their security clearances. The two soldiers refused, commenting that "the era of the pink triangle [was] over."[276] Their attempts to reach some sort of compromise had been "brusquely" turned back by the two women, and the conversation ended without an agreement. This was followed (initially) by one of the two staff sergeants submitting a petition to the parliamentary commissioner for the armed forces, which essentially addressed the MAD employees' insistence on revealing his orientation to his direct disciplinary superior.[277] This led the office of the commissioner to inquire at the BMVg the extent to which "'coming out' to one's disciplinary superior and security officer could be demanded."[278]

The ministry forwarded the question to MAD, including a draft of a position paper for the service to look over. The ministry took up most of the feedback it received from MAD's Cologne office, replying to the commissioner in February 2004. It began by observing that the laws clearly made it essential for the soldier to state his (same-sex) partner and incorporate his partner into the security review process. As a result, both the soldier's immediate security officer and MAD would be informed of the same-sex partnership.

> It cannot be ruled out with all certainty that the service post head or disciplinary superior will be informed by the security officer; nonetheless no obligation to disclosure toward disciplinary superiors exists on the part of the affected party.
>
> Since superiors change frequently, the affected party could repeatedly wind up in the situation of having to share his disposition with a new superior. According to the principle of proportionality it is entirely sufficient for the individual to make a one time disclosure to his personnel office.[279]

In and of itself, homosexuality did not constitute a security risk.

---

276 Interview with Master Sergeant H., 29 March 2018.
277 First Sergeant H., complaint to the parliamentary commissioner for the armed forces, 9 November 2003.
278 BArch, BW 1/532308: parliamentary commissioner for the armed forces to the BMVg, 18 December 2003.
279 Ibid., BMVg, Org 6 to the parliamentary commissioner for the armed forces, 16 February 2004 (original emphasis).

> Homosexuality which the affected party has kept secret can, however, present a basis for a security risk under §5 (1) Sentence 1 No. 2 of the Security Review Act, if it provides actual grounds for an increased threat of attempted grooming or solicitation by foreign intelligence services, and especially worries about susceptibility to blackmail (compromising situations).[280]

An individual admitting his tendencies or relationships openly would render them ineffective as a means of coercion.

> In the event of a known and compromising personal weakness and its ongoing concealment – despite having informed the individual about his potential liability to blackmail – MAD must still rule a security risk present, as security interests take precedence over other concerns in case of doubt under §V 14 (3) Sentence 2 of the Security Review Act.[281]

The letter closed with the previously quoted assessment that the new legal situation and regulations on handling homosexuality in general, and homosexual soldiers in particular, were irrelevant to the security review process.

As for the two soldiers under MAD review, things would escalate in time. The written exchange reveals a steadily growing series of misunderstandings and mistrust on the part of the two men toward MAD, and actual missteps – or at least unfortunate actions – on the part of multiple MAD employees which only worsened the soldiers' lack of confidence. Two supplements to the petition reflect the soldiers' burgeoning impression in April 2004 that MAD was looking to pressure them into outing themselves to their superiors. Both rejected the possibility outright; one stood shortly before review, and had also applied to enter career service. Under no circumstances did he want to jeopardize either venture by revealing his homosexuality to his superior. For its part, MAD protested that it had not been pressuring either soldier but merely called attention to the current legal landscape regarding concealed homosexuality. The soldiers finally struck upon a way out of the dilemma, at least for the time being, declaring their intention to wait until the matter of the ongoing petition to the parliamentary commissioner had been settled before complying with the supposed requirement of speaking with the superior. The security review dragged on; two years later the two soldiers filed a further petition with the parliamentary commissioner, among other things reproaching a MAD officer for revealing his own homosexuality to them in the course of their security review. The petition quoted the officer as saying there was no problem in "coming out," and expressing his willingness to accompany the two soldiers to speak with the disciplinary superior and security officer. Since grown skeptical of MAD and

---

280 Ibid.
281 Ibid.

convinced the organization was acting in bad faith, both soldiers had considered it a trick to win their trust. Even if the MAD man were homosexual, they continued, it was both improper and objectionable to deploy one's own homosexuality in order to reach a desired goal.[282] In its reply to the commissioner, the BMVg clarified that the conversation had merely been conceived as a "well-intentioned comradely tip" on the part of the MAD employee, and was not at all meant as a "provocation under a false flag."[283] The officer was in fact homosexual, but "no strategy in the sense of a targeted deployment" could be derived on that basis. The BMVg fully dismissed any possibility of a "tactical calculation on the part of MAD [...] to feign the sexual orientation of a MAD employee in order to manipulate third-party behavior."[284] The author interviewed numerous former MAD officers for this study – one made a chance reference to the case sketched here, and turned out to be the MAD officer in question. Like the BMVg, he stressed that his revelation to the soldiers had not been "a trick at all"; he really was homosexual and had only set out "with good intentions to help as a comrade."[285]

Amid all the misunderstandings and the unfortunate twists and turns, the events leave the impression that the mistrust homosexuals felt toward the Bundeswehr and MAD in particular, a mistrust that had developed over decades of repression, did not simply vanish with the new millennium. Prior personal experience or bad memories shared by older comrades had taken root in soldiers' minds and continued to have an effect.

This impression was bolstered in conversation with another eyewitness – today a master sergeant. When filling out a security level 2 questionnaire in 2010, the man found himself faced with the question of whether to follow the requirements and state that he lived at home with his partner, or better not. Reading through the form gave the senior NCO doubts as to whether he could trust "a secret service with private, intimate information." He decided for himself in the negative.[286] His own concerns grew out of memories of the Kießling affair, which lay more than twenty-five years in the past but was (and is) still quite alive in the minds of many homosexual soldiers. To answer truthfully, the officer thought, would provide the secret service with the same information that had brought official ruin to a general in 1983.[287]

---

282 BArch, BW 1/532308: First Sergeant H., Complaint to the parliamentary commissioner for the armed forces, 15 September 2006.

283 Ibid., BMVg, Org 6 to the parliamentary commissioner, 30 November 2006.

284 Ibid.

285 Interview with Captain H., 12 June 2018.

286 Interview with Master Sergeant H., Berlin, 2 July 2018.

287 Ibid.

The comparison was off, however, if only because Kießling never gave MAD any information about a male partner, nor could there have been any in the absence of his being homosexual. At the time, however, the senior NCO was unaware of such details. He brought up the matter with a security officer in his unit in confidence, who had even less of an idea – Kießling's name meant nothing to him. This led the NCO to explain the 1983 scandal to the officer, or at least what he knew about it, though it was not merely the NCO's memories but worries about his future that were troubling him in 2010. At the time he assumed that from now on his security files would carry a "pink tab," i.e. a "homosexual mark." If the winds changed course in the future and intolerance toward gays returned, it would be possible to identify every soldier registered as homosexual simply by calling up the data. While the prospect gave the NCO a considerable "stomachache," he had nevertheless filled out the form truthfully as requested. As of 2018 MAD had not shown any interest in his homosexuality or life partner and his "stomachache" had also since subsided, as MAD "certainly had other, more important things to do."[288]

Soldiers' reluctance to communicate about their partners and thus their sexuality with their disciplinary superiors, personnel leadership and even when it was required with MAD, shows an understandable caution and concern about ultimately falling victim to hidden antipathy. Building trust takes time, and time alone can heal old wounds.

Wounds can reopen though, even after a long time has passed and when least expected. MAD does not forget all that quickly, as one older career lieutenant colonel was forced to discover. Throughout all his years in the service had kept his homosexual orientation a secret, never once naming his companion of many years during mandatory security reviews. It was not until fourteen years after the service relaxed its position that the officer finally resolved to declare his partner during an upcoming re-examination by MAD, a significant step out of the shadows taken with a confidence in the military's new position. The officer had not reckoned with MAD, however, whose employees now came calling to question him. It was not his homosexuality that was at issue, but the false statements he had provided in previous security reviews. By the standards of the service this gave cause for serious doubt as to the officer's reliability, resulting in the withdrawal of his security clearance.[289] The staff officer hired a lawyer, whose interventions at least succeeded in getting his client's security clearance reissued, albeit subject to conditions. Among them was one stipulating that he submit to semi-annual reliability assessments by

---

288 Ibid.
289 Interview with Lieutenant Colonel D. of Berlin, 12 February 2018, subsequently verified in conversation on 7 August 2019.

the security officer at his post, and that MAD receive the results. Making matters more interesting was the fact that the security officer was a staff sergeant directly subordinate to the officer himself. The conditions continued to vex the staff officer even after he retired in 2018, when he agreed to take part in a reservist exercise for the BMVg. He had no other choice but to reveal the background for his conditional security clearance and thus "let his pants down,"[290] as he put it, outing himself as homosexual eighteen years now after the Bundeswehr altered its position. The shadows of the past and the old restrictions continue(d) to make themselves known.

290 Ibid.

VI A New Millennium – a New Era

Subject Heading: Personnel management of homosexual soldiers [...] Homosexuality does not constitute a reason for restriction regarding assignment or status, nor therefore does it require special consideration as a criterion in eligibility.[1]

Despite great expectations for the two parties and especially new Defense Minister Rudolf Scharping, the change in government to a Green and SPD-led coalition in 1998 did not initially bring about any improvements in the collective lot of gays and lesbians. Late that year the Gay Federation in Germany (SVD) congratulated Scharping on his new appointment, tying its well wishes to hopes for a "prompt change in current personnel policy regarding sexual identity."[2] German gays and lesbians hoped in particular for effective measures against continued discrimination, including (and especially) in the Bundeswehr.[3] Scharping, however, stuck to the hardline position of before. Parliamentary State Secretary Walter Kolbow (also of the SPD) wrote back for the minister that it was "neither legally nor factually objectionable to avoid assigning homosexually oriented soldiers, be they gay or lesbian, as troop leaders or instructors as soon as their tendency is known."[4] While Kolbow drew on arguments that his institution had been advancing for decades, his answer did contain a novelty: For the first time, the secretary's response included mention of lesbian soldiers, making it clear that the same restrictions would apply for them. Both the Social Democrats and the Greens were known to set great stock on granting women equal rights in their communications, a principle that now meant restrictions against gay soldiers would hold equally for women. Otherwise, all the old arguments stood present and accounted for: Even if "growing tolerance [could be] registered" in society, "a general level of tolerance could not be assumed [among soldiers] in principle, especially among conscripts." Instead, the working premise should be that "one part of young conscript-bound soldiers themselves or their families would have no understanding for...employing homosexually-inclined superiors." Knowledge of a superior's homosexuality in the line of duty could "shake" his authority, which was, however, "indispensable" for operational

---

1 BMVg, PSZ III 1, 3 July 2000.
2 BArch, BW 2/38358: Gay Federation in Germany, State Chapter Berlin/Brandenburg, to Rudolf Scharping, 25 November 1998.
3 BArch, BW 2/38357: Gay Federation in Germany, Speaker Manfred Bruns to Rudolf Scharping, 4 December 1998.
4 BArch, BW 2/38358: BMVg, Parliamentary State Secretary Walter Kolbow to SVD, 26 February 1999, in what follows as well.

readiness. In brief, even with an SPD minister at the helm no change in course came down from Hardthöhe – except for the mention of lesbian soldiers.

The soldiers working at BASS made little secret of their disappointment in Scharping and the Red–Green coalition government. In an open letter to the minister, they wrote that the change in government and Scharping's post had "lit a spark of hope in many gay soldiers."[5] In July 1998 Scharping himself had still been saying after all that the SPD would actively implement "policies to dismantle discrimination and hardship for lesbians and gays." Instead, the letter continued, the BMVg was fighting "tooth and nail against gays receiving equal treatment in the Bundeswehr." The soldiers also went public with their complaints, as with a first sergeant fighting for acceptance into career service cited in *Focus* in August 1999. For the soldiers, Scharping had been the "greatest disappointment [...] Before the vote he announced he would do away with every form of discrimination against homosexuals in the event they won. Yet he barely had set foot in office when his tail went between his legs. His ministry wo not tolerate any more gays in career service. Scharping is an electoral fraud."

1. The European Dimension: The 1999 ECHR Verdict against the British Armed Forces

In fall 1999 more ominous news arrived for the BMVg and its minister, this time from Strasbourg. Like a dark cloud, a weeks-old decision at the European Court of Human Rights (ECHR) hung over the ministry – would the politicians, officials and officers simply be able to ignore it, or would lightning strike on Hardthöhe as well? Three years before, in 1996, the ECHR (incorrectly listed in BMVg papers at the time as the European Court of Justice, or ECJ) had taken up a series of complaints filed by British soldiers.[6] Now, in September 1999, the Strasbourg judges issued their verdict: The dishonorable discharge given in 1994 to four members of the British armed forces based on their homosexual orientation stood in violation of the European Convention on Human Rights, as did the "extraordinarily invasive" interrogation of their sexual lives prior to dismissal. In the view of the court,

---

5 All quotes from *Focus*, "Schwule in die Bundeswehr."
6 The court's ability to accept and rule on the petitions was a direct consequence of the European Convention on Human Rights' reform taking effect the previous year. Supplementary protocol 11 strengthened the convention's protective mechanism and marked the birth of the ECHR in its present form. From now on, individual complaints could be filed directly at Strasbourg, which in turn had sole jurisdiction over them. The reform led to a marked increase in petitions in the coming years.

the British armed forces' methods constituted an unjustifiable intrusion into the private sphere, as was protected by Article 8 of the Convention.[7]

The London government's argument relied on a report from the Homosexuality Policy Assessment Team (HPAT), which had foreseen issues for fighting power and operational readiness "in animosity on the part of heterosexuals." For its part, the court had doubts as to the validity of HPAT's findings; the authors were not outside experts but employees working at the Ministry of Defense and within the armed forces, nor had their survey of soldiers been anonymous but included names, and contained leading questions. Even working under the assumption that the survey results were accurate, the negative attitudes that had been registered among heterosexual soldiers toward homosexuals would not justify the harsh restrictions any more than "similarly negative attitudes toward people of another race, ethnicity or skin color."[8] London had also failed to present a convincing account of the damage it feared would be inflicted on troop morale and fighting power. To the Strasbourg court, this meant there existed "no weighty or convincing grounds" that might have justified the soldiers' dismissal. Accordingly, the intrusion into the soldiers' private lives over the course of their dismissal and interrogation was incompatible with Article 8 of the Convention.[9] The judges did not rule in favor of the plaintiffs' reinstatement into service, but they did find the discrimination grounds for financial compensation. The British government accepted the verdict and suspended current dismissal proceedings against homosexual soldiers pending further review of the ruling.[10]

The German Ministry of Defense pored over the Strasbourg decision with a magnifying glass; the day after the ruling State Secretary Peter Wichert promptly ordered his legal staff to draw up possible consequences for personnel leadership in the Bundeswehr. The legal department had an initial assessment ready two days later that sounded the all-clear for the BMVg's stance:

> 8. Overall environmental effects on interested circles notwithstanding, the decision does not demand any change in the going practices of the Bundeswehr [...]

---

7 ECHR ruling from 27 September 1999. See also BArch, BW 1/502107, no pagination: BMVg, R I 1 to State Secretary Wichert, 30 September 1999. For a contemporary legal assessment of the ruling see Schmidt-Radefeldt, "Streitkräfte und Homosexualität." *Bundeswehr aktuell*, a weekly newspaper put out by the BMVg also reported extensively on the ruling: *Bundeswehr aktuell*, 4 October 1999, 4.
8 ECHR ruling from 27 September 1999, compare to BArch, BW 1/502107: Report from Doctor of Law Armin Steinkamm, Bundeswehr University Munich, 25 January 2000, here 5–6, quote on 6.
9 Ibid.
10 BArch, BW 1/502107, no pagination: BMVg, R I 1 to State Secretary Wichert, 30 September 1999.

9. The issue of the disconcerting interrogations is irrelevant if only because Bundeswehr personnel leadership does not carry out similar sorts of inquisitions.

10. The ruling cannot be applied to the Bundeswehr anyway, since it does not make homo sexuality automatic and absolute grounds for dismissal, which is what the ruling hinges on. Moreover, the court only uses the argument of homosexuals' undue and prejudiced rejection by heterosexuals to justify its decision regarding the serious intrusion on the professional freedom of the persons concerned [...]

12. In light of the European Court of Justice's [sic] emphasis on finding the human rights violation to consist in the degree of interference in status law, First Lieutenant Stecher's prospects for success before the European Court of Justice, where he could appeal fol lowing a negative decision at the Federal Constitutional Court, should likely be assessed as low.

13. Court approval of Bundeswehr practices around accepting soldiers for career service, on the other hand, cannot be predicted as having the same prospects for success [...] To support these practices the court would ultimately have to follow the argumentation that it is not the established legal position of an existing employment relationship that is being interfered with, but rather the expansion and continuation of a legal relationship there is no basis to claim as one's own.[11]

The jurists concluded their report to the secretary by recommending that current practices be kept in place. The personnel department's evaluation came several days later; its employees agreed that the German practice of not assigning known homosexuals to positions as troop leaders or instructors was unaffected by the Strasbourg ruling. They did, however, view the "practical exclusion [of homosexual soldiers] from the status of career soldiers" as being in far greater "jeopardy" than the jurists.

> The ECJ [sic] has, however, also ruled as immaterial the principal argument used by the Bundeswehr in justifying its restrictive assignment practices [regarding homosexuals] as well as [their] practical exclusion from the status of career soldiers. [In the court's view] this is founded exclusively on prejudices within the heterosexual majority, and could be answered by appropriate regulations on conduct and discipline such as those the British Army used to counter racial prejudice and reservations toward women. Against this backdrop, in the event a concrete individual case were referred to the court, our practice of accepting soldiers for career service would be jeopardized at the very least.[12]

More than their counterparts in the legal department, the officials and jurists in the personnel department no longer thought it possible to bar homosexual soldiers generally from career service after the court ruling. One such case was already on its way through the courts after Lüneberg Administrative Court had ruled ini-

---

11 Ibid. See chapter 7 for greater detail on the British armed forces.
12 BArch, BW 1/502107, no pagination: BMVg, PSZ III 1 to department head at PSZ, 4 October 1999.

tially in favor of a first lieutenant; the case would be in Karlsruhe at the Federal Constitutional Court before too long, and potentially wind up in Strasbourg. If the internal conversation reveals anything, it is that the ECHR ruling brought significant worries to the BMVg. For some in the ministry, it gave even greater cause for concern than the upcoming decision in Karlsruhe on First Lieutenant Stecher's constitutional complaint regarding his removal as platoon commander.

The personnel department's paper mentioned another lawsuit filed by a gay officer that was pending at the administrative court in Berlin; First Lieutenant Schmid had filed the motion after he was transferred out of his post as platoon leader in a mechanized infantry battalion and had a firm offer of a military career withdrawn.[13] While this third lawsuit was just beginning to make its way through the courts in late 1999, the personnel department was already warning that here too, "the legal path might be exhausted" all the way up to Karlsruhe and Strasbourg.

It was not only in offices at Hardthöhe that the potential implications of the Strasbourg ruling on the Bundeswehr were reverberating but in the opposing camp as well, among advocates for gay soldiers, where hope for change was growing. Meanwhile the advisory panel on leadership development and civic education within the Bundeswehr tasked Armin Steinkamm, a professor of public law at Bundeswehr University Munich, with preparing a legal report as to what the Strasbourg court's ruling might portend for the current suits. The ECHR had dealt exclusively with the question of terminating an already existing service contract, leaving aside for the present matters of reinstatement and promotions within existing contracts. The court's predecessor, the former European Commission on Human Rights, had consistently ruled that there was no legal entitlement to be hired or taken on as a public employee. The commission had similarly denied all legal claims to promotion or particular assignments in the armed forces based on the European Convention on Human Rights. The ECHR ruling, by contrast, had now made it clear that "national armed forces would not be allowed to exist in a 'legal vacuum'" but fell subject to "the same convention standards as any other sovereign authority." Strasbourg also did not concede any "expanded leeway for assessment due to reasons of national security policy where intimate areas of private life are concerned."[14] The European court opinion took such a general tack that "the ECJ [could be expected] to perceive all forms of discrimination against homosexuals in public office that were justified by prejudice as irreconcilable with Article 8 [of the European Con-

---

13 BArch, BW 1/502107, no pagination: BMVg, PSZ III, 5 January 2000. See chapter 4 for a full account.
14 BArch, BW 1/502107: Report by Doctor of Law Armin Steinkamm, Bundeswehr University Munich, 25 January 2000, here 9–10.

vention on Human Rights]."[15] This principle was in turn brought to bear in the suits the Bundeswehr soldiers had filed, based as they were on the plaintiffs' exclusion from particular assignments. Steinkamm's report echoed a sentiment coming from other corners that "the postulates of democratic European society such as pluralism and tolerance [must not be allowed to] stop 'outside the barracks gate,' but find special relevance, here of all places."[16]

Steinkamm also set the Strasbourg decision within the context of Articles 3 and 33 (2) of Germany's Basic Law, the relevant domestic conventions for the soldiers' legal complaints regarding their rejection for career service and assignment restrictions. The latter statute states that "every German shall be equally eligible for any public office according to his aptitude, qualifications and professional achievement"; by Steinkamm's reading, the Strasbourg decision made barring homosexual soldiers from career or fixed-term service *solely* on the basis of their homosexual disposition incompatible with the article.[17] At the same time, not assigning or promoting homosexual soldiers as superiors or instructors solely on the basis of their homosexual disposition violated Article 3 of the Basic Law. The law professor closed out his report by appealing to "the Bundeswehr's interests in adopting appropriate measures, to avert legal developments in a timely fashion that ran contrary to the European community's efforts at fighting discrimination."[18]

Christina Schenk and the PDS faction had already submitted a minor inquiry on "Gays and the Bundeswehr" in October 1999, asking among other things whether the justifications given for the ECHR ruling against the British armed forces did not also apply to the Bundeswehr, and whether the federal government would revise its position toward homosexuals in the Bundeswehr in light of the verdict. The inquiry also wanted to know whether the government would withdraw the legal steps it had already taken against the decision from Lüneberg Administrative Court in favor of the staff sergeant, and take the plaintiff back as a troop instructor.[19] The defense ministry's answer, as might be expected for most opposition inquiries, was brief: The ruling against the British armed forces was not transferable "without further ado," since the Bundeswehr did not tie homosexuality to "any automatic

---

15 Ibid., 20.
16 Ibid., 11.
17 Ibid., 17.
18 Ibid., 21.
19 BArch, BW 2/38358: Deputy Christina Schenk and the PDS Faction, Minor inquiry to the federal government, 1 October 1999 (emended by hand to 5 October 1999), Bundestag printed material 14/1750.

and absolute grounds for dismissal." This made it pointless for the BMVg to answer any of the following questions.[20]

Even if the BMVg did not see it that way, at least outwardly, the ECHR ruling took on a highly-charged aspect when a Bundeswehr officer filed suit at the Federal Constitutional Court – would he end up in Strasbourg as well?

2. The Legal Dimension: A First Lieutenant's Complaint and Questions from Karlsruhe for the BMVg

> I hereby file a constitutional complaint against [...] the decision of the Federal Ministry of Defense [...] for violating the general right to personality (Art. 1 (1) in conjunction with 2 (1) of the Basic Law), the principle of equality before the law (Art. 3 of the Basic Law) and the right to equal access to public office according to aptitude, qualification and professional achievements (Art. 33 of the Basic Law).
> I submit the following motions:
> 1.) The decisions named are repealed.
> 2.) [...] The Federal Ministry of Defense is obligated to reassign the plaintiff to his former service post as platoon head in Squadron 3 of the air force base battalion.[21]

In a rationale the lieutenant's lawyer characterized as a "constitutional appraisal," she explained that the BMVg was relying on the "valid legal position" by which "an officer who admits his homosexuality will not be assigned a position in which he is directly responsible for leading, educating or instructing subordinate soldiers." Yet what exactly did "[admitting] his homosexuality" mean in this instance? "Would the plaintiff have had to dispute his homosexuality, contrary to the truth, and lie to his commander and squadron chief to be able to continue to serve as an instructor?"[22]

When the Federal Administrative Court referred to the fact that "homosexually inclined men were still broadly rejected by heterosexual men, potentially resulting in an unacceptable loss of authority," this was "a mere supposition in 'a vacuum'." The court deserved to be "fundamentally reproached for not concerning itself in the slightest with the concrete situation within the ranks."[23] In the lieutenant's case "everyone involved, subordinates and superiors alike, had spoken out in favor of

---

20 BArch, BW 2/38358: BMVg, Parliamentary State Secretary Walter Kolbow, 14 December 1999.
21 BArch, BW 1/502107, sheets 65–118: Constitutional appeal by First Lieutenant Stecher from 23 December 1998, here sheets 65–66.
22 Ibid., sheet 74.
23 Ibid., 77–78.

[his] staying on [...] in his post as a platoon leader."[24] Personnel measures such as those taken "would be absolutely unthinkable in any other public post today." The Bundeswehr laid claim to an "exceptional position [...] that appears more and more questionable in an age of increasing social acceptance of homosexuality."[25]

Looking back, it is remarkable that Lieutenant Stecher's appeal was the first to reach Karlsruhe. Every suit preceding it had ended at the latest before the Supreme Administrative Court. It remains anyhow a matter of speculation whether, and in any event highly unlikely that, constitutional judges would have ruled in favor of a gay soldier filing suit in the 1970s or 1980s. Societal values change over time, and courts require an even longer time to render this shift into rulings. A defeat at constitutional court in Karlsruhe in 1980 or 1990 would likely have done a disservice to the cause of homosexual soldiers; by 1999 the signs pointing toward a successful constitutional appeal were much more favorable. First, however, the lieutenant would have to cope with rejection: On 31 August 1999 the constitutional court (BVerfG) rejected an express appeal from the lieutenant's lawyer to return her client to his former post. There was no pressing need to act since the plaintiff had been given leave from service for a longer period to complete specialized training.[26]

In October 1999, the court ordered the federal government to draft a position paper concerning the main proceedings by 28 January 2000. The court president, Jutta Limbach, gave the government a general opportunity to comment, but also asked specifically after the "underlying factual basis of the contested decision by the Federal Ministry of Defense for assessing a possible disruption to service operations," and how the government would view the "constitutional objections raised against the backdrop of the Federal Constitutional Court's ruling history." The court was also interested in how other NATO members dealt with the matter: "Are homosexually disposed soldiers entrusted with direct supervision, education and training of subordinates in allied NATO forces?"[27]

In a draft response composed on State Secretary Wichert's letterhead, Legal Section II 2 opened by stressing that it held "the established legal tradition at the Federal Constitutional Court [...] to be correct." The same could not be said for the plaintiff's claim in the case at hand, namely that he had been transferred to a posi-

---

24 Ibid., 75.
25 Ibid., 79.
26 BVerfG, 17 August 1999, 2 BvR 2276/98.
27 BArch, BW 1/502107, no pagination: Bundesverfassungsgericht, Az 2 BvR 2276/98, from 6 October 1999.

tion on squadron staff that was ill-suited to his qualifications and expertise. On the contrary, he had been "handed a position that entailed responsibility."[28]

The legal section proposed by way of response to the court's first question that "determining a lack in fitness in the plaintiff for his former position [had not been] based on disruptions caused to service operations, issues with acceptance [n]or specific incidents that otherwise called his fitness into question." Rather, the decision had been based on the *"abstract danger* to his authority as a military leader and troop instructor coming from the revelation of his same-sex tendency in the meantime."[29]

To account for this anticipated loss in authority, the jurists cited the same lack of social acceptance they had trotted out continuously before administrative courts since the 1970s, even repeating it word for word: "There is moreover much to suggest that even today, behavioral patterns that would not draw any attention among heterosexuals might lead to gossip, suspicion, and rejection [when coming] from homosexually inclined superiors, potentially leading to a considerable loss of authority for the superior and thus a disruption to service operations."[30]

As proof the legal section pointed to a survey of conscripted soldiers this study has previously discussed at several points, conducted by the Bundeswehr Institute of Social Sciences in 1992. A mere one in three of the recruits found homosexuality "acceptable," while nearly one half considered it "negative" or "very negative." (Another 20% chose the further alternative of "unacceptable." It is worth noting here that the survey results showed a two-thirds majority rejecting homosexuality.)[31] "Assertions about the increasing acceptance of homosexuality [on the other hand] must be examined."[32] In raising the specter of "abstract dangers," the legal division introduced a new argument concerning deployment abroad. The lieutenant's platoon had not been deployed yet, and "it is precisely the particular trials of endurance [...] a small fighting group [would experience] [...] abroad under meager living conditions" that the unit had not been forced to undergo to date. Specifically, the ministry cited "confined living quarters" and the "highly restricted range of possibilities to engage in sexual activity." The section went farther still:

---

28 BArch, BW 1/502107, no pagination: BMVg, State Secretary, Draft response to the BVerfG, Az 2 BvR 2276/98, undated, drafted by R II 2, 21 December 1999. All quotes below from the same document. Original emphasis.
29 Ibid.
30 Ibid.
31 See chapter 4 for a full account of the study.
32 BArch, BW 1/502107, no pagination: BMVg, State Secretary, Draft response to the BVerfG, Az 2 BvR 2276/98, undated, drafted by R II 2, 21 December 1999. Quoted as well in what follows.

Even an accepted and well-respected superior can wind up in borderline situations where the formal principle of the chain of command on its own cannot provide a sufficient basis for him to prevail over his subordinates [...] Particularly with a view to the exceptional strains of [foreign] deployment, a homosexual officer's given track record of assessment and achievement during peacetime operations on national territory loses its validity in refuting the problems of acceptance outlined above.[33]

The regulations cited in response to the court president's second question about other NATO member states will be considered in closer detail in the following chapter. The third question, which contained Karlsruhe's request to assess the "constitutional objections raised against the backdrop of the Federal Constitutional Court's ruling history," prompted the BMVg jurists to reach deep into the desk drawer for previous administrative court verdicts, including one from 1975 analyzed closely above in chapter 4 – the case of Reserve Lieutenant Rainer Plein from Münster. It seems that in early 2000, the lawyers in Bonn could not actually think of much more than to underpin their argument than to draw and quote extensively from a twenty-five-year-old ruling.[34] They suggested the BMVg emphasize to the court the considerable discretion the military had in making assignments.

The federal government is of the opinion that acceptance of homosexual superiors in the armed forces has not yet reached a state as to preclude making *known* homosexuality the deciding factor in assignment decisions. On the one hand, a homosexual soldier has the option of living out his sexual orientation in private, outside of service. On the other, the armed forces' constitutional mandate and the existential danger to which soldiers are exposed if the military does not counteract disruptive factors are sufficient grounds to justify the requirement that soldiers accept certain restrictions on their official eligibility based on their personal sexual tendencies.[35]

When the draft was circulated for approval, the otherwise routine procedure drew significant protest from some corners as a result of differences between sections and departments. The back and forth reveals that by early 2000, the BMVg's restrictive stance was no longer shared by every official and officer at the ministry. Section III 5 at the Personnel, Social Services and Central Affairs Department did not sign off on the draft without also suggesting to leave out the 1975 verdict entirely. In its

---

33 Ibid.

34 Ruling at North Rhine-Westphalia Superior Administrative Court on 4 September 1975, Az I 4 1108/74. Incidentally, the jurists in Bonn wrongly attributed the ruling to Rhineland-Palatinate Superior Administrative Court in Koblenz.

35 BArch, BW 1/502107, no pagination: BMVg, State Secretary, Draft response to BVerfG, Az 2 BvR 2276/98, undated, drafted by R II 2 (original emphasis on "discovered").

place they proposed a more recent short-term SOWI study so as to "arrive at more sound argumentation."[36] The staff at another legal section also thought their colleagues might like to revise their remarks on the 1975 verdict; the arguments that had been drawn from the case no longer reflected current case law. "References to older jurisprudence might sooner weaken the position of the federal government during proceedings."[37] They also criticized the argument about the lieutenant's potential rejection while on deployment as inapplicable, since his subunit had not yet been deployed.[38] Section PSZ III 6 meanwhile declined to cosign the draft, clearly articulating to the legal department as to why: Karlsruhe would find the draft responses "unconvincing."[39] Drawing on the study from Britain's Homosexuality Policy Assessment Team was "simply counterproductive." The British had made out "animosity on the part of *hetero*sexuals, as well as attacks against homosexuals – their harassment and molestation as well as their ostracization and being shunned" to be problematic for fighting power and operational readiness. If this argument were presented before the court, it would logically follow that "soldiers from outside Europe, for example, might just as well be seen as 'disruptors' with implications for the Bundeswehr's operational readiness in the event that fellow soldiers did not accept them. 'That cannot be true!'"[40]

The personnel department also criticized the fact that the ministry's own legal staff was still relying on a survey from 1992. Assuming a continued lack of acceptance would have to be "substantiated again by facts." The letter from the common soldiers in the platoon led by the lieutenant spoke a different language than the survey. Nor did the section mince words about the draft response to Karlsruhe's third question. "In light of the more than 3,000 female soldiers [in the military] at present, it was not tenable" to argue before the Federal Constitutional Court in the year 2000 that "other soldiers entered consideration as sexual partners for homosexuals, unlike for heterosexuals," and that therefore the behavior of the former toward comrades or subordinates might be "influenced by sexual motives" – all while referring to a verdict from 1975 at Koblenz Superior Administrative Court.[41]

PSZ III 6 was not alone in its forceful criticism. Section III 1 at the Personnel, Social Services and Central Affairs Department shared "unreservedly" in the

---

36 BArch, BW 1/502107, no pagination: BMVg, PSZ III 5 to R II 2, 18 January 2000. Also in BArch, BW 2/38358.

37 BArch, BW 1/502107, no pagination: BMVg, R I 1, 18 January 2000. Also in BArch, BW 2/38358.

38 Ibid.

39 BArch, BW 1/502107, no pagination: BMVg, PSZ III 6 to R II 2, 11 January 2000 (emphasis in original). Also in BArch, BW 2/38358.

40 Ibid.

41 Ibid.

concerns that had been voiced, although it did not withhold its signature. "Since, however, we manifestly do not have any other or better arguments at our disposal, we have no choice but to rely on the reasons you have chosen in the hopes that the Federal Constitutional Court will work them into its decision in our favor."[42]

Why, if hopes did not seem to run all that high in the personnel department, did it nevertheless sign on to the draft and thus endorse it? The answer comes in the first few sentences of the department's response: "Personnel leadership must take its direction from the intentions of the public agencies as recently laid out in the new MFR draft proposal from Section FüS I 4 and maintain the current restrictive line," a goal which the legal department, too, "ultimately served."[43] The "public agencies" mentioned here were the military service branches, the army, air force and navy. MFR is the abbreviation for "Militärischer Führungsrat" or Military Command Council, in which the chiefs of the individual service branches and the chief of defense consult and reach internal agreement. The paper from the personnel division speaks to the pressure applied by military leadership on other departments in the BMVg, and likely political leadership, in order to maintain the stance, it had kept to date.

The draft response never reached Karlsruhe. BMVg sections were not the only ones that either refused to sign or reported serious concerns; both the Federal Ministry of the Interior and the Federal Ministry of Justice did the same.[44]

Karlsruhe insisted on an answer. The draft response was circulated to the ministries of the Interior, Justice and Family for cosignature; all three declined, holding the defense ministry's position to be "no longer appropriate to the times or constitution." The Federal Ministry for Family Affairs, Senior Citizens and Women and Youth, led by Social Democrat Christine Bergmann, further viewed the draft as violating the coalition agreement between the SPD and the Greens. When the BMVg section responsible for the draft asked again, all three ministries stated that "there was no room for convergence [even] at a working level."[45] The reply indicates that the ministries' respective positions had been coordinated by political leadership at the institutions; the Justice Ministry's negative response was later shown to have been decided in conjunction with the head of the ministry, Herta Däubler-Gmelin. Instead the "divergence of opinion" should be resolved at the "leadership level," i.e.

---

42 BArch, BW 1/502107, no pagination: BMVg, PSZ III 1 to R II 2, 18 January 2000. Also in BArch, BW 2/38358.
43 Ibid.
44 BArch, BW 2/38358: BMVg, FüS I 4, speaking notes for the chief of defense at a council meeting on 24 January 2000.
45 BArch, BW 1/502107, no pagination: BMVg, R II 2 to State Secretary Wichert, 20 January 2000.

between ministers.[46] All this led the government to request an extension until the end of March 2000. The clock had begun to tick; the BMVg had two months' time to answer Karlsruhe – or change its stance. The hour for a political decision from Minister of Defense Rudolf Scharping had come.

3. The Political Dimension

First Lieutenant Stecher's transfer also took on political dimensions in 1999. The fight drew a line through the governing coalition and the SPD itself, escalating amid public clashes between Scharping and his fellow cabinet ministers and in some cases those within his own party.

In May of that year, Minister for Economic Cooperation and Development Heidemarie Wieczorek-Zeul took up Stecher's cause with Scharping, asking the minister to explain his position on soldiers' sexual orientation and the case at hand.[47] Scharping thanked her for the "opportunity to correct a number of recent unfounded publications." "Most of the one-sided depictions in the media," Scharping wrote, "give the impression that the Bundeswehr is ignoring the repeal of homosexual behavior's criminality, and refusing to take account of societal developments. In truth, the Bundeswehr – more than many other armies – has continually been open to shifts in society."[48]

Yet "a different assessment had shown itself" among troop leaders and instructors, "namely that despite greater tolerance within society, a general level of acceptance cannot be [accepted as] the working premise." This explained the risk a superior ran of losing the confidence of and authority over troops in the event he or she were found to have a homosexual "inclination." Tolerance could not be ruled by decree. The personnel desk drafting the minister's response went on to paraphrase extensively from the familiar litany of administrative court rulings, echoing their emphasis on the unacceptable risks to operational readiness. They further cited Stecher's recent promotion to first lieutenant as evidence that it did not attach "moral opprobrium" to a soldier leading a same-sex lifestyle. Rather, the ministry

---

46 BArch, BW 2/38358: BMVg, FüS I 4, Speaking notes for the chief of defense for a council meeting on 24 January 2000.
47 BArch, BW 1/502107 and BW 2/38357: Federal minister for economic cooperation and development to the BMVg, 19 May 1999.
48 BArch, BW 2/38357: BMVg, Minister, to Federal Development Minister Wieczorek-Zeul, 24 June 1999, cited as well in the following. The draft response of the minister's letter by PSZ III 1 is available in BW 1/502107.

took its cues from "social reality and its implications for the mission of the armed forces."[49]

Yet the question of whether or not the Bundeswehr was attuned to "social reality" in 1999 was precisely what gave more and more people cause for serious doubt. The parliamentary state secretary at the justice ministry, Eckhart Pick (SPD), clearly thought this, refusing to sign on to a BMVg draft response to Deputy Christina Schenk (PDS). In doing so he referred explicitly to the coalition agreement, which stated that "Nobody [...] may [...] be discriminated against due to their sexual orientation as gay or lesbian."[50]

Federal Minister for the Environment Jürgen Trittin (Alliance 90/The Greens) also engaged on behalf of the forcibly transferred lieutenant.[51] Tritten did not leave the matter at a letter to a fellow cabinet member but took sides publicly, issuing a passionate reminder to Scharping that the governing coalition had made it its business "to protect minorities and help bring about their equality and participation in society."[52] Trittin labelled Scharping's contention that homosexual superiors were not sufficiently accepted in the Bundeswehr "out of touch,"[53] and he stressed that "simply giving into antigay sentiment and thus bolstering it" was clearly out of step with the Bundeswehr's principle of leadership development and civic education.[54] Fellow Green Angelika Beer took Scharping's ministry still more sharply to task, noting the coalition's express agreement that nobody should suffer disadvantages based on their sexual orientation. She was "appalled that this sort of discrimination should now simply carry on, even drawing on alleged reservations among the population to do so."[55] Beneath the headline "Red and Green Fight over Homosexual Soldiers," the *Frankfurter Rundschau* quoted Scharping's press spokesperson in June 1999 with the words "The Bundeswehr bases itself on laws, not coalition agreements."[56]

In Koblenz, the site of the largest Bundeswehr installation at the time, the *Rhein-Zeitung* ran a piece that announced a "Fight between Trittin and Scharping: Gay Officer Forcibly Transferred."[57] Scharping himself was cited in the piece; the

---

49 Ibid.

50 BArch, BW 2/38357: BMJ, Parliamentary State Secretary Eckhart Pick to the BMVg, Parliamentary State Secretary Brigitte Schulte, 15 June 1999.

51 Ibid., Federal Minister Deputy Jürgen Trittin to Defense Minister Scharping, 21 January 1999.

52 *Rhein-Zeitung*, "Streit zwischen Trittin und Scharping: Schwuler Offizier zwangsversetzt."

53 *Frankfurter Rundschau*, "Rot und Grün streiten über homosexuelle Bundeswehrsoldaten."

54 "Streit zwischen Trittin und Scharping: Schwuler Offizier zwangsversetzt."

55 "Rot und Grün streiten über homosexuelle Bundeswehrsoldaten."

56 Ibid.

57 "Streit zwischen Trittin und Scharping: Schwuler Offizier zwangsversetzt." Cited as well in what follows.

only thing that occurred to him was to repeat the arguments that had seemingly been carved in stone since the 1970s. "Homosexuality raises considerable doubts regarding fitness [to become a superior], and prevents assignment to positions tied to leading, educating and instructing soldiers." The Bundeswehr had "opened itself to societal change more than many other armies." It would, however, be "missing the point of social realities to want to ascribe a leading role to the armed forces where serious conflicts with the values of many citizens loom."

In its own piece entitled "Homosexual Soldiers: Sager criticizes Scharping," *Die Welt* reported that Krista Sager, a Green party member and senator for equality in Hamburg had also come out against discrimination against homosexual soldiers.[58] Society's acceptance of gays in the military, including those in positions of leadership, had grown considerably.

Yet it was not only from the Greens that Scharping found himself under increasing pressure throughout 1999 – members of his own party applied it too:

> The SPD's best critics still come from within the SPD itself. So it was that the chairman of Schuwsos [the LGBT wing of the SPD] for Lower Saxony, Achim Schipporeit, called on the chancellor to put his foot down [...] If he remained silent, he would be "partly to blame for violating the human dignity of gay soldiers." In Schipporeit's words, "How much longer will the Red–Green coalition let Scharping lead it around by the nose on the matter?"[59]

In an interview for this study, the parliamentary state secretary for the BMVg at the time, Brigitte Schulte (SPD), recalled the increasing pressure coming from within and outside of the SPD: "There was an arrangement in the [Red–Green] coalition agreement to end discrimination against homosexuals across the board." Schulte herself operated under the assumption that the subject had not been broached in the SPD faction, as "there would have been a fuss otherwise."[60] There turned out to be a fuss within the SPD faction after all. The second parliamentary state secretary, Walter Kolbow, was forced to deal with the anger, "defending himself against a barrage of recriminations from the entire faction."[61]

In a *FAZ* article from September 1999, a defense ministry spokesperson found himself repeating his ministry's position yet again beneath the headline "Homosexuals are not allowed to instruct." Homosexuality still was not "well received by society at large, and thus was not accepted by all the soldiers," which meant a loss

---

58 "'Homosexuelle Soldaten'."
59 *Rosa Rauschen*, "Schwule bei der Bundeswehr."
60 Interview with retired Parliamentary State Secretary Brigitte Schulte, Wachtberg, 16 April 2019.
61 BArch, BW 2/38357: BMVg, FüS I 4, 11 November 1999, referring to a 9 November 1999 session of the SPD parliamentary faction's working group on security policy.

in authority over troops had to be expected. That loss was unacceptable, however, "since the Bundeswehr's defense mandate demands unconditional trust in superiors and unimpeded operational readiness." Soldiers could not simply be told to accept homosexuality "by decree."[62]

In October 1999, gay and lesbian soldiers received renewed support from the FDP in the form of a motion introduced by the faction: "The German Bundestag calls on the federal government to guarantee that soldiers are not discriminated against based on their sexual orientation within the working operations of the Federal Ministry of Defense."[63] When Minister Scharping and State Secretary Wichert explained that homosexuality "raised lasting doubts about soldiers' suitability for the task of leadership as their authority might suffer" the Liberals countered that the armed forces had since allowed women to join the ranks:

> It has long been self-evident that female and male superiors alike will have subordinates of the opposite sex. As such, the Federal Ministry of Defense's call for homosexual and heterosexual superiors to receive different treatment can only be the result of the prejudice-riddled notion that homosexual superiors might sooner tend to give into the possibility of sexually motivated desires within the official line of duty than would be the case with the majority of superiors who are heterosexually inclined. Yet there is no set of experiences that would justify such an assumption. It may be accurate to say that revelation of a superior's homosexuality may initially lead to inappropriate reactions that are the consequence of young soldiers' being insufficiently educated. In that case, however, it falls to the superiors on site to provide young people with the right kind of information and help them learn how to deal with homosexuality. The Bundeswehr cannot shrink back in the presence of ready discrimination, much less confirm and strengthen it through conscious discrimination of its own. The German Bundestag fully commits itself to demanding a Bundeswehr free from discrimination. No member of the Bundeswehr may be discriminated against in any way on the basis of race, religion, sex, the national affiliation of his countrymen or sexual orientation. On the contrary, it is the task of the Bundeswehr to fight against prejudices that may exist among its members when necessary and take on an informative role.[64]

The FDP motion was taken up by the full Bundestag in March 2000, where the matter was referred to the Defense Committee.[65] Scharping viewed the motion and

---

62 *Frankfurter Allgemeine Zeitung*, "Homosexueller darf nicht ausbilden."
63 German Bundestag, 14th legislative period, Document 14/1870. Motion by Deputies Hildebrecht Braun (Augsburg), Günter Nolting, Jörg van Essen, other deputies and the FDP faction: "Bekämpfung jeder Art von Diskriminierung in der Bundeswehr."
64 Ibid.
65 German Bundestag, 14th legislative period, typed transcript of the 95 Session on 23 March 2000, plenary transcript 14/95, 8844–45.

its redirection to committee as "a good opportunity to speak calmly with each other about these issues, and not try to resolve them based on some form of agitation."[66]

Press reports also credited the SPD Minister of Defense with commissioning a study from the ultra-conservative group "Christians on the Offensive" and its associated "Institute for Youth and Society" in Reichelsheim that had sought to cast homosexuals as unfit to lead or instruct Bundeswehr troops. The alleged commission caused a significant stir in the press in January 2000; *taz* spoke of "dubious numbers from the 1950s," with one article in the paper entitled "Scharping's Bundeswehr Study: Gays are sick."[67] The *Berliner Zeitung* meanwhile reported "Gays demand apology from Scharping,"[68] while Bundestag deputy Volker Beck (Alliance 90/The Greens) accused Scharping's ministry of circulating "homophobic pamphlets."[69] According to the taz report, the study still proceeded to understand homosexuality as an illness even though same-sex desire was no longer seen as requiring treatment. "Still, there was evidently no desire for close analysis at Rudolf Scharping's ministry. Given such advice, it is small wonder that the Federal Ministry of Defense continues to look to prevent gays from entering the military," the paper concluded.[70]

What was the study under discussion? Had it in fact been commissioned by the BMVg, even directly by the minister himself? The truth proved to be quite different than what the headlines suggested. As it turned out, the "Institute for Youth and Society" in Reichelsheim had sent the report to the BMVg on its own initiative in September 1999, where it was shelved by the press and information staff. When an editor from *MAX* magazine sent in an inquiry to the BMVg about homosexual soldiers in late December 1999, an official on the press and information staff had responded briefly by fax, summarizing the ministry's stated position and including the Reichelsheim study, expressly (as was later explained) to show how outside forces sought to influence the ministry. The last page of the letter however included a typed closing phrase from the official and her signature – directly beneath the Reichelsheim study. The editor at *MAX* used it in turn to present the otherwise obscure study as the BMVg's own, securing a media sensation in the process.

---

66 Ibid.

67 Lange, "Scharpings Bundeswehr-Studie."

68 "Schwule fordern Entschuldigung von Scharping," available as a copy in BArch, BW 1/582743.

69 The BMVg press review likely falsely attributed the article "Defamation of homosexuals," which was based on an AP news report, to the 28 January 2000 edition of the *Berliner Morgenpost* (a copy is available in BArch, BW 1/582743). *taz* further quoted Beck as saying it would be a "grave insult" if a study for the Ministry of Defense "vilified" the lifestyles of gay and lesbian citizens "as an illness and thus an illegitimate, less-worthy form of life." Lange, "Scharpings Bundeswehr-Studie."

70 Ibid.

Inquires from *Spiegel* and other editorial boards followed shortly after *MAX* came out with its piece "Pink Army Faction."[71] The BMVg clarified the misunderstanding and was able to put out the fire, at least temporarily;[72] a week later, the flame rekindled. On 26 January 2000 the tabloid *B.Z.* made its report, followed the next day by taz and other newspapers. The press and information staff now had its hands full trying to get the story under wraps. On 28 January *Berliner Morgenpost* reported "Homophobic study not from the Bundeswehr"[73]; *taz* followed with a correction the day after.[74] Independently of the subject at hand, the incident demonstrates the importance of exercising particular care and caution in dealing with the press. In the hands of a media outlet with its own interests, a matter as simple as a wrongly placed signature can provide cause for scandal.

4. The Internal Military Dimension: "The Service Branches' Position on Homosexuality Rock Solid"

Scharping had not wanted to take charge of any federal ministry in 1998, least of all defense.[75] Visibly a stranger to the task, the new minister had next to no experience with the Bundeswehr, relying instead on the state secretaries (especially on the seasoned Peter Wichert, who had been with the BMVg since 1989) and military leadership's counsel. Scharping led the ministry and armed forces under the principle "the apparatus must be trusted in," as one contemporary involved at ministry leadership level stressed. The interviewee, who wished to remain anonymous, recalled that similarly to Helmut Schmidt the new minister had first wanted to "tune into the Bundeswehr to find out what the hot topics were for soldiers, what was on their minds."[76]

In the course of speaking with soldiers the subject of homosexuality had not come up once.[77] Another eyewitness, a former officer on staff at the Center for Leadership Development and Civic Education in Koblenz, was still able to recall why. One of the roundtable discussions had been intended to address the question of minorities; the BMVg had not initially planned on it but the eyewitness had been

---

71 Baum, "Rosa Armee Fraktion."
72 BArch, BW 2/38358: BMVg, Press/Information Staff, 21 January 2000.
73 "'Schwulenfeindliche Studie' nicht von der Bundeswehr." A copy is available in BArch, BW 1/582743.
74 *taz*, "correction," 29 January 2000. A copy is available in BArch, BW 1/582743.
75 Letter from retired Parliamentary State Secretary Brigitte Schulte to the author, 2 June 2019.
76 Interview by telephone (anonymized), 13 May 2019.
77 Ibid.

able to convince the minister of the need for an additional session on the topic. As planned, the conversation was meant to invite homosexual soldiers, but the BMVg struck it – and with it the topic in general – from the ministerial conversation. Thus in early 1999 Scharping met with Muslim, Jewish and Russian–German soldiers; a Sikh had even been in attendance. To the interviewee's mind, no decision-maker at the BMVg had wanted to raise the thorny issue of homosexual soldiers in the minister's presence. "And this when from a purely statistical perspective, homosexuals far and away made up the largest group of minorities in the armed forces with a normal distribution of five to ten percent of the population, much larger than Muslims, Jews, Russian–Germans and [as of 1999] women combined."[78]

The eyewitness, who worked directly within Scharping's sphere, recalled the minister himself as having "no fears about broaching the subject, but not seeing any urgent need to act either."[79] The "topic had bobbed along" at the ministry, "landing from time to time on the [minister's] desk in the form of ongoing proceedings, especially legal complaints." While homosexual soldiers presented a "serious topic in certain circles," those circles were "tightly constricted."[80] In obvious contrast to the soldiers who were themselves affected, the public at large did not view homosexuality as a decisive topic for the Bundeswehr. SPD member Brigitte Schulte, who entered the ministry with Scharping as a parliamentary state secretary, recalled that

> the case of First Lieutenant Stecher must have been presented to him [Scharping] by State Secretary Dr. Wichert and the general who was still leading the personnel department after [Scharping] took office in 1998–99. They sought to obtain the most agreeable answer from the new minister, who had to familiarize himself with the enormous set of responsibilities involved in defense in a fast-track procedure. That was unfair and ill-advised![81]

When she realized that a lieutenant was going to be dismissed because he was homosexual, Schulte's immediate reaction had been that "It was simply impossible! The time for that is truly past."[82] "That's how we've always done it," had been State Secretary Wichert's response. Personnel matters fell under his purview. Schulte recalled she had been "left completely speechless that this was still going on in the Bundeswehr in the year 1999. I would have thought that the liberal coalition had cleared up the matter. It was something we [SPD defense politicians] should have

---

78 Interview with Reserve Lieutenant Colonel Joachim Meier of Karlsruhe, 16 July 2018.
79 Interview by telephone (anonymized), 13 May 2019.
80 Ibid.
81 Letter from retired Parliamentary State Secretary Brigitte Schulte to the author, 2 June 2019.
82 Interview with retired Parliamentary State Secretary Brigitte Schulte, Wachtberg, 16 April 2019.

done better at earlier on."[83] And still, Scharping let more than a year slip by before he began to consider revising the ministry's position.

Close colleagues of the minister recalled that homosexuality had not been the "dominating topic" at the BMVg, "not by a long shot." Nor had Scharping viewed it as a key topic; it "was not part of the priorities on his agenda when he arrived at the ministry." They explained Scharping's hesitation in terms of his conviction that things usually had to ripen until they were ready for decision. From that perspective the ongoing suits had "been quite helpful," putting the BMVg under pressure to decide specifically whether to "clear up the matter or let the suits continue."[84] Peter Wichert recalled something very similar. Minister Scharping himself had been quiet on the subject, thinking "Why change the regulations when there's nothing to regulate?" Scharping and he (Wichert) had both had pursued the maxim "Let it be!" and sought to keep the practice of "tacit acceptance." Yet "tacit acceptance" was no longer enough for those who were directly impacted, and who by now had a strong lobby in politics and the media, allowing them to build up "tremendous social pressure."[85]

A good year after taking office Scharping made a first approach on the subject of homosexuality, reminding colleagues during a council meeting on 22 December 1999 that he had been tasked with "developing a position on the subject of homosexuality for the armed forces and briefing on it."[86] (The council, whose meeting was archived internally, was composed of the institution's top members – the minister [abbreviated to BM from *Bundesminister* in the archives], the state secretaries and the chief of defense.[87]) The minister insisted on an update by January 2000; he did not consider new internal studies or surveys necessary.[88]

Military leadership responded with a call for a new empirical study about soldiers' attitudes toward homosexuality. Presumably this was a play for time; soldiers learn the combat style of delay during tactical training, when one's own forces either are not sufficient for linear defense or the opponent is too powerful. Evidently, the generals in Hardthöhe were now employing a similar tactic to hold up the show of political will.

---

83 Ibid.

84 Interview by telephone (anonymized), 13 May 2019.

85 Interview with retired State Secretary Peter Wichert, Bad Münstereifel, 10 April 2019.

86 BArch, BW 2/38358: BMVg, deputy chief of defense, notes from 23 December 1999 concerning the 22 December 1999 council session.

87 BArch, BW 2/21537, no pagination: BMVg leadership council, April 1983.

88 BArch, BW 2/38358: BMVg, deputy chief of defense, notes from 23 December 1999 concerning the 22 December 1999 council session.

Whether or not such a study and new survey of soldiers should be commissioned had been a perennial source of debate between BMVg sections in the late 1990s. Advocates for change were the first to issue demands for a new survey; the last empirical study had been conducted in 1992 and they expected data from the Bundeswehr to reflect greater tolerance in light of the societal changes that had since occurred. The chiefs of the joint staff and the individual service branches, meanwhile, dismissed a new survey as unnecessary to date, loathe as they were for an uncomfortable topic to come to the fore. In 1999 the staff department head at FüS I postponed a decision about the study until the Federal Constitutional Court had decided on First Lieutenant Stecher's case.[89] By January 2000, the tables had turned: Now it was the generals who were fighting for a new study, while the faction seeking change within institutional leadership no longer viewed it as necessary.

On 6 January 2000 FüS I 4 invited representatives from a total of ten branches of the service staffs, the personnel department and the legal department to a coordinating session in advance of a Chief of Staff Council (MFR) meeting fixed for 19 January.[90] "Homosexuality in the Armed Forces" was listed as the third point on the agenda, with the stated goal of reaching a "common state of knowledge" regarding homosexuals in roles of authority and determining whether there was room for maneuver in the current position. To come straight to the point, the answer was there was none; the army, air force and navy all stonewalled: "The [service branches'] adherence to the current position does not allow for a change in stance on homosexuality within the armed forces at present."[91] A personnel section had briefly summarized the possibilities in advance of the coordinating session "without prejudice to the outcome": Sharpening restrictions would give "cause for legal concern" and was "impossible to implement politically."[92] Lifting current restrictions depended on the "public agencies," i.e. the armed forces changing their position. There was no leeway for "practicable interim solutions," which meant it would have to be clarified with service branch representatives at the meeting whether their leadership wanted to "maintain or lift the restrictions." The "favorable jurisprudence from the courts" to date did not place the ministry under any pressure to stick to its practices. The personnel section also warned that if the

---

89 BArch, BW 1/502107, no pagination: BMVg, PSZ III 1, 5 January 2000.

90 The Military Command Council "served to formulate overall military demands and objectives." Chaired by the chief of defense, the council was made up of the three chiefs of the services and the surgeon general, along with the deputy chief of defense.

91 BArch, BW 2/38358: BMVg, FüS I 4 to the chief of defense, 14 January 2000. Also available as a draft in BArch, BW 1/502107.

92 BArch, BW 1/502107, no pagination: BMVg, PSZ III 1, 5 January 2000. Also available in BArch, BW 2/38358.

Federal Constitutional Court ruled the assignment policy unconstitutional, it would make it untenable to continue rejecting homosexual soldiers for career service.[93]

A further comment from Section FüS I 1 in February 2000 conveys the ministry's awareness of the problem with remarkable clarity: "The Bundeswehr cannot prove homosexual soldiers' lack of fitness for assignment as direct superiors in the troops either generally or in individual cases. Rather, the point of departure for the position is the assumption that a like superior would be rejected by their subordinates and considerable segments of the population."[94] This led the section to draw clear conclusions: "A supreme court ruling against the Bundeswehr would force it to abandon its previous position. A ruling against assignment decisions would also take down our position on [not] accepting soldiers for career service."[95]

FüS I 4 made an effort to garner support among the other sections and departments involved in the discussion to draw the necessary consequences, but it was not able to convince them. The coordinating session opened in typical fashion for military decision-making, with a situational report. The BMVg's stance was well-known to all: "not an illness, not a breach of service," but restrictions on assignment and status. "The position regarding homosexual superiors is based on anticipated problems with acceptance and as a result authority, touching on operational readiness."[96] This position was politically disputed, coming under "tremendous" criticism from deputies within Alliance 90/The Greens and the SPD (as well as the SPD working group on security policy), backed by the approval of Parliamentary State Secretary Schulte. "The federal minister's task must be seen against this backdrop; he wants a tenable position, i.e. one that the Bundeswehr also accepts." Using the diction typical of a military situational assessment, FüS I 4 saw "three possibilities for acting: Maintain current position until forced to change if necessary by court ruling; abandon current position; maintain current position while at the same time pursuing an informational and educational campaign in the direction of greater tolerance."[97]

All those present shared the opinion that the cases involving First Lieutenant Stecher, First Lieutenant Schmid and another staff sergeant would cause a "considerable stir in public"; all three soldiers were in good standing.[98] "Their 'unsuit-

---

93 Ibid.

94 BArch, BW 2/38358: BMVg, FüS I 4 to the chief of defense, 24 February 2000.

95 Ibid., BMVg, FüS I 4 to the chief of defense, 17 February 2000. In draft form from 20 January with slightly different wording.

96 BArch, BW 2/38358: BMVg, FüS I 4, introductory statement on 6 January 2000.

97 Ibid.

98 BArch, BW 2/38358: BMVg, FüS I 4 to the chief of defense, 14 January 2000, in what follows as well. Also available in draft form in BArch, BW 1/502107.

ability' for assignment to leadership roles arose exclusively from an expectation of their potential rejection by subordinates and assumed limitations on operational readiness, for which, however, there is no proof in the specific cases." Speaking behind closed doors, they openly assessed the BMVg's chances of prevailing over Lieutenant Stecher before the Federal Constitutional Court as "doubtful." A decision from the high court would "in any event force the previous position to be abandoned." Those gathered also showed open self-criticism in their assessment that, in Stecher's case, a ruling against the BMVg would also bring an end to its stance on (not) accepting homosexual soldiers for career service.

While there was consensus regarding the situation at hand, no single proposal for a way out of the anticipated dilemma followed. FüS I 4 sought for one in vain, proposing a shift in the restrictive position from general exclusion to case-by-case inspection. "Non-assignment or transfer would then only occur in 'conspicuous cases' under the same criteria as with heterosexual soldiers."[99] The section had already introduced individual case decisions as a path forward in September 1994, in a letter to a staff surgeon who later successfully petitioned for acceptance into career service. Yet in practice nothing changed; due consideration of the circumstances at hand had even been explicitly rejected as a policy. The same was seen in January 2000:

> The other sections pointed out that this essentially meant abandoning the current position. The representatives from the service branches were not ready to do so. The branches operate under the assumption that significant segments of society, as well as soldiers in the Bundeswehr, would reject a personal encounter with homosexuality [...] They argue specifically that the mere presence of a risk/supposition of a restriction on assignment or cause for worry justifies the current stance.[100]

The assessment bordered on resignation as it continued: "The lack of fitness that the service branches assume cannot be substantiated, either generally or in specific instances."[101] Society's increased acceptance of homosexuals, cited by advocates for changing the regulations, was "doubted by those responsible for operational readiness [the armed forces]." "The Minister's (implicit) wish for the armed forces to disengage from the current position cannot be reconciled with such a view." The armed forces would "potentially" be open to new regulation only if new studies

---

99 Ibid.

100 BArch, BW 1/502107, BMVg, FüS I 4, draft of the nearly identical presentation to the chief of defense on 14 January 2000 (the presentation is available in BArch, BW 2/38338).

101 BArch, BW 2/38358: BMVg, FüS I 4 to the chief of defense, 14 January 2000. Also cited in what follows; a draft is available in BArch, BW 1/502107, 688.

and surveys registered a change in soldiers' stance on the matter. The minister, however, did not view new studies or surveys as necessary, leading FüS I 4 to conclude in summary that "the [service branches'] adherence to the current position does not allow a change in stance on homosexuality within the armed forces at present." "The expected path through the courts will make a recurring problem of the topic, and places the armed forces under constant pressure to justify itself." The BMVg ran the risk of its position "holding no legal standing," and the Bundeswehr exposed itself to the "accusation of taking social developments into account only under tremendous pressure."[102]

The true scope of the dilemma unfurled itself in a proposal from the office of the chief of defense that the MFR maintain its current position, leaving any changes in regulation to first come about "either as a consequence of investigative results [a study or survey], ministerial orders or a decision at the supreme court." The final version of the document also proposed that the chief of defense "conduct an empirical investigation into the acceptance of homosexual instructors/superiors."[103] As noted before, this was the idea that the military chiefs of staff finally struck upon in their fight to delay the matter. After the 6 January meeting, the head of FüS I 4 noted with resignation that the "[service branches'] position on homosexuality in my meeting was rock solid: Maintain current policy."[104]

The notes prepared for the chief of defense in advance of the MFR meeting on 19 January still had to make the normal ministerial rounds for cosignature. One section in the personnel department suggested articulating more clearly that calls by FüS I 4 for case-by-case inspections did not constitute an "interim solution" but a "complete rejection of the current position."[105] The section in charge of key personnel issues at Army joint staff signed the document, albeit contingent on essential notes and revisions being taken into account. On the one hand, the Army questioned the pessimism regarding the BMVg's chances of success in the ongoing suit, as well as whether the results of a new study or survey would "necessarily lead to a readiness to change."[106] Most important, however, was the note to strike the FüS I 4's suggestions without any replacement, presumably in the unspoken hope that no suggestions would mean no changes. Section R II 2 also signed, thought it emphasized in doing so that in its view "a readiness to comply with the minister's orders

---

102 Ibid.

103 Ibid.

104 Ibid., BMVg, FüS I 4, 6 January 2000.

105 BArch, BW 1/502107, no pagination: BMVg, PSZ III 1 to FüS I 4, 13 January 2000.

106 Ibid., BMVg, FüH 1 to FüS I 4, 11 January 2000.

does not have to be mentioned. That is to be taken for granted. The same holds for the obligation to implement court rulings."[107]

At the Military Command Council meeting, the army, air force and navy chiefs all backed the chief of defense in his insistence on maintaining the current line. Change was possible only "if forced by court decision" or on orders from the minister.[108] Thus reinforced, Chief of Defense General Hans Peter von Kirchbach went into a council session on 24 January. FüS I 4 had given him an idea ahead of time of the positions he could expect from the other participants: Minister Scharping was aware of the armed forces' stance but expected a "departure from [their] previous position"; the insistence of the chief of defense was not likely to meet Scharping's expectations.[109] State Secretary Schulte was "vehemently opposed to the Bundeswehr position" and could potentially push for the military to rapidly abandon its current practices. State Secretary Kolbow, also of the SPD, was a supporter of the Bundeswehr's position in his party, for whom "a matter of this sort could not be solved by going against the attitude within the armed forces." Kolbow was under "heavy criticism" within his party. The permanent state secretary Peter Wichert supported the armed forces; the stance of the other participants was unknown to FüS I 4.[110]

In speaking with the author of this study, Wichert repeatedly stressed that the antipathy he, the chief of defense and the service branch chiefs had shown toward fully opening the armed forces to homosexuals had not been guided by homophobia but constantly out of concern for the troops. He had "never once met a chief of defense, service branch chief or general who struck him as homophobic."[111] "Our, and my own concern," Wichert recalled in retrospect, had been that if the position on homosexuality were changed, openly homosexual officers or NCOs might then draw attention through cases involving sexual harassment or assault. It would have brought significant damage to the Bundeswehr as an institution had this occurred, or even been linked to the armed forces' acceptance of outwardly gay soldiers. It had been his and military leadership's steady aim to "protect the institution of the Bundeswehr from harm in the event it came to incidents like that."[112]

---

107 Ibid., BMVg, R II 2 to FüS I 4 and others, undated.
108 BArch, BW 2/38358: BMVg, FüS I 4, recommended language for MFR meeting on 19 January 2000, TOP 3.
109 Ibid., BMVg, FüS I 4, speaking notes for the chief of defense for the council session on 24 January 2000.
110 Ibid.
111 Interview with retired State Secretary Peter Wichert, Bad Münstereifel, 10 April 2019.
112 Ibid.

While Scharping did not let the chiefs deter him from the changes he sought, the minister's well-known caution and sense of balance brought him to hesitate before a decision against armed forces' leadership, and he continued to search for a way to bring the generals on board and involve them. In this spirit he invited them to a retreat in late February 2000 with the sole set topic of "Assigning homosexual soldiers leadership, educational and instructional roles."[113] Chief of Defense General von Kirchbach arrived at the retreat bearing the by-now familiar position of considering the "vote of the chiefs responsible for operational readiness in their service branch" to hold "weight." In the course of debate, he returned to the idea of commissioning an empirical study as a path out of the entrenched positions, "so that we no longer have to proceed based solely on assumptions."[114] In this case, too, the written record tallies with the memories of those involved at the time. Former State Secretary Wichert recalled it simply as a matter of the respect Kirchbach held as the chief of defense for the official responsibilities each service branch chief bore toward their respective branch.[115]

As the new millennium approached, back and forth the BMVg went about whether a new survey regarding soldiers' tolerance of homosexuality made sense or would be useful for the ministry's own position. While political leadership ultimately decided against it, the Bundeswehr Institute of Social Sciences proceeded to act in the meantime. It was not the soldiers who were asked their opinion, however, but the general population, within the context of the institute's annual general survey. In December 1999, researchers consulted around 2,700 people over the age of 16 as to their attitudes toward homosexuality in general, and homosexuality in the armed forces in particular. The numbers that came back showed an ideal distribution as might be found in a textbook: exactly one quarter showed a positive attitude, exactly one quarter had a negative attitude; the remaining half gave "differentiated" answers.[116] These results hardly let the BMVg make out sensible arguments for deciding the matter at hand. The Bundeswehr sociologists had the foresight to ask for respondents' age, and the ministry itself was primarily interested in acceptance among younger people – the age-range containing those required to

---

113 BArch, BW 2/38358: BMVg, FüS I 4, speaking notes for the chief of defense for retreat with the federal minister of defense on 25 February 2000.

114 Ibid.

115 Interview with retired State Secretary Peter Wichert, Bad Münstereifel, 10 April 2019.

116 BArch, BW 2/38358: Bundeswehr Institute of Social Sciences (SOWI), Report No. 2/2000: "Einstellungsmuster gegenüber Homosexuellen in der deutschen Bevölkerung," March 2000, here p. 3. A copy is available in BW 1/502107, SOWI to BMVg, 3 July 2000.

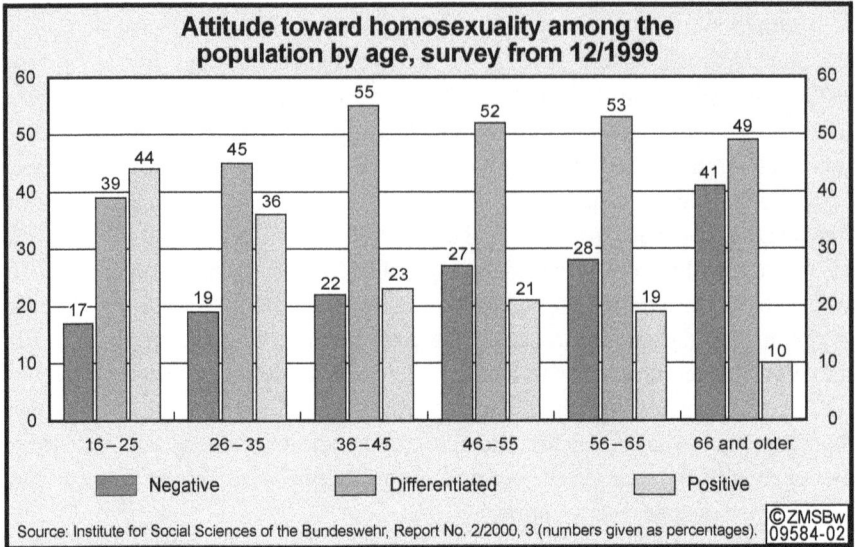

Attitude toward homosexuality among the population by age, survey from 12/1999

16–25: Negative 17, Differentiated 39, Positive 44
26–35: Negative 19, Differentiated 45, Positive 36
36–45: Negative 22, Differentiated 55, Positive 23
46–55: Negative 27, Differentiated 52, Positive 21
56–65: Negative 28, Differentiated 53, Positive 19
66 and older: Negative 41, Differentiated 49, Positive 10

Legend: Negative, Differentiated, Positive

Source: Institute for Social Sciences of the Bundeswehr, Report No. 2/2000, 3 (numbers given as percentages). ©ZMSBw 09584-02

perform military service and the pool of potential fixed-term soldiers. And it was in fact age that proved the decisive factor.[117]

Younger people, the key group for the Bundeswehr, showed unmistakably greater tolerance toward gays and lesbians, with acceptance predominating up to the age of forty-five. It was only within the age groups of forty-six and over that negative attitudes took over, increasing with age. Among sixteen to twenty-five-year-olds – young soldiers, conscripts and possible fixed-term soldiers from the Bundeswehr perspective – 44 percent registered a positive attitude toward gays and lesbians, with just 17 percent holding a negative opinion. Twenty-six to thirty-five-year-olds, making up the lion's share of active fixed-term and career soldiers, showed 36 percent holding a positive attitude of gays and lesbians and 19 percent negative. This was telling data for the decision the ministry was facing; the relevant groups for active service or as potential soldiers were clearly favorable toward homosexuals.

While it is important to recall that it was not soldiers who were being surveyed in this case but the general population, the numbers still provided ample firepower at the time for those calling on the Bundeswehr to perform an about-face. Faced with the data now in 2000, their arguments lay more clearly on the table than ever before. The Bundeswehr presented itself as a mirror to society; the armed forces were recruited from the population. And the age groups that were relevant to the

---

117 Ibid., 6.

armed forces showed an undeniable trend toward tolerance of gays and lesbians. The SOWI researchers drew equally clear conclusions from the results. One quarter of survey participants showed a "markedly positive attitude" toward homosexuals and favored equality, viewing homosexual soldiers as an "expression of normalcy" and disapproving of professional obstacles. The tolerance on display within this group was "unstable in parts, but could be stabilized by political decisions that lead toward opening social institutions reserved for heterosexuals, such as marriage."[118]

At the other end of the spectrum stood a quarter of the population that clearly disapproved of homosexuality. A "personal, even physical distaste" came through in answers to the many further questions, only some of which can be reproduced here. The distaste manifested itself in strong positive reactions to statements like "Homosexuals make me uncomfortable," "Homosexuals are not fit for military leadership" or "I cannot imagine working alongside a homosexual." Less marked but still significant was the approval that this quarter of respondents showed for the statement "Homosexual soldiers damage the reputation of the Bundeswehr."[119] The "deep distaste" that nearly 25 percent of people felt fed on "fears about the potential erosion of traditional social structures that provide security if 'abnormality' were promoted."[120] In SOWI's analysis, "this group believed homosexuals should not take on military leadership roles under any circumstances. [Homosexuals] serving in the Bundeswehr is generally viewed critically, and it is assumed that their presence in the armed forces damages the reputation of the Bundeswehr."[121]

It bears repeating that the age of the respondents in the groups where these opinions prevailed ultimately made them irrelevant for the inner workings of the armed forces. That was not the case with younger survey participants, a majority of whom affirmed statements like "It does not matter to me whether somebody is homosexual," "I can imagine working alongside homosexuals" or "Homosexuals should have the same career opportunities in the Bundeswehr." The statement "Homosexual soldiers damage the reputation of the Bundeswehr" met with clear rejection.[122] With age left out of the question, a total of 54 percent of participants considered homosexuals holding leadership roles to be "problematic."

At the same time, a 57 percent majority of respondents opposed "obstructing the career" of homosexual soldiers. The pattern of response was "doubtless inconsistent" as SOWI rightly observed, especially among those who "did not want to

---

118 Ibid., 15.
119 Ibid., 3–4.
120 Ibid., 15.
121 Ibid., 5.
122 Ibid., 3.

see homosexuals' careers blocked while still rejecting them for positions of leader-ship."[123] When it came to homosexuality and the Bundeswehr, aspects and opinions came together "that were in part diametrically opposed." In this case the Bundes-wehr found itself in no-man's land, caught between fronts; it was "one of the cul-minating points where traditional institutions came up against alternative living styles."[124] The number of those showing tolerance, or the "positively inclined" would rise in the future as "adherence to traditional values linked to age" weak-ened and was "overtaken" by generations whose attitude toward gays and lesbians ranged from indifferent to positive. The moment for the armed forces to act was "already here"; they could either "wait to repeal restrictions on giving homosexuals [military] assignments until other social institutions like marriage and child-rear-ing opened to homosexuals" or it could lift them now, thereby "demonstrating that the Bundeswehr assesses an individual based on his accomplishments and not against the backdrop to his life." In the first scenario, the future shift in public opinion would force the Bundeswehr to act; the second would allow the Bundes-wehr to mitigate the "image of [itself as] an instance of conservative socialization" and "prove that it could come to terms with societal change."[125] In their choice of phrasing and analysis of the survey data, the SOWI researchers left a clear recom-mendation for the latter option.

By January 2000 the initial results of the SOWI study lay on the minister's desk; 53.2 percent of survey participants regarded homosexuals as (tending to be) unfit for military leadership, 44.7 percent tended to disagree.[126] That June, Section FüS I 4 presented the complete survey results to the minister along with two conclu-sions: First, conscripts' age meant they could be assumed to be relatively toler-ant toward homosexuals, although the share of conscripts with a "conservative opinion" and "less education" "may be above average" "due to the realities of con-scientious objection."[127] This led FüS I 4 to conclude that tolerance was "likely to be lower than average for the age group." It could be assumed for officers and longer serving NCOs, on the other hand, that "they would disapprove more strongly than conscripts of homosexuals" due to their seniority and "overwhelming conserva-tive values." "Issues in accepting homosexuals [might] grow virulent" with the shift Scharping announced in the BMVg's position. All this brought FüS I 4 to repeat its recommendation that a survey on attitudes toward homosexuals be conducted spe-

---

123 Ibid., 11.
124 Ibid., 15.
125 Ibid., 15–16.
126 BArch, BW 2/38358: BMVg, FüS I 4, 20 January 2000, emended by hand to 15 February 2000.
127 Ibid., BMVg, FüS I 4 to the defense minister, 9 June 2000.

cifically within the armed forces. "Such an investigation ought to be independent and anonymous, and carried out with the utmost discretion and care."[128]

There were was no question that the survey proposed by military branch leadership and the chiefs of services was being set up against the clearly articulated will within political leadership at the ministry. It represented a last-minute attempt by military leadership to put the brakes on the minister's impending decision. State Secretary Schulte spotted the intention, noting "This cannot be real!!" on the FüS I 4 document. Scharping evidently saw things similarly, writing "Internal armed forces investigation *not* required!"[129]

There was no need for a study, then, in the eyes of BMVg political leadership. Yet it may have been more decisive still that by the summer of 2000, it was already too late – in late March, the minister had already decided (or been forced to decide). For all the while the clock had been ticking, specifically at the Federal Constitutional Court, which was expecting an answer from the federal government by the end of March when its extended deadline came up. Scharping found himself in a corner. Forced to decide, he took the political decision to reach an agreement with Lieutenant Stecher and thus initiate a general shift in the armed forces' position on homosexuality. The decision was thoroughly discussed in the "knitting circle," as Brigitte Schulte dubbed it twenty years later (the "knitting circle" was the inner circle of political leadership, the minister and the four state secretaries).[130]

5. "The Dam Has Broken!"

To announce the change in course, Scharping selected the most important forum available to a German politician: a full session of the Bundestag. With it, the minister surprised everyone – his party, the opposition and the media alike. The generals in Hardthöhe may have been especially startled; there are no signs of the minister informing military leadership of his decision ahead of time.

Scharping began his speech before the Bundestag deputies with words perfectly suited to his cautious, diplomatic character. It was, he said, an *"imperative of wise leadership* to make a view one holds to be correct, bearable, palatable and understandable in reasonable fashion." It had become necessary to take account of what in his view were "outdated prejudices or reservations." One could not "just

---

128 Ibid.
129 BArch, 2/38358, handwritten note with the initials BS [Brigitte Schulte] on the document BMVg, FüS I 4, 9 June 2000 (original emphasis).
130 Interview with retired State Secretary Brigitte Schulte, Wachtberg, 16 April 2019.

simply decree" a change in course; tolerance had to be "made possible to understand, develop and [...] learn."[131]

> As you are aware, to date *same-sex orientation among members of the Bundeswehr* has led to
> conclusions regarding their fitness and qualifications in the role of instructors and leaders.
> It would at most be correct to draw conclusions based on how a person pursues their sexual
> orientation – be it heterosexual or homosexual – but not the orientation itself.[132]

There had not been a single case during his tenure as minister, Scharping continued, in which a soldier's sexual orientation had led to conclusions automatically
being drawn. (The transcript registers a "Shout from the SPD: Very good!") The
cases that had sparked public debate had originated in the time of his predecessor
in office. Scharping's self-defense checked out; Lieutenant Stecher had been dismissed as platoon commander in April 1998; another suit filed by a first sergeant
after he was rejected for career service dated back to 1997; and First Lieutenant
Schmid had been dismissed as a platoon commander in 1996, when he also had a
firm offer of acceptance into career service retracted. Still, it was under Scharping's command that midway through 1999 the ministry appealed Lüneberg Administrative Court's ruling in favor of the first sergeant, a contradiction subsequently
pointed out by Deputy Christina Schenk (PDS) in a minor inquiry.[133] Parliamentary
State Secretary Kolbow replied that the federal government did not share her view;
the case in Lüneberg had "unquestionably come about in the time of his predecessor in office."[134] Kolbow's was a characteristic response to an opposition query:
wrong neither in form or content, but circumventing the question. It was true after
all that the BMVg had appealed the decision under Scharping's aegis.

Deputy Günther Nolting of the FDP asked the minister whether it would be
"better to reach a *political decision* here in the Bundestag [...] and to do so now?"
Scharping replied that the deputy was "somewhat impatient." Nolting persisted,
contending that "we should not constantly let ourselves be driven around by the
courts" as had been the case with the ECJ decision about opening the armed forces
for women.[135] Before the full Bundestag, Scharping announced he would seek to

---

131 German Bundestag, 14th legislative period, typed transcript of the 95th Session on 23 March
2000, plenary transcript 14/95, 8844–45 (original emphasis).

132 Ibid. (original emphasis).

133 BArch, BW 2/38358: Deputy Christina Schenk, inquiry to the federal government, 27 March 2000.

134 German Bundestag, Document 14/3275, response from Parliamentary State Secretary Kolbow.
A copy is available in BArch, BW 2/38358.

135 German Bundestag, 14th legislative period, typed transcript of the 95th Session on 23 March
2000, plenary transcript 14/95, 8845 (original emphasis).

"settle the present case [First Lieutenant Stecher] *without dispute.*" "I'm certain I'll achieve that."[136] Looking beyond the case at hand, he further stated his intention to "give orders for a code of conduct that rules out any automatic procedures based on the mere fact of sexual orientation, and sanctions any form of discrimination due to sexual orientation."[137] The minister elaborated:

> We have to stop drawing conclusions based on the mere fact of sexual orientation. I'll say it again: Whether it is a man harassing a woman, a man with a same-sex orientation harassing another man, or a woman with a same-sex orientation harassing another woman, it is the same behavior that must be reproved, and from which conclusions in the specific case can, and when in doubt must, be drawn regarding fitness or qualification.[138]

As the Minister of Defense, Scharping would "come to a comprehensive, well-considered, calm and logical decision so that as many people as possible can enter the armed forces and nobody has to feel pushed aside or tricked." This too he considered "leadership development and civic education, and an aspect of smart political caretaking."[139]

"Victory on all fronts," ran the euphoric headline in Berlin's *taz* in response to Scharping's announcement.[140] The editors did not forget to point out who the plaintiff had to thank for his victory, however – the European Court ("of Human Rights," it would be correct to add here).

The following morning, the minister's office head forwarded the text of the late-afternoon speech Scharping had delivered before the Bundestag to the joint chiefs of staff. The text was then passed along to the chief of defense, the chiefs of the services, and the Surgeon General of the Bundeswehr along with the announcement that on 27 March 2000 the minister would address "the topic of homosexuality in the armed forces" in council with the chiefs.[141] The deadline Karlsruhe had imposed was set to expire three days after the scheduled meeting; on its own, the minister's announcement did not change things at first for the court.

The council convened on 27 March. One participant (who wished to remain unnamed) recalled that the prospect of Lieutenant Stecher's stated intention to appeal to the ECHR had loomed over the meeting; Scharping himself described the

---

136 Ibid. (original emphasis).
137 Ibid. The protocol records applause from the SPD and Alliance 90/The Greens as well as FDP deputies.
138 Ibid., 1845–46.
139 Ibid., 1846.
140 Feddersen, "Sieg auf ganzer Linie."
141 BArch, BW 24/37667: Internal BMVg emails from 24 March 2000.

"risk of litigation [as] very high." "How," the minister asked those gathered, "can we appease the man?" State Secretary Wichert's response came just as succinctly: By reassigning the lieutenant to his former post as platoon commander. The anonymous participant recalled that the three chiefs of the services and state secretary all spoke out against this option, however, instead making a case to maintain the current line. The council and minister reached an agreement to await the outcome of the legal proceedings in Karlsrhue and Strasbourg as necessary, and thus accept defeat (albeit tacitly) before both courts. Then, however, "quickly and without further consulting the three chiefs of the services," Scharping had acted on his own initiative and made the u-turn.

A written note confirms the eyewitness recollection; First Lieutenant Stecher should be "appeased by an offer. Since he wants to become an instructor again, 'the dam' has broken!"[142] Now everything came very quickly. That same day, 27 March, Scharping instructed State Secretary Wichert via his office manager to coordinate with the Bundeswehr personnel office and come up with a solution for the first lieutenant.[143] They were to do so moreover without involving the chief of the air force or leadership, as a high-ranking officer in Air Force Command at the time noted in 2018, still with a discernible lack of understanding. A proposal lay on the table the very next day. Once the lieutenant completed his ongoing training in summer 2000 he would be given command of a platoon in his old squadron, though not his original platoon, as the post was already occupied. Since the two posts were "absolutely equal in value," the "measure" would "take care of" the current lawsuit in Karlsruhe, removing the cause for complaint. There was still the off-chance, however, that the Federal Constitutional Court would rule on the main proceedings if "cases of fundamental importance" had to be clarified or the "breach of constitutional rights [appeared] particularly grievous." This meant that the plaintiff and his lawyer had to be persuaded at all costs to withdraw the constitutional complaint, which would retroactively eliminate the "legally pending" nature of the constitutional complaint and was binding for the court.

The comment reveals once again the level of worry at the BMVg about a potential defeat in Karlsruhe even after it came to an agreement with the first lieutenant (or the "most awkward of malcontents," as the magazine *Gigi* described Stecher).[144] Wichert recalled that he had not feared a possible loss at Karlsruhe or Strasbourg as a state secretary at the time but wanted to "let it depend." Even if the courts did rule against the ministry, their written opinions would have provided the BMVg

---

142 BArch, BW 2/38358. BMVg, handwritten note for FüS I 4, 27 March 2000.
143 Ibid., BMVg, PSZ III 1, 28 March 2000. Also in what follows.
144 Heilmann, "Helm ab zum Sex!"

with a basis for new regulations. Scharping was a politician, however, and the politicians wanted to avoid defeat in Karlsruhe or Strasbourg if at all possible, not least out of concern about negative headlines in the press.[145] A note from 11 April 2000 confirms an agreement with the officer.[146] This meant there was never a decision from the supreme court, although it is still generally portrayed that way in the media today.[147]

It is worth noting that even after reaching an agreement with the service and returning to his old post, Stecher gave up on his ambition of entering career service. The years-long dispute had left behind scorched earth, and the armed forces lost a highly talented officer. What remains to be said? It was the lieutenant's lawsuit and the work of his exceptional lawyer, Maria Sabine Augstein, that forced the BMVg to perform an about-face. This represents Winfried Stecher's great and enduring legacy; not the first, but certainly the best-known known case of a homosexual officer petitioning for his rights. Those who know the man, his military career and his attitude toward a soldier's life will know Stecher would have gladly spared himself the fame and continued to serve in the air force with daring and courage, if without drawing attention to himself. Yet personnel leadership and the ministry, its legal staff and administrative judges stood opposed.

It now remained for the two other suits still pending before administrative courts to be settled in a comparable way. Section PSZ III6, the office in charge of the affair at the BMVg, rated the trial prospects in both cases as "extremely poor, and will worsen further still in the case of the first lieutenant in the reserve if PSZ III 6 does not immediately enter into extrajudicial negotiations with the aim of conciliation/settlement."[148] There was a risk of demands for compensation and press reports "to public effect." While the settled suit pertained to an assignment decision and not, as with the other two suits, to a decision on status, the BMVg had applied the same argument in every case: "Lack of fitness due to homosexual tendencies." Following Scharping's decision it was no longer possible to use a lack of fitness blocking acceptance as a career soldier as the working premise. Ministry documents reveal that the signature of the joint chiefs of staff was not sought in deciding on the other two cases as was customary, i.e. they were not involved.

---

145 Interview with retired State Secretary Peter Wichert, Bad Münstereifel, 10 April 2019.
146 BArch, BW 2/38358: BMVg, FüS I 4, 11 April 2000.
147 For example: "In 2000 an officer filed suit before the Federal Constitutional Court against his discrimination. The supreme German judges ruled in his favor." Friederichs, "Homosexualität als militärischer Makel."
148 BArch, BW 2/38358: BMVg, PSZ III 6, 12 April 2000. Also in what follows.

In early May 2000 personnel advised leadership to settle the lawsuits amicably and avoid a decision in court.[149] That July, the first sergeant from Münster was reinstated as a career soldier, and later accepted into the career track of a specialist officer; he has since gone on to become a staff captain.[150]

First Lieutenant Schmid, whose suit lay before Berlin Administrative Court, was also offered a career post in the military;[151] personnel leadership set the process in motion immediately following on the BMVg's "change in heart" toward homosexuals. Schmid was given a spot, quite belatedly, in the staff officer training course at the Bundeswehr Command and Staff College.[152] Yet Schmid did not enter career service either, turning the offer down at the last moment during a ceremony in the office of his commanding officer.

> I was supposed to receive my letter of acceptance for career service on Friday morning, practically one day before the course began. I had been ordered to report to the head of Berlin command, my battalion commander was present. But in the moment I refused to accept. Even before the surprising turn of events, I had already come to terms with the fact that I no longer had any real chances at a career and started to look elsewhere. During the (brief) preparations for the staff officers' training course, it became quite clear to me that I would not experience fair treatment "as the first of my kind," there would always be exaggerations in one direction or the other. And somehow I was already over it. What mattered to me was to use the unique position of my case to finally do away all the established practices, connected with the hope of finally scoring a breakthrough.[153]

It was self-evident to the offices involved in the matter at Hardthöhe that the three precedent cases would hold a "normative function for subsequent cases."[154] The same ministry orders from March 1984 prescribing different treatment for homosexual and heterosexual soldiers was still in effect, though the policy unit for military personnel noted that their continued existence should not be made public knowledge. Rather, their abolition was necessary. That did not make new ministry orders necessary from the section leader's point of view, however, as they would (now) constitute "an undesirable form of unequal treatment."[155] Going forward,

---

149 BArch, BW 2/38358: BMVg, PSZ III 1, 15 May 2000, with a reference to a decision template from PSZ III 6 from 2 May 2000.
150 BArch, BW 1/503302: BMVg, PSZ I 8, 20 June 2002.
151 Ibid.
152 Email from Erich Schmid to the author, 15 November 2018.
153 Ibid. Erich Schmid added the final sentence later.
154 BArch, BW 2/38358: BMVg, FüS I 4, 11 April 2000.
155 Ibid., BMVg, PSZ III 1, 17 May 2000, signed by Colonel Ohm, as well as an eyewitness interview with Ret. Colonel Dieter Ohm, Meckenheim, 17 April 2019.

"separate consideration of homosexual soldiers" so as to develop "case-by-case per-spectives on suitability" could not be reconciled with Scharping's statements before the Bundestag. The minister had willed that in the future homosexuality would "no longer be specially regarded as a criteria for suitability."[156]

The next time the top leadership circle at Hardthöhe convened on 4 July 2000, Scharping had set homosexuality as the top agenda item, ahead of problems with field post delivery abroad, improving fueling aircraft and security in the Caspian region.[157] The council meeting resulted in the note "BM-decision: 1.) No SOWI study 2.) Prepare a code of conduct."[158]

The dice had finally been cast, the minister had decided. On 3 July 2000, the day before the council meeting, the BMVg repealed the old decree issued by P II 1 on 13 March 1984. As revolutionary as it was for those it affected, the paper was composed only of two tight-lipped sentences. Beneath the subject heading "Person-nel management of homosexual soldiers" stood the phrase "Homosexuality is not grounds for restrictions with regards to assignment or employment status, and as such does not represent a suitability criteria requiring separate examination."[159] The paper was drawn up and signed by Colonel Dieter Ohm, head of the section PSZ III 1 responsible for policy matters.

On 1 July 2000 Chief of Defense General Hans Peter von Kirchbach made his departure. Regarding the timing, it seems obvious at least not to rule out a connec-tion to Scharping's shift on homosexuality. Yet even if von Kirchbach's retirement did fall exactly in the same period as Scharping's change in course, multiple eye-witness recalled the two events as not having any causal connection. Other weighty differences between the Bundeswehr's top soldier and the minister underlay the general's retirement.[160]

So what did dictate the BMVg's change in position? The timeframe clearly sug-gests First Lieutenant Stecher's suit before constitutional court as a deciding factor. Internal papers leave no doubt as to the pressure the federal government was under from Karlsruhe, a pressure that only increased with the deadline Court Pres-

---

156 BArch, BW 2/38358: PSZ III 1, 17 May 2000, signed by Colonel Ohm.

157 Ibid., BMVg, Office of State Secretary Biederbick, 29 June 2000, daily council agenda on 4 July 2000.

158 Ibid., written note from 4 July 2000 from BMVg, FüS I 4 to the chief of defense, 30 June 2000.

159 BMVg, PSZ III 1, 3 July 2000, as well as an interview with retired Colonel Dieter Ohm, Mecken-heim, 17 April 2019. Copy is in possession of the author.

160 Among others, this was Peter Wichert's firm belief in an interview with the author (Bad Mün-stereifel, 10 April 2019). Kirchbach's release was known about by 24 May 2000. "Tensions between Scharping and Kirchbach had been reported for weeks." See *Der Spiegel*, "Scharping entlässt Gene-ralinspekteur Kirchbach"; Leersch, "Scharpings falsches Spiel."

ident Jutta Limbach set for answering the questions. When Federal Minister of the Interior Otto Schily and Justice Minister Herta Däubler-Gmelin refused to cosign the BMVg's draft response, insisting as it did on the ministry's well-trodden position, Scharping was forced to convince his cabinet members of the defense ministry's stance – that, or bring about change in his own institution. Time ran out at the end of March 2000. This meant it was likely no coincidence that Scharping made his surprise announcement on 23 March, before coming to a last-minute agreement with Lieutenant Stecher. While the decision initially pertained to an individual case, it had a signaling effect.

A number of leading politicians, civil servants and officers involved in the March 2000 decision, by contrast, did not view the pending constitutional complaint as a make-or-break scenario. On its own, Stecher's case would have been unlikely to bring about any fundamental changes in the BMVg's attitude toward homosexuals; the ministry could have reached an individual agreement with the plaintiff if necessary without redirecting the general course of ship, operating under the motto "That's how we've always done it."[161] Weighing more heavily for those interviewed was the European Court of Justice's ruling from January 2000, which had mandated that the Bundeswehr fully open to women. Present-day Navy Commander Alexander Schüttpelz put it succinctly in an interview for a book from 2014: "Strictly speaking we have four British soldiers, one German woman and the European courts to thank for the sudden improvement in the legal standing of homosexual soldiers in the Bundeswehr at the dawn of the new decade."[162] Another staff officer in active service, Torsten Rissmann, took a similar view in retrospect, commenting aptly in 2010 on the change from ten years' previous:

> all of a sudden everything went very quickly, the Bundeswehr was out in front of society. Even without any sort of European anti-discrimination regulations being put in place or implemented at the national level, the Bundeswehr reacted to changes in society. One reason in part was certainly every [military] career group and assignment opening to women soldiers.[163]

Rissman's reference to women gaining access to the full range of military career tracks is crucial in understanding the BMVg's shift. A fact nearly forgotten today, in 2000 both the public and the military were much more preoccupied with the question of women in the military than how homosexual soldiers were treated.

---

161 For example, interview with Ret. Colonel Dieter Ohm of Meckenheim, 17 April 2019.
162 Schadendorf, *Der Regenbogen-Faktor*, 69–70.
163 "Obama: Bald 'Ask and Tell'?"

The Bundeswehr first began to admit women in 1975, adopting previously trained female doctors and pharmacists into its ranks. Starting in 1989 young women were able to apply for the career of officer in the medical corps without restriction, and after 1991 permitted to join as volunteer NCOs and enlisted soldiers in the medical corps, as well to serve in the music corps and soldier–athletes.[164] Yet outside of these three specialized and smaller fields, women remained excluded from every other branch of troop category and assignment. When a woman applied and was rejected for service as a fixed-term soldier, she filed suit at Hannover Administrative Court, claiming her right to equal professional treatment had been violated under EU law. The court referred the case to the European Court of Justice in Luxembourg for review. In January 2000, the court found the Federal Republic of Germany in breach of the provisions of the European equal treatment directive. In the wake of their defeat in Luxembourg, the BMVg and German lawmakers had been forced to create legal and organizational parameters for female volunteers within every arena of the armed forces. Many of the decision-makers from 2000 interviewed by the author for this study confirmed that the armed forces' approach to women serving in the future had been the key matter. It, not the question of homosexual soldiers' treatment, had occupied the center of attention,[165] demanding the creation of legal and internal regulations to fully open the armed forces to women volunteers.

The Bundestag voted in favor of the necessary legislative packet in June 2000; that December Article 12a of the Basic Law was emended. On 2 January 2001 the first 244 women entered voluntary service as NCOs and enlisted soldiers, followed on 2 July 2001 by the first female officer cadets outside the medical corps and music corps. Women have been able to serve in every troop category and assignment since then; by May 2005 the percentage of women in uniform had risen to 5.4% (16,830 female soldiers in absolute numbers) and as of 2020 the share was 12.55%).[166]

The farsighted had immediately read the ECJ ruling as a signpost indicating the future of homosexual soldiers: "While it may largely have gotten lost or overshadowed in the initial reactions to the Luxembourg ruling, homosexual soldiers also spoke up, demanding an end to their discrimination."[167]

As one staff officer serving at the time at the Center for Leadership Development and Civic Education told the author, the ECJ ruling made the Bundeswehr's policy toward gays and lesbians "a complete absurdity." It was a "crying injustice"

164 Biesold, "Der Umgang mit Sexualität in der Bundeswehr," 6–7.
165 Among others, interview with Ret. General Harald Kujat, Neuruppin, 30 January 2019.
166 Biesold, "Der Umgang mit Sexualität in der Bundeswehr," 7.
167 Kümmel, Klein and Lohmann, "Zwischen Differenz und Gleichheit," 76.

if women were now allowed to volunteer and make a career in the service without having to perform military service, while gays still had to perform basic service but were blocked from any career. It left the latter "good enough to serve at the bottom, but unfit for anything higher up."[168] At the time, the eyewitness had assessed the Bundeswehr's position as one "of maximum discrimination." It had been clear to him that the Bundeswehr would "now quickly have to open itself up to homosexuals, and could not wait for Karlsruhe or Strasbourg to force the issue." The armed forces should show its own soldiers and the public that it had the "courage to change of its own accord." The major himself at least had the courage to share his conviction "loudly and audibly," though his initiative had run up against a "solid wall of rejection" at the Center for Leadership Development and Civic Education and the BMVg alike. "Everything was rejected regardless of how good the arguments were – there was not even a response." From his point of view in Koblenz, the Bundeswehr and its political leadership had lost all credibility where homosexuality was concerned, "not simply as an institution but each individual politician, jurist, civil servant, general and officer who for years, for decades, had kept silent about their comrades' discrimination. None of them did anything, they kept silent and looked the other way." At his center he had at least managed to create the first seminar on minority treatment in the Bundeswehr, giving homosexual soldiers a chance to have their say. Lesbians seem never to have come up as a topic.

Looking back on his time as section head for policy issues in the personnel department, a now retired colonel also saw the ECJ's ruling on women in the military as decisive:

> With the [Bundeswehr] opening to women, [there were also] good arguments for fundamentally changing how homosexuals were treated [...] When the Bundeswehr opened to women, the question of sexuality in the armed forces came up again [...] the topic of homosexuality now had to be reevaluated from the [new] standpoint. Those opposed to opening to homosexuals thus ran out of their previous arguments [...] it was all so simple and logical that nobody at the BMVg could escape it, in fact.[169]

An employee in the minister's immediate circle, on the other hand, remembered Lieutenant Stecher's pending suit as providing the sole focus.[170] Otherwise, the witness (who wished to go unnamed) confirmed the impression written sources give, that the agreements reached with the plaintiff soldiers and the fundamental

---

168 Interview with Ret. Lieutenant Colonel Joachim Meier, Karlsruhe, 16 July 2018. Meier's views are given in further quotes below.
169 Interview with Ret. Colonel Dieter Ohm, Meckenheim, 17 April 2019.
170 Interview by phone (anonymous), 13 May 2019.

shifts within the BMVg that followed in tow had not "gone uncontested, not by a long shot."

> The three chiefs of the services and the chief of defense had all clearly made their objections known to the minister. What use could cosignature from the service branches bring still if the chiefs had already voiced their reservations to the minister? Nor could the armed forces be expected to simply follow the minister on the matter without any protest after representing a different stance for decades and up to the last minute. It would have come across as opportunistic had they done an about-face overnight.[171]

Yet neither the consent of the chiefs nor that of the ministerial "apparatus" was necessary to begin with. Instead, Scharping made a political decision, then implemented it at the ministry level and the Bundeswehr as a whole. The much-cited "primacy of politics" in Germany meant that as the one holding the power of command, Scharping was not dependent on approval from the generals or the "institution." "There was no change in position at the BMVg. The BMVg apparatus and military leadership stuck to their position and Rudolf Scharping enacted his decision politically."[172]

This raises still other questions, why for example did not Scharping assert the primacy of politics earlier and more quickly? Why did not he act after moving into the minister's office in fall of 1998? Why wait a year and a half, thereby bolstering the impression of an indecisive and irresolute politician? Yet it also raises questions as to the BMVg's decision-making process in 1999 and 2000. Every high-ranking employee within Scharping's orbit interviewed for this study, all the generals and officers asserted that during those two years, homosexuality had not been at the center of the ministry's focus. The thoughts and actions of the minister, those of the state secretaries and the apparatus itself had been taken up by other, more pressing concerns – for example, to name but a few, the ongoing deployments to Bosnia and Macdeonia, the Kosovo crisis, and especially the bombing of Yugsolavia from February to June 1999 and the following Kosovo Force mission in Kosovo.

And yet: Scharping's display of hesitation and reticence before military leadership did not leave a good impression where the primacy of politics was concerned. It was also a case of a weak minister demonstrating a lack of leadership on the matter for too long. Scharping preferred exposing himself and his party to the accusation of broken campaign promises over letting things deteriorate with the generals. The weakness, even lack, of political leadership did not simply exacerbate the issue, it "frightened" many an observer and citizen. One Munich man found

---

171 Ibid.
172 Ibid.

unequivocal words in October 1999. Mr. S. drew on a radio interview with State Secretary Brigitte Schulte in which she painted a general picture of Scharping as desir-
ing change but being slowed by the joint chiefs of staff. The man reported Schulte
as saying: "A minister cannot simply disregard it if commanding officers take this
sort of stance."[173] Scharping was "more liberal in his positions" Schulte had said in
the interview, and a possible court clarification of the matter "was not the worst
thing."[174] S. was horrified. "It is not for the joint chiefs of staff to decide on political
issues but lawmakers and the elected government." It gave "cause for concern" if
"the supreme commander of the armed forces was neither able nor willing to push
his ideas through in such a hierarchical organization." So long as the military "is
supposed to be led politically as the constitution provides, the minister cannot let
himself be told what to do by those he is supposed to lead."[175]

Even with a good twenty years' hindsight one could not formulate it anymore
clearly. Incidentally, when the state secretary received the ministry's draft response
to Karlsruhe representing the familiar line of the BMVg to date, she dismissed it
with an emphatic line drawn across the page, accompanied by the remark "no –
not like this!"[176] Instead, beneath the new version of the response composed on her
behalf, Schulte added in writing that she would "fight resolutely against any form
of discrimination of homosexuals, you can count on that."[177]

Still, it was not the growing pressure from the media and public, or even the
outrage from the governing SPD and Green parties that was ultimately able to
change the position of the BMVg and Minister Scharping. It was only under the
pressure of European court rulings and the anticipation of similar decisions in
Karlsruhe that Scharping, against the bitter resistance of the military leadership,
changed course and steered the ship in the opposite direction. In reaching an out-
of-court settlement, Bundeswehr jurists succeeded at the last minute in preventing
the BMVg's previous practices from being classified as unconstitutional. Lieutenant
Stecher's settlement turning into a policy decision, "a breach in the dam," likely
had to do with the fact that two further lawsuits were pending. Had BMVg jurists
insisted on the old line, loss in court was practically a foregone conclusion, at least
by Karlsruhe. The prospect of further defeat on the horizon made it impossible to

---

173 BArch, BW 2/38357, Letter from Mr. S. to the BMVg, Parliamentary State Secretary Brigitte
Schulte, 5 October 1999.

174 Ibid.

175 Ibid.

176 BArch, BW 2/38357: BMVg, FüS I 4, draft response from 3 November 1999, Military Disciplinary
Code and Military Complaints Code with handwritten remark from Parliamentary State Secretary
Brigitte Schulte, 15 November 1999.

177 Ibid., BMVg, Parliamentary State Secretary Brigitte Schulte, 27 December 1999.

isolate Stecher's case. Under sober consideration, by the end of March 2000 the BMVg was left with no other choice but immediately to initiate a turnabout.[178]

6. New Working Principles: Tolerance and Privacy Protection

A paper put out on 3 July 2000 represented a first step in the paradigm shift. The second followed soon thereafter in December 2000,[179] when the new Chief of Defense General Harald Kujat issued "Leadership assistance in dealing with sexuality." Scharping's previous announcement in parliament of a military code of conduct toward homosexual comrades never came about; instead, the ministry opted to draft a general guide that did not focus on homosexuality alone. "This guide is intended to help break down uncertainties in conduct in light of the armed forces' continued opening to women, changes in the Bundeswehr's previous stance toward female and male soldiers with a same-sex orientation and the problems active-duty soldiers encounter when 'dealing with sexuality'."[180] The introduction to the guide laid out the general legal principles that also applied to the armed forces: The "intimate and sexual life of a person [...] [stood] under constitutional protection as a part of their private life" under the Basic Law (Article 2 Section 1, in conjunction with Article 1 Section 1). The principle of equal treatment under Article 3 of the Basic Law and the ban on discrimination under Article 14 of the European Convention on Human Rights protected further against "unequal treatment based on sexual orientation." The direct reference to Article 14 of the convention came as a clear acknowledgment of the ECHR rulings in 1999 and 2000. It was no coincidence for the guide to expressly state that "a ban on discrimination is fixed in European law by Article 14 of the European Convention on Human Rights and is legally binding for the Federal Republic of Germany." This obviously applied only insofar as normal barracks operations and one's comrades were not disrupted or otherwise bothered; couples holding hands while walking through the barracks should still be avoided. It was demanded of soldiers that they show "tolerance toward different, non-criminal sexual orientations," explicitly mentioning homosexually oriented

---

178 A similar position is represented in Schadendorf, *Der Regenbogen-Faktor*, 72. Schadendorf also cites the law governing civil partnerships, adopted by the Bundestag in November 2000 and taking effect on 1 August 2001, as evidence for a shift in how homosexuals were treated. Ibid.

179 Multiple witnesses viewed the ministry orders as a "paradigm shift" or "minor explosion." Biesold also views the orders from December 2000 as a shift in paradigm in Biesold, "Der Umgang mit Sexualität in der Bundeswehr," 4.

180 BMVg, FüS I 4, Az 35-04-09 from 20 December 2000, also cited in what follows. The author holds possession of a copy.

male and female soldiers. While the ministry thus overnight ordered tolerance among the troops by decree "from on high," a change in regulations did not also mean a change in soldiers' minds. This led the chief of defense to call on superiors to remain "sensitive to sexually motivated tensions and disruptions in cohesion in the areas under their command." "It is moreover particularly important to demand tolerance of other sexual orientations."[181]

The convention of "Leadership assistance" is one tool the chief of defense has at his disposal to influence troops directly, and the one Kujat elected to use. The origin and occasion was the armed forces' scheduled opening for women volunteers at the start of 2001, a transition that necessitated legal as well as internal regulatory frameworks, among them for determining how sexuality between female and male soldiers would be treated in the future. The joint chiefs of staff composed an initial draft that revolved exclusively around the practical aspects of life together, including the possibility of sexuality between men and women. Kujat found the draft too conservative and said as much; homosexuality, for example, was not mentioned once. Kujat discarded the proposal, and one weekend before Christmas 2000 sat down in the peace and quiet of home to compose a new paper himself. His wife had encouraged him "to be progressive."[182]

Kujat took her advice. The new set of orders broke new ground in referring to soldiers' homosexuality, both individually and between them. The former chief of defense recalled that numerous conversations within NATO circles at the national and international level had drawn his attention to the importance of homosexuality among soldiers as a topic, and he decided to take the opportunity to "clear up the matter at once." The statement that held most weight for the general was that "intimate and sexual life" belonged to "a person's private sphere," and was thus a private matter. That went for soldiers as well, and showed up expressly in the document for homosexual soldiers.[183]

When the press found out about the leadership assistance document it gladly shortened it to "Sex Orders," and *Bild* struck up a campaign against the guide. It was not homosexuality within the ranks that bothered the editors, however, nor heterosexual issues for that matter. Rather, it was the ban on pornographic photos in soldiers' lockers that drew their ire, and they now responded to the chief of defense by running a new image of a naked woman daily. While it was nothing exceptional for the tabloid, *Bild* still had the cover girl asking the general "What do you have

---

181 Ibid.
182 Interview with Ret. General Harald Kujat, Neuruppin, 30 January 2019.
183 Ibid.

against me?" in accusatory fashion.[184] The newfound tolerance of homosexual soldiers either drew no attention whatsoever in the newspaper, or the editors did not see any potential for agitation. The lack of a media sensation over the topic, even at *Bild*, shows just how strongly public opinion toward gays and lesbians had shifted, even normalized, by the new millennium.

Gay officers still clearly remember just how pivotal the chief of defenses decree was. "With him [Kujat], sexuality was taken up as a topic for the first time. Before it was taboo. And for the first time it was mentioned that homosexuality between soldiers existed."[185] For one present-day navy commander, General Kujat had been the "great role-model" in 2000–01; the chief of defenses guide had been of tremendous importance to him as a lieutenant at the time. It had been a sign of encouragement for an chief of defense to set his signature beneath the orders, instilling in the eyewitness a new sense of self-confidence as a homosexual officer.[186] Other former officers and NCOs interviewed for the study found the orders "liberating"; some, looking back over a distance of eighteen years, lumped Kujat's orders and Scharping's decisions beforehand into one, referring to them as the "Scharping decree" for short. A captain in special service today recalled that the orders had "freed him from the heavy burden of having to hide and conceal his private life in service." Although he had "otherwise been able to take little" from Scharping's record as minister, he had been quite grateful for the minister's decision and would have "liked to hug him and said 'Rudi, you really did well by this!'"[187] Other contemporaries share the sentiment: "Now appeal was possible if I was discriminated against for being gay (I was never discriminated against, or noticed it). Now I could live openly and my partner could go with me even to official events."[188] Still, the "sex orders," as the media dubbed them, do not seem to have attracted a broad audience. One major general recalled the guide was "completely unknown" at Military District Command IV (comprising Bavaria and Baden-Württemberg) when he took command there. He responded at the time by setting it on the meeting agendas for commanders and company chiefs, and presenting on the subject himself.[189]

The next step in bringing regulations to the armed forces' new position up to speed came in February 2002, following on the new personnel department orders and the guide of the chief of defense. Annex B 173 to Joint Service Regulation 14/3

---

184 The *Bild* campaign came to an end once Kujat agreed to be interviewed on the matter. Interview with Ret. General Harald Kujat, Neuruppin, 30 January 2019.

185 A retired Lieutenant Colonel, Berlin, to the author, 30 January 2019.

186 Interview with Navy Commander Alexander Schüttpelz, Berlin, 24 January 2019.

187 Interview with Captain H., 12 June 2018.

188 Email from First Class Sergeant in the Reserve S. to the author, 5 April 2018.

189 Email from Ret. Major General Justus Gräbner to the author, 12 July 2017.

(of the Military Disciplinary Code and the Military Complaints Code) regulated every last service-related detail regarding "sexual conduct of and between soldiers." From the outset, the 2002 version now stated categorically that

> a person's intimate life, as a part of a soldier's right to personality, is fundamentally excluded from influence by the service. As such, a soldier's relationship to his sexuality is only relevant under service law in the event that it complicates joint work in the line of service or negatively impacts cohesion among comrades and thus brings about lasting disruptions to official order. Sexual orientation as such, whether heterosexual or homosexual, is irrelevant.[190]

The regulations also paved the way for heterosexual and homosexual relationships between superiors and subordinates in principle, albeit qualified with the "if" and "however" clauses typical of German legalese:

> Regarding the general acceptance of non-conjugal domestic partnerships, long-term heterosexual relationships, including those between soldiers of different rank, is fundamentally irrelevant in a disciplinary context. This applies, however, only insofar as no negative impacts on working operations touching on the respectability or trustworthiness of the superior result, or circumstances otherwise intervene that are liable to gravely detract from the public reputation of the Bundeswehr. The same applies – despite lower thresholds of tolerance within society and the line of service – for homosexual domestic partnerships between soldiers of different rank. As a rule, consensual heterosexual or homosexual activity between soldiers of different rank outside the context of a long-term domestic partnership is likewise irrelevant in a disciplinary context [...] The existence of a direct superior–subordinate relationship between those involved in a consensual heterosexual or homosexual relationship may entail risk of causing serious damage to the respectability and trustworthiness of the superior, especially if such a relationship is clearly not intended to last.[191]

In March 2002, the alternative leftist magazine *Gigi: Zeitschrift für sexuelle Emanzipation* devoted its cover story to the Bundeswehr's newfound liberal streak in a piece whose title played on a dog food ad: "A Whole Man Thanks to Scharping." The piece tied equal treatment for gay and lesbian soldiers to the armed forces' opening fully to women. The publishers found off-kilter titles for other pieces as well, such as "Helmet off for sex!" or "Fucking for Volk and Fatherland."[192]

That liberal streak still had its limits, however, applying in the same measure for heterosexual and homosexual soldiers alike:

---

190 ZDv 14/3 Military Disiciplinary Code, Appendix B 173, revision from 20 February 2002.
191 Ibid.
192 *Gigi* no. 18, March/April 2002. Title page and pages 14–16.

Sexual activity among female or male soldiers cannot be tolerated while on duty, even if consensual. It is irrelevant whether the relationship is heterosexual or homosexual. Service operations must unfold in a 'sexually neutral' manner. As a rule, sexual activity while in service shall be regarded as a disruption to service operations that must be stopped and subjected to disciplinary assessment. The same holds for sexual activity that may occur outside service hours but on military property.[193]

In short, no sex during service and no sex after service in the barracks.

Two years later in June 2004, a new version of ministry orders entitled "Dealing with Sexuality in the Bundeswehr" also permitted "sexual activity" during leisure time spent in the barracks. From now on, "sexual activity within service accommodations and facilities [...] was fundamentally irrelevant in terms of disciplinary law."[194] The rule from two years previous ordering "no sex during service, and no sex after service in the barracks" now no longer applied, at least during one's free time in the barracks. The deciding factor in this case had been the increasing number of foreign deployments. The narrow confines of private life in military camps in Afghanistan, Kosovo and Bosnia or onboard the navy's fleet were common knowledge. Tours of duty often lasting four to six months had regularly resulted in intimate contact between soldiers, including those of the same sex, and encounters could not always be concealed with close confines hardly offering a chance to withdraw. This gave rise to a latent risk of disciplinary punishment for breach of service, whether for heterosexual or homosexual contact.

The 2002 leadership guide's reference to "lower thresholds of tolerance within society and the line of service for homosexual domestic partnerships" was struck from the 2004 version. Heterosexual and homosexual encounters were set on equal footing in every context; "heterosexual as well as homosexual partnerships and activity outside the line of duty are as a rule of no disciplinary relevance," including situations in which "the partners are of different rank."[195] "Bundeswehr tolerates sexual relationships," *FAZ* announced in a pithy headline.[196]

The new approach to "homosexual and bisexual members of the Bundeswehr" also drew the attention of the parliamentary commissioner for the armed forces. In his annual report for 2003, Wilfried Penner found that despite every Bundeswehr member's obligation "to refrain from and stand up against sexual discrimination," "intolerance, fear of contact or simple uncertainty and a lack of knowledge was

---

193 ZDv 14/3 Military Disciplinary Code Appendix B 173, revision from 20 February 2002.

194 Ibid., revision from 30 June 2004.

195 Ibid.

196 The FAZ article from 18 August 2004 is cited in Lutze, "Sexuelle Beziehungen und die Truppe," 193.

present in everyday troop life."[197] In a statement on the commissioner's report, the BMVg clarified again in September 2004 that sexual orientation generally formed "part of Bundeswehr soldiers' right to personality and was irrelevant under disciplinary law." Soldiers' duty to camaraderie ruled out discrimination and demanded tolerance. The troop instructors' guide on "dealing with sexuality" from 2000 had already required superiors to show particular sensitivity toward sexually-motivated tensions within the areas under their command, and to demand requisite tolerance toward different sexual orientations. "Although there is no evidence that superiors are not fulfilling their duties," the BMVg's response continued, "it should be assumed that deep-seated prejudices continue to exist within society, and thus among individual members of the Bundeswehr."[198]

One master sergeant was forced to learn as much in 2007 when his immediate superior, also the officer directing personnel affairs at the post, chanced upon a photograph of the sergeant's partner and exclaimed "But that's no woman that you have there!? I have to know. That has to go in your personnel file! That's a breach of duty!"[199] Surprised and taken aback, the master sergeant referred his superior to the revised ministry orders from 2000, explaining he did not have to provide any further information about his private life or sexual orientation – in fact, these were the very questions that were no longer permissible. The run-in had left an already tense relationship between the sergeant and his superior in tatters. Over the following two years the senior NCO recalled he had experienced the "power of bullying"; in the end he transferred to another barracks.[200]

It should be noted here in passing that while open discrimination was (and remains) prohibited and legal recourse was/is available, informal sanctions that could only be challenged with difficulty continued to run their course. This might include negative assessments or personnel measures such as transfers or removal from a service post or course, as well as personnel selection, general staff officers' training, for example. This kind of rejection is obviously no longer justified along the lines of the candidate's sexual orientation but by means of other, "watertight" alibis, making them extremely difficult, and often impossible to counter. Within any hierarchically organized group, measures that lie at the discretion of superiors or personnel leadership form a gray-zone for informal sanctions and covert discrimination. One gay master sergeant confirmed that while open discrimina-

---

197 "'Umgang Mit Homosexualität in Der Bundeswehr'", https://www.queerbw.de/ahsab-ev/der-verein/historie (last accessed 3 April 2017).
198 Ibid.
199 Interview with Master Sergeant H., Berlin, 2 July 2018.
200 Ibid.

tion is no longer an issue in everyday military life, "every person [naturally] had their own view on any number of topics, including homosexuality and 'marriage for all'."[201] "Subliminal, furtive forms of discrimination" still exist, as in the form of "words spoken behind one's back." Assessments represent another shadowy realm in which superiors might still give free, "subliminal" reign to a concealed antipathy toward homosexuals within the realm of their discretionary powers, making successful appeal impossible.[202]

In 2006, the Act on Equal Opportunities for Female and Male Military Personnel, while implementing broader European guidelines regarding the principle of equal treatment, also wrote a ban on discrimination based on sexual identity into the Soldier's Act.[203] Since then, Section 3 has stipulated that "sex, sexual identity, ancestry, race, belief, worldview, religious or political views, country of origin [and] ethnic or other extraction" cannot be taken into account as deciding criteria for appointments and assignments.[204] The act's adoption in 2006 finalized the legal framework for ensuring homosexual soldiers' equal treatment.

The framework in place since the change in millennium guarantees all men and women the same legal standing regardless of whether they are heterosexual, homosexual or bisexual, with all assignments and career prospects equally open to everyone. Yet equality before the law did not mean that complete acceptance set in among the troops overnight. Acceptance, or tolerance at least is always up to the individual. Tolerance may, however, be demanded of all soldiers as a professional duty. The ban on discrimination and the regulatory canon described above provide a secure basis for each and every soldier to live out his or her sexual identity. Practically every interview conducted for this study revealed a slow and steady growth in homosexual soldiers' self-assurance after the millennium, and their increasing trust in the Bundeswehr's newfound liberalism as inscribed in ministry orders and regulations. The question of potential rehabilitation and compensation for damages suffered, on the other hand, remains unresolved.

---

201 Interview with Master Sergeant H., 29 March 2018.
202 Ibid.
203 §§1 (1) and 3 (1) in the Equal Treatment Act for Soldiers (SoldGG), http://www.gesetze-im-internet.de/soldgg/SoldGG.pdf.
204 The present commentary emphasizes with a view to the past that "by introducing sexual identity in section one [of §3 SG] (in 2006) as a further characteristic that cannot be considered in appointing and assigning soldiers, lawmakers put a line through a contrary practice that until recently was condoned by the highest courts." Walz, Eichen and Sohm, Kommentar zum Soldatengesetz, 73.

7. Lindner v. the Federal Republic of Germany: A Former Captain's Struggle for Restitution

In April 2018 AHsAB, the Working Group for Homosexual Members of the Bundeswehr, wrote a letter calling on the Minister of Defense to annul "verdicts reached [by military service courts] against soldiers of all ranks merely on the basis of consensual homosexual activity". To do so the letter continued, the existing law on criminal rehabilitation should be revised and expanded to include court decisions. The working group also demanded financial compensation for soldiers who had not received further assignment as fixed-term or career soldiers due to their homosexuality prior to 2000, while also encouraging the BMVg to issue an "apology that was long overdue" to those affected by past policies.[205]

In responding to the group's demands for financial compensation the ministry legal department acknowledged the career disadvantages homosexual soldiers had suffered. Yet it "was not homosexuality as such that had primarily been seen as the problem" but "fears about the affected parties losing their authority as superiors based on the general views of society" as well as their "susceptibility to blackmail." This explained why the soldiers had been excluded from "certain assignments," a practice from which Bundeswehr had "distanced itself considerably". Nonetheless, "regardless of the injustices that were doubtless inflicted, the legal system does not anticipate any individual compensation."[206] Claims of that nature presupposed a "criminal breach of duty on the part of those acting," which the legal department did not view to be the case. "As much as the prevailing practices at the time disregarded the rights of those impacted from today's perspective, the parties involved cannot be blamed. The Bundeswehr's approach was established within the context of contemporary societal values and the applicable laws, and was regularly upheld by court decision at the Federal Administrative Court."[207]

The legal press also supports this view. The rehabilitation act explicitly excluded career measures in the past "such as a loss of professional position," instead serving "exclusively to remove the taint of criminality suffered as a result of previous conviction." Legal scholars stressed explicitly that the law does not view prior convic-

---

205 Letter from the Working Group for Homosexual Members of the Bundeswehr to the federal minister of defense, 16 April 2018.
206 BMVg, R I 5 to the Working Group for Homosexual Members of the Bundeswehr, 16 August 2018.
207 Ibid.

tions as unconstitutional, which would contradict the 1957 and 1973 rulings at the Federal Administrative Court.[208]

To date, one officer at least has succeeded in managing to wrest financial compensation from the BMVg. When the BMVg fundamentally revised its position toward homosexual soldiers in 2000, Captain Michael Lindner, in retirement since 1982 for health reasons, spotted a chance to have his own case reassessed and ruled on anew. He applied for reappointment into career service, simultaneously submitting a petition to the parliamentary commissioner for the armed forces and the Bundestag petitions committee.[209] The personnel section reported to the state secretary that the retired captain was "the first former soldier to apply for reappointment based on the shift in the BMVg's position regarding the personnel management of homosexual soldiers."[210] After reviewing the case, the section head found reappointment "unwarranted," noting that "we would have to use the legal landscape from twenty years ago as the basis for evaluation."[211] Personnel informed the petitioner that his 1982 retirement was "final, and that no official interest in reappointment existed."[212] The ministry determined that Lindner had already exceeded all age groups eligible for retirement, making reappointment impossible from a legal perspective. The alternative petition for raising his pension entitlement had "no legal basis for support."[213] Military administrators likewise came to the conclusion that Lindner was not entitled to compensation; his retirement in 1982 had been lawful. Military District Administration West nevertheless recommended "weighing the possibility of reaching an accommodating one-time decision without acknowledgment of a legal obligation."[214] Lindner did not give up, and after ten years of countless petitions, complaints and finally lawsuits, his claim was finally acknowledged: The Bundeswehr had accommodated Lindner on two previous occasions; designating him major in the reserve in 2004, and two years later promoting him to lieutenant colonel in the reserve.[215] In 2004 Lindner,

---

208 Rampp, Johnson and Wilms, "Die seit Jahrzehnten belastende Schmach fällt von mir ab," 1146.

209 BArch, BW 1/503302, Petition from Lindner to the BMVg, 30 March 2001, along with petition to the parliamentary commissioner, 31 March 2001 ibid., parliamentary commissioner for the armed forces to Defense Minister Scharping, 4 April 2001; the author is in possession of Lindner's petition to the Bundestag petitions committee. Thanks to Michael Lindner for sharing this and numerous other documents pertaining to his legal battle for restitution.

210 BArch, BW 1/503302: BMVg, PSZ III 6 to State Secretary Biederbick, 29 June 2001.

211 Ibid., Head of personnel office, 2 May 2001.

212 Personnel office to Ret. Captain Lindner, 15 May 2001.

213 BArch, BW 1/503302: BMVg, PSZ III 6 to State Secretary Biederbick, 29 June 2001.

214 Ibid., Military District Administration West.

215 Certificates from the personnel office from 30 April 2004 and 28 July 2006.

who had gone on to complete a degree in geography after his time in the service, was accepted as a senior civil service employee at the Bundeswehr geoinformatics office in Euskirchen, where he received a collective pay rate until reaching retirement age in 2009.[216]

Lindner's culminating legal battle aimed at adjusting his pension. After six German lawyers had found his case stood little chance of success under German law, Lindner finally met a lawyer in Vienna who saw better prospects in his lawsuit under European law and was also authorized to argue before the ECJ in Strasbourg. Thus prepared, Lindner submitted a request that he receive the same pension beginning in 2009 that he would have received had he remained in regular service as an officer after 1982 and reached pay grade A 14 (lieutenant colonel).[217] On this matter too, Lindner, now a retired captain and lieutenant colonel in the reserve, persevered with his inborn tenacity. Hamburg Administrative Court heard Lindner's case against the Federal Republic of Germany in June 2012. The court found that while the action was likely to prove unsuccessful based on the current facts and laws in the case, as German law did not provide for compensation claims,

> the legal situation before the ECHR is likely to be different, based on the European Convention for Human Rights. In the view of the court there is much to speak for the fact that having exhausted the national legal process, the plaintiff [in light of the English cases] could be awarded compensation under Article 41 of the convention [...] The [plaintiff's] 1982 retirement could be viewed as a violation of Article 8 as well as Article 2 paragraph 1 in conjunction with Article 1 paragraph 1 of the Basic Law. Both norms protect the plaintiff's right to sexual self-determination. This was interfered with by the defendant without justification [...] The blanket policy that prevailed in the Bundeswehr at the time whereby homosexual soldiers were not promoted or allowed to work as instructors is likely to constitute a sufficiently intensive form of discrimination. Through this policy homosexual soldiers were, in the view of the court, at least indirectly forced out of the Bundeswehr solely on the basis of their sexual orientation. The plaintiff was impacted by the policy, as it ultimately led to his being determined unfit to serve.[218]

The presiding judge strongly suggested a settlement during the hearing. The BMVg acceded with surprising speed.

216 Military District Administration West, testimonial from 2 July 2009.
217 Lindner to the BMVg, 30 January 2008 and 13 January 2009.
218 Hamburg Administrative Court, Az 20 K 3130/09, 19 June 2012. The author holds a copy in his possession.

VII What of the Others? The Practices of Other Armed Forces

> Men who consistently engage in homosexual activity pose a serious problem for the armed forces of any country. The solution depends on each country's moral and ethical attitudes, as well as its criminal laws.[1]

In managing its approach to homosexuality, the BMVg kept one eye steadily trained on the practices of other counties. Those who have served in the military will be familiar with using "the neighboring situation" as a reference point when giving orders or assessing a situation. Comparing policies of one's own to those of other armed forces presented (and presents) an obvious choice, as gay and lesbian soldiers are present in every army throughout the world.

1. European Armed Forces by Historical Comparison

An already-discussed 1966 work conference organized by the Surgeon General of the Bundeswehr provides one historical context for comparison. Aside from homosexuality's medical aspects, the conference considered the phenomenon's appearance in the policies of other armed forces. "Even in states in which homosexuality is not criminal, as in France, Italy, Sweden, England and the U.S.A. and elsewhere, illicit same-sex activity committed by soldiers is not tolerated but subject to disciplinary action. As a general rule it occurs [...] exclusively for disciplinary reasons."[2]

The BMVg also took interest in other North American and European regulations in its 1969 efforts to prevent homosexual activity being struck from the books as a criminal offense, at least for soldiers. The military attachés at German embassies made official inquiries at the respective ministries of defense, often supplementing these unofficially through personal channels. While the summarized reports give a clear overall view of how other armed forces proceeded with gay soldiers in 1969, they also provide a glimpse of the criminal laws prevailing in other countries at the time. Here the results are reproduced for a selection of armed forces.

---

1 BArch, BW 24/3736: Surgeon General Dr. Finger, "Einführende Bemerkungen zu BMVg" InSan: "Beurteilung der Wehrdiensttauglichkeit und Dienstfähigkeit Homosexueller," 1966, here sheet 4.
2 Ibid., "Erfahrungen mit homosexuellen Soldaten in der Marine." In BMVg, InSan: "Beurteilung der Wehrdiensttauglichkeit und Dienstfähigkeit Homosexueller," 1966, sheets 64–77, here 64.

Unlike its neighbor north of the Rhein, Switzerland no longer brought legal action for homosexual activity, although it was not tolerated in the Swiss Army. Conscripts were expected to refrain from all "homosexual practices" during their three months of service, as well as military exercises that could last up to four weeks.[3] While Swiss law did not consider sexual acts between adult males a criminal offense, a strict military penal code applied in the Confederacy that, in contrast to nearly every other country, held for soldiers, state officials, salaried employees and contractors in the military administrative complex at both the federal level and the cantons, as well as for civilians who worked for the armed forces. Article 157 of the code prescribed prison sentences for sexual activity between people of the same sex (expressly including women), and disciplinary measures in less serious cases. The laws stipulated a minimum sentence of one month in prison in the event that a relationship of dependence or a case of hardship was found to have been exploited.[4]

Belgian law likewise did not recognize sexual activity between adult men as a criminal act. What the BMVg found of particular interest in 1969 was Belgium's lack of any special legal regulations for soldiers. Same-sex activity pursued by soldiers was subject to disciplinary measures if it jeopardized discipline, including dismissal under special circumstances.[5] A similar situation applied in Sweden, where no special regulations existed for the military or in the civil criminal code. In practice, medical examiners and troop physicians would release homosexual conscripts from service "under the pretext of one illness or another."[6] The same held for neighboring Denmark: Consensual sex between adult men was not punishable by law, nor did any regulations regarding homosexual activity appear in the military criminal code or disciplinary regulations. Homosexual conscripts were ruled unfit for service but sometimes drafted for the Home Guard. Active soldiers would likewise be released from service as unfit.[7]

---

3 Ibid., Lt. Col. (MC) Dr. Rudolph Brickenstein, "Probleme der Homosexualität in der Sicht des InSan in BMVg." In BMVg, InSan, "Beurteilung der Wehrdiensttauglichkeit und Dienstfähigkeit Homosexueller,"1966, sheets 22–34, here 23. An identical formulation later found in Brickenstein, "Probleme der Homosexualität im Wehrdienst." The BMVg jurists likely took their phrasing from the article.

4 BArch, BW 1/187212: German Embassy in Bern, Air Force, Army and Navy attachés, 13 February 1969.

5 BArch, BW 1/187212: German Embassy in Brussels, Air Force, Army and Navy attachés, 17 February 1969.

6 BArch, BW 1/187212: German Embassy in Stockholm, Air Force, Army and Navy attachés, 13 February 1969.

7 BArch, BW 1/187212: German Embassy in Copenhagen, Air Force, Army and Navy attachés, 15 April 1969.

Italy's criminal code did not recognize sex between men as a criminal act either unless it occurred in public, nor did any special criminal laws apply in the armed forces, although there were internal disciplinary measures. Homosexuality was grounds for being declared unfit for service during entrance screenings.[8] In the case of a first offense, Portugual's "Código Penal" prescribed a fine, described as bail, for "exercising a desire contrary to nature," with prison sentences being awarded only in particularly severe cases.[9] In most cases "officials kept their eyes closed," a fact the Portuguese attaché registered as noteworthy given the authoritarian government in Portugal at the time.[10] The armed forces for their part did not keep their eyes closed but, as in Italy, would bring disciplinary proceedings. In cases where "troop morale" was seriously impaired, the soldier in question would without exception be demoted to the lowest rank, and in extreme cases be kicked out of the armed forces.[11] West Germany's military attaché to Spain, the kingdom without a king, reported that the common criminal code did not feature any regulations specific to homosexual activity – and this under the rule of dictator Francisco Franco. Soldiers were, however, subject to Article 352 of the military criminal code, under which "dishonorable actions with people of the same sex" were punishable by a prison term ranging from six months to six years, along with mandatory expulsion from the armed forces. It is worth noting that the paragraph threatened all same-sex activity pursued by soldiers with punishment and dismissal, including with civilians, and applied to all service ranks.[12]

The flow of information concerning soldiers' homosexuality in other armies did not constitute a one-way street; neighboring and allied armed forces were just as curious "about the others" and would make inquiries at ministries of defense in partnering countries, including Germany. The BMVg's archives include written

---

8 BArch, BW 1/187212: German Embassy in Rome, Air Force, Army and Navy attachés, 24 March 1969.

9 Portuguese Penal Code, Article 71 No. 5. In: BArch, BW/187212: German Embassy in Lisbon, head of military attaché staff 25 February 1969.

10 Ibid.

11 BArch, BW/187212: German Embassy in Lisbon, Head of military attaché staff 25 February 1969.

12 BArch, BW 1/187212: German Embassy in Madrid, Air Force attaché, 6 March 1969.

requests for information sent to German military attachés by defense ministries in Australia,[13] Greece,[14] the UK[15] and repeatedly from the U.S.[16]

As the new millennium drew near, the BMVg put out a revised summary of the current practices in other NATO armed forces based on attaché reports. The reports came about in the wake of inquiries Hardthöhe made regarding stipulations in criminal and disciplinary law as well as any assignment or career restrictions, prompted in turn by a June 1997 inquiry from the FDP fraction in the Bundestag.[17] Even without the FDP inquiry, comparing the BMVg's own position to other allies' armed forces represented an important way of identifying any possible need for change, as retired State Secretary Wichert recalled.[18] By international comparison, there had not been any need for changes in German practices, Wichert continued; German policies were entirely respectable when measured up against other NATO militaries.[19] As Colonel Dr. Brickenstein reported previously in a psychiatric "evaluation" from 1980, "we [the Bundeswehr] are the most liberal in NATO" – something *he* had personally ensured.[20]

Differently from Germany, in Belgium it was possible for homosexual soldiers to serve as immediate superiors, provided no activity relevant to criminal or disciplinary law was in evidence.[21] The military attaché in Copenhagen similarly reported no restrictions on homosexual soldiers serving in leadership roles, nor for that matter any sanctions against homosexual behavior, criminal activity notwithstanding. Gay men were not drafted until 1979, but since then homosexuality had not been grounds for exclusion and no longer factored into entrance examinations. Homosexuality in general "was not a topic" in the Danish military.

---

13 BArch, BW 2/31224: Embassy of the Federal Republic of Germany in Canberra A.C.T., defense attaché, 26 June 1992; parallel inquiry from the Australian defense attaché in Bonn and the BMVg's reply from FüS I 4 on 2 July 1992, ibid.

14 BArch, BW 2/31224: Inquiry from the Greek defense attaché in Bonn from 18 July 1985 and reply from the BMVg on 4 October 1985.

15 Among others, BArch, BW 1/546375, Inquiry from the British defense attaché in Bonn on 26 July 1990 and reply from the BMVg on 21 August 1990; inquiry from the British defense attaché on 9 September 1991, the BMVg's reply from 5 November 1991 is in BArch, BW 1/531592.

16 For example, BArch, BW 2/31224: Embassy of the Federal Republic of Germany in Washington, D.C. Navy attaché, 20 December 1989 and the reply of the BMVg, FüS I 4 on 17 January 1990, ibid.

17 See chapter 4 for more on the FDP inquiry.

18 Interview with retired State Secretary Peter Wichert, Bad Münstereifel, 10 April 2019.

19 Ibid.

20 Interview with Michael Lindner, Hamburg, February 2017.

21 BArch, BW 1/502107, BW 2/38357 and BW 2/38358: BMVg, state secretary, draft response to the Federal Constitutional Court, undated.

There were no restrictions on assignment, including aboard ships.[22] In Norway as well, homosexual soldiers were eligible for all service posts, positions of leadership included; homosexuals' broad acceptance in society did not allow for distinctions to be drawn between their treatment in civil society and the military.[23]

The Greeks also seemed to take a highly pragmatic approach to the subject. Homosexuality was not grounds for being mustered out of the military; homosexual men performed military service like the others. Joint staff in Athens reported that whether or not homosexuals remained in the armed forces "was not assessed based on their sexual preferences"; the "rules that applied for the rest of military personnel" prevailed. The joint staff reckoned that the majority of homosexuals did not disclose their sexual preferences while in service.[24]

Catholic Italy struck a line similar to the Greeks in the late Nineties; homosexuality was neither talked about nor debated within the armed forces, "it does not occur outwardly."[25] The Ministry of Defense had not issued any legal regulations or decrees pertaining to the matter; cases were considered and decided on an individual basis and soldiers had access to legal means of recourse. The deciding criteria in Italy was the distinction between "egosintonico" and "egodistonico." "Egosintonico" was used for a homosexual soldier who was "at peace with himself and did not bother anyone." In that case, his sexual orientation held no implications for his service, assignments or career prospects – psychological stability proved the determining factor. While they were not mentioned, the same was understood to apply for conscripts. A man recognized as "egodistonico," on the other hand, might prove a liability in stressful situations and was immediately dismissed from the armed forces as unfit for service. In 1997 a petty officer appealed his dismissal and won, earning the right to be reinstated with compensation for loss of earnings and professional disadvantages.[26]

The military attaché in Warsaw reported that homosexual soldiers did not come up for discussion in Poland, though not out of tolerance or liberal politics but because the subject was strictly taboo, due in no small part to the strong influence of the Catholic Church. Soldiers identified as homosexual were initially put on leave then released from the armed forces after medical appraisal, a policy that

---

22 BArch, BW 2/38358: German Embassy in Copenhagen, defense attaché, 10 July 1997.
23 BArch, BW 2/38358: BMVg, annex to FüS I 4, 27 July 1998, unchanged in 1999.
24 BArch, BW 2/38358: General Staff, head of protocol for foreign relations to the German Embassy in Athens, defense attaché, 11 August 1997.
25 BArch, BW 2/38358: Germany Embassy in Rome, defense and army attaché, 8 August 1997.
26 BArch, BW 1/502107, no pagination. BMVg, state secretary, draft response to the Federal Constitutional Court, undated. Also in BArch, BW 2/38358.

also meant they were excluded from positions of leadership.[27] The Czechs meanwhile struck an exceptionally liberal tack with their homosexual soldiers. In 1999 the BMVg noted no restrictions on leading, instructing or educating subordinates, nor was homosexuality grounds for excluding conscripts from service or acceptance as a fixed-term soldier, provided that no problems in adjusting to military life or other psychological problems presented themselves.[28] This made the former Eastern Bloc state far more progressive on the issue than its neighbor to the west, Germany. The change in heart at the Ministry of Defense in Prague seems to have unfolded between 1997 and 1999: in 1997 the German military attaché had still been reporting that homosexuals were turned down as volunteers, and eligible conscripts released from their obligation to serve, while already active soldiers were dismissed.[29] In contrast to the Czech Republic, the Hungarian armed forces dismissed part-time or career soldiers if they came out as homosexual, based on a lack of fitness to serve as leaders, educators and instructors. Gay soldiers were also not spoken about or debated as a topic in public.[30]

Similarly to Poland and Hungary, the Portuguese armed forces replied that discovery of a soldiers' homosexuality resulted in immediate, dishonorable discharge. Leadership positions were ruled out entirely. Reporting in 1999, the military attaché could not make out any social pressure for change.[31] Neighboring Spain took a decidedly more relaxed approach to homosexuality than Portugal; homosexuals were "hardly stigmatized" in the armed forces. The military would "hold on" to the officer even if the "tendency" should "happen to be" discovered. In the case of "decent and neutral conduct," the officer would retain his leadership position in the service and remain eligible for promotion. Legal consequences followed only in the event of official breaches of duty or criminal acts.[32]

---

27 Ibid.
28 Ibid.
29 BArch, BW 2/38358: BMVg, annex to FüS I 4, 27 July 1998.
30 BArch, BW 1/502107, no pagination. BMVg, state secretary, draft response to the Federal Constitutional Court, undated. Also in BW 2/38358. The German military attaché reported further in 1997 that homosexuality "wasn't a topic" in the armed forces of Hungary, Slovenia and Albania. BArch, BW 2/38358, German Embassy in Budapest, military attaché, 9 July 1997.
31 Ibid.
32 BArch, BW 2/38358, German Embassy in Madrid, defense attaché, 9 July 1997.

Societal Acceptance of Homosexuality from 1 (never) to 10 (always)

West Germany	4.46
Belgium	3.88
France	3.92
United Kingdom	3.43
Northern Ireland	2.42
Ireland	3.15
Italy	3.63
The Netherlands	7.20
Portugal	2.35
Spain	3.43

Source: Fleckenstein, "Homosexuality and Military Service in Germany," Appendix, Table 2, 1993. Survey results undated. ©ZMSBw 09585-02

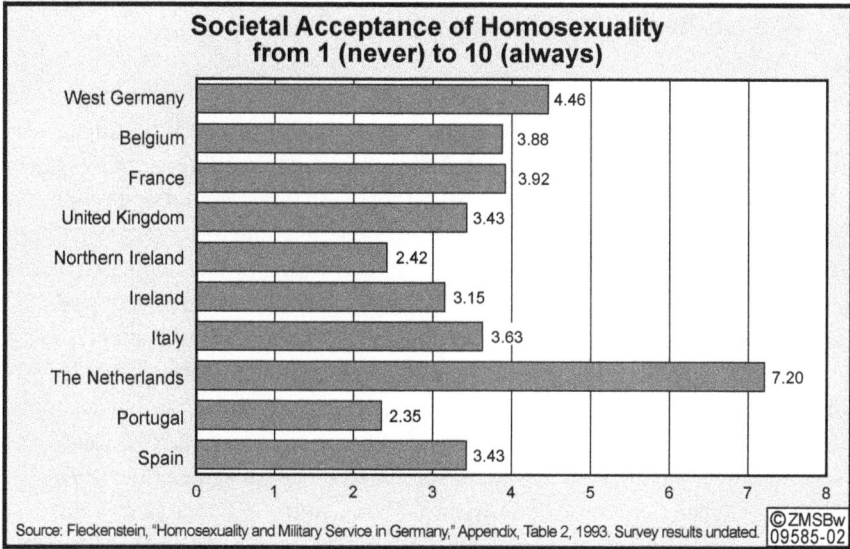

Laying reports from the various capitals side by side, one encounters a mosaic of opinions that could not be more different. The liberalism on display in Denmark and the Netherlands hardly surprises for example, matching the broad tolerance in those countries and societies. The survey results from the Allensbach Institute shown above reveal the degree of social tolerance different European countries showed toward homosexuality in the early 1990s, with participants asked to rank their acceptance on a scale of 1 (never) to 10 (always).[33]

The restriction of survey results to West Germany is noteworthy, almost certainly indicating that Allensbach collected the data before German unification in 1990. The SOWI study was published in 1993 yet gives no mention of the survey's timeframe, and thus no information as to how current it was. Setting aside these gaps, the West German population fell somewhere in the middle in terms of acceptance. Aside from Northern Ireland, Portugal showed the lowest rate of acceptance at 2.35 out of 10. By direct comparison, there is a surprisingly higher show of tolerance in the other Catholic countries of Italy (3.6) and Spain (3.4).[34]

---

33 Fleckenstein, "Homosexuality and Military Service in Germany," appendix, Table 2.
34 Ibid.

2. The Netherlands: "It Goes without Saying"

In the Netherlands, consensual sex between men had not constituted a criminal act since 1969. Still, for soldiers, teachers and others, illicit sex with subordinates was punishable by up to six years in prison. The current military criminal code began by establishing that the full scope of regulations in the general criminal code applied to soldiers. Conversely, this meant that there were no separate regulations governing homosexual activity, which evidently included disciplinary law; in 1969 the West German military attaché stressed that homosexuality did not pose "any problem" within the armed forces.[35] It remains an open question whether the attaché meant to say here that it did not exist, was not relevant or was not seen as an issue. In 1969, young Dutch men who were identified as homosexual or showed similar "conduct" were still being ruled unfit for conscription and as volunteers, with soldiers who were already in the military released as a consequence. This meant the Dutch regulations matched those in West Germany – at least until 1974. Five years before the Federal Republic changed its own entrance regulations, the Netherlands declared that on its own, a "diagnosis" of homosexuality neither "could nor should" serve as grounds for rejecting a person from service. The Minister of Defense explained the new policy on the grounds of social views shifting away from stigmatization and toward recognition of "two forms of sexual orientation."[36] That did not mean that all homosexuals automatically qualified for service, however. It would still have to be evaluated on an individual basis whether it would harm the psychological and "mental health" of the soldier in question for him to remain in the service.[37] Working in reverse, this meant that outside of exceptions nothing stood in the way of homosexual soldiers remaining in service.

The Ministry of Defense document from The Hague did not contain any clause denying homosexuals' ability to serve as fixed-term or career soldiers, or blocking their right to serve in leadership. Access to confidential or classified material remained the only restricted arena, though here too a policy of case-by-case evaluation replaced the former blanket policy of gay soldiers' disqualification from receiving security clearances. Previously, the same regulations had applied on this point as in the Bundeswehr, rationalized along very similar lines: Social intolerance

---

35 BArch, BW 1/187212: German Embassy in The Hague, Air Force, Army and Navy attachés, 17 February 1969.

36 BArch, BW 4/839: Dutch Minister of Defense to the Defense Committee of the Lower Chamber of Parliament, 15 February 1974. Available as a copy in the Embassy of the Federal Republic of Germany in The Hague to the BMVg, 19 June 1985.

37 Ibid.

of homosexuality had made it impossible for gays to be open about their sexual orientation in the past, leaving them exposed to blackmail attempts and forcing them to associate with "criminals or people at the edge of society." Society's growing acceptance of gays now enabled them to stop "hiding" and pursue relationships openly, increasingly undercutting the reasoning behind denying them security clearance. Soldiers who were open about their homosexuality but had no relationships with those at the margins of society or criminals were now granted access to confidential material.[38] With the introduction of the policy in 1974, the Dutch armed forces preceded West Germany by more than ten years. There was a crucial difference, however: The Netherlands made it easy for their officers and NCOs to be open about their sexual orientation. Unlike the Bundeswehr, no restrictive personnel measures generally followed an "outing." Put succinctly, beginning in 1974 Dutch soldiers could go about openly with their sexual orientation and serve as officers and NCOs unlike their West German counterparts – remarkably early by comparison with other NATO forces.

The West German defense attaché voiced his misgivings about the path taken by the Netherlands in a 1987 report:

> The [...] initiative moves yet another marginal group issue in Dutch society into the military spotlight [...] What remains is a tolerant stance within the Ministry of Defense toward liberal expressions of life from members of an emancipated society – that and the consternation and far-reaching rejection of the trend among the troops themselves. Yet criticism only comes in private conversation, as with the problem of mixed warship crews in the navy.[39]

The simple fact that criticism was only voiced in private among officers attests to how far the acceptance of Dutch society had worked its way into the Army. The armed forces were clearly under pressure from the social, and subsequently political, trend toward tolerance. Yet unlike in West Germany, the Ministry of Defense in The Hague did not make an effort to slow the trend but rather asserted the primacy of politics to prevail over the military on this issue as well. Here too, (West) Germany and its Ministry of Defense were still a far cry from the position ten years later. In 1995 the German defense attaché sent off another report to Bonn on the current state of the Netherlands' liberal policies based on conversations with the personnel department at the Dutch Ministry of Defense. Legal provisions forbade discrimination "against homosexuals and lesbians" in the armed forces, including placing any

---

38 Ibid.
39 BArch, 2/31224: Embassy of the Federal Republic of Germany in The Hague, defense attaché, 17 February 1987. Also available in BW 4/1530.

career restrictions on homosexual soldiers. Quite the contrary – in the meantime they had been "fully accepted and integrated" into society and military alike.[40] The attaché also sent over a photocopy of a brochure put out by the Dutch Ministry of Defense in 1992 entitled "Homosexuality and Defense." The brochure opened with the question "Gays in the armed forces, is that allowed?" "Yes, of course it's allowed. Much more than that, it goes without saying that it's possible. Military personnel are a reflection of society, after all." The brochure ended quoting then Defense Minister Relus ter Beek that he was able only "to exercise limited influence on the conduct of my personnel," but viewed it as his mission to create the preconditions so that "no differences in conduct based on homosexuality" came about.[41]

The liberal policies within the Dutch armed forces were not simply of interest to the Bundeswehr for its own edification; they had practical consequences. Beginning in 1995, German and Dutch soldiers served in a joint corps, with staff headquarters located in Münster. Just weeks after the corps staff began operations the BMVg found itself confronting problems arising out of the "extraordinarily liberal" stance the Dutch armed forces took toward homosexual soldiers, which barred sexual orientation from leading to "any restrictions on assignment or professional disadvantage."[42] As of June 1996, Hardthöhe found that policy differences on the matter had not led to any problems within the joint corps,[43] although the working group on "Deep Integration" should see to it that "homosexually inclined Dutch soldiers should not be put in command of German soldiers, if at all possible."[44] The archives are silent as to whether this actually occurred or not.

Soldiers in the German Air Force training regiment located in the Dutch town of Budel still recalled the astonishing openness that reigned among the Dutch Army in the early Nineties in comparison to the Bundeswehr. The Dutch Air Force took out ads for future pilots in gay magazines that showed the cockpit of a fighter jet bearing the catchphrase: "There are more exciting places than the darkroom." The relaxed attitude the Dutch took to homosexuality had an effect on the German soldiers stationed there. One contemporary eyewitness recalled his swearing-in at Budel in 1990. A conscript had invited his long-term partner to the event – the two greeted each other with a kiss in plain sight, directly in front of the company build-

---

40 BArch, BW 2/38353: Embassy of the Federal Republic of Germany in The Hague, defense attaché to the BMVg, 21 December 1994. Previously issued with the same wording in ibid., I. (GE/NL) Corps, German division G1 to the BMVg, 19 December 1995.

41 Ibid., photocopy and translation of the brochure "Homosexualiteit en Defensie" from May 1992.

42 BArch, BW 2/38353: BMVg, FüS I 4, 20 June 1996.

43 Ibid.; and previously in ibid., I. (GE/NL) Corps, German division G1 to the BMVg, 19 December 1995; ibid., BMVg, State Secretary Wichert to Deputy Ruprecht Polenz, 14 February 1996.

44 BArch, BW 2/38353: BMVg, FüS I 4, 20 June 1996.

ing. The German soldiers present had been flummoxed; there were no negative reactions to speak of. "Wow, he's got guts!" had been the words of one.[45]

3. Great Britain: "Immediate Dismissal as Unfit to Serve"

Winston Churchill is credited with one famous saying about "traditions" in the Royal Navy: "Naval Tradition?" He reportedly said as the First Lord of the Admiralty in 1911 (other sources put it in 1913), "Monstrous. Nothing but rum, sodomy, prayers and the lash."[46] A closer look at the sources reveals the attribution to be spurious. Churchill's personal assistant, Anthony Montague Browne attested to asking Churchill about the quote, to which Churchill replied: "I never said it. I wish I had."[47]

Writing in 1908, Karl Franz von Leexow noted the strict line British armed forces took against homosexuals in their ranks "to promote discipline and morality."[48] Yet Leexow also quoted "one of the best-known English generals" (Lord Kitchener, by Magnus Hirschfeld's account) as saying, "If we run out of officers in the Sudan, I'll use the retired homosexuals."[49] Rumors about Herbert Kitchener's own homosexuality swirled about the Army officer during his lifetime (1850–1916), reaching back to his time as commander of the Egyptian Army between 1892 and 1899.[50] "Is a soldier married a soldier spoiled?" the women's magazine *Home Chat* asked on a 1910 cover in reference to one of Kitchener's statements, picturing the officer alongside.[51] The reality was different: During World War I, 22 officers and 270 NCOs or enlisted soldiers were sentenced by court martial for homosexuality. Dubbing it a "German perversion," the press campaign against actual or alleged homosexuals as German agents reached a highpoint in 1916.[52]

Homosexuals also (predictably) served in the British Army, Royal Navy and Royal Air Force during World War II, among them highly-decorated officers and

---

45 Interview with Winfried Stecher, Hamburg, 25 January 2018.
46 Hewlett, "When and why did Winston Churchill say: 'The traditions of the Royal Navy are rum, sodomy and the lash'?"
47 Churchill, *Churchill by Himself.*
48 Leexow, *Armee und Homosexualität*, 100.
49 Ibid., 101; Hirschfeld, *Von einst bis jetzt*, 152.
50 Bourne, *Fighting Proud*, 5–11.
51 Reproduction of the cover and the article in Bourne, *Fighting Proud*, 109–11.
52 Schwartz, *Homosexuelle, Seilschaften, Verrat*, 153–57. Among those who fell victim to suspicion were economist John Maynard Keynes, employed at the time in London's Ministry of Finance. Ibid., 154.

war heroes. Wing Commander Ian Gleed (1916–1943) was one; Gleed entered the Royal Air Force in 1936, fought in the "Battle of Britain" in 1940, was twice honored by King George VI and became a Wing Commander in 1941 before being shot down and fatally wounded in Tunisia in 1943. In *Arise to Conquer*, an autobiographical account of the "Battle of Britain" that came out in 1942, Gleed alluded to a secret lover named Pam at the advice of his publisher. There never was a Pam, but there was a Christopher.[53] Christopher Gotch (1923–2002) entered the Royal Air Force at nineteen, receiving pilot training in a squadron led by Wing Commander Gleed. The two quickly became lovers, with the twenty-five-year-old Gleed initiating the relationship by Gotch's account. Gleed was taking a risk; sex between men stood under special threat of punishment for being considered morally corrosive, or a "load of rubbish" as Gotch put it. Gotch publicly disclosed his relationship to Gleed for the first time in 1997, in the BBC documentary "It's not unusual."[54]

Nothing changed after World War II; in 1997 the air force, army and navy all still had just a single word for an officer whose homosexuality became public knowledge: Out. Homosexuals were sought out by means of the intelligence services. In 1967, or two years before West Germany, the "Sexual Offences Act" altered sex crimes in Great Britain, decriminalizing consensual sexual activity between men over the age of twenty-one.[55] The provisions in the new law drew an explicit exception for soldiers and other members of the armed forces, for whom service branch law continued to apply.[56] Article 66 of the 1955 Army Act, like its counterparts in the air force and navy, made "disgraceful conduct of a cruel, indecent or unnatural kind" liable to punishment, prescribing up to two years in prison. Article 64 also saw to it that any officer who "behaves in a scandalous manner, unbecoming the character of an officer and gentlemen, shall, on conviction by court-martial, be cashiered." Under the two articles, Her Majesty's Armed Forces also made homosexual activity punishable by at least twenty-eight days' arrest. NCOs would as a rule be demoted to the lowest possible rank, officers would be dismissed. Simplified disciplinary measures did not exist. Less serious offenses might be "regarded and treated as medical cases" by troop physicians and wind up in transfer or dismissal.[57]

---

53 Bourne, *Fighting Proud*, 97–104.
54 Ibid., 102–3.
55 BArch, BW 1/187212: Germany Embassy in London, head of the military attaché office, 20 February 1969. For a full account of the debates about decriminalization in the House of Commons see Ebner, *Religion im Parlament*, 42–94. On the 1967 Sexual Offences Act in particular see 94–95.
56 BArch, BW 1/187212: German Embassy in London, head of the military attaché office, 20 February 1969.
57 Ibid.

BMVg jurists returned to take another look at other armed forces' policies in 1970. With a volunteer Army, the British did not accept men with homosexual "tendencies" for service. If the fact were "recognized" once they had already entered the military, the soldier would be immediately dismissed as "unfit for service."[58] Yet by all accounts there were exceptions to the stringent policies, especially with high-ranking officers. One military historian close to General Johann Adolf Graf von Kielmansegg recalled the general telling him in 1967 or '68, while Kielmansegg was serving as NATO's Commander in Chief of Allied Forces in Central Europe and living in Bad Krozingen outside Freiburg, that the British kept "both eyes closed" for generals whose homosexual orientation was an open secret.[59] A retired naval officer had something similar to report. A former commander with years of training England, he laconically interjected at one point that "the transition from camaraderie to homosexuality was fluid on the island."[60]

In contrast to the impression these individual accounts might give, the legal landscape was quite unambiguous: Up until 1994 homosexuality constituted a criminal act within the British armed forces. In 1997 the German Army attaché reported from London that the British government had "made it clear that homosexuality would not be tolerated in the armed forces [...] in the future either." The armed forces "had reserved the right to distinguish themselves from society." Simply put, the position of the British Ministry of Defense was that "homosexuals exercise a bad influence on morale in the armed forces."[61] An internal survey had shown soldiers strictly opposed to accepting homosexuals into the armed forces, while those who were identified as homosexuals were generally dismissed. Between 1990 and July 1997, 417 soldiers were released from service, with the annual figure ranging between 42 and 65. That included a surprisingly high number of women; in 1996, for example, 43 men and 22 women were dismissed, with similar numbers for the previous year. In summary, the German military attaché found "the UK Ministry of Defense resolved neither to adhere to ECJ legislation nor give in to what was currently somewhat subdued social pressure on the delicate issue, [and] prepared to risk action before the ECJ with the backing of the government."[62]

Such was the state of things in July 1997. Initially at least, Tony Blair's Labour government showed as little will to change as Germany's Red–Green coalition would the following year. Two years and two months later, the European Court

---

58 BArch, BW 24/7180: BMVg, VR IV 1, 29 September 1970.
59 Interview with Dr. Georg Meyer, Freiburg im Breisgau, 7 September 2019.
60 Letter from Ret. Navy Commander Heinrich Franzen in *Die Bundeswehr* 11, 2020, 120.
61 BArch, BW 2/38358, Germany Embassy in London, deputy army attaché, 29 July 1997.
62 Ibid.

of Human Rights brought an end to the persecution and prosecution of homosexuals in the British armed forces. The lawsuit revolved around four former career soldiers, both women and men, who had been dismissed from the armed forces for their sexual orientation. The final ruling on 27 September 1999 found that the current personnel policy as it pertained to homosexuality was not "legally sustainable," as Defense Minister Geoff Hoon conceded in parliament. The court opinion made it clear that the existing rules would have to change, the minister continued frankly, calling on the head of the joint staff to make an urgent review of current regulations.[63] On 12 January 2000 Hoon presented a revised code of conduct to the House of Commons that had the armed forces' operational readiness – but not differences in lifestyle – at the center of its focus. The second sentence of the code explicitly addressed itself to all members of the armed forces "regardless of their gender, sexual orientation, rank or status." "Personal relationships do not lend themselves to precise prescription," the document continued, nor was it practicable to list every possible inappropriate form of behavior individually.[64] Instead, the new orders put a test question, or "service test" at the heart of evaluating conduct: "Have the actions or behavior of an individual adversely impacted or are they likely to impact on the efficiency or operational effectiveness of the service?" Before the House of Commons, Hoon explained that since operational effectiveness would be the lone criteria in assessment going forward, there were no longer any grounds for rejecting homosexuals from military service. In consequence, the ministry had decided to repeal the existing ban against homosexuals. The revisions took effect that same day, 12 January 2000.[65] Twenty years later, on 12 January 2020, the central Ministry of Defense offices and Royal Navy HQ in Portsmouth were lit up by rainbow flags, celebrating the opening of the military to LGB personnel.[66]

---

63 "Homosexuality and the Armed Forces," speech by Defense Minister Geoff Hoon before the House of Commons on 12 January 2000, forwarded in the original English by BMVg Section PSZ III 1 on 3 April 2000 to the joint chiefs of the armed forces, BArch, BW 24/37667.

64 British Ministry of Defense: The Armed Forces Code of Social Conduct Policy Statement. An English-language copy was also forward by PSZ III 1 on 3 April 2000 to the joint chiefs of the armed forces, BArch, BW 24/37667.

65 Speech of British Defense Minister Geoff Hoon before the House of Commons on 12 January 2000, BArch, BW 24/37677.

66 "Ministry of Defense lit in rainbow colours to celebrate LGB personnel."

4. The U.S.: "No Queens in the Marines"

So many queens think everybody's gay, and John Wayne is gay, and Gary Cooper is gay, and he's a cocksucker even though he's got a wife and two kids. But a square guy is a square guy, and there were no queens in the Marines.[67]

Such was the account one paratrooper gave of serving in the U.S. Marines in the Pacific theater during World War II, going on to recall the intimacy that developed in the course of the fighting and everyday life in between battles. "But the closeness there had absolutely nothing to do with the gay thing at all. Because if you were gay you were kicked out of the goddamned Marine Corps immediately. Even if they *thought* you were gay you were kicked out of the Marine Corps. It was not a common thing like it was in the fucking navy. If a guy were gay he normally went in the navy, because of clean living aboard ship and everything, and the nice white uniform."[68]

Criminal legislation of sexual behavior in the U.S. occurred at the state level, with a number of states criminalizing sexual activity between men as "sodomy." For the armed forces the Uniform Code of Military Justice (UCMJ) applied, whose §925 Article 125 also made "sodomy" punishable by law.[69] In 1969, the German Army attaché in Washington reported that the death penalty could be imposed in such cases, but generally sexual activity between adult men where force was not involved brought four years' "hard labor," i.e. a labor camp. Convicted soldiers would receive dishonorable discharge from the armed forces.[70] As in the UK, homosexual soldiers were sought out in the U.S. using intelligence methods, with gays and lesbians who had been identified as such by one means or the other dismissed "without honor." This was not the same as dishonorable discharge, which incurred "disgrace" and held grave social consequences for the future, as Colonel Dr. Brickenstein described in 1966.[71] Even so, Dr. Brickenstein continued with palpable regret, "U.S. armed

---

67 Bowers, "No Queens in the Marines," 80.
68 Ibid., 82. For a full account of the situation facing gay and lesbian U.S. soldiers during World War II see Bérubé, *Coming Out Under Fire.*
69 The offense of "sodomy" also made heterosexual anal intercourse punishable: "Any person [...] who engages in unnatural carnal copulation with another person of the same or opposite sex or with an animal is guilty of sodomy. Penetration, however slight, is sufficient to complete the offense." Available online at https://ucmj.us/ and in BArch, BW 1/187212: German Embassy in Washington D.C., military attaché, 17 February 1969.
70 Ibid.
71 BArch, BW 24/3736: Lt. Col. (MC) Dr. Rudolph Brickenstein, "Probleme der Homosexualität in der Sicht des InSan im BMVg," in BMVg, InSan: "Beurteilung der Wehrdiensttauglichkeit und Dienstfähigkeit Homosexueller," 1966, sheets 22–34, here 24.

forces' infiltration by homosexuals could not be prevented entirely."[72] Unlike in Germany or Great Britain where "the problem chiefly [played out] in the navy," the U.S. largely encountered the problem in the air force. In making this claim, Brickenstein drew on a study attributed to Arnold Mysior, a psychologist working for the U.S. Air Force.[73] According to Brickenstein, Mysior saw the causes for this as lying in the broad mobility of soldiers in the air force; like his German colleague, Mysior was certain that homosexuals formed "sociological groups of their own [in the Army], with shared jargon, near unerring recognition of one another and a widespread system of mutual acquaintanceship linked to treason, addiction and criminality."[74] In order to investigate homosexuals more effectively the U.S. military had created the Office of Special Investigations, which sought to track down gays secretly serving in the military via intelligence, "eyewitness testimony and verifying biographical as well as hereditary anamnesis."[75] (Here Brickenstein was likely overly focused on homosexuality. The Air Force Office of Special Investigations pursued all kinds of leads related to security, by no means only those linked to homosexuality.)

Homosexuals were requested to report other soldiers they knew to be homosexual, a practice mentioned explicitly in U.S. Army service regulations. To follow Brickenstein's account, Mysior was convinced that "true homosexuality" was present only when sex between men "was the expression of psychological experience."[76] The phrasing, which is not elaborated on, may echo a distinction the Bundeswehr also attempted to draw between true, consistent homosexuality and sexual "slip-ups" that were context dependent (e.g. excess alcohol consumption by someone who was "actually" heterosexual). The service regulations in the U.S. Armed Forces evidently followed a somewhat different definition: Only a person who actually engaged in homosexual activity should be regarded as such. This

---

72 Ibid., 25.

73 Ibid. Starting in 1947 Arnold Mysior (1921–2015) worked counterespionage in the Air Force Office of Special Investigations. After retiring in 1965, Mysior became Director of Psychological Services at Georgetown University, where he taught until 1977. http://arnoldmysior.com/bio (last accessed 6 March 2019).

74 BArch, BW 24/3736: Lt. Col. (MC) Dr. Rudolph Brickenstein, "Probleme der Homosexualität in der Sicht des InSan im BMVg," in BMVg, InSan: "Beurteilung der Wehrdiensttauglichkeit und Dienstfähigkeit Homosexueller," 1966, sheets 22–34, here 25.

75 Ibid. Brickenstein's mention of "hereditary anamnesis" is chilling, recalling the darkest eras of German medicine, and German psychiatry in particular. The era lay just twenty years in the past; the doctors were often the same.

76 Ibid.

pregnant point was not elaborated on either in 1966, prompting the obvious question of whether it applied conversely that a soldier who abstained sexually but was
homosexual by all outer appearances was not seen as such, and thus did not have
any restrictions to fear – i.e. dismissal. If so, did it constitute a further parallel to
the position taken by the Catholic Church? The jurist presenting for the German
Navy at the same work conference in 1966 also took a look over the pond; the U.S.
Navy did not simply crack down on homosexuality in its ranks with "severe punishment," "but by consciously promoting a natural sex-cult."[77] The navy lawyer put
it more concretely. By "promoting the distribution of risqué depictions of pin-up
girls," the navy strove to "channel soldiers' sexuality along natural courses and
avert homosexual deviations," although "the extent to which the American Navy
has succeeded in these methods with true homosexuals unfortunately could not be
determined."[78]

The Naval Military Personal Manual in use in 1983 contained the following:

> Homosexuality is incompatible with naval service. The presence in the naval environment
> of persons who engage in homosexual conduct or who, by their statements, demonstrate a
> propensity to engage in homosexual conduct seriously impairs the accomplishment of the
> naval mission. The presence of such members adversely affects the ability of the Department
> of the Navy to maintain discipline, good order, and morale; foster mutual trust and confidence
> among service members; ensure the integrity of the system of rank and command; facilitate
> assignment and worldwide deployment of service members who frequently must live and
> work under close conditions affording minimal privacy; recruit and retain members of the
> Department of the Navy; maintain the public acceptability of the Department of the Navy; and
> prevent breaches of security.[79]

The corresponding passage in the U.S. Army Manual featured the same wording.[80]
At least on individual occasions, soldiers who were taken into custody for activities
of the sort were also subjected to physical violence by military police. One witness
speaking for a television documentary recalled the German police and the Military
Police Corps appearing suddenly outside his hotel room in the 1960s. A U.S. soldier
had rented the room to spend the night with the German, who was sixteen at the

---

77 BArch, BW 24/3736: "Erfahrungen mit homosexuellen Soldaten in der Marine," in BMVg, InSan:
"Beurteilung der Wehrdiensttauglichkeit und Dienstfähigkeit Homosexueller," 1966, sheets 64–77,
here 66.

78 Ibid.

79 BArch, BW 2/31224: Embassy of the Federal Republic of Germany in Washington D.C. naval
attaché, 24 November 1989, containing a copy of SECNAVINST 1910. 4A from 27 December 1983.
Identical wording in the Naval Military Personal Manual, 3630400.

80 Ibid., containing a copy of the Army Policy of Homosexuality.

time. The eyewitness recalled that the soldier had been dragged out of the room and later "been savagely beaten with a rubber club."[81]

Beginning in the late Eighties, a glimmer of hope appeared on the horizon in the U.S. for gays and lesbians in the military, a development that can also be gleaned from reports and newspaper articles sent to Bonn by the German military attaché in Washington.[82] One of the first signs came in a study put out by the Pentagon's Personal Security Research and Education Center in Monterey, California. The increasingly liberal and open stance toward gays and lesbians within the broader population, paired with homosexuality' decriminalization, had decreased the pressure on homosexuals to conceal and hide themselves. This meant that gay and lesbian soldiers were no longer susceptible to blackmail and thus no longer presented a security risk. For the researchers in Monterey, it also meant the time had come to consider how homosexuals might be integrated into the armed forces. The German Navy attaché added that the Pentagon "continued to be as steadfastly opposed as before. Homosexuality was incompatible with the living conditions that military service entailed; it disturbed soldiers' coexistence, undermined order and discipline and thus detracted from the armed forces' ability to fulfill its mission."[83]

While the Pentagon's arguments read similarly to Hardthöhe's, the consequences were different. In the U.S. armed forces, any soldier identified as gay or lesbian was unfailingly discharged without honor; their West German counterparts on the other hand were allowed to keep their uniforms and serve out the remainder of their term (with the exceptions described earlier). It is worth noting in this context that a military draft had not existed in the U.S. since the 1970s, meaning all U.S. soldiers were either fixed-term or career. The German Navy attaché included a personal take on the issue with his report. To date, the U.S. military had made use of "the easily understandable argument of homosexuality as a security risk almost exclusively, and too vehemently." This let other, "equally weighty" arguments sooner be classified as "as excuses from a group of conservatives reluctant to apply societal changes they did not like to their own sphere of activity." The risk of political or legal decisions against the military's position was on the rise, as the

---

81 Reported in the television documentary "Der Schwulen-Paragraph," broadcast 10 October 2019 at 11.15 p.m. on HR-Fernsehen.

82 For example, BArch, BW 2/31224: Embassy of the Federal Republic of Germany in Washington D.C., naval attaché, 24 November 1989, containing copies of multiple newspaper articles, among them Schneider, "Rethinking DOD Policy on Gays"; Sciolino, "Report Urging End of Homosexual Ban Rejected by Military."

83 BArch, BW 2/31224: Embassy of the Federal Republic of Germany in Washington D.C., naval attaché, 24 November 1989. For a more complete analysis of U.S. gay and lesbian soldiers in the 1970s and 1980s see Shilts, *Conduct Unbecoming* and Wells-Petry, *Exclusion*. Both works came out in 1993.

end of general conscription meant that fewer and fewer "members in the legislative and judicial spheres" would be familiar with life in the armed forces from personal experience.[84]

The Navy attaché's prognosis proved correct; in 1993, newly elected President Bill Clinton enacted a new policy on homosexual soldiers. (In line with the attaché's warning, Clinton had no personal experience in the military.) Clinton had promised to grant all citizens access to the armed forces on the campaign trail in 1992, but even as president had not been able to prevail over the resistance he met from the Pentagon and military commanders. U.S. generals' skepticism emerged in casual remarks as well, such as one voiced by an old guard in the military to State Secretary Wichert: "As long as it was forbidden nobody could agree more than me, now that it is tolerated I can live with it, as soon as it gets mandatory I'll quit the service."[85]

As the internal discussion surrounding Clinton's planned revisions progressed, U.S. politicians consulted with the BMVg about its own approach. Aside from the crisis posed by the collapse of Yugoslavia, U.S. Senator John Warner had homosexuality high on his agenda when he came to visit Bonn in April 1993.[86] Warner was not a run-of-the-mill senator; a widely respected military expert, he had been tasked with resolving the conflict between Clinton's campaign promise and the military's resistance to lifting restrictions against gay and lesbian soldiers. The Warner Commission, which took its name from the senator, landed on a compromise in the phrase "Don't ask, don't tell." The new policy essentially mirrored the approach the Bundeswehr had taken since the 1970s. It is possible that Warner got the idea for it on his visit to Hardthöhe. The parallels were self-evident to Peter Wichert – the Bundeswehr unspokenly followed the principle the U.S. later set about implementing.[87] Even at the time, the BMVg viewed it in a similar light: "Upon initial review, the relevant reforms in the U.S. armed forces aim at a procedure comparable to the [Bundeswehr]."[88] The parallels also presented themselves to *Der Spiegel* in an article from February 1993 that asked "Gays in the Army? In the U.S. Bill Clinton wants to let homosexuals in the military – nothing new for the Bundeswehr."[89] Compared with U.S. practices to date, the German military was not so bad after all. "If homosexual tendencies are discovered within officers already in service,

---

84 BArch, BW 2/31224: Embassy of the Federal Republic of Germany in Washington D.C., naval attaché, 24 November 1989.

85 Email from retired State Secretary Peter Wichert to the author, 26 April 2019.

86 BArch, BW 2/38355: BMVg, Staff officer for the chief of FüS staff, 31 March 1993.

87 Interview with retired State Secretary Peter Wichert, Bad Münstereifel, 10 April 2019.

88 BArch, BW 2/32553: BMVg, FüS I 4, 3 February 1993. Also available in BW 24/14249.

89 "'Versiegelte Briefe'."

military intelligence does not intervene, as in the U.S."[90] (Of course, this study has shown the Bundeswehr absolutely did intervene.)

President Barack Obama made a new attempt at removing restrictions against gays and lesbians in the U.S. military, issuing a clear pronouncement in his 2010 State of the Union address: "This year, I will work with Congress and our military to finally repeal the law that denies gay Americans the right to serve the country they love because of who they are."[91] Chairman of the Joint Chiefs of Staff Admiral Mike Mullen gave the green light himself at a congressional hearing: "I personally believe it is right to allow homosexuals and lesbians to stop hiding. Current practice forces young men and women to deny their identity so that they can defend their fellow citizens. For me personally, this is ultimately about integrity. That of the soldiers and that of our institution."[92] In 2011, President Obama lifted all restrictions against gay and lesbian soldiers.

U.S. soldiers took advantage of their newfound freedoms. Particularly on foreign assignment they were now able to strike up new friendships and meet sexual partners, both within their own ranks as well as among soldiers from other countries. German soldiers stationed in Afghanistan reported especially frequent and intimate contact with U.S. soldiers, who as of 2011 were now able to move about freely and easily with their sexuality, at least as a general rule. One German NCO recalled an unusual encounter with another sergeant in Camp Mazar-e Sharif in 2011. The sergeant did not appear alone to the date the two had fixed for sex, but came with yet another sergeant in tow. Contrary to the German's sudden expectation that the date would turn into a threesome, the second sergeant did not take part at all but remained seated on a chair, without the least interest in the sex that was taking place directly in front of him. The unusual observer explained that the sergeant had brought him along as a witness in order to respond to any potential accusations or complaints that might arise about sexual misconduct, even rape. The trepidation and fear regarding lawsuits of the sort led some U.S. soldiers to reach for reassurance – the sergeant certainly was not alone in the practice, and it seems to have been even more widespread among heterosexual U.S. soldiers.[93]

Up to this point in the study, one country and Army have been left out that present perhaps the most obvious point of comparison: The GDR and its National People's Army (Nationale Volksarmee, NVA). Though it may be astonishing, while the Ministry of Defense in Bonn kept regular tabs on the regulations of every mil-

---

90 Ibid.

91 McGreal, "Barack Obama promises to end gay army recruit ban."

92 Rissman, "Obama: Bald 'Ask and tell'?"

93 Interview with H., Berlin, 2 July 2018.

itary conceivable from Norway to Portugal, it never did so for the NVA. No document turned up in the Hardthöhe archives pertaining to how the GDR armed forces handled the subject of homosexuality.

5. The NVA and GDR Border Troops: Operational Personal Checks by the MfS

After 1950, the previous, more lenient version of §175 StGB as it appeared in the constitution of the German Empire applied in the GDR. The high court in East Berlin ruled that the more stringent version had been a "Nazi" form of injustice, recommending at the same time that legal proceedings allowed by the version of the paragraph from the National Socialist era be discontinued due to the minor nature of the crimes involved. This explains why research literature consistently refers to the fact that the GDR legal system stopped using §175 in the Fifties. Court rulings from the archived files of the East German military prosecutor's office and the Ministry for State Security (Ministerium für Staatsicherheit, MfS), however, belie this assumption, at least up through 1968.[94] That year (one year before the Federal Republic revised its own criminal code), the new GDR criminal law book did in fact abandon §175 and cease to prosecute homosexual activity between grown men. In its place, the new §151 now criminalized homosexual acts by adults of both sexes with youth under eighteen in the GDR. (This included consensual activity, though it was listed in the new GDR criminal law book under the section "Sexual Abuse of Adolescents."[95]) In 1987 the East German high court ruled that homosexual people

---

94 In 1959, for instance, Magdeburg District Court sentenced two men to one and three years' penitentiary respectively for "illicit sex contrary to nature – crimes pursuant to §175 StGB" (in addition to another five years for other crimes). BStU, MfS, AU 647/59, a copy of Magdeburg District Court ruling from 3 October 1959. In 1961, Berlin-Lichtenberg City District Court sentenced a man to eight months in prison for "continuing illicit sex pursuant to §175 StGB." BStU, MfS, GH 70/61 volume 2 contains a copy of the ruling from 3 October 1961. In January 1968, Rostock Military Court sentenced a twenty-one-year-old People's Police cadet to six months' prison on probation for "illicit sex contrary to nature pursuant to §175 StGB." The cadet had performed consensual masturbation on and active anal intercourse with a fellow cadet on multiple occasions. BArch, DVW 9/35646 b: Ruling at Rostock Military Court on 3 January 1968.
95 §151 StGB of the GDR: "An adult who engages in sexual conduct with a juvenile of the same sex shall be punished by imprisonment for not more than three years or sentencing on parole," http://www.verfassungen.de/ddr/strafgesetzbuch74.htm (last accessed 22 January 2020). For a detailed legal history of the paragraph in question see Burgi and Wolff, *Rechtsgutachten*, 22–25. Könne gives a good overview of homosexual men and women's situation in the GDR in Könne, "Schwule und Lesben in der DDR."

did not stand "outside of socialist society" but were "entitled to the same civil rights as all other civilians."[96] Likely as a result, the criminal laws were amended in December 1988, and §151 was formally struck from the GDR criminal code on 1 July 1989 along with the other remnants of separate criminal status for homosexuals of both sexes.[97] (The 2017 criminal rehabilitation act for those convicted of consensual homosexual acts after 8 May 1945 also repealed any GDR rulings that came about based on consensual homosexual activities under §151.)

a.) "Not an Issue"

Even with the repeal of the old version of §175 in 1968, trepidation still prevailed among homosexuals in the GDR "as though it were still a crime that could be prosecuted." Looking back, one contemporary recalled that "homosexuality was so hushed up in society people [in the GDR] simply couldn't deal with it."[98] The same was true to an even greater extent for the armed forces. A former senior midshipman in the People's Navy remembered that being gay had been an "absolute no-go" in the GDR even as a civilian, not to mention the Army. "I myself wouldn't have even dreamed of thinking to tell somebody." The fact coming to light in service would have brought one's career to a full stop. The professional, personal and social consequences were unforeseeable; they could not be reckoned on. Even for conscripts it had been "downright dangerous" to be identified as homosexual.[99] A profoundly coarse tone reigned among many of the conscripts at the time, as confirmed by another former soldier looking back on his days in Pontoon Regiment 3 in Dessau. When one soldier tried to avoid military service by wearing women's underwear to show that he was gay, "it totally backfired. The attempt was immediately revealed as shirking military service in his barracks. There was tremendous pressure in the barracks. It ended with a plunge from the second floor of the company building. No serious injuries."[100]

Up through the end of the 1980s, homosexuality was just as taboo in the East German armed forces as it was in the Bundeswehr.[101] Practically none of the former NVA officers interviewed for this study could think back to a single instance of

---

96 Backovic, Jäschke and Manzo, "Werd endlich ein bisschen Mann."
97 Ibid.
98 Ibid.
99 Email from Andreas T. to the author, 7 December 2017.
100 Email from Wulfried G. to the author, 30 June 2017.
101 See Smith, "Comrades in Arms: Military Masculinities in East German Culture," published after the German manuscript of this study was completed in early 2020.

homosexuality during their time in the service. The subject as a whole was hushed up. One former NVA officer later accepted into the Bundeswehr as a lieutenant colonel offered freely that homosexuality had not "been an issue" among the troops he led.[102] After long pause for reflection the officer did end up recalling one incident: In 1978, a relationship between a captain from the staff of a pioneer battalion and a conscript had been observed and admitted to. The two men had been "caught" during a walking inspection of a technical facility – of all people by the officer responsible for state security, a position that existed within every unit. In search of a simple solution to an uncomfortable problem, the battalion commander settled on issuing the captain a warning and transferring the conscript to another unit. The officer got off very lightly in this case, with an embarrassing incident cleared up informally. This allowed the captain to continue his career without further complications, something that would have been unthinkable in the Bundeswehr at the time. "The topic of homosexuality wasn't much liked in the NVA; you avoided it if at all possible. If there was a need for regulation it was decided with extraordinary leniency, and people often got off surprisingly lightly. The main thing was no scandals."[103] Other reports seem to confirm that avoiding scandal had been the primary objective of commanding NVA officers.

Two medical examiners were not able to recall a single case of a young man stating his homosexuality in their interviews. Their replies do not lay any claim to being representative, as both physicians worked in rural Western Pomerania and there certainly would have been cases of gay soldiers announcing themselves as such in larger cities. The entrance regulations from 1987 listed the rules for handling instances of homosexuality in chapter 7 (Neurology/Psychology) under section 9 (after alcoholism): "Homosexuals should [...] be rated as fit for service. They are not fit, however, to serve as fixed-term soldiers, fixed-term non-commissioned officers, fixed-term officers, career NCOs, ensigns or career officers. If homosexuality appears in connection with a severe personality abnormality or neurosis, assessment should proceed according to paragraphs 8 or 11 of this appendix."[104]

This meant the homosexual men were as a rule fit for service, as they had been in the Bundeswehr since 1979. The exception made for "severe personality abnormality or neurosis" further matched the Bundeswehr's phrasing; homosexuals' exclusion from longer-term service as NCOs or officers presents another note-

---

102 Interview with Ret. Lieutenant Colonel B. (of the Bundeswehr and formerly the NVA), Potsdam, 26 January 2018.
103 Ibid.
104 MfNV, Ordinance 060/9/002 concerning the work of the NVA medical assessor commission in the field of military medical assessment (assessor order) from 5 August 1987, here 110.

worthy similarity. As with the 1984 BMVg personnel guidelines, the NVA even ruled out homosexual soldiers' reassignment to the ranks of the enlisted (referred to in the NVA as fixed-term soldiers). For both German armies, then, the same principle applied for homosexual men: Conscription yes, career no.

Homosexuality had been "completely taboo" in day-to-day life within the East German armed forces, with gay soldiers unanimously stressing that they never discussed their "personal secret" up through the end of their time in the service.[105] Still, a handful of incidents surfaced, whether from observers or involved parties. One colonel recalled his time as a student at the former "Ernst Thälmann" Officers' College for Ground Forces in Löbau, where he and a friend had boxed together in the Army sports club. After both becoming company commanders in a division in the early 1970s, he learned "to his complete surprise" that his former boxing companion had been dismissed without notice; the man was rumored to have carried on a sexual relationship with a soldier. "He had always been an excellent comrade in my mind, an exceptional boxer and certainly a highly qualified officer."[106] A young officer in a paratrooper division in the early 1960s offered a similar recollection; during the GDR skydiving championship (probably in 1963), he had learned that one of his former classmates from officers' college had been dishonorably discharged as a lieutenant for homosexuality, whether purported or actual. "I was surprised, but that was probably due to my naivety about the topic at the time. Back then I thought that homosexuality was a 'professional disease' for hairdressers and ballet dancers, and wouldn't show up outside those groups."[107]

Another contemporary recalled multiple incidents of homosexual soldiers "coming on" to him sexually during his time as an NCO and later as a staff sergeant in the NVA. One time it had been a young lieutenant, after a party with heavy drinking in the singles' dormitory in the barracks, years later it was a first sergeant one night while at home. The witness had rejected the advances in both cases, keeping his own homosexuality a secret. He had not reported either incident, "of course not."[108] In general, the memories are striking for how rarely minor incidents with a homosexual motivation were reported to superiors (almost never in fact). This applied in equal measure for the Bundeswehr as for the NVA. The taboo seems to have reigned even more strictly in the NVA, with the positive outcome for homosexual soldiers that any advances did not raise the proverbial alarm, or even merit

---

105 Interview with Ret. Master Sergeant R., 7 February 2018.
106 Email from Ret. Colonel L. (NVA) to the author, 13 February 2018.
107 Email from Peter G. to the author, 9 February 2018.
108 Interview with Ret. Master Sergeant R., 7 February 2018.

a report to the commanding officer. They were hushed up instead, partially out of a sense of camaraderie, partially out of shame.

Soldiers who were dismissed for their sexual orientation also experienced shame, but bit their tongues – how could they have defended themselves? Administrative courts did not exist in the GDR, "there was no legal protection worthy of the name in administrative affairs."[109]

Still, there were cases of those who had been convicted, dismissed or demoted looking to put up a fight. One involved a staff sergeant accused of "having greatly damaged the reputation of the Army in the public view by [carrying on] homosexual relationships with different persons."[110] He was dismissed from active service in 1964 and demoted to the lowest rank of pilot by order of the head of the Air Force and Air Defense. As was customary, he was also expelled by party procedure from the SED ("struck as a member"). The staff sergeant filed a complaint with the SED Central Committee. The party control commission at Air Force Command conducted a "detailed investigation" and reached the conclusion that "M. had neither violated the law nor brought harm to the public reputation of the NVA." As a result, the disciplinary measures – his demotion to the lowest service rank – were repealed, although his dismissal was not. Instead, a new justification was found, namely "exceedingly difficult personal circumstances," as per §24 Paragraph 1 of the service career regulations.[111]

A twenty-two-year-old petty officer 2nd class in the People's Navy also fought back after he was arrested under warrant in 1964 for "crimes under §175a StGB" (abuse of a relationship of subordination). The officer stood accused of "three counts of masturbation and one count of oral intercourse" with a twenty-year-old staff seaman under his command. The 2nd Criminal Senate at the superior military court in Neubrandenburg upheld the officer's appeal; Wolgast District Court had not "thoroughly examined [the facts of the case before issuing the arrest warrant], as the present investigation findings do not justify pressing suspicion of a violation of §175a StGB." The aggrieved staff seaman had been heavily under the influence of alcohol and was asleep when "the accused was said to have performed illicit acts on him [the seaman]." "If, however," the criminal court continued, "illicit acts are committed against a sleeping male person under twenty-one years of age, that does not meet the elements of a crime under §175a numbers 2 and 3 of the StGB, as no

---

109 Ramsauer, "150 Jahre Verwaltungsgerichtsbarkeit."
110 BArch, DVW 1/17043: MfNV head of LSK/LV to the Minister, 15 January 1965.
111 Ibid. The repeal of the disciplinary measures took effect on 22 January 1965 by orders of the minister of defense, signed personally by Army General Heinz Hoffmann. Ibid., Order of the Minister No. 5/65.

'abuse of a relationship of subordination' (Number 2) or 'seduction' (Number 3) [...] have occurred." Nor were there any criminal elements in further acts that had occurred once the sleeping sailor woke up. The petty officer had further stated that he too was heavily under the influence of alcohol, and had not been conscious of the "illicit acts" in his state of "total inebriation."[112] West German judges ruled and reasoned in similar fashion.

b.) 1988 and On: "Equal Rights and Duties for All"

1988 saw a new line of thinking take root on the matter at the East German Ministry of National Defense in Strausberg. A memo prepared for the defense minister found that the preceding years had seen "repeat decisions that cannot be justified by medical circumstances" when it came to determining the military eligibility of homosexual men.[113] Against regulation, homosexual men had not been "admitted" to military service or had themselves succeeded in being mustered out of the military. So as to "clearly delineate" the factors in conscripts' medical assessment, the document recommended striking the current stipulation that homosexuals "are not fit [...] to serve as fixed-term soldiers, fixed-term non-commissioned officers, fixed-term officers, career NCOs, ensigns or career officers."[114] The memo was issued and signed by the minister's deputy and head of rear services, Lieutenant General Manfred Grätz, according to whom it had been coordinated with all the minister's other deputies, which would have included the chiefs of the joint staff and service branches. On closer inspection, the document's wording reveals a gap between its content and reasoning, the latter of which sought to enable homosexuals to perform military service, or alternatively block their intention to avoid it.

Flanking the document in both date and subject, the head of the administrative cadre commissioned a series of "principles for working with applicants, professional cadres and members of the NVA in fixed-term positions in instances of homosexuality" and presented it to the minister. This document also expressly stated that homosexuality was not grounds for exclusion from the NVA; everybody was "granted the right due to them to protect the socialist fatherland." An assessment as to military eligibility should only be made for cases "where problems arose out

---

112 BArch, DVW 9/13935: Neubrandenburg Superior Military Court, 2nd Criminal Senate, ruling on 31 December 1964.
113 BStU, MfS, HA I 15318: MfNV, Chief Kader to Administrative Head 2000, 7 July 1988 containing the memo cited here, Lieutenant General Manfred Grätz to the defense minister, undated.
114 Ibid.

of sexual-erotic differences."[115] Point 1 of its preceding section on "social views of homosexuality" stated that the "capabilities, accomplishments and social properties" of homosexual people were "neither better nor worse than those of heterosexuals."[116] Point 2 contended that "from a moral political standpoint, every citizen has the right to live and [...] enter partnerships in accordance with his sexual orientation." Yet the consequences one might then expect to find based on these grand expressions of tolerance did not follow. On the contrary, the armed forces still intended to block volunteers who were known homosexuals from longer-term service. Applicants that fell into this category "should have it explained to them in confidential meetings that pursuing a civilian career would be more expedient for them due to the particularities of military life," and should not be admitted either as fixed-term or career soldiers.[117]

The 1988 paper did introduce a novelty, however. "If no complications arose," soldiers identified as homosexual who were already serving in the NVA in a fixed-term or career capacity would now be able to continue to serve. This was expressly made to apply for the duration of training at military teaching facilities as well. The paper cited "material or financial dependency, disturbances to the superior–subordinate relationship and educational issues" as potential complications; their presence would result in dismissal. Soldiers affected by the policy should hear explicitly that the reason for their dismissal "was not homosexuality but the complications arising from it."[118] The paper was still in draft form, although the final version approved by the defense minister in September 1988 does not show any emendations. The minister's imprimatur also endorsed prospective officers and NCOs recognized as homosexual continuing to train and serve, again provided none of the complications cited came about, and further affirmed that "great care, tact and

---

115 BStU, MFS, HA I 16634: Border Troop Command, deputy head of border troops and chief of staff to the chief of Administration 2000, 21 October 1988, containing a copy of MfNV, "Grundsätze für den Umgang mit homosexuell veranlagten Bewerbern Berufskadern und NVA-Angehörigen auf Zeit" ("Principles for handling homosexually inclined applicants, professional cadres and NVA members in fixed-term positions"). The MfS received multiple copies of the same MfNV paper from different senders, among them the chief of staff for the border troops. Major General Dieter Teichmann explicitly drew attention to the fact that the responsible department in the NVA only required verbal instruction on the new regulations.
116 BStU, MfS, HA I 15318 and HA I 16634: Copy of MfNV, "Grundsätze für den Umgang mit homosexuell veranlagten Bewerbern Berufskadern und NVA-Angehörigen auf Zeit."
117 Ibid.
118 Ibid.

consideration" would be exercised with all decisions and "any form of discrimination" avoided.[119]

By 1988 the NVA had thus pulled even with the Bundeswehr's practice of not terminating existing service relationships early, i.e. not dismissing homosexuals from service. Anyone who was already a fixed-term or career soldier could now serve out the remainder of his time in service (provided "no complications arose"). East German forces even outdid the Bundeswehr in tolerance on one count in 1988. Though the new orders did not explicitly mention it, outwardly homosexual officer and NCO candidates were allowed to continue their training as before, and eventually graduate into the ranks as full officers or NCOs. This mean that differently from the Bundeswehr, the new regulations opened the door for homosexuals to become NCOs, officers and even career officers in the GDR. The NVA's weekly paper *Die Volksarmee* wrote about the new regulations in January 1990: "Up until September 1988, a regulation existed under which homosexuals were unfit for a military career. This rule was repealed in order to guarantee equal rights and duties for all." Still, "making the right military decision is one thing – putting it into practice is another."[120] It also deserves mention that in May 1988, the same year the NVA changed its course, the honorific title of "Ludwig Renn" was assigned to Pioneer Battalion 24. Up to his death in 1979 Renn, who had fought in the Spanish Civil War, had lived an astonishingly open life as a homosexual in Dresden. Renn had previously made it onto a short list of names for a foreign officers' training college in Prora on the island of Rügen in 1980–81, but was passed over at the time.[121]

c.)   "Beaten Up in the Washroom." NVA Soldiers' Experiences

This process of liberalization set in a year before the momentous upheaval in the GDR military, state and social order known as the *Wende*, or turning point. The *Wende* brought social liberation to gays and lesbians living in East Germany, even if the last crimes specific to homosexuality had already been struck from the books, as described. Gays serving in the NVA now began to speak out about their experiences, several of which were reported on in the first edition of the magazine *Die Volksarmee* in 1990, albeit under protection of anonymity: "Bernd, 24, non-commis-

---

119 BStU, MfS, HA I 15342, 158–161: MfNV, cadre chief to head of Administration 2000, 28 September 1988, containing a copy of the "Grundsätze für den Umgang mit homosexuell veranlagten Bewerbern Berufskadern und NVA-Angehörigen auf Zeit" as approved by the minister of defense.
120 Siemann, "Coming out in der NVA?"
121 See Storkmann, *Geheime Solidarität*, 419.

sioned officer: Jokes get made all the time. But if you're actually gay, you better keep your mouth shut. All the fun stops there; the others take offense and feel threatened. Even our superiors usually think they still might have to protect soldiers from someone like that."[122] So far, the observations might have come from the Bundeswehr in 1989. Yet what follows sets them apart entirely. NCO Bernd continues:

> The worst thing happened to me in H., where the company political officer warned everyone about me and demanded that any incidents be immediately reported to him. After that I got beaten up in the washroom, naked, they were doing their best to stick a broomstick up my butt. All the KC [company chief] said was that I had myself to blame, and it shouldn't come as a surprise.

Every experience indicates that a company chief would not have kept his eyes closed had such an incident occurred in the Bundeswehr – he would not have been allowed to. The company chief's comment would hardly have been conceivable and, if it had in fact occurred and been reported, would have resulted in severe disciplinary consequences.

One deputy political officer in a battalion reported to *Die Volksarmee* that "there aren't any soldiers like that [in my unit], I keep an eye out for that." "The soldiers have a stressful job; anyone with time for little games like that probably hasn't been used to their full capacity." The editors at the weekly publication set the officer's words in direct juxtaposition to those of a homosexual soldier, reportedly from the same battalion:

> I go along with it all here. Coming back from vacation I tell stories about my experiences with girls, I get mail from my boyfriend every three months at my home address when I go back. My boyfriend gets all the letters together and then we read them. I wrote him a letter here once on the toilet. I don't know how I'm going to make it through the rest of the year.

These experiences quickly recall those of Bundeswehr conscripts, even from as late as 1989. Andreas, an officer and secretary in the state youth group Free German Youth (Freie Deutsche Jugend, FDJ) likewise echoed the experiences of Bundeswehr officers nearly verbatim: "The worst thing is that you can't talk with anybody about it. I feel totally isolated – that's my real problem, not being gay. How am I supposed to find a boyfriend? I don't want to leave the Army, but sometimes I think it might be my only chance."

---

122 Here, and in what follows: Siemann, "Coming out in der NVA." Lesbian soldiers did not speak out in the Volksarmee piece, nor were they mentioned.

Five weeks later, *Die Volksarmee* published a letter from a major: "It is high time that the VA [Volksarmee] turned itself to the subject of homosexuality in the NVA," the major wrote. As a superior he had found himself confronted with the issue on multiple occasions.

> I have [...] always made an effort to develop a genuine relationship of trust with Army members. One part of that is human tolerance. It was also possible before the *Wende*. That was the basis for most of the gays reporting the problems they had with others to me. Most of the time I succeeded in creating a climate of acceptance. Gays are regarded as strange creatures by the others and are subject to greater public scrutiny [...] On the other side one has to tell gays openly, honestly and tactfully about where they isolate themselves socially [...] The young people in question first experience their coming-out during their time in the NVA. It isn't rejection or isolation they need but words of encouragement [...] Those stirring the pot against homosexuality are mostly sexually repressed themselves, often even ashamed of being naked. That's how they try to conceal their own problems. Gays are people like you and I. The ones who impose themselves are an absolute exception. It isn't gays who are perverse, but the people who refuse to accept their fellow humans.[123]

The GDR Ministry for State Security likewise showed little to no acceptance of gay NVA soldiers up through 1989. The MfS kept a close watch on gays or suspected cases in the NVA (as well as within its own ranks), relying on a tightly woven network of informants to do so.

d.) OPK "Lover" and other Surveillance Measures

The formidable power of the MfS was typical of the East German state, and greatly distinguished the GDR's approach to homosexuality from that of the Federal Republic. In 1984 the BMVg was reproached for keeping lists with the names of homosexuals. The ministry denied the accusation in a press release, while a state secretary went before the Bundestag to clarify that no lists were kept, nor was any surveillance conducted.[124] The MfS, on the other hand, did keep lists; they are preserved under the title "People with homosexual tendencies" or simply "Homosexuals." Twenty-three people were registered between the years 1977 and 1979 including one colonel, a naval commander and multiple majors, with NCOs and enlisted men (simply called soldiers in the NVA) predominating. After the colonel's name one finds the remark, "dismissal from post." For the majors and other service ranks (outside of conscripts and NCOs) one finds the phrase, "transferred to the reserve,"

---

123 Letter from Major Andreas T. in *Die Volksarmee* 6, 1990, 4.
124 See chapter 5.

which in plain language also meant dismissal from active service. Five new entries are listed for 1982 and seventeen for 1983, among them lieutenant colonels and majors, although once again sergeants, NCOs and enlisted soldiers make up the bulk. A note following the name of one sergeant reads, "suicide attempt."[125] The list for 1984 contains eight names, including that of a major in the Border Troops with the remark, "early dismissal." After the name of a captain studying at a military academy one reads, "summary dismissal."[126] No further notices of dismissal are found in 1985 or the following years for any service rank.[127]

Behind practically every one of these names there stood an MfS surveillance operation, or an "Operational Personal Check" (Operative Personenkontrolle, OPK) as it was termed, which nearly always came with a more or less imaginative code-name attached. The MfS generally reserved surveillance measures for officers suspected of being homosexual, but would do so for NCOs as well, and in isolated instances for enlisted soldiers in security-relevant positions.

Every OPK meant a deep intrusion into the private life and intimate sphere both of the person under surveillance as well as that of his partner. It is not the intention of this study to cast yet another light on these private stories, even if this time it is from an academic perspective. The activities of state security and their impact on those being monitored, however, are of interest.

As one example, OPK "Lover" was conducted against a lieutenant colonel, a deputy regimental commander who was slated to take full command of the regiment. This apparently led MfS to conduct a routine investigation, in the course of which "personnel reconnaissance brought references of homosexual conduct to light." The officer's sexual orientation had in fact been "brought to light" by a former classmate, who informed MfS about a relationship he had with the lieutenant colonel at military academy. State security now assigned the informant to the "target person" as an informal collaborator. After employing the collaborator for two months along with measures "26A" (phone line surveillance) and "26B" (acoustic surveillance of private residence), the MfS drafted an interim report. The lieutenant colonel in question led a withdrawn life, watched West German television and – of particular interest to the MfS – the informal collaborator was without doubt the only homosexual partner the officer had ever had. MfS passed along the report to the NVA with the goal of preventing the officer's assignment to regiment commander. The cadre department ("cadre" was the GDR term for personnel) not

---

125 BStU, MfS, HA I 12881.
126 BStU, MfS, HA I 4176.
127 1985 had nine new names; 1986, twelve; 1987, eleven (including a major as the highest service rank represented); 1988, three; and 1989 listed six names (including two majors). Ibid.

only decided against the officer's promotion, but dismissed the lieutenant colonel from active service, an action the NVA consistently couched in the phrase "transferred to the reserve." (The other officer who had informed MfS about the relationship as an informal collaborator was also dismissed.)[128]

The influence that state security wielded on military personnel decisions – forceful and direct, not only when it came to suspicions of homosexuality, though certainly on that count as well – set the NVA apart from the Bundeswehr. As has already been shown in some detail, discoveries by MAD could also lead to unfavorable decisions for Bundeswehr members. Yet the lieutenant colonel would not have been dismissed from the Bundeswehr; MAD would not have advised such harsh measures for homosexuality, and if it had, the officer would have had every legal route available to him in contesting his dismissal or early retirement before administrative court. The same could not be said for in the GDR, giving one clear example of the crucial difference between a constitutional state founded on the rule of law and its absence in the GDR. In the West, administrative judges would have had the final say (toward the end the judges at the Federal Constitutional Court nearly had theirs); in the East the arbitrary exercise of power reigned supreme, even on highly particular topics such as this one. Still, one parallel remained: Had MAD issued a similar report, it is entirely likely that the lieutenant colonel would no longer have been appointed regimental commander. Nor is it hypothetical to observe that lawsuits against a decision of this sort stood practically zero chance of success in the Federal Republic up until the turn of the millennium; the contention is supported by numerous court rulings.

Subjects of surveillance by MfS, in contrast, had no court of appeal at their disposal, as the following case shows. In the late 1980s, MfS received word from an informal collaborator that an officer directly outside a general's office at the Ministry of Defense was "most likely homosexual" and living in a committed domestic partnership. The MfS began an OPK, assigning multiple collaborators to the target. The operation also brought in the heavy artillery of technical surveillance, monitoring both the subject's work and private phones as well as his partner's home line; conducting acoustic surveillance of both men's residences; opening the mail of the target person, his partner and relatives; and investigating and monitoring the partner's family. The stated goal was to clarify "whether based on the [target's] homosexual orientation and the current contacts his partner's family has in non-socialist countries, the target offers points of approach for enemy agencies, even if he himself is entirely unaware of them." An interim report was composed after six months, and it was decided both to continue with Measures 26A and 26B and take

---

128 BStU, MfS, HA I 13148.

on new collaborators.[129] In this case too, the end of SED rule and the MfS in fall 1989 brought an end to the surveillance.

One master chief petty officer in the People's Navy was not as lucky, cropping up on the radar of state security one year too soon. The opening salvo was likely a letter from the parents of a petty officer 2nd class informing the commander that their son had had sex with his superior, the master chief petty officer, in their summer house. The NCO was demoted by one rank, although not because of this incident but another. Independently of his demotion, MfS began surveillance on the officer in May 1988.[130] In the course of monitoring his mail it came out that he had been in touch with homosexual citizens of the Federal Republic, and that the men were planning to meet in Hungary on vacation. (Before 1989, Hungary was popular as one of the only destinations where Germans from both German states could meet relatively inconspicuously.) In considering the living circumstances of the master chief petty officer "to be analyzed operatively," MfS gave an objective rendering of the pressures under which NVA members had to serve and live: "He has had to 'conceal' his homosexual tendencies from others for years now, i.e. he cannot show them openly or pursue them as a member of the NVA."[131] The officer was closed off in service and kept his distance from others. His wife had filed for divorce three years after marriage. Among other measures, the MfS assigned three informal collaborators to continue checking the subject's mail.[132] It is characteristic of the methods of the MfS and its collaborators that numerous copies of personal, even intimate letters were archived, at times even torn or crumpled up originals presumably gathered from the waste basket by an informant.[133] The OPK ended with the officer's dismissal from the Navy in December 1988; that October MfS staff had conducted an "operational clarifying talk" seeking his consent for "removal from active service." The plan worked; the officer agreed to hand in a request for dismissal. In exchange the MfS offered "help and support in a smooth dismissal from service." The former officer received an assignment at a new civilian post.[134]

A staff officer and lecturer at a prominent NVA training facility was also released from service (or "transferred to the reserve") in the Eighties. Word about

---

129 BStU, MfS, HA I 15009.

130 BStU, MfS, AOPK 344/89, sheets 96–103: MfS, HA I, Department People's Navy, Introductory Report to OPK "Wächter" from 31 May 1988.

131 BStU, MfS, AOPK 344/89, sheet 99.

132 Ibid., sheets 309–314: MfS, HA I, Department People's Navy, Implementation plan for OPK "Wächter" from 10 October 1988.

133 Ibid., sheets 114 and 117–18.

134 Ibid., sheets 347–50: MfS, HA I, Department People's Navy, Concluding report for OPK "Wächter" from 20 December 1988.

the lecturer's homosexuality had prompted MfS to comb through the man's entire military career as well as those of soldiers (or "comrades" in GDR terminology) who had served with him in the past. In its report, the MfS described the surveillance target as "holding strong homosexual inclinations" and a "destabilizing factor in the context of protecting secrets." State security recommended that the NVA transfer the lecturer to the reserve, which happened once the omnipresent state apparatus found him a suitable position as the departmental head of a civilian firm.[135]

Surveillance did not necessarily end in release. In the case of a major in 1988, the MfS decided only that he could not continue serving in his current regiment "from a security perspective." The key factor allowing the major to remain in service (and retain his rank) was his "political reliability." After fifteen months of observing the major, the MfS found his "ideological convictions and assured character" made him "uncompromisable in terms of his homosexual disposition."[136] The MfS arrived at this view after fifteen months of surveillance; in September 1987 "current information" had come together with earlier tips ("predominately suppositions and rumors") to form an "actual basis."[137] The "action plan" involved three informal collaborators and the usual measure of inspecting the target's mail. The following summer in 1988, an MfS official invited the major to an "operational discussion" and confronted him with what the state security apparatus had learned of his private and intimate life. The major "admitted to his homosexual disposition without hesitation" and "was prepared to give comprehensive information on every question without restriction."[138] As described, the OPK concluded in December 1988, with a collaborator assigned to keep an eye on the major until he was transferred to a new service post.

Surveillance of a sergeant serving in a particularly sensitive post at a communications center reached a similar conclusion in 1988. In April of the preceding year, the MfS ran a routine OPK in advance of the sergeant's assignment to a new security-sensitive position. The central department responsible for the NVA at the MfS, Central Department I, received news of the sergeant's homosexuality from its exterior Defense department; while the sergeant sought out contact with women, it found no sign of intimate relations. Rather, MfS suspected the sergeant of trying to distract from his "inclination." The sergeant also visited upper-crust wine bars and

135 BStU, MfS, HA I 15114.

136 BStU, MfS, AOPK 3769/89, sheets 186–91: MfS, HA I/Military District V, Concluding report for OPK "Palast," from 15 December 1988.

137 Ibid., sheets 4–9: MfS, HA I/Military District V, Introductory report for OPK "Palast" from 6 September 1987.

138 Ibid., sheet 183.

restaurants in Berlin and possessed foreign currency that he used to shop with at Intershop. The MfS assigned four informal collaborators to the sergeant; his immediate superior, a colleague at the communications center, a gay man who had been intimately involved with the target in the past and a fourth who lived in the same house as the sergeant. In addition to this tight network of informants the MfS relied on its usual methods of opening mail, this time the target's and his mother's.[139]

In an interim report from November 1987, the MfS "confirmed" the sergeant's "negative personal characteristics"; the informal collaborator assigned to the target, himself homosexual, had "proven [X.'s] homosexual tendency." Surveillance continued, with an additional NCO brought in for a "skimming interview" to clarify the target's circle of associates. Meanwhile the sergeant's immediate superior, himself a collaborator, made sure the sergeant did not receive access to any secret or confidential material.[140] Surveillance ended in June 1988 once the sergeant's "personality profile" had been "comprehensively" established. In addition to his sexual orientation, the MfS rated the sergeant's contacts in non-socialist countries and his unstable personality as relevant to security, and recommended that the commanding officer not assign the sergeant to the new, sensitive post.[141] The archives give no indication that the sergeant wanted to be transferred out of the communications center, much less dismissed from the NVA. In classifying the case, it is important to recall that it is standard procedure within all armed forces for intelligence services to conduct reviews before a soldier is assigned to a sensitive post; in the U.S. these go by the term "clearances."

Gay NCOs or enlisted soldiers were also generally removed from or transferred out of security-related positions in the NVA, though they were not dismissed. Such was the case for an enlisted conscript involved in logistics at the same communications center as the sergeant, who was revealed by an informant to be homosexual. Surveillance measures began in 1983 under the codename "Anus."[142] Once again, the files contain what are at times highly intimate reports and descriptions from informants. The MfS ceased surveillance after just one month; suspicions had been confirmed, but no criminally-relevant activity detected. The soldier was still rated a security risk, however, due to the frequency with which he changed partners,

---

139 BStU, MfS, HA I 16444, sheets 608–16: MfS, HA I/Department MfNV, Introductory report for OPK "Reblaus" from 26 May 1987.
140 Ibid., sheets 617–23: Interim report for OPK "Reblaus" from 26 November 1987.
141 Ibid., sheets 631–36, Concluding report from OPK "Reblaus" from 16 June 1988.
142 BStU, MfS, HA II 15932 as well as HA I 15203 and AOPK 9404/83.

including men from West Berlin, and he was transferred.[143] Here too it is essential to consider other armed forces' security review policies in situating the case.

e.) Excursus: Homosexuals in the Ranks of the MfS

Aside from the NVA, East German conscripts were also assigned to serve in the "Feliks Dzierzynski" guard regiment, which belonged to state security. One contemporary recalls serving in the battalion starting in 1985, which guarded the bunkered command and control post for state and party leadership in the forests outside Prenden (today often referred to colloquially as "Honecker's bunker"). The battalion consisted of close to 500 men between the ages of eighteen and twenty-one, with only the group leaders – holding the rank of NCO – somewhat older. In contrast to the regular NVA, a high percentage of the conscripts in the battalion had completed their *Abitur*, the qualifying exam for university entrance. This made a palpable difference on the internal climate of the battalion, the interviewee recalled; longer-serving soldiers did not harass younger soldiers as was otherwise common in the NVA. Instead, the priority lay with safeguarding prospects of a place at university by avoiding "conspicuous behavior of any sort (neglecting guard duty, alcohol)" or causing trouble for one's parents. Superiors did not act in a demeaning manner toward subordinates, as occurred in the regular armed forces. Nor did homosexuality ever come up for discussion; the eyewitness could not recall a single incident from his time in the service. If from time to time one or the other soldier was suspected or rumored to be homosexual, there was never any bullying or harassment. "With 500 soldiers you can assume at least twenty-five to thirty gays. Well? It wasn't an issue." In the rear services company, one soldier assigned as a cook had "definitely" been gay, but he was also treated "in a friendly, joking way" without any visible psychological strain: "The soldiers quickly lost interest in his case." Still, the interviewee recalls suffering feelings of loneliness and the unswerving pressure of having to constantly pull himself together and stay vigilant. He did not always manage. During his first year he had "checked out [a comrade's] package for too long" in the shower once after guard duty. The other had looked up quickly in surprise, and whispers as to his potential homosexuality had trailed briefly after the incident. Yet "at the time [1986] the World Cup made everything sink back into insignificance. The terror subsided."[144]

---

143 AOPK 9404/83, MfS, HA I, Department MfNV, Concluding report for OPK "Anus" from 28 July 1983.
144 Email from R. to the author, 1 May 2018.

The archived files of the guard regiment, however, confirm that homosexual NCOs were in fact being dismissed while the eyewitness was guarding Honecker's bunker. The Stasi files for an NCO released in 1986 open with a letter written by an acquaintance from the officer's hometown (a conscript in the NVA himself at the time). The denunciation ends with a request to treat the information confidentially. The MfS began surveillance on the soldier, and in the course of collecting data came across another report that the NCO's address had turned up with a homosexual man in a different GDR district. The NCO was ordered to the medical station in the guard regiment for assessment. The physicians confirmed the suspicions of homosexuality and the officer was released as permanently unfit to serve.[145]

If full-time members of the Stasi (short for *Staatssicherheit*, or the MfS) were discovered to be homosexual, the organization typically responded with dismissal. The policy rested on a view shared by practically all intelligence agencies, that homosexuals were susceptible to blackmail and thus presented a security risk. The same opinion prevailed in the GDR: In the late Eighties a young officer, recently graduated from a university outside the purview of the MfS and now at the start of his career in the service, became ensnared in the web of his own institution. When the MfS came up with a number of the man's sexual partners from the previous years and listed them off by name, the young officer responded "unapologetically," according to one note. "He repeatedly expressed a lack of understanding for the MfS' position of not recognizing homosexuals, and described the branch's decision [his release] as a professional ban. He was of the opinion that in a matter of years, homosexuals would be equal partners in [MfS]."[146]

State security did not take its eyes off the former officer even after his dismissal but instituted comprehensive surveillance measures, including acoustic surveillance of the subject's residence.[147] The MfS instituted similar surveillance measures in another case, assigning informal collaborators and opening the mail of a prospective officer after he was dismissed. Among other things, the archives contain the copy of a highly personal letter the officer wrote to a man he loved.[148] The sublieutenant was dismissed from his post in an MfS district administration office in 1986 as "'permanently unfit to serve' due to a dominant homosexual disposition that cannot be corrected."[149] As always with cases like his, the MfS found

---

145 BStU, MfS, BV Pdm KD Brandenburg 1076, vol. 3.
146 BStU, MfS, BV Rst Abt XX 1204.
147 Ibid.
148 BStU, MfS, BV Suhl Abt KuSch 2497, sheets 18–19.
149 The rank of Sublieutenant in the East German MfS, Armed Forces and police was of Soviet origin. It did not exist in West Germany; BStU, MfS, BV Suhl Abt KuSch 2497, sheet 7.

him a new post in the civilian workforce, where informants were still passing along rumors about his homosexuality in 1989 without knowing about their colleague's past in the MfS.[150]

The archives also document a particularly tragic case. A cadre department report from the MfS dated 16 March 1966 details a discussion conducted with a sergeant the day before at an MfS district administration branch. Accused of homosexual acts with a member of the MfS guard regiment in Berlin Adlershof, the sergeant's interrogation had proceeded in a "calm and objective atmosphere." "The causes of his deviant sexual activity could not be completely clarified, but may be sought chiefly in improper education in the parental home." It was not an option for the sergeant to remain at the MfS. The sergeant's superior informed his father, a member of the People's Police, "with the aim of continuing to exercise a positive influence on the son's development."[151] A further conversation between the sergeant and his superior had been scheduled for the start of service on 16 March, to which the sergeant had been instructed to bring a written statement. A private conversation with the father in the son's presence was planned for the same day.[152] It did not come to that, however. When the sergeant handed in the required statement at 7.45 that morning, his superior revealed the planned meeting with his parents. According to the MfS account of what happened, the sergeant

> gave the impression that he was not comfortable having a conversation with his parents. He was simply told by his superior that this was how life had to go from now on, and that he had to detach himself from abnormal sexual things by finding a girl. Comrade [X.] then inquired whether he should count on being dismissed [...] He was told that if it did come to dismissal, he would depart the body [the MfS] with honors. It was explained once again to him that he was not being pushed out under any circumstances but would leave with honors. It was necessary, however, for him to steady himself and lead an orderly life. He was advised to take his necessary personal belongings such as his shaving kit, etc. home with him.[153]

At 8.45 a.m., the sergeant was discovered lying in a pool of blood in his quarters, the result of a near-fatal head wound he had inflicted on himself with his service pistol about forty-five minutes before. He died later that day at 4 p.m., at the age of twenty-two.[154]

---

150 Ibid., sheet 20.

151 BStU, MfS, GH 194/85, sheets 9–15: MfS, HA KuSch, 16 March 1966.

152 Ibid., sheets 9–12: MfS, HA KuSch, 16 March 1966.

153 Ibid., sheets 16–17: MfS, BV Dresden, Abt. KuSch, 16 March 1966.

154 Ibid., sheet 70: MfS, HA KuSch, 16 March 1966, including Erich Mielke's handwritten endorsement, among others.

When the East German Ministry of Defense adopted a fundamentally new stance toward homosexual officers and NCOs in 1988, the MfS explicitly continued its policy of rejection: "There is no place for people like that in the MfS. They cannot work in a reconnaissance organization, the danger is too great. Such comrades must be spoken to sensibly and no confrontation allowed, they will be dismissed for reasons of health. It must be made sure in any event that no harm comes to them."[155] A list of personnel decisions at Dresden District Administration from summer 1989 includes a note from a local office reading "not-suitable/homosexual."[156]

f.)　OPK "Traitor"

On the long list of names taken down on Stasi filing cards, the case of one homosexual lieutenant in the Border Troops sticks out especially. Toward the end of 1978 the lieutenant revealed his intention to flee to West Berlin to an acquaintance, an alleged friend of his who turned out to be an MfS informant. The secret service set more informants on the job and began, under the codename "Traitor," an OPK of the man, referred to as "Schulze" in what follows. The aspiring officer was removed from his post on the border and transferred onto regimental staff; with that the state security officers believed themselves to have the lieutenant under control, assuming they had made it impossible for him to flee. They were mistaken. Putting his intimate knowledge of security installations to work, in May 1979 the lieutenant succeeded in escaping to Wannsee in West Berlin, where his partner was waiting for him. His boyfriend, here given the name "Mihailescu," was a Romanian man who, the MfS later discovered, had been in contact with the U.S. Secret Service since that month.[157] Mihailescu and the lieutenant had met several weeks before at a friend's apartment in Prenzlauer Berg in East Berlin. At his new friend's insistence, Schulze had gathered together all the Border Troop documents and papers he had access to in the days leading up to his flight, including the regimental Defense plan, its telephone directory and a list of names, as well as patterns for authorization cards to enter the property. On 25 May Schulze left the documents in a bag at the Ostbahnhof luggage office. The following day he gave the key to Mihailescu, who then returned to the GDR for the bag. According to subsequent MfS investigations,

---

155 BStU, MfS, BV Dresden, AKG 7590: MfS, BV Dresden Abt KuSch, Report from cadre leadership conference on 25 November 1988, dated 28 November 1988.
156 BStU, MfS, BV Dresden, Abt KuSch, No. 4314, MfS, BV Dresden Abt KuSch, 15 September 1989.
157 BStU, MfS, HA IX 23866, sheets 4–5.

Mihailescu smuggled the bag back to West Berlin on May 27 or 28 "by deceiving the border patrol" and promptly handed it over to the American secret service.[158] Mihailescu even had the chutzpah to ring the on-duty officer at the border company several days before Schulze deserted and ask to speak with the lieutenant. Schulze was not on site. No less astonishing is that scarcely two weeks after he did flee, the lieutenant called the on-duty officer at his old company and demanded to speak with an NCO. In the MfS report, the surprised officer let slip a spontaneous "Are you nuts?!"[159] The officer denied any private connection to Schulze under subsequent interrogation, although his name appears on later lists of suspected homosexuals.[160] Central Department I at MfS, in charge of observing the NVA and Border Troops, later "worked out that the motivation for desertion was [...] undoubtedly his homosexual disposition, in addition to political and ideological motives."[161] After meeting him in West Berlin in September 1979, the lieutenant's father also reported to MfS that his son's "only motive" had been his "homosexuality and his ideas about life."[162]

After his westward flight the lieutenant found himself back in an office, this time run by the U.S. Secret Service in Zehlendorf, where he was questioned for close to a month about his service in the Border Troops.[163] MfS later identified other enlisted soldiers, NCOs and young officers in the NVA and the Border Troops with whom Mihailescu had been in contact.

> Taking advantage of his homosexual disposition, he kept up intimate contact with the deserting officer and was instrumental in his recruitment and successful desertion. [Mihailescu] is known in homosexual circles within the GDR capital and Halle. In Halle it was [...] determined that he is purposefully recruiting people in homosexual circles and offering to smuggle them. He is said to have ties to the U.S. Secret Service [...] He regularly travels to the GDR capital. He [...] holds a West German passport and is a Romanian citizen.[164]

---

158 Ibid.
159 BStU, MfS, AOP 1761/80.
160 BStU, MfS, HA I 12881.
161 BStU, MfS, HA I, AOP 2431/79, MfS, HA I, Department of Exterior Defense, Plan for dispatching IMS [X.] into the operational territory of West Berlin from 7 September 1979, here p. 9. In June 1979 the MfS noted "a strongly pronounced homosexual disposition" as the primary cause and motivation for the flight. BStU, MfS, AOP 1761/80, vol. 1, sheets 13–17: MFS, HA I, Concept for further handling the deserting officer from the Border Troops 2nd lieutenant [X.] from 26 June 1979.
162 BStU, MfS, HA II, 32736, MfS, HA I, Department of Exterior Defense, 13 September 1979.
163 For a detailed account of the lieutenant's successful escape and the backstory, see Storkmann, "Einmal West-Berlin und zurück."
164 BStU MfS, AOP 1761/80, vol. 1, sheet 113: MfS, HA I, Department of Exterior Defense, UA 1, Opening report for developing an operation against [X.], born in Bucharest, resides in West Berlin, from 4 September 1979.

All this set off alarm bells at the MfS; the organization's suspicions about homosexual officers in the NVA and among its own seemed fully confirmed in the present case. As shown throughout this study, the stereotype of gays as untrustworthy and potential traitors has a long history, and this was not by any means only on display in the GDR secret service.

Mihailescu continued to travel to the GDR from West Berlin and meet new men, preferably soldiers, a situation that led to growing jealousy on Schulze's part. On 31 August the lieutenant called the People's Police, requested that they connect the MfS, and then divulged the time and place of his partner's next entry into the GDR, along with a precise description of his person. One day in September in 1979, the Romanian crossed the checkpoint on Friedrichstraße (better known as Checkpoint Charlie) in his VW Golf, where he was immediately apprehended. (On 17 July 1980 military judges sentenced him to seven years in prison for espionage in conjunction with an aggravated case of assisting a deserter.[165]) At 8 a.m. the same day the lieutenant's father returned to East Berlin on the S-Bahn with his son in tow, where MfS officers were waiting for them. The father had brought his son back on their behalf. The lieutenant was questioned extensively by state security in the weeks following his return; he named his love for the Romanian in West Berlin as one explicit motive for his flight, along with a general wish to live openly and freely as a homosexual in West Berlin. In the course of his deposition he revealed names from his circle of homosexual acquaintances, including officers in the Border Troops.[166]

Stasi interrogators could scarcely believe their ears as they learned about a circle of homosexual students at the Border Troop officer's school in Plauen that would meet in the apartment of a greengrocer. The names of other NVA soldiers surfaced during Mihailescu's interrogation by state security; enlisted soldiers, NCOs and officers the Romanian man knew to be gay. The number of filing cards for homosexual soldiers grew considerably in 1979. The interrogations resulted in a detailed list of names entitled "Information on officer affiliations jeopardizing the security of the armed forces," and was presented to the NVA chief of staff in October 1979 by the head at MfS Central Department I (which went under the pseudonym of "Administration 2000" in its dealings with the NVA). Among the information the MfS gathered from the Romanian was the name and address of a first lieutenant from Cottbus. The Air Force officer had met Mihailescu at a pub in East Berlin –

---

165 BArch, DVW 13/65439: Senior military prosecutor for the GDR, reference file M, containing the ruling from Berlin Superior Military Court on 17 July 1980.

166 On the subsequent twists in this gripping and somewhat dizzying tale about the shadowy world of borders, secret services, love and jealousy, see Storkmann, "Einmal West-Berlin und zurück."

a "meeting point" for homosexuals, as MfS characterized it. The first lieutenant had promptly "revealed his affiliation with the NVA and place of service in Cottbus to the U.S. agent, knowing that he lived in West Berlin."[167] Both men made their way to a border crossing upon leaving the pub; the Romanian drove into West Berlin only to return a short while later to the GDR, where the lieutenant was waiting in a taxi. They then drove on to the lieutenant's NVA residence in Cottbus, where the NVA officer slipped his acquaintance through the backdoor and past the guard. The Romanian returned to West Berlin after spending the night. The MfS noted down the "strong homosexual tendencies" of the first lieutenant as a motive.[168] The MfS also reported to the NVA chief of staff on another lieutenant in the Border Troops with whom the Romanian had been in contact, who carried on "homosexual relationships with civilians and military personnel in frequent succession," often in parks and at times while in uniform. In the eyes of the MfS the lieutenant posed a "considerable threat for the security of the armed forces" and should be dismissed "on short notice."[169] The Romanian was also reported to have had contact with a Navy sailor in Stralsund.[170]

Meanwhile, despite exoneration from criminal charges, Lieutenant Schulze grew increasingly dissatisfied with his new old life in the GDR. The MfS had also arranged work for him as a waiter at an Interhotel and found him an apartment, while setting him under renewed surveillance with an operation simply entitled "Gay".[171] The thickly assembled circle of MfS informants kept Schulze in view at all times. In October 1980 he tried again to flee to West Berlin, this time not by climbing over the border fence with a rope ladder but with deception. His plan was to pass himself off as a permanent representative of West Germany in the GDR who had lost his papers, presenting a monthly transportation pass he had kept from West Berlin as evidence. The pass had long since expired, so he falsified its period of validity and thus "armed" set off on 16 October 1980. He did not make it far. The People's Police detained him in front of the entrance to the Permanent Represen-

---

167 BStU, MfS, AOP 23179/80, vol. 2, sheets 292–93. Chief of Administration 2000 to Deputy Minister for National Defense and Chief of Staff at the NVA, 10 October 1979, as well as AOP 23179/80, vol. 3, sheets 7–9: Interrogation protocol for the Romanian from 25 September 1979.
168 Ibid.
169 Ibid. For one comprehensive account of the Ministry for State Security's hold over the NVA see Wenzke, *Ulbrichts Soldaten*, sheets 540–46.
170 BStU, MfS, AOP 1761/80.
171 Ibid., vol. 4, sheets 232–33: HA I, Department of Exterior Defense, Resolution to create Operation "Gay" from 20 September 1979; ibid., vol. 1, sheets 207–8: HA I, Department of Exterior Defense, Information on Operation "Gay" from 30 September 1979; Ibid., vol. 4, 229–31: HA I, Department of Exterior Defense, Concluding Report on Operation "Gay" from 22 November 1979.

tative Mission and brought him to the station "to clarify the facts of the matter," in the well-known GDR phrase. That same day an arrest warrant was issued on suspicion of attempted unlawful border crossing.[172] The previous investigation into the lieutenant's desertion was also reopened, and on 10 September 1981 the judges at Berlin Military Court announced their decision – or more likely the ruling that state security had fixed ahead of time. "The accused is sentence to eight years imprisonment for the crime of espionage – §97 (1) StGB – aggravated desertion – §254 (1) and (2) [...] StGB – aggravated premeditated unlawful border crossing – §213 (1) and (3) [...] StGB – and unauthorized possession of a weapon – §206 (1) StGB."[173] Schulze had to serve out his sentence to the last day, until his release in October 1988. One year later, SED rule and its omnipresent secret service came to an end.

g.) "You'll Be Here at Eight!" Rulings on Sexual Assault

Cases involving sexual assault among soldiers were subject to court discipline in the GDR. Unlike the Federal Republic, East Germany possessed a code of military law that handled all criminal proceedings involving soldiers, including those occurring outside of service.[174] Just like their counterparts in the Bundeswehr or the U.S., soldiers serving in the NVA experienced sexual assault and violence, which in the vast majority of cases involved a soldier abusing his position of authority. During the first four months of 1956 internal statistics registered a total of eight "crimes against morality," among them four cases of rape against women and three cases of "illicit sex between men that exploited a relationship of dependence," as laid out in §175a StGB.[175] In what follows, a handful of the numerous cases involving sexual assault or abuse that have come down through investigative documents from the office of the GDR military prosecutor are sketched briefly.

In 1959 an NCO in the Border Police (the institutional forerunner to the Border Troops) was sentenced to two years and three months in prison under §174 StGB for continued illicit sex, exploiting a relationship of dependence for what at times was consensual, and at times non-consensual, sexual activity with other soldiers.[176]

---

172 BStU, MfS, HA IX, sheets 1–19.

173 BArch, DVW 13/48246: Berlin Military Court, 1st Military Criminal Senate, ruling on 10 September 1981.

174 On military law, justice and courts in the GDR see Wenzke, *Ulbrichts Soldaten*, 527–32, as well as a more detailed analysis in Wenzke, *Ab nach Schwedt!* 50–109.

175 Senior prosecutor for the People's Police, 30 May 1956: "Analyse über Strafverfahren gegen Offiziere im Dienstbereich des MfNV 1.1. bis 30.4.1956," classified material.

176 BStU, MfS, AU 31/60. The MfS had complete control of the case, i.e. the investigations, as the

That same year, a staff sergeant charged under the same paragraph received two years in prison for sexually assaulting five direct subordinates in his company.[177]

An arrest warrant was issued for another staff sergeant by Rostock Military Court in July 1978.[178] The sergeant stood accused of, starting in November 1977, having ordered around fifteen NCOs in training under his command to his quarters then forcing them to expose themselves. In the majority of the cases the sergeant had also demanded that the NCOs masturbate in front of him, with some acceding. One NCO was ordered to insert a matchstick into his penis, with the sergeant threatening he would do it to the NCO himself if he did not comply. In October 1978 the Rostock court sentenced the sergeant to two years and two months in prison on multiple counts of attempted and completed sexual abuse, as well as multiple counts of insulting subordinates.[179] The remainder of the staff sergeant's sentence was suspended in June 1979 after just under a year spent in prison including pretrial detention; the sergeant had already been ordered dismissed from active service before the trial began.[180]

Prior to that, in December 1976, a sergeant in the reserve who had previously been discharged from service likewise stood trial at military court in Halle/Saale on charges of coerced sexual activity and abuse. The inditement accused him of having, once in February of 1976 and again on two separate nights in September, forced an NCO to engage passively and actively in sexual activity under threat of violence, even punching him in the jaw.[181] The court gave the sergeant one year in prison and three months on probation.[182]

In one case that stands slightly apart, an active-duty sergeant was arraigned before military court in Schwerin in 1977 on multiple sexual acts against several soldiers while they were sleeping, and thus Defenseless. In bringing charges, NVA investigators ultimately had to base their inditement on the statements of the accused duty sergeant. The centerpiece of the investigation was an NCO who, having grown suspicious, was only feigning asleep when the sergeant stole up to his bed one night. When the sergeant's hand grazed the NCO's genitalia, the NCO shot

---

NCO also worked as an informal collaborator for state security.

177 BStU, MfS, AU 77/60. The MfS took over investigations itself, as the staff sergeant was an informal collaborator for state security and threatened to reveal as much if he was investigated.

178 BArch, DVW 13/64809: Rostock Military Court, arrest warrant from 17 July 1978.

179 Ibid., Rostock Military Court, ruling on 13 October 1978.

180 Ibid., Rostock Military Court, ruling on 19 June 1979.

181 BArch, DVW 13/54795: Leipzig military prosecutor, inditement from 22 November 1976.

182 Ibid., Leipzig military court, ruling on 8 December 1976.

up and struck the sergeant with his fist. The court punished the unwanted touching with one year on probation.[183]

Another example from 1982 shows just how much enlisted soldiers could fear the direct superiors in a platoon or company, usually NCOs or sergeants.[184]

> I was forced to put up with [X.'s] sexual fondness for me so as not to suffer any disadvantages during my time in the service, and also so I could have my vacation and leave. From what I knew of Sergeant [X.], he absolutely had the power to inflict those sort of disadvantages if I turned him down [...] In my opinion [X.] acted like that in part for sexual arousal, and in part to demonstrate his power over us as soldiers.[185]

This was how one conscript responded when asked in his witness statement why he had not defended himself more resolutely against a master sergeant. Within the space of two months in 1982, the accused had sexually abused direct subordinates on five separate occasions, each time by fondling their genitalia against their will until ejaculation. Witness statements had the sergeant "really ordering [the soldiers] to him" with the words "You'll be here at eight!"[186] In each case he had either threatened to withdraw vacation time that had already been approved, or tempted the individual soldier by promising a leave-slip despite the company chief's ban. As one conscript serving under the master sergeant at the time later said, "It was generally known in the unit that [X.] held the keys to vacation and leave [...] He would use expressions like 'I'm going to fuck you till the water boils in your ass.'"[187] Other soldiers in the company gave a similar account on questioning.

> You want to go on vacation don't you, well why don't you show how hard you've got it, prove it to me [...] 1. He threatened that I should bring him a vote of confidence or he would [...] make life hard for me. 2. I wouldn't receive any more time off or vacation [...] on the evening of February 8 he wanted to try again and showed me the leave slip. I should at least accept being touched. I didn't go along that time either. I asked him why he was doing it. He got agitated wondering what I was thinking and tore up the leave slip. He let me pick up the snippets [...] The master sergeant flaunted the fact that he could cancel vacation approved by the colonel. I was in such a state at that point that I said: It's all the fucking same to me, the main thing is it'll

---

183 BArch, DVW 13/54475: Schwerin Military Court, ruling on 8 March 1977.
184 For a detailed account of the internal conditions in the NVA see Wenzke, *Ulbrichts Soldaten*, 451–526 as well as Rogg, *Armee des Volkes?*
185 BArch, DVW 13/86440, Military state prosecutor, investigative files Az Str. II-23/83 (Bln.-Gr.), Witness examination of B., 15 March 1983.
186 Ibid.
187 Ibid.

be over soon, preferably quickly and painlessly. I was disgusted the whole time [...] Sometimes I didn't get to bed until after midnight.[188]

The highly restrictive policies in the GDR armed forces regarding vacation and leave should be kept in mind when assessing the extortion potential for denying either. NVA soldiers were strictly barracked and usually had to remain on standby even in the evenings and on weekends. Unlike the Bundeswehr, going out at night and weekend leaves were subject to authorization from the commanding officer, making the threat of denying vacation time particularly effective.[189] The master sergeant abused one private fifteen times within a two-month window. One of the soldier's roommates later recalled it had been "awful" how often the soldier had been ordered to the sergeant. The other soldiers in the room had laughed at first when the sergeant ordered other soldiers to him before bed. "We didn't think anything of it, we assumed there was a service context." Yet the private had always been "pretty beat" after returning to the barracks dormitory without ever saying why, another witness stated.[190]

Another private recounted the master sergeant as saying: "Think it over, I've got power and a lot can happen." The sergeant abused this soldier as well, touching him intimately on four occasions. When asked why he had not reported anything, the soldier replied that he had been warned by another private "just not to mess with the sergeant," things could "get dangerous and he wanted to be left in peace until he was dismissed."[191] The master sergeant had "so much power in the company that I did not know how I was supposed to act." Other soldiers had been ordered to appear before the sergeant dressed only in their underwear. The sergeant had threatened one soldier who suspected the sexual motivations behind the orders and refused that "he wouldn't let me on leave for six to eight weeks and let me stew the whole time in the service." "You want to go on vacation, don't you," the sergeant told another conscript to his face. "Well prove to me that you need it." Then he grabbed the soldier by his genitals and said "You know what that's there for!"[192]

The military prosecutor summarized the results of his investigations in an inditement in late March 1983: Between December 1981 and February 1983 the accused had "coerced subordinates to sexual acts in abuse of his official post," on

---

188 Ibid., Witness examination of S., 1 March 1983.
189 For more on "military discipline as [a form of] repression," see Wenzke, *Ulbrichts Soldaten*, 533–34.
190 BArch, DVW 13/86440: Witness examination of K., 10 March 1983.
191 Ibid., Witness examination of W., 1 March 1983.
192 Ibid., Witness examination of S., 1 March 1983.

at least twenty-five separate occasions, each time in his service quarters.[193] In early April 1983, before main proceedings were set to open in military court, the sergeant was demoted to the lowest service rank and dismissed from the NVA by personnel order for "gross violation of orders and regulations, abuse of official authority and jeopardizing combat readiness."[194] Other researched cases reveal that the accused was nearly always dismissed from the NVA before a case went to trial. This spared the People's Army from having to haul active-duty soldiers in uniform before the courts for such serious crimes. A similar method would have been inconceivable in the Bundeswehr, where military service courts only ruled on dismissal after hearing the evidence.

Military court sentenced the now former master sergeant to one year and three months in prison for "coercion to sexual acts, in partial conjunction with repeated failure to follow orders" (referring here to the defense ministry's ban on consuming alcohol in the barracks). The court ruling again listed the twenty-five proven crimes in detail. The NVA judges surprisingly stuck to the lower end of the range of punishment when determining the sentence, as they themselves emphasized.[195] The sergeant's appeal was rejected by superior military court in Berlin.[196] The former sergeant began to serve his sentence in civilian prison in June 1983, and was released early on good conduct by March 1984.[197]

As elsewhere, sexual misconduct in the GDR was not always sexually motivated, but could also be a show, or rather abuse, of power. In examining the interrogation transcripts, it is striking that nearly every culprit stubbornly denied any sort of sexual motivation, instead putting a desire to exhibit their boundless power over subordinates in the foreground. Evidently this seemed more advantageous to them than being considered homosexual.

Multiple eyewitnesses agreed on how coarsely superiors had treated their subordinates. Soldiers recall occasionally suspecting that a concealed or subconscious sadistic streak was being expressed. Thinking back to his second year of service in 1983–84 as a young NCO, one man described his superior, a captain and later a major, as being "very severe" with him and "mistreating" him by different means on at least seven separate occasions within the space of a single year, all without the NCO knowing or being told what he had done wrongly. One weekend the captain

---

193 Ibid., Berlin military prosecutor, inditement from 22 March 1983.
194 Ibid., Border Troops, Border Command Center, cadre order from 6 April 1983.
195 BArch, DVW 13/86440: Berlin Military Court, 2nd Military Criminal Division, ruling on 22 April 1983.
196 Ibid., Berlin Superior Military Court, 3rd Military Criminal Senate, ruling on 6 May 1983.
197 Ibid., Berlin, 2nd Military Criminal Division, ruling on 3 February 1984.

had ordered the NCO to his residence and had him "stand at attention" in his apartment. This had struck the NCO as "odd," "but you don't ask questions as a nineteen-year-old NCO, and especially not in the NVA." No sexual advances came about in this instance, but in retrospect the eyewitness recalled suspecting at the time that the superior was "compensating for some kind of secret sexual preferences" with his orders and punishments. "It wasn't normal behavior." This suspicion only grew when the officer, by now a major, forced his wife and child out of their shared apartment after the *Wende* in early 1990 and moved in with a man in his NVA service apartment.[198]

It was not always possible for investigating bodies to fix, beyond all shadow of a doubt, the border between treating subordinates roughly and in an uncouth way, between inhumane behavior on the part of superiors and acts with a sexual motivation. The archives of the SED Central Committee contain a complaint received in 1979 from a married couple living in Dresden that accuses a military superior, "given to drink and usually bellowing," of having attempted "to approach soldiers indecently and set after them homosexually." A son of relatives, a private, had been repeatedly grabbed on the backside and bit on the back by the sergeant. "The private had defended himself so far, but feared the revenge of the spurned."[199] The couple now turned their accusations toward higher authorities: "It's inconceivable to us how such a corrupter of youth could stay in our socialist Army [...] Not a single superior knows about the abnormal passion? Inconceivable! Is there no check on superiors that fear could be permitted to spread in such a way?"[200] The senior military prosecutor began an investigation and presented the results to the Central Committee's division for security affairs. No crime had been confirmed, including in the opinion of the private himself, "to whom it had never occurred to regard the improper actions of the ranking officer as sexual."[201]

A conscript similarly assumed there was a proper, official backdrop to a phone call he received from a captain on regimental staff one evening in June 1989. The conscript arrived at the captain's quarters as requested at 7 p.m. When the captain locked the door from inside and laid out an alleged affadavit binding the soldier not

---

198 Interview with retired Master Sergeant R., 7 February 2018.
199 SAPMO-BArch, DY 30/IV B 2/12/261: Hans and Gerda D. to "General state prosecutor at NVA Supreme Court in MfNV" (they intended the senior military prosecutor) dated 11 January 1979, likewise as a complaint submitted to the SED Central Committee, forwarded to Senior Military Prosecutor Major General Leibner by the committee's Division of Security Affairs on 1 February 1973. The author is grateful to Dr. Christoph Nübel at the ZMSBw for directing him to this source.
200 Ibid.
201 SAPMO-BArch, DY 30/IV B 2/12/261: Senior military prosecutor to SED Central Committee Division of Security Affairs, 21 February 1973.

to speak about the following conversation, the soldier assumed he would likely be interviewed about other soldiers. (On its own, this seemingly obvious assumption is revealing of the conditions in the NVA.)

Instead, the captain, still dressed in uniform, showed him heterosexual and homosexual pornographic images and presented him with a questionnaire containing thirty questions about the conscript's private life, including intimate questions about his own body-build and sex life. The soldier answered every oral and written question, still believing there was a professional context for the "review" of his "sexual conduct." "Inwardly I was waiting to find out what it all meant, the meaning wasn't clear to me yet. The officer [...] was ultimately a kind of confidante for me."[202] Yet the soldier grew increasingly circumspect, and when the officer ordered him to get undressed and masturbate in front of him, the soldier rebuffed him forcefully. The officer then spent nearly two hours trying to convince the soldier, with the soldier rejecting his advances. The soldier was finally allowed to leave the captain's quarters around 9.30 p.m. The following day he told an NCO about what had happened, who advised him to report the incident. "After some hesitation," the soldier did four days later.[203]

When interrogated by the military prosecutor, the captain initially denied any homosexual intent. "I wasn't aware that [...] images where men show themselves naked and pleasure themselves [...] was itself an indication of homosexuality. I neither can nor could imagine that to be the case." The officer justified his avid interest in the soldier's genitals on near biological grounds: "What do his genitals look like, and most of all what does it look like if he pleasures himself nearly every day?"[204] (The military prosecutor's office did not accept this overly simple excuse, and later obtained a confession from the captain that the soldier was such a "pretty young man."[205]) Once again, a line of Defense disputing any and all homosexual interest emerged here that was equally familiar in the Bundeswehr as in the NVA. In a distressing turn that would have been unthinkable in the Bundeswehr, the military prosecutor brought in the captain's wife to ask her details about the sexual life of the married couple.[206]

The captain freely confessed to pressuring soldiers who showed a conspicuous lack of discipline by verbally upbraiding them or threatening them with NVA

202 BArch, DVW 13/48584: Erfurt military prosecutor's office, question protocol for Soldier B., 28 June 1989.
203 Ibid., Complaint of Soldier B., 27 June 1989.
204 Ibid., Statement of Captain [X.], 8 July 1989.
205 Ibid., Additional statement of Captain [X.], 17 July 1989.
206 Ibid., Question protocol for Mrs. [X.], 6 July 1989.

military prison in Schwedt, all with the long-term goal of cowing soldiers into submission and "making them docile" in order "at a later point to somehow come into sexual contact with them."[207] One opportunity presented itself when a Bible was found in a soldier's living quarters, and the soldier had initially viewed his conversation with the captain and the unusual questions in this context.[208] The case never reached military court; instead the military prosecutor passed "the matter" along for the regimental commander to apply the disciplinary code.[209] The Ministry of Defense ordered the captain to be dismissed from active service and demoted to lieutenant in the reserve.[210]

Another investigation was likewise called off in 1980 after a captain tried to seduce two NCOs in training in his residence hall. One of the two quickly withdrew; the other stayed, at first. Subsequently, under the pretext of having to take a leak, he was able to inform the residential officer on duty of the captain's intention "to perform sexual acts on him." For whatever reason, the NCO then went back into the captain's room, where he was later "fetched" by a loud knock on the door. The military prosecutor eventually discontinued his investigation into suspected coercion to sexual acts under §122 (1) of the GDR criminal code when the criminal elements for force could not be shown to be present. The NCO could have "freed" himself from the situation at any point, nor was any relationship of military subordination in effect at that hour in the evening in the residence hall. On its own, the difference in service rank was not enough to satisfy the crime of abusing one's professional position.[211] Nevertheless, the captain's behavior had been "politically and morally reprehensible to a high degree," all the more so as the investigation had turned up previous, albeit consensual homosexual activity with NCOs in training, NCOs and officers. The matter was left to the commander to apply the disciplinary regulations. The investigations also prompted disciplinary action against another captain and company head who was likewise reported to have engaged in (consensual) homosexual activity with NCOs in training, NCOs and the already accused captain.[212]

Dismissals linked to criminal convictions under Section 151 of the GDR Criminal Code also merit special consideration. Introduced in 1968, the section crimi-

---

207 Ibid., Concluding examination by the office of the state prosecutor, 17 July 1989. The mere threat of "Schwedt" was enough to frighten soldiers. For more on the Schwedt prison see Wenzke, *Ulbrichts Soldaten*, 539–40, and a full account in Wenzke, *Ab nach Schwedt!*

208 BArch, DVW 13/48584, Complaint of Soldier B., 27 June 1989.

209 Ibid., Military prosecutor at Border Command South, order from 4 August 1989.

210 Ibid., MfNV, orders of the minister from 29 August 1989.

211 BArch, DVW 13/66204: Löbau military prosecutor, order from 21 March 1980.

212 Ibid.

nalized all same-sex activity, consensual or not, between adult men or women and youth under the age of eighteen. GDR military prosecutor archives record twelve investigations under §151 after the law was passed, with sentences ranging from a year on probation to two years and eight months in prison. Two sets of legal proceedings were suspended. Before drawing any conclusions about these numbers, however, it is essential to distinguish between consensual and non-consensual acts in reviewing court opinions. To give one example, in 1988 the military court in Dresden sentenced an *Oberfähnrich* to seven months in prison under §151(in the NVA the position *Oberfähnrich* did not refer to an officer candidate as in the Bundeswehr, but a separate career track between NCO and officer, comparable to a specialist officer). Accused of sexually coercing and abusing a seventeen-year-old, the officer had already been dismissed from the NVA by order of the personnel department before court proceedings began, as was custom.[213] This ruling does *not* fall under the 2017 act rehabilitating people convicted of consensual homosexual acts under §151.

h.) An East German Military Career

As for the Bundeswehr, to conclude this chapter, the service career of one NVA soldier will be sketched in its entirety. Born in Saxony in 1952, the soldier had thirteen years in the service behind him when he was dismissed for his homosexuality in 1984.[214] It could not have been the first time his sexual orientation came to the Army's attention; as a young man, the soldier remembered giving a feminine impression, coming across as somewhat "of a swish" in his own words. Devoted to ballet, he had already passed his entrance exam for the state ballet school in Dresden when military conscription struck a cross through his future plans.

His feminine style had not given rise to any problems when he was mustered into service in 1971; more than simply being declared fit to serve, he was asked at Army district command whether he wanted to commit to career service. (Unlike the Bundeswehr, ten years in the service sufficed to achieve the status of career soldier; fixed-term soldiers served between three and four years.) While the young Saxon did not harbor any future ambitions beyond eighteen months of basic service, the

---

213 BArch, DVW 13/70093: Dresden Military Court, 2nd Military Criminal Division, ruling on 14 October 1988.
214 This section is based on an in-person interview in Dresden and multiple conversations with the former soldier over the phone.

rejection he had received from ballet school due to his impending conscription made "it all the same" to him at the time, and he signed on for ten years as an NCO.

Even during basic training at the "Paul Fröhlich" school for non-commissioned officers in Zwickau, he held a singular reputation among comrades for his noticeably "camp" appearance. At one point, the school commander told him point blank that "Normally you shouldn't have been allowed to be confirmed as a career soldier in the first place."

Looking back today, the former soldier still attributes his acceptance as a career NCO to an error or omission on the part of Army district command. Yet it may not have been an error at all but basic need; the NVA was wanting for longer-term volunteers. It likely occurred the way it has for armies the world over in every era: Need creates fitness for service. The whispers continued when the NCO was put in charge of the mess hall at Reconnaissance Battalion 7 in Dresden; "Here comes the ten-year-homo" fellow soldiers would say of the NCO, and later warrant officer, referring to the amount of time to which he had committed. "I had to put up with idiotic comments," the retiree recalls. When a friendship developed between him and another soldier, the latter was warned by other superiors that he should take care, the cadet was gay.

In 1973 the warrant officer was assigned to the task force in Pioneer Construction Battalion 22 in Biesdorf outside Berlin, to assist with constructing the Palace of the Republic and other projects planned for the capital. At night and on the weekends, the soldier took advantage of his post in the city to immerse himself in the small gay scene in the East Berlin neighborhood of Prenzlauer Berg, recalling them as his "vagabond days." Yet all throughout his exploits, he was constantly on the lookout not to be discovered by other soldiers. "Nobody, and I mean nobody could get wind of it." The thought "Hopefully nobody sees you!" constantly ran through his mind. "More than enough!" the witness answered when asked whether he knew other gays in the NVA. He had met a number of gay soldiers in his Biesdorf battalion, though there had not been any sexual contact. "I couldn't afford that." The conscripts themselves were quite free in their sexual encounters; the witness had caught two soldiers in *flagrante delicto* more than once while walking through the barracks dorms at night. "It wasn't forbidden, which meant they weren't dismissed from service for it." One gay soldier from Plauen openly told him who he had been "in the sack" with. For commanding officers like him, however, sexual escapades in the barracks were taboo. Gays were also at risk of being exposed by their immediate families. This happened to one master sergeant in the construction battalion, whose wife caught him with another man and reported him. The sergeant was subsequently demoted then dismissed.

Aside from the prattle and half-witted comments of other soldiers, the former soldier stressed that he did not experience any career obstacles while serving in the

NVA, and was promoted to master sergeant according to plan, the highest service rank for an NCO. In 1982 he extended his contract to fifteen years and switched over to the career track for prospective officers. The obvious discrepancy with the regulations, between the soldier's reassignment and promotion on the one hand and knowledge of his homosexuality on the other, once again demonstrates the gap between claim and reality in the NVA.[215]

In 1984 the now warrant officer experienced a rapid and unexpected end to his career. He himself had provided the impetus; while drunk he had "tried to get into the pants" of a young conscript. The conscript, who was drunk himself, had refused and punched the warrant officer, a significantly higher-ranking and senior soldier, "right in the trap." The company commanders could not turn a blind eye to an attack on a superior, and a talk was set up between the deputy battalion commander responsible for the mess hall, the battalion political officer, the SED party secretary and the liaison officer for the MfS in the battalion.

The group decided to dismiss the soldier for reasons of health, referring him to the psychiatric unit at the Army hospital in Bad Saarow. (As shown, the Bundeswehr also looked regularly to psychiatric evaluation as the "royal road" for "getting rid of" homosexual soldiers.) At the hospital a physician showed the soldier erotic images of women to gauge his level of arousal – all in vain. The medical diagnosis avoided the term homosexuality, speaking instead of "sexual deviation" or "abnormal sexuality," as the doctor phrased it simply. "Sexual deviation" also went down as the diagnosis in the warrant officer's personnel form.[216] His personnel file (or cadre file, in the language of the NVA) lists "insufficient pre-qualifications for a military career," prompting the battalion commander to request dismissal from active service.[217] This meant the warrant officer, still a soldier, now had to find a civilian post; once he had found one in the gastronomy sector he was dismissed from the NVA. By way of a side-note – in clear contradistinction to West German service court rulings on similar cases, no demotion in rank was associated with the dismissal. Upon dismissal the warrant officer received a final evaluation that was entirely positive in tone to accompany him on his way into the civilian job market (a "friendly and open-minded nature, respected in the group of career NCOs as a

---

215 *NVA: Anspruch und Wirklichkeit* (NVA: claims and reality) was the name of a 1993 book about the history of the NVA edited by retired General Klaus Naumann.

216 Personnel form, medical evaluation from 22 August 1984. (The author would like to thank the witness for sharing a copy of this and other documents.)

217 Suggested dismissal from active service from 28 August 1984.

comrade, polite and disciplined toward superiors"). The report did not contain a single reference to the incident or its underlying causes.[218]

It was only after the GDR and its Army ceased to exist that the witness learned from former comrades from Biesdorf that nobody in the battalion had been told the reasons why he, well-known in the barracks as the cook, had disappeared so suddenly. While the other soldiers had been at a loss, they had not asked any questions, as was characteristic in the NVA. Still, word had gotten round about the incident in the barracks with the young soldier, letting the soldiers put two and two together.

The numerous rulings in West German service courts this study has considered give an idea of how the Bundeswehr might have proceeded in the event of a similar incident within its own ranks. During the 1980s, the period in question, military service courts would commonly have settled on a reduction in rank for a comparable case – a one-time instance of minor sexual assault against a lower-ranking soldier from the same unit. On rare occasion the company chief might decide to dismiss the solider in question. Strictly speaking, the warrant officer was not legally dismissed from the NVA for his infraction but released as unfit for service based on a psychiatric evaluation by a military physician. Standard procedure in the Bundeswehr would have involved a formal disciplinary hearing; in Biesdorf it was the commander, deputy political officer and party leadership in conjunction with state security opting for a discreet solution. The unpleasant incident was silently "swept under the rug"; the chosen path not only for sexual incidents but anything that did not fit the ideal image of the NVA as a socialist Army. The key was no unrest in the troops, no scandals that might eventually make their way into the public sphere. In the Biesdorf case, the fact that other soldiers in the battalion did not learn anything of the warrant officer's fate speaks to the motives underlying the matter's quiet resolution without disciplinary proceedings. Not that the Bundeswehr would have posted its disciplinary measures on the bulletin board or announced it by loudspeaker; data privacy laws and the personality rights guaranteed to all soldiers stood in the way. At the same time, it is safe to assume that word would have gotten out about the measures, even become public in the case of a reduction in rank. The true aim of any disciplinary measures within the Bundeswehr was their corrective influence on the accused, after all, as well as on the comrades in his orbit. The crucial difference between the case in Biesdorf and a comparable incident in the Bundeswehr lies in the presence of formal procedures in the West that followed clear rules and guaranteed rights to the accused. Nonetheless, the Bundeswehr also had the "solution" of having military physicians evaluate soldiers whose sexuality had drawn notice with a view to their fitness to serve, then potentially dismissing

---

218 Final evaluation from 28 August 1984.

them as unfit. "That's exactly what happened with me!" was the former warrant officer's spontaneous reaction when reading about similar cases in the Bundeswehr in the context of his interview.[219]

Postscript: In 1988 the warrant officer, now in the reserve, was called up for "reserve service" (the East German term for a reserve duty training exercise). He refused the call. however, thinking "first they kick me out and now they want me back? I don't think so!" In 1989 he received a second inquiry from Dresden Army District Command asking whether he would join the draft board. This time he did not say no, and served from March to August 1989 in his previous service rank.

---

219 Interview on 5 January 2018.

Conclusion

The following conclusion is presented in the form of succinct theses, based on the questions formulated at the outset of the study.

1. Male Homosexuals' Fitness for Military Service

During the first two decades of the Bundeswehr, men who either declared themselves to be homosexual or were identified as such during their mustering were consistently rejected for military service. It was not until the end of the 1970s, when low birth-rates in the years coming up for conscription combined with a greater availability of alternative national service programs to raise the number of conscripts, that homosexuality ceased to constitute a reason for ineligibility from military service on its own – much to the surprise of actual or alleged homosexuals themselves. From that point on, homosexual conscripts were considered in essence fit for service unless a medical, that is psychiatric, report attested to a given conscript's inability to integrate into a "male society within confined quarters." Throughout the 1980s and 1990s, homosexual men could expect to perform basic service, but could not expect a professional military career.

2. Personal Recollection and Experience

Eyewitnesses provided vivid and credible reports as to the intense pressure under which they served for years, even decades, as homosexual NCOs and officers. *Die Zeit* spoke to the heart of the matter in commenting that the armed forces drove their homosexual soldiers to "psychological self-mutilation." The sword of Damocles hovered perpetually over the heads of gay officers and NCOs, threatening to come down at any moment and end their career. Gay soldiers, both former and current, gave compelling accounts of how acutely aware of the danger they were, and how much it weighed on them psychologically and restricted their lives, including their private lives. On the other hand, there are the many eyewitnesses who reported a much greater degree of tolerance existing among troops than the regulations in fact permitted. Especially by the 1990s, there was no lack of officers and NCOs serving at all levels of leadership whose homosexuality was an open secret.

3. Male Homosexuality in Criminal and Disciplinary Law

After 1949, the Federal Republic maintained the more stringent version of § 175 adopted in the National Socialist era. Soldiers who were found guilty in criminal court faced additional charges from military prosecutors and conviction in the military service courts. Homosexuals who "drew attention" to themselves were routinely dismissed from the armed forces up through the late 1960s. The social misfortunes soldiers experienced went beyond their civil conviction to include the loss of their profession and social milieu, which often concentrated exclusively around their company and fellow soldiers. If they returned home to a rural area or smaller city, the subsequent stigmatization and exclusion often required a fresh professional start elsewhere, in a different place "where nobody knew them." In comparing criminal court rulings with those of the disciplinary courts, it is significant that the latter arrived at much harsher decisions, although again one cannot deduce a miscarriage of justice in disciplinary proceedings on that basis. Different interests count in criminal proceedings compared to disciplinary proceedings; it is a well-known fact that the same matter can be unobjectionable in criminal court and still constitute an official misdemeanor. It was not uncommon for cases involving consensual sexual activity between soldiers to be punished in a disciplinary court even after criminal proceedings had been abandoned by the state prosecutor or court.

Criminal prosecution of homosexual activity reflected social – as well as ethical, moral and religious – values (or prejudices). Until 1969 any conviction under §175 automatically triggered disciplinary proceedings that often resulted in the dismissal of the accused, with the same applying to soldiers as for civil servants at the federal, state and district levels. The violation of any criminal law or prevailing moral standard was usually punished as an official misdemeanor, with homosexual activity ranking among "the most serious."[1] On this count, the laws for civil servants were the same as for the Bundeswehr. "A great deal of politics is contained within this assessment; as a public employer, the state accedes to the concepts and demands held by the majority of its citizens. In this way, civil service law becomes a means of enforcing and maintaining collective expectations regarding conduct by way of example."[2] Behind the laws stood the image of the civil servant as a representative of the state, a quality that applied not only during work but after hours as well, at all times and universally. It did not just apply to higher-ranking administrative posts, police officers or teachers but more "minor" positions as well – post

---

1 Gollner, "Disziplinarsanktionen gegenüber Homosexuellen im öffentlichen Dienst," 105.
2 Ibid.

office clerks, firemen, train engineers and ticket inspectors.[3] This point also reveals another a clear parallel to the expectations the Bundeswehr had for its soldiers, particularly for NCOs and officers as reflected in § 17 (2) of the Soldier's Act, which governed their behavior both on and off duty.

Court rulings that lay thirty or forty years in the past should not be evaluated by today's standards. At the time, reservations toward homosexual men existed among the broad majority of the population and were reflected in the way soldiers and their commanding officers thought, as well in employees' and jurists' work at the Ministry of Defense and in the court system. "Most historians fail to situate themselves vis-a-vis the decisions facing their period of study, or fully comprehend them. All too often, they want to accommodate the current *Zeitgeist*, which is highly pernicious for being so emotionally laden. Historians who write in the spirit of the *Zeitgeist* are essentially looking at the present, not at history."[4] Yet still they pretend to be investigating the historical record. The disciplinary law internal to the armed forces had (and still has) other interests to weigh than the criminal justice system at large. The actions and decisions of Bundeswehr officials and jurists, those of legal advisors, military prosecutors as well as the judges themselves were bound by law and justice as a matter of course. Yet the law and the laws followed different norms in the 1960s and 1970s than they do in 2020.

Up through the late 1960s, military service judges set an explicit emphasis on the "cleansing effect" of their rulings for crimes that might have jeopardized "troop cleanliness." Yet those same "purifying disciplinary measures" were imposed for all kinds of other official offenses – it both was and remains a common form of expression among jurists. Beginning in the 1970s, "troop cleanliness" was supplanted by the softer, more technical-sounding phrase "jeopardizing troop order and discipline," which was then used repeatedly to justify disciplinary punishment in cases of outed homosexuality under the new versions of §175 adopted in 1969, then again in 1973. The Bundeswehr and its jurists were following general legal norms when applying disciplinary law. In 1970 a military service senate ruled logically that since simple homosexuality had been decriminalized, it no longer constituted an official breach of duty when it occurred between soldiers – unless, that is, there was a connection to the chain of command. Still, the Bundeswehr reserved its own discretionary power of interpreting what exactly constituted a connection to the line of duty. In 1970 that could be taken to mean two soldiers simply carrying on sexual

---

3 In the TV documentary "Der Schwulen-Paragraph," Günter Landschreiber describes a letter he received dismissing him as a prospective postal employee after he was taken into custody in Gelnhausen in Hessen when his ex-boyfriend's mother reported him.

4 Ret. Surgeon General Dr. Horst Hennig in an interview, Cologne, 20 June 2018.

relations, even if it took place exclusively in private and the soldiers had no official contact. This strict framework was steadily relaxed in the service courts over the years, although sexual relations between superiors and subordinates continued to be handled strictly, with even an abstract relationship of command sufficing under the directive governing superior–subordinate relations. Sexual activity between soldiers in the same unit was also subject to disciplinary action, independently of service rank. The ban on sexual activity inside the barracks was lifted in 2004.

Dismissals under § 55 (5) of the Soldier's Act present a blind spot; intended for official misdemeanors that posed a serious threat to military order, the paragraph allowed soldiers within the first four years of their service to be summarily dismissed from the Bundeswehr in a simplified procedure that did not involve a ruling at disciplinary court. This study managed to identify only a handful of isolated instances through chance findings or eyewitness tips. What remains is the suspicion that the number of soldiers affected by the provision is far higher than the number of soldiers dismissed by ruling at the service courts.

The study drew a clear distinction between consensual sexual activity and cases involving sexual assault. Sources attest to the high rate of sexual assault or similar attempts by officers and NCOs against lower-ranking, often younger soldiers. Up to the present day, such cases would be (and are) punished under disciplinary law, and potentially criminal law, independently of the question of homosexuality. In early January 2000, a personnel section at the Bundeswehr determined once again that homosexual activity did not hold any fundamentally different relevance for disciplinary action than heterosexual activity.

4. Unfit to Command?

Even below the threshold of disciplinary action, until 2000 the Bundeswehr considered homosexuality a severe stigma, with it usually entailing serious consequences for military service. Even an officer or NCO with a flawless service record did not stand a chance of being appointed to career servicer if he had been identified as homosexual. The Bundeswehr usually blocked any such soldier from reassignment, denying even willing conscripts the chance to continue to serve in the ranks of enlisted men.

Still, commencing in the 1970s, soldiers of every service rank who were known to be homosexual were generally no longer subject to early dismissal, as remained standard practice in the British and U.S. armed forces. Rather, the Bundeswehr allowed soldiers to serve out their military contracts, while anyone already in career service would likely be allowed to remain until he reached retirement age.

The same degree of protection was not extended to prospective officers and NCOs. If a soldier in one of these groups came out as homosexual, he was dismissed in simplified proceedings as allegedly unfit for service.

Even if soldiers identified as homosexuals were no longer subject to early dismissal (with the named exceptions), the BMVg usually deemed them ineligible to serve as immediate commanders or instructors, through a blanket policy that expressly ruled out case-by-case decisions. The deciding factors in this context were an anticipated loss of authority and the associated risks for troop discipline; the Bundeswehr saw its combat readiness threatened. Ensuring full combat readiness in turn laid the groundwork for the armed forces to fulfill its mission to defend, and national defense ultimately had constitutional priority. These were the arguments grounding the ministry's belief that it was well equipped for a lawsuit at the Federal Constitutional Court, a lawsuit that looked increasingly likely as the years passed. The judges at the high court never actually reached a decision on the matter; when they were first called to in 2000, the BMVg conceded at literally the last possible minute, thus avoiding a ruling. For the thirty years leading up to 2000, each and every attempt to bring about looser restrictions through legal action was stone-walled in the administrative courts. In the 1980s and 1990s, the Ministry of Defense noticeably tightened its restrictions against homosexual superiors serving in the military, adhering undeterred to its strict path into the new millennium, and often prompting gay men to refrain from petitioning or applying of their own accord.

The Bundeswehr missed out on a large pool of potential personnel in pursuing its policy. After completing their studies, some officers would take advantage of the personnel guidelines to cut short the time they had left in the service either as genuine or apparent homosexuals, thereby securing a quicker exit to the broader jobs market. In terms of effective personnel policy, these were ultimately own goals. Former Parliamentary State Secretary Brigitte Schulte looked back in wonder at "how misinformed and narrow-minded [...] civilian and military leadership in the Bundeswehr and our society were up into the twenty-first century."[5] The reference to society is key here; up through the late 1970s, the Bundeswehr was little more than a mirror to society, although the reflection grew more and more distorted as time wore on.

Numerous examples, on the other hand, show that as long as homosexual officers or NCOs simply lived their lives without any grand pronouncements, they were able to make their way through the ranks of the armed forces and achieve prominent positions with astonishing ease.

---

5 Letter from Ret. State Secretary Brigitte Schulte to the author, 2 June 2019.

Here too, it is crucial not to assess decisions that lay decades in the past exclusively by today's standards. In the minds of the officers in charge, jurists and officials, the age-old wisdom about the military as a school for masculinity lived on.

The Bundeswehr was not alone in discriminating against homosexuals. At least in the first decades of its existence, it acted in accordance with traditional cultural values and norms held by large portions of mainstream society in which tolerance toward homosexuals was not an outstanding feature. Homosexuals who came out as such would likely have suffered professional consequences in practically any line of work. The social consensus came out in untold numbers of jokes and sayings about gays, such as CSU Chairman Franz Josef Strauss' quip that he "would rather be a cold warrior than a hot brother."[6]

Whether or not something can be spoken aloud is the deciding measure of its acceptance in society. The same applies in the armed forces. Openly announcing oneself as gay was a common topos within the homosexual movement; in the military it was a major step after which regulations usually took hold. Courageous activists opted for this stony path consciously, likely in the knowledge that they would not achieve anything (yet) except the end of their career and defeat in court.

Despite the well-known restrictions, homosexual men still opted for a military career. During public talks, audiences have occasionally asked the author of the present study in disbelief how a person could even think about becoming a career soldier in the Bundeswehr as a homosexual, knowingly exposing himself to such a "homophobic environment." Yet for anyone who did want to take up the career of a soldier, whether because he was convinced of the Bundeswehr's mission or simply because he wished to be a soldier, turning back from such a decision would have amounted to a form of self-abandonment or self-discrimination. Looking back, a staff officer involved in personnel matters who was not affected by the policies himself recalled his attitude to the situation in 1999: "We denied homosexuals any sort of career, even when the vast majority were already cowering and withdrawn so as not to attract any attention to themselves. And these men consciously chose to serve in the armed forces as officers or NCOs despite this rejection and all the discrimination."[7] One way or the other, the armed forces' approach to homosexuality exerted a considerable influence on the lives of those it affected.

---

6 Franz Josef Strauß cited in the *Neue Osnabrücker Zeitung* on 6 March 1970. Strauß repeated the same line nearly verbatim at a CDU election rally the year after in West Berlin, cited in *Der Spiegel*, 12, 1971, p. 21.
7 Interview with Lieutenant Colonel (of the Reserves) Joachim Meier, Karlsruhe, 16 July 2018.

5. Homosexuality as a "Security Risk"

Into the 1980s, internal security clearance guidelines generally rated homosexuality and other forms of sexual conduct considered "abnormal" as security threats. The regulation was not specific to the Bundeswehr, however, but stemmed from the Federal Ministry of the Interior, and applied in equal measure to all departments in the federal government. New regulations drafted in 1983 stipulated that homosexuality was no longer liable to blackmail when practiced openly, and as such no longer posed a security risk. The new security clearance regulations took effect in 1988. If officers and NCOs kept their homosexuality to themselves (in service), MAD classified them as potentially susceptible to blackmail and thus in jeopardy of "being approached by [enemy] intelligence contacts."

Contrasting this are the accounts of numerous gay soldiers from a wide range of ranks and branches of service, who insist they never experienced any problems with MAD. Still, the restrictions in place against homosexual officers and NCOs made it nearly impossible for them to come out to the personnel leadership – except, of course, at the cost of their professional future. *Die Zeit* addressed this virtually inescapable conflict directly in January 1984, quoting Michael Lindner at the height of the Wörner–Kießling affair: "It is discrimination that creates susceptibility to blackmail in the first place," and "the Bundeswehr is creating its own security risks."[8] There is only one way to avoid this sort of situation, which is refusing to grant the categories of heterosexual, homosexual, bisexual and transsexual any relevance in the matter. An open and tolerant atmosphere that permits everyone to be open about their sexual orientation is the only means of combatting malicious gossip and suspicion by removing any cause for secrets in the first place; only then will homosexuals no longer be liable to blackmail, and thus not a threat to security. The particular irony in the tragedy of the Wörner–Kießling affair lies in the fact that this realization should have to come with the downfall of a man who – according to everything his close friends had to say and what his own writing expresses – was not homosexual to begin with. The only way out of the endless loop was a change in the Bundeswehr's stance toward homosexuality. It was a step that was both long hoped for and long called for, and was finally taken in 2000.

---

8 "Homosexualität – ein Sicherheitsrisiko?"

6. A New Millennium – a New Era

Such a change was only possible from "on high" as it were, at the ministrial level, and then only when coming from the political leadership. While Rudolf Scharping's hesitation and timidity before the military leadership does not leave a good impression where the primacy of politics was concerned, it was in keeping with the minister's cautious nature and his intermediary role. Scharping did not want to steamroll the military leadership, but rather include them on the path to change. As Scharping himself said to the Bundeswehr, it was an "imperative of wise leadership to make a view one holds to be correct, bearable, palatable and understandable in reasonable fashion [...] tolerance had to be made possible to understand and develop, and in this way to learn."[9] Scharping showed greater willingness to open himself and his party up to the accusation of breaking a campaign promise than let things deteriorate with the generals. It was only under heavy pressure, including from a pending decision at the Federal Constitutional Court, that the minister changed course in 2000 and steered the ship in the opposite direction, prevailing over the bitter resistance of the military leadership. Scharping's decision allowed the BMVg to avoid a ruling in Karlsruhe that might have established the unconstitutionality of the Bundeswehr's previous position toward its homosexual soldiers. The chiefs of the services, the chief of defense and their staffs, on the other hand, preferred – to draw an admittedly inappropriate analogy to the fleet in November 1918 – to go down fighting. Scharping, however, had no interest in running the ship aground at Karlsruhe. He was a politician and made a political decision, even if at the last minute. It resulted in a historical break, and the abandoning of a line that had been held for forty-five years.[10]

In 2000 the German armed forces opened fully to women by court order, a development that ran in parallel to the end of restrictions on homosexuals. In the public perception and in the troops' own self-image, the two combined to paint the picture of a rapidly changing Bundeswehr. While each chain of events occurred independently of the other, they remain inseparable. The answer as to why, after decades, the Bundeswehr suddenly became accommodating toward its homosexual soldiers and threw every last long-standing principle overboard within a few short months, is found primarily at the European level, in the course of changing European concepts regarding human rights and freedom from discrimination.

---

9 German Bundestag, 14th legislative period, typed transcript of the 95th Session, 23 March 2000, 8844–45.
10 In other words, "The break with tradition could hardly have been more dramatic." Schadendorf, *Der Regenbogen-Faktor*, 72.

7. Historical and Lateral Views of other Armed Forces

Homosexuality has been and remains a topic within armed forces all over the world. This means the Bundeswehr's own approach has to be assessed within a greater, transhistorical and international context; comparing the Bundeswehr to other armed forces helps situate its methods within a broader framework. At times, Bundeswehr practices closely resembled those revealed by sources from the Imperial Navy, the Prussian Army in the time of the German Empire and the Reichswehr. Yet, after due consideration, the fact comes not so much as a surprise as typical of the armed forces as such.

Historically, the Bundeswehr does not rank all that negatively by international comparison: unlike the armed forces of the U.S., British, and other NATO states, starting in the 1970s, officers and NCOs known to be homosexual were no longer generally subject to dismissal, and certainly not immediate dismissal, from the Bundeswehr. It was not until 1993 that the U.S. introduced similar regulations, though admittedly not under such a pointed policy title. Granted, the U.S. policy of "Don't ask, don't tell" did not give carte blanche to gays and lesbians in the armed forces; soldiers who were open about their sexual orientation were still in danger of being thrown out of the military. U.S. armed forces did not open fully to homosexuals until 2011, eleven years after the Bundeswehr.

In the UK, homosexuals were likewise subject to immediate dismissal from the armed forces. While Great Britain ceased criminal prosecution of male homosexuals one year before the Federal Republic, in 1968, Her Majesty's Armed Forces stayed the course, maintaining a harsh and restrictive line thirty years after the laws had changed. The British practice of summarily dismissing homosexual soldiers first ended in 1999 by a court ruling at the European Court of Human Rights. Still, in the context of NATO it was not the armed forces of West Germany who stood at the forefront of tolerance toward homosexuals. That role was reserved for the Dutch.

Homosexuality presented just as great a taboo in the East German armed forces as it did in the Bundeswehr. The BMVg itself did not take an interest in NVA practices, as shown in the lack of relevant documentation. If it had, the jurists and officers in Bonn would have found that much like the BMVg, NVA personnel guidelines ruled homosexuals out for any further assignment (laid out explicitly in mustering regulations), never mind acceptance for career service as an NCO or officer. Both German armies took the same position on homosexual men: military service itself was possible, but not a career. Looking back, nearly every former NVA officer interviewed for this study recalled the topic had been "hushed up." Some were nonetheless able to recall a handful of related incidents, whether as observers or participants. The individual case studies indicate that there was no uniform response to a fixed-term or career soldier in the NVA being identified as homosexual. Decisions ran the gamut, ranging from dismissal from active service by personnel order (described consistently as "transferred to the reserve"), dismissal for alleged medical reasons following on the "results" of medical inspection by military physicians, transfer to another place of service, to no discernible (written) restrictions.

The heavy hand that state security had in military personnel decisions – by no means only in cases of suspected homosexuality, although definitely in these cases – set the NVA apart from the Bundeswehr. The MfS placed soldiers from every service rank suspected of homosexuality under surveillance operations termed "Operational Personal Checks." If those suspicions were confirmed, the MfS generally advocated that officers be dismissed or "transferred to the reserve." This demonstrates once again the crucial differences between a state founded on the rule of law and its absence in the GDR. In the West, administrative judges would have had the final say (and toward the end the judges at the Federal Constitutional Court nearly had theirs), while in the East the arbitrary exercise of power reigned supreme concerning this particular topic. In 1988 the NVA stance toward homosexual soldiers shifted; if before it had rejected homosexuals for service as volunteers and conscripts, it now stated explicitly that homosexuality did not constitute grounds for exclusion from the military. Fixed-term or career soldiers already serving in the NVA whose homosexuality came out could continue in active service "as long as no complications" arose, a policy that applied explicitly for teaching positions as well. Unlike the Bundeswehr at the time, the regulatory shift in 1988 opened the door for homosexuals to serve as NCOs, officers and even career officers.

8. The Matter of Lesbian Soldiers

In the past, it was always male homosexuality that was meant when the topic surfaced for discussion in the Bundeswehr. Aside from two exceptions in 1999 and 2000, no documents concerning lesbian soldiers were discovered within the extensive archives of the BMVg and the armed forces for the period under consideration. The same holds true for decisions in military court, and for that matter any other disciplinary measures based on sexual activity between two female soldiers. Lesbian soldiers first received mention in February 1999 in a BMVg response to the Gay Association in Germany, which noted it was "neither legally nor factually objectionable to keep homosexually oriented soldiers, whether they be gay or lesbian, at a remove from assignment as troop leaders or instructors as soon as their tendency is known."[11] Yet a lack of sources can be revealing in and of itself, in this case of the fact that lesbian women were not perceived as a significant factor or any sort of a problem by the Bundeswehr or the BMVg.

It remains to be seen whether this was out of ignorance or tolerance. Multiple officers who dealt with the subject in a professional capacity summed it up in hindsight by saying "Lesbians? They were never an issue." It almost seems as though lesbian soldiers did not appear on the radar of the defense ministry, military leadership or Bundeswehr jurists until the new millennium. There are two possible explanations for this. It is possible, on the one hand, there was a problem of perception in the sense of a total ignorance about women loving other women, which would have meant that the Bundeswehr did not see it as a problem. Yet it is also possible that male conceptions of sexual activity between women were at work, which have not always regarded that activity as a form of homosexuality but a sort of sexual game, even an object of male fantasy.

Criminal law followed the Bundeswehr and BMVg in not giving serious consideration to female homosexuality, incidentally; § 175 only ever applied to male homosexuality. On the other hand, the proportion of lesbian soldiers may have been so small based alone on the minuscule number of women accepted into the Bundeswehr and their restriction to two areas of service up until 2000 that the BMVg saw no need for regulation. This would partially explain the ministry's perceptions, or lack thereof. This does not mean of course that it was easy for lesbian soldiers to live openly with their sexuality, or that it did not lead to problems in individual cases. In either case, the lack of written sources meant that research on the subject only came about via eyewitnesses, whose recollections of serving in the 1990s show, for example, that women in uniform encountered the same issues with security clearance checks. At the same time, interviewees attested to widespread tolerance in the troops, in spite of any number of sexist, dim-witted or at the very least ill-considered comments.

9. "We Have to Betray the Essence of Who We Are"

Speaking to *Der Spiegel* in 1993, a BMVg spokesperson declared that there was no "injunction to prosecute or witch burning" in the Bundeswehr.[12] "What soldiers do 'off duty' does not interest us," the spokesperson continued. Things looked differ-

---

11 BArch, BW 2/38358: BMVg, Parliamentary State Secretary Walter Kolbow to the SVD, 26 February 1999.
12 "Versiegelte Briefe," 54.

ent in reality. True, gay soldiers were not being burned at the stake, but in the first years of the Bundeswehr they were most certainly subject to legal prosecution, and were still experiencing discrimination at the turn of the millennium.

To the extent that freedom is also the absence of fear, homosexuals had not been free in Germany for centuries, not in the first decades of the Federal Republic, and not up until the new millennium in the case of the Bundeswehr. Throughout the first four decades of the Bundeswehr, as in armed forces the world over, the situation was as actor Simon Curtis summed it up in the fallout from the public scandal surrounding sexual assault and the widespread, but perpetually concealed, homosexuality within the U.S. film industry: "Gay men aren't allowed to be who we are. In order to work and follow our dreams we have to betray the essence of who we are."[13] In the Federal Republic, homosexual soldiers were considered unfit for their profession up to the end of the 1970s, and thus ineligible to serve in positions of leadership. Instead, they were placed under general suspicion by military intelligence, had allegations brought against them by state and military prosecutors, and were alternatively shunned and tolerated by fellow soldiers.

Part of any objective appraisal must include setting earlier decisions within their historical context. The Bundeswehr was a mirror of society. As incomprehensible as it may appear from today's perspective in 2020, up until the late 1980s the jurists, officials, officers and politicians at the BMVg knew themselves to be operating in harmony with mainstream society. Discrimination was not specific to the Bundeswehr; society at large did the same, as numerous court rulings against suits filed by homosexual soldiers can attest. Society opened up to sexual minorities over the course of the 1990s, showing increasing levels of tolerance and acceptance. Neither the BMVg nor Bundeswehr followed suit until 2000, and then not on its own initiative or out of conviction, but only when forced to do so by politicians, the constitutional court and the media – in short, the public opinion of a changing society. In March 2020 Minister of Defense Annegret Kramp-Karrenbauer expressed her regret for the unjust treatment homosexuals had received from the Bundeswehr. "They have been subjected to considerable discrimination on the basis of their sexual orientation, not least in the consequences they suffered in their professional development."[14] Until the year 2000, Kramp-Karrenbauer continued, homosexuals had been put at a "structural disadvantage in the Bundeswehr," with the regulations "repealed at far too late a date," in the minister's opinion.[15]

---

13 Diez, "Er ist so nett."
14 Federal Ministry of Defense, "Vielfalt im BMVg: Jeder Einzelne wird wertgeschätzt," (BMVg communication) from 3 March 2020.
15 Ibid. The defense minister directed her ministry to "draft proposals for a new legal basis that

Today all of this lies in the past for the Bundeswehr, even if the not all-too-distant past. To this day, many soldiers in other armies, both female and male, are still forced to deny the essence of who they are. In 2018 a master sergeant looked on the hitherto unimagined degree of freedom and tolerance that prevailed in the contemporary Bundeswehr with satisfaction, viewing it as a "gift" to soldiers, "to all soldiers, regardless of whether they're gay, lesbian, hetero, bi, transgender, or part of another sexual minority."[16] The soldiers of decades past could not have dreamt of a similar sort of openness and liberalism. At present the Bundeswehr was "even a social pioneer in matters of accepting minorities."[17]

The growing self-assurance among homosexual women and men in uniform is also reflected in the activities of the national group *QueerBw* (known until March 2020 as AHsAB, the Working Group for Homosexual Members of the Bundeswehr). In response to the group's demands of legal rehabilitation and compensation for homosexual soldiers who had suffered disciplinary measures and other professional setbacks, the Ministry of Defense wrote in 2018 that while the clock could not be turned back, it was a personal concern of Minister Ursula von der Leyen "to direct public attention to the dire experiences of those affected." In saying so, the minister also made it clear that "everyone both male and female, regardless of whether they are gay, lesbian, trans- or heterosexual, is welcome in the Bundeswehr today."[18] Within the Bundeswehr, she continued, every individual was valued and respected. Discrimination would also be made subject to punishment, as Defense Minister Kramp-Karrenbauer stressed in March 2020.[19]

---

would do more justice to the legitimate concerns of those left at a disadvantage than has been the case to date."

16 Interview with Master Sergeant H., Berlin, 2 July 2018.

17 Ibid.

18 BMVg, R I 5 to the Working Group for Homosexual Members of the Bundeswehr, 16 August 2018.

19 Federal Ministry of Defense, "Vielfalt im BMVg: Jeder Einzelne wird wertgeschätzt," (BMVg communication) from 3 March 2020.

Postscript

In January 2017, then Minister of Defense Ursula von der Leyen requested that the ZMSBw undertake the present study. On 17 September 2020 her successor, Annegret Kramp-Karrenbauer, presented the results from Potsdam to the press and public. The minister spoke in unambiguous terms: "For decades after its founding in 1955, the Bundeswehr [...] systematically discriminated against homosexual soldiers. The Bundeswehr's stance was wrong. It was wrong even at the time, lagging behind society, and is all the more so from today's perspective." She then spoke the words that soldiers who had experienced discrimination must have been waiting decades to hear: "I deeply regret these practices. And for all those who were made to suffer from them, I ask for forgiveness."

In closing, the minister laid the groundwork for an act of rehabilitation. "We are not indifferent to how people were treated in the past," Kramp-Karrenbauer affirmed. "Even if we are not able to do justice to every fate, we are going back into it now and will correct as much as possible." On 25 November 2020, the Federal Cabinet resolved to set the legislative gears in motion for the Rehabilitation Act for Homosexual Soldiers Discriminated against in the Bundeswehr and the National People's Army.

On 20 May 2021, the German Bundestag voted unanimously and without abstention to pass the Rehabilitation Act for Soldiers Adversely Impacted under Civil Service Law Due to Consensual Homosexual Activity, Homosexual Orientation or Sexual Identity.

It took effect on 23 July 2021.

Sources and Bibliography

1. Archival Sources

a.) Federal Military Archives (BArch), Freiburg im Breisgau

BH 1	Federal Ministry of Defense – Army Joint Staff
BM 1	Federal Ministry of Defense – Navy Joint Staff
BW 1	Federal Ministry of Defense – Leadership, Joint Staffs and Civilian Departments
BW 2	Federal Ministry of Defense – Chief of Defense and Joint Chiefs of Staff
BW 4	Military attaché staffs
BW 24	Federal Ministry of Defense – Office of the Surgeon General
BW 31	Office of Military Counterintelligence
BW 32	Subordinate Agencies of Military Counterintelligence
DVW 1	GDR Ministry of National Defense
DVW 9	NVA, Military District Command III
DVW 13	NVA Senior Military Prosecutor for the GDR
N 818	Dieter Wellershoff Estate
N 851	Günther Kießling Estate
No Signature	BMVg, Minister, VR I 1, New Ministry Ordinance, 7 February 1964, Annex 2
Pers 1	Personnel files for career and fixed-term Bundeswehr and Wehrmacht soldiers
Pers 6	Personnel records of members of the Reichswehr and the Wehrmacht
Pers 12	Court files from the military service court
RH 12–1	Reichswehr, Army Personnel Office
RM 31	Baltic Navy Headquarters of the Imperial Navy

b.) Federal Commissioner for the Records of the State Security Service of the former German Democratic Republic (BStU)

MfS BV Dresden, Abt. KuSch	Ministry of State Security, Dresden District Administration, Cadre and Training Department
MfS BV Pdm, KD Brandenburg	Ministry of State Security, Potsdam District Administration, County Unit Brandenburg/Havel
MfS BV Rst	Ministry of State Security, Rostock District Administration
MfS BV Suhl, III	Ministry of State Security, Suhl District Administration Department III (Radio reconnaissance/counterintelligence)
MfS BV Suhl, Abt. KuSch	Ministry of State Security, Suhl District Administration, Cadre and Training Department
MfS HA I	Ministry of State Security, Head Department I (NVA and Border Troops)
MfS HA III	Ministry of State Security, Head Department IIII (Radio reconnaissance/counterintelligence)
MfS HA IX	Ministry of State Security, Head Department IX (Investigative Branch)
MfS HV A	Ministry of State Security, Main Directorate for Reconnaissance
MfS ZAIG	Ministry of State Security, Central Evaluation and Information Group

∂ Open Access. © 2025 Klaus Storkmann, published by De Gruyter. (cc) BY This work is licensed under the Creative Commons Attribution 4.0 International License.
https://doi.org/10.1515/9783111082691-015

c.) **Stiftung Archiv der Parteien und Massenorganisationen der DDR im Bundesarchiv (SAPMO-BArch)**
DY 30/IV B 2/12 Zentralkommitee der SED, Abteilung für Sicherheitsfragen

d.) **North Rhine-Westphalia State Archives (NRW)**
Holdings Westfalen, Q 222
Holdings Westfalen, Q 926

e.) **Witten City Archive**
Holdings Witten-Alt, 2.25b.300, files Robert M.

f.) **Bundeswehr Center of Military History and Social Sciences (ZMSBw), Potsdam, Research Department Military History after 1945**
Jörg Schönbohm Estate (VJS 07)

2. Service Regulations

Federal Ministry of the Interior, Guidelines for the security clearance process of federal employees as of 15 January 1971
Federal Ministry of the Interior, Guidelines for the security clearance process at federal agencies as of 10 November 1983
Federal Ministry of Defense, Chief of Defense of the Bundeswehr – FüS I 4 Az 35-04-09 – Leadership assistance for "Handling sexuality" from 20 December 2000
MfNV (Ministry of National Defense), Ordinance 060/9/002 Regarding the work of the NVA medical assessor commission in the area of military medical assessment (assessor order) from 5 August 1987
Secretary of the Navy Instructions 1910. 4A from 27 December 1983, Navy Military Personal Manual, 3630400
ZDv (Joint Service Regulation) 2/30: Security in the Bundeswehr, BMVg, Bonn 1988
ZDv (Joint Service Regulation) 14/3: Military Disciplinary Code and Military Complaints Code, Annex B 173, Revision as of 30 June 2004, published as elsewhere by the Gay and Lesbian Federation in Germany: https://www.lsvd.de/fileadmin/pics/Dokumente/Recht3/bwsex03.pdf (last accessed 29 March 2021)
ZDv (Joint Service Regulation) 14/5: Soldiers' Law. Confidential Electoral Act
ZDv (Joint Service Regulation) 46/1: Guidelines for performing medical examinations at muster and entry into service of conscripts, accepting and hiring voluntary applicants and dismissing soldiers, BMVg, Bonn 1979

3. Court Rulings and Correspondence

BMVg, P II 7 to Münster Administrative Court, 16 July 1973
BVerfG, 17 August 1999 – 2 BvR 2276/98
BVerfG, Ruling on 15 December 1983, Az. 1 BvR 209, 269, 362, 420, 440, 484/83
BVerwG, 1st Military Service Senate, Az 1 WB 152/84 on 11 April 1985
BVerwG, 1st Military Service Senate, Court opinion, WB 48.97 on 18 November 1997
BVerwG, 1st Military Service Senate, Ruling on 19 November 1998 – BVerwG 1, WB 54.98

BVerwG, 2 WD 63/67: Federal Administrative Court, 2nd Military Service Senate, Ruling on 8 June 1988
BVerwG, 2 WD 69/87: Federal Administrative Court, 2nd Military Service Senate, Ruling on
    11 November 1988
BVerwG, 21 WB 73/83: Federal Administrative Court, 1st Military Service Senate, Ruling on 29 May 1984
BVerwG, 2nd Military Service Senate, Ruling on 11 May 1982, Az 2 WD 4/82
BVerwG, Decision 16 February 1976, Az VI B 83.75
Düsseldorf Administrative Court, Disciplinary Division, Az 15-0-12/79, Ruling on 28 June 1979
ECHR, Ruling on 27 September 1999
Hamburg Administrative Court, Az 20 K 3130/09, 19 June 2012
Law firm F. to Hamburg Administrative Court, 14 November 1980
Lower Saxony Superior Administrative Court (Lüneburg), Decision on 16 December 1998, Az 2 M
    4436/98
Lüneburg Administrative Court, Decision on 7 September 1998, Az 1 B 53/98
Lüneburg Administrative Court, Ruling on 3 June 1999, Az 1 A 141/97
Military District Administration I to Hamburg Administrative Court, 11 August 1980
Military District Administration I, Muster Division 2, notice of appeal from 28 May 1980 against the
    decision of the draft board from 10 March 1980
Military Service Court C1, Az C 1 VL 46/63 on 20 February 1964
Military Service Court South, 1st Division, Ruling on 7 October 1980, Az S 1–VL 10/80
Military Service Court South, 1st Division, Ruling on 17 November 1981, Az 1 VL 15/81
Münster Administrative Court, Ruling on 10 June 1974, Az 4 K 338/73
North Rhine-Westphalia Superior Administrative Court, Disciplinary Senate, AzpV–11/79, Ruling on
    7 October 1980
North Rhine-Westphalia Superior Administrative Court, Ruling on 4 September 1975, Az I 4 1108/74
Plein, Rainer, to Münster Administrative Court, 23 March 1973
Saarland Regional Social Court, Az S 17 Vs 43/87, Ruling on 11 May1989
Saarland Regional Social Court, Az L 2 V 21/89, Ruling on 11 September 1990
Stade public prosecutor's office, decision on 19 September 2017

Court Rulings found on jurion.de (Now wolterskluwer-online.de)
Military Service Senate decisions at the Federal Administrative Court, and previously at the Federal
Disciplinary Court with file reference numbers:
    BVerwG WD 5/59, WD 8/62, I WD 69/64, II WD 35/64, I (II) WD 129/64, II (I) WD 121/64, II WD
    44/66, II WD 60/67, I WD 33/66, II WD 57/75, II WD 59/68, II WD 73/69, II WD 18/69, II WD 67/70,
    I WD 4/70, 2 WD 80/79, 2 WD 6/88, I WD 54/68, II WD 19/66, 2 WD 69/87, II WD 8/66, II WD
    27/66, II WD 35/63, II WD 39/68, 2 WD 15/98, 1 WB 113/78, 1 WB 61/90, 2 WB 60/79

4. Autobiographical Sources

Buzan, Werner. www.wernerbuzan.de (Last accessed 29 March 2021)
Kluss, Heinz. "Kein Versöhnungsbier in Moskau. Die Affäre Kießling und der Militärische Abschirm-
    dienst: 30 Jahre danach als Lehrstück von einem mitverantwortlichen Akteur ausufernd erzählt."
    Unpublished manuscript
Koch, Dierk. "Meine unvergessenen Freunde." Unpublished manuscript of the author's life
    experiences, as well as an email from Dierk Koch to the author, 6 September 2019
Lindner, Michael. "Das halbe Leben halb gelebt." Unpublished manuscript, 1985
Mysior, Arnold. www.arnoldmysior.com/bio (Last accessed 29 March 2021)

5. Conversations and Interviews with Contemporary Witnesses (alphabetically by surname)

Retired General Wolfgang Altenburg, Lübeck-Travemünde, 11 June 2014 and 7 August 2014, and by phone on 5 July 2017

Retired Surgeon General Dr. Horst Hennig, Cologne, 14 February 2018, 20 June 2018 and 22 November 2019

Retired Colonel Heinz Kluss, Wachtberg, 13 February 2018

Dierk Koch, Hamburg, 22 February 2018 then again by phone on 7 September 2019

Retired General Harald Kujat, Neuruppin, 30 January 2019

Michael Lindner, Hamburg, 7 February 2017, 14 February 2017, and at other times

Reserve First Lieutenant Joachim Meier, Karlsruhe, 16 July 2018

Dr. Georg Meyer, Freiburg im Breisgau, 7 September 2019

Dr. Michael Müller, Berlin, 1 August 2019

Retired Colonel Dieter Ohm, Meckenheim, 17 April 2019

Reserve First Sergeant Martina Riedel, Hamburg, 23 January 2020

Erich Schmid, Berlin, 5 December 2017 (by email)

Retired Parliamentary State Secretary Brigitte Schulte, Wachtberg, 16 April 2019

Navy Captain Alexander Schüttpelz, Berlin, 24 January 2019

Winfried Stecher, Hamburg, 25 January 2018

Retired State Secretary Peter Wichert, Bad Münstereifel, 10 April 2019

An additional fifty-four conversations or interviews were conducted in person, over the phone or by email that will remain anonymous here at the wishes of those spoken to.

6. Sources from the German Bundestag (All accessed 29 March 2021)

Document 10/6333 from 4 November 1986, Minor inquiry from Deputy [Herbert] Rusche and the Green Party faction, "Diskriminierung von Homosexuellen im Berufsleben," https://dserver. bundestag.de/btd/10/063/1006333.pdf

Document 11/1734 from 29 January 1988, Inquiry from Deputy Jutta Oesterle-Schwerin, https://dserver. bundestag.de/btd/11/017/1101734.pdf, Nos. 6 and 7, p. 4

Document 11/2586 from 24 June 1988, Major inquiry from Deputy Oesterle-Schwerin, Deputy Schmidt-Bott and the Green Party faction, "Rosa Listen. Beeinträchtigung des Rechtes auf informationelle Selbstbestimmung von Homosexuellen durch den Homosexuellen-Sonder-paragraphen (§175 StGB) und die Sicherheitsrichtlinien," https://dserver.bundestag.de/ btd/11/025/1102586.pdf

Document 13/8676 from 2 October 1997, Minor inquiry from Deputy Heinrich Graf von Einsiedel and the PDS group, "Gewalt gegen Schwule und Diskriminierung von Schwulen in der Bundeswehr," https://dserver.bundestag.de/btd/13/086/1308676.pdf

Document 13/8950 from 7 November 1997, "Antwort der Bundesregierung auf die Kleine Anfrage des Abgeordneten Heinrich Graf von Einsiedel und der Gruppe der PDS," Document 13/8676, https:// dserver.bundestag.de/btd/13/089/1308950.pdf

Document 14/1750 from 5 October 1999, Minor inquiry from Deputy Christina Schenk and the PDS faction, "Schwule und Bundeswehr."

Document 14/1870 from 27 October 1999, Inquiry from Deputies Hildebrecht Braun et al., and the FDP faction, "Bekämpfung jeder Art von Diskriminierung in der Bundeswehr," https://dserver. bundestag.de/btd/14/018/1401870.pdf

Document 14/3275 from May 5 2000, "Schriftliche Fragen mit den in der Zeit vom 25. April bis 5. Mai 2000 eingegangenen Antworten der Bundesregierung," https://dserver.bundestag.de/ btd/14/032/1403275.pdf, pp. 38–39, Nos. 70 and 71

Document 14/4894 from 6 December 2000, "Beschlussempfehlung und Bericht des Rechtsaus-schusses (6. Ausschuss)," https://dserver.bundestag.de/btd/14/048/1404894.pdf

9th legislative period, 45th Session, 24 June 1981, transcript, https://dserver.bundestag.de/ btp/09/09045.pdf

10th legislative period, 47th Session, 19 January 1984, transcript, https://dserver.bundestag.de/ btp/10/10047.pdf

10th legislative period, 52nd Session, 8 February 1984, transcript, https://dserver.bundestag.de/ btp/10/10052.pdf

10th legislative period, 207th Session, 20 March 1986, transcript, https://dserver.bundestag.de/ btp/10/10207.pdf

11th legislative period, 57th Session, 3 February 1988, transcript, https://dserver.bundestag.de/ btp/11/11057.pdf

14th legislative period, 95th Session, 23 March 2000, transcript, https://dserver.bundestag.de/ btp/14/14095.pdf

7. Sources from the German Reichstag

Protocol of the 61st Session of the German Reichstag on 29 November 1907, https://www.reichstags protokolle.de/Blatt_k12_bsb00002839_00213.html (last accessed 29 March 2021)

8. Secondary Literature

(all links accessed 29 March 2021 if not otherwise stated)

Allmeier, Michael. "Schwul zu sein Bedarf es Wenig." *Frankfurter Allgemeine Zeitung*, August 1, 1998.

Army Act. 1955. https://www.legislation.gov.uk/ukpga/1955/18/pdfs/ukpga_19550018_en.pdf.

ATÜ (Student periodical of Bundeswehr University Munich). "Homosexuelle an Der HSBw," 1979.

"Augenzeugenbericht Hans. G." In *Rosa Winkel, Rosa Listen: Homosexuelle und "Gesundes Volks-empfinden" von Auschwitz bis heute*, edited by Hans-Georg Stümke and Rudi Finkler, 301–6. Reinbek bei Hamburg: Rowohlt, 1981.

"Augenzeugenbericht Harry Pauly." In *Rosa Winkel, Rosa Listen: Homosexuelle und "Gesundes Volks-empfinden" von Auschwitz bis heute*, edited by Hans-Georg Stümke and Rudi Finkler, 312–16. Reinbek bei Hamburg: Rowohlt, 1981.

"Augenzeugenbericht Hermann R." In *Rosa Winkel, Rosa Listen: Homosexuelle und "Gesundes Volks-empfinden" von Auschwitz bis heute*, edited by Hans-Georg Stümke and Rudi Finkler, 325–30. Reinbek bei Hamburg: Rowohlt, 1981.

"Augenzeugenbericht Johann-Rudolf Braehler." In *Rosa Winkel, Rosa Listen: Homosexuelle und "Gesundes Volksempfinden" von Auschwitz bis heute*, edited by Hans-Georg Stümke and Rudi Finkler, 316–24. Reinbek bei Hamburg: Rowohlt, 1981.

Backovic, Lazar, Martin Jäschke, and Sara Maria Manzo. "'Werd endlich ein bisschen Mann': Verfolgung Homosexueller in Deutschland." *Der Spiegel*, June 4, 2014. https://www.spiegel.de/geschichte/schwulenparagraf-175-homosexuelle-in-der-ddr-a-972887.html.

BASS. "Printed Advertisement and Invitation to Regional and Federal Meetings." *Die Bundeswehr*, 1999

Baum, David. "Rosa Armee Fraktion." *MAX*, 2000.

Berliner Morgenpost. "'Schwulenfeindliche Studie' nicht von der Bundeswehr," January 28, 2000.

Berliner Tageszeitung. "Soldaten Dürfen Keine Männer Lieben," June 30, 1992.

Berliner Zeitung. "Schwule fordern Entschuldigung von Scharping," January 30, 2000.

Bérubé, Allan. *Coming out Under Fire: The History of Gay Men and Women in World War II*. Chapel Hill, NC: University of North Carolina Press, 1990.

Biesold, Karl-Heinz. "Der Umgang mit Sexualität in der Bundeswehr (1955–2005): Vom Verbot der Homosexualität bis zum Sexualerlass 2004." Sexuologie: *Zeitschrift Für Sexualmedizin, Sexualtherapie und Sexualwissenschaft* 1–2 (2007): 2–8.

Bormuth, Maria. *"Ein Mann, der mit einem anderen Mann Unzucht Treibt [...], Wird mit Gefängnis Bestraft" § 175 StGB – 20 Jahre Legitimiertes Unrecht in der Bundesrepublik am Beispiel des Strafvollzugs in Wolfenbüttel*. Wolfenbüttel: Gedenkstätte in der JVA Wolfenbüttel, Stiftung niedersächsische Gedenkstätten, 2019.

Bösch, Frank. *Öffentliche Geheimnisse: Skandale, Politik und Medien in Deutschland und Großbritannien 1880–1914*. Munich: Oldenbourg, 2009.

Botsch, Kerstin. *Soldatsein: Zur sozialen Konstruktion von Geschlecht und sexueller Orientierung in der Bundeswehr*. Wiesbaden: Springer, 2016.

Bourne, Stephen. *Fighting Proud: The Untold Story of the Gay Men Who Served in Two World Wars*. New York: I.B. Tauris & Co., 2018.

Bowers, Scotty. "No Queens in The Marines." In *My Buddy: World War II Laid Bare*, edited by Dian Hanson, 79–96. Cologne: Taschen, 2014.

Brickenstein, Rudolph. "Probleme der Homosexualität im Wehrdienst." *Wehrmedizinische Monatszeitschrift* 13, no. 5 (1969): 149–53.

Bruhns, Meike. "Homosexualität Wird Bei Outing Zum 'Eignungsmangel': Bundeswehr will Schwulen Offizier nicht übernehmen." *Berliner Zeitung*, June 27, 1998. Accessed 24 March 2017.

Brühöfener, Friederike. "Contested Masculinities: Debates about Homosexuality in the German Bundeswehr in the 1960s and 1970s." In *Gendering Post-1945 Germany History: Entanglements*, edited by Karen Hagemann, Donna Harsch, and Friederike Brühöfener, 295–314. New York: Berghahn Books, 2019.

"Sex and the Soldier: The Discourse about the Moral Conduct of Bundeswehr Soldiers and Officers during the Adenauer Era." *Central European History* 48 (2015): 523–40.

Bundeswehr aktuell. "Urteil EuGHMR," October 4, 1999.

Burgi, Martin, and Daniel Wolff. *Rechtsgutachten zur Frage der Rehabilitierung der nach Paragraph 175 StGB verurteilten homosexuellen Männer: Auftrag, Optionen und verfassungsrechtlicher Rahmen*. Baden Baden: Nomos, 2016.

Churchill, Winston. *Churchill by Himself: The Definitive Collection of Quotations*. Edited by Richard M. Langworth. New York: PublicAffairs, 2008.

Clarke, Kevin. "Das Militärhistorische Museum Dresden." *Männer*, 2012, 32–35.

Claussen, Christine. "Schwule werden abgesägt." *Der Stern*, June 18, 1981, 188.

Criminal Code of the North German Confederation (1870), 46. https://www.deutschestextarchiv.de/book/view/unknown_strafgesetzbuch_1870?p%20=56.

Denninger, Erhard. "Entscheidungen Öffentliches Recht: Soldatengesetz §§ 3, 4, 10, 11." Juristische Zeitschrift, 1976, 444–46.

Diez, Georg. "Er ist so Nett." *Der Spiegel*, November 10, 2017, 122–123. https://www.spiegel.de/kultur/er-ist-so-nett-a-448af13a-0002-0001-0000-000154232702.

Domeier, Norman. "'Moltke als Schimpfwort!' Der Eulenburg-Skandal, der Moltke-Mythos und die Moralische Rechtfertigung eines 'großen Krieges.'" *Militärgeschichte: Zeitschrift Für Historische Bildung* 2 (2015): 14–17.

Drescher, Jack. "Gender Identity Diagnoses: History and Controversies." In *Gender Dysphoria and Disorder of Sex Development: Progress and Care and Knowledge*, edited by Baudewijntje P.C. Kreukels, Thomas D. Steensma, and Annelou L.C. de Vries, 137–50. New York: Springer, 2014.

Drobinski, Matthias. "Römisches Doppelleben." *Süddeutsche Zeitung*, February 20, 2019.

Ebner, Katharina. *Religion im Parlament: Homosexualität als Gegenstand parlamentarischer Debatten im Vereinigten Königreich und in der Bundesrepublik Deutschland (1945–1990)*. Göttingen: Vandenhoeck & Ruprecht, 2018.

Ernst, Roland, and Cornelia Limpricht. "Der organisierte Mann." In *"Verführte" Männer: Das Leben der Kölner Homosexuellen im Dritten Reich*, edited by Cornelia Limpricht, Jürgen Müller and Nina Oxenius, 56–66. Cologne: Volksblatt, 1991.

Feddersen, Jan. "Infames Diskretionsgebot: Das Outing des Berliner Regierungschefs Klaus Wowereit hat der Homosexualität etwas von Ruch des Peinlichen Genommen." *taz Magazin*, July 7–8, 2001. https://taz.de/!1163573/.

"Sieg Auf Ganzer Linie." *taz*, April 8, 2000. https://taz.de/!1239102/.

Federal Ministry of Defense. "Vielfalt Im BMVg: Jeder Einzelne wird wertgeschätzt," March 3, 2020.

Federal Ministry of Defense, ed. *Weißbuch 1985: Zur Lage und Entwicklung der Bundeswehr*. Bonn: Bundesminister der Verteidigung, 1985.

Federal Ministry of Justice and Consumer Protection. "Gesetz zur Rehabilitierung verurteilter Homosexueller tritt in Kraft." July 21st, 2017. Accessed 16 April 2018. www.bmjv.de/SharedDocs/Artikel/DE/2017/072117_Rehabilitierung_Paragraph_175.html.

Féron, Élise. *Wartime Sexual Violence Against Men: Masculinities and Power in Conflict Zones*. Lanham: Rowman & Littlefield International, 2018.

Fh. "Das Tabu: Bundeswehr Und Homosexualität." *Nürnberger Nachrichten*, January 26, 1984.

Fischer, Sigmar. "Bewegung zwischen Richtungsstreit und Stagnation: Die Deutsche Aktionsgemeinschaft Homosexualität (DAH)." In *Politiken in Bewegung: Die Emanzipation Homosexueller im 20. Jahrhundert*, edited by Andreas Pretzel and Volker Weiß, 236–272. Hamburg: Männerschwarm, 2017.

"Er organisierte Deutschlands erste Schwulendemo: Gedenken an Rainer Plein." *www.queer.de*, November 26, 2016. https://www.queer.de/detail.php?article_id=27600.

Fitschen, Klaus. *Liebe zwischen Männern? Der deutsche Protestantismus und das Thema Homosexualität*. Leipzig: Leipzig Evangelische Verlagsanstalt, 2018.

Fleckenstein, Bernhard. "Homosexuality and Military Service in Germany." SOWI Working Paper 84. Munich: Sozialwissenschaftlichen Instituts der Bundeswehr, 1993.

Focus. "Schwule in die Bundeswehr," August 2, 1999.

Frankfurter Allgemeine Zeitung. "Der Fluchtgrund des MAD-Manns," April 4, 1968.

Frankfurter Allgemeine Zeitung. "Homosexueller darf nicht Ausbilden," September 1, 1999.

Frankfurter Rundschau. "Den Haag gibt wegen AIDS nach," April 22, 1988.

Frankfurter Rundschau. "Rot und Grün streiten über homosexuelle Bundeswehrsoldaten," June 4, 1999.

Friederichs, Hauke. "Homosexualität als militärischer Makel." *Die Zeit*, February 1, 2014. https://www.zeit.de/politik/deutschland/2014-01/bundeswehr-homosexualitaet-soldaten-tabu.

Gast, Wolfgang. "Neonazi Michael Kühnen gestorben." *taz*, April 26, 1991. https://taz.de/Neonazi-Michael-Kuehnen-gestorben/!1722115/.

Gay Journal. "Homodiskriminierung in der Bundeswehr," 1984.

GDR Criminal Code, §151 (January 12, 1968). http://www.verfassungen.de/ddr/strafgesetzbuch74.htm.

Gebauer, Gunter, and Christoph Wulf. "Soziale Mimesis." In *Ethik der Ästhetik*, edited by Christoph Wulf, Dietmar Kamper, and Hans Ulrich Gumbrecht, 75–85. Berlin: Akademie Verlag, 1994.

German Bundestag. "Diskussion und Feststellung des Deutschen Bundestages in Sachen Kießling, Bericht und Empfehlung des Verteidigungsausschusses als 1. Untersuchungsausschuss." (Kießling Investigative Committee) published by the German Bundestag, Bonn 1984.

Gesetz über die Gleichbehandlung der Soldatinnen und Soldaten (SoldGG). http://www.gesetze-im-internet.de/soldgg/.

Gesetz über die Rechtsstellung der Soldaten (SG). http://www.gesetze-im-internet.de/sg/.

Gesetz zur Änderung des Strafgesetzbuchs (June 28, 1935). https://www.servat.unibe.ch/dns/RGBl_1935_I_839_G_Strafgesetzbuch.pdf.

Glade, Clemens. "In Reih und Glied!" *Magnus*, 1996, 10–11.

Gollner, Günther. "Disziplinarsanktionen gegenüber Homosexuellen im öffentlichen Dienst." In *Seminar: Gesellschaft und Homosexualität*, edited by Rüdiger Lautmann, 105–24. Frankfurt am Main: Suhrkamp, 1977.

Grau, Günter. *Lexikon zur Homosexuellenverfolgung 1933–1945: Institutionen-Kompetenzen-Betätigungsfelder*. Berlin: LIT Verlag, 2011.

Graw, Ansgar. "Echter Schlagabtausch oder höfisches Ritual?" *Die Welt*, February 20, 2019, 4.

Greer, Germaine. *The Boy*. London: Thames & Hudson, 2003.

The Guardian. "'Not Acceptable': Indian army backs gay sex ban despite decriminalisation," January 11, 2019. https://www.theguardian.com/world/2019/jan/11/not-acceptable-indian-army-backs-gay-sex-ban-despite-decriminalisation.

Hammerich, Helmut Rudolf. *"Stets am Feind!": Der Militärische Abschirmdienst (MAD) 1956–1990*. Göttingen: Vandenhhoeck & Ruprecht, 2019.

Haring, Claus, and Karl Heinz Leickert. *Wörterbuch der Psychiatrie und ihrer Grenzgebiete*. Stuttgart: F.K. Schattauer, 1968.

Haubrich, Wolfgang. "Schwul und beim Bund?!" Heer, 1991. Appeared in service branch magazines *Luftwaffe* and *Blaue Jungs* in identical form in September 1991.

Hecht, Alexander. "Gay ORF?! Das ORF Fernsehprogramm durch die rosa Brille betrachtet – ein Streifzug durch das Archiv." *Medien Und Zeit* 4 (2007): 16–21.

Heer. "Reader reactions and statements on the article 'Schwul und beim Bund?!' (Issue 9/91)," 1991, 34–35. Identical in *Luftwaffe* and *Blaue Jungs*.

Heilig, René. "Alexander der Große wäre heute nicht mal Feldwebel." *Neues Deutschland*, November 22–23, 1997.

Heilmann, Andreas. "Helm ab zum Sex! Zur Führungshilfe für Vorgesetzte der Bundeswehr im Umgang mit Sexualität." *Gigi: Zeitschrift für Sexuelle Emanzipation*, April 2002. http://www.gigi-online.de/inhalt18.html.

Hemicker, Lorenz. "'79 Zentimeter sind Schwul': Homophobie in der Bundeswehr." *Frankfurter Allgemeine Zeitung*, January 9, 2014. Accessed 27 March 2017. www.faz.net/aktuell/politik/inland/homophobie-in-der-bundeswehr-79-zentimeter-sind-schwul-12744050.html.

Heß, Michael. "Der ungeliebte Aktivist: Münster tut sich schwer mit der Ehrung Homosexueller." *Straßenmagazin Draußen*, 2015.

Hesse, Max René. *Partenau*. Frankfurt am Main: Rütten & Loening, 1929.

Hewlett, Edward. "When and why did Winston Churchill Say: 'The traditions of the Royal Navy Are Rum, Sodomy and the Lash'?" *The Guardian*. https://www.theguardian.com/notesandqueries/query/0,,-1433,00.html.

Hildebrand, Hans, Albert Röhr, and Hans-Otto Steinmetz. *Die deutschen Kriegsschiffe: Biographien – ein Spiegel der Marinegeschichte von 1815 bis zur Gegenwart.* Vol. 3. Herford: Koehler, 1981.

Himmler, Heinrich. *Geheimreden 1933 bis 1945 und andere Ansprachen.* Edited by Bradley F. Smith and Agnes F. Peterson. Berlin: Propyläen, 1974.

Hirschfeld, Magnus. *Die Homosexualität des Mannes und des Weibes.* Berlin: Marcus, 1914.

"Sexualpsychologie und Volkspsychologie: Eine epikritische Studie zum Hardenberg-Prozeß." *Zeitschrift Für Sexualwissenschaft* 4 (1908).

Von einst bis jetzt: Geschichte einer homosexuellen Bewegung 1897–1922. Edited by Manfred Herzer and James Steakley. Berlin: Rosa Winkel, 1986.

Hussey, Andrew. *The French Intifada: The Long War between France and Its Arabs.* London: Granta, 2014.

Jentzsch, Christian. *Vom Kadetten bis zum Admiral: Das britische und das deutsche Seeoffizierkorps 1871 bis 1914.* Berlin; Boston: De Gruyter Oldenbourg, 2018.

Junge Freiheit. "Bundeswehrunis: Spiegelbilder Der Gesellschaft," December 22, 1995, 10.

"Keine gleichgeschlechtlich veranlagten Soldaten als Ausbilder." *Neue Zeitschrift Für Verwaltungsrecht Rechtsprechungs-Report* 4 (1998): 244–45.

Knuth, Christian. "Bundesverteidigungsministerin Dr. Ursula von Der Leyen im Interview." September 21, 2017, printed in *Leo* August 2017. https://www.maenner.media/gesellschaft/bundesvertei digungsministerin-ursula-von-der-leyen-interview/.

Koelbl, Susanne, and Alexander Szandar. "'Im Kosovo noch lange Benötigt'. Der neue Wehrbeauftragte Willfried Penner über die Armee-Reform, Auslandseinsätze und Frauen in den Streitkräften." *Der Spiegel,* July 3, 2000. https://www.spiegel.de/politik/im-kosovo-noch-lange-noetig-a-1afef55f-0002-0001-0000-000016810588.

Kohrs, Ekkehard. "AIDS-Spezialist Gauweiler Sorgt Sich Um Die Bundeswehr." *Bonner Generalanzeiger,* August 13–14, 1988.

Könne, Christian. "Gleichberechtigte Mitmenschen? Homosexuelle und die Bundesrepublik Deutschland." *Deutschland Archiv,* September 7, 2018. https://www.bpb.de/themen/deutschland archiv/275113/gleichberechtigte-mitmenschen/.

"Schwule und Lesben in der DDR und der Umgang des SED-Staates mit Homosexualität." *Deutschland Archiv,* February 28, 2018. https://opus4.kobv.de/opus4-euv/frontdoor/index/index/start/2/ rows/10/sortfield/score/sortorder/desc/searchtype/simple/query/K%C3%B6nne/docId/344.

Kramar, Konrad, and Georg Mayrhofer. *Prinz Eugen: Heros und Neurose.* Vienna; Salzburg: Residenz Verlag, 2013.

Krause, Tilman. "Max von Baden: Der schwule Totengräber des deutschen Kaiserreichs." *Die Welt,* December 3, 2013. https://www.welt.de/kultur/literarischewelt/article122489282/Der-schwule-Totengraeber-des-deutschen-Kaiserreichs.html.

Krause, Wilfried. "Da Spiel' Ich Denen Eine Komödie Vor." *Der Stern,* January 19, 1984.

Krebs, Albin. "Roy Cohn, Aide to McCarthy and Fiery Lawyer, Dies at 59." *New York Times,* August 3, 1986. https://www.nytimes.com/1986/08/03/obituaries/roy-cohn-aide-to-mccarthy-and-fiery-lawyer-dies-at-59.html.

Kulke, Ulli. "Lieber Homosexuell als zur Bundeswehr." *Die Welt,* October 26, 2010. https://www.welt.de/ politik/deutschland/article10540126/Lieber-homosexuell-als-zur-Bundeswehr.html.

Kümmel, Gerhard, Paul Klein, and Klaus Lohmann. "Zwischen Differenz und Gleichheit: Die Öffnung der Bundeswehr für Frauen." SOWI Report 69. Strausberg: Sozialwissenschaftlichen Instituts der Bundeswehr, 2000. https://opus4.kobv.de/opus4-zmsbw/frontdoor/deliver/index/docId/159/ file/15010181.pdf.

Küthe, Jörg. "Bundeswehr = Mittelalter." *Berliner Tageszeitung,* June 30, 1992.

Lange, Nadine. "Scharpings Bundeswehr-Studie: Schwule sind krank." *taz*, January 27, 2000. https://taz.de/Scharpings-Bundeswehr-Studie-Schwule-sind-krank/!1251335/.

Lautmann, Rüdiger. *Der Zwang zur Tugend: Die gesellschaftliche Kontrolle der Sexualitäten.* Frankfurt am Main: Suhrkamp, 1984.

Leersch, Hans-Jürgen. "Scharpings Falsches Spiel: Der neue Mann des Ministers." *Die Welt*, May 25, 2000. https://www.welt.de/print-welt/article515563/Scharpings-falsches-Spiel-Der-neue-Mann-des-Ministers.html.

Leexow, Karl Franz von. *Armee und Homosexualität: Schadet Homosexualität der militärischen Tüchtigkeit einer Rasse?* Leipzig: Spohr, 1908.

Lindner, Michael. "Homosexuelle in der Institution Bundeswehr: Wehrpsychiatrische, Rechtliche und Sozialpsychologische Aspekte eines Dilemmas." In *Sexualität als Sozialer Tatbestand: Theoretische und Empirische Beiträge zu einer Soziologie der Sexualitäten*, edited by Rolf Gindorf and Erwin Haeberle, 211–32. Berlin: De Gruyter, 1985.

"Nicht mehr mein Weg." In *Unbändig männlich: Ein Lesebuch für halbstarke Väter und Söhne*, edited by Rudi Finkler and Nikolaus Hansen, 88–102. Reinbek bei Hamburg: Rowohlt, 1983.

Lorenz, Gottfried. *Todesurteile und Hinrichtungen wegen homosexueller Handlungen während der NS-Zeit: Mann-männliche Internetprostitution und andere Texte zur Geschichte und zur Situation der Homosexuellen in Deutschland.* Berlin: Lit, 2018.

Lüders, Christine. "Vorwort zur Veröffentlichung eines Rechtsgutachtens zur Frage der Rehabilitierung der nach der nach §175 StGB Verurteilten Homosexuellen Männer," 2016. Accessed 17 April 2018. https://www.antidiskriminierungsstelle.de/SharedDocs/downloads/DE/publikationen/Rechtsgutachten/rechtsgutachten_burgi_rehabilitierung_175.pdf?__blob=publicationFile&v=3.

Lutze, Christian. "Sexuelle Beziehungen und die Truppe." *Neue Zeitschrift Für Wehrrecht* 5 (2007): 192–201.

Machtan, Lothar. *Prinz Max von Baden: Der letzte Kanzler des Kaisers; Eine Biographie.* Berlin: Suhrkamp, 2013.

Magnus. "Niederlande: Schwuler Leben," 1996, 14.

Magnus. "Streifzug NATO-Länder," 1996, 15.

Männer. "Schwule in der Bundeswehr: Für den Dreck gut genug," 1999, 28ff.

Marquez, Hugo. "Persecution of Homosexuals in the McCarthy Hearings: A History of Homosexuality in Postwar America and McCarthyism." *Fairmount Folio: Journal of History* 12 (2010): 52–76.

Martel, Frédéric. *Sodom: Macht, Homosexualität und Doppelmoral im Vatikan.* Frankfurt am Main: S. Fischer, 2019.

Mauz, Gerhard. "Warum so und später Anders...?" *Der Spiegel*, July 13, 1970, 74–75.

McGreal, Chris. "Barack Obama promises to end gay army recruit ban." *The Guardian*, January 28, 2010. https://www.theguardian.com/world/2010/jan/28/obama-usa-military-gays.

Meisner, Anja. "Minderheiten in den Streitkräften: Homosexuelle in der Bundeswehr." Thesis, Potsdam University, 2001.

Meyer, Steffen. "Lebacher Soldaten-Morde: Haupttäter will im Knast sterben." *Bild*, April 20, 2016. https://www.bild.de/regional/saarland/saarland/haupttaeter-der-lebacher-soldaten-morde-will-im-knast-sterben-45295336.bild.html.

Mildenberger, Florian. "Vögeln für Volk und Vaterland." *Gigi: Zeitschrift Für Sexuelle Emanzipation*, March/April 2002, 14–16.

"Ministry of Defense lit in rainbow olorcolors to celebrate LGB personnel," January 10, 2020. https://www.gov.uk/government/news/mod-lit-in-rainbow-olorcolors-to-celebrate-lgb-personnel-2.

Moll, Albert. *Berühmte Homosexuelle.* Wiesbaden: Bergmann, 1910.

Möllers, Heiner. *Die Affäre Kießling: Der grösste Skandal der Bundeswehr.* Berlin: Ch. Links, 2019.

"Die Kießling-Affäre 1984: Zur Rolle der Medien im Skandal um die Entlassung von General Dr. Günter Kießling." *Vierteljahrshefte Für Zeitgeschichte* 63, no. 3 (2016): 517–50.

Mosely, Olaf. Was Admiral Lord Nelson gay? https://bryanhemming.wordpress.com/2013/09/14/was-admiral-lord-nelson-gay/.

Müller-Jentsch, Ekkehard. "Schwuler Offizier darf nicht Chef sein." *Süddeutsche Zeitung*, April 18–19, 1998.

Naumann, Klaus, ed. NVA: *Anspruch und Wirklichkeit nach ausgewählten Beiträgen*. Berlin: Mittler, 1993.

Neuberg, Sophie. "Großbritannien: Zutritt Verboten." *Magnus*, 1996, 13.

"USA: Nichts Fragen, Nichts Sagen." *Magnus*, 1996, 15.

Nicolai, Walter. *Geheimdienst und Propaganda im Ersten Weltkrieg: Die Aufzeichnungen von Oberst Walter Nicolai 1914 bis 1918*. Edited by Michael Epkenhans, Gerhard P. Groß, Markus Pöhlmann, and Christian Stachelbeck. Berlin: De Gruyter Oldenbourg, 2019.

Nieden, Susanne zur. "Der homosexuelle Staatsfeind – Zur Geschichte einer Idee." In *Ideen als gesellschaftliche Gestaltungskraft im Europa der Neuzeit: Beiträge für eine Erneuerte Geistesge-schichte*, edited by Lutz Raphael and Heinz-Elmar Tenorth, 397–427. Munich: Oldenbourg, 2006.

Noack, Rick. "As Trump attempts a transgender military ban, Germany celebrates its first trans commander." *Washington Post*, November 11, 2017. https://www.washingtonpost.com/news/worldviews/wp/2017/11/11/as-trump-attempts-a-transgender-military-ban-germany-celebrates-its-first-trans-commander/.

"Panzergrenadierbrigade 17 Hamburg." Accessed February 12, 2019. https://pzgrendiv6.de/brigaden/panzergrenadierbrigade-17.html.

Phillips, Dave. "More than 100,000 Men Have Been Sexually Assaulted in the Military in Recent Decades." *The New York Times*, September 10, 2019.

Pieken, Gorch, ed. *Gewalt Und Geschlecht: Männlicher Krieg – Weiblicher Frieden?* Dresden: Sandstein, 2018.

Polednik, Marc. "Israel: Wo Jeder Gebraucht Wird." *Magnus*, 1996, 12–13.

Pretzel, Andreas, and Volker Weiß, eds. Vol 1., *Ohnmacht und Aufbegehren: Homosexuelle Männer in der frühen Bundesrepublik. Geschichte der Homosexuellen in Deutschland nach 1945*. Hamburg: Männer-schwarm Verlag, 2010.

Quick. "Die Moral Der Truppe," 1984.

Ramge, Thomas. *Die grossen Polit-Skandale: Eine andere Geschichte der Bundesrepublik*. Frankfurt am Main: Campus, 2003.

Rampp, Matthias, Christian Johnson, and Yvonne Wilms. "'Die seit Jahrzehnten belastende Schmach fällt von mir ab': Rehabilitierung und Entschädigung der Wegen einvernehmlicher homosexueller Handlungen Verurteilten." *JuristenZeitung* 23 (2018): 1143–50.

Ramsauer, Ulrich. "150 Jahre Verwaltungsgerichtsbarkeit – Jubiläum einer Unvollendeten." *BDVR Rundschreiben* 3 (2013): 124–27. https://www.verwaltungsgerichtsbarkeit.de/allgemeines/07_geschichte/index.php.

Range, Thomas. "Irgendwas mit ü." *Die Zeit*, October 23, 2003. https://www.zeit.de/2003/44/A-Kie_a7ling.

Reichardt, Jürgen. *Hardthöhe Bonn: Im Strudel einer Affaire*. Bonn: Osning, 2008.

Rhein-Zeitung. "Streit zwischen Trittin und Scharping: Schwuler Offizier zwangsversetzt," June 6, 1999. Accessed 16 August 2019.

Rimscha, Robert von. "Offen gestanden: Der Sozialdemokrat Klaus Wowereit, Berlins neuer Regierender Bürgermeister, hat sich als schwul geoutet." *Der Tagesspiegel*, June 22, 2001. www.tagesspiegel.de/kultur/homosexualitaet-in-der-politik-offen-gestanden/235686.html.

Rissmann, Torsten. "Obama: Bald 'Ask and Tell'?" *Die Freie Welt*, February 20, 2010. https://www.freiewelt.net/blog/obama-bald-ask-and-tell-1511/.

Rogg, Matthias. *Armee des Volkes? Militär und Gesellschaft in der DDR.* Berlin: Ch. Links, 2008.

Roos, Peter. "Der bittre Ritter: Prinz Eugern." *Die Zeit,* October 17, 2013. https://www.zeit.de/2013/43/prinz-eugen-350-geburtstag.

Rosa Rauschen. "Schwule Bei Der Bundeswehr." Accessed August 16, 2019. http://rosarauschen.de/archiv/themen/bundeswehr.html.

Schadendorf, Jens. "Hauptmann Uhlmann ist Schwul." *Die Zeit,* June 10, 2014. www.zeit.de/gesellschaft/2014-06/bundeswehr-homosexualitaet-tabu/komplettansicht.

Der Regenbogen-Faktor: Schwule und Lesben in Wirtschaft und Gesellschaft; "Von Außenseitern zu selbstbewussten Leistungsträgern." Munich: Redline Press, 2014.

Scheck, Roman, and Karsten Utess. "Was wir damals gemacht haben, war kein Verbrechen." *Bild,* August 30, 2019, 7.

Schmidt-Radefeldt, Roman. "Streitkräfte und Homosexualität: Anmerkungen zur Entscheidung des Straßburger Gerichtshofs für Menschenrechte vom 27. September 1999: Lustig-Prean und Beckett gegen Großbritannien und zur Rechtsprechung deutscher Verwaltungsgerichte." *Neue Zeitschrift Für Wehrrecht* 42, no. 4 (2000): 141–50.

Schneider, Howard. "Rethinking DOD policy on gays." *Washington Post,* November 6, 1989.

Schomers, Bärbel. *Coming-out: Queere Identitäten zwischen Diskriminierung und Emanzipation.* Opladen: Budrich UniPress, 2018.

Schulz, Bernhard. "Der Multikulti-Prinz: Eugen von Savoyen." *Der Tagesspiegel,* April 9, 2010. https://www.tagesspiegel.de/kultur/ausstellungen/eugen-von-savoyen-der-multikulti-prinz/1785396.html.

Schwalm, Georg. "Die Streichung des Grundtatbestands homosexueller Handlungen und ihre Auswirkungen auf das Disziplinarrecht." *Neue Zeitschrift Für Wehrrecht* 1 (1970): 81–98.

Schwartz, Michael. "Entkriminalisierung und Öffentlichkeit: Mediale Reaktion zur Reform des Homosexuellen-Strafrechts in der Bundesrepublik Deutschland 1969–1980." In *Gewinner Und Verlierer: Beiträge zur Geschichte der Homosexualität in Deutschland im 20. Jahrhundert,* edited by Norman Domeier, 79–93. Göttingen: Wallstein, 2015.

Homosexuelle, Seilschaften, Verrat: Ein transnationales Stereotyp im 20. Jahrhundert. Berlin; Boston: De Gruyter Oldenbourg, 2019.

Sciolino, Elaine. "Report urging end of homosexual ban rejected by military." *New York Times,* October 22, 1989.

Shilts, Randy. *Conduct Unbecoming: Lesbians and Gays in the U.S. Military; Vietnam to the Persian Gulf.* New York: St. Martin's Press, 1993.

Siemann, Holger. "Coming out in der NVA?" *Die Volksarmee,* 1990, 5.

Der Spiegel. "Die Bekenntnisse des Krull," July 25, 1961, 13–16. www.spiegel.de/spiegel/print/d-43366138.html.

"'Berufliches': Michael Lindner," July 6, 1981, 176.

"Ein schmaler Grat," September 9, 1985, 221–223. www.spiegel.de/spiegel/print/d-13515078.html.

"'New York Times': Zehntausende Männer im US-Militär sollen Opfer sexueller Übergriffe geworden sein," September 12, 2019. https://www.spiegel.de/politik/ausland/usa-tausende-maenner-im-militaer-sollen-opfer-sexueller-uebergriffe-geworden-sein-a-1286424.html.

"Scharping entlässt Generalinspekteur Kirchbach," May 24, 2000. https://www.spiegel.de/politik/deutschland/bundeswehr-scharping-entlaesst-generalinspekteur-kirchbach-a-78007.html.

"Soldaten als potentielle Sexualpartner," January 16, 1984, 22–23. www.spiegel.de/spiegel/print/d-13509064.html.

"Späte Milde," May 12, 1969. https://www.spiegel.de/politik/spaete-milde-a-2be75b59-0002-0001-0000-000045741408?context=issue.

"Versiegelte Briefe," February 15, 1993, 47–54. https://www.spiegel.de/politik/versiegelte-briefe-a-0a4b648f-0002-0001-0000-000013855325.

"Wörner - 'der Lächerlichkeit preisgegeben'," January 30, 1984, 17–28. www.spiegel.de/spiegel/print/d-13510423.html.

Smith, Tom, *Comrades in Arms: Military Masculinities in East German Culture*. New York: Berghahn Books, 2020 (published after the German manuscript of this study was completed in in early 2020).

Spiewak, Martin. "Schwule beim Bund." *JS: Das Magazin für Leute beim Bund*, 1994, 12–13.

Der Stern. "Justin Trudeau entschuldigt sich unter Tränen bei Homosexuellen," October 19, 2017. https://www.stern.de/lifestyle/leute/justin-trudeau-entschuldigt-sich-unter-traenen-bei-homo sexuellen-in-kanada-7767968.html.

Storkmann, Klaus. "20. January 1969: Der Soldatenmord von Lebach." *Militärgeschichte: Zeitschrift für historische Bildung* 4 (2015): 29.

"'79 cm sind schwul': Homosexuelle Soldaten in der Bundeswehrgeschichte." *Militärgeschichte: Zeitschrift Für Historische Bildung* 1 (2018): 4–9.

"Cui bono? Entscheidungen und Hintergründe des Wörner-Kießling-Skandals 1983/84 im Spiegel neuer Forschungen." *Österreichische Militärische Zeitschrift* 6 (2014): 716–721.

"'Don't Ask. Don't Tell' – Auf Deutsch?" *Zeitschrift Für Innere Führung* 3 (2017): 12–21.

"Einmal West-Berlin und Zurück: Die ungewöhnliche Fahnenflucht eines Offiziers der DDR-Grenz-truppen." *Gerbergasse 18: Thüringer Vierteljahrshefte für Zeitgeschichte und Politik* 2 (2020): 11–17. (An abbreviated version also appears in *Militärgeschichte: Zeitschrift für historische Bildung* 3 (2020): 14–17.)

"'Ein widerwärtiges Schmierenstück': Die Wörner-Kießling-Affäre." *Militärgeschichte: Zeitschrift Für Historische Bildung* 4 (2013): 18–21.

Geheime Solidarität: Militärbeziehungen und Militärhilfen der DDR in die "Dritte Welt." Berlin: Ch. Links, 2012.

"Der General-Verdacht: Wie das Bundesverteidigungsministerium 1983/84 einen General verfolgte, dem Homosexualität nachgesagt worden war." In *Gewalt Und Geschlecht: Männlicher Krieg – Weiblicher Frieden?*, edited by Gorch Pieken, 294–307. Dresden: Sandstein, 2019.

"Das große Tabu: Homosexuelle Soldaten in der Bundeswehr von 1955 bis zum Jahr 2000." In *Gewalt und Geschlecht: Männlicher Krieg – Weiblicher Frieden?*, edited by Gorch Pieken, 288–299. Dresden: Sandstein, 2019.

"The 'Most Liberal in Nato'? How the (West) German Ministry of Defense Looked to Other Armed Forces' Regulations Concerning Homosexuality (1966 to 1999)." *International Journal of Military History and Historiography* 42 (2022): 70–105.

Storkmann, Klaus and Jacqueline E. Whitt, ed. "The long fight for fighting with pride: LGBT Soldiers in the Military History of Australia, Germany, Israel, the Netherlands and the United States," Special issue *International Journal of Military History and Historiography* 42 (2022).

Süddeutsche Zeitung. "Steinmeier bittet Lesben und Schwulen um Vergebung," June 3, 2018. https://www.sueddeutsche.de/politik/homosexuelle-steinmeier-bittet-lesben-und-schwule-um-vergebung-1.4000315.

Stümke, Hans-Georg. *Homosexuelle in Deutschland: Eine politische Geschichte*. Munich: C.H. Beck, 1989.

Stümke, Hans-Georg, and Rudi Finkler. Rosa Winkel, *Rosa Listen: Homosexuelle und "Gesundes Volksempfinden" von Auschwitz bis heute*. Reinbek bei Hamburg: Rowohlt, 1981.

Der Tagesspiegel. "'Die Angst der Lehrer, sich zu outen.' 40 Jahre AG Schwule Lehrer: Interview mit Detlef Mücke," March 7, 2019. https://www.tagesspiegel.de/gesellschaft/queerspiegel/40-jahre-ag-schwule-lehrer-noch-immer-haben-lehrer-angst-sich-zu-outen/24073050.html.

taz. "'Männerliebe gefährdet die Bundeswehr': BVG bestätigt ein Urteil gegen Analverkehr im Dienst," June 3, 1992.

Theyssen, Andreas. "Heißer Tip." *Abendzeitung*, July 1, 1992.

Thomas, Hans. "MAD kann Schwulen-Hatz nicht lassen." *taz*, May 5, 1998. https://taz.de/!1849446/.

Tresckow, Hans von. *Von Fürsten und anderen Sterblichen: Erinnerungen eines Kriminalkommissars.* Edited by Hermann Syzygos. Berlin: F. Fontane, 1922.

Tümmers, Henning. *AIDS: Autopsie einer Bedrohung im geteilten Deutschland.* Göttingen: Wallstein, 2017.

"'Umgang Mit Homosexualität in Der Bundeswehr' von der Gründung der Bundeswehr bis heute." https://www.queerbw.de/ahsab-ev/der-verein/historie.

Vehse, Carl. *Geschichte des Östreichischen Hofs und Adels und der Östreichischen Diplomatie.* Hamburg: Hoffmann und Campe, 1852.

Waeger, Stefan. "Sexuelle Ausrichtung und Führungsverantwortung." Thesis. Munich, 2001. https://www.grin.com/document/103977.

Walz, Dieter, Klaus Eichen, and Stefan Sohm. *Kommentar zum Soldatengesetz mit Vorgesetztenverordnung und Reservistinnen- und Reservistengesetz.* Heidelberg: C.F. Müller, 2016.

Weidinger, Rudolf. "Homosexuelle Neigungen eines Militärischen Vorgesetzten." *Truppenpraxis*, 1981, 21.

Wells-Petry, Melissa. *Exclusion: Homosexuals and the Right to Serve.* Washington, DC: Regnery Gateway, 1993.

Die Welt. "'Homosexuelle Soldaten': Sager kritisiert Scharping," November 9, 1999. www.welt.de/print-welt/article589831/Homosexuelle-Soldaten-Sager-kritisiert-Scharping.html.

Wenzke, Rüdiger. *Ab nach Schwedt! Die Geschichte des DDR-Militärstrafvollzugs.* Berlin: Ch. Links, 2016.

Ulbrichts Soldaten: Die Nationale Volksarmee 1956 bis 1971. Berlin: Ch. Links, 2013.

Wickel, Horst Peter. "In einer Männergesellschaft nicht hinnehmbar." *taz*, August 21, 1986.

"Männer im Schatten: Schwule beim Bund" *JS: Das Magazin für Leute beim Bund*, 1986, 4–5.

Willemsen, Roger. *Das Hohe Haus: Ein Jahr im Parlament.* Frankfurt am Main: S. Fischer, 2014.

Wolfert, Raimund. *Homosexuellenpolitik in der jungen Bundesrepublik: Kurt Hiller, Hans Giese und das Frankfurter Wissenschaftlich-humanitäre Komitee.* Göttingen: Wallstein, 2015.

Wörtz, Tilman. "Beim Fummeln erwischt." *Der Spiegel*, January 30, 1984, 17–28. www.spiegel.de/spiegel/print/d-13510423.html.

Die Zeit. "Helden wie wir," April 29, 1999. www.zeit.de/1999/18/199918.er_war_der_held_.xml/komplettansicht.

"Homosexualität – ein Sicherheitsrisiko?," January 20, 1984. www.zeit.de/1984/04/homosexualitaet-ein-sicherheitsrisiko.

"Ein kleiner fall Dreyfus," January 27, 1984. https://www.zeit.de/1984/05/ein-kleiner-fall-dreyfus.

"Steinmeier bittet Homosexuelle um Vergebung," June 3, 2018. https://www.zeit.de/gesellschaft/zeitgeschehen/2018-06-festakt-berlin-verfolgung-homosexuelle-nationalsozialismus-frank-walter-steinmeier.

9. TV Documentaries

"Sachsenspiegel," aired 27 April 2018, on MDR-Fernsehen.

"Der Schwulen-Paragraph," aired 10 October 2019, 11.15 p.m., on hr-fernsehen.

"Der Soldatenmord: Die Schüsse von Lebach," a part of the series "Die großen Kriminalfälle," aired 6 February 2001, on ARD.

List of Abbreviations

ABC	Atomar, biologisch, chemisch (Nuclear, biological, chemical)
AHsAB	Arbeitskreis Homosexueller Angehöriger der Bundeswehr (Working Group for Homosexual Members of the Bundeswehr)
AIDS	Acquired Immune Deficiency Syndrome
ASBw	Amt für Sicherheit der Bundeswehr (Bundeswehr Security Office)
BArch	Bundesarchiv (Federal Archives)
BASS	Bundesweiter Arbeitskreis schwuler Soldaten (Federal Working Group of Gay Soldiers)
BM	Bundesminister (Federal Minister)
BMVg	Bundesministerium für Verteidigung (Federal Ministry of Defense)
BStU	Bundesbeauftragte/r für die Unterlagen des Staatssicherheits- dienstes der ehemaligen Deutschen Demokratischen Republik (Federal Commissioner for the Records of the State Security Service of the former GDR)
BG	Bezirksverwaltung (District Administration)
BVerfG	Bundesverfassungsgericht (Federal Constitutional Court)
Bw	Bundeswehr
BWK	Bundeswehrkrankenhaus (Bundeswehr hospital)
CDU	Christlich-Demokratische Union (Christian Democratic Union)
CSU	Christlich-Soziale Union (Christian Social Union)
DM	Deutsche Mark (German Mark)
d.R.	der Reserve (reserve)
ECHR	European Court of Human Rights
ECJ	European Court of Justice
FAZ	Frankfurter Allgemeine Zeitung (Frankfurt General Newspaper)
FDJ	Freie Deutsche Jugend (Free German Youth)
FDP	Freie Demokratische Partei (Free Democratic Party)
FüH	Führungsstab des Heeres (Army Staff)
FüL	Führungsstab der Luftwaffe (Air Staff)
FüM	Führungsstab der Marine (Naval Staff)
FüS	Führungsstab der Streitkräfte (Armed Forces Staff)
GenInsp	Generalinspekteur der Bundeswehr (Chief of Staff, Bundeswehr)
GG	Grundgesetz (Basic Law)
GDR	German Democratic Republic (Deutsche Demokratische Republik)
HIV	Human Immunodeficiency Virus
HR	Hessischer Rundfunk (Hesse Broadcasting)
InSan	Inspektion des Sanitäts- und Gesundheitswesens (Office of the Surgeon General, Bundeswehr)
JS	Junge Soldaten (Journal: Young Soldiers)
LGBT	Lesbian, Gay and Bisexual and Transgender
Lt. Col.	Lieutenant Colonel
MAD	Militärischer Abschirmdienst (Military Counterintelligence Service)

MC	Medical Corps
MdB	Mitglied des Deutschen Bundestages (Member of the German Parliament)
MFR	Militärischer Führungsrat (Chiefs of Service Council)
MfNV	Ministerium für Nationale Verteidigung (Ministry of National Defense)
MfS	Ministerium für Staatssicherheit (Ministry for State Security)
NCO	Non-commissioned officer
NRW	Nordrhein-Westfalen (North Rhine-Westphalia)
NVA	Nationale Volksarmee (National People's Army)
OPK	Operative Personenkontrolle (Operational Personal Check)
P	Abteilung Personal (Personnel Directorate)
Parl.	Parliamentary
PDS	Partei des Demokratischen Sozialismus (Party of Democratic Socialism)
PersABw	Personalamt der Bundeswehr (Bundeswehr Personnel Office)
PSABw	Personalstammamt der Bundeswehr (Bundeswehr Central Personnel Office)
PSZ	Abteilung Personal-, Sozial- und Zentralangelegenheiten (Personnel, Social Services and Central Affairs Directorate)
R	Abteilung Recht (Legal Affairs Directorate)
SED	Sozialistische Einheitspartei Deutschlands (Socialist Unity Party of Germany)
SG	Soldatengesetz (Legal Status of Military Personnel Act; Soldier's Act)
SOWI	Sozialwissenschaftliches Institut der Bundeswehr (Bundeswehr Institute of Social Sciences)
SPD	Sozialdemokratische Partei Deutschlands (Social Democratic Party of Germany)
SS	Schutzstaffel (Protection Squadron)
StGB	Strafgesetzbuch (Criminal Code)
StRehaHomG	Gesetz zur strafrechtlichen Rehabilitierung der nach dem 8. Mai 1945 wegen einvernehmlicher homosexueller Handlungen ver urteilten Personen (Act to Criminally Rehabilitate Persons Who Have Been Convicted of Performing Consensual Homosexual Acts After 8 May 1945)
StS	Staatssekretär (State Secretary)
SVD	Schwulenverband Deutschlands (Gay Federation in Germany)
TSK	Teilstreitkraft/-kräfte (Armed Service)
ZAIG	Zentrale Auswertungs- und Informationsgruppe (Central Evalua tion and Information Group, MfS)
ZDv	Zentrale Dienstvorschrift (Joint Service Regulation)
ZMSBw	Zentrum für Militärgeschichte und Sozialwissenschaften der Bundeswehr (Bundeswehr Center of Military History and Social Sciences)

Index

www.ingramcontent.com/pod-product-compliance
Lightning Source LLC
Chambersburg PA
CBHW030311100426
42812CB00002B/664